D1603698

Monographs of the Hebrew Union College

Monographs of the
Hebrew Union College
Number 18

———

"Your Voice Like a Ram's Horn":
Themes and Texts in
Traditional Jewish Preaching

An I. Edward Kiev
Library Foundation Book

"Your Voice Like a Ram's Horn"

Themes and Texts in Traditional Jewish Preaching

Marc Saperstein

Hebrew Union College Press
Cincinnati

© Copyright 1996 by the Hebrew Union College Press
Hebrew Union College-Jewish Institute of Religion

Library of Congress Cataloging-in-Publication Data

Saperstein, Marc.
　　Your voice like a ram's horn : themes and texts in traditional Jewish preaching / Marc
Saperstein.
　　　　p.　　cm. -- (Monographs of the Hebrew Union College ; 18)
　　Includes bibliographical references and index.
　　ISBN 0–87820–417–2 (alk. paper)
　　1. Jewish preaching--History.　　2. Jewish sermons--History and
criticism.　　3. Jewish sermons.　　I. Title.　　II. Series : Monographs
of the Hebrew Union College ; no. 18.
　　BM730.A3S25　1996
　　296.4'2--dc20　　　　　　　　　　　　　　　　　　　95–41647
　　　　　　　　　　　　　　　　　　　　　　　　　　　　　CIP

Printed on acid-free paper
Manufactured in the United States of America
Distributed by Behrman House, Inc.
235 Watchung AVenue, West Orange, NJ 07052
1–800–221–2755

In memory of
Nancy Louise Grant
1949–1995

Her music departed far too soon
from this world

Contents

TEXTUAL STUDIES

Preface

I began working on the history of medieval and early modern Jewish preaching around 1980, when *Decoding the Rabbis*, the book based on my doctoral dissertation, was completed. During this period, I began to reflect upon my experience in the homiletics courses offered as part of my rabbinical training at the New York school of the Hebrew Union College–Jewish Institute of Religion. It occurred to me that while many referred to the "traditional Jewish sermon," I had never been asked to read one, even in courses intended to teach future rabbis how to prepare and deliver sermons of various kinds. We were never expected to listen to a recording or watch a video-tape of a distinguished preacher, nor asked to undertake a critical evaluation of a sermon delivered at any of the synagogues in New York. In retrospect, it seemed to me that this was like teaching aspiring playwrights to write drama without ever requiring the students to read a play or go to the theater.

Without any clear sense of where the venture might lead, I undertook to find and read sermon texts, including many in manuscript. Largely ignored by modern scholarship, the genre, I came to believe, was a central expression of Jewish literature, an untapped resource for understanding Jewish history, Jewish spirituality, and Jewish thought. My first goal, then, was to make some of the classical texts available to serious students of the Jewish past and to contemporary practitioners of the homiletical art. *Jewish Preaching 1200–1800*, published in 1989, was the result. In that volume, a lengthy introduction reviewed what I had learned about the texts of sermons and the situations in which they were actually delivered. I then presented annotated translations of sermons by sixteen preachers from the High Middle Ages to the beginning of Emancipation.

While *Jewish Preaching* was in process, two important studies and translations of homiletical texts appeared: Hayim Perelmuter's edition of a sixteenth-century "Defense of Preachers" and Henry Sosland's edition of a seventeenth-century Italian "Guide for Preachers." Since then, many related publications have validated my original sense of the subject's significance. In English they include Carmi Horowitz's book on the fourteenth-century preacher Joshua ibn Shu'eib, the collection of essays on Italian Jewish preaching edited by David Ruderman, and Robert Friedenberg's survey of Jewish preaching in America. Significant work by Israeli scholars using sermons for historical investigation has appeared, mostly in Hebrew, occasionally in English. Aviezer

Ravitzky, Shaul Regev, and Dov Schwartz have published Hebrew sermons from manuscripts, and useful indices have been added to more familiar texts.

At the same time, my own investigation of various aspects of Jewish preaching has also continued, resulting in the present collection of studies that further illustrate the use of sermons to probe different aspects of the Jewish past. The material is divided into two categories.

Thematic Studies

The first two chapters focus on the most important occasions for traditional rabbinic preaching. One was the Days of Awe: Rosh Hashanah, Yom Kippur, and the Sabbath between them. The biblical verse *Lift up your voice like a ram's horn* (Isa. 58:1) was frequently used in sermons during the Days of Awe; the ram's horn provides a connection with a Pentateuchal lection for Rosh Hashanah (see Gen. 22:13), and the Isaiah verse is taken from a prophetic lection for Yom Kippur. By exploring the ways in which the analogy between the ram's horn and the preacher was explained, we see how Jewish preachers conceived of their own responsibilities and goals. The second intense period came in the spring with the Sabbath before the holiday of Pesach. My discussion, in chapter two, of the different themes emphasized in preaching for this holiday was originally presented to a conference of the Medieval Sermon Society in Oxford during the summer of 1986.

The following two chapters are concerned with homiletical exegesis of classical Jewish texts. Most investigations of exegetical issues focus exclusively on the commentary, a genre formally dependent upon another text and devoted almost entirely to its interpretation. I argue that sermons must also be recognized as an integral part of the history of Jewish hermeneutics. My examination of typological exegesis, which presents biblical narratives as prototypes of events that would occur later, illustrates the pitfalls of generalizations based solely on commentaries—in this case, the claim that typology, used by Nahmanides, had no impact on subsequent Jewish writers. I show in chapter three that typological interpretation was widely used by Jewish preachers who wanted to demonstrate the relevance of these narratives to present and future.

Decoding the Rabbis studied exegesis of the aggadah—non-legal statements from classical rabbinic literature—as a source for Jewish intellectual history. In that book I used only commentaries on the Midrash and the aggadic passages of the Talmud. Chapter four, "Inscribed for Life or Death?" uses sermons to illustrate the problematics of aggadah, tracing preachers' interpretations of one of the central aggadic dicta pertaining to the Days of Awe. The beginning and end of this piece diverge from usual academic style in their personal and homiletical character—an example of research triggered by a real life situation producing results that transcend its point of origin.

Chapters five and six treat a subject of significant scholarly and personal interest to me: the historical interaction between Christians and Jews. A large literature focuses primarily on polemical texts produced by the two sides. In my reading of sermons and other homiletical texts, however, I began to encounter a different kind of material: the passage in which a preacher, calling his own community to account for their failings, points to the Other as an object lesson worthy of emulation. The chapter based on these passages was originally my contribution to a Festschrift in honor of Professor Krister Stendahl, my own "rebbe" in the subject of Christian-Jewish relations.

The second piece on this subject, in chapter six, begins a series of studies focused on a narrower geographical and chronological framework. It was written for a memorial volume dedicated to Frank Talmage, who devoted his considerable talent and unflagging energy to the academic study of this same subject. In it, I analyze the sermons of Jacob Anatoli, a thirteenth-century Jewish philosopher, whose presentation of Christians and Christianity highlighted aspects of spirituality with parallels in the Jewish community that he was eager to criticize.

One of the most important functions of the sermon was as an instrument for the diffusion of ideas. In an age before printing, the sermon served as a medium through which large numbers of Jews were enabled to discover how new ideas could be incorporated within the framework of their tradition. In a study originally presented to an Israel Historical Society conference on Elite and Popular Cultures, published here in chapter seven for the first time in English, I investigate the evidence in Spanish sermons from the last generation before the Expulsion for the spread of philosophical ideas and philosophical modes of reasoning in discourse intended for broad circles of Jewish society.

Italy was one of the great centers of Jewish preaching in the late sixteenth and early seventeenth century. When my colleague David Ruderman organized a series of lectures at Yale on the Italian Jewish pulpit in its diversity, he asked me to give an introductory survey of the field. The result, in chapter eight, is intended not as a complete bibliographic review of this rich literature, but rather as an overview of some of its central conceptual issues, leading toward an appreciation of both the challenges and the rewards of studying carefully the works of Italian Jewish preachers.

I first came across the sermons of Saul Levi Morteira, rabbi in the Portuguese community of Amsterdam from ca. 1619 until his death in 1660, quite by accident. The Warsaw 1912 edition of *Giv'at Sha'ul* was one of the books that had belonged to my great-grandfather, Rabbi Hyman Lasker of Troy, New York. When I found this volume and began reading Morteira's printed sermons, I sensed that this was the work of a master preacher. The sermon I included in *Jewish Preaching*, "The People's Envy," is one of my favorites in the entire literature. Chapter nine, a study of the artistic craftsmanship of the sermons in *Giv'at Sha'ul*, was my first published effort to present these texts as literature. Considerable subsequent work on Morteira, including extensive analysis of hundreds of manuscript sermons recently discovered (see below), has served to confirm the conclusions reached in this piece.

In addition to their function as mediators of a tradition, preachers are also frequently cast in the role of social critics, responsible for exposing the failures of a community when judged by its own standards. What are the shortcomings for which preachers criticize their congregations, and how reliable are these criticisms as evidence for the social and religious realities of a Jewish community? These are questions I addressed in a conference at Harvard devoted to a reassessment of Jacob Katz's classic *Tradition and Crisis*. In chapter ten, I take as a test case the community of Prague in the second half of the eighteenth century, one of the outstanding centers of Jewish homiletical activity at the time, analyzing the sermons for their evidence of a traditional community in crisis.

From the same period, I look at a different issue: the relationship of Jews in central Europe to their national governments. A new genre of Jewish sermon appears in the middle of the eighteenth century: the occasional sermon generated by an event not in the Jewish community but in the political life of the nation state in which Jews are living. In chapter eleven, originally an address delivered at the Leo Baeck Institute in New York, I argue that by analyzing such sermons preached between the start of the Seven Years' War and the Congress of Vienna, we can find evidence of a developing sense of patriotic identification with the state even before the Emancipation changed the legal status of the Jews.

Textual Studies

The second part of this book continues my project, begun in *Jewish Preaching*, of making accessible translations of little known but significant examples of Jewish homiletical art. Although I attempted to provide ample annotation for the texts presented in *Jewish Preaching*, the format of that book did not allow for a complete discussion of matters raised by the sermons included. Here I have used the individual homiletical work as a way of exploring a full panoply of issues relating to historical context and genre. Most of these texts are my own discoveries. All but the last are manuscripts that have never before been discussed in scholarly literature. The final one is listed in bibliographies, but has never been analyzed. They are all published for the first time with my annotated translation accompanying the Hebrew original.

When *Jewish Preaching* appeared, I still believed that the earliest theoretical discussion of Jewish homiletics was Joseph ibn Shem Tov's "'Ein ha-Qore" from the middle of the fifteenth century, and I included several passages from this as yet unprinted work. During the summer of 1993, Ari Ackerman of the Hebrew University called my attention to Moscow Hebrew Manuscript 926, one sermon from which was the basis of his M.A. thesis. In addition to numerous philosophical sermons, this manuscript contains an unexpected gem: a short anonymous text written as a "Guide for Preachers," similar to dozens of contemporary Christian *artes praedicandi* but, as far as we know, unique in medieval Jewish literature (chapter twelve). I date it to the early part of the fifteenth century. The conventional nature of its content makes it especially valuable as an expression of medieval Jewish attitudes toward the art of preaching.

The following year, Avraham David of the Institute for Microfilmed Hebrew Manuscripts in Jerusalem informed me that a new microfilm of a manuscript of sermons in the St. Petersburg Library had just arrived. This turned out to be related to the Moscow manuscript mentioned above, with several sermons in common. One sermon not known from any other text, however, was delivered to a voluntary association of Jews (*hevrah*, or confraternity) committed to special devotion in the areas of prayer and study, probably at Saragossa in the early fifteenth century (chapter thirteen). This is a fine example of a sermon discussing halakhic or legal material—in this case the vow—in a moderate philosophical manner. The texts in this manuscript are clearly transcriptions of sermons delivered on specific occasions; their existence requires a modification of my assertion, made in *Jewish Preaching*, that the earliest such texts date from the middle of the fifteenth century.

Two sermons, appearing in chapters fourteen and fifteen, come from the fateful generation of the expulsion from Spain. I published the first, on the "Binding of Isaac," in a Festschrift for one of my teachers at the Hebrew University, Professor Haim Beinart. This sermon raises significant historical issues about martyrdom. Most striking is an otherwise unknown quotation attrib-

Your Voice Like a Ram's Horn

uted to Rabbi Hasdai Crescas stating that those who are unwilling to die as martyrs and offer their own children as sacrifices like Isaac are not from the "seed of Abraham." This is particularly poignant because Crescas's own son perished in Barcelona during the riots of 1391. His extreme position seems to be part of an ongoing Jewish debate over whether the Binding of Isaac was a unique event or a paradigm worthy of ongoing emulation.

The importance of the second sermon lies primarily in the realm of Jewish religious thought. Written for the Sabbath between Rosh Hashanah and Yom Kippur by one of the leading halakhic authorities of the generation, Rabbi Isaac Aboab, it is devoted to the theme of repentance. This central Jewish doctrine was apparently under attack by philosophers at this time, and Aboab explores several pertinent problems at length. The sermon is notable for its form—the use of the scholastic "disputed question" as an integral component of Jewish homiletics—and for its content, including strong social criticism and the unexpected use of Kabbalistic material.

The most exciting development since the publication of *Jewish Preaching* has been the discovery of the manuscript sermons of Saul Levi Morteira of Amsterdam. While *Jewish Preaching* was in press, Yosef Kaplan of the Hebrew University informed me that microfilms of Morteira's sermons had recently reached the Institute for Microfilmed Hebrew Manuscripts in Jerusalem. The manuscripts, located in the Rabbinical Seminary in Budapest, had not been known to outside scholars, never having been described in any bibliography or catalogue. I worked on the microfilms during the first half of 1989, when I was privileged to be a fellow of the Institute for Advanced Studies at the Hebrew University, and made a quick trip to Budapest to consult the actual volumes.

Altogether, there are some 1,150 folio pages (counting both sides of the page as one) written by Morteira himself. Totalling about 550 different sermons, it is the largest extant repository of Jewish homiletical art from any preacher before the nineteenth century. I hope to devote a separate monographic study to this material, and also to participate in a joint project of multivolume publication. Here, in chapters sixteen and seventeen, I have included the texts of three of the most important historical sermons I discovered in this treasury: two eulogies delivered by Morteira near the beginning of his career for the noted former New Christian physician Dr. David Farar, and the eulogy delivered in 1657 for his brilliant younger colleague, Rabbi Menasseh ben Israel.

The final text, in chapter eighteen, is also a eulogy delivered by the leading rabbi of a major Jewish community, in this case Ezekiel Landau of Prague. The text is an example of what librarians call "ephemera": it was printed rapidly (actually in three different versions) within a few months of delivery as a pamphlet that was read and later discarded. The person being eulogized is a non-Jew, the Empress Maria Theresa, and the text presents the apparent paradox of a rabbi lavish in his praises of a monarch whose policies and personal style made her known as one of the most antisemitic rulers of the age. It thereby provides a test case for some of the issues of developing Jewish patriotism explored in chapter eleven.

Several underlying principles characterize my approach to the history of Jewish preaching in these studies. The starting point is the text of the individual sermon. There can be no substitute for the painstaking effort to identify those texts, whether in manuscript or in print, that reflect the core preaching event: the oral communication, usually within the context of a public religious ceremony, in which a speaker expounds the meaning of classical Jewish texts in a manner intended to address the intellectual or spiritual needs of the listeners. The attempt to locate, identify, and present such texts in accordance with the standards of modern scholarship has been a major preoccupation of my research.

The present book reveals three ways in which I try to situate these texts within a broader framework. The first is the immediate context: What was the situation in which the preacher and the listeners came to the sermon? What were the problems being addressed? What resonance would allusions within the sermon have had for a contemporary audience that may well be lost on us? Second is the broader contemporary context: How does this text relate to issues and concerns expressed in other sermons by the same preacher, or by other preachers—Jewish or Christian—in the same community or the same region, at roughly the same time? Third is the diachronic element: How does this text fit into the centuries-old tradition of Jewish preaching? What elements of the sermon are conventions and topoi? And where is the preacher consciously modifying, or departing from, such conventions? The studies in Part One focus more on the second and third dimensions; those in Part Two, more on the first. But all of these questions must inform any responsible analysis.

In preparing for this new collection studies that have already appeared in print, I have resisted the temptation to indulge in substantial rewriting. Changes have been introduced into the main text only as they were necessary to avoid repetition, incorporate cross-references to other chapters in the book, and modify statements that subsequent research has shown to be inaccurate. I have imposed a common format on all footnotes, added references to more recent scholarly literature, and cited English translations of books that were at the time of original writing available only in Hebrew.

Israel Bettan's path-breaking *Studies in Jewish Preaching: The Middle Ages* was published by the Hebrew Union College Press in 1939. For almost fifty years, this remained the only book on an otherwise empty shelf of literature in English on the Jewish sermon and those who delivered it. I will be gratified if my own studies—though quite different in methodology and approach—stand next to his as a resource for those who would learn and for those who will continue to map this still largely uncharted territory.

Serious research is stymied without access to materials. By far the most important resource for any scholar working on Hebrew manuscripts is the Institute for Microfilmed Hebrew Manuscripts in the National Library of Jerusalem. Avraham David and Benjamin Richler of the Institute have been consistently helpful to me over the years, in ways ranging from informing me about new manuscript discoveries of sermon texts to helping decipher an apparently illegible passage. I have consulted manuscripts in the libraries of Oxford and Cambridge Universities, the British Library, Harvard's Houghton Library, and the Jewish Theological Seminary of America. I spent a particularly exhilarating and fruitful week at the Rabbinical Seminary of Budapest working on the massive manuscripts of Morteira's sermons, and I am deeply grateful to Rabbi Jozsef Schweizer, Director of the Seminary, for giving me access to the manuscripts and permission to publish selections from them. Washington University's Olin Library has been my base for general research, and Harvard's Widener Library has continued to provide me with the opportunity to consult more specialized Hebrew texts. Final details were rechecked at the Library of the Center for Judaic Studies at the University of Pennsylvania.

I have used microfilms of the Hebrew text of Ezekiel Landau's Eulogy for Maria Theresa from the British Library and the National Library in Jerusalem, and of German and Judeo-German texts from the Klau Library of the Hebrew Union College-Jewish Institute of Religion in Cincinnati.

Several of the chapters in this book grew out of research during a sabbatical stay at the Hebrew University's Institute for Advanced Studies as part of a team of scholars, organized by Moshe Idel, working on various aspects of biblical exegesis. My gratitude to this Institute for the opportunity to spend six months in Jerusalem in an ideal working environment, stimulated by outstanding colleagues, is deep and enduring. The Research Fund attached to the Gloria M. Goldstein Chair of Jewish History and Thought at Washington University has supported further visits to Israel and led to new discoveries described herein.

The Newsletter of the Medieval Sermon Society continues to be an invaluable resource for bibliography on medieval Christian preaching, and two conferences of this Society that I have attended provided an opportunity for fruitful exchange of a comparative nature.

A number of Amercan colleagues were helpful in preparing for initial publication articles later incorporated into this book. They include Steven Schwarzschild *z"l* (chapter 3), David Ruderman (chapter 8), Alan Mintz (chapter 9), and Bernard Cooperman (chapter 10). Joseph Davis was extremely helpful in reviewing my annotation of manuscript material, especially for the sermon of Isaac Aboab. I have also benefited from the opportunity to discuss various aspects of my work with colleagues in Washington University's History Department and Program for Jewish and Near Eastern Studies, including Solon Beinfeld, Nancy Berg, James Diamond, Pinchas Giller, Tom Head, and Joseph Schraibman. I am grateful to Yom Tov Assis, Reuven Bonfil, Joseph Dan, Lois Dubin, Gad Freudenthal, Moshe Idel, Paul Mandel, Steven McMichael, Dov Noy, Shaul Regev, H. P. Salomon, Dov Schwartz, and Isadore Twersky, all of whom helped on specific issues of interpretation.

Aileen Rabushka patiently prepared some of the material in a word processing format appropriate for publication. Dafna Lautmann and Hannah Hashkes typed Hebrew texts by Morteira and Landau with efficiency and precision.

At the Hebrew Union College Press, Michael Meyer, Chair of the Publications Committee, provided encouragement and guidance at all stages of the process that transformed an idea into the book at hand. Barbara Selya's fine sense of style and meticulous attention to detail helped improve even material that had appeared in print before. Kelby Bowers supervised with professional expertise the technical preparation and layout of Hebrew material.

My wife Roberta and our daughters Sara and Adina have remained tolerant of the countless hours I have spent trying to make sense out of manuscripts containing words spoken from distant pulpits centuries ago. Without their consistent support and enthusiasm for my work this project would have been considerably more burdensome.

Just before receiving page proofs of this book, I learned of the death from cancer of Nancy Grant. A cherished colleague in the History Department of Washington University specializing in African-American history, she was also a superb violinist; we spent many special hours together recreating the wonders of violin-piano music. This book is dedicated to her memory.

1

"Your Voice Like a Ram's Horn": Conceptions of Jewish Preaching

Of the various ways in which the Hebrew Bible helped to mold traditional Jewish literature, not the least significant was its impact as an unending inspiration for Jewish preaching. It was an established tradition for Jewish sermons to begin with a biblical verse, and much of their texture was exegetical. Whether the center of gravity was a theological problem, a historical event, or a tension point in the society, the discussion generally flowed from the interpretation of some passage in the Bible.

Furthermore, particular verses recurring frequently throughout the homiletical literature signaled central issues relevant to the preachers' self-conception and their understanding of the problems they faced. For example, the mocking barb of the Hebrew slave to Moses—*Who made you chief and ruler over us?* (Exod. 2:14)—regularly appears to express the resistance encountered by those who used their sermons to criticize imperfections in Jewish behavior. No other words could articulate so succinctly the ambiguous nature of the preacher's authority and the hostility often generated in listeners who were not reticent in challenging a preacher's right to tell them how they should live.

Perhaps the verse most extensively used to express the preachers' view of their own vocation was Isaiah 58:1: *Cry aloud, do not hold back, raise your voice like a shofar, declare to My people their transgression, and the house of Jacob their sin.* That such a verse was used for this purpose is in itself significant. Jewish preaching was not generally deemed to be a continuation of prophecy. Whatever claims to authority Jewish preachers could make, and this was by no means a simple issue, they rarely claimed direct divine inspi-

Originally appeared in *Conservative Judaism* 38 (1985): 83–90. Reprinted with permission of *Conservative Judaism*, copyright 1985, by the Rabbinical Assembly. Published by the Rabbinical Assembly and the Jewish Theological Seminary of America.

ration or asserted that they were uttering the word of God.[1] The preacher played many roles—educator and entertainer, articulator of the people's hopes and fears, defender of the tradition and purveyor of novel insights, representative of the establishment and critic of the status quo—but the congregation did not ordinarily look for the mantle of prophecy in the pulpit.

Yet especially in the preaching of ethical and religious rebuke, which peaked during the forty-day period ending with Yom Kippur, this verse seemed particularly appropriate to the preachers' task, expressing at least an implicit claim that they were continuing what the Prophets had done, and that God's instruction to the Prophet defined their own role. Further, beyond this assertion of continuity with the biblical tradition, the verse, and especially the comparison with the shofar, functioned to provide guidance on virtually the entire range of problems that the preacher confronted.[2] The following sources, exploring the various connections between the shofar and Jewish preaching, have been selected not from biblical commentaries, which might indeed be speaking about the Prophet in ancient times, but from preaching manuals, homiletical treatises, and the actual texts of sermons, in which the identification with contemporary preaching is explicit.

One lesson drawn from the comparison with the shofar applied to the occasion for preaching: Ephraim Luntshitz, one of the giants of the Polish homiletical tradition, noted that the series of verses in Isaiah beginning with the preaching mandate ended with the phrase, *Refrain from trampling the Sabbath* (Isa. 58:13). Putting the two together, he concluded that the opening verse taught that preaching was particularly appropriate "on the Sabbath

---

1. Contrast the Christian claim of divine inspiration in preaching, as in Grasso, pp. 33–34. This was viewed as a distinctive aspect of Christian preaching by Abravanel in his comment on Zechariah 13:2 (Abravanel, *Prophets* 3:241b).

2. The importance of this image has been noted by Mendel Piekarz in his seminal work *Bi-Ymei Tsemihat ha-Hasidut*, pp. 116–20. Furthermore, between the original publication of the article and the present book, there appeared Piekarz, *Ide'ologiyah,* the fifth chapter of which, entitled *Ha-Adam ki-Keli Bi-Ydei ha-Elohim* ("Man as an Implement in God's Hands"), contains an extensive discussion of the shofar (and other implements such as the organ, hammer, axe) as an image for the human being's proper relationship to God in the religious life in general, with material pertaining specifically to preachers. Piekarz's sources are drawn from eighteenth-century eastern Europe; I have expanded his treatment through earlier sources and eighteenth-century texts from central Europe, especially Prague.

Christian preachers did occasionally use this verse, but the Vulgate translation of the simile did not have the resonance for them that the Hebrew word "shofar" had. See Philip of Harveng, "On the Training of the Clergy," VI:20, in *Medieval Rhetoric*, pp. 219–21, and Michel Menot, sermon in Petry, pp. 301–8.

day, when the shofar is not sounded." This refers both to the Sabbath preceding Rosh Hashanah, and to Rosh Hashanah itself when it occurs on the Sabbath. In both cases, the shofar would not be heard, and "the voice [of the preacher] should take the place of the shofar."[3]

In the eighteenth century, Ezekiel Landau, chief rabbi of Prague, applied the verse to the sermon to be delivered each Rosh Hashanah, whether or not it came on the Sabbath: "From the first day of Rosh Hashanah, when the blast of the shofar is heard in the city and the people tremble in awe at the Day of Judgment, then you too must raise your voice." A contemporary argued that the preacher must not make the mistake of assuming that a sermon on one day of the holiday would suffice: "Just as the shofar must be blown on both the first and second day of Rosh Hashanah, so you must preach words of ethical instruction on both days."[4]

This presumes a particular conception of the primary purpose of preaching. At least at this time of the year, the sermon was to be not essentially an appeal to the intellect, but rather a fervent rebuke and a call to repentance. The connection was made by Joseph ibn Shem Tov, whose manual on preaching written in the middle of the fifteenth century in Spain, an early Jewish *ars praedicandi,* is partly structured on the pattern of Isaiah 58:1. "The purpose in the sounding of the shofar is to make the hearts of sinners quake. The Prophet said, *If the shofar is sounded in the city, will the people not tremble?* (Amos 3:6), showing clearly that its effect is to instill fear. . . . So the sermon should be such that it instills fear and awakens the hearts of sinners so that they will return to God and be forgiven."[5]

Again in late eighteenth-century Prague, the point was expanded, this time by Eliezer Fleckeles. He based his point upon a halakhic ruling, attributed to the Jerusalem Talmud by Asher ben Yehiel and Nissim Gerundi: One who blows through the wide end of the shofar has not fulfilled the obligation, for the verse says, *"From the narrow straits (min ha-meitsar) I called unto God"* (Ps. 118:5). Playing upon a series of Hebrew words linked with the root *tsar* and bearing the cluster of meanings "narrow, anxiety, enemy, oppression," Fleckeles insisted that the preacher must "raise his voice from the narrow straits . . . not with weak homilies that broaden the mind, but following the model of the shofar . . . the preacher must publicly declare the

---

3. Luntshitz, *'Olelot,* II,27,180; II,31,210; II,32,219.

4. Landau, *Derushei,* p. 29b. *'Ir Damasek Eliezer,* quoted in Piekarz, *Bi-Ymei,* p. 166.

5. " '*Ein ha-Qore,*" fol. 14v; see Saperstein, *Jewish Preaching,* p. 387.

sins and transgressions of evil people."[6] It was a time when the sermon should produce anxiety and distress.

The comparison with the shofar was also used to illustrate the proper technique of preaching. Jewish preachers frequently complained about the heterogeneous nature of their audience, ranging from noted Talmudic scholars to Jews capable of little more than mechanical reading of Hebrew. This made the task of pleasing everyone an impossible challenge. Joseph ibn Shem Tov, addressing this problem through the Isaiah verse, noted that the two primary sounds of the shofar were *teqi'ah,* "a simple, straightforward sound," and *teru'ah,* "wavering and staccato." The third sound, named by the sages *shevarim,* is a combination or composite of the other two. These three sounds, we are told, represent three kinds of sermons, depending on the nature of the audience.

If the congregation consists of ordinary Jews, the preacher should speak about simple matters, so that the audience will understand and the benefit he hopes for will be received. This corresponds to the *teqi'ah,* a simple sound. If there are learned and knowledgeable people there, he should speak of profound and original matters, not straightforward truths that are known to all. This corresponds to the *teqi'ah,* a complex sound. If both categories are present together, his speech should be composed of both kinds of material, corresponding to the *shever,* intermediate between *teqi'ah* and *teru'ah.* He may divide his sermon into separate parts appropriate for each group, or he may give one unified sermon appropriate for everyone.[7]

Three centuries later, Zerah Eidlitz, one of the leading preachers of Prague, used the various sounds of the shofar to address a different issue, relating not to the discourse of instruction but to the sermon of ethical and religious rebuke. According to the Talmud (B. RH 33b–34a), the shofar must first issue a simple sound, then a sound of groaning, then a sound of wailing, and finally a simple sound again. "So the sermon of ethical rebuke should begin with simple thoughts. Then the preacher may say things that break the heart, such that all who hear them will sigh and groan, and then he may say things that impel people to weep. But he should conclude with a thought that is positive and straightforward."[8] Rather than using the sounds to designate different kinds of sermons, Eidlitz employed the halakhic progression to indicate the structure of a single sermonic call to repentance.

6. Fleckeles, *'Olat,* p. 7a–b. Cf. R. Asher on M. RH 3,4 (end), and R. Nissim on Alfasi, Rosh ha-Shanah, p. 6b.

7. "'Ein ha-Qore," fol. 15r–v; *Jewish Preaching,* pp. 388–89.

8. Eidlitz, p. 17b; cf. Alsheikh, *Mar'ot* on Isaiah 58:1, p. 60b.

A contemporary of Eidlitz, Issachar Bloch, derived from the technique of blowing the shofar a lesson for effective preaching. Everyone knows that "if a person immediately begins to blow into the shofar with all his strength, he will find it difficult to complete his task." The expert begins to blow as if in a whisper, letting the air enter the shofar gently, and then he gradually increases his effort until at the end he is at full strength. This should be the technique for the sermon of rebuke.

> If the preacher begins in full force at the outset, saying "*Hear now you rebels* (Num. 20:10), you have done this and that," his rebuke will not be sustained. He should rather begin quietly, saying, "My brothers and friends, let us return to God. Put away your evil doings." Later, in the middle of the sermon, he may specify the ways in which they have acted faithlessly with God. This is the meaning of the verse, *Raise your voice like a shofar:* lift it step by step. Then afterward, *Tell My people their sin* (Isa. 58:1), not immediately at the beginning.[9]

The problem of how to criticize religious shortcomings without merely arousing hostility and anger weighed heavily on the minds of many Jewish preachers. Here is a call to approach the task of criticism with sensitivity and tact and an awareness of how listeners might react to what is said.

Others used the shofar analogy to make a point about the qualifications of the preacher. The simplest interpretation of the phrase *Raise your voice like a shofar* is that it refers to the preacher's voice. Thus, Judah Messer Leon, author of a well-known treatise on rhetoric, took the verse to mean "that the voice, when expressing reproof, should be loud."[10] A more subtle explanation was suggested by Eliezer Fleckeles of Prague. He contrasted the simile "like a shofar" with other possibilities, such as "like a harp." Had a more beautiful-sounding instrument been mentioned, the implication might have been that only those blessed with a pleasing, resonant voice are entitled to preach. Instead the verse teaches that the quality of voice is unimportant; only the content of what is said has significance to God.[11]

One frequently discussed issue dealt with the dynamics of a preacher criticizing fellow Jews for their imperfections. If he was a man of unquestioned piety, his message might be dismissed as holding up an impossible standard for the community. If his own spiritual achievements were not obviously outstanding, listeners were quick to question by what right he came to censure them. Expressions by preachers of their own sense of unworthiness are

---

9. Bloch, p. 4d; cf. Benjamin ben Elhanan, p. 26d, and Piekarz, *Bi-Ymei,* p. 116 at n. 71.
10. Judah Messer Leon, *Nofet Tsufim,* in Rabinowitz, pp. 128–29.
11. Fleckeles, *'Olat .*

not always conventional commonplaces; sometimes they express the genuine anguish of a sensitive personality in an ambiguous position. One eighteenth-century preacher turned to the shofar for guidance on this issue: just as the shofar, the horn of a lowly beast, summons Jews to repentance, so the preacher should not refrain from his task because he considers himself unworthy. Humble implements can bring about great results.[12] On the other hand, the shofar is something more than just an animal horn; it may not be used until properly scoured and cleansed. So the preacher must look to his own conduct and cleanse himself of sin before rebuking others.[13]

Another recurrent theme was the social status of the preacher and his position vis-à-vis the powerful figures of the community whom he was sometimes called upon to rebuke. This was frequently addressed in the works of Ephraim Luntshitz. "The form and shape of the shofar is intended to apply to the sermon of rebuke, providing guidance for those who deliver it. We learn this from the words of Isaiah, *Raise your voice like a shofar, and tell My people their sin.*"[14]

Luntshitz then proceeded to apply the halakhic requirements for the shofar to the personality and position of the preacher. The first is humility. "Just as the shofar must be bent, so one who rebukes another must speak with a heart that is bent, broken, and contrite. He must not be one of the deceitful, who speak high-sounding words and preach for their own glory, borne aloft by their own hot air, with ambitions for power." Such men, concerned more with their own reputation than with the efficacy of their message, are to be abhorred.

But humility should not be identified with a lack of the courage to say what needs to be said. The shofar also reminds us that the preacher must be "strong enough to prevail over the high-handed. . . . He must not fear anyone, nor be obsequious toward the wicked, no matter how powerful they may be. For this reason, the shofar may not be decorated with different colors, for that would symbolize a hypocritical sycophant," who says whatever he thinks the listeners want to hear.

The preacher who is obsequious toward the wealthy overlooks their manifest imperfections because he is secretly envious, fully aware of the pleasure money can bring. Luntshitz turns to this point with a different halakhic statement: "The sages said that when a shofar is plated with gold, if its sound changes it is disqualified from use (B. RH 27b). So with the preacher: be-

---

12. Elijah ben Moses, p. 101b; cf. Benjamin ben Elhanan, p. 26b.
13. Elijah ben Moses, p. 101b; cf. Piekarz, *Bi-Ymei*, pp. 116–17.
14. Luntshitz, *'Olelot*, II,31,210–11; see the full passage in *Jewish Preaching*, pp. 403–5.

cause they plated him with gold, his voice changed, and he tells the wicked that they are righteous." Such a person clearly fails to fulfill his task.

The challenge of originality was yet another crux for those who delivered sermons. No one addressing a congregation week after week could hope to be consistently both novel and cogent. Many preachers were therefore conscious of facing a difficult dilemma. If they used the best interpretations of biblical verses and rabbinic statements in the traditional literature or in the published sermons of others, they could be criticized by knowledgeable members of the audience, who felt that listening to familiar material was a waste of time. But if the preachers constantly sought to present original interpretations, they were in danger of being criticized for excessive ingenuity and for straying from any plausible meaning of the texts.

Luntshitz criticized both extremes, but in the present passage he is more disturbed by the plagiarists.

> If fragments of different shofars are glued together so that it may be sounded, it is disqualified (B. RH 27a). This teaches us about the preacher who does not cite the source for the material he uses, wrapping himself in someone else's prayershawl. All that he says is stolen, fragments broken off from various compositions, a little from here and a little from there, as if this made a complete discourse.

Merely collecting material from what others have written is not enough to produce a true sermon.

Whereas Luntshitz treated the general problem of the preacher facing the wealthy and the powerful, eighteenth-century figures addressed the specific problem of itinerant preachers who delivered sermons in return for a fee. Some argued that since anyone who accepted such payments must obviously be insincere, the message of such preachers was unworthy of serious consideration. The itinerant *maggidim* vehemently defended themselves against such charges.

Zerah Eidlitz, further developing the ideas of Luntshitz, once again drew guidance from the rabbinic laws governing the shofar.

> The rabbis said, "A shofar plated with gold in the place where the mouth is set is unfit. If plated on the inside, it is unfit; if on the outside, it is unfit if its sound is changed from what it was, but if its sound is unchanged, it is fit" (B. RH 27b). Now we find that the Bible compares the preacher to a shofar, saying *raise your voice like a shofar*. Thus a shofar "plated in the place where the mouth is set" means that the preacher sets his mouth because they give him money. Such a man is unfit to preach a sermon of rebuke.

Similarly, "plated on the inside" means that inwardly the preacher cares only about the money, and has no religious concerns. He too is unfit. "Plated on the outside" refers to one who is inwardly pure, unconcerned about money, but who accepts money for another reason—because he has no other source of sustenance and is like a poor man wandering from place to place. Of such a person it says, "If its sound is changed from what it was," meaning that because of this he refrains from rebuking those who pay him lest they become angry at him, he too is unfit, for he should trust in the Lord and cast his burden upon God, who will provide for his need. But "if his sound does not change," he is fit.[15]

The precarious position of an impecunious preacher standing before the powerful and criticizing their behavior led in the eighteenth century to the development of a doctrine of preaching not usually identified with the Jewish context. Scholars have recently analyzed the emergence within certain Hasidic circles of an ideology of quietism, emphasizing the total passivity of the human being, whose individuality all but disappears as he becomes little more than a vessel of God. The metaphor of the shofar was used to express this passivity in ordinary speech: "*Raise your voice like a shofar,* that is to say, just as the sound of the shofar issues from the person who blows it and not from the shofar itself, so a person should see to it that the speech issuing from him is no more than the sound of the shofar, and that it is of the Holy One, blessed be He." But the metaphor also applied to the preacher: "Just as the shofar does not exult in the sound that comes from it no matter how fine and pleasant it may be, so the preacher and the one who raises his voice to preach ethical rebuke does not at all exult [in his eloquence]."[16]

Paradoxically, the doctrine of quietism could be transformed into a justification for an activist preaching of social criticism. If the preacher is no more than the passive instrument of God's word, he could, at least in theory, criticize the conduct of the most powerful without fear for his own popularity or well-being. This doctrine is expressed as follows by Eidlitz:

One who preaches rebuke out of pure motivation must think that the sermon is not his at all, but that he is as dead as a trampled corpse, and that whatever

15. Eidlitz, pp. 27b–c; see *Jewish Preaching,* pp. 423–24.

16. Joseph Weiss, "Via Passiva in Early Hasidism," in Weiss, *Studies,* pp. 72–73, material emanating from the circle of the Maggid of Mezritsch. This imagery is similar to that used by Christian preachers, such as Vicente Ferrer: "When a musician plays a horn, to which does the melody belong, to the horn or to the musician? Surely to the musician. So with a good preacher, who lives a good life: he is the instrument, but Jesus Christ is the musician who inflames the will to love, the intellect to discern, the memory to recall." Grasso, pp. 33–34.

he says comes from God. If so, there is no reason why he should hold back on his ethical instruction, or fear any person. He is just like a shofar: something comes in one end and goes out the other.

So God places in his heart the words of ethical instruction that he will speak, and each word burns fiercely within, impelling him to utter them. . . . If, on the other hand, he thought that he spoke his own mind, giving of his own knowledge and wisdom, he would refrain from speaking critically when he feared someone. This is the meaning of Cry *aloud* (Isa. 58:1). . . . The heart is like a shofar: What goes in comes out. So with all who speak: What God puts in your heart, you are compelled to utter aloud.

Attributing the content of his speech entirely to divine inspiration, the preacher is able to disclaim responsibility for what he says and protect himself against the wrath of the powerful, even as his words continue to denounce the imperfections of Jewish life.[17]

We began with a biblical verse addressed to a Prophet, which Jewish preachers seized upon as an essential description of their own role. The biblical image of the shofar, fraught with associations particularly powerful during the period surrounding Rosh Hashanah, was explored by these men in all its implications, leading them beyond the Bible to talmudic material, some of a rather technical halakhic nature, homiletically interpreted to apply to themselves. What we find is a self-conscious effort to delineate the challenges and pitfalls of Jewish preaching by leaders who were prepared to criticize not only their audiences, but also those colleagues who failed to measure up to the standards implied by God's charge.

---

17. Schatz Uffenheimer, pp. 198–99. Piekarz, *Bi-Ymei,* p. 117, warns against pressing such a passage too far as evidence for a kind of social activism. However, it should be noted that this passage appears to have been adumbrated in a 1745 sermon by Jonathan Eybeschuetz (Eybeschuetz, 1:80d), where the message is clearly that the preacher should not fear punishment in criticizing the sins of the people. Piekarz, *Ide'ologiyah,* p. 83, cites this passage to argue that the conception is not necessarily bound up with mystical quietism.

2

Preaching for Pesach

No less than today, the unique rhythm of the holiday calendar provided special challenges and opportunities for medieval Jewish preachers. The autumn, with its rapid procession of holy days, festivals, and intermediate Sabbaths, taxed the energies and ingenuity of the most dedicated *darshan* (and undoubtedly the patience of many congregants). After this, the preacher could settle into a more leisurely schedule of a weekly sermon on the Sabbath, until the tempo picked up once again in the spring with the approach of Pesach.

The Sabbath preceding this holiday, called *Shabbat ha-Gadol,* was one of the most important preaching occasions of the entire year. In many communities, particularly in northern and eastern Europe, the rabbi was obliged to preach only on this Sabbath and on the Sabbath between Rosh Hashanah and Yom Kippur, while men of lesser stature (though often of greater homiletical ability) assumed the responsibilities of the pulpit for the rest of the year.

Among the explanations for the honorific name *Shabbat ha-Gadol* was the fact that all rabbis, whether or not they were accustomed to preach regularly during the rest of the year, ascended the pulpit on this day. Indeed, it was considered to be an obligation not only for rabbis to preach, but for the entire congregation to attend the service and listen. As one fourteenth-century preacher put it, "All Jews are required to gather in synagogues and houses of study on this day called *Shabbat ha-Gadol . . .* to hear words of Torah, as they did in the Rabbinic period . . .; even women and even small children are to come." [1]

Originally appeared in *Journal of Reform Judaism* 34 (1987): 25–36. Reprinted with permission from *Journal of Reform Judaism,* copyright 1987, by the Central Conference of American Rabbis.

1. Anonymous, "Disciple of R. Asher," fol. 92r; cf. Ibn Shu'eib, *Derashot* (1583), p. 38a, Ibn Shu'eib, *Derashot* (1992), 1:204. Another explanation was that this Sabbath was called "great" because the sermons delivered on it were longer than usual; the Italian preacher Azariah Figo continued, "Therefore, my lords, if these words of mine go beyond the measure of my accustomed brevity, let it not be burdensome to you" (Figo, Sermon 23, p. 68a).

In addition to *Shabbat ha-Gadol,* the first and eighth days of Pesach were regular preaching occasions, while the second and seventh days and the intermediate Sabbath might have their sermons as well. Although the subject matter was somewhat more restricted than in the great holidays of the fall, there was still ample opportunity for variety and innovation. At least four different categories of material appear in these sermons: legal discussions associated with the commandments pertaining to the holiday, exegeses of traditional texts, analyses of philosophical problems, and responses to contemporary historical events.

Legal Discussions

Throughout the centuries, a predominant subject for the Pesach sermons, particularly the sermon for *Shabbat ha-Gadol,* was the laws relating to the festival. Because of the rather complicated nature of these laws, many rabbis felt the need to remind their congregants year after year what they were expected to do. This material, often repetitious and somewhat routine, was not always recorded in the written versions of sermon texts. In one manuscript of a sermon that the thirteenth-century philosopher Jacob Anatoli identified as suitable for *Shabbat ha-Gadol* or the first day of Pesach, we find the remark, "Here is a place where one may preach about the laws of leavened and unleavened bread and their ramifications. At the end, one should say that all this comes to remind us of the marvelous redemption that follows after harsh service."[2] On the other hand, the practical legal conclusions might be all that a disciple felt impelled to record from the sermons of his mentor.[3]

Preaching about the rules for proper observance of the festival could indeed be carried to excess. One early fifteenth-century rabbi from Saragossa was lampooned with the charge that "on *Shabbat ha-Gadol* he would ascend the pulpit and preach for six hours on the laws of *ḥaroset* and parsley."[4] But if not often on a very high artistic level, these sermons were an important educational tool, explaining what was not fully understood or reminding of what might otherwise have been forgotten from year to year.

In addition to its pedagogical purpose, the Pesach sermon frequently had

---

2. Anatoli MS, fol. 83c.

3. See, for example, the report by a disciple of the Shabbat ha-Gadol sermon delivered by Rabbi Jacob Weil in 1432; Spitzer, *Derashot,* esp. pp. 24–30. Some of the earliest extant Jewish sermons from Europe are primarily legal in content; cf. Hurvitz, "RABaD," pp. 34–42.

4. Schirmann, "Pulmus," p. 19.

a hortatory function. The Polish moralist Ephraim Luntshitz explained the need for repeated emphasis on even the most basic observances:

> This supports the custom of the rabbinical scholars in our own age to preach publicly each year on *Shabbat ha-Gadol* about the laws of Pesach. [They include in their sermons] simple rules that have become widespread customs among the masses, known to all. Most will also preach about the same laws they have discussed on many previous years. Some may wonder about this, thinking that there is no need for such repetition. However, since most of the laws of Pesach involve an expenditure of money—for example, purchasing new utensils and getting rid of all kinds of leaven, and on Pesach itself there are considerable additional expenses such as buying wines and grains, and other expenses as well—we have to worry that people will become confused.[5]

Here is a penetrating psychological insight—that people are more likely to "forget" the law when remembering it will cost them money, and that the preacher's role is more demanding when his exhortations entail expenditures.

Many preachers were not content with repeating the laws and urging their people to obey them. In the manner of homiletical artists throughout the ages, they probed these laws for hidden significance, uncovering levels of meaning that applied to the inner life as well as the outer forms of behavior. A good example is the Talmudic use of the phrase "the yeast in the dough" (B. Ber 17a) as a metaphor for the "Evil Urge."[6] At the end of the thirteenth century, the author of *Kad ha-Qemah*, a reference book for preachers, described as "well known" the idea that "the prohibition of leaven contains an allusion to the Evil Urge, over which man is obligated to make the Good Urge dominant."[7]

Generations of preachers seized upon this motif for the homiletical extension of the Pesach laws into the moral realm: the principle of cleaning out all yeast and leaven from one's possession was to be applied as well to the inner transformation of the individual. There were, of course, variations on this theme. For an unknown fifteenth-century preacher, leaven represented the vegetative and animal parts of the soul while matzah referred to its intellectual components; for MaHaRaL of Prague in the sixteenth century, unleavened bread alluded to the soul and leaven to the body with its drives; for Ezekiel Landau in the eighteenth century, it was a commonplace among preachers of

5. Luntshitz, *'Olelot*, II,2,38.

6. Rashi explains: the Evil Urge in our hearts makes us turn acidic (*mahmitsenu*). Cf. I Corinthians 5:7–9, and the review of early material by Abrahams, *Studies* 1:51–53.

7. Bahya ben Asher, *Kad ha-Qemah*, p. 312; Bahya ben Asher, *Encyclopedia*, p. 504. Cf. the esoteric interpretation of the leaven in Zohar 1:226b.

rebuke that "leaven alludes to pride . . . , for the nature of leaven is to rise up-ward."[8] But the technique of using familiar Pesach laws as a springboard for homiletical moralizations was so common as to be almost predictable.

Philosophers and mystics offered other interpretations. The virtuoso six-teenth-century Italian preacher, Judah Moscato, found in the command-ments relating to leavened and unleavened bread an allegorical hint of a the-ological doctrine. Yeast, which produces ordinary bread through a chemical interaction occurring over a period of time, represents the ordinary pattern of cause and effect that governs our world. Matzah, produced quickly from dough without fermentation, represents Creation. According to the preacher, the obligation to eat matzah applies only to the first night of the holiday because creation *ex nihilo* occurred only at the very beginning of the Creation week. However, the prohibition against eating bread during the en-tire seven days of the holiday (alluding to the seven days of the primal week) is a reminder of the severe punishment for anyone who denies the funda-mental doctrine of creation.[9]

Kabbalistic interpretations also existed, although there was a greater reluc-tance to discuss this material in public. The first Jewish preacher known to have included Kabbalistic material in his sermons was the early fourteenth-century rabbi Joshua ibn Shu'eib. In a sermon for the first day of Pesach he discusses the essential commandments: paschal lamb, unleavened bread, bit-ter herbs. While their exoteric function is to serve as a reminder of the Exo-dus, they also have a meaning that is "esoteric, exalted, wondrous . . . con-cealed for those in possession of the true doctrine." This significance, however, mentioned but not systematically explained in the sermon, remains accessible only to those already initiated into the doctrine.[10]

---

8. Regev, "Derashot," p. 232; Leib ben Bezalel of Prague, "Derush na'eh le-Shabbat ha-Gadol," in MaHaRaL, 3:224–25; Landau, *Derushei*, p. 50a; cf. also Alkabetz, fol. 5r. This theme is a point of contact between Jewish and Christian preaching. Christians, expanding the metaphor of leaven as corruption in I Corinthians 5, frequently made homiletical points quite similar to those of their Jewish counterparts. See for example, Chrysostom, *Homilies*, pp. 85–86. (I was informed by specialists at the Medieval Sermon Society Colloquium, where a form of this chapter was delivered as a paper in July of 1986, that the motif is common in medieval Christ-ian preaching for Easter.) The fundamental difference is that Jewish preachers insisted that in addition to the ethical message underlying the commandment, all leaven must actually be re-moved from the house, while Christians assumed that the ethical message replaced the act.

9. Moscato, nu. 4, p. 10d.

10. Ibn Shu'eib, *Derashot* (1593), p. 41b–c; Ibn Shu'eib, *Derashot* (1992), 1:220. On the re-luctance to divulge Kabbalistic doctrines in sermons, cf. "Dover Meisharim," fol. 60v (on a dif-ferent subject): "[T]he Kabbalists have given the true interpretation of it, but it is not appro-priate to say it to the masses." Moscato also refers to a "deep esoteric" (i.e. Kabbalistic) meaning of unleavened bread, but states that he will not discuss it in his sermon (Moscato, nu. 4, p. 10c).

Exegesis of Traditional Texts

The exegesis of traditional texts, always a staple of Jewish homiletical art, frequently led the preacher away from purely legal material. Although the texts could be drawn from different sources, the Torah was paramount. Three different pericopes from the middle of Leviticus could be read on *Shabbat ha-Gadol,* and it was always a challenge to relate the subject matter of these chapters to the theme of the season. Less difficult were the chapters from Exodus read on the first and seventh days of the holiday. Indeed, since the overriding theme was the miracle of redemption, much of the material in the narrative part of Exodus, including the many exegetical problems bound up with the Ten Plagues, was appropriate.[11]

In addition to passages from the Torah and the prophetic readings mandated by the liturgy, the Song of Songs is traditionally read in the synagogue either on the intermediate Sabbath or on the seventh day of the Pesach week. Although its thematic connection with the holiday is tenuous at best (the only clear link was Song 1:9), some preachers made this book a basis for their homilies. For example, Joshua ibn Shu'eib used it in his sermon for the last day of the holiday. Accepting the standard rabbinic interpretation that the love poetry was an allegory for the relationship between God and the people of Israel in history, he presented a selective summary of rabbinic interpretations of the book. But as in the case of the commandments in his earlier sermon, he pointed to a deeper level: "In the way of Kabbalah, these are esoteric matters, about which it is forbidden even to think, relating to the supernal chariot, above the chariot of Ezekiel, namely the realm of the *sefirot.*" His sermon reached a climax with a messianic exegesis, deriving from the language of the Song of Songs the conclusion that the Messiah was to be expected during the first two hundred years of the sixth millennium, i.e., no later that the year 1440.[12]

Besides the *tanakh,* the most important source of exegetical material for Pesach preaching was the text of the Haggadah. The substantial literature of commentary on the Haggadah becomes even more impressive when supplemented by the homiletical exegesis that pervades the sermons. Sometimes the preachers actually elucidated the inner dynamics of the text, but

---

11. Anatoli devotes much of his Pesach sermon to discussing the order of the Ten Plagues: Anatoli, pp. 96a–b; cf. Schwartz, "Yetsi'at Mitsrayim," pp. 277–80. In the margin of "Dover Meisharim," it is noted: "the matter of the Ten Plagues, good for Pesach" (fol. 79r).

12. Ibn Shu'eib, *Derashot* (1593), pp. 42a–44a; Ibn Shu'eib, *Derashot* (1992), 1:231–34. Cf. Silver, pp. 97–98.

frequently they pushed further, using the text as a springboard for their own messages.[13]

A sermon of Ephraim Luntshitz provides an illustration of a familiar passage exploited for an unexpected criticism of his audience. Taking up the conventional identification of "night" with "exile," Luntshitz translates the introduction to the "Four Questions" into historical terms: "Why is this present exile different, in its length and its bitterness, from all previous ones?" His answer, based on interpretation of the rest of the passage, is a commonplace of homiletical-ethical literature: the current exile is prolonged because of the failures of Jewish society—particularly the prevalence of contention and strife within the Jewish community, the feverish pursuit of money, the compulsion to fulfill hedonistic desires, and the arrogant pretensions of the powerful.[14]

The homiletical legerdemain deriving these qualities from the four sentences of the passage—for example, playing upon two different meanings of matzah (unleavened bread; strife)—need not detain us. We should note, however, what the preacher has done with his source. In the original text, the four sentences expand the general question by specifying four examples of behavior unique to the first night of Pesach. The preacher transforms them into four answers to the original question, the reasons for the prolonged exile. For example, the third and fourth sentences originally referred to practices that represent the meal of the free and prosperous, thereby celebrating the antithesis of Egyptian servitude. Luntshitz turns these acts into negative symbols: the dipping of the herbs represents the hedonistic pursuit of gastronomic pleasures, and reclining represents an arrogance ("like kings in their palaces") totally inappropriate for contemporary Jewish life. The preacher thus indulges in a rather remarkable editorial freedom, pushing and squeezing the familiar words to the point where their meaning has been totally transmuted. Whether or not this technique made his criticism more effective is open to conjecture.[15]

Analysis of Philosophical Problems

The Pesach season could also provide an occasion for the investigation of rather abstract theological problems, sometimes in a form not usually asso-

---

13. See, for example, the extensive homiletical discussion of the Four Sons passage in Regev, "Derashot," pp. 232–36.

14. Luntshitz, 'Olelot, II,7,75.

15. For a contemporary attack on this technique, see *Jewish Preaching*, pp. 399–400.

ciated with Jewish preaching. A striking example appears in a sermon for *Shabbat ha-Gadol* by Hasdai Crescas, a rabbi and philosopher known for his critique of Aristotelian physics and one of the intellectual leaders of Spanish Jewry at the end of the fourteenth century.[16] The problem or *derush* (the medieval Hebrew equivalent of the Latin *quaestio*) is "whether the miracle creates a new opinion or belief in the human soul without the assent of the will, or not?" Although the very formulation of the question would seem to show the Scholastic influence—we might compare it with Part II-II Question 6, Article 1 of St. Thomas' *Summa Theologica*—it is not difficult to see the appropriateness of the subject to the season commemorating the Exodus.

Following the format of the "disputed question," the preacher offers four arguments for the claim that the assent of the will is required for faith. Each argument points to a contradiction implicit in the opposite assertion. For example, if the miracle necessarily produced faith independent of human choice, there would be no basis for reward or punishment in relation to one's belief, but we know that belief is rewarded. Furthermore, faith generated necessarily by the sight of a miracle would never waver, nor would it be susceptible to change—but we see the opposite in the Bible. This is followed by four arguments to support the claim that miracles cause faith without the assent of the will. For example, if faith were dependent on the will, no firm and lasting faith could ever be produced, for the will is subject to constant change. Moreover, it would be possible to will to believe two contradictory propositions, which cannot be done.

At this point the preacher proceeds to resolve the apparent conundrum. The text may not be complete, and the different versions are not fully consistent. One version employs a *ḥilluq* or *distinctio,* arguing that the word *emunah* can be used in different ways, only one of which, the true faith where no contradictory assertion can even be imagined, is the faith in which the will plays no role. There is also a response to the arguments against the thesis that is ultimately sustained. The problem of God's rewarding faith that is necessarily imposed rather than freely chosen is resolved by identifying an attendant quality—joy—in which the will is active. Whether or not a person *rejoices* in his faith is, indeed, a matter of free decision. Thus it is this joy, rather than the faith itself, that occasions the reward.

Leaving aside the technical aspects of the discussion, it is interesting to note that Crescas incorporated the same problem into his classical theologi-

---

16. Anonymous, Harvard, fol. 194v–203r. This sermon and its influence upon subsequent texts were discussed in Ravitzky, "Ketav," "Zehuto," and in his book-length study, *Derashat ha-Pesaḥ*. On the philosophical issue, see Ravitzky, "Hitpatḥut" and Feldman, "Determinism."

cal work, *Or ha-Shem*, "The Light of the Lord." In a surprising reversal of what might have been predicted, however, in the book he merely presents the arguments sustaining the second position, that faith is not dependent on the will. Since the sermon was apparently written before the book was completed, Crescas apparently considered the "disputed question" form to be appropriate for his public preaching, but overly sophisticated and in need of simplification for his book—known to be one of the most difficult texts in all of Jewish religious philosophy.[17]

The very same question, in much the same form, also appears in a number of different homiletical texts from the late fourteenth century and into the fifteenth: a sermon for *Shabbat ha-Gadol* by a contemporary of Crescas, Joseph ben David of Saragossa; a manuscript containing sermons by Michael Balbo of Crete from the middle of the fifteenth century; and a manuscript of sermons by an unknown Spanish preacher from the end of the century. This last author introduces it as follows: "There is in the writings of the ancients a profound question, a great investigation. . . ; I want to speak about this question on this Sabbath [*ha-Gadol*] because of the miracle publicized at this season."[18] Also in the generation of the Expulsion, Isaac Abravanel incorporated the dispute into his Torah Commentary.[19] Apparently the question whether we are free to believe or to doubt, with its corollary whether faith engendered by a religious experience is strong enough to withstand the onslaught of rationalistic skepticism or the pressures to accept a different faith, continued to preoccupy preachers in the Sephardic tradition. Perhaps it even continued to intrigue their audiences.

Reactions to Contemporary Events

Some of the most compelling sermons of the Pesach season are those that deal with contemporary historical events. These are not very common; the extant texts of Jewish sermons are more often concerned with halakhic, ethical, or conceptual problems than with current affairs. Even monumental events such as the issuing of the Edict of Expulsion from Spain left no recorded sermonic reactions. A contemporary chronicle states that the Edict was publicized shortly before the holiday of Pesach in 1492, and "in place of

---

17. Crescas, Or II,v,5, pp. 219–23. Crescas does use the disputed question form in his book: II,v,1–3, pp. 206–14. On the dating of the sermon in relation to *Or ha-Shem*, see Ravitzky, *Derashat ha-Pesaḥ*, pp. 25–26.

18. "Dover Meisharim," fol. 81v.

19. Abravanel, *Torah*, 3:21 (Question 24 on Exodus 3).

the Haggadah there was weeping of bitterness and horror over the unleavened bread and bitter herbs; the people wept on that night, for there was great sorrow."[20] It is inconceivable that Spanish rabbis failed to respond to the crushing news in sermons delivered that Pesach, perhaps along the lines of the poignant rhetorical question in the Haggadah Commentary of Don Isaac Abravanel: "What have we gained by the Exodus and redemption from Egypt, if we are now in Exile?"[21] But nothing of that nature has been preserved.

Some extant Pesach sermons that do address contemporary events were recorded in an incomplete form. Solomon Levi of Salonika interrupts the texts of his published sermons to report:

> The day of *Shabbat ha-Gadol,* the tenth day of Nisan, 5333 [March 14, 1573]. I did not preach, nor did the other sages of the city [Salonika] preach in their congregations, for we were in emergency session all day long, discussing the crisis attendant upon the building of the walls, brought upon us by that enemy and adversary . . . the regional Judge Muslih al-Din, may his name and memory be blotted out! Members of the various congregations had been thrown into prison. But praise be to God, a great miracle was performed for Israel, and on the first night of Pesach, at midnight, God smote him dead, and *There was light and joy for the Jews* (Esther 8:16).

The text then continues, "The first day of Pesach, 5333 [March 19, 1573], I preached: *It is the Pesach sacrifice to the Lord* (Exod. 12:27)." The first part of the sermon is recorded, discussing the theoretical question why, when most commandments entail actions rather than words, the observance of Pesach requires a retelling of the events surrounding the Exodus. But then it breaks off abruptly: "And I explained the theme verse as applying to the miracle performed for us in the death of the adversary."[22] Apparently the application to the situation of the moment, which was no doubt immediate and moving to his listeners, was simply not considered by the preacher to be of sufficient permanent interest to include in the published text of his sermon.

In later periods, however, we do have Pesach sermons that connect the holiday and its liturgy with contemporary events. Ezekiel Landau, in a sermon for *Shabbat ha-Gadol,* referred to an uprising of the Bohemian peasants, which had recently been suppressed by Imperial forces. The Jews of Prague, know-

20. "Hashlamat Sefer ha-Qabbalah le-R. Avraham mi-Terrutiel," in David, *Shetei Kroniqot,* p. 37.
21. Abravanel, *Zevaḥ Pesaḥ,* p. 76a.
22. Levi, *Divrei Shelomoh,* pp. 191c–192a.

ing that they were usually the first victims of such popular revolts, had been terrified as the peasants approached their city. Viewing their deliverance from danger as a sign of divine providence, Landau expressed gratitude in a contemporary version of the song *Dayenu* ["It would have been enough for us"]:

> Had He saved our lives and not saved our houses and our possessions, but [the peasants] had burned our homes and all that is in them, *dayenu*, for *skin for skin, all that a person has will he give for his life* (Job 2:4). Had He saved our houses and not saved our possessions, but they had come and plundered us, *dayenu*. Had He saved our lives and our houses and our possessions and not saved us from the anxiety and terror that they would come to the city, *dayenu*. How many more times, then, since He saved life and home and possessions and preserved us from all terror and fear, are we obliged to be grateful and praise and extol His great Name.[23]

In 1782, the Habsburg Emperor Joseph II issued his Edict of Toleration. This Edict ended discriminatory legislation against the Jews and encouraged them to learn the German language and master the various trades and crafts that would make them useful subjects of the State. Though ambivalent about the potential dangers of Jews reading German philosophy and literature, Landau approved of the Edict; in his sermon for *Shabbat ha-Gadol* of that year, he praised the Emperor as a benevolent ruler, the antithesis of Pharaoh. This point is made in another homiletical interpretation of the Four Questions. Why is the "night" of Egyptian Exile different from the "nights" of other Exiles; why the celebration over the Exodus from Egypt, when Jews remain in Exile even at present?

> The answer is that there is a great difference, for then in Egypt, "we were slaves to Pharaoh," a cruel king, a king who made us suffer without benefit to himself, solely in order to humiliate us. But now there is a gracious and compassionate king. Even though we are subjects, he has removed from us the stigma of bondage, removed all externally recognizable signs of servitude.[24]

The present was obviously better than the past.

One hundred and sixty years later, that was hardly the case. Rabbi Israel Spira, the Hasidic Rebbe of Bluzhov, described in retrospect the observance of Pesach in the concentration camp of Bergen Belsen. In the homiletical in-

23. Landau, *Derushei,* Sermon 42, p. 55d. On the peasant uprising, see Wright, pp. 48–49.

24. Landau, *Derushei,* p. 53a; *Jewish Preaching,* p. 364 (the entire sermon is translated and annotated in that book).

terpretation of the same Four Questions that he shared with his fellow inmates, he also resorted to the exegetical tradition, but with a poignantly different conclusion:

> Night means exile, darkness, suffering. Morning means light, hope, redemption. "Why is this night different from all other nights?" Why is this suffering [under the Nazis] different from all the previous sufferings of the Jewish people? . . . "On all other nights we eat bread and matzah." Bread is leavened; it has height. Matzah is unleavened and is totally flat. During all our previous sufferings, during all our previous nights in exile, we Jews had bread and matzah. We had moments of bread, of creativity and light, and moments of matzah, of suffering and despair. But tonight [the night of the Holocaust] we experience our greatest suffering. We have reached the depths of the abyss, the nadir of humiliation. Tonight we have only matzah, we have no moments of relief, not a moment of respite for our humiliated spirits."[25]

Whereas Landau in 1782 located the unique horror of enslavement in the distant past, Spira in 1942 located it in the present. Such are the vagaries of Jewish historical experience.

But this was not the only mode of sermonic response to the nightmare of Pesach in Hitler's Europe. One of the leading rabbinic authorities of the age was Ephraim Oshry, whose legal responsa to questions arising from heart-rending situations are a classical expression of religious leadership tempered by humane vision. The book containing these responsa includes three sermons for *Shabbat ha-Gadol*, delivered in the Kovno Ghetto before Pesach in 1942, 1943, and 1944. An annotation to the last states that only one week before the sermon was delivered, the Nazis had carried out a particularly brutal massacre of Jewish children.[26]

One searches in vain for reference to the situation of the preacher and his audience. With all the potential for drawing upon the themes of the festival either for contrast or for hope, there is not even the faintest allusion to the events of the hour. Instead, Oshry delivered talmudic lectures, exploring problems relating to the laws of Pesach as if he and his listeners were studying in a talmudic academy during the most peaceful of times. In their content, virtually the same sermons could have been delivered one hundred or four hundred years before.

25. Eliach, pp. 19–20. According to the chronology provided by Eliach, pp. 283–84, this must have occurred in the spring of 1944. The report of the sermon was recounted by Rabbi Spira thirty-one years later (Eliach, p. 21).

26. Oshry, 2:226–63. On the "children's action" at Kovno on March 27–28, 1944, see Gilbert, pp. 664–65.

How could a preacher appear to be so insensitive to the world around him? Perhaps an analogy may be found in Sir Arthur Quiller-Couch's lectures on *The Tempest*, given at Cambridge University in the midst of the First World War. In his introduction to these lectures, the Shakespearian scholar justified his analysis of art in the midst of bloodshed with the claim that this enterprise provided a "double anchor" for the soul:

> There is the lesser anchor of pride, that, happen what may, here is something our enemy can as little take from us as he can imitate it: that the best part of revenge is to be different from our enemy and hopelessly beyond his copying, whatever he may destroy. But there is also the better anchor of confidence, that in a world where men just now seem chiefly to value science for its power to slay, we hold to something as strong as it is benign, and careless of death, because it is immortal.[27]

Oshry's sermons from the Kovno Ghetto would seem to reflect the preacher's own form of defiant resistance: a refusal to recognize the reality of the Nazis and the world they created, even by allusion or hint. Beyond the details of rigorous talmudic analysis, the underlying message communicated to Oshry's listeners in the Kovno Ghetto celebrated a timeless world of Jewish mind and spirit that even the Nazis could not touch—a world that the preacher believed would endure, embodied in a mode of discourse from the past, long after the Nazis had disappeared from the earth. At a time when there was little ground for comfort or encouragement, the traditional form itself of the halakhic Pesach sermon may well have meant more to the listeners than anything "relevant" the preacher could have said.

---

27. Quoted in Stiernotte, p. 180. Cf. the recent analysis of this strategy in the Warsaw Ghetto sermons of Rabbi Kalonymos Kalman Shapira in Polen, *Holy Fire,* pp. 17–21, esp. 20–21, 54, 124, 133. Polen describes a Pesach sermon by Shapira on p. 73.

3

Jewish Typological Exegesis
After Nahmanides*

Typological interpretation is the intersection of exegesis and historiography. Serving to connect a classic literary text with historical events that lie beyond that text—whether in past, present, or future for the interpreter—it is both a way of reading a piece of literature and a way of understanding what happens in the world. The use of typological interpretation by early Christian thinkers in order to demonstrate the continuity between the Hebrew Scriptures and the central Christian story is obvious to every reader of the New Testament[1] and the Church Fathers.[2] Its status within the Jewish tradition is somewhat more problematic.

By "typological interpretation," I do not mean the claim that certain ambiguous, open-ended biblical prophecies were or are being fulfilled by a par-

---

Originally appeared in *Jewish Studies Quarterly*, vol.1 (1993/94), pp. 158–70. Reprinted with permission.

*This chapter was originally written in the spring of 1989 for presentation at a colloquium in memory of Frank Talmage while I was a fellow at the Institute for Advanced Studies of the Hebrew University, participating in the seminar on biblical exegesis.

1. E.g., Mt. 12:40: "Even as Jonah was in the belly of the fish three days and three nights, so will the Son of Man be three days and three nights in the bowels of the earth." Most scholars consider this to be a late statement attributed to Jesus after his death, as it does not appear in the parallel versions (Mk. 8:11–12, 11:29–30). This would make it a fine example of the function of typology discussed at the end of this article. Cf. also Heb. 7:1–3 on Melchizedek.

2. E.g., Isaac carrying the wood to the top of Mt. Moriah where he is to be sacrificed is a type for Jesus bearing the cross to Golgotha. This typology, which somewhat surprisingly does not appear in the New Testament, was used by the Church Fathers; see Daniélou, "Typologie d'Isaac," and in general, Daniélou, *Shadow*. Cf. also the use of Joshua as a type for Jesus (the names are the same in Greek) in Justin Martyr: Joshua distributed the "holy land," a temporary posession; Jesus will distribute the spiritual "land" as an eternal possession. Robert L. Wilken, *Land*, 57–58. A different kind of patristic typology is St. Augustine's use of Cain as a type for the Jewish people: see his "Reply to Faustus the Manichean," bk. 12, paragraphs 9–13, in Talmage, *Disputation*, pp. 28–32.

ticular event. That kind of interpretation, exemplified by the *Pesher Habakkuk* of the Qumran community and by no means uncommon among medieval Jews, responds to a biblical passage that clearly refers to the future. The starting point for typological interpretation cannot be a prophecy; it must be a passage, usually a narrative, that, seemingly complete in its own terms, is shown to be an adumbration of something beyond itself.[3]

In addition, that "something" must have a historical character. The medieval Jewish philosophical interpretations of Sarah and Abraham as representing matter and form, or the four kings and five kings (in Genesis 14) as the four elements and five senses—interpretations that scandalized some of those who heard about them—are not typology but allegory.[4] Nor do the Kabbalistic explications of biblical narratives as dynamic events within the Godhead qualify.[5] True typological interpretation requires that events recounted in the Bible, appearing to be unique occurrences consigned to the past, be shown to prefigure analogous events that will subsequently occur on the stage of history. I use the term in this narrow sense so that the force of my argument will not be dissipated.

This approach to the Bible appears in several midrashic works, often (but not always) introduced by the phrase *Ma'aseh avot siman le-vanim.*[6] It was later cultivated by one of the most powerful and influential Jewish thinkers of the Middle Ages, Moses ben Nahman (RaMBaN, Nahmanides), in his commentary on the Torah. RaMBaN's typological exegesis has been subjected to a penetrating study by Amos Funkenstein, who explored its relationship to Christian typology.[7] In that context, Funkenstein made several generalizations about the status of this mode in Jewish exegesis: typological interpretation, "rich and dominant in the Christian purview" remained "peripheral and unimaginative" within Judaism.[8] Even

---

3. Ezra-Zion Melamed lists Nahmanides' interpretations of Lev. 26:16, Deut. 28:42, and the *Ha'azinu* poem (Deut. 32) together with the examples of true typology, thereby blurring an important distinction. See Melamed, *Mefarshei ha-Miqra,* 2:950–52.

4. Accusations about these interpretations played an important role in the conflict over the study of philosophy at the beginning of the fourteenth century. See Saperstein, *Jewish Preaching,* pp. 380–82.

5. See, for example, Tishby, "She'elot u-Teshuvot le-R. Moshe de Leon be-Inyenei Qabbalah," in *Ḥiqrei Qabbalah,* 1:40–75.

6. Tanhuma, *Lekh Lekha,* 9. Cf. also Gen. Rab. 40,6; Tanhuma, *Va-Yeshev,* 4 and *Va-Yiggash,* 10; *Pesiqta Rabbati* 33,4

7. Funkenstein, "Parshanuto"; Funkenstein, "Nahmanides"; Funkenstein, *Perceptions,* pp. 98–121. I have quoted from the English version of the article but used both versions.

8. Funkenstein, "Nahmanides," p. 129.

RaMBaN, the "exception which proves the rule," showed extreme caution in his use of this approach, limiting it to the patriarchal narratives and never applying it to obvious candidates such as the story of Joseph. And RaMBaN's idiosyncratic exegesis had little influence; indeed, "it is astonishing how seldom Jews used typologies creatively, even for polemical purposes."[9] In the last part of his article, Funkenstein offers several explanations for that neglect.

In a brilliant article on Jewish allegorical interpretation of the Bible, Frank Talmage points to a typological commentary on the Book of Ruth by a Spanish rabbi from the generation of the Expulsion, thereby indicating that Funkenstein's premise was somewhat overstated.[10] My work on the history of Jewish preaching in the late Middle Ages and early modern period had led me independently to a similar conclusion. Indeed, I am struck by the extent to which Jewish preachers seem to have considered typology a natural and popular technique for linking biblical narratives with subsequent Jewish history.[11] This material suggests to me that such interpretation was neither "peripheral" nor "unimaginative" in the hands of medieval Jews living after Nahmanides. The subject deserves a more encompassing study than is possible in the present framework, but I will concretize my conclusion by reference to several individuals from different historical milieux.

In the generations immediately following RaMBaN, a use of typological interpretation that was not at all peripheral can be seen in the sermons on Genesis by David ha-Nagid (the grandson of Maimonides)[12] and by Joshua ibn Shu'eib.[13] The technique is especially prevalent in the works of ibn Shu'eib's contemporary, Jacob ben Hananel Sikili, who wrote an important collection of model sermons, most of which remain unpublished. Typological interpretation was clearly central to his understanding of the patriarchal narratives, appearing in almost every *parashah* from *Lekh Lekha* (Gen.

---

9. Ibid., pp. 141–42.
10. Talmage, "Apples of Gold," 1:314.
11. See *Jewish Preaching*, p. 141, n. 9.
12. David ha-Nagid. He interprets typologically the four kings of Genesis 14 (p. 60), the wells dug by Isaac (pp. 107–108), and Jacob's nocturnal wrestling match (p. 143), all of which had been given similar interpretations by RaMBaN. He also uses typology in the Joseph story (p. 162), which RaMBaN had not done. All of these are based on midrashic sources. It is not clear to me that he used RaMBaN at all; he may have developed the approach independently, using the same sources that RaMBaN did.
13. On Joshua ibn Shu'eib, see *Jewish Preaching*, pp. 137–55, esp. p. 141, and Horowitz, *Jewish Sermon*, p. 176.

12:1–17:27) to *Va-Yeḥi* (Gen. 47:28–50:26). He also demonstrated imagi-
nation and creativity, going considerably beyond merely recapitulating interpretations familiar from the Midrash and RaMBaN.[14]

For example, the appearance of three mysterious messengers to Abraham
at the beginning of *Va-Yera* (Gen. 18:1–22:24) prefigures the "three re-
deemers, Elijah, Messiah ben Joseph, and Messiah ben David," who will appear to the Jewish people in the most painful period of their exile. The author
notes here, "If need be, you may interpret homiletically the entire passage describing Abraham's meal in relation to the messianic era," a remark that suggests such interpretations were by no means unusual.[15] The three descents of
Joseph's brothers into Egypt are the "types" (*dugmot*) for the three exiles of the
Jewish people; Joseph's weeping three times in their presence "hints to them
of what would occur to them and their descendants in the future."[16]

A fuller statement of the assumptions undergirding the typological
hermeneutic appears in the sermon on *Va-Yetse* (Gen. 28:10–32:3):

> When God saw the righteousness and piety of the patriarchs, He wanted to
> show them what was fundamentally real: that the nation He would single out
> from all peoples to be His own unique treasure would emerge from them, and

---

14. On Jacob ben Hananel, see *Jewish Preaching,* p. 65 n. 4; I should have included there
a reference to Hurvitz, "Torat ha-Minhah." That article demonstrates the dependence of
Jacob ben Hananel on David ha-Nagid, and indeed some instances of his typological interpretations (though not all) may be derived from David. While less original than I had once
thought, Jacob's use of typology remains relevant evidence for my case about the prevalence
of this type of exegesis, especially in sermons, after RaMBaN.

There are many manuscripts of "Torat ha-Minḥah"; I have used Vienna MS 37. Some of
his interpretations may be called "weak typology," based not on the events but on the words
that describe them. For example, *The life of Sarah was 127 years* (Gen. 23:1) refers to the years
of suffering (*tsarah*) experienced by Israel in their exiles (the *sin* and the *tsaddi* are said to be
interchangeable); *Sarah died in Kiryat Arba* (Gen. 23:2) refers to the end of the suffering
(*tsarah*) caused by the four (*arba'*) kingdoms; *Hebron* (Gen. 23:2) refers to the gathering of
all the nations (*nithabberu*) against Jerusalem in messianic times (fol. 40r). Similarly, *The time
of Israel to die drew near* (Gen. 47:29) means "the suffering of exile was so strong that [the
people of Israel] almost reached the gates of death" (fol. 76r). Such passages frequently contain calculations of the messianic advent derived from hints in the wording. Funkenstein does
not consider this to be genuine typological exegesis ("Naḥmanides," pp. 139, 142–43), and I
will therefore not consider it further.

15. Jacob ben Hananel, fol 40r. The passage describing the appearance of the three
strangers to Abraham was used by Christians as a biblical base for the doctrine of the Trinity;
see Berger, *Jewish-Christian Debate,* pp. 362–65. The usual Jewish response was defensive, arguing that it cannot refer to the Trinity (see ibid., pp. 48–51). Jacob ben Hananel's typological interpretation turns the tables, using the passage for a positive purpose.

16. Jacob ben Hananel, fol. 70r–v.

that all their activities would be signs and hints of what would occur to their descendants. God therefore showed this to Abraham, and again to Isaac and to Jacob, the three patriarchs, corresponding to the three exiles, the three re-demptions, and the three temples.

After this general introduction, the technique is applied to a section that RaMBaN had not interpreted typologically:

> Jacob did not leave [the house of Laban] until Joseph was born, hinting that Israel would not be redeemed until all the souls of the storehouse are used up (B. Yeb 62a) and then the Messiah ben Joseph would come forth. Laban op-pressed and burdened him . . . and he tricked him, changing his wages ten times (Gen. 31:7), alluding to the burden and oppression Israel would suffer in exile and the tricks the Gentiles would play upon them. Jacob's fleeing from Laban is a hint of the ingathering of the exiles. Laban's pursuit after him and his attempt to destroy him completely hints of the nations' persecution of Is-rael with Gog and Magog. . . . After all the suffering experienced by Jacob, he separated from that wicked man and escaped without harm. Then the mes-sengers of God met him (Gen. 32:2), alluding to the messengers who will in the future appear to Israel: Elijah, and King Messiah.[17]

We have here a fully developed typology that is both central to the preacher's reading of the text and imaginative in going beyond the earlier sources. In this conception, the reason for the type is to provide information to the original protagonist—the patriarchs—about the destiny of their off-spring. But the rhetorical function within the context of the sermon is, of course, quite different. By sharing information originally intended for the patriarchs, the preacher can strengthen his listeners' belief that history is not random or meaningless, and comfort them in their sufferings with the as-surance that a happy ending is encoded in the very beginnings of the annals of their ancestors. In virtually all of these passages, the messianic element is pronounced. Thus the sermons of Jacob ben Hananel, which served as homiletical models, reveal typology as a powerful tool for reading the patri-archal narratives as messianic texts.

Other preachers understood the function of typology somewhat differ-ently, emphasizing not so much the historical as the ethical nature of the bib-lical narrative. In this approach, the stories of the patriarchs disclose infor-mation not just about what will happen, but about how Jews should conduct themselves. The behavior of the protagonists provides a model to be emu-

17. Jacob ben Hananel, fol. 47b, 48b. This messianic typology is cited verbatim in its en-tirety in an anonymous collection of sermons in the Spanish tradition from the sixteenth cen-tury: Anonymous, JTSA, end of *Va-Yetse*.

lated (or in some cases avoided) by their descendants in the circumstances prefigured by the type.[18]

Both uses of typology can be found in the sermons of one of the great Ottoman Jewish preachers of the sixteenth century, Solomon Levi of Salonika, who enthusiastically recommended Nahmanides' typological exegesis to his listeners and developed it in original ways himself. He used the technique to convey historical information in a discussion of RaMBaN's view that Abraham's giving of his wife to Pharaoh was a sin that caused the exile of his descendants in Egypt.

> In my view, it was not RaMBaN's intention to say that this sin was sufficient to cause the exile in Egypt, but that this was a sign to his descendants that they would fall into the power of Pharaoh and emerge from his power without faltering or harm. . . . In short, all that happened to the patriarchs was a sign to their descendants. That is why this information was disclosed to Abraham: to show him that he was a sign for his descendants, not that the matter would be absolutely decreed because of this act.[19]

More often, however, Solomon Levi employed typology to draw a moral lesson. A good example is the sermon on *Va-Yetse* (Gen. 28:10–32:3) delivered in 1573, which provides an interesting contrast with the *Va-Yetse* sermon of Jacob ben Hananel, cited above. Here too, the preacher begins with a general introduction: "I have already said, citing RaMBaN,[20] that the foundation upon which most patriarchal narratives are built is that all of them are a sign of that which would happen to their children. God's intent was to inform Jacob's offspring so that they would recognize and know that because of the presence of divine providence over this seed, they will endure forever, never to be destroyed as many other nations have been." The information here is intended not primarily for the patriarchs, as in Jacob ben Hananel, but for their descendants.

Solomon Levi then applied the typology to the story of Jacob:

---

18. An example of the negative model is Jacob's sending of emissaries to Esau, which may have reminded Esau of quarrels long forgotten. See Gen. Rab. 75,3, B. AZ 8b, Nahmanides on Gen. 32:4, and Ibn Shu`eib in *Jewish Preaching,* pp. 141–42.

19. Levi, *Divrei Shelomoh,* p. 172b. On this preacher, see *Jewish Preaching,* pp. 240–52, including references to the studies by Joseph Hacker in the notes. The problem addressed in this passage is that RaMBaN's comment on Gen. 12:10 seems to waver between typology (in Abraham's descent into Egypt, God "hints to him that his descendants would go down into Egypt") and the quite different view that Abraham sinned in leaving the land of Canaan and giving his wife to Pharaoh, thereby causing Egyptian exile to be decreed (as a punishment) upon his descendants. The ambiguities of this comment inspired many subsequent discussions.

20. The reference would seem to be to his sermon on *Toledot* (Gen. 25:19–28:9), delivered on the previous Sabbath; see the translation in *Jewish Preaching,* p. 244.

The narratives of our father Jacob come to teach that he was persecuted by the wicked Esau, who hated him, because of which he was forced to flee from Esau's presence. He went to another wicked man who hated him, undoubtedly arriving there stripped of all worldly goods, because of the expulsions which made him sneak away. This second hater welcomed him warmly. During the relatively few years he remained there he grew in strength and in industriousness. This would have been impossible without God's close support, as the Bible says, *The Lord blessed you because of me* (Gen. 30:30). Ultimately, because he grew powerful and wealthy, Laban began to hate him, desiring to trick him and take all that he had. All this is an instructive sign that our people would be expelled and persecuted, moving from kingdom to kingdom, from one ruler who hates them to another. Within a relatively few years they would become more powerful and wealthier than the native inhabitants of the land, who would eventually come to despise them, so that they would have to flee from that land to yet another. Such would be the pattern until the messianic age. For God would arrange it that when they were persecuted by one who hated them, as was the case with Esau, they would find another who would welcome them warmly, as was the case with Laban.

We learn also that the industriousness of our people, [enabling them] to earn money and acquire wealth is similar to that found in our father Jacob. But his industriousness was rooted in justice and truth. . . . That is not the case among our people in this evil generation, for they are *filled with lies and violence* (Ps. 10:7). The meaning [of this passage] is that our people should not be blamed because they are so energetic and devote such effort to acquire wealth and capital in a land not their own, so long as they amass it justly and equitably, for this is what our father Jacob did, and this is what has preserved us among the gentiles. At first, they see that God brings them blessing because of us. But later on, they begin to despise us and think of taking it all from us. They therefore trump up charges against us in order to enslave us. Such events have occurred to our people throughout the thousands of years we are in exile, many, many times, as history reveals.[21]

The contrast between this and the sermon of Jacob ben Hananel is clear. Unlike the earlier passage, this one is fully within the parameters of history. Prefigured is not the messianic drama but the dynamics of Jewish life in exile. Listeners may well have understood the preacher to suggest that Jacob's fleeing from the domain of Esau to the domain of Laban prefigures the mass migration of Jews from the Iberian peninsula to the Ottoman Empire, but this movement is then divested of its uniqueness and treated as one instance of a recurring pattern.

Furthermore, unlike the fourteenth-century sermon, this one draws spe-

---

21. Levi, *Divrei Shelomoh*, p. 231a; the passage is discussed in the context of Solomon's thought by Hacker, "Yisra'el ba-Goyim," pp. 81–82.

cific lessons for conduct. The preacher was obviously attempting to define a middle ground for his social doctrine. There were Jewish leaders who condemned all economic initiative leading to the accumulation of wealth as inappropriate for the condition of exile.[22] But there were undoubtedly also some who regarded all forms of economic activity as exempt from the imposition of ethical and religious standards. Jacob might seem to be a rather ambiguous paradigm for the message that wealth must be acquired "justly and equitably," but his forceful denial of Laban's charges (Gen.31:36–42) provides enough of a basis for the preacher to contrast Jacob's conduct with that of "this evil generation." The typology thus may serve to affirm not only the legitimacy of acquiring wealth in a land not one's own, but the need for honesty and justice in that pursuit. Here the technique becomes a vehicle for social criticism and rebuke as well as for comfort.

The final figure to be considered in this brief survey is the noted preacher of the Portuguese community in Amsterdam, Saul Levi Morteira. The printed sermons of *Giv'at Sha'ul* (Amsterdam, 1645) contain little typology; indeed, they leave the impression that Morteira was not at all interested in this kind of interpretation. The massive collection of his manuscript sermons,[23] however, reveals that this was not at all the case. In fact, Morteira turned to typology in his preaching on many occasions.

A sermon on *Va-Yetse* (Gen. 28:10–32:3), preached near the beginning of his career (in 1619 or 1620), is entirely devoted to the typological significance of the patriarchal narratives, working out in elaborate detail the principle that they prefigure "the entire history of this people."[24] The stories of Abraham

---

22. See, for example, the sermon of Saul Levi Morteira translated in *Jewish Preaching,* esp. pp. 274 (which may have been influenced by this passage), 275, 276.

23. Five bound volumes, containing more than 550 of Morteira's sermons have recently come to light in the Rabbinical Seminary of Budapest (see Preface, above). On Morteira, see the bibliography cited in *Jewish Preaching,* p. 270, n. 1.

24. The sermon, entitled "Avot 'al Banim," is the fourth in vol. 3 of the manuscript. He referred approvingly to this interpretation in a later sermon, the fifteenth in vol. 5 (fol. 29r–v). The typological principle that the three patriarchs correspond to the three major periods in the history of the Jewish people, drawn from RaMBaN's comments on Gen. 12:10, 26:1, and 32:4, was commonly used by subsequent writers (see Jacob ben Hananel, above). Morteira's sermon should be compared with the work of Mordecai Dato published by Isaiah Tishby in "Demuto shel Rabbi Mosheh Cordovero be-Ḥibbur shel Rabbi Mordecai Dato," in Tishby, *Ḥiqrei Qabbalah,* 1:131–76, especially pp. 159, 161, 165–72 (and cf. Dato, "Derashot," fol. 41b, the Hebrew formula appearing in the midst of a vernacular Italian text). It should also be compared with Ephraim Luntshitz's treatment of *Toledot* (Gen. 25:19–28:9) in *'Ir Gibborim* (Luntshitz, *'Ir,* p. 17b–d). Each author applies the underlying typological principle in his own way; despite some striking similarities, I see no evidence of direct influence.

correspond to the First Temple period; those of the adult Isaac, to the Second Temple. With the second famine (Gen. 26:1) the current exile begins.

> *Isaac sowed seed in that land . . . and God blessed him* (Gen. 26:12) hints of the material success enjoyed by the Jews in exile. Then it says, *for all the wells dug by the servants of Abraham,* namely the fine traits of character and intellect, *the Philistines stopped up,* meaning, exile did not allow the Jews to cultivate fine traits, *and filled them with the earth* (Gen. 26:15), referring to the destruction of books, and [the development of] repugnant traits, for they assimilated with the gentiles and learned their ways. After that, Abimelech said, *"Go away from here, for you are too strong"* (Gen. 26:16). This is an allusion to the expulsions, all caused by arrogance and wealth. Then it tells that they dug wells and quarreled over them, and then they dug another but did not quarrel over it, and they said *"For now God has given room"* (Gen. 26:19–22). This hints that one will cast us out and another will take us in. . .[25] After this it says that *Esau married Judith* (Yehudit) *daughter of Beeri the Hittite and Basemath daughter of Elon the Hittite* (Gen. 26:34). This is an allusion to the religion of the Christians, who profess the Jewish Scripture (*Torat Yehudit*) but pervert it and append their claims to it, "Hittite interpretations" (*be'erei ha-Ḥitti*). *This was a bitter grief to Isaac and Rebecca* (Gen. 26:35): to the Jews and to their land.[26]

In the sermon by Solomon Levi, the paradigm and prefiguration for contemporary Jewish experience is Jacob's sojourn with Laban. In Morteira's sermon it is located earlier, in Genesis 26. Nevertheless, the similarities of approach are obvious. In both, typology becomes a vehicle for the preacher to express not merely information about history but social criticism. Exile produces negative character traits among the Jews. All expulsions are caused by Jewish arrogance and wealth, a theme to which Morteira would return in a powerful sermon two years later.[27] In the present sermon, the typology also provides an opportunity for an anti-Christian barb that, although occupying a small part of the whole work, would not have been lost on the congregation composed largely of those who had been born into Christianity and repudiated that faith.

The sermon then continues with the story of Jacob. After a brief comment pertaining to contemporary realities ("The Bible tells of the conflict between Jacob and Esau, hinting of the conflict over faith, which remained

---

25. Cf. Nahmanides on Gen. 32:9, and Solomon Levi, above. Each finds the prefiguration of the insecurities of Jewish life in exile in a different biblical text.

26. Morteira, "Giv'at Sha'ul," vol. 3, fols. 7v–8r. Cf. also the sermon on *Toledot,* fol. 174r.

27. The sermon is translated in *Jewish Preaching,* pp. 272–85.

to Israel; Esau sought to kill him, but he was saved, just like us"), Morteira shifts to a messianic scenario.

> It tells that when Jacob had twelve sons he said, "Let me go," hinting that when the Jewish people pay their debt, they will return to their land. Just as Laban tried to prevent his return, so they will want to prevent us, but God will help us. Then the messengers of God met him (Gen. 32:1): so Elijah and the Messiah will meet us. . . .[28] *Jacob came unimpaired* (Gen. 33:18) hints of the ingathering of the exiles. The taking of Dinah hints of Gog and Magog, when the *women will be ravaged* (Zech. 14:2). The killing of the men of Shechem hints of the killing of those Gentiles. After this they removed the foreign gods from their midst (Gen. 35:4), a hint of the idols which will totally disappear (Isa. 2:18). *He called the place El Beit El* (Gen.35:7) hints of the third Temple, which will be strong (the meaning of *eil* in 2 Kings 24:15). There *Deborah, Rebecca's nurse dies* (Gen. 35:8), an allusion to the evil impulse, which nourished the Jews in their exile. *God appeared to Jacob again* (Gen. 35:9) hints of the return of prophecy. . . . And *kings will emerge from your loins* (Gen. 35:11) alludes to the son of David.[29]

This passage, which draws from the biblical narrative prefigurations of future events beyond the experience of any contemporary listeners, is closer to the sermon of Jacob ben Hananel than to the sermon of Solomon Levi. This and similar messianic uses of typology, both by Morteira and by others,[30] raise serious doubts about the validity of Funkenstein's statement, "It is astonishing how seldom Jews used typologies creatively even for polemical purposes." Indeed, the demonstration by so many Jewish preachers that the traditional messianic scenario was encoded in the most familiar biblical narratives reveals a creativity arguably more pronounced than in Christian typologies of Jesus. It is as if Morteira and his colleagues were saying, "We can play this game as well as you, and even better."

It is important to note that Jewish typological reading of the Bible was not limited to the patriarchal narratives. RaMBaN himself, apparently drawing from a midrashic tradition that "like the first redeemer [Moses] will be the last redeemer [the Messiah]" (Numbers Rabbah 11,2, Pesiqta Rabbati 15,10), made Moses' confrontation with Pharaoh into a prefiguration of the Messiah's coming to the papal court.[31] RaMBaN also noted, "All that Moses

28. Exactly the same interpretation of the verse is given by Jacob ben Hananel (see above).
29. Morteira, "Giv'at Sha'ul," vol. 3, fol. 8r.
30. See above, n. 17.
31. Nahmanides, "Disputation of Barcelona," in RaMBaN, *Writings,* 2:666, 671, 676. For a fuller development of this typology, see my *Decoding,* pp. 103–5. Cf. also Abraham Abulafia's use of this motif in Berger, "Abulafia," p. 57, n. 8. See also below, n. 33.

and Joshua did with them [Amalek] the first time, Elijah and Messiah ben Joseph will do with their descendants."[32] Morteira devoted considerable attention in his sermons to Joshua as a type for the Ephraimite Messiah.[33]

Typological thinking reached a pinnacle of imaginative creativity within the Sabbatian movement, particularly in its moments of greatest stress.[34] Despite the phenomenological parallel with early Christian typology, the sustained effort by Sabbatians to find biblical prefigurations of an apostate messiah appears to have been not the result of Christian influence, but rather the natural response of believers to a situation of spiritual crisis, in the spirit of messianic typological interpretations common in Jewish writings of previous generations.

Typological exegesis was thus anything but an idiosyncrasy of RaMBaN. Although some eyebrows were raised about its appropriateness in certain cases,[35] it became almost a universally accepted vehicle for Jewish understanding of the book of Genesis, and other parts of the Bible as well. Shem Tov ibn Shem Tov began his sermon on *Va-Yishlaḥ* (Gen. 32:4–36:43) by saying, "It is a well-known fact that all that occurred to the patriarchs is a sign for their descendants."[36] Ephraim Luntshitz wrote in *'Ir Gibborim* that although "all of the books are filled with this doctrine, as water covers the sea, namely that the tribulations of Jacob with Esau hint of the tribulations that we encounter in this bitter exile, I will not refrain from adding my own to theirs."[37] And Morteira describes it as "an accepted view of the sages, and after them all the commentators, that what occurred to the patriarchs is a

---

32. Comment on Exod. 17:9. Cf. Morteira 1912, end of sermon on *Va-Yeshev,* p. 90. The same statement is made in a sermon for Purim from the early fourteenth century, Anonymous, "Disciple of Rabbenu Asher," fol. 71v–72r.

33. E.g. Morteira, "Giv'at Sha'ul," vol. 3, sermon on *Ve-Zot ha-Berakhah,* fol. 242r.

34. See Scholem, *Sabbatai Ṣevi,* pp. 585–86, 704–28, 743. Scholem's statement on p. 586, "Although the concrete details of [Abudiente's] typology are derived from midrashic literature, the idea of taking an Old Testament figure such as Moses as a type of the messiah seems to be Christian," is remarkable in light of the use of this motif in Nahmanides' "Disputation," above, n. 31. See also Scholem, *Meḥqarim,* pp. 243–45, 270–71 (Nathan of Gaza), 308 (Cardozo). Based on the typology of Moses (above, n. 31), believers in Sabbatai Zevi expected his reappearance forty years after his apostasy, in the year 1706. See Carlebach, p. 90.

35. We sense a reservation in a remark by Abravanel on the story of the wells in Genesis 26. RaMBaN could find "no benefit and no honor for Isaac; that is why he turned to interpret it typologically (*'al-derekh ha-tsurah*) about our Temple. In my view there is great honor for Isaac; that is why it is written here" (Abravanel, *Torah* 1:303b). This view, which would limit the typological interpretation to narrative passages that seem to have no other positive function, would indeed consign it to the periphery of Jewish exegesis.

36. Shem Tov, *Derashot,* p. 17b. In a different sermon, Shem Tov cites this principle and uses it in interpreting the story of Cain and Abel (p. 7b).

37. Luntshitz, *'Ir,* beginning of *Va-Yishlaḥ.*

sign for their descendants."[38] Such writers would have been most surprised to hear that this mode of exegesis was peripheral in Judaism.

At the end of his article, Funkenstein attempts to explain why, as he posits, typological exegesis was neglected by Jews before and after RaMBaN. One of his explanations is that Jews were "never compelled to demonstrate the unity-within-diversity of two or more successive revelations. Yet throughout the history of Christian typologies, the *concordia veteris ac novi testamenti* remained the main methodological paradigm."[39] I would argue precisely the reverse, not only about the Jewish "neglect" of typology, but about its use by Christians.

The fundamental purpose of typological exegesis in Christianity was not to demonstrate the unity of two Scriptures, for typology is found within the Gospels and Epistles of the New Testament itself, which were written at a time when there was only one Scripture, the Hebrew Bible. The original Christian typology attempted to show continuity between the Bible and the life and meaning of Jesus, that is, between a sacred book and events beyond that book. The Church Fathers continued to elaborate new typological interpretations for polemical reasons: to prove the truth of their faith to Jews, to disciples of Marcion, and to pagan thinkers. But for Christianity as it ultimately crystallized, the central story was in the past. After its triumph on the stage of history, most Christians had no inner need to develop creative typologies that would link the Hebrew Bible with the events of the present or the future.[40] Therefore, typological exegesis remained "peripheral and unimaginative" among most Christian writers of the Middle Ages.

38. Morteira, "Giv'at Sha'ul," vol. 3, sermon on *Toledot*, fol. 320v. The second sermon in Judah Moscato's *Nefutsot Yehudah* is based on a typological interpretation of the Jacob story that refers to RaMBaN but develops the typology further (Moscato, pp. 5c, 7c–d). Cf. also Ibn Shu'eib, *'Olat Shabbat*, p. 31a.

39. Funkenstein, "Nahmanides," p. 142.

40. Exceptions to the general rule would be the use of typological exegesis by Christians seeking to comprehend baffling events in times of crisis (e.g., the response to the conquest of Jerusalem by the Persians in 614 [Wilken, *Land*, pp. 325–26]), and its use by non-establishment Christian groups that felt a need to establish their legitimacy by connecting biblical events with their own story. Thus, for example, the Israelite exodus from Egypt, sojourn in the wilderness, and entrance into the land of Canaan became important types in the preaching of New England Puritans who had made the transition from the Old World to the New; see Stout, pp. 45, 54, 73, 173; cf. also pp. 138–39. The same would be true for the use of Moses and the Exodus as types in the preaching or political rhetoric of Irish nationalism (e.g., John F. Taylor's speech as incorporated into James Joyce's *Ulysses* [New York, 1961], pp. 142–43), of Afro-Americans (in relation to figures such as Marcus Garvey and Martin Luther King, Jr.), and of "Liberation theologians" (see, e.g., Croatto, pp. 15–18). In these cases, a typological hermeneutic is engendered to demonstrate not the *concordia veteris ac novi testamenti*, as Funkenstein maintains, but rather the providential connections between ancient event and contemporary historical experience.

This was not the case in Judaism. The story to which the experiences of the patriarchs were linked was an ongoing story, the story of exile and redemption. Preachers who discussed the pericopes of Genesis and Exodus felt it imperative to show that these narratives were not merely part of an ancient past, but that they bore a historical message for the present and the future. Therefore, typological exegesis was cultivated by Jewish preachers more than it was by their Christian contemporaries. After Naḥmanides, the gates were opened. His interpretations were cited and discussed,[41] but more important, they were expanded upon and his approach applied in innovative and imaginative new ways. It might indeed be argued that in the entire commentary of RaMBaN, with all its wealth and profundity, there is nothing that had a greater impact on subsequent generations than his typological exegesis of biblical narratives.

---

41. And sometimes criticized. For example, Morteira rejected one of RaMBaN's typological interpretations in a sermon on *Va-Yishlaḥ* devoted to a discussion of the Ephraimite Messiah. As an appendage to the manuscript text, he writes, "I added [apparently in the delivery of the sermon], that RaMBaN on the lesson *Va-Yeḥi* (on Gen. 47:28) wrote that the deep mourning for Jacob at the threshing-floor of Atad (Gen. 50:10–11) hints of the mourning the nations will engage in because of our salvation. This is not correct, for if it were, would Israel, the children of Jacob, be mourning and grieving with [the Egyptians]? It is more correct to say, in accordance with our subject, that it is a hint of the mourning for the killing of the Ephraimite Messiah, for then the Gentiles will mourn with [the Jews]" (Morteira, "Giv'at Sha'ul," vol. 3, fol. 99v). Here the criticism is that the typological interpretation of RaMBaN is inappropriate for the simple meaning of the verse. Not every typology is acceptable.

4

Inscribed for Life or Death?

Some years ago, during the morning service of Rosh Hashanah, I was conscious of a pretty eleven-year-old girl sitting near the front of the sanctuary. Her mother, who had not yet reached her fortieth birthday, was in the hospital, dying of cancer. There was at this point no realistic hope for a remission. (She actually died just a week later; the funeral service was held on the morning preceding Yom Kippur). I had spent a considerable amount of time with this woman; she had been very much in my thoughts during the previous few months. But now I was thinking about the daughter. How would she respond when the inevitable occurred?

I had always been moved by the power of the *U-netaneh toqef* liturgy, but this year, with the child sitting in front of me, I found it difficult to say the words, *"U-teshuvah u-tefilah u-tsedaqah ma'avirin et ro'a ha-gezeirah."* Max Arzt wrote in his commentary on the liturgy for the Days of Awe, "The prayer . . . reaches its climax when it assures us that it is within man's power to annul an evil decree."[1] Did this mean that it was within the power of that child, or her mother, to arrest the cancer through penitence, prayer, and charity? Would the mother's untimely death after an agonizing struggle prove that she and the members of her family had not engaged sufficiently in penitence, prayer, and charity, and that they were therefore at least partly responsible for the consequences? I was quite certain that I did not want the girl to leave the synagogue with such a message. But was that what the liturgy truly meant?

Not at all certain that the Hebrew words affirm that "it is within man's power to annul an evil decree," I resolved to look for discussions of the passage to see how it was traditionally understood. While I have not found very much interpretative material specifically on *U-netaneh toqef,* I did find considerable literature on a well-known aggadah relating to Rosh Hashanah,

Originally appeared in *Journal of Reform Judaism* 28 (1983): 18–26. Reprinted with permission from the Central Conference of American Rabbis.
    1. Arzt, p. 166.

which raises a similar problem. The rabbinical attempt to grapple with the implications of this aggadah turned out to be quite instructive.

The passage is found in B. Rosh Hashanah 16b:

> Said Rabbi Kruspedai, in the name of Rabbi Yohanan: Three books are opened on Rosh Hashanah, one for the wholly righteous, one for the wholly wicked, and one for the intermediates. The wholly righteous are at once inscribed and sealed for life; the wholly wicked are at once inscribed and sealed for death; and the intermediates are held suspended from Rosh Hashanah until Yom Kippur. If they are found worthy, they are inscribed for life; if unworthy, they are inscribed for death.

Discussions of this statement appear in many medieval sermons dealing with Rosh Hashanah, as well as in the exegetical literature on Talmud and Aggadah.

Virtually every figure who discusses the passage begins by noting that it raises an obvious and serious difficulty. In his Sermon for Rosh Hashanah, RaMBaN articulated this problem with force. "How could R. Yohanan have said such a thing," he asks rhetorically. "Do all the righteous indeed live and all the wicked die [each year]? Is not the world and all its desirable things given over to the wicked? Biblical verses cry out against him [citing Eccles. 7:15 and 8:14, Jer. 12:1, Hab. 1:3–4]. Has this sage never seen the book of Job?" And he goes on to quote several rabbinic statements that seem blatantly to contradict R. Yohanan's assertion.[2] Other preachers and commentators felt it unnecessary to document the problem by citing Bible and Talmud. They point simply to empirical evidence and common experience: everyone knows that some righteous people die untimely deaths and wicked ones often live many years in tranquility.[3] Assuming then that R. Yohanan was not totally blind to the realities of life, his statement clearly required interpretation.

One approach focused on the terms "inscribed for life" and "inscribed for death." After formulating the problem raised by the statement, the Tosafist answered simply, "All that is called here 'death' for the wicked and 'life' for the righteous refers to the life of the world to come."[4] This interpretation

---

2. Sermon for Rosh Hashanah, in RaMBaN 1:224–45; cf. 2:264–65.

3. See, for example, Arama, *'Aqedat*, nu. 63, 2:171a: "The senses testify to the opposite of what is maintained here"; Morteira 1912, p. 291: "Experience shows that many wicked people live long lives in their evil, and many righteous people are cut down in the midst of their days as would be appropriate for the wicked."

4. Tosafot RH 16b, *Ve-neḥtamim*. The Tosafot rarely comment on purely theological problems in the aggadah; here it is the apparent conflict between this assertion and another in B. Qid 39b that occasions the comment.

was expanded by later writers—in particular Samuel Edels (MaHaRSHA) and Judah Moscato—in accordance with the rabbinic statement, "The righteous are called 'alive' even in their death, while the wicked are called 'dead' even while they are alive."[5] The ultimate significance of life and death pertains not to this world but to the fate of the soul in eternity. Therefore, when the righteous become sick or impoverished, these apparent evils may still lead to the ultimate good of eternal life. As they would be rewarded with eternal bliss, even when suffering physical death, they may be subsumed under the rubric "inscribed for life." On the other hand, long life, health, and prosperity only lead the wicked more certainly toward the destruction and death of the soul. In this sense, despite their physical fortune, the wicked are said to be "inscribed for death."[6]

Is it true that the judgment occurring on Rosh Hashanah refers to the fate of the soul in eternity rather than to the course of one's life in this world? Most Jewish thinkers rejected this conclusion. They argued that the judgment of eternal life or eternal death should be a one-time event, appropriate immediately after the death of the body. There is no reason why such a judgment should occur each year. Furthermore, statements in the Rosh Hashanah liturgy clearly indicate that what is at issue are the affairs of this world: "On it, sentence is pronounced upon kingdoms—which is destined to the sword and which to peace, which to famine and which to plenty." To interpret "inscribed for life" in such a manner as to include physical suffering and even death during the ensuing year is therefore forced and improper.[7]

A second mode of exegesis concentrates on the meaning of the terms "wholly righteous" and "wholly wicked." A radical reinterpretation of these terms was suggested by Isaiah of Trani the Elder, and picked up by RaMBaN and later by Nissim b. Reuben Gerundi. These scholars maintained that the terms refer not to the person's overall nature, but to his status in the particular judgment of each Rosh Hashanah. An evil person brought to trial may be, for one reason or another, acquitted; with regard to this trial, he could therefore be described as "wholly innocent." Similarly, God may decide on Rosh Hashanah to grant a year of life and health to a scoundrel in order to reward a single good deed and reserve unmitigated punishment for the world

5. B. Ber 18a–b; cf. RaSHI on Gen. 11:32.

6. MaHaRSHA, ad loc.; Moscato, nu. 41, p. 123. Moscato claims to have arrived at his interpretation independently of the Tosafot, and to have seen the Tosafot only after he had wrestled with the problem and reached the same conclusion.

7. See, for example, Ibn Shu'eib, *Derashot* (1583), p. 90c, *Derashot* (1992), p. 497; Josiah Pinto in *'Ein Ya'aqov*, ad loc.

to come. Such a person is called "wholly innocent" (*tsaddiq gamur*) with regard to this judgment. By contrast, a saint may be judged worthy of death
as punishment for a single sin so that he may attain unabated reward in the
world to come, and he will therefore fit into R. Yohanan's category of
"wholly guilty" (*resha'im gemurim*). In this manner, RaMBaN concludes, the
statement can be understood to have been said "with wisdom and logic."[8]

This view too was subjected to scathing criticism by later writers. The
Spanish preacher Isaac Arama contended, "All these words [of RaMBaN] fail
to bring satisfaction; indeed they are most astonishing. Is it acceptable to the
mind that the Patriarchs and Prophets and the other pious men who lived
full and noble lives should, when it came time for them to ascend to the
presence of the Lord, be referred to as *resha'im gemurim* inscribed and sealed
immediately for death? Or that a malicious rogue who lives a long and evil
life be described [each year] as one of the *tsaddiqim* inscribed and sealed immediately for life?"[9] Linguistic legerdemain fell by the wayside as Jews re-
coiled before RaMBaN's assertion that Moses himself was once included in
the category of *resha'im gemurim,* and Ahab could be described as a *tsaddiq
gamur.*

One of the most impressive attempts to interpret the aggadah comes from
Arama himself. Insisting that the judgment of life and death on Rosh
Hashanah applies to this world, Arama drastically reduced the scope of that
judgment. Perhaps most significant is his argument that the annual Day of
Judgment does not determine death from natural causes, which is part of the
human condition, but only special modes of death that are clearly punishments for the sins of the individual. This allowed Arama to avoid the para-
doxical conclusion apparently required by the aggadah that every person, no
matter how good, must in some year be included in the category *resha'im.*

Now it could be maintained that a righteous man who lives to an old age
dies not because of a decree on Rosh Hashanah, but simply because of the
nature of the human body.[10] Furthermore, Arama argued that the truly

8. Isaiah di Trani, p. 127; RaMBaN 1:225, 2:264–65; Nissim ben Reuben, *Ḥiddushim,* p.
6a. All three justify their interpretation of *tsaddiq* and *rasha'* as meaning "innocent" and
"guilty" by citing Deut. 25:1.

9. Arama, *'Aqedat* 2:171a.

10. Josiah Pinto (in *'Ein Ya'aqov,* ad loc.) carries this idea further. He maintains that the
life span of each human being has been determined by God from the beginning of time (and
therefore independently of the person's actions). The righteous, inscribed for life, are allowed
to live out their allotted days, although this may not necessarily mean a long life; the wicked
may be given their full allotment as recompense for a single important deed of goodness, or
their life may be cut short of what was allotted to them.

wicked man, who is doomed to eternal destruction, is not included at all in the judgment of Rosh Hashanah. He may therefore live a long life if he is endowed with a naturally strong constitution. The death ordained on Rosh Hashanah must enable an individual to atone for an outstanding sin, leaving him worthy of life in the world to come.

Finally, Arama maintained that the judgment of Rosh Hashanah is not irrevocable. It reflects the situation at one point in time, and it may be reversed by subsequent actions. Being inscribed and sealed for life with the righteous is no guarantee that someone will live throughout the following year, and not only because of death through natural causes. A person may decide to give up his life as a martyr, or to jump off a high roof, or to ignore warnings of danger, or to commit a capital crime. In each of these cases, despite having been inscribed for life on Rosh Hashanah, the individual may die. The same is true of a judgment for death. This does not mean instant execution of all sinners, but simply that God's providential protection is removed and the individual given over to the dangers of chance. The story of Hezekiah proves that if the person returns to God in repentance a few months later, the sentence may be reversed.

In this way, Arama introduced an element of dynamism into what might appear to be an all-encompassing and irreversible judgment, thereby explaining the absence of correlation between moral character and the timing of death in a manner different from either the Tosafot or RaMBaN. The most serious objection to his view was anticipated by Arama himself. The reader might say, "According to these assumptions of yours, you have nullified the entire principle of judgment on Rosh Hashanah. For if the judgment can change each day according to the actions of the individual, wherein is this day different from others, that we call it a day of the shofar blast and set it apart as the Day of Judgment?"

In answer, Arama suggested the analogy of a physician who attends to specific illnesses in his patients as they occur, but who sets aside a special time in the spring to promote a general health campaign. So God deals with His people: the most serious sins are adjudicated right away; the lesser sins, which in themselves would not merit a death sentence, are adjudicated on Rosh Hashanah.[11] It was an answer that failed to satisfy Saul Levi Morteira, the rabbi of young Spinoza's Amsterdam.

After reviewing earlier interpretations and noting several additional problems with the aggadah, Morteira placed the entire matter in a different perspective by introducing a distinction between two kinds of judgment. In ad-

---

11. Arama, *'Aqedat*, 2:173b.

dition to the judgment of the individual, there is the judgment of an entire group—a community, a city, a nation, or the entire world. It is this collective judgment that occurs on Rosh Hashanah; the individual, as Arama had maintained, may be judged anew each day in accordance with his deeds. The divine calculus underlying the collective judgment is described by Morteira as follows. On Rosh Hashanah,

> God judges the deeds of each person individually at first, not in order to find that person innocent or guilty as an individual, but to determine whether or not to bring him into the general account. That is, God weighs the deeds of Reuben alone, and finds on Rosh Hashanah that his merits exceed his faults in quantity and quality (for God alone can judge in this matter: One transgression may be equivalent to a thousand merits, and one mitsvah equivalent to a thousand sins; blessed is He who knows the true criterion). The merits of Reuben will then be inscribed among the merits of the community, and he will be called "wholly righteous." If it should be the opposite, his sins will be inscribed among the sins of the community, and he will be called "wholly wicked."
>
> The few sins of the *tsaddiq* will be punished by God and will not be included among those of the community; the few merits of the *rasha'* will be rewarded by God and will not count for the community. According to their nature, they will be inscribed immediately on Rosh Hashanah, whether for good or for evil. The intermediates, whose deeds are balanced, are held suspended until Yom Kippur. If they are worthy, they are inscribed in the manner of the wholly righteous, so that their deeds will not harm the community at all; if they do evil, they will be inscribed in the category of the wholly wicked, so that their merits will bring the community no benefit.[12]

In this manner, Morteira was able to solve a number of problems concerning the aggadah. He brings it into harmony with the formulation of the Rosh Hashanah liturgy: "Sentence is pronounced upon kingdoms—which is destined to the sword and which to peace." He explains why an individual with a preponderance of good deeds and some bad ones is called "*wholly righteous*": only the good deeds are efficacious within the context of the collective judgment.[13] He resolves what he considers to be "an enormous problem that earlier writers never imagined": How can Yohanan's statement that

12. Morteira 1912, pp. 292–93.
13. The comment of the Tosafot had already explained that the terms "wholly righteous" and "wholly wicked" had to include those who were for the most part righteous or wicked, otherwise the term "intermediates" would include virtually everyone. It did not explain why the adjective *gemurim* was used in the statement at all.

the righteous are immediately inscribed and sealed for life be reconciled with the prevalent view that the sealing of judgment does not occur until Yom Kippur? The answer is that the decision for the righteous and for the wicked is made on Rosh Hashanah, but the collective judgment must wait until Yom Kippur, so that the actions of the intermediates can be entered into account.

Most important for our investigation, Morteira allows for the possibility of a righteous individual suffering while insisting on the efficacy of his good deeds *in the context of this world.* "It is possible that a *tsaddiq,* who is inscribed for the life of the community [that is, his deeds help insure that the community will survive and prosper] will die because of a minor sin that he committed, or because his time has come, or for another reason."[14] But there is a close interrelationship between the welfare of the community and that of the individual. If the group prospers, partly because of the efforts of a particular individual, then even if that individual suffers because of a minor sin or because of purely natural circumstances, he cannot fail to benefit from the success of the community in which he lives.

Whether or not this interpretation of Morteira can be said to be the simple meaning of the rabbinic statement, and whether or not it is a theological stance satisfactory after Auschwitz, it is not my purpose to decide. What I have attempted to demonstrate is that many generations of leading Jewish thinkers refused to accept the notion that the judgment on Rosh Hashanah implies a causal link between goodness and life, and between wickedness and death in the following year. Using various techniques in their sermons and other writings, they reinterpreted a well-known rabbinic assertion so as to account for the painful reality of their own experience, while retaining the belief in a just God and a day of accountability.

This brings us back to the *U-netaneh toqef* passage. My own suggestion concerning the meaning of that affirmation differs from the common understanding precisely in that it is more literal. It should be noted that the source of the climactic sentence is a statement appearing in several midrashim: "Three things annul the decree (*mevattelim et ha-gezeirah*): they are prayer, charity, and penitence."[15] The word *gezeirah,* taken over into the liturgy, is not identical with *din* or *gezar din* (judgment, verdict); it does not necessarily imply the outcome of a trial administered by a just judge. It is often used (for example, in the phrase *gezeirat ha-melech*) to mean the arbi-

14. Morteira 1912, p. 294.
15. Gen. Rab. 44,5; see the extensive notes in the Albeck edition for parallel readings in other midrashic texts.

trary decision of a powerful ruler, a decision that has no apparent rational basis. What is inscribed on Rosh Hashanah and sealed on Yom Kippur may be a *gezeirah* unconnected with the individual's moral or religious stature.

Furthermore, the two changes introduced into the wording of the liturgical sentence are of utmost importance. Where the midrash says *mevattelim* (annul, cancel), the liturgy says *ma'avirin* (literally, cause to pass). And where the midrash says *ha-gezeirah* (or in one version, *gezeirot ra'ot*) the liturgy says *ro'a ha-gezeira* (the evil of the decree). The midrashic source asserts, to use Arzt's formulation, that "it is within man's power to annul an evil decree," but the liturgical passage tells us something quite different: that penitence, prayer and charity "make the evil of the decree pass."

Death, sickness, impoverishment, tragic as they may be, are not identical with evil. They do bear a potential for truly evil consequences. They can poison, embitter, fill us with self-pity, destroy a marriage, blind us to the needs of others, turn us away from God. But the evil consequences of even the most fearsome decree are not inevitable. If penitence, prayer, and charity cannot change the external reality, if they cannot arrest the malignant cancer, they can indeed ensure that the evil potential in that reality will not become actual and enduring, but will pass. They can enable us to transcend the evil of the decree. This, I believe, is the simple meaning of the Hebrew words.[16] And this is a meaning that we can, in conscience, share with that eleven-year-old girl.

---

16. I would therefore reject all translations that imply that the external reality of the decree can be altered through penitence, prayer, and charity; my argument is that such translations, in addition to raising the theological problem I have noted, distort the simple meaning of the Hebrew text.

5

Christians and Jews:
Some Positive Images

The dean of contemporary Jewish historians, S. W. Baron, has persuasively argued that many modern conceptions of Jewish experience in medieval Christian Europe suffer from a fundamental distortion. Writing history was not a natural vocation for medieval Jews: most Jewish historiography was inspired by calamities that generated the impulse to record and, if possible, to explain. Most medieval Jewish chronicles are little more than accounts of the massacres and attacks suffered by various communities at different times. The tendency to assume that these historiographical sources present a full picture of reality resulted in what Baron called the "lachrymose conception of Jewish history"—viewing medieval Jewish experience as a succession of tragedies in a vale of tears.[1]

A similar danger of distortion exists in reconstructing the perceptions of the Other held by Christians and Jews in the past. A number of rigorous studies of Christian and Jewish polemical texts have been published during the past generation.[2] But since this literature is by nature composed of attacks on a rival community and its faith, it tends to convey the impression that the discourse between the two communities was entirely limited to such attacks and to imply that the leaders of Christianity and of Judaism conceived of each other solely as the enemy to be refuted or vanquished. Similarly, eloquent and thorough treatments of the history of anti-Jewish teachings have been produced by both Christian and Jewish scholars.[3] But by

Reprinted from *Christians Among Jews and Gentiles,* edited by George Nickelsburg and George W. MacRae, copyright 1986 by the President and Fellows of Harvard College, by permission of Augsburg Fortress Press.

1. Baron, *History,* pp. 84, 96, and frequently elsewhere in his work.
2. Of the many possible examples perhaps the most important are Lasker, *Philosophical Polemics;* Berger, *Jewish-Christian Debate;* Kimhi, *Covenant;* Talmage, *Kitvei Pulmus;* Trautner-Kromann.
3. E.g. Trachtenberg; Ruether; Cohen, *Friars;* Almog.

selectively focusing on negative images, these studies often project a picture that is overly dismal and bleak.

There can be little doubt that Christians and Jews often viewed each other as less than fully human and sometimes even worse, although the complete history of the "demonic" conception of the Gentile that pervades classical texts of the Jewish mystical tradition has yet to be elucidated. What deserves attention, however, is that more positive perceptions existed as well. Particularly striking are those occasions when religious leaders, addressing their own people in a context of ethical and religious exhortation and rebuke, recognized in the other community positive qualities worthy of emulation.

This use of the outsider as a model with which to admonish one's own people has a long history as a powerful weapon in the arsenal of the rhetoric of self-criticism. We find it in the prophet Malachi *(For from the rising to the setting sun, my Name is great among the nations, . . . but you profane it—* Mal. 1:11–12) and in the exemplum of the "good Samaritan" (Luke 10:30–37). But it is more than merely a rhetorical ploy. To be effective, listeners must find verisimilitude in such presentations and respond, "Yes, it's true, those people for whom we have such contempt are actually better than we are in this respect." While such passages must not be taken simplistically as accurate descriptions of either community, they may serve to indicate the attitudes of the author, and to some extent also of the audience being addressed. That a full collection of such passages would be a valuable complement and corrective to the picture presented by the literature of polemic and contempt will, I hope, be demonstrated by the following illustrations.

Despite widespread antipathy, there were certain qualities that Christian moralists respected in their Jewish contemporaries. First, Jews were known for their devotion to the Sabbath and to the holy days of the festival calendar. Some of the most virulent anti-Jewish preachers conceded this point and identified that devotion as an area in which their own listeners frequently fell short. Few religious leaders exceeded the venomous antisemitic rhetoric of John Chrysostom. But even he recognized that Jewish commitment was worthy of emulation:

> You Christians should be ashamed and embarrassed at the Jews, who observe the Sabbath with such devotion and refrain from all commerce beginning with the evening of the Sabbath. When they see the sun hurrying to set in the west on Friday, they call a halt to their business affairs and interrupt their selling. If a customer haggles with them over a purchase in the later afternoon, and offers a price after evening has come, the Jews refuse the offer because they are unwilling to accept the money.[4]

4. The text is quoted from Wilken, *Chrysostom*, p. 66.

This theme was frequently reiterated in the Middle Ages. Berthold of Regensburg, one of the great popular preachers of the thirteenth century (whose sermons reflect some of the worst anti-Jewish stereotypes of that age) told his flock:

> Now you see very well that a stinking Jew, whose odor is offensive to all, honors his holy days better than you. Bah! As a Christian you should be ashamed of yourself that you do not trust in God as much as the stinking Jew, by believing that if you spent the holy day in His praise as He commanded you, He would certainly reward you.[5]

The gratuitous insults, drawn from the common medieval notion of *fetor judaicus,* only heightened the shame of the congregation in failing to meet the religious standards set by their despised neighbors.

John Bromyard, author of a monumental fourteenth-century anthology of homiletical materials, reported that a Jew successfully challenged his Christian neighbors with the charge that "You say that you have festivals in your law, but I do not see how you observe them. What I do see is armored chariots, and horses with packs going to the woods, and merchants, and such kinds of activity on those days you call holy, just like those on other days." Therefore, says Bromyard, "because of our bad conduct the verse from Lamentations has been fulfilled in us Christians: *Her enemies have seen her and mocked at her Sabbaths* (Lam. 1:7)."[6] A similar point is made at the end of the fifteenth century in Sebastian Brant's *Ship of Fools.*[7]

Related to this is the devotion to God expressed through a constant

---

5. Berthold von Regensburg, 1:270. Cf. Trachtenberg, p. 277 n. 18; Cohen, *Friars,* pp. 228–38. In different sermons, Berthold maintained that the Jews "honor their fathers and mothers better than you" (1:164) and pointed to the "stinking, offensive Jew" who is able to remain continent during the period of his wife's menstruation, contrasting the lack of self-control in his Christian listeners: "And so should you act at that time": (1:323, cf. Iannucci, p. 29).

6. Bromyard, 1:281a. The Lamentations verse is, of course, cited from the Vulgate (viderunt eam hostes, et deriserunt sabbata ejus), which has read the Hebrew *mishbatteha* as "Sabbaths." Cf. Lam. Rab. on this verse (*Midrash Rabbah,* 4, Lamentations, p. 108). To my knowledge, the only scholar to call attention to the positive image of the Jew in Bromyard's work was Owst, *Preaching,* pp. 177, 418–19.

7. "Die Juden spotten unser sehr,/ Das wir dem Feirtage thun solche ehr,/ Das sie noch halten also steiss,/ Das ich sie nicht ins Narrenschiff,/ Wolt setzen." Brant, *Narrenschiff,* p. 162 ("Jews jeer at us with words that flay,/ That we neglect the holiday/ Which they observe with heart and lip,/ So that into the dunce's ship/ I would not place them": Brant, *Ship of Fools,* p. 308). Elsewhere in this work Brant uses the Jews as a negative model (*Ship of Fools,* pp. 127, 290).

awareness of God and the divine commandments. Bossuet, the great French preacher of the seventeenth century, conceded that the religious ideals expressed in Deuteronomy 6:4–9 were more readily accepted by contemporary Jews than by most Christians.

> Don't tell me that this attentiveness [to God] pertains only to the cloisters and is relevant only to the life of withdrawal [from the world]. This formal precept has been written for the entire people of God. The Jews, carnal and coarse as they are, recognize even today that this indispensable obligation is imposed upon them. If we pretend, Christians, that this precept has less validity under the law of grace, and that Christians have less of an obligation for such attentiveness than do the Jews, we dishonor Christianity and shame Jesus Christ.[8]

The idea that Jews could take their religious obligations more seriously than Christians was a scandal to more than one Christian leader, but it was an idea that seemed to reflect their genuine perception of Jewish life.

A second theme was the Jews' abhorrence for blasphemous language and profanity in speech. One of the most influential popular preachers of the early thirteenth century, Jacques de Vitry, reproaching his audience for their frequent profanity, related the following incident:

> I have heard that a certain Jew, while playing at dice with a Christian, heard that Christian swearing and blaspheming God because he was losing. The Jew stopped up his ears and, leaving the money behind, got up from the game and fled. For the Jews not only refuse to blaspheme God, they are unwilling to hear anyone blaspheme.

According to the preacher, Jews

> would never tolerate it, but rather become infuriated, if anyone were to say about their own wives, or their parents, or any member of their family, the shameful things that Christians say about the blessed Virgin, and the saints, and even about God.[9]

---

8. Bossuet 2:151a. Bossuet continues to use the same kind of rhetorical comparison with Muslims: "The false prophet of the Arabs, whose paradise is entirely sensual, and whose religion is pure politics, did not neglect to command his miserable sectarians to worship five times each day, and you see how precise they are in this observance." For a general statement that Jews, Muslims, and even pagans observe their laws "though they are now of no avail for the salvation of souls" while Christians do not, see Gregory VII, p. 194.

9. Crane, p. 91.

This theme is taken up by Bromyard in several places of his magnum opus. The Jews, he writes, "rarely swear, for one hardly ever hears them take an oath, except in accordance with their law. . . . When they hear a blasphemy, they rend their garments . . . and cover up their ears." And "They do not blaspheme, nor do they willingly hear someone blaspheme or swear falsely. But we laugh when we do this, or when we hear it done by others."[10] There is no mistaking the pointed suggestion that the Jewish standards of decorum might well be taken as a model for Christians.

Thirdly, the Jewish commitment to education was recognized and admired by at least some Christians. A contrast between the two communities is drawn in a commentary written by a pupil of Abelard:

> If the Christians educate their sons, they do so not for God, but for gain, in order that the one brother, if he be a cleric, may help his father and his mother and his other brothers. They say that a cleric will have no heir and whatever he has will be ours. . . . A black cloak and a hood to go to church in and his surplice will be enough for him. But the Jews, out of zeal for God and love of the Law, put as many sons as they have to letters, that each may understand God's Law. . . . A Jew, however, poor, would put even ten sons to letters, not for gain, as the Christians do, but for the understanding of God's Law, and not only his sons but his daughters.[11]

It is not only the value Jews place on education, but the purity of their motives that the Christian writer finds so impressive.

Perhaps most poignant is the recognition of Jewish willingness to suffer for their faith. The assertion placed into the mouth of Peter Abelard's fictional Jewish participant in dialogue, that "surely no nation is known or is even believed to have suffered so much for God as we constantly endure," is more than an attempt to create a realistic character; it strikes a chord of genuine empathy.[12] Just as eloquent is John Bromyard, conceding the Jews' loyalty even as he denies the validity of their faith:

> In many countries where the Jews live, certain offenses are punished according to local custom by the Jew's being hung by the feet between two dogs, just

---

10. Bromyard, 1:419c, 2:235a–b. The same idea appears in French Reformation sermons: see Taylor, p. 154.

11. Smalley, p. 78. The statement about daughters receiving a Torah education is striking in light of Jewish ambivalence on this point. In general, girls were not included in a formal educational program; cf. the preliminary remarks in Kanarfogel, pp. 10–11.

12. "Nulla quippe gens unquam tanta pro deo pertulisse noscitur, aut etiam creditur, quanta nos jugiter pro ipso sustinemus." Cf. Abelard, p. 32. The entire passage in which this sentence appears is noteworthy; cf. Liebeschutz.

as they hanged Christ between two thieves, or by being buried alive. Before the sentence, they may be offered their lives if they would be willing to accept our faith and baptism. Yet they prefer to suffer those punishments and death rather than to deny their faith.

Thus, according to Bromyard, "many Jews frequently suffer the most excruciating punishments and ultimately the most horrible deaths for their faith, clearly much more painful than many martyrs for the Christian faith." Although the absence of divine miracles on behalf of the Jewish martyrs was taken as proof of the falsity of their religion, there was clearly something in the phenomenon of Jewish martyrdom that impressed the preacher deeply.[13]

Positive views of Christian behavior are similarly to be found in the Jewish literature. Various aspects of Christian intellectual life were identified by Jews as exemplary. Joseph ibn Kaspi, passionately devoted to a philosophical exposition of Judaism, lamented the paradox that Christian scholars honored and studied Maimonides' *Guide for the Perplexed* while Jews, for whom the book had been written, neglected it.[14] Solomon ibn Verga, author of a groundbreaking historical work, praised his Christian neighbors for their "active desire to learn about ancient things in order to draw moral instruction from them," a quality he considered to be a sign of their enlightenment.[15]

The values and institutions of Christian education were often admired. In the early seventeenth century, a German Jewish author conceded in an apological work that "almost all the Christians of our time study, and they value learning, while among us it is the opposite: only a few engage in the study of Torah, while most are eager to make money."[16] In the middle of the eighteenth century, a rabbi preaching to the Ashkenazic congregation in London drew a painful contrast between the educational activities of his own community and those of the country where he lived:

> Look and see how many schools of higher learning (*battei midrashot*) they have throughout this realm, which they call "Academies." Whosoever seeks wisdom may go and study; all is provided. As for us, we do not have even one school worthy of being called by the Name of God.[17]

13. Bromyard, 1:290a. On the humiliating mode of execution, see the sources cited by Roth, "European Jewry," p. 159 and the picture in Hsia, p. 28. Cf. the passage cited by Oberman, p. 99.

14. Joseph ibn Kaspi, in Abrahams, *Ethical Wills,* 1:149–50, 154.

15. Ibn Verga, p. 21.

16. Zalman Zevi Openhausen, *Der Judischer Theriac,* chaps. 2 and 7, quoted in Assaf, 1:74.

17. Levin, "Derashot," fol. 19b; cf. Duschinsky, p. 18.

Christian devotion to the church is emphasized in an extraordinary work of self-criticism written near the beginning of the fifteenth century in Spain, after the devastating pogroms of 1391 and the wave of apostasies that followed in their wake.

> Those in whose country we live bring tithes and give generously to their scholars from the first produce of their fields. They place these portions before them graciously, giving their very best possession, so as to make their religion strong. Their nobles and lords yearn to have their sons enter holy orders and attain a position of honor in their church. But affluent Jews and Jewish communal leaders give our own scholars meagre bread and scant water. To their shame and disgrace, they eat like princes and dress like nobles, while scholars eat the bread of toil and languish. . . . This is why the Torah is dishonored and forgotten by us. The leaders of our community have no desire for their sons to enter the discipline of serious Torah study and be dependent upon it for their livelihood.[18]

Here it is the Christians who want their children to devote their lives to their faith, while influential Jews do not—precisely the opposite of the point made in the passage from Abelard's student, quoted above.

The same Jewish author criticized his coreligionists for not behaving in the synagogues more like their Christian neighbors.

> Look what happens when a congregation [of Jews] gathers to hear words of Torah from a sage. Slumber weighs upon the eyes of the officers; others converse about trivial affairs. The preacher is dumbfounded by the talking of men and the chattering of women standing behind the synagogue. If he should reproach them because of their behavior, they continue to sin, behaving corruptly, abominably. This is the opposite of the Christians. When their men and women gather to hear a preacher, they stand together in absolute silence, marvelling at his rebuke; not one of them dozes as he pours out his words upon them. They await him as they do the rain, eager for the waters of his counsel. We have not learned properly from those around us.[19]

Nor was this the only aspect of Christian preaching that Jews found admirable. In the middle of the fifteenth century, the author of a Jewish treatise on homiletics contrasted the courage of Christian preachers with the sycophancy of their Jewish counterparts: "A Gentile may preach against

---

18. Alami, p. 26.

19. Alami, p. 27. Very much the same point was made a century later, following the Expulsion, by Yabetz, *Ḥasdei ha-Shem*, p. 56.

kings and nobles, proclaiming their sins for all to hear. But in our own nation, no one will raise his tongue against any Jew whatsoever, and certainly not if the man is wealthy or a potential benefactor."[20] One of the best known Jewish preachers in the generation of the Expulsion from Spain traced the impetus for his own creativity to popular recognition of the high level of Christian preaching, which left his people dissatisfied with most of the sermons they heard in the synagogues.[21]

Except for the apostates, medieval Jewish writers were unambiguous in asserting the inferiority of the Christian religion to their own. Yet the devotion of many Christians to their faith was recognized, admired, and even envied by more than a few. Critics of rationalism frequently asserted that Christians believed in God and in the fundamental teachings of the Torah—such as creation, prophecy, miracles, and immortality—more genuinely than did those Jews who were influenced by corrosive philosophical skepticism.[22]

A thirteenth-century German text criticizes, in fairly commonplace terms, the absence of genuine religious devotion in synagogues at the time of prayer. The contrast it draws, however, is not at all unusual. "Look at the fear and trembling with which Christian kings fall upon their knees before the image of God in their churches," the author admonishes. "If the Christians show so much reverence before a statue, how much more should we Jews show as we stand in the presence of the Almighty."[23]

Joseph Karo's "Maggid" was obviously impressed by Christian ascetic piety, for he advised the great lawyer and mystic to "go out and learn from the Gentiles. Think of the tortures and mortifications they suffer. How much more should you be ready to suffer tortures and mortifications for the true faith."[24] From a very different cultural milieu, we hear a similar sentiment in a seventeenth-century Polish moralist:

> We should learn a lesson from the Christian priests and monks. They cast off their sleep every midnight, and also perform other great acts of self-abnegation on certain days, even though they dwell in peace and tranquility. . . .

20. "'Ein ha-Qore," fol. 20r; Saperstein, *Jewish Preaching*, pp. 391–92.

21. Jews "heard the [Christian] preachers and found them impressive; their appetites were whetted for similar fare. This is what they say: 'The Christian scholars and sages raise questions and seek answers in their academies and churches, thereby adding to the glory of the Torah and the prophets. . . . But our Torah commentators do not employ this method that everyone admires.'" Arama, introduction, 1:8a; *Jewish Preaching*, p. 393.

22. E.g. Abraham Abulafia, quoted in Scholem, *Major Trends*, p. 129; Arama, *Ḥazut*, Gate 8, p. 11c; Abravanel, *Prophets* 1:53b, on Joshua 10; Yabetz, Or *ha-Ḥayyim*, pp. 20a, 15b.

23. *Sefer Ḥasidim* (Bologna), section 18, p. 9a; cf. *Sefer Ḥasidim* (Parma), section 1189, p. 389.

24. Werblowsky, *Karo*, p. 163.

How much more should be, the holy people, dwelling in this bitter exile. . . .
Yet even in the hour especially appropriate to set our souls in order and to
bring the redemption near, we are too lazy to awaken.[25]

Jewish authors also pointed with grudging admiration to aspects of Christian behavior in the secular realm. One of the strongest arguments in Hebrew polemical literature was the superior ethical standards of Jewish society.[26] But in the homiletical literature, a different view was sometimes
offered. Solomon ibn Verga maintained that the Christians, who were lax in
their observance of religious rituals, were scrupulously honest in business,
while Jews, meticulously observant in the ritual domain, were not always
ethical in their business affairs.[27] His contemporary, Joseph Yabetz, chastised
his contemporaries even more directly:

> If you open your eyes, you will be envious of them, for you will see them ful-
> filling the rational commandments—*doing justice, and loving mercy* (Mic.
> 6:8)—better than we do. Their nobles take pride in the mitzvah of charity and
> compassion for the poor, which they themselves perform, in all their grandeur,
> out of love for God. Their sages are civil to each other, while some of ours are
> jealous and try to destroy each other; modesty and humility are to be found
> among them, while among us is insolence and pride.[28]

In 1747, Rabbi Jonathan Eybeschuetz rebuked his congregation in Metz by
reminding them that certain commandments, required by reason as well as
by revelation, were better observed by the Gentiles than by the Jews—for example, "honoring of father and mother and [the prohibitions against] rob-

---

25. Judah Pukhovitzer, *Da'at Ḥokhmah,* 1:39d–40a, cited in Tishby, *Netivei,* p. 125.

26. E.g. Kimhi, *Covenant,* pp. 32–35; the passage is also in Talmage, *Disputation,* pp.
11–13. Cf. the use of this claim in the context of Christian self-criticism by Bromyard,
1:289c–d.

27. Ibn Verga, p. 45. Cf. the statement in *Sefer Ḥasidim,* "There are places where the Gentiles judge truthfully and the Jews do not" (*Sefer Ḥasidim* [Parma], nu. 1301, p. 321, cited,
with similar material, in Baer, "Ha-Megamah," p. 37).

28. Yabetz, *Ḥasdei ha-Shem,* p. 56. In the eighteenth century, Hirschel Levin, rabbi in
London, contrasted the humane and compassionate way in which the Christians treated their
poor with the humiliating practices of his own people, concluding "Would that we might
learn from them in this matter" (Levin, "Derashot," fol. 19r, 21v). Yet in the Middle Ages,
the Jewish commitment to charity was praised by Christian preachers, to the denigration of
their Christian audience: "Predico eciam contra iniusticiam quorundam diuitum qui paupe-
rum Christi fratrum suorum minus miserentur quam Iudei vel Saraceni. Probatur. Principes
Iudeorum colligunt a diuitibus unde pauperes nutriantur. Principes vero Christianorum colligunt a pauperibus ut diuites in sua superbia foueantur." Brinton, 1:197; cf. Muntzer, p. 69:
"The Jews help their brothers, we take from ours."

bery and fraud, and many like them."[29] Perhaps the most impressive statement of this thesis comes at a climactic point in a sermon by Morteira, who
cites the Talmudic dictum, "You have followed them in their corruption, you
have failed to emulate their good" (B. Sanh 39b).

The dictum is applied by the preacher as follows:

> Look at the Gentiles among whom we live. We learn from them styles of
> clothing and haughtiness, but we do not learn from them silence during
> prayer. We are like them in consuming their cheeses and their wine, but we
> are not like them with regard to justice, righteousness, and honesty. We are
> like them in shaving our beard or modeling it in their style, but we are not
> like them in their refraining from cursing or swearing in God's Name. We are
> like them in frequenting underground game rooms, but we are not like them
> in turning from vengeance and refraining from bearing hatred in our hearts.
> We are like them in fornicating with their daughters, but we are not like them
> in conducting business affairs with faithfulness and fairness.[30]

We cannot know whether this passage was delivered in thunderous cadences
or in hushed, understated restraint, whether in biting sarcasm or in painful
anguish, but we may imagine the effect it must have produced upon the listeners. Measured not only against the high standards of their own tradition,
but against the actual behavior of the Christian neighbors, they were found
wanting.

Read in isolation, the passages cited above would suggest a perception of
the Other no less distorted than the usual list of negative characterizations. It
is certainly not to be suggested that the material collected here represents the
normative view on either side. Rather, it may be taken as a clue that there was
more in the mutual perceptions of Christians and Jews than unmitigated hostility and contempt, just as there was more to Jewish history than uninter-
rupted persecution and suffering. Taken together with the more prevalent
negative images, these positive glimpses express the ambivalence that impelled
each side to view the other frequently as a demonic adversary, but occasionally also as a challenge to creative competition in ethical and religious living.

---

29. Eybeschuetz, p. 99a. Note that Berthold of Regensburg had said precisely the opposite about the honor of father and mother (above, n. 5), and John Bromyard had pointed to
the Jews as a model in their handling of monetary matters because of their careful observance
of the prohibition against taking interest from their "brothers," a prohibition that not all
Christians observed (Bromyard, 2:235a).

30. Morteira 1912, p. 129a.

6

Christians and Christianity
in the Sermons of Jacob Anatoli

Sermons preached in medieval Christian churches and public places were often a vehicle for the expression of the most virulent anti-Jewish sentiments. Although the texts of these sermons resemble other theological treatises when they are bound together in someone's Collected Writings, the difference in genre is significant. Unlike the treatise, which was (until the sixteenth century) expensive to reproduce and then accessible only to individual readers, the sermon could reach a multitude of listeners simultaneously. Its power to excite heightened by a charismatic delivery, it could appeal to the emotions of the crowd and provoke immediate action. While the best-known anti-Jewish sermons of antiquity—by Melito of Sardis and John Chrysostom—do not seem to have had direct and immediate consequences, those of popular medieval Christian preachers often did. Such figures as Berthold of Regensburg in Germany, Ferrant Martinez and Vicente Ferrer in Spain, and Bernardino da Siena, John Capistrano, and Bernardino da Feltre in Italy attest to the power of the preacher to spread negative views, sometimes with devastating results.[1]

What contemporary Jewish preachers were saying about Christians and Christianity is less well known. Obviously, the power structure made incitement to violence inconceivable. The ground rules of toleration rendered explicit attacks on Christian beliefs from the pulpit problematic and potentially dangerous. Nevertheless, the texts of Jewish sermons from the Middle Ages and early modern period do contain references to Christians and their doctrines. These are important for several reasons. Unlike openly polemical

Reprinted with permission from *Jewish History* 6 (1992): 225–46, by the Haifa University Press.

1. On Berthold of Regensburg, see Cohen, *Friars,* pp. 229–36. On Ferrant Martinez and Vincent Ferrer, see Baer, *History,* 2: 95–96, 166–71; Ben-Shalom, pp. 28–30, 35–38. On the Italian preachers, see Cohen, *Friars,* pp. 238–40; Cassuto, *Firenze,* pp. 56–59; Poliakov, *Bankers,* pp. 140–42, 148–49; Toaff, pp. 45–50, 57–64, 69–71; Hughes, esp. pp. 17–28, 51–54.

writings, where the content was defined by an external challenge and the purpose to present a one-sided, negative picture of the Other, sermons reflected the preacher's own agenda. Since the sermon as a genre necessitated no mention of Christianity at all, the references that occurred indicate the significance of the rival religion in the preacher's presentation of his own commitments. The occasional polemical passages reveal what was viewed to be most threatening; where a homiletical or rhetorical purpose was served by a reference that does not denigrate, ridicule, or attack, we get a glimpse of what in the neighbor's faith was deemed worthy of attention. As sermons were undoubtedly the most effective form of mass communication before the advent of printing, it is worth trying to discover what those who delivered these sermons thought their people needed to know about Christian practices and beliefs. This chapter focuses on the presentation of Christianity in the sermons of Jacob Anatoli, a rationalist preacher who flourished in southern France and southern Italy during the first half of the thirteenth century.

Anatoli's *Malmad ha-Talmidim* consists of a series of model sermons on most of the weekly Torah lessons.[2] While they cannot be regarded as direct transcripts of sermons Anatoli actually delivered, they undoubtedly reflect some of the preaching experience described in his introduction. A matter of conjecture is whether his references to Christianity would be more likely to appear in the oral sermon or in the written text. Since the sermon was undoubtedly delivered in the vernacular while the text was written in Hebrew, it might be argued that a preacher who considered it discreet not to talk about Christianity in the language shared by Christian neighbors would feel less constrained when writing in a language to be read only by Jews. In addition, a preacher in a small community would presumably know those in his audience and refrain from delicate and controversial matters if Christian guests were present. On the other hand, a written text could get into the hands of a trouble-making apostate, and it could be argued that a preacher might be more likely to speak about Christianity than to transcribe his remarks in a book. Thus while it cannot be proven that the references to Chris-

---

2. On Anatoli as a preacher, see Saperstein, *Jewish Preaching*, pp. 15–16, 111–23, and the studies noted on p. 111, n. 4. In the introduction to his work, Anatoli asserts that the Christians make a concerted effort to investigate the Bible according to their belief, "constantly preaching in public," with the result that their lie is held to be the truth, whereas Jews are lazy in this regard, with many rabbis content to have the Torah read without delving into its meaning. Could this be a reaction to the preaching of the early Mendicant Friars? Elsewhere, Anatoli suggests that the absence of Jewish preachers willing to rebuke their people without fear results in the prolonging of the exile (Anatoli, p. 151a).

tianity in *Malmad ha-Talmidim* were actually included in the sermons Anatoli delivered, there is no reason to assume that they were not.

Anatoli apparently began to deliver sermons as a young man in southern France. His book was written after his collaboration with Michael Scot in the court of Frederick II in Naples, for he cites interpretations of Scot at least twenty times and twice refers to the Emperor himself.[3] It is therefore impossible to date the material precisely or even to be certain whether the proper context for any particular passage was southern France or southern Italy. What is certain is that Anatoli had an opportunity to learn about Christianity directly by living and working in an environment of sophisticated Christian intellectuals. Indeed, we may assume that he knew considerably more about Christianity than appears in the book. We will return to the question of selectivity later.

Some of the references pertain to Christian attitudes toward Jews and Judaism. Medieval Jews frequently perceived that Christians made fun of their rituals. In a passage criticizing some Jews' mechanical, unthinking observance of the commandments, Anatoli addresses the effect of such behavior on Christian neighbors: "We have become an object of mockery among the nations: they laugh at us because of the sounding [of the shofar] and many other such commandments, because we do not know how to respond to them and to explain their true reason. They therefore think that we are a foolish people and that our Torah, as we understand it, is foolishness" (177a).[4] This is, of course, precisely the opposite effect that

---

3. The sermon for Sukkot was written when Anatoli was 55 years old (Anatoli, p. 186b); it is not known exactly when he was born, but his father-in-law, Samuel ibn Tibbon, is thought to have been born ca. 1160. Anatoli's references to Scot as "the scholar with whom I collaborated" implies that the collaboration has ended; Scot died before 1236. Thus 1236–1240 is a reasonable estimate for the composition of the book, and the 1220s as the period of Anatoli's preaching in southern France. For one aspect of Michael Scot's work, see Thorndike, *Magic,* 8 vols. (New York, 1923–1954), 2:307–337 and Thorndike, *Scot* (London, 1965). Neither Thorndike nor Charles Haskins, who devoted several brief studies to Scot, were much interested in Scot's biblical exegesis. A comparison of the passages in which Anatoli reports his colleague's interpretations of biblical verses with Scot's voluminous unpublished works has yet to be done.

4. All page references in parentheses are to the Lyck, 1866 edition of *Malmad ha-Talmidim.* I have compared the quoted passages with Anatoli, MS (cf. *Jewish Preaching,* pp. 121 n. 26 and 122 n. 29). It happens that all passages containing even moderately negative references to Christianity or Christians have been erased from the British Library MS, so that the printed edition is far preferable to the manuscript for the subject of this study. However, in a few cases, passages erased have been omitted from the printed edition as well. I have been able to decipher only one of these passages with ultra-violet light; see below, n. 45. A critical edition of the *Malmad ha-Talmidim* is a true desideratum.

the commandments are intended to have on the nations.[5] A proper understanding of the reasons for the commandments—and conscious awareness of those reasons during their performance—is therefore crucial. The
argument functions both on the level of apologetics and within the context of Jewish spirituality.

A second passage compares Christian conceptions of Jews with the analogous Jewish conception of Christians. Discussing the phrase *tselem Elohim*
(Gen. 1:27), which he understands, following Maimonides, to mean the intellect with its capacity for reason, Anatoli notes that this is a matter in
which "all the nations are equal. We should not say that only Jews have a soul
[*nefesh*], as the foolish Gentiles say that Jews have no soul. This is just an expression of their arrogance and foolishness. The truth is that all possess the
tselem, for this is what God desired" (25b).[6] Anatoli's formulation ("we
should not say," *lo she-nomar*) implies that some Jews were guilty of this
error. Perhaps he was referring to circles of the early Kabbalists who may
have been exploring doctrines, later incorporated into the Zohar, that denied

---

5. That the Gentiles make fun of Jews for their observance of seemingly foolish rules was
a commonplace of medieval Jewish literature; see, e.g., Maimonides, *Code, Me'ilah* 8,8. It is
not easy to find evidence of medieval Christians ridiculing the sounding of the shofar, although this was a theme in the sermons of John Chrysostom; see his *Discourses,* 1.7.2, 4.7.4–6
("What do you go to see in the synagogue of those God-fighting Jews anyway? Men blowing
trumpets. . . . Don't you see that today, instead of serving the purposes of worship, the trumpets merely provide music?"), 7.1.2. Anatoli takes this as a paradigm for the mechanical performance of the commandments; see p. 9 of the Introduction to the *Malmad,* where he also
reports the Christians' claim that Jews observe only the externals. (Anatoli's own criticism of
the mechanical, unthinking observance of the commandments is one of the central themes of
the book; see, e.g., pp. 9–10 of the introduction, 148b, 163b.) The intended effect upon the
nations of the Jewish observance of the divine decrees (*ḥuqqim*) is expressed in Deut. 4:6, as
understood by Abraham ibn Ezra (commentary ad loc.) and Maimonides, *Guide* 3,31 (In an
unpublished lecture, Isadore Twersky has noted this as an apparent example of Ibn Ezra's influence on Maimonides).

6. The Hebrew text seems to be saying not that all Gentiles hold this foolish view, but that
the fools among the Gentiles do. While some Christian writers in rhetorical contexts raised
questions about whether the Jew was fully human (see, e.g., Peter the Venerable, in Williams,
p. 387), Anatoli certainly knew that most Christian theologians who discussed the "image of
God" and the soul did so in universal terms, without excluding the Jews. See, for example,
Aquinas, *Summa theologica* Ia, 93. 1 and 2. Cf. the papal bull of Gregory IX from April 1233,
which rather eloquently portrays the Jew as a human being: "They bear the image of our Savior, and were created by the Creator of all mankind" (qui Salvatoris nostri habens ymaginem,
et ab universorum Creatore creati): Grayzel, *Church and Jews,* pp. 200–201. It must be noted
that Anatoli denies that women were created in the *tselem Elohim*; on the background of this
issue, see Horowitz, "Image," pp. 175–206.

at least the higher soul to Gentiles.[7] The conclusion of this passage combines the openness of the rationalistic world-view with the ethical rebuke of the preacher: "A non-Jew who engages in the mode of study appropriate for him is greater than one of our own people who does not engage in what is appropriate for him" (25b).

A third reference to Christian attitudes toward Jews pertains to the situation of Jews in exile. A sermon on *Toledot,* beginning with the Haftarah verses on God's love for Jacob (Mal. 1:2), asserts that this statement by the last of the Prophets is intended "to refute a great confusion that has taken hold concerning the length of the exile, to the point where many have thought that this punishment results from God's hating us more than any other people, and in His love for the Gentiles He has given them sovereignty at present" (23b)—a concise formulation of Christian triumphalist theology. The preacher returns to this theme in his sermon on *Va-'Ethanan,* explaining the verses beginning with Deuteronomy 4:25 as a clear statement that the current exile was caused by our failure to worship God alone with all our hearts. "The reason for the length of our exile is not the claim they burden us and mock us with. . . . It is not that our faith is bad and their faith is good" (161a). Here we have a classic theme of Jewish apologetical literature. Though the response to the Christian claim was sharp, it was primarily a call for his own people to rally to a pure service of God based on belief in God's absolute unity and incorporeality.[8]

In addition to references to Christian attitudes, there are a number of references to Christian doctrines, often compared with Jewish beliefs. In a sermon for the Sabbath of Repentance, the "goat for Azazel" (Lev. 16:26) leads to a discussion of the belief in demons. In this context, Anatoli notes that "some of the Gentiles" believe

7. The Zohar states that the souls of the Gentiles are "from the side of defilement" (1:131a: *mi-sitra' mesa'ava iyt lon nishmatin*; cf. 1:13a, 47a). Cf. Wijnhoven, pp. 120–40; Yehudah Liebes, *Zohar,* p. 244 n. 92. It is not clear to me whether this doctrine can be documented in the texts of Kabbalists from the time of Anatoli, but the absence of such documentation would not prove that it was not maintained by Jews in his environment. For an illuminating discussion of the general issue in Jewish thought, see Greenberg, pp. 67–76.

8. Cf. also p. 136a on Jewish despair about redemption. Anatoli's statements about exile and redemption are discussed by Azriel Shochat, "Beirurim," pp. 58–60. Note in particular Anatoli's explanation of the positive role of the Diaspora (p. 97a), cited by Rosenberg, "Exile" p. 408. As for the passage on pp.160b–161a, I have read it many times without being able to decide how much is directed simply at the paganism of antiquity, how much at the Christian adoration of images, and how much (if any) at the symbolic language of early Kabbalist circles, which speaks of God in corporealist terms. The passage may be intentionally ambiguous and meant to depend upon its resonance with the listeners.

that the order of angels that was supreme over all others fell from heaven because of its pride, and turned into the order of demons: they entice human beings and are responsible for causing all evil, and they ruled over Hell until the advent of their Redeemer. They based their faith on this, and used it in their interpretation of the chapter about Sennacherib, saying that Samael was called "Day-star son of the morning" (Isa. 14:12) [i.e., Lucifer]. This entire matter is extremely far-fetched; it is not worth thinking about it, let alone writing it down, except that this delusion spread so far among the nations that many of our people believe in the existence of demons (182b).

This fairly accurate presentation of Christian belief[9] is criticized rather vehemently. But its function within the sermon is not to attack Christianity, but rather to explain the origins and power of Jewish superstition concerning demons, and this is what the preacher goes to some pains to ridicule and denounce.[10]

Anatoli seems to have been rather interested in Christian penitential practice and refers to various aspects of it. Discussing the verse *Guard your foot when you go to the house of God* (Eccles. 4:17) at the beginning of a sermon on *Shemot* (Exod. 1:1–6:1), he maintains that it has a simple meaning: one should clean one's feet when coming to a house of prayer. He develops the principle in contemporary terms, reflecting an age of unpaved, muddy streets:

> In those countries where it is the practice to wear narrow shoes which can be untied only by hand, the shoes must be cleaned before coming [to the house of prayer], for they should not be untied because of the cleanliness of the

9. The fundamental elements of this presentation—that the fall occurred among the highest order of angels (or that the Devil was originally supreme among the angels), that the cause of their fall was pride, that the fallen angels were transformed into evil demons, that Satan ruled over hell until the "harrowing of hell" by Jesus—can be found in many Christian texts culminating in the formulations of the Fourth Lateran Council and the discussion of Aquinas. See Russell, *Lucifer,* pp. 94–95, 152, 173–76; Foster, 9:306–21; Quay, pp. 20–45. For a broader treatment in Jewish and Christian sources, see Bamberger. Cf. Talmage, "Hebrew Polemical Treatise," pp. 334–35; Talmage, *Sefer ha-Berit,* p. 95.

10. Later in the sermon he complains that "most of our people, even well-known sages among them, harbor this corrupted belief, and to this day they stumble in the inanities of demons" (184b). For others in the same intellectual context who tried to convince their fellow Jews that demons did not indeed exist, see Talmage, *David Kimhi,* p. 80; Saperstein, *Decoding,* pp. 26–27; Septimus, pp. 86–87. Anatoli's colleague, Michael Scot, did apparently believe in the existence of demons; see Thorndike, *Magic,* 2:320–21, 323; Thorndike, *Scot,* pp. 93–94, 116–17. Two generations later, Solomon ibn Adret thought of the German Pietists as the ones preeminently engaged in various activities concerning demons (Adret, I, nu. 413), but whether Anatoli could have been thinking of them when he referred to "well-known sages" cannot be determined. See below, n.33.

hands. In countries where it is the practice to wear sandals and the like, they are removed from the feet.[11] The *kohen* who ascends to bless the congregation must remove his shoes. . . . Of the same nature is the prohibition against wearing a sandal on Yom Kippur, when clean clothing is required. All of this is intended to inspire us to the way of repentance. And the nations who imitate our righteous laws[12] have similar customs for their penitent, forbidding the wearing of sandals and requiring the wearing of white garments.[13] All of this inspires the appropriate emotions in one who is in the presence of the King (45a–b).

Here we have a totally neutral reference to Christianity as deriving its practices from ancient Jewish traditions; its inclusion serves merely to underscore the authenticity and rationality of Jewish ways.

Another reference to Christian penitential doctrine comes in a discussion of repentance in a sermon on *Nitsavim* (Deut. 29:9–30:20). The preacher argues that repentance is actually not that difficult for a Jew to achieve:

It is considerably easier for a Jew than it is for the peoples who imitate the Torah in their laws. Do you not see that they require the penitent to undergo many afflictions, such as traveling beyond the sea or to other distant places.[14] Not so the Torah of Moses, which commands only the confession of the mouth and of the heart" (174b).

---

11. This apparently refers to the difference in practice between Muslims, who remove their shoes before entering their place of worship, and Christians, who do not. Jewish law does not require Jews to remove their shoes in the synagogue (see Maimonides, *Code, Tefillah* 11,9 based on B. Ber 63a).

12. That Christianity was in many respects an "imitation" of Judaism is a recurring theme in the sermons; cf. pp. 15b (ritual immersion for converts), 98b (forbidden foods), 174b (penitential acts), 180a (fasting). See also Saperstein, *Decoding,* pp. 189, 195, and Maimonides, "Yemen," pp. 99–100.

13. For the Christian requirement of going barefoot as an act of penance, see Robert of Flamborough, pp. 212, 218, 223, ranging from a period of forty days to ten years. White apparel, however, was not the usual dress of Christian penitents.

14. On the journey to a distant land as a penitential act in Christianity, see Lea, *Auricular Confession,* 2:131–35; McNeill and Gamer, pp. 34, 252, 367. Lea points out that the newly established Inquisition imposed the penance of pilgrimage to the Holy Land on so many suspected of heresy in Languedoc in the 1230s that this practice was forbidden by the Vatican out of fear that the faith of the Holy Land would be contaminated (2:133–34). That this form of penance was endorsed by the German Pietists can be seen in *Sefer Ḥasidim* (Parma), nu. 175, p. 71: "A murderer must become a 'fugitive and wanderer' for five years"; the following paragraph shows that the penitential life of exile was considered to be the norm and a deviation from it had to be justified. It is obvious that Anatoli was not sympathetic to German Pietistic traditions of penance; see below. Cf. Green, pp. 267–68, n. 15.

Here too, the preacher's purpose is not to criticize the Christian practice, but rather to overturn the Pauline claim that the Law is an impossible burden. The passage culminates in an appeal to his listeners not to fail in what is after all less demanding than the requirements for their neighbors.[15]

In other passages, Anatoli's reference to Christian practice is more critical. Occasionally he introduces a Christian belief as part of his argument against a similar doctrine held by Jews that he feels compelled to attack. The prophetic verse *I will pour out My spirit upon all flesh* (Joel 3:1) seemed to imply that everyone, even the most ignorant and uneducated, would become prophets in the messianic age. This raised serious problems for the philosophical doctrine of prophecy, which held that intellectual preparation was a prerequisite. Anatoli tried to defuse the verse through a reinterpretation of the word *basar* (flesh):

> God will pour out His spirit on all flesh, namely, the living flesh, which is a metaphor [*kinnui*] for all who are wise of heart.[16] It is not that God will pour out His spirit upon the ignorant. Heaven forbid that we believe this foolishness that has spread in our time, to the point where those whom the masses think of as the pious of our generation [*ha-ḥasidim she-be-dorenu*] maintain this. They think that they are increasing God's glory with this doctrine, but whoever affirms it shows contempt for the awesome dignity of the Name (150a).

So far we are in the realm of internal Jewish debate, rooted in Maimonides' discussion of the various views of prophecy (Guide, 2,32). Anatoli first takes on that "multitude of fools," including some Jews, who held that

---

15. Cf. his statement, "There is nothing in all God's commandments that is distant or difficult, not in thought or word or deed, but everything is accessible, so that the good may be attained" (p. 104a). Elsewhere, in a passage of powerful rebuke about laxness in synagogue attendance, Anatoli insists that the commandments are not a burden but an expression of God's love (109b). By contrast with the Torah, Christianity legislates an extreme ethic, the benefit of which is not accessible to the entire people (58b).

16. Anatoli refers to his sermon on *Shemini* (99b bot.), where he interprets the apparently universalistic expression "all flesh" in Isa. 66:23 as referring to "the good and holy human beings," arguing that the word can refer either to the entire human race (as in Gen. 6:12) or only to the good (as in Ps. 145:21). The phrase "all flesh" is discussed in more detail on pp. 10a–b, and the passage from Joel on p. 100a. Note that RaDaQ commenting on Joel 3:1 interprets "all flesh" to refer to Israel, not all human beings; like Anatoli, he insists that "not all will prophecy," but only "some of them, in whom the intellect is purified and the rational power is strengthened"; cf. Talmage, "Rationalist Tradition," p. 187, 191–92 n. 72. Cf. Abravanel's first question on Joel 3:1 (Abravanel, *Prophets* 3:71a) for a review of different interpretations of the verse.

God can select anyone He wants to be a prophet, even if that person is totally ignorant. The vehemence of Anatoli's polemic, however, shows that he was responding not just to a view recorded by Maimonides, but to a belief held by some of his own contemporaries. Who were these Jews "whom the masses think of as the pious—or perhaps the Pietists—of our generation," who looked to the universal restoration of prophecy as a characteristic of the messianic age? It is tempting to associate this position with the view recorded more than a generation later in the Zohar, that in messianic times even children will have the gift of true prophecy—an idea explicitly repudiated in the *Guide*.[17] How prevalent this belief was among Kabbalists in the generations before the Zohar, and how widespread in the general Jewish population, cannot at present be determined.

But Anatoli continues to attack this doctrine by associating it with a Christian teaching:

> There is no doubt that this is of the same category as the error of the nations, and those of our own people who imitate them, who say that the exalted God, in His great humility, makes His presence rest [*mashreh shekhinato*] upon everything, paying no attention to the degradation of the lowliest things (150a).

We cannot be certain which term in Christian theology corresponds to the Hebrew *shekhinah* and to which doctrine he was referring. The context (the discussion of prophecy) suggests that he could be alluding to the heretical teaching of a group such as the Amaurians, who seem to have held to a mystical antinomian pantheism and were accused of stating that "Within five years all men will be Spirituals, so that each will be able to say, 'I am the Holy Spirit.'" On the other hand, Anatoli may no longer be talking about prophecy in the messianic age, but about a Christian teaching of divine immanence even in the basest of environments, a concept crucial (at least from the Jewish perspective) to the doctrine of the Incarnation.[18]

---

17. Zohar 2:170a; 2:22b–23a; see Baer, *History,* 1:269–70; Goetchel, pp. 236–37. For apparently uneducated Jews in late thirteenth-century Spain actually claiming to be prophets of the messianic age, see Baer, "Ha-Reqa'," pp. 40–42; Baer, *History* 1:280, and the discussion in Adret, 1, nu. 548.

18. On the Amaurians or Amalricians, see Cohn, pp. 152–62; also, Lerner. The doctrine of the Incarnation affirms that God, in humility, entered the womb of a woman to be born as a human being; for Jewish horror at the idea that God "entered a woman with a belly full of feces," see Berger, *Jewish-Christian Debate,* pp. 44, 68, 350–54. One of the Christian responses to this objection was that God fills everything, and is therefore in all sinners, yet remains pure; therefore God could remain uncontaminated in the womb (p. 351). Cf. also Lasker, *Philosophical Polemics,* pp. 111–12.

Here, however, much to our surprise, Anatoli associates this teaching with contemporary Jews who, he claims, have been overly influenced by the Christians; where usually it was the Christians who imitated the Torah, here the process was reversed. His formulation is strikingly reminiscent of Moses Taku's denunciation of the doctrine of God's immanence, which he believed came to some of the German Hasidim from Saadia Ga'on, whom Taku attacks as having been influenced by non-Jewish scholars during a thirteen-year imprisonment.[19] Anatoli is critical of the Christian doctrine, but his fundamental purpose in this passage is not to refute Christianity but to attack analogous beliefs in his own camp.

On several occasions, he compares Christian with Jewish practices, arguing that the innovation made by Christianity was not an improvement, as they claim, but a change to something inferior to the original. The sermon on *Lekh Lekha* (Gen. 12–17) contains a philosophical discussion of circumcision. Turning to the use of circumcision in conversion to Judaism, he notes, "As for the nation that patterns itself upon us and our Torah, when they baptise and convert people to Christianity [*mesha'ammedim*],[20] they bring the convert into the covenant of their faith. But they have exchanged a good sign for a bad one, for their sign is only temporary, while ours, part of the body, endures permanently" (15b).[21]

The same sermon contains an attack on Christian attitudes toward procreation. Abraham's decision to take Keturah as a wife (Gen. 25:1) shows his commitment to human procreation, a commitment expressed in the rabbinic statement, "Whoever does not engage in procreation is as one who diminishes the divine likeness" (B. Yeb 63b). "This is unlike the opinion of the Christians, who set apart some of their children to be barren to their deaths, as if God hates the human race" (15a). This appears to be an attack on the ideal of celibacy espoused by the Christian clergy, but the formulation is general and may have broader resonance as well: in feudal society many younger

19. Taku, pp. 66–67, 69, 82–83; cf. Dan, *Torat ha-Sod* pp. 171–83. The implication would be that the doctrine of immanence, as held by the Hasidim, is influenced by the Christians and undermines one of the Jewish arguments against the Incarnation. One would not have predicted that Anatoli and Taku would have agreed on anything, but they apparently took similar positions on this matter of immanence.

20. The word used by Anatoli, *mesha'amedim,* is extremely unusual; Ben Yehudah cites this passage as one of two references, along with Judah ibn Tibbon's translation of the Kuzari 3:65 (Ben Yehudah, *Millon* 7:3406). See also Roth, *Conversos,* p. 6.

21. The relative merits of circumcision and baptism were a topos in Jewish-Christian debates. This particular argument, of course, does not apply to the Jewish ritual of conversion for a woman, which is overlooked here.

sons of nobles were expected not to marry and have children themselves, in order to guard against the proliferation of heirs.[22] In any case, it clearly represents Anatoli's perception of a fundamental difference in values between Christians and Jews.

In a passage critical of the ascetic practices of Christians, particularly those involving excessive fasts, Anatoli argues that God desires a healthy body. That is why the Torah does not command many fasts, but only "one a year, as atonement for our souls." Coming but once a year, the fast has a curative effect, whereas excessive fasting endangers physical health (98a).[23] The preacher goes on to contrast Jewish and Christian dietary and sexual practices in a rich passage that deserves to be quoted at length:

Look at the foods the Torah has forbidden to us. It does not prevent us from eating meat during a certain period of the year the way the nations who imitate the laws of our sacred Torah do. They avoid eating meat and cheese and eggs for part of the year. This is the opposite of the living words of God; they have made the bitter sweet and the sweet bitter. For with regard to the enjoyment of food, which is always necessary for physical sustenance, they discontinue beneficial foods for a period of time—precisely the period that is most important for a healthy regimen. Whereas with regard to the enjoyment of sexual activity, which is not a constant need, but actually harmful much of the time, they do not interrupt it for any set period; [they forbid it only] between certain persons based on consanguinity, even if the relationship is extremely distant, while it would be better to encourage such relationships in order to keep the inheritance intact and to promote the health of the offspring.[24] Our Torah, in its perfection, has denied us the enjoyment of sexual activity during a considerable period of time, as its purpose is procreation. This denial is in such a way that the prohibition, in addition to the benefit [to our health, to to the health of the offspring], produces intense pleasure, and release, and great joy, and increased love between husband and wife, virtually achieving each month the delight of a new bridegroom with his bride. However, re-

22. See Duby, *Knight,* pp. 104–6. For a summary of Jewish (and some Christian) attitudes toward procreation, see Cohen, "*Be Fertile.*"

23. Anatoli overlooks the additional fasts commemorating historical events, which are in the category not of a Torah commandment but of custom (Maimonides, *Code, Ta'aniyot* 5,5). In this context, Anatoli compares the annual fast with the eating of asparagus, which he says has a medicinal function if taken once a year, but can result in sudden death if eaten regularly. He returns to this theme in a sermon on *Nitsavim,* explaining that asparagus is administered once a year as a diuretic "to cleanse one of all the fluids that have degenerated in him because of decay" (179a); this is compared with Yom Kippur. Cf. Rosner, p. 81.

24. For the tendency among medieval Jews to seek marriage partners within the extended family, see the sources noted by Shatzmiller, *Shylock,* p. 182, n. 9.

garding the enjoyment of food, we are not deprived of it for a particular period during the year; the Torah deprives us only of certain kinds of food, making us abandon what is superfluous (98a).

As a text of Jewish intellectual history, this passage is part of the tradition
of the rational explanation of the commandments based on the philosophical value of moderation. Maimonides' classical treatment in part 3 of the
Guide spawned an abundance of treatments by philosophically oriented disciples who repeated his insights and applied his basic approach to topics he
had not explicitly covered. The negative assessment of sexual activity comes
directly from Maimonides' Aristotelian tradition;[25] the description of the effect of periodic self-denial on the quality of the sexual experience and the en-
hancement of marital love has altogether different roots.[26]

Placed in the context of Jewish-Christian debates, we see once again the
effort to convince Jews that the Pauline critique of the Law is misguided.
The argument is made on two fronts: first, that the Church itself does not
reject the principle of law regulating behavior but merely substitutes its own,
patterned after those of the Jews; and second, that the laws of the Church
are not nearly as rational as those of God's own revelation. The contrast between the two kinds of prohibition—of foods and of sexual activity—is
neatly and effectively drawn.

How much knowledge does this passage reveal about Christian observances? Anatoli deals with three major areas. First, the refraining from the
eating of meat, eggs, and cheese during Lent was indeed an important
component of medieval Christian spirituality.[27] Even among the
Catharists, who were opposed to eating meat at all times, there were some
who felt that eating it during Lent was worse than at other times of the
year.[28] Secondly, Anatoli shows an awareness that the prohibited degrees of
consanguinity according to canon law were considerably more extensive

---

25. See the discussion in Saperstein, *Decoding*, pp. 91–101.

26. The starting point is R. Meir's statement in B. Nid 31b, which, despite its apparent
usefulness in the context of *ta'amei mitsvot*, does not seem to have been widely cited by later
authorities. Anatoli quotes the statement on p. 102a in a similar discussion.

27. See Bynum, *Holy Feast*, p. 40: "Throughout the Middle Ages, the Lenten fasts and
weekly fast days, especially Fridays, remained basic marks of the Christian" (cf. p. 323 n. 47);
her discussion on pp. 33–49 is the best recent summary of Christian fasting traditions (although it does not do justice to the fasting of the Cathars). On the requirement to abstain
from meat, cheese, and eggs, see Aquinas, *Summa theologica* II–II, 147, 8, where, despite a variety of local customs, he concludes that "the Lenten fast lays a general prohibition even on
eggs and milk foods" (2:1792).

28. Ladurie, *Montaillou*, p. 314.

than in biblical or rabbinic law, and that these presented real problems for medieval Christian society.[29]

The third area is more problematic. It is simply untrue that the Church did not prohibit sexual activity according to time but only according to category, as Anatoli maintains. Christians were expected to refrain from marital relations during the period of the wife's menstruation, during pregnancy and for some time after birth, and even during periods of the year and days of the week.[30] There was debate over the seriousness of the sin in the case of infractions, and there is little question that Jews considered sexual relations during and soon after the wife's menstruation a greater taboo than did their Christian neighbors. But Anatoli's assertion misrepresents the reality of Christian doctrine and practice. Whether this was an indication of ignorance, or a deliberate distortion for the sake of his symmetrical scheme and homiletical purpose, is unclear.

The above passages can be seen as part of a larger polemic against extreme forms of asceticism. This is a recurring theme in the sermons; indeed, it appears so frequently that it seems to be one of the problems uppermost in Anatoli's mind. Drawing on the commonplace analogy with the cures of physical ailments through medications, Anatoli insists that ascetic self-renunciation must be used sparingly and only to remedy a spiritual illness. Otherwise it is harmful (79a, 127b). The Nazirite must bring a sin-offering, lest other Jews conclude that his self-renunciation is desirable in itself.

> It is like one who takes sharp and bitter drugs as medicine for his body, which, if eaten while healthy would bring about his sudden death. So it is with those who cause pain to their soul and mortify their body in the manner of the saints of the nations, who separate themselves from the world—such [Jews] are sinners and cruel (127b).

Similarly,

> God does not hate the body, but loves it out of His love for the soul, so that the individual may thrive and the human species endure. This is unlike the view of the Gentile saints, who imagine that they can achieve perfection by going to the extreme in all kinds of self-affliction. They are cruel and deceived (79b).

---

29. On the laws of consanguinity and affinity (considerably liberalized by the Fourth Lateran Council of 1215), see Baldwin, 1:333–37; Duby, *Knight*, pp. 35–36, 208–9.

30. See Duby, *Knight*, pp. 29, 67; Noonan, pp. 165, 281–82; Brundage, pp. 242, 451. Thirteenth-century thinkers tended to repeat earlier prohibitions without as much emphasis on the seriousness of the infraction.

In a third sermon, Anatoli reiterates the argument that Judaism and the commandments of the Torah do not constitute a heavy burden, unlike "the various religions of the nations who impose upon themselves fasts and the affliction of journeys and other kinds of affliction, to the point where some of them burn their children with fire, and perform other such abominations that God detests [cf. Deut. 12:31]" (145b). This extreme charge also appears in a sermon on *Qedoshim* (Lev. 19–20), where he argues that the sole path to holiness is the observance of God's commandments,

> not through different kinds of difficult service that the other peoples have seized upon, involving affliction of soul and body, and dwelling on mountains and other [such] places, until they even burn their sons and daughters by fire. God does not require this or anything like it from us, only that we abandon all that is superfluous. . . for God does not hate the body at all, but desires that it fulfil His words justly in order to bring life to the soul (104a).

In some of these passages, it is clear that Anatoli was using extreme examples of Christian (and possibly Muslim) asceticism in order to remind his listeners of a point we have seen before: that God's requirements for the Jewish people are not excessively rigorous. In this context, criticism of the practice of the Other is incidental to the homiletical purpose, becoming pronounced only with regard to the accusation, appearing in two different sermons, that the ascetics of other faiths were responsible for the burning of their children. To what could he have been referring? No Christians were accused of burning their own children; the only conceivable way this phrase could be understood literally is as an allusion to the dramatic spectacle of more than four hundred Catharist "heretics" burnt at the stake at Minerve, Lavaur, and Casses in 1210 and 1211, the news of which must have made a lasting impact on all living in Languedoc at the time.[31] But these were not children who were burnt, nor was the burning a direct consequence or an intended result of ascetic activity.

A more likely interpretation, then, is that Anatoli was using the verse the way it was used in *Sefer Nitsaḥon Yashan*. Rejecting the literal meaning, the author maintains that the "burning" of children denounced in the biblical verse "refers to the priests and nuns who burn up in their lustful desire but are unable to consummate it." This polemical reading uses the metaphor in the celebrated formulation of Paul—*It is better to marry than to burn* (I Cor. 7:9)—and applies it in denunciation of the practice of celibacy. Anatoli's ar-

---

31. See Oldenbourg, pp. 141, 149.

gument would be that the ideal of ascetic renunciation, pressuring children into a celibate life, imposes an unconscionable burden not desired by God.[32]

On the other hand, at least one of the passages indicates that the preacher was arguing against Jews who themselves were engaging in acts of excessive self-renunciation and affliction of body and soul, analogous to those of the Christians. This attack would seem to apply most appropriately to the penitential practices of the German Hasidim, although it is not clear to what extent these practices were actually known in southern France at the time Anatoli was writing.[33] Alternatively, he could have been referring to tendencies among those in his own community— tendencies not necessarily formulated in a book or crystallized in a movement.[34] His emphatic insistence that "God does not hate the body" seems to be in response to the then current view, similar to one articulated later in the Zohar, that the body is the creation of Satan, belonging to the realm of the Other Side, and that God "crushes the body in order to give supremacy to the soul."[35] That a traditionalist, antirationalistic moralist such as Jonah Gerundi could agree with Anatoli in condemning the asceticism of excessive fasting among Jews indicates that this must have been a tendency causing Jewish leaders some concern, a trend perhaps influenced by a psychological challenge to the Jewish self-image of moral superiority

32. Berger, *Jewish-Christian Debate*, p. 70. On the practice of abandoning children to the care of monasteries and the debate over whether such children retained any right to withdraw at a later date, see Boswell, *Kindness*, pp. 228–55, 296–321. See also below, n. 36. Fire was also used by Christian writers as a metaphor for ascetic fasting, a meaning that would fit well in this context; see Bynum, *Holy Feast*, p. 39.

33. See Marcus, *Piety*, pp. 43, 79, 125–26 and passim. How much was known about German Pietists in southern France during Anatoli's time remains an intriguing problem. Abraham ben Nathan ha-Yarhi referred to *Ḥasidei Alemanyah* in his *Sefer ha-Manhig* in the late twelfth century (Marcus, *Piety*, p. 147, n. 3). Joseph Dan has shown that the esoteric writings of the Pietists were known to the Kohen brothers in Castile in the third quarter of the thirteenth century (Dan, "Goralah" pp. 96–97), and it is not unreasonable to assume that reports of distinctive practices would have circulated in southern France considerably earlier. Recently, Haym Soloveitchik has argued for an early redaction of *Sefer Ḥasidim*, before 1225 (Soloveitchik, "Ta'arikh," pp. 383–88). It is thus not at all impossible that Anatoli could be responding to aspects of Judah Hasid's program.

34. On ascetic ideals in early thirteenth-century southern France, see Scholem, *Origins*, pp. 229–33; Scholem maintains that Jews in this region were "undoubtedly inclined toward the more radical demands of German Hasidism" (p. 230); cf. also Twersky, *Rabad*, pp. 25–29. Even before the thirteenth century, there is evidence of ascetic tendencies in southern France; according to Benjamin of Tudela, R. Asher of Lunel was "a recluse [*parush*], who dwells apart from the world; he pores over his books day and night, fasts periodically and abstains from all meat" (Benjamin of Tudela, p. 60).

35. Zohar 1:180a; see the discussion of negative attitudes toward the body by Tishby, *Wisdom* 2:764–65.

posed by the newly invigorated monastic ideal.[36] The ascetic impulse appears to be the aspect of Christianity that provoked Anatoli most deeply—perhaps an indication of the power of its appeal.

Malmad ha-Talmidim also contains references to dualistic beliefs that the Church considered heretical. In a sermon for Shavuot, Anatoli reminds his audience of a standard Jewish observance and its theological implications: "As we say a blessing over good, so do we over evil [cf. M. Ber 9,5], to repudiate the idle opinion of those who speak libel, namely, the heretics who say that the perishable matter of the elements and all that is composed of it is the work of Satan" (118b). He returns to the subject in a sermon on *Nitsavim* (Deut. 29:9–30:20), giving as the paradigm for the word *sikhlut* "the idea of some people about Satan: they think he is a unique spiritual being who rules over the world to do evil. Heaven forfend that we believe this, for this leads to the belief of the Dualists, who believe that there are two gods, one good and one evil" (173b).

In an extensive discussion of false beliefs relating to demons and fallen angels intended for the Sabbath of Repentance, Anatoli cites a belief of "total heresy: that God created a group [of demon-angels] to rule over man and cause him to sin and bring about evil and destruction. This is just like the position of those who say that there are two gods, one good, one evil" (183a). Although this latter belief is said to be of ancient origins, beginning in Egypt before the giving of the Torah, there can be little doubt that he was alluding to a contemporary notion. Juxtaposing from these passages the elements of the good and the evil gods and the identification of the physical world as the creation of Satan, we have in a simplified, popular form the most distinctive outlines of Catharist theology.[37]

Perhaps the most intriguing reference to Christian heresy is a somewhat obscure passage in a sermon on *Be-Midbar* (Num. 1:1–4:20). The verse *She did not know: it was I who bestowed on her the new grain and wine and oil* (Hos. 2:10) is taken to allude to those who believe that God has abandoned

---

36. Jonah Gerundi, *Sha'arei Teshuvah*, section 82, p. 82. On the psychological impact of the monastic ideal, see Berger, *Jewish-Christian Debate,* p. 27. Cf. the presentation and repudiation of the monastic ideal in Kimhi, *Covenant,* pp. 34–35 and n. 21.

37. Cf. the statement by Meir ben Simeon, cited by Shatzmiller, "Kefirah," p. 343. Shatzmiller also cites the second and third passages from Anatoli. Cf. the simple assertion by a Catharist believer, "There are two Gods! One good, the other bad," Ladurie, *Montaillou,* p. 238. For a summary of Catharist theology and the circumstances surrounding the establishment of Catharist religion in southern France, see Moore, *Origins,* pp. 139–240; Oldenbourg, pp. 28–81.

the earth. "And even if they do not say this explicitly, they understand that the active God is the evil God, because of the corruptibility inherent in the material realm, and these evil people also say that the fornications of the land [*zenunei ha-arets*] bring forth new grain and wine and oil. This is the position of those evil heretics called Patarini" (115a). "Patarini," actually the name of an eleventh century movement in Italy, was used in the thirteenth-century as a general term for the Catharists.[38] What is not entirely clear is the thrust of the phrase *zenunei ha-arets,* which could conceivably refer to some kind of sexual fertility rite, or to a mythical doctrine explaining how the earth, the creation of the devil, produced that nourishment which, since the Catharists abstained from all products of animal procreation (meat, eggs, dairy products), was absolutely essential for their survival.[39] In either case, it seems to be an indication of a Catharist teaching on a more popular level than the official theology.

I conclude with a passage of considerable historical interest. Rebuking his audience for a laxity of sexual standards, the preacher admonishes:

> We should avoid the songs of the uncircumcised, which are nothing but lechery and obscenity; their entire purpose is to lead women astray. It would be absolutely amazing for a woman grown accustomed to these lecherous words from the time she was small not to sin. *Can a man conceal fire in his breast without burning his clothes?* (Prov. 6:27). If we condemn those who linger over the wine, how much more should we condemn those who sing these lecherous songs! Woe to the foolish father and the seducing mother who raise their daughters in this way, leading them in the path of harlotry (cf. Lev. 19:29). There is no doubt that this is a terrible custom, which has come to us from the practices of the Gentiles in whose midst we live (126b).[40]

---

38. Moore, op.cit., p. 246.

39. On popular Catharist attitudes and beliefs about the harvest, see Ladurie, *Montaillou,* pp. 293–96, which records considerable ambivalence and uncertainty.

40. The issue of Jews singing secular songs arose first in the Islamic environment; cf. Maimonides, *Responsa,* nu. 244, 2:399–400; Maimonides, *Guide* 3,8. Anatoli's passage, however, seems to be more than merely a repetition of Maimonides' strictures. Cf. *Sefer Ḥasidim* (Parma), nu. 344, 346–47 (on lullabies), 348 (on using Christian melodies in Jewish worship); Guedemann, 1:32; Baron, *SRHJ* 7:205–6. From his own environment, see Abraham ben Nathan, pp. 20–21 (part of which is cited in Harris, p. 199), where the target is not the parents who allow their daughters to sing Gentile songs but the Jews who write lewd poetry in Hebrew. Jewish mystics had a much more positive attitude toward music and singing than expressed in this passage; see Idel, *Mystical Experience,* pp. 53–71, especially the description on p. 61 of the singing of "two young French girls in the city of Montpellier." Their song, however, was not a troubadour poem but the "love song" Psalm 45.

Note that this is an attack not on Christianity, but rather on the inroads made by the troubadour ethos within the general society—about which many leaders of the Church were just as upset.[41]

This passage, together with many of the others cited, should help dispel the simplistic views that the Jewish rationalist in the generations after Maimonides was necessarily an assimilationist, and that the intellectual who worked with Christians in the study of philosophical texts would naturally have a weaker sense of Jewish identity and be more likely to abandon his people for the majority faith. Here we see Anatoli speaking as a stern moralist, denouncing that aspect of assimilation that he judged to be most offensive to traditional Jewish moral standards. His thorough-going commitment to a rationalistic presentation of Judaism is beyond question, but so is his loyalty to the conscientious observance of the commandments, to the superiority of Judaism over its rival faiths, and to a distinctive Jewish survival despite the pressures of a prolonged exile.[42]

What can be concluded about Anatoli's presentation of Christianity? There are, to be sure, elements of a more traditional polemical character in his sermons. He acknowledges and responds to some of the standard Christian arguments—that the suffering of the Jewish people in exile is proof of their rejection by God and the truth of the Christian faith (23b, 161a), that Jews are unable to attain salvation for their souls in their exile because the sacrifices are no longer possible (91a), that no spiritual reward is promised in the Torah (124a–b), that the Messiah has already come (189b), and that the commandments of the Torah should be understood only according to a hidden meaning (192a). The end of the final sermon interprets the last three verses of the Torah as "two strong responses against the adherents of the religions that imitate the goodness of our Torah" (192a). But these are clearly not at the heart of the sermons, and the distance between these texts and the Hebrew polemical literature of the thirteenth century is great.

Although Anatoli was certainly equipped to respond to Christian polemics (and in his translation of Aristotle's *Organon* he proclaims the need for Jews to master logic in order to do so),[43] the texts of his model sermons, unlike the writings of his contemporaries, contain no philosophical analysis and refutation of the central theological doctrines of the Trinity, the Incar-

---

41. For Christian opposition to secular love poetry and songs, see Whicher, p. 1; Nelli, pp. 221, 236, 247–51; Kendrick, pp. 60, 222 n. 23.

42. Note that Anatoli's evaluation of Islam and the Quran is considerably more negative than his image of Christianity (58b: "The religion of Ishmael is worse than all because of its monstrous laws and the inferior reward it promises"; cf. 183a: "Its laws are base").

43. See Saperstein, *Jewish Preaching*, p. 111.

nation, the Eucharist, or original sin. There is no response to the standard messianic interpretation of biblical verses. There is no criticism of Jesus and the apostles, or attack on the ethical standards of contemporary Christians. There is little use of irony or scorn. Christian teachings are frequently presented for the purpose of elucidation through comparison, without any polemical agenda.[44] Even where there is an unambiguous critique, the tone is generally one of respect.[45]

The most important references to Christianity in his sermons are incorporated for a homiletical purpose of an internal nature. His comparison of Jewish practices and beliefs with their Christian counterparts leads him to conclude that "ours are better," or "ours are easier," and that therefore there is no excuse for our failure to observe them. It also leads him to identify certain contemporary Jewish beliefs (e.g. in demons) and practices (e.g. of an ascetic nature) that should be repudiated because they are dangerously close to undesirable Christian beliefs and practices. Thus the references to Christians and Christianity in the sermons turn out to be reflections of the preacher's evaluation of the religious health of his own people.

Part of what bothers him is the religious laxity and the mechanical per-

---

44. For example, Anatoli refers to the Vulgate's translation of *Elohei 'olam* (Isa. 40:28) as "*el nitsḥi*" (*Deus sempiternus*) rather than "God of the Universe," and similarly with *Melekh 'olam* (Jer. 10:10) (10b); he cites the Vulgate's rendering of *'aluqah* in Prov. 30:15 as "leech" (*sanguisuga*) (5a), and the translation of *kavod* (Ps. 149:5) as *gloria* (174b). He also reports the Christian etymology of "Jerusalem" as *re'ut shalom* (cf. Isidore of Seville, *Etymologies,* in Migne, Patrologia Latina 82:295—*nam Jerusalem "visio pacis" interpretatur*) and its interpretation as "the glory in place for the righteous" (171b, cf. the anagogical interpretation by Guibert de Nogent in *Medieval Rhetoric,* p. 171). In none of these cases is there an attack or refutation of the Christian interpretation. He also cites a statement from "the books of the Gentiles" that "the Greeks chose wisdom, the Jews abstinence, which they call *regula,* and the Romans heroism" (103b). I have not been able to identify this quote; cf., however, Abraham ibn Ezra in Schirmann, *Shirah* 1:578. The word *regula* in this context must be based on the "rule" governing monastic life.

45. There are several exceptions. Repudiating the claim that the exile is proof that God now hates the Jewish people, Anatoli shoots back that "those hated by God are the ones who hate Him by denying His unity" (*son'av ha-koferim be-yiḥudo,* 26a). A harsh passage erased from Anatoli, MS fol. 153d is also missing from the printed text on p. 189b. The printed text, line 10, reads "If so, it is not as they say that the Redeemer has already come." I was able to decipher most of the erased passage with the aid of ultra-violet light; it reads, "If so, what the Christians say—that the Redeemer has already come—is a lie. Woe to those who see but do not know what they see. For they say that that Redeemer is God, and that he [one Hebrew word indecipherable] and died a violent death after horrible tortures and great afflictions. To distinguish the sacred from the profane, was not Moses. . ." (as in printed text, contrasting the peaceful death of Moses). The sentence "Woe to those who see. . ." (B. Hag 12b) is a stunning reversal of the common Christian attack upon Jewish "blindness."

formance of the commandments—objects of attack by preachers of rebuke
in every generation. But what seems to exercise him the most are certain patterns that we have identified with German Hasidism and with the Kabbalah.
Dating from the second quarter of the thirteenth century, these sermons may
provide significant details about the process—as yet not fully documented—
by which Hasidic tendencies were spreading and Kabbalistic tendencies beginning to crystallize. These two "movements" have been associated by modern Jewish historians with developments generally seen as among the most
positive of medieval Christianity: the resurgence of Cluniac monasticism
and the flowering of Franciscan spirituality.[46] *Malmad ha-Talmidim* reveals
a Jewish rationalist repudiating the new currents in the Jewish environment
by associating them with those elements of contemporary Christianity that
he considered most negative: asceticism, fanaticism, and superstition.

---

46. On the purported influence of Cluniac monasticism, see Baer, "Ha-Megamah," p. 3,
repeated by Katz, *Exclusiveness,* p. 3 and Scholem, *Major Trends,* pp. 83–84. On affinities with
Franciscan spirituality, see Baer, "Ha-Megamah," pp. 7, 21, 49 and Baer, *History* 1:270–71,
274.

7

Sermons as Evidence
for the Popularization of Philosophy
in Fifteenth-Century Spain

In a seminal article published in 1981, Aviezer Ravitzky raises an important distinction between the history of technical philosophical ideas and the role of philosophical study in the history of the Jewish people and of Judaism. In order to reach a proper assessment of the second, we are told,

> we must investigate not only the content of the philosophy . . . but also the scope of engagement in philosophy. Is the philosophical enterprise always confined to the realm of individuals, an enterprise whose legitimacy is in question, so that it remains by its nature alien and external, or does this enterprise sometimes penetrate into the synagogue, the Talmudic academy, the curriculum? For example, the identification of a philosophical sermon delivered in the synagogue by the rabbi, and the analysis of the content and the sources of this sermon, are relevant not only to research in the history of certain ideas. Its significance transcends the internal history of philosophy.[1]

My research into the history of Jewish preaching confirms these sentiments about the importance of the sermon as a bridge between the elite culture of leading intellectuals and the general Jewish society in which they lived.[2]

Despite evidence that significant numbers of Jews in, let us say, fourteenth-century southern France had considerable interest in extremely technical philosophical works (such as ibn Rushd's commentaries on Aris-

---

1. Ravitzky, "Derekh Ḥiaqiratah," p. 9; the essay has been reprinted in his book, *'Al Da'at ha-Maqom.*
2. See Saperstein, *Jewish Preaching.* In the present study, I am concerned only with the diffusion of philosophical ideas and not with other kinds of material pertaining to elite culture, such as halakhah and Kabbalah. Certain sermons can serve as evidence also for more popular culture; a good example from a later period is the sermon of Elijah ha-Kohen of Izmir, translated in *Jewish Preaching,* pp. 303–26.

totle, which have been preserved in an impressive number of Hebrew man-uscripts[3]), the philosophical book remained throughout the Middle Ages an elitist instrument. Since it had to be copied by hand, it was expensive to produce. It could be read by only one individual at a time. Its content could be as difficult and challenging as the author wanted to make it. A history of Jewish philosophy based on the standard printed works is there-fore deep but narrow, limited to a relatively small number of individual authors.[4]

The sermon, by contrast, was by its nature a much more popular medium. It had no economic constraints, for it cost nothing to prepare, de-liver, or hear. Generally given in the vernacular on public or semipublic oc-casions, it was accessible to dozens of listeners at a time. Since the audience ordinarily included Jews of different educational backgrounds and intellec-tual levels, and since listeners had various ways of expressing displeasure at what they were hearing, the sermon had to be pitched at a level that would not exclude most of the congregation.[5] Whereas a difficult passage in a book could be studied at length, the sermon as an oral medium had to be intelli-gible at a single hearing. It was thus not a medium for profound probing of original ideas, but rather an instrument for their simplification, application, popularization, and diffusion.

When, therefore, philosophical modes of argumentation were employed from the pulpit, when philosophical formulations were asserted as self-evi-dent, and when we find in sermons references to philosophical works by Jew-ish, Greek, and Arabic writers alongside quotes from the Talmud and Midrash, we can conclude that philosophy was establishing itself as an inte-gral part of the Jewish cultural milieu. The sermon both served as a vehicle for this diffusion and—by revealing the preacher's assumptions about what his audience already knew and what it was prepared to hear—provides evi-dence that the process had already taken place. And when we find resistance to the incorporation of such ideas, we see a society grappling with the limits of its toleration for potentially unorthodox thought.[6]

To be sure, significant methodological problems need to be addressed.

---

3. See Harry Wolfson, "Plans for the Publication of a Corpus Commentariorum Averrois in Aristotelem," in Wolfson, *Studies* 1: 431–32; Saperstein, *Decoding*, p. 272, n. 9.

4. Husik, for example, treats some twenty thinkers spanning more than five centuries; only four of these thinkers lived in Christian Europe.

5. On the challenges of addressing audiences composed of Jews with different levels of ed-ucation, see *Jewish Preaching*, pp. 51, 388–39, 410; on ways of expressing displeasure, pp. 54–58.

6. For examples of such resistance, see *Jewish Preaching*, pp. 380–86.

There is the problem of sample: only a minuscule percentage of the sermons delivered by Jews in the Middle Ages have been preserved in a form that is available to us.[7] The sermons that were the most popular were probably the least likely to have been written in a permanent form. Sometimes we learn about the use of philosophy by popular preachers through written statements of their opponents; in most cases, the original sermons have been lost forever. I see no reason to assume, however, that a philosophically inclined preacher would have been more likely to record his sermons for dissemination than someone whose works were confined to the tradition of "rabbinic ethics."[8] Indeed, one might argue that the more radical the philosophical doctrine, the less likely it was to have been preserved in written form. I therefore see no reason to suspect that the extant written texts over-represent the influence of philosophy in the Jewish pulpit.

A second problem is reliability: Do extant sermons represent what was actually said? The Hebrew texts available to us are certainly not stenographic transcriptions: certain transformations inevitably occurred in the shift from oral message to written text.[9] A specific reference to a work of Aristotle, for example, may have been added to the written version—it might have been more important to a reader than to a listener. But philosophical ideas and arguments that appeared as integral parts of the sermon's structure were probably what the congregation actually heard. With these caveats in mind, I shall review some of the evidence for the popularization of philosophy in the sermons of Spanish preachers of the fifteenth century.

Let us begin with three statements by contemporary Jewish observers. The first is in the famous letter of Hayyim ibn Musa (ca. 1380–1460), written in the middle of the fifteenth century. The author described a sermon he heard in his youth, in which the preacher attempted a philosophical demonstration of the unity of God through a *reductio ad absurdum* of the antithesis: "If God is not one, then such and such must necessarily follow." It is not the content of the philosophical doctrine but the preacher's technique of logical reasoning that aroused the ire of his listeners and impelled the author to conclude that the sermon was inappropriate. He goes on to describe the

new type of preacher. They rise to the lectern to preach . . . and most of their sermons consist of syllogistic arguments and quotations from the philoso-

---

7. Cf. ibid., pp. 5–7.

8. On this category, see Dan, *Sifrut ha-Musar*, pp. 146–66.

9. For a general discussion of this problem, see ibid., pp. 35–36; *Jewish Preaching*, pp. 7–9, 20–24.

phers. They mention by name Aristotle, Alexander, Themistius, Plato, Averroes, and Ptolemy, while Abaye and Raba are concealed in their mouths. The Torah waits upon the reading stand like a dejected woman who has prepared herself properly by ritual immersion and awaits her husband; then, returning from the house of his mistress, he glances at her and leaves without paying her further heed.[10]

Second, from the same generation, we have the as yet unpublished treatise on preaching by Joseph ibn Shem Tov (ca. 1400–ca. 1460), in which the author complains about "most of the preachers of our time. . . . Some speak about false doctrines in the fashion of debaters[11] or sophists, using these two arts— dialectics and sophistical arguments, . . . or they speak confusingly with syllogistic arguments, benefiting no one. They think that they excel in syllogistic proofs,[12] but for the most part they preach about things that neither they nor their listeners understand."[13]

Finally, a generation later, there is Isaac Arama's introduction to *'Aqedat Yitshaq,* in which he praises the level of contemporary Christian preaching:

> In every city their scholars master all branches of knowledge, their priests and princes stand at the fore in philosophy, integrating it with their theological doctrine. They have written many books, on the basis of which biblical texts are expounded before large congregations. Each day their preachers give important insights into their religion and faith, thereby sustaining it. For some time now, calls have gone out far and wide, summoning the people to hear their learned discourses. . . . Among those who came were Jews. They heard the preachers and found them impressive; their appetites were whetted for similar fare.[14]

Although these three texts indicate an ambivalent attitude, they affirm that it was not uncommon for Jewish preachers to use philosophical mater-

---

10. Ibn Musa, pp. 117–18; translated in *Jewish Preaching,* pp. 384–87.

11. Hebrew: *mitvakhim,* referring to the use of "disputed questions," as will be discussed below.

12. An untranslatable pun in the Hebrew: these preachers think they are *anshei mofet* (outstanding men) because they discuss *'inyanim moftiyim* (matters involving logical proofs).

13. " 'Ein ha-Qore," fol. 17r–v; translated in *Jewish Preaching,* p. 340. The passage continues, "I once heard people tell of a man who thought much of his own intellectual abilities. He began a sermon . . . by saying that his sermon would be divided into three parts: the first part would be comprehensible to him and to them, the second part comprehensible to him but not to them, and the third part neither to him nor to them. Indeed, I would think that many sermons of our time are of this third category."

14. Arama, *'Aqedat,* Author's Introduction, p. 15; translated in *Jewish Preaching,* pp. 392–93.

ial in their sermons in the fifteenth century. While such material may have aroused opposition in some circles (including those who were themselves not unsympathetic to philosophy), it was perceived by others as serving a cultural need. What do we find in the writings of the preachers themselves?

A first step is to identify all references to and citations of philosophical works by preachers.[15] The large number of such citations in the extant literature reveals that that in many synagogues, Aristotle marched alongside the luminaries of medieval Jewish thought—Maimonides, Gersonides, Albo— as an authority. References to "the Philosopher" abound; I would estimate that after the Bible, rabbinic classics, and perhaps the *Guide for the Perplexed,* Aristotle's *Ethics* was the most widely cited work in the sermons of the period, and other Aristotelian works were frequently quoted as well.[16]

Sometimes the preacher became quite technical, as in the following passage by Isaac Aboab, from the generation of the Expulsion:

On this matter, Thomas said in the Commentary on the Seventh Book of the Metaphysics in the name of ibn Rushd that [Aristotle] held the position that the essences of species and their definitions reside entirely in the form. Yet in many other places in the philosophical literature we find explicitly that [Aristotle] says that the essences of species and their definitions reside in both matter and form. How then could he have said the opposite?[17] The answer: it is known that all accidental properties have an essential aspect. They are called "accidents" because they cannot exist without a subject (*nose*). Thus, he said that the essences of species and their definitions reside entirely in the form because it is the source of accidents as accidents, which need a subject. He said that they are in both matter and form because his investigation of accidents revealed that they have an essential aspect. Whoever thinks deeply

15. The full panoply of names mentioned by ibn Musa can be documented in the extant records of fifteenth-century sermons if we include *'Aqedat Yitsḥaq.* (On the problem of the relationship between this book and sermons actually delivered in the synagogue, see *Jewish Preaching*, pp. 17–18.) Sarah Heller-Wilensky identified places where Arama mentions or cites Plato, Aristotle, Alexander of Aphrodisias, and Themistius: see Heller-Wilensky, pp. 37–39. For another citation of Alexander, see the manuscript "Anonymous 'Bibago,'" fol. 107 (David Sassoon, *Ohel David* [London, 1932], p. 72). For citations of Ibn Rushd, see below.

16. For references to Aristotle in a collection of sermons from the early fifteenth century (pre-dating ibn Musa), see n.6 to chap. 13 below.

17. Cf. Aquinas, *Metaphysics* 2:556, on *Metaphysics* VII 10, 1034b–1035a. This work was translated into Hebrew by A. Nahmias, apparently in the year 1490, in the city of Ocaña; see Steinschneider, p. 485. If so, it would appear that R. Isaac Aboab, who lived not far from Ocaña in Guadalajara, acquired the translation, studied at least part of it, and incorporated a section into his sermon at some time between the completion of the translation in 1490 and his death in 1493.

about what I have said will find that it is true, especially if he is anointed with
the oil of wisdom.[18]

Aboab was famous as one of the last great Talmudists in Spain. Yet here is a
passage—the conclusion of a sermon—that could have come from a lecture
at the University of Paris. Introduced as part of the discussion of an aggadic
statement, this is material that at least one preacher considered compatible
with sermonic discourse.

On the whole, philosophers were not cited by the Spanish preachers in
order to refute them or contrast their teachings with those of Torah. Philosophy was commonly used to furnish established truths, self-evident principles, universally accepted doctrines, that could be used as building blocks for
subsequent assertions. A preacher such as Shem Tov ben Joseph ibn Shem
Tov, a contemporary of Aboab's, frequently referred to philosophical doctrines as axiomatic: "It is known in natural science that. . . ," "It has already
been explained in political science that. . . ," "It has already been explained
that man is by nature political."[19] Here, for example, is the introduction to
Shem Tov's sermon on the scriptural lesson *Bereshit* [Gen. 1:1–6:8]:

> It is beyond doubt that every science has its own axioms, on the basis of
> which the investigations of that science may be carried out. The knowledge
> of these axioms eliminates the uncertainties that arise in this science. If the
> axioms of each science are not discovered, nothing can be known about it, as
> is explained in Chapter 2 of [Aristotle's] Book of Demonstration (*Sefer ha-
> Mofet*). If someone denies the axioms of a particular science, the expert in
> that science cannot discourse with him, as is explained in Book One of the
> Physics. . . .[20]
>
> As the divine Torah includes all kinds of perfection and encompasses all the
> sciences, it must contain well-known axioms. . . . Now the creation of the

---

18. Aboab, *Nehar Pishon,* p. 32d, compared with the first edition (Venice?, 1538), p. 84.
In both editions, the sermons appear in a totally arbitrary order; by contrast, in the manuscript Aboab, "Nehar Pishon," they appear in the order of the Torah readings. However, this
manuscript contains nothing that is not in the printed editions, and lacks some material that
is included in the printed editions. In the passage cited, obvious errors occur in the manuscript text (fol. 150a), which should not be used as a reliable source. By contrast, the manuscript Aboab "Qetsat Parashiyot" contains important and interesting homiletical material that
does not appear at all in print. See below, chap. 15.
19. Shem Tov, *Derashot,* pp. 37c, 28a. 63b.
20. See Aristotle, *Posterior Analytics* I 10, 76a–b; *Physics* I 1, 185a; cf. Irwin, p. 3, and
Kellner,"Torah," citing Albo, 1,17; 1:145–46. Albo's passage may have been the source for
Shem Tov.

world *ex nihilo,* without any change in the Agent, which created it in accordance with His eternal will, is the foundation of the entire Torah.[21]

The doctrine asserted is not a radical philosophical challenge to tradition but rather an affirmation of tradition against the Aristotelian challenge of the world's eternity. But note that the sermon begins with propositions taken from Aristotle's corpus, presents them as self-evident, then applies them to the subject matter of the *parashah.* The Aristotelian teaching about the axioms of each science is the foundation of the argument, presented as incontrovertible, and the doctrine of Creation is then defined in terms of this teaching. The purpose of such preaching is not to teach philosophy; it is to justify tradition to an audience that is already philosophically literate.

Philosophy also served the preachers as an exegetical tool. I refer here not to the well-known phenomenon of allegorical interpretation,[22] but to the use of philosophical reasoning to solve textual problems.[23] Several preachers complained about the ignorance of logic in their communities and attempted to teach it in the course of their sermons. Here, again, is the Talmudist Isaac Aboab, speaking in a eulogy: "Death is the cause of human perfection in the one who attains it. Death is not the goal of the human being, as many think because it is the end. And they think that the premise 'Every goal is an end' can be made into its converse.[24] This is false; every goal is an end, but not every end is a goal."[25]

The preacher continues to develop his lesson in logic by citing a passage from "the Philosopher" with his most influential commentator, Ibn Rushd:

That is why Aristotle said in Book 2, chapter 3 of the *Physics,* "This is the statement of the poet about going to death: you see why this statement is absurd." Ibn Rushd explained this passage in a manner similar to what I just said, namely, that Aristotle was opposing a certain poet who belonged to the

21. Shem Tov, *Derashot,* p. 1a; cf. the beginning of the sermon on the lesson *Ki Tissa,* p. 35b, and the lesson *Pequdei,* p. 37c.

22. For an outstanding summary, see Talmage, "Apples of Gold."

23. On the use of logic in biblical exegesis during the generation of the Expulsion, see Gross, "Pulmus," Hebrew section pp. 6–8.

24. *Ve-ḥashvu ki haqdamat kol takhlit hu sof mithapekhet.* This last word is a technical term in logic. Its meaning here is not what appears in Maimonides' "Millot ha-Higayon," 4:2 ("contrary"): cf. Fox, "Maimonides' 'Method of Contradictions,'" in *Interpreting Maimonides,* esp. pp. 68–69. It is rather the reversal of subject and predicate ("converse"). Aristotle discusses the rules of such conversions in *Prior Analytics* I 3, 25a; cf. Rosenberg and Manekin, pp. 271–72, and Rosenberg, "*Sefer ha-Hata'ah,*" pp. 284–85.

25. Aboab, *Nehar Pishon,* p. 38c (corrected on the basis of the 1538 edition).

school of those who said that the premise "Every goal is an end" can be made into its converse. If so, seeing as death is an end, the goal for which every human being exists must be death. Aristotle said [according to ibn Rushd] that this statement is absurd because the goal of every human being is not to die, but rather the perfection of his soul.[26]

There is no indication in the text of anything problematic or even unusual in a distinguished rabbi using Aristotle and Averroes as part of a eulogy.

An unknown preacher from the generation of the Expulsion named Israel, the author of a manuscript of sermons entitled "Dover Meisharim," cites Ecclesiastes 3:19, *The superiority of man over the beasts is nothing,* and comments:

> All have expressed astonishment over this statement, for it appears that its meaning is to assert that there is no superiority of man over the beasts. They come to this conclusion only because they have not studied logic, which teaches that there is a great difference between a negative statement and an affirmative statement. Thus if the verse had said "Man has no superiority over the beasts," this would be a negation of any superiority. However, the actual verse is an affirmative statement, indicating that there is superiority, but that this counts for nothing.

Israel interprets "man" in the verse as referring to the corporeal aspect of the human being, as in Genesis 2:7. In that regard, man is superior to the beasts, for the human is capable of providing for his food and all his needs. "But this superiority is nothing, for in comparison with the ultimate goal, all is vanity. Man does not attain immortality by means of this superiority over the beasts."[27] Thus a distinction, derived from logic, enables the preacher to help his audience through a well-known exegetical crux by defusing the radical implications of the apparently simple meaning.

---

26. Cf. Aristotle, *Physics,* II 2, 194a: "That is why the poet was carried away into making an absurd statement when he said, 'He has the goal [death] for the sake of which he was born.' For not every stage that is last claims to be a goal but only that which is best." Note that the text of our sermon appears to assume that the listeners are familiar with this passage in Aristotle. For the commentary of Ibn Rushd on *Physics* II, 2, 3, see Harvey, "Averroes," pp. 220, 296. Ibn Rushd wrote, "If so, it is not logically necessary that whatever is an end must be a goal, unless the end is most worthy of praise. Thus death is an end, but it is not a goal."

27. "Dover Meisharim," fol. 64a. Corresponding to the Hebrew words *shuliyi* and *ḥiyyuviyi* in text, the words *negativa* and *affirmativa* appear in Hebrew letters in the margin. This passage is based upon Albo, 3,2, 3:22, and the preacher refers to this work explicitly. However, his interpretation of the verse is different from that of Albo, on which see Piekarz, *Idéologiyah,* pp. 30, 295.

Here is the same preacher giving another lesson in elementary logic to his listeners:

> If someone should say that whoever did not enter the synagogue did not hear a word of what the preacher said, it may be deduced from this that they did not understand anything, for if they did not hear it, how could they understand? But if he should say the opposite, namely, whoever did not enter [the synagogue] did not understand, it may not be deduced from this that they did not hear. That may not be true. It is possible that someone may hear all that the preacher says from the entrance to the synagogue, or from the [women's] chamber, without understanding it.

This distinction is used to explicate the precise formulation of Moses' statement in setting the challenge for Korah [*If these men die as all men do . . . then it was not the Lord who sent me* (Num. 16:29)], rather than "then they have not spurned the Lord (cf. Num. 16:30)." The deduction works in one direction, but not the other.[28]

It is particularly interesting to see how philosophy influenced the modes of thought and forms of argumentation in the sermons. Hayyim ibn Musa's complaint about the inappropriate use of syllogistic arguments is abundantly corroborated in the sermon literature. Here, for example, is Isaac Aboab beginning a sermon on the pericope *Va-Ethanan* [Deut. 3:23–7:11] with a surprising exegesis of a well-known verse:

> *You who cleave to the Lord your God live* (Deut 4:4). This thesis is based upon true premises, which we shall state. The first is, Whoever cleaves to God lives. The second is, You cleave to God. The necessary conclusion is, You live. This is a syllogism of the first form. . . .[29] Now the major premise[30] I have taken can be established first from experience, for we see that the closer anything approaches God, the greater the portion of life it attains.[31]

---

28. "Dover Meisharim," fol. 123v.

29. *Heqesh ba-temunah ha-rishonah*, a technical term in Aristotelian logic. See *Prior Analytics* I 4, 25b–26a; Patzig, pp. 91–100. In a syllogism of the first form, the common element of the two premises (in our case, "cleave to God") is in the subject of one and the predicate of the other.

30. *Ha-haqdamah ha-gedolah*, the major premise of the syllogism. Such a premise may be established in the preacher's world by quotation of an "authority" (a biblical verse, a rabbinic statement, a passage from Aristotle), by a rational argument, or by appeal to conventional knowledge known by all from experience (here, *mi-tsad ha-metsi'ut*). It is noteworthy that the preacher assumes his congregation knows these technical terms from Aristotelian logic and can follow and appreciate this mode of argumentation.

31. Aboab, *Nehar Pishon*, p. 23a. An *Ars praedicandi* by a fourteenth-century French abbot, John of Chalons, begins "Hec est ars brevis et clara faciendi sermones secundum formam sillogisticam." See Rouse and Rouse, p. 191.

Although the second part of this brief sermon is based on a rabbinic comment about the verse, its parsing as an Aristotelian syllogism could hardly be further from traditional rabbinic hermeneutics.

A second example is the sermon by another contemporary, Joel ibn Shu'eib, on the pericope *Be-Ḥuqqotai* [Lev. 26:3–27:34]. Shortly after the beginning, he states:

> We shall explain that intellectual pleasure is more distinguished [than sensual pleasure] by three arguments. The first: the more choice pleasure is that derived from the more choice faculty. But that is [the intellect]. If so, etc. [QED]. The major premise is established because pleasure is dependent upon the activity of the appropriate faculty, as is written in the eighth chapter of [Aristotle's] *Ethics*. . . . The minor premise is established because the intellect is superior to all other faculties for its activity is the apprehension of metaphysical matters, essences abstracted from matter. . . . Therefore, the proper pleasure is the one specific to this faculty.[32]

Two other arguments are given in precisely the same form, each linked with a different meaning of the theme verse from the scriptural lesson.

In both of these examples, the conclusion is totally unremarkable; indeed, it is quite commonplace. But the syllogistic form of the argument indicates that this was a mode of thinking that could be readily followed in an oral discourse and that many found convincing. Clearly, the recent translation into Hebrew of Aristotle's works on logic effected a new manner of Jewish preaching.[33]

Perhaps its most impressive formal development was the use of the "disputed question." This was, of course, one of the most characteristic modes of medieval scholastic discourse, and it had an elegantly simple form: a) a question, formulated in such a way that the possible answers were antithetical; b) a trial answer, with supporting arguments usually drawn from authorities of various kinds; c) the antithetical answer, with similar supporting arguments; and d) a resolution of the apparent conundrum, usually in favor of the second answer, demonstrating that the arguments that seemed to support the first answer were not cogent.[34] Needless to say, this was not a form of reasoning used in rabbinic literature, or by the Tosafists; nor was it char-

---

32. Ibn Shu'eib, *'Olat Shabbat,* p. 105a–b.

33. For other examples of contemporary use of syllogisms in sermons, see "Dover Meisharim," fol. 71v ("From this premise we can make a logical syllogism that will produce for us a conclusion. . . ."), and 191r–v.

34. See Chenu, pp. 94–96.

acteristic of the Jewish philosophers writing in an Islamic environment, or of the earliest medieval sermons preserved for us. This makes its appearance in the late fourteenth or early fifteenth century Jewish sermon all the more striking.

Aviezer Ravitzky has published an excellent study of a fine example of this form that appears in several works beginning with a sermon (probably for *Shabbat ha-Gadol*, the Sabbath preceding Pesach) by Hasdai Crescas (see the discussion in chapter 2).[35] The question is "whether or not the miracle creates faith in the human soul without the concurrence of the will." It would be well worth collecting the other "disputed questions" found in the homiletical literature of Spanish Jewry.[36]

One of the most interesting and important is on the efficacy of *teshuvah*: "Whether God forgives the penitent." Like the question on faith, this question appears in several different sermons of the period.[37] The sermons show that the doctrine of repentance was under philosophical attack at the time, and preachers felt the need to acknowledge the problematic nature of the tradition and defend it philosophically. One recurring argument against the traditional doctrine was that the belief that God intends at one point in time to punish a sinner and then decides not to punish the same person after his repentance implies a God who changes. Here is how the argument proceeds, as formulated in the sermon contained in "Dover Meisharim":

---

35. Ravitzky, *Derashat ha-Pesaḥ;* see the discussion in chap. 2 above. Ravitzky provides a thorough analysis of the intellectual content of the sermon, but he does not emphasize its innovation in form.

36. A perfect example of the form in an early fifteenth-century sermon is "Whether an act performed by means of acceptance of a vow is more praiseworthy, acquiring for the one who performs it greater merit than would be acquired for him by the very same act done without acceptance of a vow?" (MS Anonymous, St. Petersburg, fol. 23r–24v; see below, chap. 13). From the generation of the Expulsion: Whether human perfection requires isolation from society? (Shem Tov, *Derashot,* pp. 5c–6c); Whether one who professes a religion may investigate his faith rationally to determine if it is divine? ("Dover Meisharim," fol. 54v; cf. Albo, I,24, 1:187–95); Whether it is permissible to discuss Creation in public? (Bibago, "Zeh Yena ḥamenu," p. 1d). A fine example from a speculative work that was undoubtedly discussed in sermons is: Whether perfect immortality of the soul is attainable under conditions of exile? (Shalom, book 11, chap. 3).

37. "Dover Meisharim," fol. 175r; Aboab, *Nehar Pishon,* p. 25a; Zarfati, p. 275c. In an interesting unprinted sermon for the Sabbath of Repentance, Isaac Aboab analyzes a different question relating to the doctrine of *teshuvah*: "Whether it is a root, like the other roots of the Torah, or a branch like the other commandments? On this matter there are arguments that make it appear that it is a root of the entire Torah, and arguments that make it appear the opposite. . . .(Aboab, "Qetsat Parashiyyot," fol. 15v; see below, chap. 15). Cf. the apocopated discussion of this question in *Nehar Pishon,* p. 56b.

It is an established axiom that all change entails movement, from place to place or from category to category, and so forth. Now all movement is dependent upon time, for it cannot occur except in time.[38] Thus if we assume that God changes, then we must conclude that God is subject to time. And whoever assumes this is a complete heretic, for God created time, just as He created everything else. A biblical verse explicitly teaches this: *For six days God made the heaven and the earth* (Exod. 20:11), where we would have expected it to say "For in six days."[39] And if God created time, how can we say that He is subject to something that He Himself made?. . . Thus, the assumption that God accepts the penitent entails the conclusion that He changes, and this is total heresy. Therefore, we must necessarily conclude that He does not pardon and does not accept the penitent.[40]

Of course, in accordance with the rules of the form, authorities on behalf of the efficacy of repentance were later provided, and the argument eventually refuted.

Aware of the obvious danger in this kind of sermon, the preacher began by defending his use of the disputed question form, anticipating the argument that "whoever does this must necessarily buttress the position that is opposed to the truth, and this is difficult for the masses." In other words, in order to fulfill the requirements of the genre, a preacher would have had to give a sophisticated and apparently convincing argument to defend positions that conflicted with the tradition. He thus ran the risk that some of the listeners would refuse to listen to the continuation and accuse the preacher of heresy, or be convinced by the argument and remember it, forgetting the subsequent refutation. Nevertheless, the preacher in "Dover Meisharim" insisted that the form was appropriate, based on precedents in the Bible, the Talmud, and medieval literature, and he affirmed that it was impossible to know the truth without knowing the arguments supporting its opposite, for "truth becomes clear only through disputation."[41]

---

38. Cf. Aristotle, *Physics* IV 14, 222b–223a; Maimonides, *Guide* 2,13; Klein-Breslavy, pp. 106–27.

39. I.e., the absence of a preposition with the phrase "six days" allows us to consider this phrase as a direct object of "made," along with "the heaven and the earth." Cf. the commentaries of Nahmanides and Bahya ben Asher on Exodus 20:13; Adret, I, nu. 423; Kasher, "Musag ha-Zeman," p. 807.

40. "Dover Meisharim," fol. 175v.

41. Ibid., fol. 175r: *mi-tokh ha-masa u-matan yitba'er ha-emet*; for a translation of the introductory passage, see *Jewish Preaching*, pp. 395–96. Cf. also Aboab, *Nehar Pishon*, p. 32c: "It is known that every sage must know the arguments for falsehood as well as the arguments for truth. There are two reasons for this. First, one must know in order to save himself from falsehood; if one does not know it, how can he save himself from it? Second, so one will be

We have thus seen that sermons from the generation of the Expulsion provide strong evidence for the penetration of philosophy into the world of the preachers and their listeners—evidence in the form of direct citations, accepted premises, and new forms of argumentation. But these sermons provide little indication that philosophy was working in Jewish society as a corrosive, destructive force leading to apostasy. Rabbi Isaac Aboab, in whose homiletical works we have found the most technical philosophical content, represents a type that was by no means rare: a leader totally faithful to Judaism, expert in its traditional literature, who turned to philosophy in a natural way, as an integral part of his thought, responding to a popular demand to present the traditional faith—both in formulation and in content—a manner compatible with the power of reason.

---

able to guide a person who is tending toward falsehood toward the truth, as Aristotle explained at the end of the seventh book. . . ." For another defense of argument by means of the disputed question, though not in a homiletical context, see Leon Joseph of Carcassonne, Renan, "Écrivains," p. 773. For opposition by Spanish Christians to disputed questions in the pulpit, see Diego de Estella, 2:123, 312–13; Smith, p. 25.

8

Italian Jewish Preaching: An Overview

On a day between Rosh Hashanah and Yom Kippur, probably in the year 1593, Rabbi Samuel Judah Katzenellenbogen of Padua delivered a eulogy for Judah Moscato. As befitted the time of year, he began with a discussion of repentance and proceeded to argue that one of the primary functions of the eulogy was to inspire the listeners to repent. He went on to discuss the qualities of a great scholar: perfection of intellect and behavior; the capacity to communicate wisdom to others; the ability to capture the listeners' attention with appealing homiletical material; and the skills to teach them the laws, the observance of which were essential for the true felicity of the soul— even though most contemporary congregations did not enjoy listening to the dry halakhic content. At this point the printed text of his sermon reads, "Here I began to recount the praises of the deceased, and to show how these four qualities were present in him to perfection, the conclusion being that we should become inspired by his eulogy and allow the tears to flow for him, look into our deeds, and return to the Lord."[1]

This passage encapsulates for me something of the challenges and frustrations of studying Italian Jewish preaching, and to some extent Jewish preaching in general. Here is a leading Italian rabbi eulogizing perhaps the best known Jewish preacher of his century. We are given important but general statements about the function of the eulogy, the proper content and

Reprinted with permission from *Preachers of the Italian Ghetto,* edited by David Ruderman, copyright 1992, by University of California Press.

1. Katzenellenbogen, p. 21b (page references are to the "Arabic" numerals). (For a reason that escapes me, the Warsaw, 1876 edition identified the author as "MaHaR"I Mintz," leading to confusion with the fifteenth-century Talmudic scholar R. Judah Mintz.) Cf. p. 58a, a eulogy for R. Joseph Karo: "After that I went into a recounting of the praise of the deceased *ga'on,*" and p. 61a, a eulogy for R. Zalman Katz of Mantua: "After that I began to recount the praise of the deceased *tsaddiq.*" Despite its elliptical character, the eulogy for Karo contains some important historical information. Cf. Bonfil, *Rabbis,* p. 303. That the elimination of material about the deceased from the written eulogy was not unique to Katzenellenbogen can be seen from Azariah Figo's eulogy for Abraham Aboab, Figo, p. 122c: "I spoke at length on some other such aspects of his personal behavior; I have not written it at length."

structure of the sermon, the expectations and taste of the average listener. Then we come to the climactic point, where the preacher turns to Moscato himself. We expect an encomium of the scholarship and piety of the deceased and, what is more important for our purposes, a characterization of his preaching, an indication of his contemporary reputation, an evaluation from a colleague who apparently had a rather different homiletical style. All of this is missing. This crucial section of the eulogy was deemed unworthy of being recorded, presumably because of its specificity and ephemeral character. What for us (and perhaps for at least some of the listeners) was the most important section has been lost forever.

In *Kabbalah: New Perspectives,* Moshe Idel argues that even after the life work of Gershom Scholem and two generations of his disciples, the literature of Jewish mysticism is by no means fully charted: important schools may never have committed their doctrines to writing, significant works have been lost, certain texts may have arbitrarily been given undue emphasis at the expense of others no less important, and there is as yet no comprehensive bibliographic survey of the literature that does exist.[2] How much more is this true for Jewish sermon literature, which has had no Gershom Scholem to chart the way. The history of Jewish preaching in general, and that of Italy in particular, may best be envisioned as a vast jigsaw puzzle from which ninety percent of the pieces are missing and seventy-five percent of those that remain lie in a heap on the floor—and for which we have no model to tell us what the finished picture should look like. Generalizations about trends or characteristics of the homiletical tradition are like speculations about the design of the puzzle based on individual pieces or small clusters that happen to fit together. And without a clear map of the conventions and continuities of the tradition, all assertions about the novelty or even the significance of a particular preacher or sermon are likely to be precarious and unfounded.

The magnitude of what we lack is astonishing. Leon Modena's *Autobiography* informs us that he preached on three or four places each Sabbath over a period of more than twenty years, and that he had in his possession more than four hundred sermons. But only twenty-one from the early part of his career were published, and the rest, except for a few in manuscript, have apparently been lost.[3] When we think of the pinnacle of Italian Jewish preaching, Judah Moscato is probably the name that comes first to mind. Yet a sixteenth-century contemporary nominated David Provençal, the author of the

---

2. Idel, *Kabbalah,* pp. 18–21.

3. Modena, *Autobiography,* pp. 95, 102. The extant manuscript sermons by Modena have recently been discovered by Benjamin Richler; see Richler, p. 169.

famous appeal for the founding of a Jewish University, as "the greatest of the Italian preachers in our time." Like most of Provençal's other works, all of his sermons (if recorded at all) have apparently disappeared, leaving us no basis for evaluating the claim.[4] It does, however, give us pause to consider that our standard canon of important Italian Jewish preachers may be highly arbitrary.

The record before the sixteenth century is entirely blank, save for one manuscript by a mid-fifteenth century preacher, Moses ben Joab of Florence, described and published in part by Umberto Cassuto more than eighty years ago.[5] We have no known extant sermon reacting to the popular anti-Jewish preaching of such Franciscan friars as Bernardino da Siena, John Capistrano, and Bernardino da Feltre; or to the notorious ritual murder charge surrounding Simon of Trent; or to the arrival on Italian soil of refugees from the Iberian peninsula; or to the exploits in Italy of the charismatic David Reubeni, which included an audience with Pope Clement VII; or to the burning in Rome and Venice of the magnificently printed volumes of the Talmud; or to the arrest, trial, and execution of former Portuguese New Christians who had returned to Judaism in Ancona and the attempted boycott of that port; or to the papal bull *Cum nimis absurdum* and the establishment of the Ghetto in Rome.

There can be little question that Jewish preachers alluded to, discussed, and interpreted these events in their sermons, nor can it be doubted that the records of these discussions would provide us with precious insight into the strategies of contemporary Jews for accommodating major historical upheavals to their tradition, and conversely, for reinterpreting their tradition in the light of contemporary events. But it apparently did not occur to these preachers that readers removed in space and time from their own congregations would be interested in learning about events in the past. They therefore had little motivation to write what they said in a permanent form.[6]

---

4. Portaleone, p. 185c. "Miqnat Kesef" was a collection of sermons written "by one of the scholars from the Provençal family in Mantua" and acquired by Leon Modena in Venice in 1595. While some are not without interest, they do not seem to be the work of a master preacher of Moscato's rank, and there were many other members of the family who could have written them.

5. Cassuto, "Rabbino;" cf. Cassuto, *Firenze,* pp. 249–57.

6. For a general discussion of the tendency to omit historical references from sermon texts prepared for publication, or to refer to events generally in a manner that assumes knowledge by the listener but raises problems for the historian, see Saperstein, *Jewish Preaching,* pp. 80–84 and the passage by Azariah Figo cited on p. 86. Cf. also the historical events mentioned by Moses ben Joab of Florence: Cassuto, "Rabbino" 3 (1906):117–18, and his statement cited in *Jewish Preaching,* p. 18.

Much of the material that exists has yet to be studied. The name of Isaac Hayyim Cantarini of Padua does not appear in any of the lists of great Italian preachers known to me. Yet he left behind what appears to be the largest corpus of Italian Jewish sermons in existence, although no one has thus far taken a serious look at this homiletical legacy. The *Sefer Zikkaron* of Padua gives the number as "more than a thousand," and a substantial percentage of these are to be found in six large volumes of the Kaufmann Manuscript collection in Budapest (Hebrew MSS 314–319), each one devoted to the sermons for a complete year between 1673 and 1682. There may be more such volumes as well. In many cases there were two sermons for each scriptural lesson, one delivered in the morning, the other at the afternoon *Minḥah* service. The sermons were written in Italian, in Latin letters, with Hebrew quotations interspersed.[7]

I once thought of looking through the 1676–77 volume to see if I could find any reaction to the news of the death of Sabbatai Zevi, but I soon realized the enormity of the task: that volume alone runs to 477 pages, and there is no guarantee that the preacher would have referred to the event explicitly as soon as the news reached his community. Needless to say, for someone interested in intellectual or social history during this period, not to mention the history of Jewish preaching or the biography of a multi-talented man, these manuscripts may well repay careful study with rich dividends.

The first desideratum is therefore bibliographical—to compile a complete list of all known manuscripts of Italian sermons—let us say through the seventeenth century—to complement the printed works identified by Leopold Zunz and others. Then there is need for a data base that would include a separate entry for each sermon, including the place and approximate date of delivery, the genre (Sabbath or holiday sermon, eulogy, occasional, etc.), the main biblical verses and rabbinic statements discussed, the central subject or thesis, and any historical connection with an individual or an event. This would at least spread out all the known pieces of the puzzle on the table before us and facilitate the process of putting them together.

In addition to actual sermons, related genres need to be considered. Henry Sosland has given us a fine edition of Jacob Zahalon's *Or ha-Dar-*

---

7. On Cantarini, see Shazar, especially pp. 13–15, 18. Another massive manuscript (376 folios) of sermons that, to my knowledge, has not been studied is Portaleone, MS. Eliezer Nahman Foa, a disciple of Menahem Azariah of Fano, left four manuscript volumes entitled "Goren Ornan," but these are closer to homiletical commentaries than actual sermons; cf. Bonfil, *Jewish Life*, pp. 236–37. The only extant collection of Jewish sermons larger than Cantarini's from before the nineteenth century are the manuscripts of Saul Levi Morteira of Amsterdam.

shanim, a manual for preachers from the third quarter of the seventeenth century.[8] But the "Tena'ei ha-Darshan," written by Moses ben Samuel ibn Basa of Blanes is no less worthy of detailed analysis.[9] Nor should the various preaching aids be overlooked: works intended to make the preacher's task easier by collecting quotations on various topics, alphabetically arranged, analogous to a host of such works written by Christian contemporaries.[10]

Once the material has been charted, we can define the questions that need to be addressed. Perhaps the most obvious deal with the sermons as a reflection of Italian Jewish culture, as documents in Jewish intellectual history. To what extent do they present evidence for the continued vitality of philosophical modes of thought, for the popularization of Kabbalistic doctrines, for the influence of classical motifs or contemporary Christian writings? These questions have been addressed by colleagues in a volume based on presentations made for a colloquium on Italian Jewish preaching at Yale,[11] so I will not pursue the theme further here.

What can we say about the native Italian homiletical tradition and the impact upon it of Spanish preaching in the wake of the Sephardic immigration? We can outline the broad contours of the Spanish homiletical tradition as it crystallized in the late fifteenth century, and trace its continuity within the Ottoman Empire.[12] The manuscript sermons of Joseph ben Hayyim of Benevento, dating from 1515 until the 1530s, provide an example of preaching on Italian soil very much in the Spanish mold: a verse from the scriptural lesson and a passage of aggadah (often from the Zohar) as the basic building blocks, an introduction including a stylized asking of permission (*reshut*) from God, the Torah, and the congregation, followed by a structured investigation of a conceptual problem, sometimes accompanied by an identification of difficulties (*sefeqot*) in the pericope.[13] But the paucity of Italian material from the fifteenth century and the first half of the sixteenth century makes it very difficult to construct a norm for Italian preaching and thus delineate the process by which Spanish Jewish preaching influenced home-grown models.

---

8. Zahalon.

9. Ibn Basa, "Tena'ei ha-Darshan"; the text was written in Florence in 1627. Cf. Bonfil, *Rabbis,* p. 300; Sosland, *Guide,* pp. 82–83n.

10. Examples from Italy include Segal, "Kol Ya'aqov" (cf. Bonfil, *Rabbis,* p. 301; Zahalon, pp. 83–84n), Leon Modena's "Beit Leḥem Yehudah," an index to *'Ein Ya'aqov* (see *Autobiography,* p. 226), and Jacob Zahalon's alphabetical index to *Yalqut Shim'oni* (see Zahalon, pp. 73–76). For other such preaching aids by Jews, see *Jewish Preaching,* pp. 16–17, 286.

11. See Ruderman, *Preachers.*

12. See *Jewish Preaching,* pp. 66–78.

13. Joseph ben Hayyim, "Derashot."

What is the relationship between Jewish and Christian preaching in Italy? I am referring not to a rehashing of the debate about the influence of Renaissance rhetorical theory,[14] but to an assessment of the more immediate impact of published Christian sermons and actual Christian preachers. Did the notorious conversionist sermons affect Jewish preaching style, or conversely, did conversionist preachers learn from Jewish practitioners the most effective ways to move their audiences?[15] Nor should we forget that Italian Jews did not always need to be coerced to listen to Christian preachers, as we learn from a passing reference to "educated Jews" (*Judei periti*) at a sermon delivered by Egidio da Viterbo in Siena on November 11, 1511.[16]

That Christians attended the sermons of Leon Modena is known to every reader of his *Autobiography*.[17] Not as widely known is the passage in which he refers to his own attendance at the sermon of a Christian preacher,[18] and the fact that he owned at least one volume of Savonarola's sermons and an Italian treatise on "The Way to Compose a Sermon."[19] His letter to Samuel Archivolti describes the sermons in *Midbar Yehudah* as a blending of Christian and Jewish homiletics, and he uses the Italian terms *prologhino* and *epi-*

---

14. Bettan, p. 196; Barzilay, pp. 168–69; Messer Leon, pp. liv–lx; Altmann, "Ars Rhetorica"; and Zahalon, pp. 105–7, n. 14; all emphasize the citations of classical rhetoricians by Jewish writers. Dan, *Sifrut ha-Musar*, pp. 190–97 argues that Moscato's sermons should be seen more in the context of the internal Jewish homiletical tradition. I tend to agree with Dan; see the example of continuity in *Jewish Preaching*, pp. 71–72. The position taken by Moshe Idel on the extent of influence by Renaissance Christian Kabbalah (in Ruderman, *Preachers*, pp. 47–59) focuses on the ideas, not the rhetoric and form of the sermons.

15. On the forced conversionary sermon in Italy, see Baron, *SRHJ* 14:50–51 and 323–24 n.47; Stow, *Catholic Thought*, pp. 19–21. I am not aware of any study of the actual rhetorical techniques of these sermons that would clarify whether the preachers tried to draw upon Jewish homiletical traditions in order to convince their Jewish audiences.

16. Rowland, pp. 250, 260. Cf. Isaac Arama's description of Spanish Jews impressed by the sermons of Christian preachers and demanding a higher level from their own rabbis: introduction to *'Aqedat Yitshaq*, cited above, p. 78.

17. Modena, *Autobiography*, pp. 96, 117. Cf. *Jewish Preaching*, pp. 26, 51 n. 19, and Isaac min ha-Leviyim, p. 80. For Montaigne's description of a Jewish sermon he heard in Italy, see *Jewish Preaching*, p. 9; for Giordano Bruno's praise of a contemporary Jewish preacher, see Roth, *Renaissance*, pp. 36, 343n.

18. In the Church of San Geremia: Modena, *Autobiography*, p. 109; cf. his letter cited by Yerushalmi, *Spanish Court*, pp. 353–54.

19. *Modo di comporre una predica*, by Panigarola (Venice, 1603); see Ancona, pp. 265–66. I am grateful to Howard Adelman for bringing this article to my attention. Joanna Weinberg's paper at the Yale colloquium discussed the influence of this text on Modena (see Ruderman, *Preachers*, pp. 110–15); except for the use of the word *prologhino* (p. 111), I found the evidence for such influence rather meager. Modena himself claims to have written a work called "Matteh Yehudah" "on how to compose a well-ordered sermon" (Zahalon, p. 82, n.1).

loghino to characterize the first and last sections of his discourses.[20] All of this bespeaks an openness to what was happening in the pulpits of nearby churches. Extremely important work has been done during the past two decades on various aspects of the history of Italian Christian preaching.[21] The task of integrating this with the Jewish material remains to be accomplished.

Another aspect of this subject relates to the use of Italian literature by Jewish preachers. Extravagant claims have been made; an *Encyclopedia Judaica* article asserts that "Like Petrarch, Dante was widely quoted by Italian rabbis of the Renaissance in their sermons."[22] I do not know what evidence could support such a statement. Extant texts contain few examples of Jewish preachers using contemporary Italian literature, and there is no reason to assume that such references would be included in the oral version and eliminated in the written, or that those who quoted Italian authors would be predisposed not to record their sermons. Nevertheless, the few examples we have are instructive. Joseph Dan has discussed Moscato's citation of Pico della Mirandola which, though incidental to the preacher's main point, shows that there was apparently nothing extraordinary about using even a Christological interpretation for one's own homiletical purpose.[23]

More impressive are stories used by Leon Modena. The allegory he incorporates into a sermon on repentance, in which Good and Evil exchange garments so that everyone now honors Evil and spurns Good, is presented as one he "heard," probably from a Christian or a Jew conversant with Christian literature. A story used in the eulogy for a well-known rabbinic scholar tells of a young man who tours the world to discover whether he is truly alive or dead. The answer he receives from a monk is confirmed in a dramatic di-

---

20. See *Jewish Preaching* 1200–1800, pp. 411–12.

21. Examples of book length studies include O'Malley; Rusconi; Delcorno; Lesnick; Paton. There have also been monumental editions of sermons by the greatest preachers, such as Bernardino da Siena (Bernardino, *Prediche*). The index to this work enables one to evaluate how important contemporary Jews were as a theme in Bernardino's preaching; it is striking how little attention the preacher seems to have paid to this topic.

22. Sermoneta, "Dante," *EJ* 5:1295. This was apparently based on Cecil Roth's assertion that "Any person with the slightest pretext to education was familiar with Dante and with Petrarch. Rabbis quoted them in their sermons" (Roth, *Renaissance*, p. 33; note the addition of "widely" in the *EJ* statement). But Roth does not provide a single example of a sermon in which either Dante or Petrarch was quoted. For a more balanced treatment of Jewish knowledge of Italian literature, but which does not address its use in sermons, see Shulvass, pp. 230–31, and, in a still broader sense, Bonfil, *Jewish Life*, pp. 237–39.

23. Dan, "Sifrut ha-Derush," p. 108; cf. the discussion of the same passage by Moshe Idel in Ruderman, *Preachers*, p. 48–49.

alogue with the spirit of a corpse in the cemetery. Modena attributes this story explicitly to a "non-Jewish book." Although its direct source is as yet unidentified, it certainly reflects the late medieval and Renaissance preoccupation with death and dying that produced not only the various expressions of the *danse macabre* motif but a host of treatises on good living and good dying, including dialogues involving a nonthreatening personification of Death.[24]

What do we know about the training of Jewish preachers in Italy? For no other country is there such ample evidence for the cultivation of homiletics as an honorable discipline in the paideia. The kinds of evidence range from the exemplary sermon of Abraham Farissol dating from the early sixteenth century to the letters of Elijah ben Solomon ha-Levi di Vali almost three hundred years later.[25] There seems to have been a special emphasis on students accompanying their teachers to services to listen to sermons, especially on major preaching occasions. In addition, preaching was actually taught in the schools.[26] Public speaking and the delivery of sermons was to be part of the curriculum in David Provençal's proposed Jewish college in Mantua.[27] The preaching exercises in which Modena participated when he was no older than ten, though apparently not unusual, must have been impressive;[28] the delivery of a sermon by a precocious child may well have had the effect that the playing of a concerto by a young prodigy would have in the age of Mozart. But the actual methods for instruction—whether printed collections of sermons were studied and sermons by noted preachers critiqued, and what written guidelines for the preparation of sermons were used in the schools—remain to be fully investigated.

A work like *Medabber Tahapukhot* by Leon Modena's grandson Isaac provides dramatic evidence of the tumultuous politics of the pulpit. Indeed, the

---

24. For the stories of Modena, see Modena, *Midbar,* pp. 15a, 76b–77a; Saperstein, "Stories," pp. 105–6; *Jewish Preaching,* pp. 98–99, 342–43. The literature on Christian attitudes toward death in the fifteenth and sixteenth centuries is enormous; see Tenenti and Delumeau. While the idea that this world was the "land of the dead" was something of a topos (e.g. Delumeau, pp. 352–53, 459), Modena's story is different from most in that it does not use the macabre (involving the putrefaction of the corpse), or the theme of *memento mori,* but simply the claim that death is true life as its summons to renunciation of this world. Cf.Innocenzo Ringhieri's *Dialoghi della vita e della morte* (Bologna, 1550), set in a cemetery, in which Death serves as a guide to eternal bliss (discussed by Tenenti, pp. 270–71).

25. Ruderman, "Exemplary Sermon;" Bonfil, "Iggerot," pp. 167, 184–85.

26. Assaf, 2:157, 177.

27. See the text in Assaf, 2:119, paragraph 12, translated in Marcus, *Jew,* p. 386.

28. Modena, *Autobiography,* pp. 85–86; cf. *Jewish Preaching,* pp. 405–6.

ways in which the selection of preachers for various occasions could reveal a hierarchy of prestige, unleashing bitter quarrels, appears as one of the central subjects of the book.[29] Conflicts over the limits of acceptable public discourse—what content could and could not be properly addressed from the pulpit—were part of the same cultural milieu that produced the battles over the printing of the Zohar and the publication of de' Rossi's *Me'or Einayim.*[30] Sometimes these issues were adjudicated by legal authorities, who issued formal responsa, but in addition to evoking decisions from the scholarly elite, they reflect the sensibilities and tastes of the listeners in the pews. A full range of such nonsermonic texts is necessary for an adequate reconstruction of the historical dynamic of Italian Jewish preaching.

A final set of questions relates to the writing and printing of sermon collections. Although sermons were undoubtedly delivered in the vernacular throughout the Middle Ages, Italy seems to have produced the first texts of Jewish sermons actually written in a European language.[31] Why did some Jewish preachers begin to write in Italian in the late sixteenth and seventeenth centuries? What does the transition from Hebrew to Italian in Hebrew characters (Dato) to Italian in Latin characters (Cantarini) reveal about contemporary Jewish culture? Interestingly, despite the new linguistic variety in the manuscripts, printed collections remained in Hebrew. The number of such books published in Venice between 1585 and 1615, both by Italian and by Ottoman preachers, is an indication of the astounding public demand for this kind of literature. Modena decided to prepare a selection of his sermons for publication, hoping that the proceeds would help ease his financial pressures. In this, as in so many other pecuniary matters, he was apparently disappointed.[32]

In addition to the economics of sermon publishing, the format seems worthy of attention. Although most collections of Spanish and Ottoman sermons were arranged in accordance with the weekly scriptural lesson, most Italian collections were not. We have relatively few ordinary Sabbath ser-

---

29. For example, Isaac min ha-Leviyim, pp. 48–50, 62–63, 74–76, 78–79, 82–83, 104–6.

30. Kaufmann; cf. the responsa of Leon Modena on philosophical and Kabbalistic content in sermons, *Jewish Preaching,* pp. 406–8.

31. The manuscript sermons of Mordecai Dato; see Robert Bonfil, "Dato;" *Jewish Preaching,* p. 41 (and the reservation in n. 41).

32. Modena, *Autobiography,* pp. 101–2, 209 n. r; and the letter translated in *Jewish Preaching,* p. 411. In his introduction to *Midbar Yehudah,* Modena speaks of a glut of sermon collections on the market that diminishes their value in the eyes of potential buyers (p. 3a–b, cited in Rosenzweig, p. 45).

mons, particularly in print; most of them are for special Sabbaths, holidays, occasions in the life cycle or in the life of the community. Yet there is abundant evidence that weekly preaching on the pericope was the norm throughout Italy. Could there have been a conscious avoidance of the Sephardic format? We have no answer as yet.

I turn now to a more detailed discussion of certain aspects of Italian preaching. Among his other roles, the preacher appeared to be a guardian of moral and religious standards, and therefore a critic of the behavior of his listeners. Frequently this was just the kind of material the preacher would omit when editing his words for publication, assuming that readers in distant cities would have little interest in the local issues he had addressed.[33] But some of this social criticism has been preserved. If we are careful to distinguish generalized complaints—the stock themes of the genre of rebuke that recur in almost every generation—from attacks that target a specific, concrete abuse, we may find clues to the stress lines within that Jewish society, clues that become more persuasive when the sermon material is integrated with the contemporary responsa literature.[34]

The proper assessment of the sermonic rebuke is not always obvious. I am not quite certain what to make of the accusation, made both by Samuel Katznellenbogen and by Jacob di Alba, that among those who leave the synagogue after the *tefillah* and therefore miss the sermon are congregants who hurry to return to their business affairs.[35] Could they be talking about Jews who engage in work on the Sabbath after attending only part of the Saturday morning service? This would be a violation so serious that one wonders why any rabbi would focus on the much more trivial offenses of missing the sermon or insulting the preacher.

Is it then merely a rhetorical device used to discredit those who walk out early by suggesting to the remaining congregation that the exiters *might* be going to work? If so, it could not be used to prove that serious Sabbath violation was actually occurring, but only that the possibility of such violation was plausible enough for the listeners not to dismiss the suggestion as absurd. Or could the entire passage be referring not to the Sabbath but to the weekday morning service? If this is the case, it would be evidence of a very different dynamic: the cultivation of the practice of an informal daily homily or *devar Torah,* and the resistance on the part of Jews who were committed enough to attend the service, but resented the homiletical accoutrement as an imposition

---

33. See the examples cited in *Jewish Preaching*, p. 22.
34. See my discussion of the methodological issues in chap. 10, below.
35. See *Jewish Preaching*, p. 52 and n. 23.

on their time. As with the Moscato eulogy, Katzenellenbogen leads us to the brink of something rather important but fails to give us quite enough to use it with confidence.

Other passages of rebuke are more straightforward. Cecil Roth wrote that "the employment of adventitious aids to female beauty was a perpetual preoccupation of Renaissance [Christian] preachers and moralists, and it is certain that Jewish women followed (or anticipated) the general fashion."[36] He provided no documentation for this, or for the subsequent assertion that "in Italy generally no sort of ornament was more common than false hair, generally blond, . . . and the wealthy Jewess was able to keep abreast of fashion simply by remodeling her wig."[37] Nevertheless, sixteenth century Jewish literature does reveal the concern of Jewish moralists with this practice.

In a sermon for the Sabbath of Repentance, Katzenellenbogen turned to the women in the congregation and raised a rather sensitive issue. Women, said the preacher, must heed the moral instruction of the religious authorities even when they do not like it. The precept chosen to illustrate the point was one in which the preacher claimed the women of his city were particularly lax: the prohibition against uncovering their hair or adorning themselves with a Gentile wig, which was indistinguishable from their own hair. "In all the Ashkenazi communities, for generations, our ancestors have protested that women must not wear even a silk ribbon that has the color of hair"; the preacher was referring to a lengthy legal decision of his in which he argued against authorities who permitted these practices. But this was not, as Cecil Roth suggested, simply a matter of Jewish women being influenced by their surroundings. Katzenellenbogen was arguing that the hair fashions of Jewish women were particularly scandalous "in a place where the Gentile women are accustomed to cover their hair, and the nuns strictly prohibit adorning themselves with a wig." For him, the Christian environment was mentioned not merely to explain why some had strayed from normative Jewish practice; the preacher used his Christian neighbors as a rhetorical goad to bring the listeners back to their own tradition.[38]

Preachers were also exercised by what they considered to be a deterioration of sexual mores. Israel Bettan cited a passage by Azariah Figo condemning the practice (perhaps more widespread in Italy than in other countries?) of recreational gazing at women, both married and single, "an

---

36. Roth, *Renaissance*, p. 48.

37. Cf. Izbicki, esp. pp. 215–16, 219 on hair styles and false hair.

38. Katzenellenbogen, p. 9b; cf. Nigal, p. 82. For other examples of Christian behavior used by Jewish preachers as a model worthy of emulation, see chap. 5, above.

indulgence that must inevitably lead to graver offenses."[39] But this was at most a minor infraction of the traditional code of Jewish norms. A far more serious charge was leveled by Figo elsewhere:

> From then [the destruction of the second Temple] until now, the first two of these sins, namely idolatry and murder, have ceased from the people of Israel. Thank God, there are no reports of a pattern or even a tendency to commit these two sins among our nation—except as a result of compulsion, or in a rare individual case. But the third sin, adultery and incest [*gilluy 'arayot*], has not been properly guarded against. Jews have violated the rules in these sinful generations in various ways, engaging in all kinds of destructive behavior publicly, out in the open, without any shame or embarrassment.[40]

Unlike the more concrete condemnations by the preachers in Prague 150 years later,[41] this passage remains too vague to be of much value to the social historian, although listeners in the audience may well have thought of specific examples. Nevertheless, the contrast drawn between what the preacher did not consider to be a real problem (the attraction of Christianity, crimes of violence) and what he did (the more serious kind of sexual sins)—plus the claim that such behavior was tacitly condoned by many Jews, that it could become public knowledge without serious repercussions for the perpetrators—may point to a genuine sense of breakdown in the core of the traditional Jewish ethos.[42]

Financial arrangements also had the potential to create deep conflicts. In powerful language, Azariah Figo addressed the complex problem of impermissible loans. The poor were forced to seek loans from the rich, who "de-

39. Figo, nu. 64, p. 93d; cf. Bettan, p. 237. A different sermon (nu. 13, p. 47b), in which Figo complains about the same common phenomenon, goes a step further by noting a rationale intended to justify the practice from traditional sources. "Let them not heed deceitful chatter (cf. Exod. 5:9) which claims, 'On the contrary, by this they increase their merit by subduing the erotic impulses [aroused], like those who said, "Let us go on the road leading by the harlots' place and defy our inclination and have our reward" (B. AZ 17a–b).'" Figo concedes that traditional ethical theory recognizes a great merit in overcoming the temptation to sin, which might lead some to conclude that arousing the temptation might play a positive religious role. But "in this generation of ours, with our sins, this is not the way; the motivation of the young men is not pure, their purpose is only to see what they can see; the practice must therefore be condemned."

40. Figo, nu. 48, p. 43b.

41. See the discussion of sexual mores in chap. 10, below.

42. Needless to say, such passages from sermons need to be integrated with other types of literature, especially the contemporary responsa, before responsible conclusions about actual Jewish behavior (as opposed to the consciousness of the religious leadership), can be drawn.

vour their flesh with several forms of clear-cut, open interest." Even worse, in his eyes, was that the sense of sinfulness about such forbidden arrangements had been lost.

> If a group of Jews were to be seen going to a Gentile butcher and were then seen publicly eating pig or other forbidden meat, they would be stoned by all, although this entails only on negative prohibition, for which the punishment is lashes. Yet here we see those who lend money on interest, which involves six transgressions for the lender, as well as others for the borrower, the guarantor, the witnesses and the scribe, and all are silent.[43]

Like the passage about sexual immorality cited above, this one also reflects a serious gap between the values of the community and the standards of its religious leadership. The prevalent social norms deemed the dietary laws to be crucial to Jewish identity, even though from a legal standpoint they did not entail the most serious of sins. Taking interest from a fellow Jew had greater legal consequences, but ordinary Jews considered it innocuous. Those who were aware of the prohibition, we are told, showed deference to the tradition by hypocritical attempts to avoid the appearance of transgression, through ruses such as an arrangement by which the creditor was allowed to live in an apartment without rent. As for the *cambio* [exchange contract], some may have been permissible, but many others were totally forbidden, so that even the well-intentioned merchant may have unwittingly erred. "My quarrel with them is this," the preacher concluded: "Why don't they consult with experts in these matters, who can provide them with proper guidance?"[44] The passage is extremely rich, revealing the frustrations of religious leaders in the face of economic and social forces they were unable to control.

In addition to areas of major conflict, the sermons reveal aspects of the norms of social life and mentality. Wedding sermons can hardly avoid reflecting the attitudes of the preachers toward women and marriage. The earliest Italian preacher whose sermons are preserved, Moses ben Joab of mid-fifteenth century Florence, speaking at a betrothal celebration of a certain Abraham of Montalcino, delivered himself of what reads today like a misogynist diatribe, but must have seemed to him like a conventional assessment of woman's limitations and perils. He then proceeds,

---

43. Figo, nu. 10, p. 33d; cf. Bettan, p. 239.

44. Figo, nu. 10, p. 33d. On the complexity of the legal issues relating to the *cambio,* see Passamaneck. For fifteenth- and sixteenth-century Italian Christian moralists and preachers and their distrust of "letters of exchange" as an attempt to camouflage illicit interest-bearing loans, see Delumeau, pp. 224–25; for the earlier period, cf. Lesnick, pp. 119–21.

What can a man do who wants to find himself a wife? All around him are "brokers of sin," who find something good to say about those who have no merit. Today they tell him one thing, tomorrow another, until their combined efforts wear him down. In order to lead him into their trap, they tell him, This woman who is coming into your home will bring some dowry! . . . Whoever escapes from the snares of these people like an energetic bird or deer, and finds himself a decent woman has indeed *found something good* (Prov. 18:22).

The use of the occasion of a betrothal celebration to incorporate into a religious discourse an attack against the prevailing standards of marriage brokers shows that Italian preachers, though frequently ponderous, were not without humor.[45]

A passage in a sermon by Katzenellenbogen gives us a glimpse of child-rearing practices and might be added to the burgeoning scholarly literature on attitudes toward children and private life. At issue was an aggadic statement (B. Hag 3a) that small children should be brought to hear sermons, even though they cannot understand them. But this is obvious, the preacher says: if the small children were left home alone, their parents would stand impatiently and resentfully during the sermon, not listening to what was being said but wishing it would end, afraid that their children might be harmed. Thus, "even if parents were not commanded to bring their preschool children, they would bring them of their own accord out of fear lest they be harmed if they are left at home with no adult around." The preacher does not address the problem of concentrating on the sermon if the infant or toddler is present in the synagogue, but we have here a rather moving indication of concern for the welfare of small children left without adult supervision.[46]

The fact that Italian preachers such as Katzellenbogen and Modena made eulogies a significant component of their relatively small selection of published sermons may well have solidified the prestige of that genre as a written text. No historical study of Jewish attitudes toward death and beliefs about the afterlife can be complete without consideration of this literature. Though often stylized and filled with conventions and commonplaces, the

45. Cassuto, "Rabbino," 4 (1907):226–27. The last sentence alludes to Prov. 18:22, *One who has found a wife has found something good*, frequently used as an ornament on Italian marriage contracts. The elements of humor and wit in Italian Jewish preaching (and in Jewish preaching in general) deserve careful study.

46. Katzenellenbogen, p. 10a. The study of Jewish child-rearing practices (as distinct from more formal Jewish education) and their relationship with those of contemporary Christian neighbors (for example, whether the conclusions of Philippe Ariès and his critics have any relevance to the Jewish family) has hardly begun. Pertinent to this passage would be Ariès's claim of a shift in the early modern period from a rather careless indifference toward the child to an attitude favoring regimentation and constant surveillance (Ariès, *Childhood*, pp. 94–97).

eulogies also reveal the texture and quality of interpersonal relationships: the respect of a student for his teacher (or the love of a teacher for his young student), the bonds of genuine friendship, the pain at the loss of a member of the immediate family.[47] No branch of Jewish homiletical literature is more deserving of systematic study.

I must mention one other kind of occasional preaching. Not infrequently, the sermon was used as a vehicle to raise funds for a worthy cause. Each community supported the central institutions of Jewish life through a system of self-imposed taxation, and there were standard funds for free-will offerings. But there were also unusual cases that warranted a special appeal from the pulpit. The causes deemed worthy of such special appeals reflect the shared values of the society, and the arguments used to convince the listeners to give point to a consensus about the expectations of responsibility in Jewish life, in addition to exhibiting another aspect of the rhetorical arsenal at the preacher's disposal.

For example, Moscato devoted a significant part of a sermon for the holiday of Sukkot to an appeal on behalf of the impoverished sick. He notes that this has been "imposed upon me by the [lay] leaders of our people to make known in public their suffering, for their numbers and their need are greater than usual, etc." After dwelling on the importance of charitable giving and the special claim of the impoverished sick, he moves on to other exegetical material, but returns later in the sermon to remind the listeners that he expects their pledges. The entire section is an integral part of the sermon, crafted with no less artistic sophistication than the rest.[48]

Katzenellenbogen delivered a eulogy for R. Zalman Katz of Mantua "in the public square of the ghetto . . . for all the synagogues were closed because of the plague," a circumstance that repeated itself several generations later (in 1657) when Jacob Zahalon preached from the window balcony of a private home to Jews standing in the street below.[49] At this time, he said, when "the line of judgment is stretched out against us," donations to charity are a traditional safeguard from harm. The eulogy ends with a direct appeal:

47. For example, Modena's eulogy for his mother delivered at the end of the thirty-day mourning period (Modena, *Midbar*, pp. 51a–55a); cf. Nave, pp. 143–44. Katzenellenbogen indicates that the prevalent taste considered it inappropriate to discuss in a eulogy the closeness of personal friendship between the preacher and the deceased, but he defends his decision to do so anyway (Katzenellenbogen, pp. 30a–31a). For recent studies of Italian Christian eulogies, see McManamon, and the articles by McManamon and Donald Weinstein in Tetel, pp. 68–104. For the Jewish eulogy, see Horowitz, "Speaking of the Dead," and chap. 16, below.

48. Moscato, nu. 36, pp. 97c–98a, 99d.

49. See Zahalon, p. 26.

> There is no need to dwell at length on these matters, for I know that your excellencies are not unaware of the great power of this mitzvah of charitable giving, particularly at this perilous time. But I beseech your excellencies to contribute speedily as much as you can, in accordance with the needs of the hour. And I will be the first to perform this mitzvah; see my example and do likewise.[50]

With that dramatic gesture, the preacher established a model not only for his congregation of listeners, but for subsequent fund-raisers as well.

Even in more normal times, the eulogy was apparently an occasion for appeals on behalf of needy members of the family of the deceased. Leon Modena excelled in this, as in so many other areas. His *Autobiography* reports that as part of his eulogy for a friend in 1616, he exhorted the congregation to take up a collection to provide a dowry for the orphaned daughter. Five hundred ducats were raised, about twice the maximum annual income of Modena's own career, though lower than the dowries he was able to provide for his own daughters, which were by no means high. The achievement was unusual enough to be taken as a model for emulation by Christian preachers, who would say on their days of penitence, in order to inspire their audiences to charity, "Did not one Jew in the ghetto raise five hundred ducats with one sermon to marry off a young girl?"[51] Unfortunately, Modena left no known written record of the eloquence of his appeal.

The Days of Awe were often an occasion for pulpit-inspired philanthropy. Azariah Figo devoted part of his sermon on the second day of Rosh Hashanah in 1643 to an appeal for funds for the impoverished Jewish community of Jerusalem. Forced to pay an enormous tax, they had sent emissaries to all the communities of the Diaspora. Figo's theme-verse was actually only a strategically chosen phrase wrenched from its syntactical context: *Ha-maqom ha-hu' Adonai yir'eh* (Gen. 22:14). This expresses both the unique providential relationship with the holy city and the hope that "God will see the affliction of that place, and bring it healing and recovery through the extraordinary kindness and generosity of your excellencies, as befits the sanctity of the place and of this time."[52] The practice of emergency appeals

---

50. Katzenellenbogen, p. 63b.

51. Modena, *Autobiography*, pp. 109, 41–42.

52. Figo, pp. 13d–14a. Cf. the Florentine preacher Jacob di Alba (Alba, p. 85a): "We might say, *How lonely does she sit* (Lam. 1:1): the city of God that descended to earth and *became like a widow* sitting on the ground, bereft of all distinction. But with regard to taxes and exactions, they perform a creation *ex nihilo* upon her; she is *great among the nations, a princess among the states* (Lam. 1:1), for she has existed only so that taxes might be taken from her, making something out of nothing. So it is, in our sins, at present: Jerusalem must pay many kinds of taxes, and if they did not send emissaries from various places, the inhabitants would not be able to endure."

on the Days of Awe for inhabitants of the land of Israel was not an innovation of the past generation.

Italian Jewish preaching, with its riches and challenges, is a topic about which much more could be said, and the reader whose appetite has been whetted may refer to other essays in the volume based on the Yale colloquium.[53] My presentation on that occasion concluded with one of the wisest sentences Leon Modena ever wrote: "In all of the congregations of Italy where I have preached, I never heard anyone complain that the sermon was too short, only that it was too long."[54]

---

53. Ruderman, *Preachers.*

54. Modena, *Ziqnei,* p. 126. The context is a halakhic question sent to him whether it was permissible for a preacher to turn over an hourglass on the Sabbath to time the sermon so that it would not be a burden on the congregation. For the use of the hourglass by Christian preachers, see *Jewish Preaching,* p. 38, n. 33.

9

The Sermon as Art Form:
Structure in Morteira's *Giv'at Sha'ul*

The study of the late medieval and early modern Jewish sermon as a branch of Jewish literature requires a careful delineation of the appropriate subject matter. Is the "sermon" the written Hebrew text that appears in a collection of *derashot*? Or is it the oral communication between preacher and congregation, an event that occurred in one place at one time, for which an extant written text serves as evidence? If it is the first, we will be concerned with the literary qualities of Hebrew homiletical writing. The genre *derashah* will have to be defined, its subdivisions and conventions explained, but there will be no need to distinguish between a *derashah* that was never intended to be spoken in a synagogue and one that reflects with some accuracy what a preacher once said.[1]

If, on the other hand, we are interested primarily in the literary dimensions not of Hebrew homiletical writing but of Jewish preaching, the task will be considerably more difficult. An integral part of the sermon in this sense is the preacher himself: his voice, gestures, animation, pace. The absence of videotapes or recordings means that this component of the sermon is irrevocably lost. Furthermore, the extant written texts of Jewish sermons are not precise accounts of what was said. They are, for the most part, neither manuscripts used by the preacher while preaching, nor transcriptions made by professional scribes during the sermon itself, but reconstructions after the sermon was delivered, in some cases made from notes only after a lapse of time. A preacher preparing a selection of his sermons for publication might eliminate passages that were once of immediate concern to his con-

Originally appeared in *Prooftexts* 3 (1981): 243–61. Reprinted with permission from Johns Hopkins University Press.

1. See Dan, *Sifrut ha-Musar*. Dan provides an extremely important discussion of the relationship between the oral and the written sermon (pp. 27–41), but his subject is defined as "homiletical literature," and it is therefore appropriate for him to analyze a work such as Abraham bar Hiyya's *Hegyon ha-Nefesh*, which does not purport to be a record of sermons actually preached (pp. 70–82). Israel Bettan's collection of essays, by contrast, is entitled *Studies in Jewish Preaching*, yet it contains little attempt to define the relationship between the written text and the oral event.

gregation, but in retrospect seem dated and unlikely to be valued by a wider reading public; he might expand theoretical points insufficiently developed in the oral presentation; he might combine parts of several sermons delivered over the years.[2]

This process is further complicated by the fact that in many cases a sermon has undergone a linguistic transformation while being prepared for publication, from a vernacular original, or more precisely a vernacular original interspersed with quotations and phrases from the traditional Hebrew literature, to a pure Hebrew text.[3] Consequently, certain literary investigations will be fraught with problems. For example, the diction or level of language in the original sermon will often be impossible to ascertain. The Hebrew text that has come down to us might be richly embellished with allusions to the classics of Hebrew literature, but what this tells us about the level of language in the vernacular original is anything but clear. The richness of the Hebrew diction may reflect an attempt to match a similar richness in the oral vernacular. But it is also possible that someone publishing a book of Hebrew sermons was expected to embellish the language no matter how simply he had spoken.[4]

On the other hand, certain literary matters remain accessible despite the

---

2. For example, Leon Modena states that he "wrote and arranged [the Hebrew sermons of *Midbar Yehudah*] from the outline notes [*rimzei rashei peraqim*] I had written." Modena, *Midbar,* p. 4b.

3. Robert Bonfil's publication of an Italian sermon by Mordecai Dato (1525–1601) (Bonfil, "Dato") provides a model of the vernacular sermon interspersed with Hebrew. Reading Bonfil's Hebrew translation of the sermon first, one might well conclude that it is so dependent upon Hebrew puns—e.g., in its explanation of the change from Avram to Abraham—that it could not have been delivered except in Hebrew. Yet the Italian original shows that the puns were no problem for a preacher addressing an audience familiar with the Hebrew text of the Bible. The relationship of Jewish preaching to the Christian "macaronic" sermon, in which Latin and a vernacular were intermingled in various ways, deserves full investigation. See Erb, p. 381, n. 4: "The text moves from one language to the other without any apparent disruption in syntax or meaning." Cf. Saperstein, *Jewish Preaching,* p. 43, n. 48 and p. 41, n. 41.

4. This would be true even if we were to assume that some sermons were preached in Hebrew. See, for example, the introduction of Joseph ben Hayyim Zarfati to *Yad Yosef* (cited in *Jewish Preaching,* p. 21). The author states that his pattern had been to write down "immediately" whatever he had said while preaching; he gives no indication of the language of the sermons. Then, when he decided to present his sermons for publication, he was tempted to rewrite them in an impressive rhetorical idiom. But he changed his mind, for two reasons. First was the tremendous amount of work involved in such a revision, "for when I wrote them originally, my only purpose was to ensure that I would not forget them, and I did not bother with rhetorical style." Second, he believed that rhetoric often distracts from the content itself. This apology for the plain style indicates that the usual pattern in preparing sermons for publication involved considerable rhetorical embellishment.

changes inherent in transforming the oral sermon into a literary text, whether or not this includes a translation. Many rhetorical features are characteristic of oral communication. When a preacher addresses his congregation with various terms of respect or endearment, asks permission of particular notables to begin his discourse, refers to the mixed level of his audience, or complains that his admonitions are rarely heeded, he may or may not be resorting to conventions and commonplaces. But it is reasonable to assume that such rhetorical devices were part of what was actually said, and unlikely that they would have been inserted as the author prepared to publish for a readership he would never know.

One of the most important literary forms used by many preachers was the parable or exemplum. These may have functioned in different ways. Parables in written texts may have been used to express and conceal a radical doctrine that the author might not have been prepared to state directly.[5] On the whole, the parables in the sermonic literature do not seem to be of this type. Their primary function is to capture the attention of the less intellectually sophisticated listeners and to dramatize in concrete and familiar terms the preacher's abstract message. It is therefore likely that such parables were part of the original sermon, and not added as the sermon was later being written in final form. Does the parable have literary merit as a story when isolated from its context? Does the preacher appear to have created the parable for his own purpose or taken it from another literary source? If it was a familiar story, did the preacher use it in a novel way and thereby modify its meaning? The answers to such questions will teach us much about the art of the sermon as oral communication.

Perhaps most important, the structure of the sermon is unlikely to have undergone a fundamental change as it was edited for publication. A lucid and logical structure is more important in a spoken discourse, which depends upon the listener's being able to follow and retain what is being said, than it is in a written work, where the reader can proceed more slowly or review the material if the train of thought has been lost. Therefore, if we find written sermons with carefully molded structure, filled with passages of recapitulation that concisely summarize what has already been discussed, the most plausible assumption is that these qualities should be attributed to the spoken message and not to the transformation from an oral to a written form.

There are other important literary questions to be considered. How do a particular preacher's sermons relate to the tradition in which he was working, a tradition based both on preachers whom he had heard and authors whose books of sermons he had read? Do the basic elements of his sermon,

---

5. Dan, *Ha-Sippur,* pp. 142–46; cf. Kermode, pp. 23–47.

the structural components of his discourse—a verse from the Hagiographa, a series of consecutive verses from the Torah reading or from the Psalms, a passage of aggadah, an introduction, a coda with a messianic conclusion—and the interrelationship of these components reflect continuity with the past or a change in the conception of how a sermon was to be composed? What were the conventions, the technical terms, and the structural parameters of the genre being used?

If the basic components of the sermon were essentially stylized, did the preacher reveal any originality in form? Did each sermon follow the same predictable pattern, or was there flexibility and the capacity for surprise within the traditional literary framework? Finally, what would have been the response of the congregation at any point in the sermon? Would an attentive listener of average education and intelligence have been able to follow the outline of the sermon as it was being preached and retain a conception of its overall structure? Might such a listener have derived intellectual and aesthetic pleasure not only from the interpretation of a particular verse, or from the establishment of an unexpected connection between two verses, or a verse and a rabbinic statement, but also from the way in which all the disparate parts of the sermon were fitted together?

Few have attempted to analyze medieval and early modern Jewish preaching from the perspective of such questions,[6] and careful study of the written legacies of dozens of Jewish preachers will be necessary before a full literary history of the Jewish sermon can be attempted. The following investigation of structure in the extant sermons of one particularly effective preacher is intended as a preliminary step in the direction of that goal.

Rabbi Saul Levi Morteira (ca. 1596–1660) was born in Venice and received his training from the colorful and versatile Rabbi Leon Modena. At about the age of twenty, he assumed a position of rabbinic leadership in Amsterdam, where he remained for some forty years. He wrote apologetical tracts in Portuguese, Spanish, and Hebrew on controversial topics such as the eternity of the soul and the duration of punishment for the unrepentant sinner, divine providence, the rabbinic aggadah, and the merits of Judaism as compared with Christianity. As the leading rabbi of the Portuguese community, he presided over the excommunication of Spinoza and was one of the signatories on the document pronouncing a *ḥerem* upon Juan de Prado.[7]

Morteira's enduring contribution to Hebrew literature was his sermons,

---

6. See especially Dan, "Tefillah ve-Dim'ah."

7. On these aspects of Morteira's writings and thought, see Altmann, "Eternality"; Mechoulan, "Spinoza"; Kaplan, "Morteira"; Melnick, pp. 29–32, 66–69; Saperstein, "Treatise"; and the massive introduction to Salomon, *Tratado*. On Spinoza, see Salomon, "Excommunication," pp. 187–88. For the writ of excommunication of Juan de Prado, see Mendes-Flohr and Reinharz, p. 51.

fifty of which were selected by two disciples and published in 1645 as *Giv'at Sha'ul*—which also contains an outline of 450 sermons not published. The disciples wrote that Morteira had preached a total of 1400 different sermons, an average of 50 per year from his arrival in Amsterdam until the book appeared. The sermons in *Giv'at Sha'ul* are relatively short, a quality intended, according to the disciples, "to appeal to the listeners of our time, who are unable to comprehend anything too long." They contain frequent recapitulations, reminding the listener of what has been discussed. With few exceptions they reveal a clarity of architectonic structure that would enable a listener both to follow the specific point being made and to see how it fit into the overall framework of the message. Insofar as such an assertion may be defensible given the still nascent state of research, these sermons would appear to represent one of the peaks of the Jewish sermon as art form.[8]

In their basic components, the sermons in *Giv'at Sha'ul* follow a tradition in Jewish homiletics traceable at least back to the late fifteenth century. A verse from the Torah pericope, called the *nose* ("theme") or *pesuq noseinu* ("our theme verse"),[9] and an aggadic passage, called the *ma'amar* ("dictum") or *ma'amarenu ha-qodem* ("our primary dictum"), were read at the beginning of the sermon, undoubtedly in the original Hebrew or Aramaic. In his choice of Torah verses, Morteira proceeded quite systematically. The first year he was in Amsterdam, he preached on the first verse of each pericope,[10]

---

8. Morteira undoubtedly preached in Portuguese, since much of his congregation was of Portuguese background. (Seven brief sermons in Portuguese, written by Morteira, were included in a verse play performed in the synagogue of Beit Ya'aqov on Shavu'ot, 1624; see Jessurun.) Though the sermons in *Giv'at Sha'ul* were published in Hebrew, they do not appear to have been substantially revised. According to the disciples, they periodically asked Morteira for texts of his sermons, secretly intending to send them to Jewish communities throughout the Diaspora, thereby to spread the wisdom and fame of their master. These were undoubtedly the Hebrew texts of the sermons preserved in the manuscript collection of the Budapest Rabbinical Seminary entitled "Giv'at Sha'ul." See above in Preface, and below, chaps. 16 and 17.

9. The technical terminology of medieval Jewish homiletics is yet to be fully investigated. I think there can be little doubt that *nose* as used here is a translation of the Latin *thema*, the technical term for the biblical verse upon which the sermon was based. It remains to be determined when and by whom *nose* in this sense was introduced in Hebrew. See *Jewish Preaching*, p. 67, especially n. 8.

10. The outline of one sermon on the first verse of each Scriptural lesson appears at the end of the *editio princeps*: Morteira 1645. The book was reprinted in Warsaw 1902 and 1912 with the following omissions: the outline of the 450 unpublished sermons (many of which are found in the Budapest MS) and ("for reasons beyond our control") the two sermons, on *Va-ethanan* (Deut. 3:23–7:11) and *Nitsavim* (Deut. 29:9–30:20), which speak most directly of Christianity. Polemical passages against Christian doctrines from the sermon on *Balaq* (Num. 22:2–25:9) were also eliminated from the Warsaw editions without any indication by the printer. Unless otherwise noted, references to the printed *Giv'at Sha'ul* (henceforth *GS*) will be to the most accessible edition, that of Warsaw 1912.

the second year he moved to the second verse, and so on. This orderly progression seems to have been something of a self-imposed discipline and challenge; at one point Morteira refers to "the theme of the verse that has come
to us following our set order." While the sermons of *Giv'at Sha'ul* are not
dated, the systematic organization of theme verses makes it possible to assign
dates to the sermons with considerable confidence: if it is the seventh verse
of the scriptural lesson, it may ordinarily be assumed that the sermon was
delivered during Morteira's seventh year of preaching.[11]

The aggadic passage was chosen from the Talmud or one of the
midrashim.[12] Unlike many earlier preachers, Morteira rarely used a midrash
on the theme verse. On the contrary, many of the *ma'amarim* read at the beginning of the sermon had no obvious connection with the Torah verse they
followed. This created a kind of tension in the mind of the attentive listener,
who knew that the preacher would somehow establish a link between *nose*
and *ma'amar* but could not yet see how this would be done. As in the classical homiletical midrash, the demonstration of unanticipated congruence
between disparate texts was an important aesthetic technique.[13]

The third basic component is the thesis or conceptual problem, called the
derush. Each sermon has its own distinctive thesis, and Morteira says quite
clearly that "it is our custom not to speak on the same subject twice" (*GS*,
269). Where the thesis is similar to that of a previous sermon, Morteira carefully explains how this one will be different. The thesis is presented in the
introduction to the sermon, which immediately follows the aggadic *ma'a-
mar*. Many of these introductions are beautifully chiseled pieces of exposi-
tory prose; some may remind the reader of the essays of Ahad Ha'am. They
often begin indirectly, raising a problem that has no apparent connection
with either *nose* or *ma'amar* but is intended to catch the listener's attention;
by the end of the introduction, however, the preacher's subject is unam-
biguously defined. Following is a representative example, partly paraphrased,
partly quoted in an abbreviated fashion, from the sermon on *Mishpatim*
(Exod. 21:1–24:18), called "Permanence on Earth":

---

11. The manuscripts of Morteira's sermons reveal that dating them is somewhat more
complicated than I originally believed; see Saperstein, "Treatise," p. 136, esp. n. 17.

12. The use of an aggadic passage at the beginning of the sermon as an integral part of its
structure is an important transformation of Jewish homiletics at the end of the fifteenth century. It constitutes a clear break from the extant thirteenth-century models, which generally
connect a verse from the Hagiographa with the Pentateuchal pericope, in the style of the older
homiletical midrash. See *Jewish Preaching*, pp. 63–67.

13. Cf. Dan, *Sifrut ha-Musar*, pp. 41–43, on linking verses from different parts of the
Bible.

Nature has implanted in all creatures the desire to preserve themselves from destruction, and the rational faculty of the human being reinforces this natural tendency. Even the pious have an aversion toward death and strive to escape it. Leaders of the Gentiles tried three ways of attaining permanence and ensuring that their name would endure in subsequent generations. The first was by making monuments and statues of wood and stone, silver and gold, which represent their physical appearance, as the Roman Caesars did, and as Alexander wanted to do in the Temple. Second was by creating lofty, awe-inspiring buildings and palaces bearing their names. . . . Third was by fixing a holiday each year on which all would play games and speak their praises; the months perpetuate the names of two Caesars, Julius and Augustus. . . .

However, when we think about this, we realize that all these techniques are of no avail; none leads to true permanence. Statues and monuments are broken, either by the ravages of time or by the person's enemies . . . buildings are destroyed, either by time or by wars or earthquakes . . . the names of months are confused and people forget their original meaning. Only God can bestow true permanence. He wanted to bestow it upon his faithful servant Moses in a manner different from these. . . . How is this? That will be our subject today, which we begin with the help of God, whose loving-kindness is for all eternity upon those who revere Him. (*GS*, 136–37)

The introduction always ends with a brief summary of the sermon subject, and an appeal for help to God in language that succinctly recapitulates what has preceded.

It was in the body of the sermon that the problem of organization and structure became paramount. Although he followed certain set rules, Morteira was by no means predictable in constructing his discourse. The number of sections in the body of the sermon ranges from three to six, and occasionally even more.[14] And the basis for the division of the sermon into sections varies: it may be the Torah verse, or the rabbinic aggadah, or it may flow from the subject matter itself. Given the preacher's adherence to the unvarying components of the sermon and his predilection toward clarity of structure, the variety in his modes of organization is quite impressive.

An example of a sermon structure dependent on a division of the Torah

---

14. For example, the sermon on '*Eqev* (Deut. 7:12–11:25) (*GS*, 257–63). The preacher maintains that there are thirteen verses in the Torah where the word *mitsvah* means not one specific commandment but a fundamental principle of the Torah, and that each such verse can be integrally linked with one of Maimonides' Thirteen Principles. The body of the sermon is therefore divided into thirteen parts. The intellectual tension in the listener is aroused by the preacher's setting up for himself a seemingly impossible task and then proceeding to accomplish it.

verse can be seen in the sermon on *Shemot* (Exod. 1:1–6:1). Entitled "The People's Envy," it is based on Exodus 1:7: *But the Israelites were fertile and prolific, they multiplied and increased very greatly, so that the land was filled with them.* The verse contains several verbs that appear to be redundant, so Morteira discusses various exegetical approaches to the general issue of apparently superfluous words in the Bible. He recognizes that the Prophets, for purely rhetorical reasons, may have repeated the same idea in different words, but he insists that each word in the Torah must have significance. The four verbs in the first part of the verse are therefore to be interpreted not as synonyms, but as four discrete actions.

The first, *paru,* indicating an increase in population, is passed over quickly; the following three provide the structure for the three major parts of the sermon. *Va-yishretsu* is interpreted to mean that the Israelites expanded, spread out, took larger houses with many rooms and excessive living space. Then *va-yirbu,* they became great, dressing like grandees, following *haute couture,* spending ruinous amounts of money to impress others with their apparel. Finally, *va-ya'atsmu,* from *'etsem,* bone, means they became corpulent by spending fortunes on lavish banquets. In this context, the preacher introduces and discusses the *ma'amar* from tractate Pesaḥim 49a, "Whoever takes pleasure in an optional banquet will eventually be exiled. . ."—a statement having no apparent connection with the theme verse, but now shown to be pertinent. Morteira argues that these patterns of excess both aroused the envy of the Egyptians and provoked God into punishing the Israelites through enslavement. The three apparently superfluous words in the verse provide the framework for an explicit and vehement denunciation of the Jews in contemporary Amsterdam for the same irresponsible behavior (*GS,* 109–14).[15]

A five-part structure based on division of the theme verse can be seen in the sermon on *Ve-zot ha-berakhah* (Deut. 33:1–34:12), called "A Delightful Treasure." The Introduction lays the groundwork for the division: "A treasure, or a collection of silver or of vessels given by one person to another to be guarded, may be lost or destroyed for one of five reasons, or for all five." First, a treasure that cannot be counted or measured may be dissipated because no one would realize if part of it was missing; second, the guardian may be lazy or incompetent; third, his attention may be diverted to something more valuable; fourth, he may be overpowered by robbers; fifth, the treasure itself may eventually be worn out or dispersed. When God gave Israel the Torah, He or-

---

15. In this sermon, translated with annotation in *Jewish Preaching,* pp. 272–85, the influence of ibn Verga's *Shevet Yehudah* and the tradition of Spanish ethical literature is especially noticeable.

dained that it would never be lost or destroyed in any of these five ways. The thesis—the eternal and indestructible relationship between Israel and the Torah—is then discussed in the body of the sermon, which is divided according to five elements in the theme verse, Deuteronomy 33:4: *Moses charged us with the teaching as the heritage of the congregation of Jacob.*

The first element of the verse, *torah,* teaches that this treasure will not be lost like something that is unquantifiable. According to a well-known homily, the numerical significance of the letters in the word *torah* suggests a specific number of commandments, and the Torah contains a finite number of verses and words; it would immediately be known if a portion were lost. *Lanu* ("to us") hints that the laziness of the guardian will not be a factor. It is in the nature of Israel to keep the Torah; "even though in many periods, Jews were idolators, they never abandoned the Torah, never wanted to make themselves into a different nation." *Mosheh* (Moses) implies that the treasure can never be replaced by something more valuable. As Moses was the supreme prophet, there can be no Torah greater than the one given through him. *Morashah* ("heritage") shows that it cannot be forcefully taken, as an inheritance cannot legally be alienated through force. "Even though several nations have compelled some of our people to abandon their faith, those who were truly children of Israel never refrained day or night from returning to the inheritance they received from their ancestors, paying no heed to dangers or misfortunes. The ones who forgot were descended from those who became mixed in with us."

Finally, *qehillat Ya'aqov* ("the congregation of Jacob") shows that this treasure can never be dissipated or dispersed. Even when the Jewish people is "*Ya'aqov,*" dispersed and subjugated in exile, it is still a *qehillah,* which comes together to study and observe the Torah. "Our gathering in the synagogue is a portent alluding to the ingathering of the exiles; just as we gather from among the Gentiles to a place of prayer, so we will be gathered from them to the Holy Land." Here the preacher introduces the *ma'amar* from tractate Berakhot 6b describing God's anger upon failing to find ten men in the synagogue, and its relevance to the theme verse and thesis is shown. The sermon ends with a recapitulation: "Just as Israel is eternal and the Torah is eternal, so the link between them is eternal, and they will not be broken apart for any of the possible reasons, as we see in our theme verse"; a succinct reiteration of the significance of each element leads to the concluding expression of a messianic hope (*GS,* 303–9).[16]

16. Parts of this sermon would have had special resonance for those in the congregation of *converso* background.

In both of the sermons discussed, the structure is provided by a division of the theme verse, and the aggadic *ma'amar* is not employed until the final section of the sermon. Sometimes the rabbinic dictum is given a more central role. As we have seen, the sermon on *Mishpatim* (Exod. 21:1–24:18) begins with an Introduction describing three techniques used by Gentile rulers to gain permanent memorials on earth. The *ma'amar* is taken from Exodus Rabbah: "Moses devoted himself fully to three things, and they were called by his name: the people of Israel, Torah, and the establishment of justice." The body of the sermon explores these three areas of Moses' activity through which he attained immortality on earth. Rather than making a statue of himself, he devoted himself to his people; rather than erecting a great edifice, he built the foundations of Torah education; rather than naming a month after himself, he exemplified in his life the ethical standards that he wanted the people to emulate.

In this sermon, it is the theme verse, Exodus 21:1, that is held in abeyance for the final section. The verse says not "which you shall say to them," but *which you shall place before them*, alluding to Moses' personal exemplification of the laws of this pericope: he showed concern for the Hebrew slave, prevented an act of homicide, intervened to end a quarrel, showed proper honor to women, lived as a shepherd. The preacher's point is that because Moses had fulfilled all these commandments himself, he was able to "place" them before the Israelites in his own person. There follows a coda of recapitulation and new homiletical flourish, linking the three words in the *ma'amar* to a new verse, Deuteronomy 33:21, and to three fundamental principles of Jewish faith (existence of God, Torah from heaven, reward and punishment), and ending with a final reference to the theme verse and a messianic hope (*GS*, 136–41).

In some of the most interesting sermons, the structure is built neither upon the theme verse nor upon the rabbinic *ma'amar*, but rather on a division intrinsic to the thesis or subject matter. Several examples will be considered. In "House of Prayer," the sermon on *Terumah* (Exod. 25:1–27:19), the problem to be investigated is formulated in the Introduction: "Why did God command that a finite house be built for Him . . . why did He not leave people to pray to Him under the heavens, wherever they may be, rather than leading them to think that His indwelling presence was restricted to a small house?" The answer is to be found in the four terms used in the Torah for the sanctuary, each of which suggests a different function, and a different meaning of the theme verse, Exodus 25:2.

The first term, *mishkan ha-Shem* (God's tabernacle), indicates that the sanctuary was a visible reminder of God's providence and a continual refutation of those who denied such providence in the sublunar realm because of an overly exalted philosophical conception of the Deity. The phrase *va-yikhu li terumah* is taken to mean, "Let them take away from Me this loftiness [*romemut*], take away from Me the claim that I watch over the supernal realm alone." Secondly, the sanctuary is called *mishkan ha-'edut* ("tabernacle of testimony"). The male and female cherubim "testify" to the marital love between Israel and the Torah, cementing the covenant with God. Because the Torah has been given to Israel, God may indeed dwell on earth. The verse is therefore interpreted to mean, "Let them take from Me the Torah, thereby removing the reason for My loftiness, and attract Me to dwell among them with My daughter."

The third phrase for the sanctuary, *ohel mo'ed* ("tent of meeting"), points to its function as a symbol of the people's unity in their worship of God. When all direct their hearts to this one place and follow a uniform standard of worship, their devotion to the one God is deepened. In this context, the verse means, "When they are all together, they will take Me as the First Cause, exalted above all." Finally, the sanctuary is called *miqdash ha-Shem* ("God's sanctuary"), alluding to God's love of holiness and revulsion toward impurity. The impurity prevalent among human beings requires that one spot be set aside as fully sacred. Therefore the verse can be taken to mean, "In this sanctified building, called *miqdash ha-Shem,* they will take away from Me My exclusive dwelling on High (which would be necessary without it), that I may come to dwell also in the lower realm." All four interpretations of the theme verse depart from the simple meaning of the verse by using *terumah* in the sense of loftiness (*romemut*) (*GS*, 141–47).

A rather impressive example of division based on extrinsic material is the sermon on *Devarim* (Deut. 1:1–3:22), "Like the Stars of Heaven." The theme verse, Deuteronomy 1:10, contains the familiar comparison of the Jewish people with the stars, but the occasion of the sermon, the Sabbath preceding the Ninth of Av, suggests a subject relating to Jewish suffering and sorrow. Therefore, at the end of the Introduction, the preacher says that he will speak about "the factors that prevent the light of the stars from reaching our eyes. It is not that any of the stars will be extinguished, for they are eternal, but their light is blocked from our eyes." In this way the motif from the theme verse is transposed into a minor key for the occasion.

Why are the stars sometimes not seen? The answer, providing the framework of the sermon, is drawn from popular knowledge. First, the stars may be below the horizon, covered by the earth, away from their proper place in the heavens. "A similar decline and fall occurred to the children of Israel when they were removed from their land and went into exile." The first part of the sermon then deals with *galut,* exile, and its concomitant sword, famine, and pestilence. Secondly, clouds in the sky may obscure the light of the stars, while leaving the terrestrial lights unaffected. The clouds represent the sins that block the light of the Jewish people; indeed, the higher the Jews reach in their aspirations for closeness to God, the more they are affected by even the slightest sin. Thirdly, stars may be rendered invisible because the light of the sun or a sudden flash of lightning overwhelms them. These competing lights allude to the nations of the world, who "claim for themselves all the good qualities of Israel."

Finally, the light of the stars may be blocked in an eclipse. This homiletical point depends on a rudimentary knowledge of astronomy, which the preacher provides. He notes that the eclipse of the moon, where the earth prevents the sun's light from illuminating the moon, is not applicable to his subject; the stars cannot be eclipsed in this manner. But the eclipse of the sun, where the moon, an alien body, blocks the source of light itself, does apply. "Even though the moon is very small in comparison with the sun, it may cover it because of its proximity to us, just as a man who places a gold coin in front of his eye may cover a great expanse of the heavens." Here the alien body represents the Christian nations, who block the light of Israel when Jews imitate the worst of their qualities. At a climactic point near the end, the aggadic *ma'amar* "You have followed them in their corruption, you have failed to emulate their good" (B. Sanh 39b) is cited, leading to a succinct but devastating critique of contemporary Jewish society.[17] As usual, Morteira recapitulates his major points as he modulates back to the major key to conclude his sermon with messianic hope (*GS,* 251–57).

In at least one case, the structure of the sermon appears to be suggested by a passage in a Christian theological work. The sermon is on *Va'ethanan* (Deut. 3:23–7:11), and the theme verse is Deuteronomy 4:2, *You shall not add to the word that I command you, nor shall you diminish from it.* The Introduction focuses on this verse, raising two problems: why the need to state *you shall not diminish,* which could be derived *a fortiore* from *you shall not add,* and why the same injunction is repeated in Deuteronomy 13:1. The first difficulty is answered immediately; the solution to the second is postponed while the preacher turns to other matters. But listeners who assumed that the sermon would be devoted to theoretical issues of exegesis were in for a surprise.

The body of the sermon signals immediately that the preacher is ventur-

---

17. The passage is cited above, p. 54. For the use of the eclipse as illustration in medieval Christian preaching, see Owst, *Literature,* p. 190.

ing onto controversial ground: "I have found in one of the Gentiles' books" the claim that Christianity initiated four improvements over Jewish spirituality: the ideal of poverty and the repudiation of material wealth, the ideal of celibacy, the ideal of love for one's enemy, and the ideal of martyrdom, implying an active pursuit of an opportunity to sacrifice one's life for God. Morteira analyzes each of these separately, arguing in each case for the superiority of the Torah doctrine as set forth by the rabbis. With a triumphant flourish, he then turns to a fundamental critique of Christian spirituality, which he sees as inherently elitist and incapable of being observed by the entire community of believers.

At this point, the aggadic *ma'amar* is introduced: R. Joshua says, "A foolish pietist, a cunning rogue, a female separatist, and the blows of the separatists bring destruction upon the world" (B. Sot 20a), and these four categories are interpreted as applying to the four Christian ideals. Finally, the exegetical problem held in abeyance from the Introduction is resolved on the basis of all that has been said: Deuteronomy 13:1, where the commandment appears addressed not to the entire community but to an individual, was necessary to repudiate the Christian addition of spiritual ideals that would apply only to a religious elite. Thus, while the four main points of the sermon are taken from a Christian source, their treatment is fully integrated with traditional Jewish texts from the Torah and the rabbinic literature in an established homiletical tradition.[18]

The relationship to Christianity is also an underlying concern in the longest and most elaborate sermon in *Giv'at Sha'ul,* and its structure deserves a more detailed analysis.[19] Preached on the Sabbath of Repentance, its theme verse from *Ha'azinu* (Deut. 32:1–52) is Deuteronomy 32:12: *The Lord led him alone, No alien god at His side.* The aggadic *ma'amar* is from tractate Shabbat 31a: "Those who are brought in to judgment are asked, 'Have you been faithful in your transaction, have you fixed times for Torah, have you

---

18. Morteira 1645, pp. 69c–71d. I have not been able to identify the Christian work to which Morteira refers. The ideals would seem to indicate a Catholic author, possibly one of the Church Fathers, and this would fit the *converso* background of many in the preacher's congregation. On the other hand, Morteira warns of the potential influence of contemporary Christian preaching on these ideals as if he were speaking about the immediate environment in Amsterdam: "In their sermons they magnify and embellish these matters with rhetorical tropes and parables that might deceive those who are insufficiently sharp-witted. We must therefore warn you to beware of these traps . . . lest we stumble" (p. 70a).

19. Morteira 1645, pp. 85c–90d. The Sabbath of Repentance, between Rosh Hashanah and Yom Kippur, on which this sermon was delivered, was a time when preachers were expected to speak at greater length; see the introduction to *GS*, pp. 38–39 and p. 290, bottom.

engaged in procreation, have you looked hopefully toward deliverance, have you engaged in the dialectics of wisdom, have you distinguished one thing from another?'"

The thesis of the sermon is God's love for the people of Israel, especially as expressed during the difficult period of exile. Morteira discusses six ways in which this love is providentially demonstrated. The sermon's content makes it a rich source for Jewish attitudes toward Christians and Christianity, but this aspect cannot be analyzed in depth here. Our concern is with the literary craftsmanship revealed in the intertwining of theme verse, aggadic dictum, and thesis to construct a sermon that, despite its length and complexity, few in the congregation would have found a burden to hear.

The Introduction to the sermon contains an extensive parable, which the listener might at first assume to be routinely familiar, but which turns out to be specially contrived to suggest a six-part structure. A king has an only son who repays his father's love and generosity with rebellious and dissolute behavior. When various imprisonments fail to reform the obstinate boy, the king prepares an elaborate plan for an imprisonment that will work. He gives the boy a drug, which makes him so different from the other prisoners that he can no longer be influenced by them. Another drug settles his disposition and temperament, a third engenders confidence that his term of incarceration will eventually end. The king commands the guards to remind their prisoner constantly why he has been incarcerated, and he impels them to hate the boy so they will not be tempted to lighten his lot. Finally, he divides the authority for guarding the boy among many men, lest one guard with exclusive power take it upon himself to put the boy to death. Only after these provisions have been made does the imprisonment begin.

The preacher continues, "The exemplification and interpretation of this parable will be our subject today, drawn entirely from our theme verse . . . ; it is a subject appropriate for this Sabbath of Repentance." The six-fold division has been indicated in the parable; the alert listener would quickly grasp at least part of its application to the experience of Israel in exile, but how it will be derived from the theme verse, how it can be related to the aggadic dictum, and how it is relevant to the special Sabbath during the Days of Awe, remain for the preacher to reveal.

The first section discusses Jewish distinctiveness. Originally, the commandments of the Torah were the antithesis of the pagan behavior in Israel's environment. Then paganism disappeared, and the nations began to imitate the Torah.[20] Christians repudiated idolatry, used prayers from the Psalms,

---

20. Cf. above, p. 61, n. 12.

observed a day of rest and holidays similar to the Jewish ones; they even used the name Israel for themselves. Muslims were even closer to the Torah: they believed in true monotheism and repudiated all images of God, prohibited meat from the pig, practiced circumcision. Since the Torah no longer separated Jews from their neighbors, there was a danger that Gentile influence upon the Jews would become excessive.

Anticipating this problem, God provided the rabbinic laws to preserve Jewish distinctiveness. The first part of the theme verse refers to this: through the legislation of the Rabbis, "The Lord led him alone, distinct, separated from all other peoples." And since God has done this, "We too must strive to carry out His will by remaining separate and recognizable and distinct from them in all matters, so that when we are asked at judgment, 'Have you distinguished one thing from another?' we will be able to answer, 'Yes.'" The preacher explains this to mean that Jews must have a distinctive appearance that will enable everyone to recognize them as Jews. But in Holland no external sign distinguished Jews as in the other lands of the exile. Therefore, "we must establish this distinctiveness by not imitating their hairstyle, by not eating their food or drinking their wine at their funerals, by praying and carrying our tefillin as we walk, so that all who see us will recognize us."[21]

The second section of the sermon begins with an extensive analysis of an aggadic passage in tractate Sanhedrin 64a concerning the uprooting of the impulse toward idolatry. It leads to the conclusion: since God saw to the protection of His people in exile by removing the temptation to worship false gods, "we must therefore strive to uproot from within us all that is similar to idolatry and lack of faith: lies . . . slander. . . unfounded gossip . . . and profanity, so that when we are asked at judgment, 'Have you been faithful in your transactions?' we will be able to answer, 'Yes.'" This section is linked with the second part of the theme verse, *no alien god at His side* (Deut. 32:12); the aggadic dictum is shifted from the realm of business affairs to the faith that must govern the Jew's entire life.

At this point, the attentive listener would have a fairly clear idea of the sermon's structure. There are six points to be made about God's providential love for the Jews in exile; these have been adumbrated by the parable in the Introduction; the *ma'amar* contains six questions, each of which is to be ap-

---

21. Morteira's sense of structure and proportion can be seen in a remark at the end of this section: "Were it not for the need to divide the time equally for all sections of this sermon, it would be possible to expatiate upon this at length. However, we will conclude this first section . . ." (Morteira 1645, p. 87b). This is a good indication of the constraints upon oral delivery.

plied to one of the major points. But what of the theme verse? It has been divided into two parts, and these have already been used for the first two sections. How will the preacher be able to use the verse for the remainder? Morteira's strategy is revealed in the third section, which deals with despair at the length of the exile. Before sending the Jews into exile, God planted confidence and trust in their hearts as a guarantee that they would never give up hope. This is linked with the first part of the theme verse, this time interpreted in a different way: *badad yanḥennu* means "He led them *secure* in their hope," as in Deuteronomy 33:28, *va-yishkon Yisra'el betaḥ badad.*

"Therefore we are obliged to repay Him by trusting in Him and not despairing of His mercy in times of trouble, by justifying His judgments in the knowledge that all is for our good, by looking at those beneath us rather than those above us, by fulfilling our vows to Him, by never overreaching or stealing but hoping that God will fulfill our permissible needs without delay, by paying hired workers at the proper time, so that when we are asked at judgment, 'Have you looked hopefully toward deliverance?' we will be able to answer, 'Yes.'" Here the link with the aggadah is obvious; the verse has been given a new and unexpected homiletical twist.

Morteira then turns to a fourth danger: because of the length of the exile, Jews might forget the Torah and what it records of their early history. Had the exile been among pagans, this might have occurred. But God providentially provided that the long exile would be among a people that itself accepts the Jewish Bible; because their Christian neighbors remind the Jews of their origins and the reason for their exile, it is impossible for Jews to forget the Torah.[22] The Talmudic statement, "Were it not for the bustling of Rome, the sound of the sun would be heard" (B. Yoma 20a), is interpreted to mean, "Were it not for Christianity, which preserves the Bible, the Jews would revert to idolatrous worship of the sun."

The second part of the theme verse is now interpreted to mean, "There was not with him a God unknown to the other nations," as was the case with Pharaoh; the Christians know God and His Torah and bear witness to it, and this helps the Jewish people to survive. Therefore, "We must set fixed times for the study of the Torah, especially in the winter season when the nights are long, so that God's teaching will be familiar to us all . . . and we must also be energetic in keeping its commandments, especially the Sabbath, both

22. Note how Morteira turns on its head the Augustinian doctrine that the Jewish people exists to preserve and testify to the authenticity of the Hebrew Scripture (and thereby to the truth of Christianity). Here it is the Christians who play a providential role as preservers of the Bible, thereby helping to testify to the truth of Jewish belief.

by studying Torah on it and by observing it in the best way possible . . . so that when we are asked, 'Have you set times for Torah?' we will be able to answer, 'Yes.'"

According to the parable in the Introduction, part of the imprisonment planned by the king for his son was to impel the guards to hate the prince. Listeners who recalled this detail would know that the preacher was now about to turn to a potentially explosive subject: Christian hatred of the Jews. But the fifth section begins rather unexpectedly with the proposition that Jews should naturally be most desirable as marriage mates. There is a rather long discussion of those Jewish characteristics that are attractive to all: wealth, lineage, intelligence, heroism. In addition, Christians should have a special attachment to Jews as the people "from which, they say, came forth their God, the savior." If nature were to take its course, intermarriage would be rampant, and the Jewish people would soon become inseparably mingled with their neighbors.

But God providentially planted an unnatural hatred of the Jews in the hearts of the Christians, a hatred that actually contradicts the Christian faith, so that Jews would not draw too close and intermarry. *The Lord led him alone* (Deut. 32:12) means not only that God ordained rules that would distinguish Jews from their neighbors, as in the first section, but that God kept the neighbors far away through unnatural anti-Jewish feelings.[23] "Therefore, we must keep far from intermarrying with them, God forbid, for this is a terrible sin . . . so that when we are asked at judgment, 'Have you engaged in procreation?' meaning, according to Jewish law, in purity, we may be able to answer, 'Yes.'"

Finally, the power of this hatred raises the danger that the Jewish people might be totally destroyed in their exile. This is why God scattered the people in many lands; dangers might occur in one, but those elsewhere would be safe. The second part of the theme verse is now interpreted to mean that God did not give His people into the power of one alien ruler (*el nekhar*); by scattering them, He retained His own exclusive control over their destiny.

And since God scattered us among the nations for our own good, so that we would not be under the power of one king, we must strive to perpetuate peace and unity among ourselves, to end all quarreling and strife among us, to re-

---

23. Cf. Spinoza's assertion that the Jewish people has been "preserved in great measure by Gentile hatred" (Spinoza, p. 55). Like Morteira, Spinoza maintains that the Gentile hatred of Jews prevents the disappearance of the Jewish people through assimilation, although Morteira speaks about a providential act of God and Spinoza of a natural reaction to the Jews' own behavior.

move from our hearts all grudges and desires for vengeance, which are qualities of Edom . . . , and also calumny, and envy, and baseless hate, which destroyed our Temple . . . so that when we are asked in judgment, 'Have you
spiced your life with wisdom?'—for wisdom and reason must be the spice of
interpersonal relations, unlike the animals who are governed solely by in-
stincts and drives—we may answer, 'Yes.'"

Characteristically, Morteira ends his sermon with a concise recapitulation of
the six sections as related to the theme verse, and a messianic hope.

This is the longest sermon in *Giv'at Sha'ul,* and it shows Morteira at his
most complex. My description of the six-part structure has passed over the
subdivisions in several of the parts. Yet while the canvas is broad, it is not un-
wieldy or unmanageable. Several strategies are employed to bind the parts
together and to help the listener retain a conception of the sermon as a
whole. First, the central thesis—God's providential care for His people in
exile, which is insufficiently appreciated by the Jews—is stated clearly at the
outset and never allowed to disappear for long. The six sections of the sermon are all clearly related to this thesis, exemplifying it and illuminating it
from different angles. Together, they build up what the preacher must have
considered to be an irrefutable case; he could be confident that the listener
would remember the thesis even if some of its manifestations were forgotten.

Secondly, the parts of the sermon, suggested by the introductory parable,
are linked together by the theme verse and the aggadic dictum. The verse
from the scriptural lesson may well have suggested the thesis. It is divided
into two parts, each of which is given three different interpretations, so that
half of the theme verse is used in connection with each of the six sections.
The rabbinic dictum, in its original context referring to the judgment of the
individual after death, is transposed to apply to the judgment of the community as a whole. This establishes a bridge between the thesis and theme
verse, which deal with matters of doctrine and theory, and the exhortative
component of the sermon—necessary because it is being delivered on the
Sabbath of Repentance—calling upon the people to examine their behavior:
"Since God has done this, we must in turn. . . ."

Although this religious and ethical exhortation represents less than one
percent of the sermon in quantity, it comes at a climactic point near the end
of each section and is obviously calculated for a maximum effect. The six
questions of the aggadic dictum, some of them interpreted in an unexpected
way, provide a stylistic leitmotif enabling the listener to recognize the end of
each section: ". . . so that when we are asked in judgment, 'Have you . . . ?'
we may be able to answer, 'Yes.'" Several interpretations may appear some-

what forced, but the overall impression is not of a preacher showing off with rhetorical games that are needlessly convoluted or artificially cute. This sermon, like the others, reflects the work of a careful craftsman, perhaps even something of an artist.

Two more general points may be made. The first pertains to literary canon. Despite new discoveries and changing tastes, there is more or less a consensus about the most important poets in the history of Hebrew literature. By contrast, with regard to the canon of outstanding Jewish preachers, whatever consensus exists today results from the selection made by one man, Israel Bettan,[24] who probably never imagined that his studies of individual preachers would virtually define the field for more than a generation. We still lack the groundwork for consensus about canon; many more historical studies of Jewish homiletics will be needed before selections can be fully defensible. To some extent these selections will be based on objective criteria: the number of sermons produced; the nature of the preacher's community and his status and popularity within it; his reputation among contemporaries and in subsequent generations. But they will also be admittedly subjective and even impressionistic: after reading the works of many preachers, one concludes that the sermons of a particular individual possess a clarity, freshness, and power that is consistently sustained. But no matter how the list of great Jewish preachers may some day be delineated, I would argue that Morteira deserves to be included among the most impressive and significant, if not among the most influential.

The second point pertains to our conception of the rabbi in late medieval and early modern times. The frequency of a rabbi's preaching during this period varied in accordance with local custom, and probably also the temperament and predilection of the rabbi himself. We do know, however, that the communities where the rabbi preached every week were by no means rare, especially in Italy and the Sephardic Diaspora. Alongside giants such as Solomon Levi in Salonika, Leon Modena in Venice, and Saul Morteira in Amsterdam, who have left clear evidence of both the frequency and the quality of their preaching, there were dozens, if not hundreds, of lesser figures about whom we know little other than that in discourses week after week, they provided ordinary Jews with a primary access to their tradition.

In addition to their other commonly recognized functions as scholars and

---

24. See above, n. 1. I hope that my own work, especially *Jewish Preaching* and the present volume, as well as the studies of colleagues published since this statement first appeared in print—1983—have succeeded in rendering it no longer true.

authors, teachers and legal decisors and public functionaries, a significant number of rabbis regularly spent a substantial portion of their time and energy in the preparation of sermons—not only in the intellectual endeavor of providing answers to problems in ancient texts, but in the literary endeavor of creating the proper fusion of form and content, the familiar and the novel, enlightenment and entertainment, encouragement and rebuke, and then communicating it to a congregation that might feel pressured to attend but had to be motivated to listen and to heed. While Morteira's finished products were undoubtedly several cuts above most, the cumulative energy and talent devoted to the cultivation of a Jewish homiletical art in the period before the emergence of the "modern sermon" must have been prodigious.

10

Sermons and Jewish Society: The Case of Prague

One of the enduring values of the sermon for the historian is its capacity to reflect the society in which it was delivered. For this purpose, it is arguably more useful than other major genres of Hebrew literature. Books of rabbinic scholarship (commentaries or novellae on the Talmud or Codes), philosophy, or Kabbalah were generally intended for an audience that was both elite, representing a small percentage of the Jewish population, and removed, living in distant cities, perhaps even in centuries yet to come. Such books reveal the minds of their authors but do not readily yield conclusions about the society in which they lived.[1]

The preacher, by contrast, addressed an immediate audience that included many groups within Jewish society. Like their Christian counterparts, Jewish listeners had many ways of expressing displeasure. If the preacher's words failed to connect with reality, their feedback was likely to be immediate and direct.[2] In a sermon of rebuke (*tokheḥah*), criticizing the ethical and religious shortcomings of the people, the preacher had to evoke a sense of verisimilitude. If the response was "What is he talking about? I don't know anyone who behaves like that," then the sermon failed by its own criteria. If successful, the response would have to be, "Yes, that's the way it is, and we should be doing better." Whether such preaching was ever effective in changing social realities is a very different question, but extrapolation from the specific rebukes of the sermon to the shortcomings of the general society is theoretically defensible. Integrated with other sources such as responsa, communal ordinances (*taqqanot*), and ethical writings, sermons contribute to the raw material of Jewish social history, as scholars such as Jacob Katz, Haim Hillel Ben Sasson, and Azriel Shochat have demonstrated.

---

1. There are, of course, obvious exceptions. Kabbalistic texts in particular sometimes contain important expressions of social doctrine. But description of the behavior of ordinary Jews is rarely part of the purpose of such texts, as it is with the sermons.

2. For examples of such critical response, see Saperstein, *Jewish Preaching*, pp. 54–59, 416–24.

Nevertheless, this use of the sermon is fraught with problems, and the caveats are worth articulating at the outset. Needless to say, we have neither tape-recordings nor stenographic transcriptions of Jewish sermons in the period under consideration. What we do have are books containing texts of sermons, usually written by the preacher some time after delivery and revised for publication. The above argument is strongest for texts of sermons actually delivered on an identifiable occasion; it is not as strong for texts that, though based on the author's preaching, were substantially recast, or for texts written in homiletical form that were never delivered to a congregation. Each text therefore requires careful evaluation to determine its relationship to a specific preaching occasion.[3]

Are we justified in assuming that the religious, ethical, and social criticism appearing in the published sermons was actually spoken to a group of Jewish listeners? A preacher who felt uncomfortable denouncing the shortcomings of Jewish society from the pulpit might conceivably have added such material in a book, supplementing what he said with what he wished he had said. Actually, however, there is more evidence of the opposite tendency—the removal of social criticism in the process of transforming the oral sermon into a text appropriate for widespread dissemination.[4] Many authors apparently felt that such material, dealing with local problems, would not be of interest to distant readers, and could therefore be eliminated. The proportion of such criticism in the delivered sermons may therefore have been somewhat greater than what is reflected in the published works.

Assuming then that the criticisms recorded in sermon texts were actually addressed to a congregation of listeners who would not readily have tolerated attacks divorced from reality, a further question arises. Even if listeners accepted the accuracy of the charges, can we conclude that the preacher's critique tells us something distinctive about his own environment? Once again, caution is in order.[5] Whenever the Days of Awe approached or a disaster befell the Jewish community, the conventions of preaching required that communal sins be identified. Nor was this merely a formal exercise. Religious

---

3. On the relationship of written text to oral sermon, see Ibid., pp. 9–15, 21–26.

4. E.g., "Here I interrupted my discourse a bit and I began to goad the people about the performance of the commandments" (Katzenellenbogen, p. 44b, cited in Bonfil, *Rabbis,* p. 303); "I spoke at length about this matter, giving ethical instruction to the people" (Levi, *Divrei Shelomoh,* p. 13b); "In this connection, I took occasion to exhort the people with reference to the sins to which all the bodily members individually are subject, but I shall refrain from mentioning them in writing" (Figo, Part II, Sermon 46, cited in Bettan, p. 236, n. 15.)

5. Some of these methodological issues are raised in Mevorakh's review of Azriel Shochat's *'Im Ḥillufei Tequfot* (Mevorakh, "Review," p. 154) and in Katz, *Halakhah,* pp. 333–39.

leaders are rarely satisfied with the behavior of their flock. The preacher's position, if not his personality, made him painfully aware of the need for improvement. The expression of dissatisfaction from the pulpit does not necessarily prove that something was fundamentally wrong with his congregants.

It is certainly tempting to conclude that a Jewish society was in crisis and about to disintegrate when its preacher thundered about divisiveness, *lashon ha-ra'* (slander), *sin'at ḥinam* (groundless hate), extravagant, ostentatious conduct, imitation of the ways of the Gentiles, insufficient commitment to charity, insincere repentance, an unwillingness to accept constructive criticism from preachers, disrespect for rabbinic leaders, excessive obeisance to the wealthy and the powerful, the arrogance of the rich who abuse their positions by oppressing the masses and insulting the learned, idle conversation during the worship service, lack of devotion in prayer, cantors who do not understand the words they sing and want only to show off their voices, a failure to fix set times for study, and a decline in the standards of Talmud Torah.

The fact is, however, that such complaints can be found in virtually every period for which Jewish homiletical and ethical literature has been preserved. They are conventions of the genre, leitmotifs that recur generation after generation. Their appearance in sermons cannot be simplistically used as evidence of degeneration or transformation in Jewish society, for the claim of degeneration was itself a *topos*. This does not mean that all rebuke was by its nature stereotyped, conventional, and therefore worthless as evidence for social history. It does mean that the analysis of sermon literature requires painstaking effort to differentiate commonplace criticisms from specific charges that point to distinctive problems and underlying change.

In order to concretize these issues, we shall examine Prague Jewry in the second half of the eighteenth century, focusing on the sermons of Zerah Eidlitz, Ezekiel Landau, and Eliezer Fleckeles, delivered during the period 1755–1785. The importance of this community has been noted by scholars, although their conclusions appear to differ. Raphael Mahler argued that the structures of traditional life remained intact at that time, and that the criticisms made by the preachers applied to relatively minor deviations.[6] On the other hand, Jacob Katz, using similar evidence, cautiously remarked in a footnote that "The situation in Prague of 1770 may already reflect a degree of secularization."[7] Thus, the first step will be to determine precisely what was being criticized by the preachers. We can then attempt to evaluate its sig-

6. Mahler, I, 2:220.
7. Katz, *Tradition,* p. 190, n. 10.

nificance and address the question of how much was new and specific to that time and place.

Not all criticisms will be useful for our purposes. Speaking during the Ten Days of Repentance, Eidlitz lambasts the usual poor attendance at synagogue services in terms that seem quite contemporary: "Throughout the year, they do not come to the synagogue at all, and as for the few who do come, most of them delay their arrival until after the Barekhu or the Kedushah" (Eidlitz, 56c, 1766).[8] Landau states that he had often complained from the pulpit about the "many heads of households who literally have not looked at a single book in the entire year" (Landau, *Derushei,* 12d, also 25b). But such attacks, colorful and suggestive as they may be, are too sweeping and conventional to serve as the kind of evidence we seek. It is the concrete, specific charge that will make the case. Four general categories will be considered.

Leisure Activities

As Jacob Katz has noted, concern about leisure activity does not fit neatly into the context of traditional Jewish morality.[9] The classical texts divided the waking hours into times for earning a livelihood and times for the fulfillment of religious obligations, including study and prayer. Other pursuits, which fall under the rubric "leisure," are intrinsically problematic, for all such activity can be considered *bittul Torah,* a waste of time that should be devoted to study. The preachers of Prague breathed new life into the old concept of *bittul Torah* by focusing on the activities to which contemporary Jews were attracted.

A well-known responsum by Landau denounces recreational hunting, but the question was asked about a single wealthy Jew, and neither the responsum nor the sermon literature suggests that this was a common practice among the Jews of Prague.[10] Other forms of recreation had a wider appeal. Some Jews were apparently intrigued by the training of soldiers, for Fleckeles expresses his displeasure at those who made it a habit to go for walks during the month of Elul to watch the military exercises of the army and cavalry (Fleckeles, *'Olat,* 73a: 1780).

---

8. Landau confirms that attendance in the large synagogues was a problem, and emphasizes the importance of synagogue prayer. The alternative seems to have been small gatherings in private houses. See the sources cited in Baron, *Community* 3:89, n. 4, and Gelman, pp. 97–98.

9. Katz, *Tradition,* p. 136.

10. Landau, *Noda'* 2, YD 10.

Fleckeles also finds his congregants' interest in the latest news unbecoming: "They show contempt for study and worship by gathering to hear about developments concerning human beings and livestock, current events which they call 'Zeitung'" (*'Olat,* 97b: 1779). In addition, the moralists tried to discourage various parlor games, apparently without much success. Landau laments the "prodigious playing of cards and other games" (*Derushei,* 29c, also *Ahavat Tsiyon,* 5c), and Fleckeles seconds the charge: "Woe for the collapse of my people, who waste their limited times in idle pursuits. If they slept away their seventy year life span, that would be better for them and for everyone else, but to squander their precious time at cards and billiards, that is an extremely serious prohibition" (*'Olat,* 78b, also 78a: 1781).

Some of the activities condemned by the preachers have greater cultural significance. This was a period of vitality in the Prague theater, when comedies and comic operas were especially in vogue.[11] How many Jews were attracted to this form of entertainment may be impossible to determine, but there were enough to disturb rabbis such as Landau, who considered it to be evidence of acculturation and seduction by Gentile values.[12] As early as 1762, he complains, "Many [Jews] go to the theaters; they envy the Gentiles and desire their pleasures" (*Ahavat Tsiyon,* 5c). In a later sermon he lists "theaters for comedy and operas" among the improper places that Jews frequent, and condemns those Jews who "listen to the sound of violin and organ, with a joy that does not pertain to a mitzvah" (*Derushei,* 36a). It is notable that in his eulogy for the Empress Maria Theresa, Landau deems it worthy of praise that "she did not participate in games or listen to music, either vocal or instrumental; she did not attend the comedy or the operas."[13] In that respect, he implies, she would have been an appropriate model for his own people.

The taste for good music apparently influenced the ambience of the synagogue service to an extent unprecedented outside of Italy. In 1768, Eidlitz, indulging in a conventional attack on cantors who are concerned more with showing off the quality of their voices than with expressing the meaning of the prayers, goes on to provide some important data:

---

11. On the cultural life in Prague, especially opera and theater, in the second half of the eighteenth century, see Schuerer, pp. 267–95.

12. On the social significance of attendance at theater, see Katz, *Ghetto,* p. 43.

13. Landau, "Derush Hesped," p. 5b. On this eulogy, see below, chap. 18. Fleckeles, preaching in 1779, criticizes Jews who go to *moshav leitsim* (97b–98a). Sometimes this is used as a Hebrew equivalent of "comedy" (e.g. Eybeschuetz, 2:29a: "*moshav leitsim* which they call 'Comic Opera'"). In other passages it is used as a general term for social gatherings characterized by frivolous banter.

> This blemish in our worship regarding cantors and singers is universal. . . . I
> know that many will protest against this criticism, for there are more than
> thirty singers in our congregations, and they will say that I am depriving them
> of their livelihood . . . but I do not care (*'Olat*, 79d).

Fifteen years later, Fleckeles bemoans the same reversal of the proper hierarchy of values: "Among the masses of Jews, what is secondary has become
paramount: women and children come [to the synagogue] to hear the
music" (*'Olat*, 5a–b).[14]

One of the most important themes in criticism of leisure activities was the
time spent in idle socializing. The term *se'udat mere'im* recurs frequently in
this literature as an expression of opprobrium for dinner parties that had no
religious function.[15] Another intriguing social reality deeply disturbing to
the preachers was the attraction of Jews to coffee houses and taverns. Eidlitz,
in 1768, describes this as a characteristic flaw of Prague Jewry:

> Here the custom prevails of sitting in the "assemblies of the ignorant which
> remove man from the world," namely, the coffee houses and taverns (*battei
> mishta'ot kafeh ve-shekhar*). This is not done in the great communities. . . . I
> have heard some of the owners of coffee houses [complain] when I said many
> times that Jews should not sit in them; they say that I deprive them of their
> livelihood, but I do not care (*'Olat*, 79d; cf. 36c).

Apparently this referred to Jewish owners, although Jewish patronage was
not limited to Jewish establishments, as can be seen in Landau's attempt to
prohibit his people from drinking coffee in Prague coffee-houses owned by
non-Jews.[16]

Taverns were a separate problem—places for drinking and listening to
gossip (Eidlitz, 86d; Landau, *Derushei*, 36a). That they could compete with
traditional Jewish obligations is seen in a rebuke by Fleckeles:

> How many times the hour for evening worship has arrived while we sat com-
> fortably, drinking wine from the bottle. . . . If someone comes and says, "Get

---

14. The question of instrumental music in the synagogue became a matter of fierce dispute a generation later when the Reformers pointed to the Prague synagogue as precedent.
Prague rabbis, including Fleckeles and Landau's son Samuel, replied that the local custom required the musicians to put away their instruments on Friday one half hour before the
Barekhu of the evening service. *Elleh Divrei ha-Berit*, p. 17; cf. Guttmann, index, s.v. Music
(Instrumental, vocal, singing). Unlike the use of choirs, instrumental music in the synagogue
does not seem to be addressed in our sermons.

15. See Katz, *Tradition*, p. 320, n. 10, citing Landau, *Derushei*, p. 18a.

16. Landau, *Noda'* 1, YD 36.

up, you drunkards, can't you see that it's dark, that it's time for *ma'ariv*?" everyone answers, "It's still light, the sun has not set, we still have time before we have to pray" (*'Olat*, 86a, 1781).

Apparently those frequenting the taverns were not completely unmindful of their responsibilities for attending daily services. But it also shows that some of those expected to join in the worship preferred to be somewhere else.

Sexual Mores

The decline in sexual morality is a common theme in the preaching of Eidlitz and Landau, appearing in virtually all their sermons of rebuke. As in the issue of leisure time, halakhic requirements created conflicts for traditional Jewish society. Buttressed by Kabbalistic sanctions, halakhic mores presupposed a society characterized by rigid segregation of the sexes and marriage soon after the onset of puberty.[17] Prague Jewry was quite different, and the moralists agonized over the resulting tensions.

The prohibition against even looking at women was certainly not universally observed. Landau was not unaware of the realities: "Not only do [the Jewish young men] look over unmarried women; even married women living with their husbands are visually examined. Thus the thought of sin is implanted" (*Derushei*, 39b, also 33c). This led to socialization. Unmarried men and women spent leisure time together, for example going on walks—a practice criticized by the preachers, but so deeply ingrained that they despaired of uprooting it (Landau, *Derushei*, 39b, cf. 13b, 29c). Mixed dancing was particularly vexing. In 1768, Eidlitz thanked God that this was not common in Prague as in other communities (*'Olat*, 79d). But not many years later Landau denounced mixed dancing as inevitably arousing the passions and thereby leading to sin, confessing that "I have become exhausted protesting with the rabbinic court" (*Derushei*, 35d). Physical and sexual contact between unmarried men and women was almost inevitable (Landau, *Derushei*, 36a, 39b).

According to Eidlitz, at least some married women of class were in the habit of socializing with men not their husbands. "There are in our community certain well-known houses," he said, undoubtedly with a pregnant pause and a knowing glance, "which I do not want to publicize . . . where men gather with dissolute women day after day to eat and play in revelry." The continuation indicates that these may have been respectable women:

---

17. Cf. Katz, "Nisu'im," and Katz, *Tradition*, pp. 166–67.

I am astonished at their husbands: how can they allow their wives to cause others to sin? Let them not make the excuse that they protested but their wives ignored them. God has judges on earth; they should lodge a complaint before their rabbi and the rabbinic court, which would enjoin them not to mingle with other men (Eidlitz, 36c–d: 1766).

The prohibition against being alone with a woman (*yiḥud*) was all but ignored by many Jews. Landau reveals his frustration in a retrospective glance:

When I first came here, I gathered together the rabbis of the court, and we decreed that no married woman should be employed as a servant in another's home, not even an elderly woman, except for a nursemaid. Nevertheless, in our sins the practice has spread so that it seems to be permissible, although it makes it impossible to avoid *yiḥud* (*Derushei*, 4a).

Eidlitz pointed to less innocent violations of the principle: "Without doubt, there are many houses in which, behind closed doors, there are only two young men and two young women in a state of *niddah* [ritual impurity], never having ritually immersed. They transgress the biblical prohibition of *yiḥud* linked with sexual sins" (Eidlitz, 98b: 1769).

Landau felt impelled to refute two misconceptions about *yiḥud*. The first was a popular misunderstanding: most Jews believed that *yiḥud* was forbidden only if it led to sin. As a halakhic and moral authority, he reminded his listeners that even if no sinful act or thought occurred, *yiḥud* itself was forbidden—by the Torah if with a married woman, and by the Rabbis if the woman was unmarried. The second error was on a more sophisticated and perhaps more subversive level: it was thought that *yiḥud* could not be forbidden to a person who had already committed a sexual misdeed, as the *yiḥud* was necessary to show that repentance was complete. After all, Maimonides' example of "complete repentance" was the case of the man who was again alone with the woman with whom he had sinned, but this time refrained from sinning. Appalled by the radical implications of this position purportedly based on classical texts, Landau rebutted it with vehemence (*Derushei*, 4a).[18]

Unable to approve of any kind of physical contact before marriage, the moralists found relations between a couple engaged to be married particularly difficult to regulate in accordance with their standards. Once, while discussing Rashi's comment (on Song of Songs 1:2) that God kissed Moses "as a groom does a bride," Eidlitz digresses: "Now I have to interrupt in the mid-

---

18. On the background of this idea, see Piekarz, *Bi-Ymei Tsemiḥat*, chap. 4; the Landau passage is cited on pp. 188–89.

dle, lest someone listening to me should erroneously conclude from the phrase 'as a groom does a bride' that this is permitted, God forbid!" Betrothed couples might erroneously infer that it was permissible to kiss before the wedding; the preacher therefore explains that the phrase pertains only to after the wedding ceremony, when the bride's ritual immersion had been completed (Eidlitz, 39a: 1766).

For the most part, the moralists denounced unsanctioned socializing between the sexes from the male perspective. Eidlitz seems almost obsessed with the problem of "improper emission of semen," devoting a large section of a long sermon to the various aspects of this theme (Sermon 1: 1766) and referring back to that sermon frequently in subsequent ones (e.g., 53a). Landau endorses the old Kabbalistic doctrine that each drop of improperly emitted semen produced a demon, all of which gather around the coffin of their "father" just before his burial (*Derushei,* 35d).[19]

But there are obvious implications for women as well. Preaching in the summer of 1769, Eidlitz states that during the previous year, "about ten" sons of unmarried women have been circumcised—an unprecedented number—while the number of girls born from such women is not even known (96c).[20] Eight years earlier, Landau had said from the pulpit that "a number of unmarried women in a state of *niddah* have given birth in these times" (*Ahavat Tsiyon,* p. 4c). Fourteen years later, in 1783, Fleckeles laments, "How many single girls have gotten pregnant this year!" (*'Olat,* 34a). This was not a mere rhetorical commonplace, for Landau, asked a halakhic question about the status of the child of an unwed mother whose father is unknown, remarks, "I must elaborate on this law [of the *shetuqi*] a bit, for in these regions the phenomenon is not uncommon."[21] Nor was it merely the lesser problem of children born to unmarried women; Eidlitz indicates that *mamzerut* (referring to the status of children born from adulterous relationships) was rampant in Prague, though only God knew the identity of all the *mamzerim* (97c–d).

There was also the scandal of Jewish women publicly known to be of loose morals. Eidlitz minces no words:

> All prostitutes are reported to the Gentile authorities, and it may well be that this year [1769] there were more Jewish girls than Gentiles. Such a thing never

19. On the background of this idea, see Scholem, *Kabbalah,* pp. 154–55.
20. The statement is used by Katz, *Ghetto,* pp. 146–47.
21. Landau, *Noda'* 1, EH 7; cf. Eidlitz, p. 47b. The birth of children out of wedlock was more than a moral and halakhic problem for the Jewish community, as the Austrian authorities sometimes seized such children for military service. See Wind, p. 73.

happened before! . . . How can we bear our shame over what happened in our congregation this year? Look how many prostitutes are known—not to mention the ones not known—in a community with less than two thousand homeowners (98a–b).

There was clearly a sense that something unprecedented and drastically wrong had occurred.

Economic Values

The sermons delivered in Prague provide a mirror for the economic life of the Jews—one that complements other more utilized sources. Community values and attitudes toward commercial activity can be discovered indirectly in the parables used by preachers to dramatize and concretize their messages. Parables drawn from the business world appear quite frequently alongside the more traditional parables of royal life. Particularly prominent is the motif of the fair, which plays a role different from what might be expected. Whereas Christian and some Jewish moralistic literature frequently uses the fair as the paradigm for the vanities of the world, which attract and seduce human beings away from their higher destiny,[22] the preachers of Prague use it quite differently.

The basic thrust is stated succinctly by Landau in a sermon for the Ten Days of Repentance: one who misses the opportunity for repentance during this season of the year is "like one who travels to Leipzig at the time of the fair, but every day of the fair he goes from tavern to tavern, until the fair ends, all his expenses have gone for naught, and he remains for an entire year without income" (*Derushei,* 29a). Eidlitz and Fleckeles turn this analogy into complex and elaborate parables involving fairs in Frankfurt am Main, Leipzig, and Constantinople, all of which present the fair as an emblem of the Days of Awe.[23] These parables cast the successful merchant as the ideal for the religious life. Drawing upon the assumption that one should prepare in advance and work hard to earn all that is possible during the time of the fair, the preacher attempts to inspire the people to make the most of the Ten

22. The best known example is "Vanity Fair" in Bunyan's *Pilgrim's Progress.* For a similar use of the fair in Hebrew literature, see Luntshitz, '*Olelot* 1, 7, 19; cf. Ben-Sasson, *Hagut,* p. 56. A modern example is in S. Y. Agnon, *Bi-Levav ha-Yamim,* chap. 4 (*In the Heart of the Seas* [New York, 1947], pp. 28–30).

23. Eidlitz, pp. 69c–d, 76a; Fleckeles, *Sheni,* beginning of sermon 5, pp. 74b–76b. Fleckeles justifies the use of this analogy on p. 76a. On the general question of attitudes toward wealth, see Katz, *Tradition,* pp. 58–61.

Days of Repentance and to take advantage of the opportunity for spiritual enrichment.

The sermons also give evidence of economic hardship and reversals. The crushing burden of royal taxes imposed upon the Jews by the government of Maria Theresa was frequently noted by the preachers. Landau suggests that these taxes may have been greater than those borne by any other Jewish community in the Diaspora (*Derushei*, 16a, cf. 50d). The result was inequity in the internal assumption of the tax burden and subterfuge by those seeking to diminish their own share (*Derushei*, 29c, 35b).

Eidlitz painted a similar picture: the taxes "devastate our wealth . . . many respectable men have become paupers" (38d: 1766, cf. 22d: 1765). Such people were faced with a terrible dilemma: if they were to divulge the true extent of their reversals, no one would lend them money. But if they concealed their desperate situations, they would be forced to pay an impossible tax assessment (38d). Many had to remove their children from school at an early age in order to send them to work (44a: 1766). Others had to leave for distant realms in search of income, and in some cases their wives became *agunot*, abandoned but unable to remarry because their husbands were still alive (47a–b: 1766). A few Jews still enjoyed abundant wealth (38c), but the preacher confessed that he knew "that there are many in our city who, because of economic oppression and meagre resources, look forward to their death" (88d: 1768).

The grievances of the poor are articulated by Landau with notable specificity in a penitential sermon. Starting with a discussion of Maimonides' "hindrances to repentance," including the despoiling of the poor, orphans, or widows (*Code, Teshuvah* 4:3), Landau builds upon the explication of this phrase by Abraham ben David of Posquières, stating,

> This offense . . . is very common in our communities of Bohemia. People lend to the poor demanding their house as collateral, and it goes on the books. Then the expenses of the poor increase to the point where they are unable to redeem the house, which is then brought to *Substatsia* and assessed for less than half its value. Now it is obvious that if the lender made the loan originally with this outcome in mind in order to take the possession of the property, he is in the category of an "evil man of guile" (*rasha' 'arum*) . . . . But even if the original loan was an honest one, if the lendor later presses the debtor and seizes the house through *Substatsia*, knowing that it is worth more, this is an act that "hinders repentance."
>
> The same is true for moveable property. I do not object to the practice of hurrying to the Gentile authorities right away, for the laws of the state give the creditor this right, and the first to make his claim should prevail. What hap-

pens, however, is that the moveable property is brought to a public auction. Expenses mount, and the debtor's property is lost, sold at half its value. This occurs because of creditors who would otherwise get nothing; they demand this expensive procedure so that prior creditors will lose as well. All this is wrong. The proper way is to have all claims recorded by the authorities, so that all will know the order of the claims. Then all should go before the [Jewish] judges, who will divide the assets according to the laws of the state, requiring no unnecessary expenses. The assets will then be sold according to their value (*Derushei,* 32c–d: 1760).

The inclusion of such material in a sermon indicates that bankruptcy proceedings in which Jews exploited the reversals of other Jews were not unknown in contemporary Prague.[24]

The accusation of dishonesty in business affairs looms large in the sermons of the Prague preachers. "Just weights and measures" was a simple and straightforward ideal that not all Jewish merchants exemplified. Fleckeles launches an attack that must have lasted close to ten minutes, beginning with the prohibition of keeping false measures in the home or the store even if they are not used to cheat, and ending with the suggestion that those who want to repent of this sin but do not know exactly whom they have cheated should make an appropriate contribution to public charities (*'Olat,* 40b–42b: 1783). Landau's published sermon is more succinct, referring to his more extensive rebuke in a Shabbat Shuvah sermon of the previous year and reminding his listeners that "at the last day of public fasting, I ordained that the shopkeepers must have standard measures. This was not done for the liquid measures of the vintners; they too must convene to establish standard measures for all" (*Derushei,* 13b; cf. 33c).

Far more complicated is the problem of interest, one of the most vexing topics in halakhic literature. Generations of legal authorities have struggled to draw the fine line between the rigor of the Torah prohibition and the exigencies of economic life.[25] Lending money at interest was an issue on which legal traditions, ethical impulses, intergroup relations, and economic pres-

---

24. From the context I assume that *Substatsia* (probably from the German *Substanz* meaning "real assets" or "actual capital") refers to a procedure of confiscation of real property in bankruptcy cases. Landau also discusses the plight of Jews who have been impoverished as a result of ill-advised loans given by greedy money-lenders (Landau, *Derushei,* p. 52b). A different sermon contains an interesting criticism of unscrupulous Jewish arendars who negotiate to take over the arendas of other Jews before they can recover their expenses. This, however, does not apply to the realm of "our duke," but rather to "other jurisdictions" (p. 13b). The criticism uses the category of *hasagut gevul* (encroachment on the rights of another), but is based primarily on an appeal to the sense of fairness.

25. See Katz, *Tradition,* p. 83–87.

sures all converged. Fleckeles refers to the problem in passing (*'Olat*, 52a–b), but several passages from the sermons of Landau focus concretely on this issue.[26]

In a sermon for the Sabbath of Repentance (1768) largely devoted to religious and ethical criticism, Landau enters the realm of finance. "I will mention another way in which some transgress the prohibition against taking interest. This is the partnership in which a wealthy man provides the capital and a poor man provides the labor. Even if they divide the profit and the losses equally, this is forbidden, unless the one who does the work is paid a fee." This, of course, is an elementary Talmudic principle that every student would have known; it is striking that Landau felt compelled to explain it from the pulpit.

> Yet here in this city I have seen documents in which it is explicitly stated that the one who furnishes the capital cannot lose, and all responsibility for the loss is borne by the working partner, but if there is a profit they will divide it. This is fundamentally forbidden, although the transgression occurs only if there is a profit (*Derushei*, 16b).

The explication of the basic halakhic principles governing partnerships and interest continues with the citation of several sources, leading to a succinct summary: "If the working partner is responsible for all losses, the entire amount is in the category of a loan, and any profit given to the other partner can only be considered interest." The preacher then returns to the realities of practice:

> This is especially true as I have seen several documents of "partnership" in which the working partner makes all of his property collateral for the entire amount invested, or he gives at the outset a handshake for the entire amount. It is clear that this is interest.

It is also clear that contemporary business practice did not always conform even to the unambiguous guidelines of the halakhah.

Landau concluded with a more complex arrangement:

> Similarly, the prohibition against interest is transgressed by those who have "Correspondance" with Jews in other places, and one agrees to pay for the other's expenses here, and the other for the first one's expenses there, until they

---

26. In addition to the passages below that deal with loans between Jews, Landau affirmed in a sermon from 1775 that it was forbidden for contemporary Jews to take interest from their Christian neighbors, "above the standard fixed by the State" (*yoter mi-tiqqun ha-medinah*) (*Ahavat Tsiyon* in Landau, *Derushei*, part 2, p. 12a).

eventually make an accounting of expenses against earnings day by day. There is no permission for such an arrangement; they transgress several prohibitions abhorrently (*Derushei,* 16d; cf. 50d).

Here we see the preacher aware of new financial arrangements such as Letters of Credit or Exchange, which he may not have fully understood, but which he knew could not be reconciled with traditional Jewish law.

Ritual Law: Clothing, Food, Sabbath

Some of the rebukes related to problems with the ritual commandments. Landau accuses his congregation of wearing *sha'atnez,* a prohibited mixture of wool and linen. They buy new clothes in honor of Rosh Hashanah, he complains, but their forbidden clothing actually enhances the power of Satan (*Derushei,* 35c). The problem arose from the purchase of clothing made by non-Jewish tailors (33d), particularly those fashionable women's clothes that came from Vienna (18a).[27] Fleckeles waxes eloquent in his denunciation: "Look how much attention you pay to your clothing—their quality, whether they are in the current mode, not too long or too short, not too full or too tight. Yet to one simple commandment, which entails a serious prohibition, the commandment of *tsitsit,* no one pays much heed." According to the preacher, the masses of Jews bought inexpensive clothing from itinerant peddlars without bothering to determine the seller's reliability. Such clothing may well have been woven by Gentiles, "for in every city, the Gentiles become more and more expert in weaving, producing clothes that are both more attractive and cheaper than those made by Jews" (*'Olat,* 60a: 1780). Furthermore, he says, the wealthy looked with contempt upon the work of Jewish tailors and gave their clothing to Gentile artisans to repair, with the result that many wore *sha'atnez* (*'Olat,* 61a: 1780).

There were also problems relating to food. Fleckeles describes ritual slaughterers in the villages who made errors while intoxicated and caused Jews to eat non-kosher meat (*'Olat,* 86b: 1781). Landau mentions a previous day's sermon in which he criticizes the practice of eating pretzels without washing the hands (*Derushei,* 33d). He notes that various confections were routinely purchased from non-Jews, some of them apparently made in pots with worms in them (36a). As for the coffee houses, "I myself have seen more than once a glob of milk in the spout of the pot, and Jews drink from this while eating meat" (51b). He questions the kashrut of products from cows milked by Gentiles without supervision by Jews (13d).

---

27. Cf. Baron, *Community,* 3:199, n. 9.

Sabbath violations are frequently enumerated. Fleckeles detects a lack of respect for the Sabbath in the practice of Jews who used their finest wines for dinner parties and the most ordinary wines for Kiddush, to the point where it became a common insult to say, "That's Kiddush wine" (*'Olat*, 85a–b: 1781). Landau addresses more serious issues, criticizing the young men and women who went for walks together outside the Sabbath limits, "carrying burdens on the Sabbath in their pockets, such as knives and keys and other small items" (*Derushei*, 13d; also 16a, 29c). He also laments the men's habit of spending too much time in the public baths on Friday afternoon, the result being that "the women, who go to the baths afterward, are unable to return home before sunset, and they light the Sabbath light [too late], thereby profaning the Sabbath" (13d).

Most of the problems relating to the Sabbath concern the use of Gentiles in various capacities. Here the homiletical material complements the legal texts analyzed by Jacob Katz, with many issues discussed in the responsa appearing in the sermons. Fleckeles, preaching as a guest in the Moravian city of Prostejov (Prossnitz) during the summer of 1780, denounces the local practice of having Gentiles come to extinguish the lights in the synagogue.[28] Summarizing the halakhic issues in the dispute among the authorities, he turns to the danger of fire. In Prague, he points out, "There are nine large, magnificent synagogues, and many small ones as well. The Gentiles do not extinguish the lamps there, and we have never heard of a fire caused by one of the synagogue lamps." By contrast, in Kojetein there had been many fires until he arrived as rabbi and ended the practice of using Gentiles; since then no fire had broken out (*'Olat*, 68b–69a). His conclusion is that fires result not from candles left burning but from the violation of the Sabbath; nevertheless, he concedes that it is permissible to hire a watchman to sit until the candles burn out. Other Sabbath violators are "some men in this country, indeed in this district, who lease their horses to a Gentile on the Sabbath. This is absolutely forbidden" (*'Olat* 21b–22a: 1783).[29]

The use of Gentiles in private homes also led to transgressions. Fleckeles attacks the custom of having non-Jews light candles on the Sabbath for social gatherings in the homes.

> They have Gentiles warm the oven in order to heat up their coffee, even though it is not cold out at all, claiming that they will catch cold if they drink their coffee cold. Many people go to the houses of Gentiles to have them

---

28. On the background of this custom, see Katz, "*Shabbes Goy,*" p. 84.
29. Cf. Katz, "*Shabbes Goy,*" p. 74.

make coffee, chocolate, and punch. And there are many other infractions as
well. Such people have no reverence for the Sabbath (*'Olat*, 30b: 1783).

Landau also criticizes a new practice of asking a Gentile to open up a fish on
the Sabbath in order to prepare it, apparently to prevent the fish from spoil-
ing (*Derushei*, 35d).

Conclusions

How do all these accusations appear in historical perspective? What do they
tell us about Jewish society in Prague between 1755 and 1785? To be sure,
the sermons provide evidence that significant numbers of Jews were doing
things not in accordance with the ideals of Jewish legal and ethical literature. They spent their leisure time in activities not recognized as legitimate
by the halakhah. They socialized and courted in ways that moralists
frowned upon. They engaged in business arrangements unsanctioned by
Jewish law. Their observance in the ritual realm left the strictest authorities
dissatisfied. It seems clear that they sought and found various kinds of social and cultural gratification beyond the more restrictive boundaries of traditional Jewish society. Jacob Katz's phrase, "a degree of secularization" is
not inappropriate.

But there are additional questions. Was such behavior unprecedented?
Did it represent something fundamentally new? Something characteristic of
this period? An adumbration of greater change to come? Or was it typical of
a certain mode of traditional Jewish society, with parallels in other communities and in earlier periods? The answers require a brief glance backward—
a review that, though obviously selective and incomplete, will provide some
chronological perspective for our survey. We will quickly touch upon the
four major categories of complaint.

The involvement of Jews in leisure and recreational activities unsanctioned by the halakhah was certainly no innovation of the second half of the
eighteenth century.[30] Fleckeles' 1779 rebuke of those who followed current
events in the "Zeitung" is paralleled in an anonymous addition to the ethical tract *Yesod Yosef*, written at least forty years earlier: "There are those who
read the *Zeitung*, and many gather to hear the news from the reader. This is
certainly forbidden." At the end of the previous century, the renowned
preacher Elijah ha-Kohen of Izmir attacked those who wasted their time

---

30. See the sources (*taqqanot* and ethical literature) cited by Katz, *Tradition*, pp. 320–21,
n. 11.

playing chess, even when justified with the claim that it sharpened their intellect. Almost a century before that, Luntshitz chastised Jews who played games with cards or dice on Yom Kippur in order to divert their attention from the pangs of hunger. Nor was the appeal of comic opera unprecedented, as can be seen in a 1745 sermon by Jonathan Eybeschuetz. And socializing at lavish dinner parties was lambasted in early seventeenth-century Amsterdam by Morteira.[31]

Similarly, the condemnation of changing sexual mores is not uncommon in earlier preachers. Eybeschuetz seems to have been as preoccupied with the problem of premarital sexual dalliance as was his disciple Eidlitz. He regularly denounced mixed dancing and the prevalence of unmarried youths embracing and kissing, leading to erection and ejaculation. He contrasted a previous era, when girls were married before they reached puberty, with the current practice common among betrothed couples, of engaging in sexual foreplay, even though the fiancée was in a state of *niddah*. A generation earlier, Elijah of Izmir was more explicit: the fiancé, overwhelmed by his passion, "finds ways to sleep with his betrothed before the marriage ceremony. This causes children conceived by women in a state of *niddah* to be born, not to mention the improper emission of semen."[32]

Business transactions that violate halakhic guidelines are also attested in previous generations. Eybeschuetz warned that businessmen needed to obtain expert rabbinic advice about loans made with a *shetar 'isqa,* for the spiritual and financial consequences of carelessness were great: "There have been many powerful and wealthy Jews in our time whose sons are now actually impoverished, all because they were not careful in the business affairs, using bills of exchange entailing interest." More than a hundred years before him, we recall that Azariah Figo denounced the circumstances that compelled the

31. Joseph ben Solomon, p. 19b; the edition containing this passage was published in 1739. Most of the original work (Frankfurt an der Oder, 1677) deals with the sin of "improper emission of semen"; see Katz, *Tradition,* p. 314, n. 10. Elijah ha-Kohen, *Shevet,* beginning of chap. 42, p. 340. Luntshitz, *'Olelot,* 2, 34, 239; for other sources on card playing, see Shochat, *Ḥillufei,* pp. 40–41. Eybeschuetz, 2:29a; cf. Shochat, *Ḥillufei,* p. 39. Jews of Mantua were deeply involved in the theater, and there does not seem to have been any protest by local rabbis; see Simonsohn, pp. 656–69, esp. p. 659 n. 285. Morteira (1912), sermon on *Shemot,* p. 57a–b, translated in *Jewish Preaching,* pp. 282–84; the emphasis here is on the wasteful expenditure of money on banquets to impress others.

32. Eybeschuetz, 1:15d, 22d, 53d, 72c; 2:2a, 22d–23a. Elijah ha-Kohen, *Eliyahu,* p. 78d. On the prevalent practice of illicitly staring at women, which the moralists were certain led to further sin, cf. Joseph ben Solomon, p. 3 and Figo, sermon 64, p. 93d, (cited in Bettan, p. 237), and sermon 13, p. 47b. A large collection of source material pertaining to the charge of a breakdown in sexual mores can be found in Shochat, *Ḥillufei,* pp. 162–72.

poor to seek loans from the rich, who "devour their flesh with several forms of clear-cut, open interest." In his judgment, the greatest tragedy is that the sense of sinfulness has been lost.

> If a group of Jews were to be seen going to a Gentile butcher, and were then seen publicly eating pig or other forbidden meat, they would be stoned by all. . . . Yet here we see those who lend money on interest, which involves six transgressions for the lender, as well as others for the borrower, the guarantor, the witnesses and the scribe, and all are silent.

Figo then proceeded to criticize hypocritical attempts to cover up the transgression through ruses such as living in an apartment without rent. As for the *cambios* or exchange transactions, some, he says, may be permissible, but many others are totally forbidden, so that even well-intentioned merchants may unwittingly err. "My quarrel with them is this: why don't they consult with experts in these matters?"[33] Like the corresponding passages in Landau's sermons, this rebuke reveals the tension between the practices of a community and the values of its religious leadership, and the frustrations of leaders in the face of economic forces they are unable to control.

Charges of laxity in the ritual realm are somewhat more difficult to come by. Like Landau but a decade or so earlier, Hirschel Levin accuses the Jews of his community, London, of "carrying burdens [on the Sabbath] even outside the City, where it is totally impermissible," and of "profaning the Sabbath by having a Gentile woman light a fire to heat water for tea or coffee."[34] But on the whole, it seems to be something of a commonplace among Jewish preachers, exemplified in the Figo passage cited above, that Jews were quite strict about their ritual observance life and more lax about the mitzvot governing interpersonal behavior.

Finally, we should glance at the earliest extant sermon of rebuke, delivered in Toledo by Todros ha-Levi Abulafia in 1281.[35] The preacher is especially

---

33. Eybeschuetz, 2:9a. Figo, sermon 10, p. 33d; cf. Bettan, p. 239. For a halakhic discussion of the *cambios* or bills of exchange, see Yehiel da Pisa, *Ḥayyei 'Olam*, in Rosenthal, chap. 15, English: pp. 122–29; Hebrew: pp. 64–70.

34. Hirschel Levin, "Derashot," translated in *Jewish Preaching*, pp. 350–58. For a comprehensive listing of the religious criticisms in Levin's London sermons, see Duschinsky, pp. 10–19. Azariah Figo's complaint about religious laxity concerns a prominent Jew who habitually ate grapes without saying a blessing (Figo, sermon 64, p. 92d, cited in Bettan, p. 238).

35. The sermon was published in *Zikhron Yehudah*, the collection of responsa by Judah ben Asher (Berlin, 1846), as section 91, pp. 43a–45b. Cf. Baer, *History*, 1:257–61. The quotation at the bottom of p. 259, not identified there, is from Todros ha-Levi, *Gan ha-Meshalim* 2,2:85; the identification of the author, made by Scholem, is based on a verbatim incorporation into the sermon of a passage from *Otsar ha-Kavod* (Todros ha-Levi, *Otsar ha-Kavod*, pp. 29b–30a).

concerned with the problem of Gentile servant women. Socially, they represent an ostentatious and offensive expression of wealth, wearing expensive embroidered garments. Religiously, they bring about the violation of the Sabbath when they perform forbidden tasks at the command of their masters, who also used them for lending money at interest in an attempt to evade the prohibitions of usury. Morally, they foment sexual dissoluteness: "In our sinfulness, a number of children have been born to servant women by Jewish fathers." Notwithstanding all the differences between late thirteenth-century Toledo and late eighteenth-century Prague, there are significant similarities in the nature of the offenses charged. In Toledo, however, this sermon apparently was part of a successful movement of reform (or of reaction, depending on one's perspective) in which Jewish leaders took specific measures to redress the problems identified by the preacher. No such action succeeded in Prague.

This is not to say that the specific complaints found in our sermons can be reproduced everywhere. There were indeed Jewish communities where examples of deviance from the halakhic and moralistic ideal are difficult to document, and were probably more unusual. The point is that other communities present a picture similar to Landau's Prague; one thinks of Metz in the first half of the eighteenth century, Amsterdam in the seventeenth, Mantua in the sixteenth, Toledo in the thirteenth—all communities dynamically adapting to their environment while still remaining within the parameters of traditional rabbinic leadership. For such communities, the phrase "a degree of secularization" might be equally appropriate.

This brings us to the nature of the challenge represented by this behavior attacked from the pulpit. The sermons indicate that the preachers themselves felt they were witnessing a crisis in the Jewish life of their community. They claim that norms were being violated as never before, and they were sure they could prove it with specific examples. More than this, these sermons, and especially those of Ezekiel Landau, the most powerful figure of the three, reveal an aura of discouragement and weariness. "My words have not been successful, nor borne fruit, for you have not accepted my ethical instruction. Worse than this: the more I continue to chastise, the more the dissoluteness grows" (*Derushei*, 8a). "All year long, public proclamations are made prohibiting games and social walks, but nobody listens" (39b). Knowing that it is their responsibility to point out the failings of their people, the preachers claim to be all but powerless to change anything. They feel that the tide is moving against them, that the forces of traditional life are being overwhelmed.

Yet on the whole, the accusations in these sermons do not seem to be of major consequence or represent a fundamental danger to the heart of the halakhic system. The Jews of Prague are accused not of working on the Sabbath, but of going for walks, carrying keys in their pockets, and asking Gentiles to perform various non-Sabbath activities that they themselves might have done but would not. They are accused not of marrying without a Jewish divorce, but of familiarity and occasional intimacy with unmarried Jewish women. They are accused not of apostasy,[36] or of establishing rival institutions, but of going to the theater and the opera and reading the newspaper. The evidence in these sermons shows the structure still intact, the underlying assumptions yet unchallenged. The critique by the preachers is in many ways analogous to the critique of modern Orthodoxy by the Ultra-Orthodox. A generation later, the complaints of Orthodox spokesmen would be fundamentally different.[37]

---

36. Landau does refer to apostates in his sermons (pp. 37b, 39a, 52b), but there is no indication that this is a common phenomenon, or that Christianity is attracting members of the community. On Landau's attitude toward apostates, see Katz, *Halakhah,* p. 268.

37. See, for example, Katz, *Ghetto,* pp. 152–54, 160.

11

War and Patriotism in Sermons to Central European Jews: 1756-1815

It was a German-Jewish scholar, Leopold Zunz, who wrote the first systematic study of the history of Jewish preaching, published in 1832,[1] but little of his material from before the nineteenth century derived from Germany. The great tradition of Jewish preaching in the Middle Ages and early modern period was not Ashkenazic, but fundamentally Sephardic, and secondarily Italian. It was in the synagogues of the Iberian Peninsula, and later of the Sephardic Diaspora in Italy, Turkey, the land of Israel, and the Netherlands, where the practice was established that a respected rabbi would deliver a sermon each Sabbath. It was the Sephardim who cultivated the sermon into an art form with a characteristic structure and a set of homiletical and rhetorical conventions.[2] Finally, it was primarily Jews from the Mediterranean basin and not from northern Europe who went to the trouble of writing the texts that enable us to know what they preached.

A late Medieval German rabbi, Jacob ben Moses Halevi Moelln of Mainz, noted that unlike Jews in Talmudic times, his contemporaries were "not accustomed to preaching."[3] Ashkenazic Jews established the custom that the rabbi would preach only twice a year—on the Sabbaths preceding Pesach and Yom Kippur—in addition perhaps to much more modest homiletical exercises on life-cycle events such as circumcisions,[4] weddings or funerals. And in many cases those Sabbath sermons dealt not with the great theme of liberation and repentance, but rather with explication of the technical laws

Originally appeared in *Year Book of the Leo Baeck Institute* 38(1993): 3–14. Reprinted with permission from the Leo Baeck Institute.

1. Zunz; the Hebrew translation is supplemented with important additions by Hanokh Albeck.

2. Saperstein, *Jewish Preaching,* pp. 63–77.

3. Jacob ben Moses Halevi Moelln, *Hilkhot Ḥol ha-Mo'ed,* in MaHaRIL, p. 25b; cf. *Jewish Preaching,* p. 27.

4. Elbaum, "Shalosh Derashot," on sermons at circumcisions in the thirteenth century.

relating to the observance of these holidays or the even more technical Talmudic disputes that bear upon them.

Nevertheless, it would be incorrect to dismiss Ashkenazic Jewry as barren of any significant homiletical creativity. It may be true that, unlike many of their Sephardic colleagues, most Ashkenazic rabbis did not view preaching as a major responsibility. But, particularly in Poland, there were some who did. Many communities there and in Central Europe appointed *maggidim*—individuals responsible for delivering a sermon each Sabbath—and by the late eighteenth century, the title "Maggid" could be almost as prestigious as "Rabbi." In addition, itinerant preachers having no contract with a particular community would travel from town to town—and sometimes to the big cities—in hopes of being allowed to preach on a fee for service basis.

These men, some of whom were extremely talented, developed an Ashkenazic preaching tradition of considerable quality. Two elements in particular seem to have been cultivated with unique success in their popular preaching style. The first was the illustrative parable, or *mashal.* Of course, the parable goes back to the Bible and the rabbinic aggadah; it was used by medieval Jewish philosophers and Sephardic preachers throughout the centuries. In the sermons of preachers like the Maggid of Dubno (Jacob Kranz), however, the parable was refined and became a supple, flexible rhetorical tool that would both entertain the listeners and drive home a serious lesson in an unforgettable manner.[5]

The second characteristic was humor—for some reason, rare in Sephardic preaching but common in Ashkenazic. Although many sources confirm the listeners' delight in the levity they heard from the pulpit,[6] some contemporaries were incensed, considering the style indecorous. "It is their foolish way," wrote a seventeenth-century Polish critic about some of his colleagues, "to mix humorous content into their rebukes so that the entire audience bursts out laughing. There is hardly any difference between them and the comedians at wedding feasts."[7] Nevertheless the style continued, and the mode of witty, semi-facetious interpretations of biblical verses and well-known rabbinic statements acquired a technical name—the interpretation *be-derekh halatsah*—and could be found in the preaching of Central and of Eastern Europe, in the preaching of Hasidim and their opponents. Unfortunately, there are indications that the humorous comments were often removed when a preacher prepared his material for publication, but this suggests that

---

5. On the controversy over the use of the *mashal* in preaching, see *Jewish Preaching,* pp. 100–103, 427.

6. Ben-Sasson, *Hagut,* p. 45; Elbaum, *Petiḥut,* p. 244.

7. The remark is quoted in Dinur, *Mifneh,* p. 138.

the use of humor in the average oral sermon was more prevalent than might be apparent from the written texts.[8]

Most such generalizations are based on the popular preaching of the Yiddish-speaking *maggidim* in Poland. (When such individuals ventured into German synagogues, they were sometimes treated with a certain contempt because of what was regarded as their all but unintelligible "jargon.")[9] Does this mean that the established rabbis of the German-speaking communities in eighteenth-century Central Europe had neither interest nor talent in homiletical endeavors? Not at all. During this period, Prague became one of the most important centers of Jewish preaching in Europe. And while German-speaking rabbis did not preach weekly, some of them were widely known for their homiletical talent, originality and power. Moreover, their sermons presented new themes, bearing on some of the most significant transformations of modern Jewish life.

The background for this development was the Seven Years' War. In a dazzling realignment of European powers, Britain and Prussia were pitted against France, Austria, and Russia, and patriotic fervor welled up in all of these countries. Did the Jews share in these sentiments? This was, it should be noted, a generation before the beginning of the Emancipation. Juridically, Jews were not yet full and equal citizens of Britain or France; in the popular consciousness they were a foreign nation, living as guests in the host country, often speaking a different language from the vernacular of the majority, restricted by special legislation, precluded from living in many cities. Their historic memory of expulsion remained powerful. They did not serve in the armed forces of any of the combatants.

In previous centuries, Jews had often lived on opposite sides of the battle lines between nations. As long as the actual fighting was far away, they did not seem to have felt much personal psychological stake in its outcome. Would the Jews of the Austrian Empire now identify with the armies of the Empress Maria Theresa, who had prohibited them from living in Vienna and had expelled them from Prague only thirteen years before the outbreak of the war? Would the Jews of Prussia identify with the armies of Friedrich der Grosse, who in the legislation of 1750 had prohibited most of them from living in Berlin, limited their economic activities, and imposed harsh tax burdens upon them?[10] In other words, would they share the attitudes of their Christian neighbors towards the "enemy?"

A partial answer to these questions may be found in a new kind of occa-

---

8. See the examples cited in *Jewish Preaching*, p. 23.
9. Heinemann, *Maggid*, p. 242, citing Abraham Flahm, *Shemen ha-Ma'or*.
10. Cf. the discussion of the Jews in Prussia in Meyer, pp. 23–25.

sional sermon.[11] There had long been special times for preaching, beyond the sermons delivered on the Sabbath and holidays and at events such as circumcisions, marriages, and funerals. For the most part, these were occasions that directly affected the Jewish community: the dedication of a new synagogue, common deliverance from a danger or threat, appointment of a new rabbi, completion of a book, even the ceremonial visit of a notable dignitary to the synagogue. Sometimes there was a summons to repentance and prayer because Jews were suffering or in serious danger, either in the community or far away. Now, for the first time, Jews participated in public expressions of mourning and celebration for events concerning the countries in which they lived. A new occasion for Jewish preaching came into being: the synagogue service on a day ordained by the government for public prayer. What was actually said in these sermons is very significant.

In the Great Synagogue of the Ashkenazic community in London, a recent arrival from Germany, originally from Galicia, was Rabbi Hirschel Levin, known in England as Hart Lyon.[12] The manuscript collection of his sermons includes four delivered on special occasions connected with the Seven Years' War. The first was delivered near the beginning of the war, when British military reverses and severe economic hardship had produced a crisis in national morale. The central theme, appropriate for a day of national fasting, was the need for repentance. Levin emphasized the obligation of Jews to serve their king through prayer, conceding that Jews could make little contribution in actual military service. He evoked the economic pressures and political turmoil caused by the war, and reflected on its causes:

> We see that sometimes kings quarrel with each other over matters that seem trivial, and eventually go to war for a reason no rational person could believe to be the actual cause of the fighting. The real reason, however, is known by the kings, about whom the wise King Solomon testified, *The mind of kings is unfathomable* (Prov. 25:3). They can foresee what will eventually develop from

---

11. There are, to be sure, methodological problems in using sermons as evidence for the attitudes and views of the community as a whole. In some cases, the points that a preacher chooses to emphasize in his sermons may be selected because he considers them to be a matter of contention and not part of a shared consensus. Nevertheless, unlike the writer of a book, who may represent no one other than himself, the preacher faces an audience that may react strongly and immediately to statements with which they disagree (see *Jewish Preaching*, pp. 54–57). We may assume, therefore, that views expressed in these sermons are not unrepresentative of those shared by many in the congregation. Particularly on public occasions, such as the ones described below, the preacher's role is to represent the congregation, not to convince it of views it rejects.

12. On Levin, see *Jewish Preaching*, pp. 347–58.

this trivial matter, and they therefore anticipate and go to war to prevent evil times.[13]

While the tone of this passage is open to different interpretations, the thrust is clearly that the sovereign must be trusted and supported even if the ordinary subject cannot understand all of his decisions.

A second sermon was delivered in a very different spirit; it was on a day "ordained by the King" as an occasion for public celebration following a military victory. In it, Rabbi Levin raises a moral issue of relevance not only in its own day:

> How can people rejoice at the destruction of their fellow human beings? Look how many thousands have died as a result of the great battles of our times. Many have been killed, many drowned in the sea, many kingdoms have been devastated, become desolate overnight, wholly consumed by terrors. Is this good in God's sight? If God did not want to destroy those pagan nations that lived in antiquity, that did not believe in God or His salvation at all . . . how much more is this true for the nations among whom we, the people of Israel, find refuge, who treat us with kindness and mercy, who are religious and act in accordance with the values of truth, justice and peace. God forbid that we should rejoice in their downfall! On the contrary, we should look out for their well-being, and pray for their peace.[14]

The nature of the occasion required the preacher to provide a solution to this question and justify the celebration: if one person is attacked by another and kills the aggressor in self-defense, it is appropriate to rejoice—not that someone has been killed, but that the endangered individual has escaped harm. This is true also of conflicts between countries. We see here evidence of a new Jewish consciousness vis-à-vis warfare between nations founded on ethical and religious principles and, on the whole, well-disposed toward the Jewish people. Although the welfare of all these nations is a matter of concern to God, some may be aggressors, and their defeat can be a legitimate cause for rejoicing. Rarely before had the battles between Gentile nations become a matter of internal Jewish concern in a context devoid of any messianic speculation.

Hirschel Levin was not the only Jewish thinker to wrestle with the implications of the Seven Years' War. After the stunning Prussian victory over the Austrian forces at Leuthen (December 5, 1757), Moses Mendelssohn

---

13. Ibid., p. 353.
14. Levin "Derashot," fol. 23b.

wrote a sermon of thanksgiving that was delivered by Rabbi David Fraenkel in Berlin, published in German, and immediately translated into English and published in London.[15] The sermon is remarkable in that it gives virtually no indication that it was written and preached by Jews. Two rabbinic statements are cited as they might have been by a knowledgeable Christian—that is, not subjected to the detailed analysis such statements usually underwent at the hands of Jewish preachers. Particularly appropriate for the context was God's rebuke of the angels for singing praises while the Egyptians were drowning in the sea (B. Meg 10b).

Throughout the discourse, this universalistic concern is combined with patriotic fervor. The sermon thus maintains that the proper form of thanksgiving for the victory of the Prussian army against the more numerous Austrian forces was to fulfill vows of benevolence for the relief of the poor, especially the widows and orphans of soldiers who gave their lives for their country. Furthermore, King Friedrich II presented a model worthy of emulation in his public expression of gratitude to God—a role played by King George II in the London sermons of Hirschel Levin. God was providentially responsible for the victory, but human beings were expected to do all they could to prepare the best possible military tactics and fight with bravery. Finally, the sermon asserts that "we are all children of the one living God. They who declare themselves our Enemies, are equally the work of his Hands, and love and fear him; and we should love them, were they not seduced by perverse Passions to disturb the Tranquility of our dear sovereign." Significantly, the publication of this work in German and English soon after its delivery shows that Jews wanted their Christian neighbors to be aware of the enlightened patriotic sentiments being expressed in the synagogues.

Needless to say, the Seven Years' War was perceived quite differently by those Jews living in the nations of the opposing coalition. At the outbreak of the hostilities (September 5, 1756), Rabbi Ezekiel Landau composed a public prayer to be used with accompanying Psalms in all synagogues of the realm, appealing to God to grant the Empress Maria Theresa and the Austrian armies good fortune in the war. A few months later (December 22, 1756), Landau and the other leaders of Prague Jewry proclaimed a ban of

---

15. This sermon is mentioned in Meyer, p. 24 and Altmann, *Mendelssohn*, p. 68. Both discuss the circumstances of the sermon but not its content, although Altmann identifies it as "the earliest known specimen of modern Jewish preaching in the German tongue." The German text is entitled *Dankpredigt über den grossen und herrlichen Sieg . . . bey Leuthen . . .* (Berlin, 1757); the English version is *A Thanksgiving Sermon for the victory [of Leuthen]* (London, 1758). I have used the copy of the English text in Harvard's Houghton Library; I have not been able to consult the German text. On the Battle of Leuthen, see Asprey, pp. 475–81.

anathema on any Jew who might harm "our most gracious Queen" in even the slightest manner by aiding the enemy as spies. The text of both the prayer and the proclamation was printed in German and distributed.[16] In June 1757, the Jews of Prague gathered in *Altneuschul* to thank God for the Austrian defeat of the Prussian forces at Kollin, which thwarted Friedrich's attempt to capture Prague.[17] In a sermon delivered at the *Hochsynagoge* in 1766, Zerah Eidlitz recalled the trauma of those days: "We were in mortal danger when we were besieged by the Prussian king; we feared for our lives night and day, and they plundered and ravaged us."[18]

Thus we see that Jews on both sides of the war that convulsed Central Europe showed a keen interest in the fortunes of their side, both when it directly affected their own welfare, as in Prague, and when it did not, as in London and Berlin. Furthermore, in each case it was the monarch who served as the embodiment of their aspirations and as a symbol of goodness and piety with which the Jews as well as their Christian neighbors could identify.

This is particularly surprising with regard to the Austrian Empress. Maria Theresa, widely known to historians as one of the most anti-Jewish monarchs of her age, was well recognized by contemporaries for her personal antipathy. In addition to her role in the expulsion of the Jews from Prague, her government imposed confiscatory taxes on Jewish subjects, at one point even considering an unprecedented levy on the *etrogim* necessary for the observance of Sukkot.

Yet when the Empress fell ill in 1767, Landau composed a prayer for her recovery and had it printed in German, together with calls for public fasting. When she recovered, he issued an extravagant prayer of thanksgiving for her return to health.[19] And when she died in 1780, Landau eulogized her in a ceremonial gathering at the Meisl Synagogue in Prague (December 10, 1780) in a sermon filled with professions of the most profound admiration and deep personal grief. He praised her abilities as a ruler, her courage as a leader in war, her capacity to inspire the dedication and sacrifice of her soldiers, her commitment to social welfare programs, even her Christian piety.

---

16. Muneles, p. 79, items 261 and 262; Kemelhar, pp. 30–35. Muneles states that it was a "Hebrew prayer," but Kemelhar makes it clear that the printed text was in German and that he had it translated into Hebrew for his book.

17. Muneles, p. 80, item 266.

18. Eidlitz, p. 22d. A translation of the full passage is in *Jewish Preaching*, pp. 86–87 (the page reference cited there in n. 18 should be corrected to 22c–d). On the siege of Prague and the Battle of Kollin, see Asprey, pp. 445–58, and Delbrueck, 4:340–44.

19. Muneles, p. 83, item 282; Kemelhar, pp. 65–68.

The eulogy was a sincere expression of Landau's recognition that the monarch was more than the source of a particular policy towards the Jews. It reflected his appreciation of qualities that were widely admired throughout the realm and was delivered, we are told, at a synagogue service attended by Christian Christian notables from the government and the army. We may assume that the eulogy was delivered in German. It was published soon thereafter in Hebrew and in two German editions, one in German type, the other in Hebrew characters.[20]

These sermons delivered in London, Berlin and Prague point to the striking psychological transformation within major Jewish communities of Central and Western Europe preceding the Emancipation, revealing what may be called an incipient patriotism. What do they show about the Jewish attitude towards armies and war? Judaism is not a pacifist tradition, and Jews of antiquity are known to have fought as bravely and as fiercely as any other people. This tradition was not abandoned in the Middle Ages: during the periods of the First Crusade, the Black Death, and, later, the Cossack uprising of 1648–1649, Jews armed themselves and attempted to defend their communities. But these were cases of Jews fighting for Jewish lives and possessions. Aggressive military activity was not a common Jewish practice. Samuel the Nagid, who led the army of the eleventh-century Berber princedom of Granada in at least seventeen campaigns, was an anomaly. Medieval Jews may have recalled ancient Jewish victories with nostalgia and turned to arms as a last resort in times of immediate danger, but most had little regard for the exploits or the values of contemporary Christian or Muslim armies, except insofar as they might figure in some eschatological scenario. Indeed, the dominant tradition in illustrating both manuscript and printed Haggadahs was to depict the "wicked son" as a soldier.[21]

The prevalent outlook is expressed in *Sefer Ḥasidim,* that fascinating compilation of the superstitious beliefs, ethical ideals, and spiritual aspirations of the German-Jewish Pietists in the High Middle Ages. "One should always think intelligently and reverently about how the ingenious ruses of the world can be honorably redeemed," we are told.

> Look how a man takes his life in his hands to go into a place of danger for his own glory. For example, knights will enter the thick of battle, ready to sacrifice their lives for their glory, to avoid being shamed. Similarly, noble women

20. Landau, *Derush Hesped;* see below, chap. 18.

21. Yerushalmi, *Haggadah,* passim. It is striking that the military exploits of Samuel ibn Nagrela (Ha-Nagid) are not mentioned in Abraham ibn Daud's *Sefer ha-Qabbalah,* written ca. 1161, a major source for our knowledge of ibn Nagrela's career.

who become pregnant from their adulterous affairs devise ingenious ruses so they will not be shamed. The same is true of thieves. If this is so for temporal glory, how much more ingenuity should be devoted to the glory of the Creator.[22]

In this passage, knights, together with adulterous women and thieves, serve as examples of human ingenuity misdirected to the attainment of personal glory and the avoidance of personal shame. The lesson is simple: if Christians devote such energy to the pursuit of ephemeral goals, it is inconceivable for Jews to slacken in their devotion to religious values, which are eternal.

This theme was developed and transformed by Jonathan Eybeschuetz in the Alsatian community of Metz. This is what he said on January 25, 1745, in a sermon delivered upon hearing the news of the expulsion of the Jews from Prague.

There are many nobles and dukes among those who serve human kings. They pay no attention at all to ordinary desires. In times of war, they lie upon the ground, ignoring the furious torrents of hail or rain. Sometimes they sleep in villages that their servants' servants would not deign to live in. They go for days without bread, meat and wine. When the war begins, they stand at the head of their troops. They deny themselves sleep. Their garments are splattered with the blood of the fallen. Yet they pay no attention to all this. On the contrary, they long for it, knowing that in this way they will be praised in the royal palace and find favor in the sight of the king and the court.

---

22. *Sefer Ḥasidim* (Parma), nu. 985, p. 242. It is worth comparing the rhetoric of this argument with the following passage by Bernard of Clairvaux:

What intolerable madness it is to fight, at vast cost and labor, for no other wages than those of death and of sin! You deck your horses with silken trappings; you put on, I know not what hanging cloaks, over your corselets; you paint your shields, your spears, your saddles; you ornament bridles and spurs with gold, with silver, with precious stones; and in such pomp, with disgraceful rage and shameless insensibility, you rush upon death! . . . Nor does anything move you to battle except an impulse of irrational wrath, or an empty thirst for glory, or the greed of earthly gain! . . . But the soldiers of Christ fight safely the battles of their Lord.

Bernard here is drawing upon an older Christian metaphor of the saints as "soldiers of Christ" and applying it to the new military orders in which the "milites Christi" are actual soldiers who combined monastic discipline with actual battle for a sacred purpose, but the contrast may illuminate part of the background for the *Sefer Ḥasidim* passage. See Bernard, *De laude novae militiae*, quoted in Storrs, pp. 570–71. I am grateful to my colleague Tom Head for this reference.

Eybeschuetz goes on to draw the appropriate religious moral: "How can one not learn from this to annul every desire for the vanities of this world in order to serve the King of Kings and find favor in His sight."[23]

The affinities with the *Sefer Ḥasidim* passage are clear, but there is also a fundamental difference. The eighteenth-century preacher devotes considerable rhetorical energy to his description of the king's officers, who are not dismissed with contempt as misguided fools, but depicted with what appears to be considerable admiration. These soldiers are motivated not merely by a desire to avoid personal shame, but by love for their king. The discipline and devotion of the soldier fighting for his country has become a positive model for the Jew to emulate in the context of the spiritual arena.

This passage points in two directions. One is an increased use of military imagery to characterize Jewish spirituality: the Jew as God's soldier— in one extreme formulation, "God's Cossacks"—who musters all the self-discipline and unquestioning obedience of army life to fight temptation and the forces of evil and impurity that Jewish mystics believed to be prevalent throughout the world—i.e., in the mystical realm of the *qelippot* ("husks"). The metaphor became part of the rhetoric of the later *Musar* movement; we find it expressed in a powerful speech in Feierberg's classic *Le-An?* (Whither?).[24] At the same time, however, the passage points to a more positive evaluation of actual armies, to a tendency to glorify military values, and to new respect for training exercises, parades, and the battlefield. There is some evidence that in the late eighteenth and early nineteenth century, Jews in Central European countries began to adopt these attitudes themselves.

Jewish leaders reacted with some ambivalence to this development. In a sermon of 1780, Eliezer Fleckeles, we recall, criticized the practice of Jews going on excursions during the month of Elul to observe military exercises of the army and cavalry when they should have been preparing for the High Holy Days.[25] But in the same year, the Chief Rabbi, Ezekiel Landau, eulogizing the Empress Maria Theresa, presented the bravery and self-sacrifice of soldiers as a value in its own right. Speaking of the devotion the Empress in-

---

23. Eybeschuetz, 1:50a.

24. Rabbi Israel Meir Ha-Kohen, the "*Ḥafets Ḥayyim*," is said to have referred to the rabbis and students of an East European yeshivah as "Gott's Kozak'n," a term he intended as a compliment. See Irving Greenberg, *Sh'ma* 10, nu. 187 (February 8, 1980): 55; cf. Feierberg, pp. 156–62. The phrase "*Tsiv'os ha-Shem*" (God's armies) has been extensively used in the rhetoric of HaBaD, especially in literature intended for children. The relationship of this metaphor with the Christian *milites Christi* as a metaphorical characterization of the saint deserves to be explored.

25. Fleckeles, *'Olat*, p. 73a.

spired within the Austrian armed forces, he said, "In times of war, we saw that all her subjects actually risked their lives for her. Those in the army, from the highest officers to the lowly privates, stood their ground and fought her battle with all their might."[26]

A few years later, Landau was confronted with a very different situation. As part of the process of improving the civil status of Jewish subjects and integrating them into the surrounding society, Emperor Joseph II declared the Jews in the Austrian Empire liable for military service—the first European ruler to do so. On May 10, 1789, Landau stood before twenty-five young Jews and their officers as they prepared to leave Prague for basic training. His German address to these young men was recorded in Hebrew characters in *Hame'asef,* the Hebrew periodical of the Berlin Jewish Enlightenment.

Most of the speech is an appeal to the novice soldiers not to forget their religion or be ashamed of their Jewish identity and to continue to observe the obligations of prayer, Sabbath, and dietary laws even in their new circumstances. But the climax, delivered, we are told, with tears running down the speaker's cheeks, makes a rather different point.

> Earn for yourselves and for our entire nation gratitude and honor, so that all will see that the Jewish people, persecuted until now, loves its sovereign and its government, and is ready, if necessary, to offer up their lives [for their sake]. It is my hope that through you—if you will behave honorably and loyally as is the duty of every subject—those remaining neck-chains that to some extent continue to oppress us will be removed.[27]

There is certainly ambivalence here, but this passage does not suggest that Landau viewed induction of Jews into the Emperor's army as an unmitigated calamity, as some writers have suggested. Military service certainly presented an obstacle and a challenge to Jewish observance, but it was also an opportunity to demonstrate the loyalty to the Emperor that many felt deeply.

Within a few months, Landau preached a thanksgiving sermon at a public gathering to celebrate the victory of Joseph II's Austrian army in their siege of Belgrade against the Ottoman Turks.[28] Landau vigorously affirmed

26. Landau, *Derush Hesped,* p. 5b; below, chap. 18.

27. *Ha-Me'assef* 5 (1789), p. 254. The full German text of the speech is given in Kestenberg-Gladstein, pp. 70–72, as part of her discussion of the first conscription of Jewish soldiers. A very free and somewhat unreliable Hebrew translation is given by Gelman, pp. 128–29.

28. Landau, *Derush ha-Shevaḥ.* On the first page Landau gave exclusive rights to publish the sermon to Abraham Kish, a poor man, in the hope that he would make a profit from it.

the high ethical standards of his sovereign and the justice not only of the Austrian cause but of its method of warfare. "Before he began this conflict, he gave warning to his enemies, as is known from his Manifesto. The Muslims were the aggressors in the war. If they did not commence against the Emperor himself, they began against his allies. . . . Thus all that the Emperor and his officers did in this war was done justly."

The ethical qualities of the "field marshals and generals" were also emphasized. Finally, the most decisive proof of divine favor for the Austrian cause was that the city was taken without Austrian casualties. "As soon as the Field Marshall gave the signal and commenced firing a heavy bombardment, they immediately surrendered and sued for peace."[29] Although there was no blatant violation of the laws of nature, this was a miracle, a "hidden miracle" like many of those in the Bible, revealing God's providence.

Very similar themes, accompanied by even greater patriotic fervor, are revealed in the sermon delivered by Ezekiel Landau's son, Samuel, in the Meisl Synagogue in Prague on July 7, 1814.[30] It was a heady, exhilarating time. The Austrian Emperor Franz I had just returned to Vienna from Paris, following the occupation of the French capital by the European allies and the abdication of Napoleon; the stage was being set for the Congress of Vienna. Not surprisingly, the transformation of European politics was placed in an explicitly providential context:

> We have seen the great victory and triumph of our sovereign king, the Emperor Franz, may His Majesty be exalted, whom God has chosen for this great work of liberation: to free kingdoms and states from their suffering.[31] We and all the inhabitants of Europe were distraught because of the chaos of war, subjugated by the power of the aggressor [Napoleon], forced to toil under a heavy yoke. Now by the enormous power of his heroic armies, he has prevailed, conquering the enemy, bestowing peace upon all the lands of Europe. God has delivered them through our sovereign, the Emperor Franz.

---

29. The victorious siege actually lasted from mid-September to October 8, 1789; see Roider, *Austria*, pp. 185–86. The war did indeed begin because of an Ottoman offensive against Russia, Austria's ally; cf. the discussion of the diplomatic background in Roider, *Austria*, pp. 169–85.

30. Landau, *Ahavat Tsiyon*, sermon 11, p. 18a–b.

31. The rhetoric of liberation played an important role as a rallying cry for the alliance forces. The order of the day sent out by the allied commander immediately before the Battle of Leipzig said, "Russians! Prussians! Austrians! You are fighting for one thing—the liberation of Europe, for the independence of your sons, for the immortality of your names." Brett-James, p. 114.

He could not simply assert that victory proved God's favor, as Napoleon himself had been astoundingly successful on the battlefield. Landau therefore argues that the proof of God's providence lies in the noble qualities of the leaders of the anti-Napoleonic forces.

> We have proof that this liberation is permanent, that cynical men will oppress us no more. For it was wrought through our sovereign, the pious and merciful ruler, who acts justly and charitably toward his servants, the subjects of his state. Furthermore, the kings who were his allies—the Emperor of Russia [Alexander I] and the King of Prussia [Friedrich Wilhelm III]—are all pious and act charitably and graciously . . .

Most of the preacher's emphasis, however, is not on the ideals of liberation or peace, but on the decisive defeat of Napoleon's forces in the "Battle of the Nations" at Leipzig, some ten months earlier.

> God has blessed our countrymen in that all of his generals are from our state—the Grand Duke Prince Schwarzenberg, through whom the victory was accomplished, for he was commander of all the armed forces, and he struck the enemy with a shattering blow and pursued him to the point of destruction. This liberation will certainly endure because the Duke, a military hero, Prince Schwarzenberg, is known to all for his noble qualities; he is outstanding in his virtues. Similarly the other generals—Prince Liechtenstein, Count Bubna, Count Nostitz, Count Klenau—and many other officers like them— are blessed by God.[32] We may rejoice that God has blessed some of our own sons— natives of Bohemia—to be worthy of being officers of our sovereign the Emperor.

In this sermon, there is no wrestling with the problem of rejoicing over the defeat of another army, as in the sermons of the Seven Years' War. Nor is there any evident awareness that Jews were among the sixty thousand French soldiers killed on the battlefield. The patriotic identification with the armies of the Austrian alliance and the sense of national pride in the glory redounding to Bohemia are unqualified; the imperial cause, morality, and God's providential plan are coequal.

We see that Jews—or at least their "spiritual leaders"—were caught up in

---

32. Prince Karl Philipp Schwarzenberg, commander of the army of Bohemia, became the supreme commander of the allied forces. On him and the other figures named in the Battle of Leipzig, see Rothenberg, pp. 178–85. The letter written by Schwarzenberg to his wife on the eve of the Battle of Leipzig does indeed reveal some rather impressive personal qualities; see Brett-James, pp. 114–15.

the military fever of these campaigns, and rabbis were not at all reluctant to show themselves knowledgeable about miliary affairs.[33] But the moralized militarism of Ezekiel Landau's praise to God for the fall of Belgrade or Samuel Landau's jubilation over the defeat of Napoleon should not be taken as the only Jewish opinion. On a different ethical level altogether is Moses Mendelssohn's 'Friedenspredigt' (Sermon on Peace), delivered by Chief Rabbi Aaron Mosessohn at a thanksgiving service in Berlin on March 12, 1763, upon the conclusion of the Seven Years' War. Rather than exulting in the achievements of military power—even justly and ethically employed— Mendelssohn caustically, with considerable rhetorical force, repudiates the notion that war can produce any virtues of value to civilization. Appealing to recent experience, he evokes the devastating waste of war, which threatens the very foundations of human culture, and expresses a genuine yearning for peace, the only true manifestation of God's purpose in creation.

> We have learned to understand that the 'vicious beasts' of human society cannot be more destructive than suspicion, hatred, jealousy, dissension, and their horrible consequence, war, with all of its barbarities. Days of sorrow are still present in our memory . . . In war, the good have no pleasure, diligence receives no reward, the worthy no prize, the honest no satisfaction; religion groans, virtue goes into hiding, and—according to the Talmudic statement the harshest curse of all—the young are arrogant towards the aged, and the dissolute toward the honorable.
>
> In war . . . cities are reduced to ashes, palaces demolished, all beneficent institutions destroyed, the laws trampled underfoot, the arts despised, and that which men have conceived and realized over a period of centuries for the betterment of their condition is quickly ruined . . . Fields are uprooted, crops are trodden down, and what does manage to grow is not enjoyed by the farmer, for the enemy consumes the fruit of his labors. That is why God, after having promised all forms of earthly happiness to those who walk in His precepts and

---

33. On the patriotism of Russian Jews during the War of 1812, see Dubnow, *Russia and Poland,* 1:355–59. On the patriotism of Prussian Jews, who volunteered to fight against Napoleon in 1813, see Meyer, pp. 138–39. Further investigation of sermons will undoubtedly fill out the picture. Israel Meshulam Solomon's *A Sermon preached . . . 13th of December, 1776 . . . for a general fast to pray for the success of His Majesty's Arms,* published in London, 1777; and Solomon Herschel's *Sermon preached . . . success of His Majesty's Fleet under Lord Nelson, off Trafalgar,* published in London, 1805 look like important texts, but I have not yet been able to trace them. Such texts were ephemeral—printed, read, and soon thrown away when they were no longer of current interest. Copies are therefore extremely difficult to find. See Roth, *Magna Bibliotheca,* pp. 325, 437.

keep His commandments, adds finally that blessing without which we can enjoy no other: *I will grant peace in the land* (Lev. 26:6). I will guide the hearts of those who have the power over war and peace to choose what is best.[34]

Although part of an occasional sermon, here is a message and a prayer that speaks to future generations as well.[35]

34. Mendelssohn, 4:407–15; passage from p. 409. The "vicious beasts" mentioned in the first sentence is Mendelssohn's allegorical understanding of the phrase in Leviticus 26:6; cf. Altmann, *Mendelssohn,* pp. 68–69, which focuses on some philosophical points in the sermon.

35. As it seemed on April 29, 1991, in the wake of the devastation wrought by the victorious American-led forces in the Gulf War, when this lecture was delivered at the Leo Baeck Institute in New York.

12

"Treatise for the Guidance of Preachers": A Newly Discovered Fifteenth-Century *Ars Praedicandi*

Moscow Gunzberg Manuscript 926, a microfilm of which has recently arrived in the Institute for Microfilmed Hebrew Manuscripts, is a miscellany, containing mainly Sephardic works from the first half of the fifteenth century.[1] These include a series of philosophical sermons by Zerahiah Ha-Levi and by Joseph ibn Shem Tov, as well as other anonymous texts produced by as yet unidentified preachers. The provenance of many of these texts was a circle of scholars deeply influenced by Rabbi Hasdai Crescas.[2] The manuscript is similar to Harvard University's Houghton Hebrew Manuscript 61, and several of the same sermons are contained in both. A colophon by the scribe, Ezra ben Solomon, is dated 10 *Marḥeshvan* 5234 (1 November, 1473).[3]

Unique to this manuscript and particularly valuable for the history of Jewish homiletics is a brief text, some 50 lines long, entitled "Seder le-Hayshir ha-Darshanim." It is a set of schematic instructions for preachers on the art of effective preaching. While dozens of such works were produced by medieval Christian writers,[4] we have no such Jewish work predating the Expulsion from Spain. The only comparable text is Joseph ibn Shem Tov's "'Ein ha-Qore," which contains considerable material on the art of preaching, as well as criticism of the failings of contemporary preachers.[5]

---

1. I am grateful to Ari Ackerman of the Hebrew University for calling my attention to this manuscript and making available to me his M.A. thesis on a sermon by Zerahiah Ha-Levi contained in it.

2. One of the sermons by Zerahiah Ha-Levi refers to Crescas's presence in the audience (fol. 149v); another sermon cites him as "our teacher" (fol. 67v). Many of the sermons cite material from Joseph Albo.

3. According to the colophon, the manuscript was transcribed for Don Moses ben Abraham Hayyun, possibly a member of the Hayyun rabbinic family in Lisbon.

4. Charland; Caplan, pp. 135–59 and the bibliographical studies listed on p. 272. For a recent scholarly edition of a representative text, see Thomas de Chobham.

5. See Saperstein, *Jewish Preaching,* pp. 387–92.

Your Voice Like a Ram's Horn

Since "'Ein ha-Qore" is far more discursive than the present text, I considered the possibility that the shorter work was the author's rudimentary sketch for his later, more complete discussion. A careful comparison, however, has led me to conclude that while there are similarities in terminology and content, there is no evidence suggesting that either work is dependent on the other. Because Joseph ibn Shem Tov is the latest known author whose work is included in the manuscript, I have tentatively concluded that our text preceded his,[6] and would thus be the earliest known *Ars Praedicandi* in Jewish literature.

It is the nature of a such a work that it reflects not so much the idiosyncracies and innovations of its author, but rather the tastes and terminology, the conventions and commonplaces of a tradition. My annotation seeks to reveal the context—both Christian and Jewish—in which the text was formulated. I have sought to identify expressions of similar ideas in Christian handbooks for preachers, particularly those produced in Spain. Although I have referred to "'Ein ha-Qore" and a seventeenth-century Italian Jewish "Guide for Preachers," most of the comparative Jewish material is drawn from actual sermons dating from the thirteenth to fifteenth centuries. In this way the value of the text as a representation of homiletical aspirations and sensibilities may be maximized.

Since systematic reflection on the art of preaching by Jews was so rare during the medieval period, the question of Christian influence upon our author naturally arises. Indeed, certain formulations appear that are commonplace in Christian homiletical treatises (e.g., biblical verse as "foundation" of the sermon: n. 8 below). To be sure, there are other subjects that can be found both in Jewish and Christian works (e.g., the need for moral rectitude in the preacher, the criticism of unnecessary length, raising doubts without resolving them: nn. 48, 37, 23 below). But many of the subjects discussed are specifically Jewish in character (problematic aggadot, relation of *peshat* and *derash*), and there is no reference, explicit or implied, to the context of Christian preaching. Thus although the author was probably aware of the existence of Christian treatises on the art of preaching, it is impossible to prove direct influence of any such text upon him. The mechanism through which medieval Christian homiletics influenced Jewish preachers remains enigmatic.

---

6. The dating of the anonymous material in the manuscript is not certain. For example, the sermon immediately following our text uses the word *thema* to refer to the opening verse (fol. 46v; the same term is used on fol. 29r). The earliest previous evidence for this word as a technical term is in sermons from the time of the expulsion (see *Jewish Preaching*, p. 67). Note that our text does not use this, or its Hebrew equivalent, *nose*, as a technical term.

The structure of the short treatise is simple: a brief introduction, ten principles of effective preaching, and a brief epilogue. Each section ends with a verse from the Hagiographa. In some cases the relevance of the verse of obvious (e.g. sections 2 and 6); in some it seems to depend upon an interpretation beyond the simple meaning (section 9). But in other cases, the relevance of the verse to the point made in the preceding paragraph is not at all obvious to me. It may be based on a convention of homiletical interpretation that is no longer accessible.

My translation includes one stylistic shift: for the most part (where there is no noun subject for the verb), the instructions have been recast from the third person to the second. Thus instead of beginning each instruction with "he should," I have used the imperative (i.e., instead of "He should be careful . . . ," simply "Be careful . . ."). This more direct style eliminates excessive verbiage not in the Hebrew yet, I believe, does not interfere with the text's intended purpose: to instruct the preachers who read it.

TREATISE FOR THE GUIDANCE OF PREACHERS[1]

One of my colleagues asked me[2] to compose a short summary[3] to teach the path of excellence in a sermon. For many have followed an unpaved path; they have spoiled the sermon's order, its splendor, dimmed its radiant luster.[4] I decided to heed him and fulfil his request, to prepare and pave the road that leads ever upward. I have divided it into ten requirements[5] [for good preaching], that it may be easily accessible to those who seek it out.[6] And as all greatness belongs to God, the source of whatever praiseworthy we may utter, I will raise a prayer that words be placed in my mouth, as the Psalmist said, *Let my lips send forth praise* (Ps. 119:171).

First: the biblical verse or statement[7] on which the preacher is to construct his sermon must be suitable to serve as the foundation of the struc-

---

1. *Seder le-hayshir ha-darshanim.* The word *seder* was used to translate the Greek *kanon* (rule, standard), as in Moses ibn Tibbon's translation of Avicenna's *Canon* (Steinschneider, p. 696). It may also reflect the Latin *ordo,* as in the work by Guibert de Nogent, *Liber quo ordine sermo fieri debeat* (A Book about the Way a Sermon Ought to be Given; Medieval Rhetoric, p. 162).

2. This may be a *topos* (see Curtius, p. 85); Joseph ibn Shem Tov similarly states that he was requested by Jewish dignitaries to write his sermons for them ("'Ein ha-Qore", fol. 2r).

3. *Klal qatsar.* The word *klal* can have the meaning "summary" (*summa*); cf. the work by Judah ibn Balat, *Klal qatsar mi-kol ha-rashum bi-ketav* (Steinschneider, p. 29). Alan of Lille wrote a *Summa de arte praedicatoria* (Compendium on the Preaching Art; *Medieval Rhetoric,* p. 228). The phrase may also reflect the term *Tractatulus,* used for at least two short medieval treatises on the art of preaching (see Caplan, pp. 135–37), or the title of the work by Raymond Llull, *Ars brevis praedicationis* (Deyermond, p. 133).

4. Cf. the introduction to "'Ein ha-Qore": "I have seen what my predecessors in these lands have done in this art: all of them have been quick to turn aside from the path of order" (fol. 2v).

5. *Tena'im:* in the sense of those characteristics required for a certain goal to be fulfilled. Cf. Ramon Llull's "De novum conditionibus sermonum" in his *Liber de praedicatione* (Llull, p. 395), and his ten "conditions" of verbal wisdom, six "conditions" of useful, fruitful and just speech (Johnston, p. 133).

6. Cf. introduction to "'Ein ha-Qore": "No one has produced an appropriately inclusive and encompassing treatise (*seder kolel u-maqif*) on the roots of this art so that it would be organized and complete, easy to derive benefit from its study, like the other arts" (Ibid.)

7. *Ma'amar* does not have the technical meaning here of a passage from rabbinic literature (see *Jewish Preaching,* p. 67). It is used by the author in the previous sentence to introduce a verse from Psalms, following the rabbinic use of *she-ne'emar.* Joseph ibn Shem Tov uses the word similarly (Regev, "Teshuvah," p. 188; Regev, "Re'iyat," p. 298–99: *lakahti zeh ha-ma'amar li-ysod mah she-omar alav*).

ture.[8] You know that a building depends upon the dimensions of its foundation.[9] Therefore the preacher should select a passage[10] or statement that encompasses most of the topics of the Torah lesson, or the specific topic he intends to preach upon, and then arrange accordingly the rabbinic midrash, if he finds one. Be careful to read the verse without any error, and explain where it is taken from and whether it is connected with what precedes it, in which case they should be presented in coherent order.[11] A reminder of this: *The mind of a wise person makes his speech intelligent* (Prov. 16:23).[12]

Second: begin by explaining the simple meaning of the verse following the gist of its words.[13] If there is more than one meaning[14] for one of the words, this should be explained. If it is a verse that has both an exoteric and an esoteric meaning, first explain the exoteric meaning, that is, the figurative text [*mashal*],[15] and then the esoteric meaning,[16] its underlying significance

---

8. Cf. Bahya ben Asher, *Kad ha-Qemaḥ*, p. 96: When the rabbis preached in public, "they would begin with a verse and use it as the foundation upon which they would construct an edifice." Cf. also Alan of Lille: "Let [the sermon] be based on a text from Scripture as its immediate foundation" (*Medieval Rhetoric*, p. 232); John of Wales, "*Thema, quod est tocius operis fundamentum*" (see *Jewish Preaching*, p. 67, n. 8); anonymous, "*Thema est quasi radix totius sermonis et per ipsum fundamentum stabilita totius aedificii fabrica consurgit*" (quoted in Charland, p. 113, n. 1).

9. This seems like a proverb: cf. Davidson, *Meshalim*, nu. 3097.

10. *Pereq*: this is used not for a biblical "chapter" in the modern sense but for a unit of meaning that can be more or less than a verse, as in the opening verses of Yizhari cited in the following note.

11. Cf. Yizhari in *Jewish Preaching*, p. 158: "These verses [Isa. 40:28–31, the theme] were spoken by the Prophet Isaiah following his initial words of comfort." This was characteristic of Yizhari's technique; cf. his sermon on *Va-Yishlaḥ*, beginning with Ps. 20:8–10: "These verses are from the same Psalm as the verse *May the Lord answer you in time of trouble* (Ps. 20:2); it is about the subject of sorrows, whatever they may be, and deliverance from them (Yizhari MS, fol. 44a). Cf. also Anatoli, beginning of *Va-Yetse*, p. 27b; Anonymous (*Derashot . . . Rabbenu Yonah*), pp. 13, 21. On the importance of context in presenting the theme, see Charland, p. 119.

12. Cf. the use of this verse in the context of rhetoric by Judah Messer Leon in *Nofet Tsufim* (Messer Leon, p. 157).

13. This is regularly done by Yizhari, often beginning his discussion with the phrase "according to the simple meaning" (*lefi ha-peshat*): e.g. fols. 44r, 52v, 137v. Cf. Zahalon, l. 586.

14. *Shittuf*: technically, equivocal or amphibolous term. Cf. ibn Tibbon, "Millot Zarot" s.v. *shem meshuttaf*, and Wolfson, *Studies* 1:455–77. For the danger of confusion by preachers in ambiguous words of a verse, see Anatoli, beginning of *Noaḥ*, p. 9a.

15. The various meanings of the word *mashal* include analogy, parable, exemplum, and allegory; see *Jewish Preaching*, pp. 93–94.

16. This translation emends an erroneous repetition of *ha-mashal*, substituting what is clearly required: *ha-nistar*.

[*nimshal*].[17] Connect the Torah lesson or the specific topic you intend to preach upon with these levels of meaning. For example, if the intended topic for the sermon pertains to the exoteric meaning, after explaining the verse, use it to support this topic, making the connection clear, and afterward explain the esoteric meaning.[18] If the topic pertains to the esoteric meaning, explain exoteric and esoteric together, and use the esoteric meaning as support for this topic.[19] A reminder of this: *Apples of gold in ornaments of silver* (Prov. 25:11).[20]

Third: avoid aggadic statements expressed in a hyperbolic or enigmatic manner incompatible with reason, unless you know an explanation or interpretation that renders them rational.[21] Do not preach about matters that are too weighty or wondrous for you,[22] or about a subject that is perplexing or raises doubts without being able to resolve such problems in his talk; otherwise, the difficulty will remain unresolved, and this is a treacherous path.[23] A reminder of this: *My words bespeak the uprightness of my heart* (Job 33:3).[24]

---

17. For an example of a sermon following this procedure, see Anatoli, *Ḥayyei Sarah*: "This entire Psalm (45) is said on two levels, just like Proverbs; the exoteric is appropriate for all, and the esoteric for select individuals, as will be explained. We shall begin by explaining the exoteric meaning . . ." (p. 12a–b). "Now we shall begin to explain the esoteric meaning . . ." (p. 21b). Cf. also the sermons on *Zakhor* (pp. 81a, 82a), *Shemini* (pp. 97a and 99a), *Shalaḥ* (pp. 138a and 140b); Joshua ibn Shu'eib, *Derashot* (1992), *Shemini*, pp. 234 and 243; Nissim ben Reuben, *Derashot*, pp. 71–72.

18. Cf. Anatoli's sermon on *Va-Yera*, where an allegorical interpretation of Lot and his wife is introduced only at the very end (Anatoli, p. 19a; also the end of *Va-Yeshev*, p. 34b).

19. For an example of a sermon following this procedure, see Anatoli, *Shemot*, explaining the simple meaning of Eccl. 5:1 (p. 45a) but then making his main point through the esoteric meaning (pp. 45b, 46a). Cf. also the beginning of *Be-Shallaḥ*, p. 56b.

20. This was the verse taken by Maimonides in the introduction to his *Guide for the Perplexed* to express the relationship between an esoteric and an exoteric level of meaning in a biblical verse (Maimonides, Guide 1, pp. 15–16. See the discussion of this passage by Joshua ibn Shu'eib at the beginning of his sermon on *Va-Yiggash* (ibn Shu'eib, *Derashot* [1992], p. 87.

21. Problematic aggadot that appeared to conflict with reason were a constant problem in medieval Jewish intellectual history. See Saperstein, *Decoding*; Hillel of Verona, pp. 179–91, especially categories 2 (pp. 183–84, enigmatic) and 5 (p. 189, line 507: hyperbolic). Accusations of inappropriate homiletical interpretations of strange aggadot abound in the controversy of 1302–1305 and in later years.

22. An apparent echo of Gen. Rab. 8,2, cited by Nahmanides at the end of the introduction to his Torah commentary. Cf. Joseph ibn Shem Tov in *Jewish Preaching*, p. 390–91.

23. An apparent echo of RABaD's critique of Maimonides, *Code, Teshuvah* 5,1. Cf. the similar sentiment expressed by Zahalon, l. 395, and in Christian homiletics, Caplan, p. 72.

24. Apparently used to mean that the preacher should speak about what he knows straightforwardly in his heart.

Fourth: be wary of preaching about matters that are accepted, popular beliefs among the people.[25] Rather, the goal should be to guide the people in beliefs that are true and based on the tradition of our ancestors,[26] and in the high ethical qualities that are desired. Be extremely careful about using all that can be found neatly organized in books. . . .[27] Rather, select from them straightforward matters that are quite beneficial to the audience and will cause it no harm.[28] Many things that can be found in books are indeed correct in the way of truth, but most people cannot understand them. They should be addressed in a sermon only by an expert speaking to other experts.[29] A reminder of this: *Put crooked speech away from you; keep devious talk far from you* (Prov. 4:24).[30]

Fifth: do not jump from one topic to another that is apparently unrelated unless some connection can be shown.[31] It is one of the great rules of this art:

---

25. It is not clear whether the author is using the terms *mequbbelet* (received from tradition) and *mefursemet* (widely known) as distinct categories or as synonyms. For the distinction between them, see Maimonides, *Millot ha-Higayon*, chap. 8.

26. Here too, it is not clear whether the author is speaking of one category (i.e., a true belief is one based on valid tradition) or two. Cf. Joseph ibn Shem Tov in *Jewish Preaching*, p. 389: "The purpose of the preacher is to convince the people only of what is true"; he should therefore be reluctant to use the art of dialectic which is based on "generally accepted opinions" (*mefursamot*). For the distinction between "widely known beliefs" and "true beliefs," see, e.g., Maimonides, *Guide* 1,2 and 2,33; ibn Tibbon, "Millot Zarot," s.v. *ma'amar hagadi*.

27. I am unable to translate with confidence the following seven words: *ve-im ḥatmu hamedabberim bo ha-de'ot ba-sefarim shonot*. One possible rendering is "especially if the experts have sealed in such books incompatible doctrines," but the syntactic and semantic difficulties of the phrase make me suspect that the text is corrupt.

28. The idea that the content of a sermon must fit the audience was commonplace; see, e.g. Joseph ibn Shem Tov in *Jewish Preaching*, pp. 388–89; Owst, p. 331; *Siete Partidas* I,5,44, pp. 228–29; Odber de Baubeta, p. 4; Smith, p. 119.

29. On the prohibition of presenting certain kinds of subject matter before a general audience, see *Minḥat Qena'ot*, p. 134, in *Jewish Preaching*, p. 382 (f). There was also a question about the propriety of Kabbalistic material in sermons; this may be the content the author has in mind here, as he uses the phrase *al derekh ha-emet* ("in the way of truth"), which was often used to introduce Kabbalistic material. See, e.g., "Dover Meisharim," fol. 60v–61r, discussing an aggadah from B. Pes 56a: "The Kabbalists have interpreted the truth in this, but it is not proper to say it to a general audience (*hamon ha-am*). My intention is to interpret it by taking the true path (*ha-derekh ha-amiti*) and disclosing what is appropriate for the entire congregation."

30. The author apparently understands *'iqshut* and *lazut* in this verse to refer to inappropriate discourse that raises doubts among listeners.

31. Cf. Joel ibn Shu'eib (cited in *Jewish Preaching*, p. 398): "The message must be connected, not amorphous and digressive". . . . (*mequshar ve-lo bilti siddur pa'am ba-ḥuts u-fa'am ba-reḥovot*), and Zahalon, ll. 468–70. For a warning against jumping from one point to another in Christian preaching, see *Siete Partidas,* I,5,44, p. 229.

a preacher must know how to structure material aesthetically, making one topic lead to another that is related to it.[32] If the sermon is intended to address a particular subject, do not begin with it at the outset. Rather, begin with another topic that fits the biblical passage, and then derive the main subject of the sermon out of the discourse, or come to it later.[33] This is a fine technique. If you have to deliver a rebuke, do so in the context of the topic being discussed, for this will provide an opening. For example, if preaching about the benevolence of the patriarch Abraham—how he gave bread and water to to his guests, running to bow down before them—after doing justice to this, you may say, "But we are guilty, for there is no one who acts with compassion," and so forth.[34] This benefits greatly those who understand; it is the right way. They will cover their mouths with their hands,[35] so stinging to them will be the rebuke. A reminder of this: *A ready response is a joy to a person* (Prov. 15:23).[36]

Sixth: do not speak too long. If you intend to explain a particular topic, do not use excessive verbiage.[37] For the topic intended is like a grain of

---

32. Cf. the early fifteenth-century Spanish sermon in Anonymous, St. Petersburg, fol. 2b: "Form is the interconnectedness of the subject matter and the constructed ordering of its parts in a proper arrangement. This is indeed the form of the sermon." On the centrality of order for the aesthetic quality of the sermon in Ramon Llull, see Johnston, pp. 125, 127. And cf. Zahalon, ll. 110–23.

33. Beginning a sermon with material not obviously connected with the sermon's main point was a common practice among Jewish preachers. Cf. Dan, *Sifrut ha-Musar,* pp. 41–44; Zahalon, ll. 340 and 517.

34. Cf. the anonymous sermons in Cambridge MS Add. 1022, fol. 40v, where first the importance of hospitality among Jews is emphasized, and then the application is made to the Torah lesson about Abraham. In Bahya ben Asher's *Kad ha-Qemah,* Abraham is presented as the model of hospitality (pp. 35–40), but there is no explicit criticism of contemporary failures in this area.

35. In an expression of dumbfounded speechlessness (cf. Micah 7:16 and Abravanel's explanation of the phrase). The idea seems to be that making the rebuke emerge unexpectedly from a discussion of the scriptural lesson heightens its psychological impact on the listener. For a similar point made later about the effectiveness of the *mashal* in introducing a rebuke, see *Jewish Preaching,* p. 103.

36. I do not see the relevance of this particular verse to the subject discussed.

37. Cf. Bahya ben Asher, *Kad ha-Qemah,* p. 363, *reshut* 4; Anonymous, St. Petersburg, fol. 2b: "Even if speech is the very essence of truth, if its quantity is too great the listeners will have contempt for it and not accept it; thus, 'whoever speaks at length brings about sin,' (M. Avot 1,17)"; Joel ibn Shu'eib (cited in *Jewish Preaching,* p. 398): "There must not be excessive or superfluous and irrelevant material, for the listeners . . . will become disgusted and fail to understand the main point. . . . Rather it should be moderate, the length of the message fitting the material and the audience." Also Zahalon, ll. 431, 590. Warnings against excessive length were common in Christian treatises. Cf. Guibert de Nogent in *Medieval Rhetoric,* p. 169; Lille, chapter 26, pp. 106–10 ("Against Loquaciousness"); Eiximenis, pp. 308–9 (*De brevitate*).

wheat, and the accompanying verbiage is like the chaff. What use is there in filling a sack full of chaff for the sake of the grain of wheat it contains?[38] Rather, be long on content and short on words.[39] Bring only those proofs and that interpretation which turn out to be true. Do not dwell at length on different interpretations, or on proofs that are subject to disagreement, of the type, "Rabbi X said this, Rabbi Y said that." It is a waste of time. Even in topics of disputation,[40] do not be too verbose. A reminder of this: *Where there is much talking, there is no lack of transgressing* (Prov. 10:19).[41]

Seventh: try to say something new in the sermon, whether concerning the simple meaning of the verse, or the interpretation of an aggadic statement, or in organizing the discussion of the central topic, for this is a great achievement for a preacher.[42] Do not speak about things that are already commonplace for the people, the learned and even the unlearned.[43] Avoid speaking about matters that will be a source of embarrassment to those who hear the sermon, such as the techniques of sexual intercourse or the woman in her menstrual period and the like, unless you speak[44] of such things in general terms, euphemistically, in order to remove obstacles from the path of the people.[45] A reminder of this: *Find favor and good sense* (Prov. 3:4).[46]

Eighth: be a decent person, following the statement of the sages, "Preach well and act well."[47] How reprehensible it is when one rebukes others for

---

38. Cf. Lille: "Loquacity is the seed which bears no fruit" (p. 108); Eiximenis: "The shorter the sermon, the more fruit it will bear within the listeners and the more they will be able to take with them." He quotes Gregory the Great: *Cibaria que minus sufficiunt, auidius sumuntur* (p. 309).

39. Cf. Maimonides, *Code, De'ot* 2,4 (quoted in *Sefer Ḥasidim* [Bologna], para. 34): "Similarly in words of Torah . . . a person's words should be few though his topics be many."

40. This refers to sermons in which opposing positions were argued before arriving at a reconciliation; see *Jewish Preaching*, pp. 75, 180, 395–96; above, pp. 84–86.

41. Cf. Anatoli, p. 140a; *Sefer Ḥasidim,* ibid.; Zahalon, l. 590. This verse is quoted by Alan of Lille in this context (Lille, p. 109).

42. On the expectation of originality, see *Jewish Preaching*, pp. 55, 400; Aboab, fol. 13v l. 11; Zahalon, l. 258, 330. In Christian preaching, see Smalley, pp. 37–38.

43. Cf. Zahalon, l. 268.

44. Reading *yiddaber* instead of the manuscript's *yarbeh.*

45. On criticism by moralists for indecencies incorporated into contemporary sermons, see Owst, *Preaching,* pp. 80–81. Our author, however, seems to be addressing the problem not of preachers appealing to a low level within the audience, but of exercising good taste in discussing marital relations. For an example of this type of discussion, see Anonymous (*Derashot . . . Rabbenu Yonah*), pp. 198–99. Cf. also Lev. Rab. 19,4.

46. The link between the idea and the verse is not clear to me. It probably applies to the second part of the paragraph, perhaps suggesting that the way to find favor in an audience is through good judgment in discussing delicate matters.

47. Cf. B. Yeb 63b, B. Hag 14b.

something about which he does not rebuke himself or control his own desires.[48] If the audience senses that he does not uphold high standards of ethical or religious behavior, they will pay no heed to his words, which will make no more impression upon their hearts than a drop of water falling upon flintstone. Sometimes a preacher will have to suppress his lofty statements, when he remembers that he himself does the opposite. But if his behavior is consistent with his words and his rhetoric, then he may speak with assurance; his audience will acclaim his message and believe in it. A reminder of this: *One who obeys shall speak unchallenged* (Prov. 21:28).[49]

Ninth: write your sermon down on paper.[50] If it is too much work to write it in its entirety, then write down its main points, and divide it into sections, and associate images with them in your mind so that you will be able to speak fluently. Go over again and again the material that you will

---

48. Cf. *Sefer Ḥasidim* (Bologna) paragraphs 5 and 38. Joseph ibn Shem Tov similarly wrote that among the requirements for a preacher is that he have "admirable ethical traits and true deeds, so that people may look and derive a lesson, as the sages said, 'Correct yourself, then correct others,'" ("'Ein ha-Qore", fol. 20r; cf. also Ephraim Luntschitz in *Jewish Preaching*, p. 403). The same theme was emphasized by Christians, e.g. Humbert of Romans, p. 221:

> Another [way in which the preacher's merit is diminished] is when the preacher does not practise what he preaches, making his deeds conform to his words. *Bind them round your throat*, as it says in Proverbs 3:3, on which the Gloss comments, "In encouraging others to live good lives, the preacher binds himself to live a good life." This is why it says, *You teach others, do you not teach yourself? You preach a ban on thieving; do you then go and thieve?* (Rom. 2:21).

Cf. also Lille, p. 143 (*Medieval Rhetoric*, pp. 234–35); Caplan, p. 129, quoting Gregory the Great: "Whose life is despised so is his preaching;" *Siete Partidas* I,5,42, p. 227, also citing Gregory; Ramon Llull, in Johnston, p. 131 and *Liber de praedicatione*, Llull, p. 401; Diego de Estella, 2:3–6, 201–3.

For an opposing perspective, see Anatoli, p. 108a: "Whoever knows how to rebuke and to chastise should do so even if he sins in the very matter that he is rebuking about; if the words that issue from those who speak them are good, truth should not be blocked because of this [that the speakers are themselves guilty]." The same point is made in Anonymous (*Derashot . . . Rabbenu Yonah*), p. 80. Cf. Alan of Lille, in *Medieval Rhetoric*, p. 232.

49. Cf. Joseph ibn Nahmias' comment on this verse, which ends, ". . . shall speak unchallenged, warning the people so that they will hear and be afraid." The editor notes that the last phrase is "superfluous" (Ibn Nahmias, p. 120 n. 1). Indeed, the interpretation up to that point applies the entire verse to the situation of the witness testifying in court. Our text may indicate a second interpretation, applied to preaching, indicating that the text of ibn Nahmias may be apocopated, with the introductory words to the final phrase having been lost.

50. On writing before delivery, see Zahalon, l. 624. In Christian homiletical theory it was considered preferable to speak not from a fully written text but from notes; see Smith, pp. 31–32.

preach,[51] so that you may bring it to life. Do not rely on your expertise; you may forget part of the structure, or stumble on your words, and you will feel humiliated when your shame is displayed for all to see.[52] When you speak in public—and all the more so at an assembly of scholars—be careful to polish and refine your words seven times over. Whatever you say that is susceptible to ambiguity must be explained and interpreted, lest the audience reproach you by attributing to you some harmful doctrine that the words might seem to imply. A reminder of this: *Then he saw, and gauged it, he measured it and probed it. And* **then** *he said to the man* (Job 28:27–28).[53]

Tenth: speak calmly and quietly—a calm manner that brings about repentance—[54] not with anger or contentiousness. If what you see and hear require you to rebuke,[55] consider well who is before you.[56] Do not take pride in your wisdom and understanding.[57] Ask permission from the congregation[58] and from the scholars in your presence,[59] even if you are more learned than they, and all the more if they are more learned than you. Let this be concise; do not bring lengthy proofs or other matters, as most of the preach-

---

51. On the importance of careful preparation before preaching in public, cf. Maimonides, *Epistles,* p. 17 (Epistle on Martyrdom); Bahya ben Asher, *Kad ha-Qemah,* p. 363, *reshut* 5, and Bettan, p. 97; also the anonymous sermons in Cambridge MS Add. 1022, fol. 76v–77a, and Zahalon, l. 639. For techniques of memorization in Christian preaching, see Diego de Estella, 2:164–65, 357–58.

52. Cf. Humbert of Romans, p. 219: "It is very unfortunate when a preacher sometimes runs out of words, whether because he has a bad memory or because he does not know enough Latin or whatever modern language it may be, or for any other reason."

53. The verses are interpreted to suggest that God prepared carefully before beginning to speak. Such an interpretation of the verse appears in the Midrash (Exod. Rab. 40,1) and applied to the context of preparation by preacher. This would seem to be the source of Maimonides (see above, n. 51); he demands a four-fold rehearsal (consistent with the Midrash); our author expands it to seven-fold.

54. Cf. Isa. 30:15 and Maimonides, *Code, De'ot* 2,5 (quoted in *Sefer Ḥasidim* [Bologna], end of section 34); Rashi on B. Ket 84b. Cf. Zahalon, l. 668.

55. Cf. Isa. 11:3.

56. Prov. 23:1, here apparently in the sense of respect for the congregation. Cf. Zahalon, l. 655.

57. Cf. Jer. 9:22 and 10:12.

58. On the *reshut,* see *Jewish Preaching,* p. 77; Zahalon, l. 524.

59. Jewish preachers occasionally addressed audiences in which noted scholars—sometimes their own teachers—were present. See, for example, the beginning of Nahmanides' "Wedding Sermon" (RaMBaN, 1:133), and the sermon by Zerahiah ha-Levi delivered in the presence of Rabbi Hasdai Crescas and other distinguished scholars: Anonymous, Moscow, fol. 149v; see Ackerman, pp. 20 and 65.

ers are accustomed to do.[60] Do not use the ready-made texts of "asking permission" that can be found in books; this is a waste of time.[61] Conclude the sermon with the verse that began it; return in order to connect the end with the beginning. Conclude with a positive sentiment, thereby bringing good at the end from the [verse at] the beginning.[62] A reminder of this: *The end of a matter is made good from its beginning* (Eccl. 7:8).

The types of sermons are three. The first is compound, such as a sermon the divisions of which are based on the divisions in the opening verse.[63] The second is simple, such as one who takes a single theme, and brings many proofs from verses and aggadot and other rabbinic statements to explore the topic.[64] The third is neither simple nor compound, but composed of questions and answers, simple interpretations of verses and [discussion of] topics.[65]

---

60. An example of a preacher who often gave an extremely lengthy *reshut* was Michael Balbo; see his "Derashot" in Balbo, fols. 79v–82r, 98r–100v.

61. As the *reshut* was a conventional part of the formal occasional sermon, handbooks contained models. An example is Bahya ben Asher's *Kad ha-Qemah*, s.v. *reshut* (ed. Chavel), pp. 357–69. Cf. also Anonymous, Moscow, fols. 37a and 37b, both entitled "*haqdamah li-kah reshut.*"

62. It was not common practice to end a sermon with the verse cited at the beginning. Anatoli does end his sermon on Korah by interpreting the verses cited at the beginning (Anatoli, pp. 141a and 145a), and cf. *Ki Tissa*, pp. 78b and 81a, and *Tazria*, pp. 100b and 102b (ending with another verse containing a key word from the opening one). It was indeed the practice to end with a positive sentiment (cf. Zahalon, l. 697).

63. Sermons structured by dividing the theme-verse are not common in extant Jewish sermons. An example is Anonymous, Moscow, fol. 25b, where the theme is Exodus 14:13: *Stand by and see the deliverance of the Lord.* The preacher begins, "I will speak on this verse and divide my speech into two parts." The first subject is the patience of Israel, which merited the Exodus and God's help (*Stand by and see*); the second is the delay in redemption (*the deliverance of the Lord*). Cf. also p. 178, below. This technique is patterned on the *divisio* of Christian homiletics; see Owst, *Preaching*, pp. 321–24; Eiximenis, pp. 336–39.

64. In this statement, the word *nose*, translated "theme," appears to be not the technical term for the verse from the scriptural lesson with which the preacher begins the sermon (see *Jewish Preaching*, p. 67), a use documented only from the end of the fifteenth century, but rather a synonym for "subject" or "topic." See for, example, the "homily on education" by Anatoli, translated in *Jewish Preaching*, pp. 113–23, and the sections of Bahya ben Asher's *Kad ha-Qemah.*

65. For "questions and answers" as a mode of Jewish homiletics (and exegesis), see *Jewish Preaching*, pp. 74–75, esp. n. 28.

סדר להישיר הדרשנים

שאל ממני אחד החברים לחבר לו כלל קצר להורות דרך הדרש המעולה שרבים דרכו בו דרך לא סלולה ושחתו סדרו והדרו וחללו יפעתו ואומ׳ לתת את שאלתו ולעשות את בקשתו ולסלול ולסקל זאת המסלה היא העולה למעלה. חלקתיו לעשרה תנאים להיות נדרש לדורשיו ונמצא למבקשיו על נקלה. ומאשר לו הגדולה וממנו מענה ותהלה אשא תפלה לשום בפי מלה, כמאמ׳ נעים זמירות תבענה שפתי תהלה.[1]

הא׳ לבאר שהפסוק או המאמ׳ שמיסד עליו הדורש מדרשו שיהיה מכוון ליסוד הבנין. וכבר ידעת לפי שיעור היסוד יהיה הבנין. על כן צריך הדורש שיבחר לו פרק או מאמ׳ כולל רוב עניני הפרשה או הענין שמכוין לדרוש בו ויסדר עליו המדרש שדרשו חז״ל אם ימצא. ויזהר בקריאת הפסוק בלי שבוש כלל ויבאר איזה מקומו ואם הפסוק נקשר עם מה שלפניו ויסדרם יחד. זכר לדבר לב חכם ישכיל פיהו.[2]

הב׳ שיפרש תחלה פשט המקרא על אפניו במלותיו, ואם יש בו שתוף ר״ל באחת מתבותיו ויבאר שתופה. ואם הוא מן הפסוק שסובל נגלה ונסתר יקדים לבאר הנגלה שהוא המשל ויאמ׳ המשל שהוא הנמשל. ויקשור הפרשה או הענין שכוון לדרוש בו עמם ר״ל שאם יהיה הענין שפתח לדרוש בו נופל על הנגלה אחר שפירש לו הנגלה יסמוך לקשרו עמו וישוב אח״כ לבאר הנסתר ואם הענין נופל על הנסתר יפרש הנגלה והנסתר כאחד ויסמוך לנסתר הענין המכוון. זכר לדבר תפוחי זהב במשכיות כסף.[3]

הג׳ שיתרחק מן המדרשות וההגדות והמדברות דרך הפלגה וגוזמא או דרך חידה שאין השכל מקבלן זולתי אם ידע להם ביאור או ציור להקריבן אל השכל ולא ידרוש בגדולות ובנפלאות ממנו או בדבר שיש בו מבוכה או ספוק ולא יוכל לדברו ולישבו ונשאר הדבר בקושיהו מסילה ודרך לא סלולה. זכר לדבר יושר לבי אמרי.[4]

1. תה׳ קיט קעא.
2. משלי טז כג.
3. משלי כה יא.
4. איוב לג ג.

הד' שיזהר מלדרוש בדברים שהם האמונה המקובלת והמפורסמת
באומה אבל תהיה מגמתו להישיר העם באמונות אמתיות ומיוסדות על
קבלת האבות ובמעלות המדות החמודות. ויזהר מאד מלדרוש כל הנמצא
מסודר בספרים ואם חתמו המדברים בו הדעות בספרים שונות, אבל
יחבר ויבור לו מהם הדברים הברים שיועילו מאד לשומעיהם ולא
יזיקום, שדברים רבים ימצאו בספרים שהם נכונים ע"ד האמת ולא
יבינום העם ואין ראוי לדרוש בהם כי אם מבין בקרב מבינים. זכר לדבר
הסר ממך עקשות פה ולזות שפתים הרחק ממך.[5]

הה' שלא ידלג מענין לענין שאינו דומה לו זולתי אם יהיה לו עמו שום
הקשר, וזה כלל גדול בזו המלאכה ר"ל שידע לסדר הדברים סדור נאה
ויסמוך ענין לדומה לו. וכשיכוין מדרשו לדבר מיוחד אל יפתח בו בתחלה
אבל יפתח בענין אחר נאות לפי הפרק והדבר המכוון ששם מגמתו אליו
ימצאהו בתוך דבריו או יאחרהו שזה נכון והגון מאד. ואם הוא מן
הראויים להוכיח יוכיח מעין הענין שדורש בו שבזה יהיה לו פתחון פה.
המשל בזה אם יהיה דורש בפרש' אברהם אבי' ע"ה שיהיה גומל חסדים
לחמו נתן מימיו נאמנים לאורחים ורץ לפניהם והשתחוה לפניהם, אחר
שיסדר הדבר יאמ' אבל אשמים אנחנו[6] שאין בנו עושה חסד וכדומה,
ובזה תועלת גדול למבין ודרך נכונה, וישימו יד על פה שתקשה בעינם
התוכחה. זכר לדבר שמחה לאיש במענה פיו.[7]

הו' שלא ירבה בדברים ר"ל שאם הוא מתכוין לבאר ענין אחד אל
ירבה עליו דברים שהענין המכוון דומה לגרגיר בר והדברים הבאים
עליו דומין לתבן ומה תועלת למלאת שק תבן בשביל גרגיר בר שהביא
בתוכו! אבל ירבה בעניינים וימעיט ויקצר בדברים, ויביא מהראיות
והפירוש המתברר שהוא האמת לבד ולא יאריך בפירושים שונים ובראיות
חלוקות כמו ר' פלו' אמ' כך ור' פלו' אמ' כך שזה אבוד זמן והפסד
ובלבוליו. גם בעניינים הויכוחיים לא יאריך יותר מהראוי. זכר לדבר ברב
דברים לא יחדל פשע.[8]

5. משלי ד כד.
6. ע"פ בר' מב כא.
7. משלי טו כג.
8. משלי י יט.

הז' שישתדל הדורש לחדש דבר במדרשו בפשט פסוק או בציירו הגדה או בסדור ענין שזה תפארת גדול לדורש, ולא ידרוש בדברים שהם כבר שגורים בפי העם היודעים והבלתי יודעים וישמיט ידו מלדרוש בדברים יקחו בושה שומעיהם לשומען כמו בדרכי המשכב והדוה ובנדתה וכדומה לזה זולתי אם ירבה בזה דרך כלל בלשון נקייה להרים מכשול מדרך העם. זכר לדבר ומצא חן ושכל טוב.[9]

החי' שיהיה הדורש נאה כמו שארז"ל נאה דורש נאה מקיים,[10] ומה מגונה להוכיח זולתו מה שאינו מוכיח עצמו ומושל בתאותו ואם השומעים יריחו בו שאינו שומר מוסר ומצוה לא יחושו לדבריו ולא יפלו בלבם אלא כנפול טפת מים על צור החלמיש ולפעמים יסתתרו אמריו בזכרו שהוא עושה הפכם ואם מעשיו מסכימים על דבריו ועל דברתו אז ידבר לבטח ואז יאשרו שומעיו דבריו ויאמינו דבריו. זכר לדבר ואיש שומע לנצח ידבר.[11]

הט' שיכתוב הדורש מדרשו על ספר ואם ילאה לכתב כלו יכתוב כלליו ויחלקהו לחלקים ויציב להם ציורים בלבו למען יהיו שגורים בפיו וישנה וישלש דברים שעתיד לדרוש ויוציאם אל הפועל ואל יסמוך על בקיאותו שמא ישכח דבר מסדריו או יכשל בדבריו ויקח לו בושת שלם בהתגלות קלונו בתוך קהל ועדה. ומאד מאד יזהר הדורש ברבים ואף כי במעמד המשכילים לצרוף וללבן ולברר ולזקק דבריו שבעתים וכל דבר שמוציא מפיו שסובל משמעיות יבארהו ויפרשהו פן יחסדהו שומע לייחס לו שום דעת נפסד שבמשמעות אותו דבר. זכר לדבר אז ראה ויספרה הכינה וגם חקרה ואז ויאמר לאדם.[12]

הי' שידבר בנחת ושובה ר"ל בנחת ותשובה בלי כעס ומריבה. ואם יוכיח למראה עיניו ולמשמע אזניו בין יבין את אשר לפניו ואל יתפאר בתבונתו ובחכמתו. וישאל רשיון מן הצבור ומן החכמים אשר לפניו גם כי יחכם מהם, ואף כי יחכמו ממנו. ויהיו דבריו בו מועטים ר"ל שלא יאריך להביא עליו ראיות ודברים כמנהג רוב הדרשנים ולא יחוש לתופש הרשויות המסודרים בספרים שזה אבוד זמן. ויחתום הדרש בפסוק

9. משלי ג ד.
10. השוה יבמות סג ב, חגיגה יד ב.
11. משלי כא כח.
12. איוב כח כז–כח.

שהתחיל בו ויחזור עליו לקשור סופו בתחלתו ויחתום בדבר טוב ר"ל
להטיב אחריתו מראשיתו. זכר לדבר טוב אחרית דבר מראשיתו.[13]

הדרכים מהמדרשות הם ג"כ שלשה: מורכב כמו הדרש מהחלקים
שבפסוק הראשון יהיו מסובבים החלקים, הב׳ פשוט כמו מי שיקח נושא
אחד ויביא ראיות רבות מפסוקים והגדות ומאמרים לנסות זו הענין, הג׳
לא פשוט ולא מורכב אלא מקושיות ותירוצים ופשטים ועניינים. תם
ונשלם שבח לבורא עולם.

13. קהלת ז ח.

13

"Make Vows and Pay Them":
A Newly Discovered Confraternity
Sermon from Spain

The Firkovitch collection of Hebrew manuscripts in the Library of St. Petersburg includes a previously unknown collection of seven Jewish sermons from early fifteenth-century Spain.[1] It contains 43 folios, written in a fifteenth-century Provencal cursive hand. At the top of the first page is the title "Sefer ha-Derashah le-Hakham . . ."; after a name that has been crossed out appears the name Astruc Hasdai.[2]

The complicated bibliographical problems relating to the collection can be indicated only in passing here. Some of its sermons appear also in other manuscripts. The first (fol. 1r–10r), a formal sermon for a wedding, is found also in manuscripts at Harvard and Moscow:[3] Houghton Hebrew MS 61 (fol. 134r–146v) and Moscow Hebrew MS 926 (fol. 157v–166v), in both of which the sermon is attributed to Zerahiah Ha-Levi. Although these other manuscripts have been studied, it has not previously been noted that the preacher refers in his sermon to his teachers present in the congregation, identifying them as *shenei benei ha-Yitshar,* presumably Mattathias Yizhari and his brother. This sermon is incomplete in the St. Petersburg MS but complete in the other two.

The second sermon, on the verse fragment *God will see* (Gen. 22:14), is also found in the manuscripts at Harvard and Moscow.[4] In this case, how-

---

1. First Series, nu. 507; a microfilm of this manuscript first reached the Institute for the Microfilming of Hebrew Manuscripts in Jerusalem during the spring of 1994, where it was catalogued under the number 51312; I am grateful to Dr. Abraham David for calling my attention to this text.

2. The name is written beginning with an *'ayin,* a highly unusual spelling. Astruc Hasdai is known from governmental records to have settled in Saragossa in the late 1360s; Baer states that "no data are available about his activities (Baer, *History* 2:61). The appearance of the name on the manuscript is not sufficient to establish Astruc as the author of all the sermons.

3. On the Moscow MS, see above, chap. 12.

4. Anonymous, Harvard, fol. 11a–20b; Anonymous, Moscow, fol. 99a–106b. Ari Ackerman has written a Hebrew University MA thesis on this sermon (see Bibliography, "Ackerman").

ever, the St. Petersburg MS is more complete than the others, containing a critical page of challenges to Hasdai Crescas' position on divine attributes that the other manuscripts do not have. In this sermon, Crescas is identified by the preacher as *morenu ha-Rav*; he says he has heard Crescas discuss the issue in his sermons and that it also appears in *Or ha-Shem*.

The third sermon, which is not known from any other source, is translated below and will be discussed in more detail. There follow three eulogies, the third of which is the same as a text appearing in an Amsterdam MS, where it is identified as a eulogy for Hasdai Crescas.[5] Finally, there is a sermon on Exodus 19:9, possibly intended for the holiday of Shavu'ot. Detailed study is required to determine whether all the sermons are by the same preacher, and who this preacher was—a project being undertaken in a doctoral dissertation by Ari Ackerman at the Hebrew University. At present, it can only be said that they emanate from the circle of disciples of Hasdai Crescas, and possibly of Mattathias Yizhari, that they reflect the full integration of philosophical material into a traditional Jewish framework,[6] and that they serve as fine examples of Jewish homiletical art and paideia at the beginning of the final century of life in Spain. No exact dates are given in the sermons, but one of the eulogies refers to the "oppression which causes us sorrow every day" (fol. 35v), and it refers to a disputation that might well be the Disputation of Tortosa.[7] The eulogy for Crescas and the references to Mattathias Yizhari are all consistent with the second decade of the fifteenth century.

The sermon translated below is a formal occasional sermon, delivered at the invitation of the leadership of the *Rodefei Tsedeq* Society, probably of

---

5. Amsterdam Ms. Rosenthal 92 (Catalogue I, nu. 39, pp. 16–17), fols. 381a–384; the description at the beginning of the eulogy is, "A sermon for the deceased, speaking about the Ten Commandments, when the light of the Rabbi En Hasdai Crescas died out." Ari Ackerman is publishing this text. Unfortunately, there is little if anything in the content of the eulogy that would enable us to identify the deceased as Crescas, as all of the references to the deceased are quite general. There are no biographical details, no concrete assessment of Crescas's achievements, and little evidence of genuine emotion or true homiletical art.

6. The sermons contain specific references to Aristotle's *Ethics* (e.g. fols. 23r, 28r, 33v), *Physics* (e.g. fol. 2r, twice), *Heavens* (e.g. fols 39v–40r), and logical works (e.g., fols. 34r, 42v). They also contain general statements such as "It is explained in the disciplines of logic that motion pertains to four categories: substance, quantity, quality, and place" (fol. 1v), and references to magnetism and number theory (below, n. 25). This circle needs to be compared with the neo-Platonic circle studied extensively by Dov Schwartz (see, with special reference to preaching, Schwartz, "Yetsi'at Mitsrayim").

7. Speaking of the Christian argument that spiritual rewards are not explicit in the Torah, the preacher notes that "recently very much has been spoken about this because of the Disputation" (fol. 35a). This was a common theme in Jewish-Christian polemic, addressed by contemporaries such as Joseph Albo, although not known to have been an important topic in Tortosa.

Saragossa, at a special event called "The Holiday of the Vigil" (*Hag ha-Mish-marah*) in the synagogue where the Society functioned.[8] The preacher himself cannot be identified with certainty, but he describes himself as holding the position of *memmuneh mursheh* in the synagogue.[9] In the introductory section, he claims to be unworthy of addressing such a distinguished audience—a commonplace expression of modesty, but unlikely to be used by a rabbi known as an outstanding scholar.

Structure

By the end of the fifteenth century, formal sermons of the Sephardi tradition began with standard texts: a verse from the Pentateuchal lesson of the week (the *nose* or "theme") and a passage of rabbinic literature (the *ma'amar* or "dictum"). Earlier, the structure had not yet been established, and extant sermons reveal a fluidity of form.[10] The Holiday of the Vigil sermon begins in the manner of the thirteenth-century sermon, with a verse from the Hagiographa. But the manner of treatment is totally different from the earlier style, which typically had its roots in the homiletical midrash. Rather than providing various interpretations of the verse and then relating it to the lesson, the verse itself provides the structure for the body of the sermon, as we shall see.

One characteristic of the fifteenth-century formal occasional sermon was an introduction in which the preacher justified his task, presenting reasons that might have impelled him to refrain from speaking and other reasons that convinced him to proceed.[11] As the nature of his material required professions of unworthiness, it could easily turn into a predictable affectation of modesty.[12] Occasionally, however, the preacher did include personal material of significant interest,[13] and in this sermon the speaker divulges some infor-

---

8. See nn. 8 and 125 to the text, below. This is the only example I know of a sermon occasioned by a confraternity celebration, an occasion that needs to be added to those I discussed in *Jewish Preaching*, pp. 26–37. The manuscript sermons of Morteira contain many linked with the confraternities of early seventeenth-century Amsterdam. For medieval Christian confraternity preaching, see *Le mouvement confraternel*, pp. 21, 148–49; Weissman, pp. 100–103.

9. See n. 9 to the text, below.

10. See *Jewish Preaching*, pp. 65–66.

11. Ibid., pp. 76–77.

12. Cf. Curtius, pp. 83–85.

13. For a striking example, see the introduction by Joseph Garçon to his first sermon in Salonika (*Jewish Preaching*, pp. 202–6)—an introduction, it must be confessed, more interesting than the rest of the sermon.

mation about his position in the community and his relationship with the voluntary society or confraternity that invited him to preach on this occasion.

In addition, there is also a substantive link between the introduction and the body of the sermon. Ideas brought into the introduction—the nature of an obligation, divesting oneself of free will by entering an obligation, compulsion as a factor that invalidates the obligation—appear at first merely to meet the needs of the expected conventional content at the beginning of the formal occasional sermon. It turns out, however, that each of these ideas reappears in the body of the sermon, integrally connected with the substantive discussion of the preacher's central topic.

The formal request for permission to speak (*reshut*) signals the conclusion of the introduction and the transition to the body of the sermon,[14] which begins with a programmatic statement that outlines the content to come:

> I will analyze the verse cited at the beginning of my speech, namely, *Make vows and pay them to the Lord your God* (Ps. 76:12). In order for the analysis to proceed in a fitting order, I shall divide the speech into four parts. The first part will be about the first term, namely *Make vows,* and in it I shall explain the essence of the vow. The second part will be about the second term, namely *and pay them,* and in it I shall explain the payment of the vow. The third part will be about the conjunction of these two terms, namely *Make vows and pay them.* In it I shall analyze the vow once it has been paid, and the relationship of an act performed as an obligation after having taken a vow with that same act performed without having taken a vow. The fourth part will be about the terms, *to the Lord your God.* In it I shall analyze that to which the vow is undertaken, and I shall explain how we should take vows and set up for ourselves commandments for the service of God beyond those written in our sacred Torah.[15]

Two aspects of this passage deserve attention. First, the division of the verse into its component terms and the structuring of the body of the sermon in accordance with these terms was not a common technique in Jewish homiletics. The "division" of the theme was, however, characteristic of the scholastic

---

14. Other sermons in the manuscript reveal the force of this convention. The first includes a discussion of form in the sermon, noting that the preacher's "first effort should be in the taking of *reshut*" (fol. 2v). The fourth indicates a diversion from the norm: "The analysis of this statement at present will not be done in the customary homiletical manner, following the custom of others who preach in public, and it will therefore be possible for me to absolve myself of the need for an introductory requesting of *reshut* and the expected asking of forgiveness [for preaching]" (fol. 28v).

15. Anonymous, St. Petersburg, fol. 21r.

thematic sermon. Thus, we seem to have here another piece of evidence in the largely untold story of Christian influence on medieval Jewish preaching.[16]

This passage also reveals a preacher who clearly liked to organize his thoughts and, even more important, cared that his listeners would be able to follow exactly where his presentation was going. This concern is manifest in the continuation, where each section is concluded with a statement announcing that a major unit has come to an end and a brief recapitulation of its content.

The first three sections of the sermon all discuss various aspects of the vow. The first is devoted to its definition, one that was not taken from any classical Jewish source but instead appears to be the preacher's own. The content of the definition will be discussed below; formally, it consists of six elements, each of which is explained in turn. Thus just as the body of the sermon is divided in accordance with the elements of the biblical verse, so the subsection is divided in accordance with an external schema: the preacher's definition of the sermon's fundamental concept.

The second section, dealing with the timely payment of vows, is quite brief; it serves the function of applying the theoretical discussion of the vow to the occasion by introducing the special vows of the Society pertaining to prayer and study. These vows are picked up later in the sermon.

The third section is in the form of a "disputed question," which requires a cogent formal argument to be made on each of two antithetical propositions before the conundrum is resolved. One of the most characteristic modes of scholastic reasoning, the appearance of this form in Jewish homiletics around the year 1400 is a dramatic example of Christian influence.[17] Indeed, the present question, pertaining to the relative value of an act performed freely without a vow as opposed to one performed as a result of a vow, is the most perfect example of the form I have found in any Jewish sermon. Again, the preacher wants the audience to follow each element of his analysis: five arguments on one side, followed by four arguments on the opposite side, then five "true premises," followed by a set of conclusions in syllogistic form, and finally a response to each of the five arguments on the side that has been shown to be false. The rigor of the intellectual exercise and the clarity of exposition must have generated some interest and even excitement in listeners who might not have responded to a technical halakhic discourse with enthusiasm.

---

16. See my comment in *Jewish Preaching*, pp. 70–71, n. 19, and p. 174, n. 63, above. On the "division" in Christian preaching, see, for example, *Medieval Rhetoric*, pp. 273–76.

17. On this form, see *Jewish Preaching*, pp. 75, 180, 395–96, and above, pp. 84–86, 171.

In the fourth and longest section, the structure is least obvious, yet the careful listener would not have had difficulty following it. It is divided into two large thematic subsections, indicated (in reverse order) by an introductory statement:

> I would say that the intent of this verse [Ps. 76:12] is to encourage and stimulate individual human beings to exercise their ingenuity to find strategies and discover ways to increase their service of God. For we, the Jewish people, are borne aloft by His acts of love, and *day by day He supports us* (Ps. 68:20) with beneficence that we do not deserve.

The preacher begins by discussing God's gracious acts of love and beneficence toward human beings in general and Jews in particular. In addition to the creation and sustaining of all existing beings, there is the bestowing of eternal life and the provision of the path to reach that goal: the gift of Torah and commandments. The discussion of eternal life, understood philosophically as the natural communion between the individual soul, removed from the dross of impure matter, and pure incorporeal intellect, leads to a fascinating digression on hidden attractions in the realms of nature and numbers. But the preacher brings the listener "back to the subject," concluding this subsection with a recapitulation of all God's kindnesses.

The second subsection is devoted to the necessary human response to these divine acts of love: a full and constant acknowledgment, including an acceptance of obligations toward service beyond those mandated by Jewish law. This leads to a discussion of the limitations of prayer in praise of an infinite Being. On philosophical grounds, the preacher, like Maimonides, seems to prefer a silent devotion that does not even attempt to articulate praises in finite and imperfect words. On the other hand, the occasion requires him to reaffirm the importance of public prayer—the special concern of the confraternity that he is addressing—as well as the intense study of Torah. A peroration urges the members of the Society to continued devotion, linking the fulfillment of vows with the messianic hope for redemption.

Content

As in every traditional Jewish sermon, there is a substantial amount of exegetical material. The art of the preacher is not merely to make assertions but to root them in the texts of the tradition, if possible through a novel yet plausible interpretation of these texts. Our preacher mobilizes verses from all over the Bible, but his favorite resource—at least for this sermon—is clearly the book of Psalms, some fifteen different verses from which are cited with homiletical commentary in the course of the discourse.[18] Because of the nature of the subject matter, it is not surprising that considerable rabbinic material pertaining to vows was included. It is usually not given much interpretation. Occasionally, the preacher uses aggadah in a homiletical fashion. One interesting example, at the end of his discussion of the world to come, is his philosophical interpretation of a statement that he describes as "strange at first glance": God "brings out the sun from its sheath" to punish the wicked and heal the righteous in the world to come (B. AZ 3b–4a).

Despite the focus on this legal material, however, the sermon is worlds away from the technical Talmudic discourse common in much north European Jewish preaching. The substance comes from Jewish law, but the form is derived from Christian scholasticism and the animating spirit not so much halakhic as philosophical.

Let us look again at the definition of the vow that the preacher provides as the structural framework for Section I of the sermon: "The vow is a binding agreement, uttered verbally, to do something or not to do it, teaching about a matter in the soul, by choice, upon which acquiescence rests." Although each element of the definition is substantiated with rabbinic sources, the actual style of definition is more scholastic than rabbinic. Compare the following definition of the *votum* from the *Code of Canon Law*: "A vow is a deliberate and free promise made to God of a good that is possible and better than its omission, the fulfillment of which obliges from the virtue of religion."[19] One can imagine a Christian preacher addressing each term in the definition and explaining it on the basis of authoritative sources just as our preacher does.

The same is true for the "disputed question" that comprises Section III of the sermon. To be sure, the argument on both sides of the question—

18. In the order in which they appear, Ps. 76:12 (the theme verse), 66:14, 132:3–4, 100:2, 145:9, 16:11, 139:14, 42:2, 84:12, 139:17–18, 65:2, 140:10, 116:18–19. This does not count verses cited in the context of their rabbinic exegesis (Ps. 132:2, 119:106, 92:3, 55:19), or phrases from Psalms used for stylistic effect.

19. *Codex juris canonici,* CIV c. 1307.1, cited in *New Catholic Encyclopedia,* s.v. Vow. An interesting basis for comparison with the material in our sermon would be the discussion of the vow in *Siete Partidas,* I,8, pp. 318–25. The vow (*votum*) was an important theme in medieval Christian thought in the context of the debate over the status of "works of supererogation," a central theme of the present sermon. See *Dictionnaire de Théologie Catholique* 15:3197. In addition to this general theological problem, there was a specific institutional problem about the use of oaths and vows by laymen to solemnify the corporate obligation of the confraternity and make the failure to fulfill such obligation into a mortal sin. In the fifteenth and sixteenth centuries, there was a strong tendency to discourage such confraternity oaths; see Weissman, pp. 97–98; Flynn, pp. 13, 36, 153 n. 66. All of this provides a broader context for the discussion in our sermon.

whether a vow enhances or diminishes the quality of a religious act—reflects the classical Jewish ambivalence about the status of vows.[20] But the mode of argumentation is not at all in the traditional Talmudic dialectical style; it is taken directly from scholastic discourse,[21] and the syllogisms that enter into the resolution of the conflicting positions reveal the impact of the Aristotelian legacy on Jewish homiletics.[22] The conclusion—that an act undertaken as the result of a religious obligation has a higher status than an act performed freely in full human autonomy—is not a surprising position for a Jew to hold, but the force of the argument against it reveals the challenge opposing views presented and the courage it must have taken to face up to them.

One of the most valuable aspects of the sermon—and one of its methodological challenges—is the evidence it provides for the nature of the audience, and thereby the level of knowledge of a particular Jewish community. This sermon does not rule out the possibility that the preacher was a serious Talmudic scholar; such a scholar may have chosen to communicate on a relatively elementary level for a particular audience.[23] What seems beyond question, however, is that the listeners could not have been an audience of scholars or advanced students, even though they were members of a confraternity devoted to Torah study. Little if anything about the vow is taken for granted; all that the listeners would need to know is presented with clarity. On the other hand, perhaps because of the forms used (the definition and the disputed question), the sermon does not come across as disappointingly superficial or trivial. Listeners might well have learned something, or felt they had been given a helpful review of what they already knew and derived aesthetic pleasure from confronting familiar material presented in a rather different way.

---

20. See, for example, the contrasting positions of R. Judah and R. Meir recorded in B. Hul 2a and Ned 9a, cited by our preacher in his sermon at n. 62 (p. 203, below), and Maimonides *Code, Nedarim* 13, 23–24.

21. We might compare a question from Aquinas's *Summa Theologica* II-II 184,3: "Whether in this life, perfection consists in the observance of the commandments or of the counsels?" Aquinas concludes that it is the commandments (love of God and love of neighbor), rather than counsels (such as selling all one's possessions and giving to the poor, Mt. 19:21), which provide the primary mode of perfection.

22. For syllogisms in fifteenth-century Jewish sermons, see *Jewish Preaching*, p. 386 n. 7, and above, pp. 83–84.

23. Some of the halakhic material in the sermons of the great Spanish Talmudist Isaac Aboab is quite elementary (see below, chap. 15). The technical halakhic discourses of Ezekiel Landau in *Doresh le-Tsiyon* suggest a totally different audience from his sermons in *Derushei ha-Tselaḥ* (cf. *Jewish Preaching*, p. 360).

If the primary category of material in the Holiday of the Vigil sermon is the vow, the second category is philosophical in nature. The philosophical orientation of the preacher is not as obvious as in the second sermon of the manuscript, with its detailed discussion of the problem of divine attributes, including a critique of Crescas's position. Although the only external philosophical work cited here is Aristotle's *Ethics,* the sermon nevertheless relies on the philosophical modes of reasoning already discussed (definition, disputed question, syllogisms) and on philosophical vocabulary used throughout. In addition, we see clear philosophical commitments in the presentation, primarily in section IV, of several classical themes of Jewish thought.

The first is the nature of eternal life, the world to come, and Gehenna. Here is the preacher's presentation of the *summum bonum,* the eternal bliss that is the ultimate goal of religious aspiration:

> This bliss is the communion of the soul with the Rock from which it was hewn (cf. Isa. 51:1). After the removal of the material component, which hinders such communion, when the soul is pure and cleansed of false ideas and evil personality traits that derive from habitual sinful acts, communion results. Between the soul and the incorporeal intellect with which it has communion there is love and desire because of the compatibility and interrelationship between them. (fol. 25v)

Not a reward bestowed by an omnipotent God for the obedient performance of irrational commandments, the *summum bonum* is the result of a natural process inherent in the cultivation of the potential in the human soul, necessarily following once the soul is purified from its contamination by the material component, as understood by the religious philosophers.

Directly connected is the philosophical interpretation of the Song of Songs as pertaining to the relationship between the individual soul and the "incorporeal intellect." It is unclear whether our preacher is referring to the "active intellect" of the philosophers or directly to God, but he clearly stands in a philosophical exegetical tradition adumbrated by Maimonides and powerfully exemplified by the fourteenth-century scholar Levi ben Gershom.[24]

---

24. This philosophical exegesis contrasts with the traditional midrashic exegesis that understood the Song of Songs as speaking of the love between God and the personified people of Israel, expressed through the events of Jewish history. The love between the *individual* and God as the esoteric content of Song of Songs is asserted by Maimonides in *Code, Teshuvah* 8,5 and exemplified in various commentaries from the thirteenth and fourteenth centuries. See Rosenberg, "Parshanut." On the commentary by Gersonides, the one most likely to have influenced our preacher, see Kellner, "Gersonides' Commentary." Kellner is preparing an edition of this work for the Yale Judaica Series.

The application of the concept of "friendly numbers" to the interpretation of two verses from Song of Songs may appear to be more mystical but is also in the philosophical tradition.[25]

Finally, the interpretation of the rabbinic concepts of "world to come" and "Gehenna" reflects the preacher's philosophical commitment. The "world to come" is simply identified with the communion of intellects that is the supreme reward; "Gehenna" is the pain caused by the absence of such communion. Rejected by clear implication here is any conception of "hell" as a positive entity in which actual punishments are meted out against soul or body.[26] This is read into an aggadic statement about God's "removing the sun out of its sheath" and using it to punish the wicked. Following the tradition of philosophical exegesis of problematic aggadot, the preacher transforms this vivid image into a metaphor for removing the soul from the body and allowing it to feel the anguish of distance from God.[27]

The second subject in which the philosophical orientation of the preacher is apparent in his discussion of the divine attributes, the apprehension of metaphysical matters pertaining to God, and prayer. For the philosopher, prayer of praise, which speaks about God in positive terms, was highly problematic, given the assumption that no human words can accurately express the divine reality, and any attempt to do so is bound to mislead. Wrestling with this problem, Maimonides concluded that the highest form of prayer is pure intellectual contemplation without words. He reinterpreted the phrase *lekha dumyah tehillah* (Ps. 65:2), usually understood to mean "to You praise is silence," referring to the *inadequacy* of human praise, to mean "to You silence is [the highest] praise," suggesting the undesirability of verbal praise.[28]

This is precisely the interpretation given by our preacher: David discovered "that the very best form of acknowledgment was silence, and so he remained silent." Yet the nature of the present occasion required that he reaffirm the significance of the public prayer undertaken by members of the confraternity, and indeed he does so. As in the original discussion of Maimonides himself, there is a tension between the philosophical conclusion that seems to subvert the importance of statutory liturgical prayer and the practical needs of a Jewish community for which such prayer served as an important cohesive force.

---

25. See p. 212 below, especially n. 91.

26. For relationship of these ideas with earlier Jewish philosophers, especially Maimonides, see n. 96 to the text.

27. See n. 97 to the text.

28. Maimonides, *Guide* 1,59.

All of this philosophical material is thoroughly and naturally integrated into the fabric of traditional Jewish texts through homiletical exegesis. While one may imagine Jews in the audience who might have been perturbed by the spiritualistic eschatology and the theoretically radical implications for prayer, it does not seem that they would have found the material—which is not at all technical or abstruse—difficult to follow.[29] And while some of the opponents of philosophy might have resented its obvious influence upon the preacher, the sermon does not obviously show philosophy as a radical threat, corrosively undermining the foundations of Jewish life.

The importance of the sermon, then, lies not in any striking new ideas, but rather in its exemplary function of demonstrating what a group of Jews gathering for a special occasion might have expected to hear. It is of historical value not because it captures a unique moment in Jewish experience, but because it reveals a preacher articulating an integrated worldview in which philosophy has been accommodated to Jewish content, structuring his presentation so that what seems to us to be a long discourse could readily be followed by his listeners, combining exegesis and exposition to reaffirm the values of prayer and study, and thereby undergirding the significance of an important voluntary society within the Jewish *aljama*. So little from this period that we can identify as a record of how tradition and new forms were mediated in the homiletical enterprise has been preserved. The present sermon is a significant addition to our evidence for this undertaking.

---

29. Contrast the material in one of Isaac Aboab's sermons, cited above, pp. 79–80.

MAKE VOWS AND PAY THEM TO THE LORD YOUR GOD (Ps. 76:12).

[Introduction]

There are two general grounds for excusing oneself: unawareness and compulsion. Unawareness is a basis for self-justification, for it totally removes and wipes away like a cloud those offenses for the intentional transgression of which there is no punishment of *karet*.[1] Indeed, with the help of a sacrifice, it removes even those sins for which *karet* applies upon intentional transgression, as is seen in the lesson *Va-Yiqra* [Lev. 1:1–5:26], and as the sages explained in the chapter beginning "It is a great principle" of tractate Shabbat.[2] However, the claim of compulsion is a stronger and more substantial basis for excuse, for it removes even the mention of the sin, restoring the person who committed the offense because of compulsion to absolute innocence of any pertinent sin and any punishment. The sages said in the chapter beginning "R. Ishmael" of tractate Avodah Zarah: "The Merciful One exempts compulsion."[3] They proved this from the verse, *But you shall do nothing to the girl* (Deut. 22:26).[4]

This being so, inasmuch as I sense in myself a transgression, having sinned by presuming to ascend to this honor of which I am unworthy, namely to speak in this select assembly, with all the fine virtues of this place—a dwelling for our sacred Torah and a house of prayer—and the virtues of the listeners, their wisdom, understanding, knowledge, and ethical qualities, I have fled for help to the two grounds for excuse that I mentioned.

As for the first ground for excuse, namely unawareness, it is a help for me; its right hand sustains me[5] in the following manner. Seeing as my importance is absolutely minimal and my knowledge altogether tiny, I was unable to imagine the extent of my limitations. This is one kind of unawareness. Furthermore, because of the great importance of the listeners and the magnitude of their wisdom, I was unable to comprehend its extent. This is a second kind

---

1. *Karet,* literally "cutting off" or "excision," is a category of biblical punishment understood by the sages as death at God's instance, and not by judgment of a human court. The language "wipes away like a cloud" is based on Isa. 44:22.

2. For the biblical material, see Leviticus 4:27–5:6 and 5:15–19; the Talmudic reference is to B. Shab 67b, 70b.

3. B. AZ 54a.

4. The biblical passage is understood to be a case of rape; the woman, a victim of compulsion, is not punished for an act that would have merited the death penalty had she performed it willingly. Cf. also Maimonides, *Code, Yesodei ha-Torah* 5,4.

5. Cf. Ps. 18:36.

of unawareness. These are but glimpses of the kinds of unawareness that have impelled me, prevailed over me, and brought me to perform this task. For if I were not ignorant of these things I have mentioned, if indeed I could (21r) imagine the utter depth of my ignorance and the full extent of the listeners' virtues, I would not have permitted myself to perform it.

Yet ignorance and unawareness are not sufficient for excuse, which sometimes requires the addition of a sacrifice in order to remove the stain of sin. We see this in the case of our ancestor Jacob. He said, *Surely the Lord is present in this place and I did not know it* (Gen. 28:16), afraid that perhaps he did not have the cleanliness and purity appropriate for the holiness of that place. And even though he had one of the categories of excuse, namely unawareness, as he said *and I did not know it,* he feared that this excuse might not suffice for him. That is why it goes on to say, *Frightened, he said, How awesome is this place! This is none other than the abode of God* (Gen. 28:17).[6] So it is for me: since I am concerned that the aforementioned excuse of unawareness might not suffice for me, I combine it with the second kind of excuse, that based on compulsion, in the following manner.

When I entered a solemn agreement with the members of this splendid Society, I divested myself of the freedom of choice that I had in all matters pertaining to the Society.[7] I surrendered my own heart and will to their will, before God. And after they insisted that I perform this task, I decided to fulfil their request, for they compelled me by saying that I am obliged to pay my vow, that *I must not change what I have uttered* (Ps. 89:35), as I said at the beginning of my speech, *Make vows and pay them* (Ps. 76:12). Furthermore, they could argue against me by claiming that since the vows that the members of this Society have taken upon themselves are remembered and fulfilled every day in this synagogue, and this Holiday of Vigil[8] is also ob-

---

6. If the excuse of unawareness were sufficient, there would have been no reason for Jacob to have been frightened, as he did not know that God was present in the place.

7. Later on in the sermon it will become clear that this is the *Rodefei Tsedeq* Society (see below, p. 221). The language "divested myself of freedom of choice" adumbrates an argument that will be presented as part of the "disputed question" in Section III of the sermon (see below, p. 201.)

8. *Hag ha-Mishmerah,* literally, "the Holiday of the Vigil," is apparently the annual event celebrating the *Ashmoret ha-Boqer* Society (*confradia de la Maytinal, d'Azmuro*), the members of which undertook to rise before dawn and pray at sunrise. See Assis, "Welfare and Mutual Aid," p. 139 with references in n. 125; Blasco-Martinez, pp. 18–19. The Society carried out its work in one of the synagogues, as contemporary Christian confraternities were based in churches, convents, and sanctuaries (see Flynn, p. 19). The annual festivities that provide the occasion for the sermon would appear to correspond to the annual celebration of the patron saint in the Christian confraternities.

served in it, bestowing unquestioned honor upon those who pray in this synagogue, and I am *memunneh mursheh,* appointed to supervise matters pertaining to the synagogue,[9] I must perforce pay close attention to its affairs, I must not avert my face from insults,[10] I must speak out even in the presence of kings without shame[11]—referring to rabbis, who are called "kings."[12]

And even though I could justify myself in this respect by saying that I am obliged to follow the teaching of our predecessors, who said in the chapter beginning "We do not teach" of tractate Hagigah,[13] "About that which is beyond you do not preach," yet they can argue back from the continuation of that statement: "That which is permitted to you (*she-hursheitah*) you should contemplate," explaining it to mean that a person should contemplate and devote his attention to a matter over which he has been appointed to a position of authority (*mursheh*).[14]

Therefore we shall rely upon these aforementioned excuses, even though they are weak in comparison with the power of the sin. With the permission, etc.[15]

[Body of Sermon]

I will analyze the verse cited at the beginning of my speech, namely, *Make vows and pay them to the Lord your God* (Ps. 76:12). In order for the analysis to proceed in a fitting order, I shall divide the speech into four parts. The first part will be about the first term, namely *Make vows,* and in it I shall explain the essence of the vow. The second part will be about the second term, namely *and pay them,* and in it I shall explain the payment of the vow. The third part will be about the conjunction of these two terms, namely *Make vows and pay them.* In it I shall analyze the vow once it has been paid, and the relationship of an act performed as an obligation after having taken a vow with that same act performed without having taken a vow. The fourth part will be about the terms, *to the Lord your God.* In it I shall analyze that

---

9. *Memmuneh* is one of the titles used for Dr. David Farar in Amsterdam; see below, chap. 16, p. 379 at n. 34. *Mursheh* was often used for communal emissaries or deputies entrusted with missions to the Court on behalf of the *aljama* (Epstein, 1:42); here, however, it seems to be an office of the synagogue.

10. Cf. Isa. 50:6.

11. Cf. Ps. 119:46.

12. Cf. B. Git 62a.

13. B. Hag 13a.

14. A play on words between the Hebrew quote from the Talmud and the Hebrew title of the preacher's position. This brings the preacher's justification to a witty conclusion.

15. The traditional *reshut,* or formal asking of "permission" to preach from the congregation and the Torah, is frequently not written out in the sermon texts. See *Jewish Preaching,* p. 77.

to which the vow is undertaken, and I shall explain how we should take vows and set up for ourselves commandments for the service of God beyond those written in His sacred Torah.[16] This is in order to *make a memorial for His wonders* (Ps. 111:4), to express gratitude for His infinite acts of love performed for us every day.

I. In the first part, pertaining to the term, *Make vows,* I have determined to explain the essence of the vow. Since the essence of something cannot be adequately explained without establishing its definition,[17] I will set forth here a definition of the vow, based on the underlying premises and root principles that we have about it, both from the verses of our sacred Torah and from the words of the sages (21v). It appears to be as follows: The vow is a binding agreement, uttered verbally, to do something or not to do it, teaching about a matter in the soul, by choice, upon which acquiescence rests. Even though this definition cannot be explained by demonstration, as are explanations in the discipline of logic, nevertheless in matters of convention such as this[18] it can be explained by using the premises we have about this subject.

a. I therefore say that the first term in the definition, namely our saying that it is a "binding agreement," serves in this definition the function of the genus.[19] This is confirmed from that which is defined, namely, the vow, for the vow is subsumed under one positive commandment, which states, *You must fulfill what has crossed your lips* (Deut. 23:24), and under one negative commandment, which states, *He shall not break his word* (Num. 30:3).[20] Since the vow is subsumed under these commandments, there can be no doubt that the vow is binding. For all the commandments bind us, for several reasons.

First, since every imperative statement from a master to a servant is naturally binding, even if the servant is not explicitly bound by it, so it is with

16. This impulse to go beyond the obligations specified in the Torah is not often associated with the spirituality of Spanish Jewish philosophers, but rather with German Pietists; see Soloveitchik, "Three Themes," esp. pp. 312–19. In the Christian context, the vow raised the problem of the value of works of "supererogation" (see note 19 to introduction).

17. Cf. Halevi, *Kuzari* 4,25: "the essence of a thing is its definition" (*mahut ha-davar gidro*); Maimonides, *Guide* beginning of 1,52.

18. *Devarim hanahiyyim*; for this terminology, cf. Albo, 3:228 (Book 3, chapter 25). The idea is that the elements of this definition will be explained on the basis of quotations from classical texts, not formally demonstrative arguments. Compare Joseph ibn Shem Tov's treatment of his own definition of "repentance" in Regev, "Teshuvah," p.198.

19. The first component of a definition is the "genus" to which that which is defined belongs (see Aristotle, *Topics* I,5,101b; *Analytica Posteriora* II,10,93b).

20. Cf. Maimonides, *Mitzvot*, Positive, 94, Negative, 157; *Code, Nedarim* 1,4.

the divine commandments, which are imperatives from the supreme Master, God, to those who serve Him, the children of Israel, as God said, *For it is to Me that the Israelites are servants* (Lev. 25:55).

Second, we have been explicitly bound to all the commandments in their entirety through one general statement at that great assembly at Mount Sinai, made by us willingly and freely, as it says in the lesson *Ve-Eleh ha-Mishpatim* [Exod. 21:1–24:18], *All that the Lord has spoken we will faithfully do* (Exod. 24:7).

There is also a third reason, pertaining specifically to the vow. This is that the words of the vow themselves denote a binding agreement. For the meaning of our saying "I vow this or that" is like the meaning of our saying "I am bound to this or that." This is the explanation of the first part of the definition.

b. The second part is "uttered verbally." Since the first part, "a binding agreement," encompasses all the commandments, it is followed by "uttered verbally," which differentiates the vow from the other commandments.[21] Now the confirmation of this is seen from that which is defined, namely the vow. In this regard, the sages said in tractate Shevu'ot, the second chapter beginning "There are two oaths": "Samuel said, If he decided in his heart, he must utter it with his lips, as the Torah says, *the clear utterance of her lips* (Num. 30:7), showing that the Merciful One made it dependent on her lips." The sages also proved this from the verse *You must fulfill what has crossed your lips* (Deut. 23:24), and from the verse, *utters with the lips* (Lev. 5:4).[22] Furthermore, we find that King David said, *I enter Your house with burnt offerings, I pay my vows to You, [vows] that my lips pronounced, that my mouth uttered in my distress* (Ps. 66:14).

And similarly with our ancestor Jacob, the one who first began with vows, as the sages said in Genesis Rabbah, "R. Abbahu said, *How he swore to the Lord, vowed to the Mighty One of Jacob* (Ps. 132:2): it did not say 'to the Mighty One of Abraham' or 'to the Mighty One of Isaac,' but rather *to the Mighty One of Jacob,* attributing the vow to the one who first began it."[23] Even though at this vision he was alone—no one with him but the glory of God that settled facing him—and it would have been enough for him to vow in the depths of his heart,[24] for *God sees into the heart* (I Sam 16:7),

---

21. In addition to the "genus," the definition contains at least one element that differentiates what is being defined from other members of the genus. See Aristotle, *Topics* 6,1, 139a; Maimonides, *Millot ha-Higayon,* 10,5, p. 71.

22. B. Shev 26b; cf. Maimonides, *Code, Shevu'ot* 2,10, *Nedarim* 2,2.

23. Gen. Rab. 70,1.

24. Language based on Job 17:1.

nevertheless in order to inform those human beings who would succeed him the proper manner regarding vows, since he was the first to begin with them, he uttered the vow with his mouth and lips, as the verse says, *Jacob made a vow, saying* (Gen. 28:20).

It is impossible to interpret the word *saying* the way we may interpret *God spoke to Moses saying*, which means that Moses should say to the children of Israel,[25] for with Jacob there was no statement from anyone else to him, and there was no one else to whom he could say this. We must necessarily say that the intent of the word *saying* was that he uttered the vow with his mouth and his lips, not that he conveyed its message in thought alone.[26] This is the explanation of the second part of the definition, which is the first of the differentiators.

c. The third part of the definition is our phrase "to do something or not to do it." Even though this is not placed in the definition in order to differentiate, it is placed there to provide information. It is not necessary that all the parts following in a definition after the genus be placed there to differentiate; some of the parts are placed there only to provide information, for the main principle and purpose of the definition is to provide information, while the differentiation is a consequence of this information.[27]

That this part is well understood, I will first set forth a proposition and say that vows are of two kinds: vows pertaining to optional matters, which are true vows, called "vows of utterance," and vows pertaining to commandments (22r) and the service of God, which are called "vows of consecration." These are analogous to oaths.[28] Since there is a great principle regarding true vows, namely that the vow take effect upon something of substance, it follows from this that the vow cannot apply to something insubstantial. There-

---

25. E.g. in a verse such as Exod. 13:1, where the word *leimor* (literally, "to say") may be interpreted to refer not to the content of what God said but as an instruction of what Moses should say to the Israelites (cf. Ibn Ezra ad loc.).

26. This is the interpretation of *Or ha-Ḥayyim* ad loc. I have not found this interpretation of *leimor* in Gen. 28:20 in an earlier commentator, although it does not seem to be an innovation of the preacher.

27. I do not know of a source for this statement that a definition may contain elements beyond the genus and specific differentiations. For the process by which a *series* of such differentiations are generated to make a complete definition, see Boethius, *De divisione*, in Kretzmann and Stump, pp. 29–31. The use of other elements (technically "accidental" properties of what is being defined) properly pertains to "designation" or "description" (Hebrew: *roshem*), not "definition." See Maimonides, *Millot ha-Higayon* 10,5, p. 71.

28. Cf. Maimonides, *Code, Nedarim* 1,1–2, using the terminology vows of prohibition and vows of consecration. The term "vows of utterance" (*neder bittui*) is derived from analogy with *shevu'at bittui: Code, Shevu'ot* 1,1.

fore, if someone says, "I take it upon myself not to sleep, or not to speak," the vow is null, for there is not here any object about which the person forbids himself. This is one of the differences between the vow and the oath. Therefore one who wants to forbid himself sleep by means of a vow should say that his eyes are forbidden from sleep.[29]

Thus we find that King David in Psalm 131 [132], which begins, *O Lord, remember in David's favor his extreme self-denial* (Ps. 132:1), followed by, *How he swore to the Lord, vowed to the Mighty One of Jacob* (Ps. 132:2), specifies two things: one that he forbade himself by means of an oath, the other by means of a vow. First he said, *I will not enter my house, nor will I mount my bed* (Ps. 132:3). In this he was not so precise, for any formulation is sufficient for a person to forbid himself something by means of an oath. However, in the second instance he forbade himself by means of a vow, saying, *I will not give sleep to my eyes, or slumber to my eyelids* (Ps. 132:4). This is equivalent to saying that his eyes are forbidden from sleep. He said it this way so that his vow would be valid, for otherwise it would have been null, that is, if he had said "I will not sleep," as he had said *I will not enter my house* (Ps. 132:3).[30]

From this root principle, namely that a vow takes effect upon something of substance, it also follows that it is impossible for the vow to be for the fulfillment of a positive act. Rather, what follows from it is always an admonition, namely, a commandment of prohibition. However, this applies only to vows pertaining to optional matters; that is, in vows pertaining to optional matters, the vow can apply only to a prohibition. Therefore, if someone were to vow and say, "By a vow I take it upon myself that I will eat today," or "By a vow I take it upon myself that I will eat this loaf," such a vow has no effect.

However, with vows of consecration, since "a statement to the Most High is like an act of transmitting property to an ordinary person,"[31] the sages treated this matter strictly, wanting the vow to be valid whether with regard to positive or negative [commandments]. Our definition therefore states "to do something or not to do it," so that it may apply to all kinds of vows, both

---

29. Cf. Maimonides, *Code, Nedarim* 3,10–11 based on B. Ned 13b and 15a. For the contrast with the oath, see *Code, Nedarim* 3,1.

30. The interpretation takes "swore [an oath]" and "vowed" in Psalm 132:2 not as "repeating the same thing in different words" but as two different legal acts, governing respectively each of the actions specified in verses 3 and 4, so that the distinctive wording of verse 4 fits the legal requirements of the vow. The same interpretation appears in Alsheikh, *Romemut El* ad loc., but I have not found an earlier source for it.

31. Cf. B. Qid 28b et al.

vows of utterance, which pertain only to negatives, and vows of consecration, which pertain to both positive and negative, like an oath. So the sages said in the first chapter of Nedarim, "'I will study this chapter or this tractate,' the person has made a great vow to the God of Israel."[32] The commentators agree that this is really an oath,[33] and it is therefore not my intention to differentiate in this definition between vows and oaths, but rather to set forth the definition in a manner that will encompass both of them.

d. Now the fourth part of the definition is our statement "teaching about a matter in the soul." This appears to be verified by that which is defined, namely from the vow. For if a person were to vow with his mouth and lips but his mind paid no heed to what he was saying, that vow is null. Even if he was thinking about something in the general category of what he accepted upon himself by his statement, if the specifics were different that vow would be null. Therefore the sages said in the second chapter beginning "There are two oaths" of tractate Shevu'ot that if a person thought of forbidding to himself a slice of wheat bread, but actually said a slice of barley bread, that oath or vow is null.[34] This would seem to be a great root principle for the sages, namely, that we need for them the consent of the mind.

It is possible that in this matter of vows and oaths the sages have a biblical basis: the phrase *the man in an oath* (Lev. 5:4). This indicates that a person must use in oaths and vows that faculty that enables him to be called "human," namely, internal speech, which is the intellect, not external speech alone. Rashi therefore interpreted this phrase *the man in an oath* (Lev. 5:4) to mean that he must be a human being at the time of the oath, even though it is mentioned with regard to the problem of compulsion.[35] This idea is transferred from oaths to vows, because the similarity between them allows the comparison to be made. This is the explanation of the fourth part of the definition, our statement (22v) "teaching about a matter in the soul."

e. Now the fifth part of the definition is our statement "by choice." This

---

32. B. Ned 8a; cf. Maimonides, *Code, Shevu'ot* 1,27.

33. See the commentary of Rabbenu Nissim ad loc: "Since by a vow a person prohibits an object to himself, it can never be in the form 'I shall do.' Rather, this is certainly an oath, and we find in many places that the sages used the term 'vow' for what was really an oath." This passage in the sermon communicates in somewhat more accessible language the idea in R. Nissim's commentary.

34. B. Shev 26a–b; Maimonides, *Code, Shevu'ot* 2,11,14.

35. I.e., the Talmudic interpretation of the phrase (B. Shev 26a) is to require that the vow be made without compulsion, as the preacher goes on to explain as his very next point. This unusual interpretation of the phrase is based on Rashi's comment not on the Pentateuch but on the biblical phrase in this Talmudic passage (B. Shev 26a, s.v. *ha-adam bi-shevu'ah*).

appears to be verified from that which is defined, namely the vow. In this regard, the sages said in tractate Nedarim, "One may make a vow to robbers, murderers, or tax-collectors," eventually saying that the vow made to such people is null.[36] They also addressed this matter in tractate Shevu'ot: that Rav Kahana and Rav Asi were arguing over what they heard from Rav, who was their teacher. Each one of them jumped to swear an oath that this was what he said. Afterward they came before Rav, who determined the law in accordance with one of them. The other one said, "Did I then swear falsely?" Rav replied, "Your heart deceived you."[37] The sages proved that the oath or vow undertaken out of compulsion is null from the biblical phrase *the man in an oath* (Lev. 5:4), saying, "excluding compulsion."[38] This is the explanation of the fifth part of the definition, our statement "by choice."

f. Now the sixth part is our statement "upon which acquiescence rests." This appears to be verified from that which is defined, namely the vow. For the sages said that even if one's mouth and heart were in accord, so that the vow was uttered with mouth and lips and the mind understood but withdrew from the vow within the time needed to make an utterance—which is the time it takes a pupil to say to his master, "Peace unto you, Rabbi!"—the vow is null.[39] It is an erroneous vow, for the second time he revealed his intent that he made a mistake. Now this is a remedy made by the sages of truth.[40] By this remedy of theirs, they provide assistance to human thoughts, which may be devoid of meaning.[41] Sometimes a person vents all that is on his mind without thinking it through, without first having consented. Therefore the sages wanted a person, within the time needed to make an utterance, to rectify his error, as he truly desires. With this I complete my discussion of the first part, namely the first term [of the verse], which is *Make vows.*

II. The second part deals with the second term, namely, *and pay them* (Ps. 76:12). We have said that there are two categories of vows. The first are vows of utterance, which are vows pertaining to optional matters. Such vows cannot be transgressed unless one fails to fulfill them at all. The second category are vows of consecration. A person can transgress these in two ways: by not

---

36. M. Ned 3,4; B. Ned 27b.

37. B. Shev 26a.

38. Ibid.

39. B. Shev 32a; Maimonides, *Code, Shevu'ot*, 2,17.

40. Note that while this term is also used to refer to Kabbalists, our author uses it to refer to the Rabbis of the Talmud. Cf. RaMBaN, 2:289 ("Sefer Ge'ulah"): "The sages of truth, by which I mean the sages of the Mishnah and Talmud, of blessed memory."

41. Echoing Ps. 94:11.

fulfilling them at all, and by delay in their fulfillment.[42] Such delay has already been defined by the sages of truth, as is mentioned in tractate Rosh Hashanah, as three festivals in their proper order or five not in their proper order, as these include three in their proper order.[43]

There is yet another category of vows, which we are obligated to pay immediately when we have made them. An example is when we make a vow to give charity. In the first chapter of tractate Rosh Hashanah we find that Rava said, "Charity becomes obligatory immediately. Why? Because it entails the subsistence of the poor."[44] I would say that the vows of this splendid Society, namely the obligations they have accepted upon themselves, are almost of this category.[45] Let me first say that as for the prayer they have accepted upon themselves, since we are obligated to pray three times a day, there is no need to say that we are obligated to do it immediately. However, we are also obligated perpetually, without interruption. The moment we finish our obligation for one prayer, we enter the obligation for the next one, which follows it.[46]

There is also a second matter which they have accepted upon themselves, namely, the study of Torah perpetually. One is obligated to this all day long. All times, all moments are appropriate for it. Look at the verse that says, *meditate upon it day and night* (Josh. 1:8). When the sweet singer of Psalms said *and pay them* (Ps. 76:12), he was speaking with the members of this So-

---

42. I.e., the transgression of delay does not apply to "vows of utterance" applying to optional matters; they may be fulfilled whenever the opportunity arises. See Nahmanides in Maimonides, *Sefer ha-Mitzvot*, Positive, 94.

43. B. RH 4a-b; cf. Maimonides, *Code, Maʿaseh ha-Qorbanot* 14,13, which codifies the position that the transgression of delay occurs after three successive holidays have elapsed no matter which comes first, not the view of R. Simeon that the preacher presents as if it is established halakhah. According to this view, the "proper order" of the holidays is Pesach, Shavuʿot, Sukkot. Therefore, for a vow made between Sukkot and Pesach, the transgression of delay would occur after the three holidays, but for a vow made between Pesach and Shavuʿot, the transgression would not occur until five had passed (Shavʿuot, Sukkot, and then the three in their proper order: Pesach, Shavuʿot, and Sukkot).

44. B. RH 6a.

45. Here the preacher applies his topic to the situation of his sermon.

46. This view is rather surprising as a statement of Jewish law. One would expect that since the afternoon prayer, for example, may *not* be said before a specified time, after one has completed the morning service, no *obligation* of prayer exists until that time arrives. Maimonides notes that "if a person wishes to pray the whole day, he may do so," but that "the prayers he adds are accounted to him as if he brought free-will offerings," for which there is no obligation (*Code, Tefillah* 1,11). It is unclear to me whether the preacher has a particular doctrine in mind, or whether he is indulging in hyperbole to make a homiletical point. He is on firmer ground when he goes on to speak about the obligation of study as perpetually binding.

ciety and their associates, in three ways. First, *and pay them*: fulfill your vows, do not transgress them. Second, *and pay them*: fulfill your vows without delay. Third, *and pay them*: a warning to the leaders of the Society that they compel the other members of the Society to fulfill their vows. The sages proved this in the first chapter of tractate Rosh Hashanah: *You must fulfill what has crossed your lips and perform* (Deut. 23:24): a warning to the court to make it be done.[47] And the leaders of the Society are a court for all its members (23r) regarding all matters of the Society.[48] With this I complete my discussion of the second part, *and pay them*.

III. Now the third part is a compound of these two terms, namely *Make vows* and *pay them*. Here I shall set forth the following disputed question.[49] Is the act performed by means of a vow and acceptance [of it as obligatory] more praiseworthy, does it acquire for the one who performs it greater merit than would be acquired for him by the very same act done without a vow and acceptance? Or is it the reverse? Now it seems here that there are aspects apparent for both antithetical propositions,[50] arguments founded on the mountains of reason, as well as arguments taken from the words of the prophets and the sages.[51]

a. I will say first that the act performed without acceptance and a prior vow is more praiseworthy and acquires for the one who does it a greater measure of merit than is acquired for him by the very same act done by means of acceptance and a prior vow. Supporting this position, there are five arguments.

The first is this. There is no doubt that the act performed with free will, out of choice, is superior to the act performed out of compulsion, and that praise and blame follow from acts performed out of choice, not from those performed out of necessity and compulsion. We see this in the third book of the *Ethics*.[52] Now the act performed without acceptance of a vow is done out

---

47. B. RH 6a; *Sifre*, Deut. 265.

48. Cf. Rivlin, pp. 196–201 on the Italian *ḥevrot*.

49. *Derush*, equivalent of the Latin *quaestio* (see *Jewish Preaching*, p. 75, n. 30). On this form, see references in n. 17 to introduction.

50. *Ḥelqei ha-soter*, a technical term in Hebrew writing of the period for the two contradictory alternative answers to the question, each of which is initially defended by various types of argument. On the term, see Klatzkin, 1:306, 3:116-17; *Jewish Preaching*, pp. 214 n. 46, 395–97.

51. The two types of arguments to be used are from reason (the Hebrew phrase "founded on the mountains" is based on Ps. 87:1), including philosophical literature such as Aristotle's *Ethics*, and from authority, subdivided into biblical and rabbinic. For such categories of arguments, cf. *Jewish Preaching*, p. 256 at note 2.

52. Aristotle, *Ethics* 3,1,1109b.

of choice, voluntarily, but the act performed by means of the acceptance of a vow is done out of necessity, for the vow binds and compels. It follows from this that the act performed without acceptance of a vow is more praiseworthy and more excellent than what is done by means of the acceptance of a vow.

The second is this. The act that we can perform without doing something else reprehensible is, beyond doubt, superior to the act that cannot be performed without doing something else reprehensible. Such is the case with the act performed by means of a vow. For it is impossible to perform it without divesting ourselves of and casting away that precious gift which God has graciously given us, namely, choice and free will.[53] This is one of the most reprehensible of acts. However, that which is performed without acceptance of a vow is done without doing that reprehensible thing, namely casting away and divesting ourselves of that precious gift. Furthermore, when we make a vow we place ourselves in danger of transgressing the vow, but if we perform the act without acceptance of a vow we do not place ourselves in this danger. From this it follows that the act performed without acceptance of a vow is more excellent, etc.

The third is this. There is no doubt that the act performed out of necessity and compulsion is done with sorrow and distress. But the service of God should not be done with distress and sighing, but rather with joy and gladness, as we see in the verse, *Worship the Lord in gladness* (Ps. 100:2).[54] Furthermore, the Bible sets out for us a punishment if we do not worship God in gladness, as is stated in a verse from the lesson *Ki Tavo* [Deut. 26:1–29:8]: *[All these curses shall befall you . . .] because you did not serve the Lord in joy and gladness over the abundance of everything* (Deut. 28:[45,]47). From this it follows that the act performed without acceptance of a vow, which can be done in joy, making it possible to serve God in this way, is better than the act performed by means of a vow which, being done by compulsion and necessity, cannot be performed in joy, and therefore cannot be used for the service of God.

The fourth argument is this. The ultimate purpose of the vow is simply that the human will should be as a peg fixed in a firm place,[55] so that the person will perform the lofty act and avoid the possibility of doing its opposite. Now it is impossible for the will to be more constant than when it is

---

53. See above, n. 7.

54. Cf. the analogous problem raised in Isaac Aboab's sermon on repentance (below, p. 324) at nn. 133 and 134.

55. Echoing Isa. 22:23.

doing something in actuality. If so, the performance of an act by means of a vow (23v) is not better than performing it without a vow.[56] And if so, performance of an act without a vow is better than performing it by means of a vow, for making the vow is superfluous, having no benefit, and we should reject that which is superfluous.[57]

The fifth argument is taken from the words of the sages. They said in the chapter beginning "One who brings in" of Tractate [Baba] Qamma, "It was taught, R. Nathan said, Whoever makes a vow is like one who has built a high place, and whoever fulfills it is like one who offered a sacrifice upon it at the time when the high places were forbidden."[58] See how they condemned this act—the vow—to the point of comparing it to one who builds a high place. This is because the person prepares himself to sin by transgressing the vow. That is why the sages said that it is a religious duty for a person to seek absolution from his vow.[59] It is in this sense that they said, "and whoever fulfills it is like one who offered a sacrifice upon it at the time when the high places were forbidden." This is because a person should derive no benefit until he has fulfilled his vow, yet he should nevertheless seek absolution from it before he fulfills it, in order not to stand in danger of transgression over it. In this regard the sages also said in [tractate] Nedarim of the Jerusalem Talmud, "Is what the Torah has forbidden to you not enough for you, that you have to forbid to yourself other things?"[60] From these arguments, it appears that the act performed without a vow is superior and more praiseworthy than the act performed by means of a vow.

b. However, the arguments for the antithesis of this part, namely that the act performed by means of a vow is superior to that performed without a vow, are four.

---

56. I.e., since the act itself is decisive, and the act is the same whether performed as a result of a vow or not, the vow is superfluous in that it does not bestow any greater merit upon the act.

57. I.e., since the vow has been deemed superfluous, there is something wasteful or inefficient about the act accompanied by a vow. Rejection of the superfluous is a central theme of medieval Jewish ethical thought.

58. This statement does not seem to appear in Tractate Baba Qamma, although it does in several other tractates (B. Ned 22a, Git 46b, Yeb 109b). The phrase "at the time when the high places were forbidden" is taken from Rabbenu Nissim on B. Ned 22a, beginning *ha-noder.*

59. On the religious duty to seek absolution: cf. R. Nissim on B. Ned 22a, beginning *ve-ha-meqayemo;* Maimonides, *Code, Nedarim* 13,25.

60. Y. Ned 29a; this is quoted by R. Nissim in his comment beginning *ha-noder.*

The first is taken from the verse which was the beginning of my speech, namely *Make vows and pay them* (Ps. 76:12). It appears from this that the sweet singer of Psalms commands and advises the vow and its payment.

The second is taken from the words of the sages. They said in the first chapter of tractate Qiddushin, "One who is commanded and does is greater than one who is not commanded and does."[61] Now one who does something by means of a vow is commanded, for it is encompassed in the positive commandment that says *You must fulfill what has crossed your lips* (Deut. 23:24), and in the negative commandment that says *He shall not break his word* (Num. 30:3). But one is not commanded about an act performed without a vow, for it is not subsumed under the commandment. It appears from this that the act performed by means of a vow is better and more praiseworthy and more meritorious for one who does it than the act performed without a vow.

The third argument is this. The sages said in the first chapter of [tractate] Nedarim, "It is taught, *It is better not to vow than to vow and not to pay it* (Eccles. 5:4), and better than both is never to vow at all: these are the words of R. Meir. R. Judah says, Better than this is to vow and pay." And the law is determined to be in accordance with R. Judah.[62] From this it seems that the act performed by means of a vow is superior to the act, etc.

The fourth argument is this. We see that our saintly ancestors, such as our father Jacob and King David, used to make vows.[63] If the act performed without means of a vow were more praiseworthy and meritorious than the act performed by means of a vow, they would have acted accordingly. That is to say, they would have done what they intended to do without a vow, so that their act would have been more praiseworthy and meritorious. Furthermore, the rabbis, commenting on the verse *Jacob made a vow, saying* (Gen. 28:20), fixed upon the word *saying* and interpreted to apply "to future generations: that they should make vows in times of trouble."[64] From this it seems that the act performed by means of a vow is more praiseworthy, etc.

c. By virtue of these arguments made for each of the antithetical propositions, our disputed question remains undecided, a matter in very great doubt.

---

61. B. Qid 31a.

62. B. Ned 9a, Hul 2a. The preacher's statement is puzzling, as Maimonides and *Tur, Yoreh De'ah* 203 take the position of R. Meir as halakhah. Cf. also Bahya ben Asher on Deut. 23:23, taking the statement of R. Meir as representing the view of "the sages."

63. See Gen. 28:20, Ps. 132:2 (discussed above).

64. Gen. Rab. 70,1; the word *leimor* is interpreted to mean "for others to say." Cf. above at n. 26.

We must now refine the analysis and remove all perplexity. To this end, I shall set forth five true underlying premises,[65] which no one would deny.

The first premise is this. With a good and lofty act, the more constant the will from which it is derived the better it is and the greater is its power to uplift. Similarly with the opposite: with an evil act, the more constant the will from which it is derived (24r) the more evil it is, and the greater is its sin. Such sins are called "malicious."

The second premise is this. Right requires that servants be obedient to their master, and creatures to their creator. It follows from this that, since our relationship to God is the relationship of servant to master and of creature to Creator, the more obedient we are to God and the more we devote ourselves to God's service, the closer we will be to what is right and to the performance of our obligations.

The third premise is this. Those who devote to God both their action and the ability they possess to choose acts devote themselves more to the service of God than those who devote only the act to God, but not the ability they have to choose what they wish. One who gives both the tree and the fruit gives more than one who gives just the fruit, and that is the case here, for acts are the fruit of the will which has the ability [to choose].

The fourth premise is this. The act performed by means of a vow is derived from a constant and unchanging will, which is not the case with an act performed without acceptance of a vow.

The fifth premise is this. Those who make a vow and fulfill it devote to God both the act and the ability they have to choose, but those who perform an act without a vow give to God only the act, not the ability [to choose] that they have.

d. From these premises that have been set forth, when placed in a proper order and arranged in a syllogistic form,[66] the verdict for this disputed question will come to light. It is this: that the good act performed by means of a vow is better and more praiseworthy than that performed without a vow.

For when one performs an act by means of a vow, this action is derived from a constant and unchanging will, as stated in the fourth premise, which

65. *Haqdamot,* presented by the preacher as self-evident truths that require no proof themselves and may be used as premises for syllogisms to derive new conclusions.

66. *Tsurah heqeshit.* For the use of syllogisms in fifteenth-century Spanish sermons, see references in n. 22 to introduction. The argument in the present sermon is not presented strictly in syllogisms, as in the examples noted in chap. 7 above, but in a syllogistic manner of deduction.

is not the case when one performs an act without a vow. And the act derived from a constant will is loftier than the act derived from an inconstant will, as stated in the first premise. Furthermore, those who make a vow and fulfill it devote to God both their action and the ability they have to choose it, as stated in the fifth premise, and those who give both act and will give more and show greater obedience to the receiver than those who give only the act, as stated in the third premise. And those who bind themselves more and become more obedient to God draw closer to what is right, as mentioned in the second premise. Thus those who make a vow and fulfill it are loftier, because they bring themselves more into the service of God, than those who perform the act without acceptance of a vow.

However, this sentence is not true as an absolute generalization unless everything is better when done by means of a vow than when done without a vow. But we should make the following distinction[67] pertaining to the generalization of this sentence. That is that this sentence is correct with regard to vows concerning religious matters, such as the vows of this Society, which pertain to prayer and study of Torah. These are matters about which we already stand commanded. Of these vows and those like them, the sages said in tractate Nedarim, "R. Giddal quoted Rav as having said, Where do we find that one may swear an oath to fulfill a commandment? From the verse *I have firmly sworn to keep Your just rules* (Ps. 119:106)." In the Gemara it is asked, "Are we not constantly foresworn since Mount Sinai? Rather, this comes to teach us that people may urge themselves on [by making vows to do what they are obligated to do]."[68]

However, as for those vows pertaining to optional matters, it is better not to make them too frequently. Of such vows, we read in [Tractate] Nedarim, "Samuel said, All those who make a vow are called sinners, even if they fulfill it. Abbahu asked, Which verse [teaches this]? *If you refrain from vowing, you incur no guilt* (Deut. 23:23). The meaning of 'refrain' is learned from the same word used elsewhere. Here it says, *If you refrain* (Deut. 23:23), and elsewhere it says, *The wicked refrain from troubling* (Job 3:17)."[69] Similarly, it says in Leviticus Rabbah:

---

67. *Le-hafrid*: the distinction is a characteristic technique of the scholastic disputed question (see Chenu, pp. 171–73), although in the present case, the distinction made by the preacher follows a traditional categorization of vows (Maimonides, *Code, Nedarim* 13,24–25.

68. B. Ned 8a.

69. B. Ned 22a. This is a classic technique of rabbinic exegesis: the context of "refrain" in the verse from Job suggests that there is something improper about the vow, for which the same word is used in Deuteronomy.

There is blunt talk like sword-thrusts (Prov. 12:18). Rabban Gamaliel says, Whoever utters a vow should be pierced by the sword, but *the speech of the wise is healing* (Prov. 12:18). For example, someone vows not to eat a loaf of bread. Woe to him if he eats, woe to him if he does not eat. If he eats, he profanes his vow; if he does not eat, he dies. What does he do? He goes to a sage to free him of the vow. This is the meaning of the verse, *the speech of the wise is healing* (Prov. 12:18).[70]

Now (24v) this is what I meant: when they said, "If he does not eat, he dies," this could not apply to vows pertaining to a religious act, for nothing evil results from them. They bring life to all who fulfill them (cf. Prov. 4:22).

e. It remains now for us to reply to the arguments which were brought first on one of the antithetical propositions.[71] They are five.

The first is that the [act ensuing from a] vow is performed by compulsion and necessity, and something done by compulsion is not as praiseworthy as something done voluntarily. The answer is that the beginning of the vow and its cause is choice and the will, which are natural dispositions of the soul from the beginning of our existence.[72] And since its beginning is an internal, not an external matter, it is not by necessity, for necessary actions or motions are those caused by something external.[73]

The second argument, fundamentally, is that by means of the vow we divest ourselves of choice, which is the precious gift that God has graciously bestowed upon us. The answer is that divesting ourselves of choice when we make it decide for the loftier of two antithetical alternatives is not reprehensible, just as it is not reprehensible to divest ourselves of choice when we actualize the superior of antithetical alternatives. Furthermore, it is contended in this argument that by means of the vow we place ourselves in danger of transgressing it. The answer is that this does not make the vow acquire an evil character, so that for this reason it must be repudiated, for the danger is not because of the vow, but rather because of a will that changes from the acquiescence that rested upon the vow when it was made.

The third argument, fundamentally, is that something done by means of

---

70. Lev. Rab. 37,3.

71. The disputed question form requires that the arguments for the position rejected must be refuted, or at least shown not to be decisive for the position actually taken. Note the preacher's recapitulation of each argument (which would not be necessary in a written text where the reader could refer back) in order to help the listener follow the point being made.

72. For the hypothetical antithesis of this position, see Maimonides, *Code, Teshuvah* 5,4.

73. Cf. Wolfson, *Crescas*, pp. 234–35 and 532–32 on "necessary" or "violent" motion (*tenu'ah hekhrehit*).

acceptance of a vow is the result of necessity and compulsion, and anything done of necessity cannot be done in joy and gladness. The answer to this argument is included in the answer to the first argument. This is that something done by means of a vow is not derived from necessity because its beginning is choice and will.

The fourth argument, fundamentally, is that the ultimate purpose of the vow is to do something in actuality, and if so, something done in actuality without a vow is as good as that which is done by means of a vow. The answer is that it is true that something done without a vow is in and of itself as good as something done by the acceptance of a vow. However, that which is done by means of a vow is better in its essence and its origin,[74] because it is derived from a constant will. And we have already said that something derived from a constant will is better than something derived from an inconstant will.

The fifth argument was taken from the words of the sages, namely their statement in tractate [Baba] Qamma that "Whoever makes a vow is like one who has built a high place," and their statement in [tractate] Nedarim of the Jerusalem Talmud, "Is it not enough for you what the Torah has forbidden to you?"[75] The answer is clear. These statements were said only about vows of prohibition, which are vows of optional matters, not vows of consecration. Vows of consecration, those which entail the acceptance of a religious act, are appropriate and permissible for a person to perform. And this is for people to urge themselves on as in the statement of R. Giddal.[76]

Here I place an end to my words[77] resolving this disputed question. This is the conclusion of my third part, which is the compound of these two terms: *Make vows and pay them* (Ps. 76:12).

IV. Now the fourth part pertains to the terms *the Lord your God* (Ps. 76:12). As these are the final parts from the opening [verse] of my speech, I shall link them together with that which preceded them, speaking a bit about the intent of the entire statement: *Make vows and pay them to the Lord your God* (Ps. 76:12).

I would say that the intent of this verse is to encourage and stimulate individual human beings to exercise their ingenuity to find strategies and dis-

---

74. The contrast is between *mi-tsad atsmo* and *mi-tsad mahuto ve-shorsho*. Here the argument is defused by means of a distinction that concedes that it is partly true and partly untrue.

75. Cf. above nn. 58 and 60.

76. See above, n. 68.

77. Echoing Job 18:2.

cover ways to increase their service of God.[78] For we, the Jewish people, are borne aloft by His acts of love, and *day by day He supports us* (Ps. 68:20) with beneficence that we do not deserve.

First, He brought us into being after total nonexistence, (25r) absolute nothingness. Second, He maintains our existence from day to day. For without God, all existing beings would be devastated in a moment (Ps. 73:19), *the heavens would melt away like smoke, the earth would wear away like a garment, and its inhabitants would also die* (Isa. 51:6). For God is not like human laborers. Once they have fashioned something, it can remain in existence without them. When a builder fashions a house, it remains in existence even in his absence. This is not the case with God; if He were to disappear, all existing beings would likewise disappear, *becoming as if they had never been* (Obad. 16). In this regard, those who ordained the liturgy said, "Who in His goodness renews each day, continually, the work of creation."[79] For since existing beings need God to give permanence to their existence, it is possible to say that each day He creates them anew, as He did in the work of creation.

God's beneficence and kindness can be seen especially in those things generated that are destructible, that contain the inception of their destruction, because the simple elements from which these things are constructed are opposed to each other.[80] Of this it is said, *The Lord is good to all, and His mercy is upon all His works* (Ps. 145:9). This means that God's goodness is made to flow upon all existing beings, both those eternal and those things generated that are destructible, and it is the cause of their continued existence. However, "His works," which are things generated that are destructible, need for their continued existence a measure of divine mercy, since they contain in

---

78. This idea of devoting one's ingenuity to increase the service of God beyond the minimum required by the traditional commandments is reminiscent of German Pietist use of the Talmudic phrase (B. Ber 18a) *'arum be-yirah,* "cunning in the fear [of God]." See Soloveitchik, "Three Themes," especially pp. 312–24.

79. In the first of the benedictions from the morning liturgy preceding the *Shema';* see Baer, *'Avodat Yisra'el,* p. 76. Note how the preacher subtly recasts the idea from what might seem to be an assertion of God's active intervention in the natural order to a continuous grounding of existence as it is; cf. Arama, chap. 4, p. 33b, criticizing the interpretation of those who claim that "the permanence in existing things can be called in a way 'renewal' (*ḥiddush*). For the interpretation of Ps. 145:9, cf. Me'iri, *Tehillim,* p. 286, interpreting the second phrase as applying to God's providing of plants and animals with the means for propagation, so that their species remains even though their individuals are destroyed.

80. Cf. Albo, 4:486 (Book IV, chapter 51) for a similar use of the term *hafkhiyut;* Albo uses it as an explanation for change, not of destruction.

their own substance the cause of their destruction; the source of their devastation and ruin derives from themselves and is within them.[81]

Those who ordained the liturgy of the "Grace after Meals" also alluded to this in saying "Who nourishes the entire world in His goodness, in grace, in kindness, and in mercy."[82] It begins with the attribute of goodness, which is in God, and from it the continued existence of everything is made to flow. This is what is meant by the expression "Who nourishes," for nourishing implies permanence. Then it said, "in grace, in kindness, and in mercy," alluding in these three attributes to the three parts into which human life is divided.[83] Even though there are indeed more parts, they are all included in these three. In the first, the force of nature is so strong that it is sufficient to provide enough to compensate for all that is broken down and also to grow. During this part of life, the quality of grace is sufficient for the continued existence of the person. In the second part, the force of nature is sufficient to provide enough to compensate for all that is broken down, but not to grow; during this part of life the quality of kindness is necessary for the continued existence of the person. But in the third part of life, the force of nature is weak, so that it is insufficient to provide enough to compensate for what is broken down; in this part of life the quality of mercy is necessary for the continued existence of the person.

There is a third aspect of God's greatness toward us. This is that He assigned for us eternal bliss. After He removes us from this world of sighs, he places us in the utmost delight; after having existed as things generated that are destructible, God makes us eternal.

Fourthly, God has acted toward us with kindness in his mercy and great love by showing us *the path to where light dwells* (Job 38:19), by means of which we may attain that eternal life. This is by giving us His sacred Torah, which is the direct path to the attainment of that eternal life. It is as the biblical verse states, *You will teach me the path of life; in Your presence is perfect joy, delights are in Your right hand eternally* (Ps. 16:11). The meaning is that eternity and perpetuity without interruption are made to flow to us from God, and delights and fullness of love. Thus He places us "in His presence,"

---

81. Echoing Isa. 49:17 in its rabbinic interpretation: those who destroy you come from your midst. Cf. Rashi on Lev. 26:17, based on Sifra: "I will set up foes from you and in your midst."

82. See Baer, *'Avodat Yisra'el*, p. 554. As with the previous liturgical passage, the preacher gives a simple interpretation of familiar language in a philosophical spirit.

83. On three stages of life, see Saperstein, *Decoding*, p. 114; cf. also p. 237 n. 89, citing a passage that interprets the Talmudic statement that God "nourishes the entire world" (B. AZ 3b) as applying to four periods of human life.

referring to the world that is entirely good,[84] He places us in utmost delight, so that we may rejoice and be glad in Him (Ps. 118:24). This is the meaning of the expression *perfect joy* (Ps. 16:11). And in this world He directs us to the path by which we may arrive at that eternal life. It is as if this verse were divided into three parts. The first two parts are on the level of premises; from them is derived (25v) the last part, which is on the level of the consequence.

Certainly God, whose power is infinite, could if He wanted give us eternal bliss without burdening us with so many commandments and requirements of service. Nevertheless every rational person will necessarily conclude that it is better for us to attain this blessing and this eternal life by means of some proofs of prior compatibility than to attain it for nothing, without the the proofs of compatibility. The practical and rational commandments placed in our sacred Torah furnish this prior compatibility. This was what R. Hananiah ben Akashyah meant when he said, "God wanted to grant merit to Israel; therefore He multiplied for them Torah and commandments."[85] This means that it is a greater merit for Jews to attain eternal bliss by means of a multiplicity of commandments and different forms of service than if they were to attain it for nothing. Linked with this is the fact that this eternal bliss is an almost natural consequence of the commandments placed in our sacred Torah, because of a wonderful special quality that God imprinted upon the totality composed of its individual components.

This bliss is the communion of the soul with the Rock from which it was hewn.[86] After the removal of the material component, which hinders such communion, when the soul is pure and cleansed of false ideas and evil personality traits that derive from habitual sinful acts, communion results. Between the soul and the incorporeal intellect with which it has communion there is love and desire because of the compatibility and interrelationship between them, until because of this the King takes delight in her; she is called daughter and beloved, and He is called lover and friend, as we see in the scroll Song of Songs.[87]

---

84. I.e., the realm of eternity where souls receive their spiritual reward; cf. B. Qid 39b.

85. M. Mak 3,16.

86. Based on Isa. 51:1.

87. Here the preacher follows the philosophical exegesis of Song of Songs, intimated by Maimonides (*Code, Teshuvah* 10,3 and *Guide* 3,51), and systematically applied by, among others, Joseph ibn Aqnin and Levi ben Gershom, in which the love described in the Song is between the individual soul or intellect and God, or the Active Intellect. Cf. n. 24 to introduction.

Speaking of this love, the Bible says, *Vast floods cannot quench this love, nor rivers drown it; if a man offered all the wealth of his household for love, He would be laughed to scorn* (Song 8:7). The intent of the first part of this verse is that when the soul is pure and cleansed of evil personality traits there is nothing that can hinder communion from it; that is the meaning of the phrase *Vast floods cannot [quench]* (Song 8:7). The intent of the second part is to inform us of the opposite of this, namely, that when the soul is not pure in its substance, that is, when its traits are not in harmony and of a superior nature, nothing of the external merits—wealth, possessions, or honor, expressed in the phrase *the wealth of his household* (Song 8:7)—will enable the person to reach this communion. Rather, that person who imagines this to be possible *would be laughed to scorn* (Song 8:7), just as people would scorn and mock someone who thought that he could purchase a precious stone worth ten thousand silver coins for something worth a penny. He would indeed be worthy of mockery.[88]

This love and desire occur between things because of the interrelationship and compatibility between them. Sometimes this interrelationship is very much hidden and concealed, and this may be the reason for actions that seem strange to us in our ignorance, as when we observe a stone attracting iron and a stone attracting grain.[89] Someone has said that there exists a stone that attracts gold. We may even say that there is nothing in the world for which there cannot be found something else that has such an interrelationship with it. One savant has said that for every thing there is a magnet that attracts it.[90]

We may also find this interrelationship even among numbers; they are the ones called "friendly." Each one of these is contained in its companion and is present in it. That is to say, the factors of each one of them add up to the

---

88. This interpretation differs from that of both Ibn Aqnin and Gersonides, who understand the verse to mean that one who feels this love would not abandon it even for a huge payment of money (RaLBaG, *Megillot,* p. 21c; ibn Aqnin, p. 437).

89. The attraction of iron by a magnet was taken by many medieval Jews as a paradigm of a phenomenon confirmed by experience that could not be explained by available knowledge; see Albo 1:148–49; Abravanel, *Prophets,* 1:468a–b. On the capacity of a mineral (amber) to attract grain (or straw), see Langermann, p. 271 n. 8.

90. Compare with these statements the passage by our preacher's contemporary, Simeon ben Tsemah Duran, in his encyclopedic work *Magen Avot*: "There are among the stones such as attract iron, and they are called *magtinas* (sic), and some flesh, and some hair, and some gold, and some silver, and some straw, and some the water that is in the belly . . ." (quoted in Patai, p. 265). The word "magnet" is used in the Hebrew original of our sermon.

other numbers. The first numbers having this property are 220 and 284.[91] The scroll Song of Songs alludes to these in the verse, *Sustain me with raisin cakes, refresh me with apples, for I am faint with love* (Song 2:5). The woman in her desire began with this, for that which is lacking should be aroused in its own behalf to seek perfection. She asked for the friendly number which is in the object of her desire, namely 284, for it is the greater, and it is appropriate to be used for the male. The verse alludes to this, saying *Refresh me* (*rapduni*), the root of which is *resh-peh-dalet,* which is numerically equivalent to 284.[92]

(26r) After this, in another verse, it says, *You have captured my heart, my sister, my bride, you have captured my heart with one of your eyes, with one bead of your necklace* (Song 4:9). This is said in the name of the incorporeal intellect, the lover. It means, my soul is bound with cords of love for you. *With one of your eyes* means with one of the faculties that apprehend, for there are many faculties in the soul, and the interrelationship and compatibility between the soul and the incorporeal intellect is not because of faculties that do not apprehend, but because of those that do. And of those that do apprehend, it is not because of all of them, for there are many: those that apprehend internally with the intellect and those that apprehend externally with the senses.[93] Rather, the interrelationship is because of one of them, namely the rational faculty. This is what is meant when it says *with one of your eyes,* referring to the eye of reason. Afterward it says *with one bead,* referring to one of your jewels and ornaments, for the faculties are the ornaments of the soul. And the word *bead* (*'anaq*) alludes to the smaller of the friendly numbers, which is 220 [the numerical equivalent of *'ayin-nun-qoph*]. It is appropriate for this to be used for the female, which is the smaller.

As these numbers are friendly, they possess the special property of bring-

---

91. The factors of 284—142, 71, 4, 2, and 1—add up to 220, while the factors of 220—110, 55, 44, 22, 11, 10, 5, 4, 2, and 1—add up to 284. The property of these two numbers was known to Greek mathematicians (See Heath, 1:75) and discussed in the "Book of Arithmetic" by the Arab writer 'Abd al-'Aziz ibn Abu al-Salt. This work was translated into Hebrew by Don Benveniste ben Lavi at Saragossa in 1395 (Oxford Bodleian Library, MS Neubauer 2774, fols. 47b–59a). It is not at all unlikely that our preacher derived his knowledge of the "friendly numbers" from this work. I am grateful to Tony Lévy for providing me a typescript of his forthcoming article "L'histoire des nombres amiables: le témoignage des textes hébreux médiévaux," to appear in the 1995 volume of *Arabic Sciences and Philosophy: A Historical Journal.*

92. I have not been able to find any source for this interpretation of Song 2:5, or the interpretation that follows of Song 4:9.

93. On the internal senses in Arabic, Hebrew, and Latin philosophical texts, see Wolfson, *Studies* 1:250–314.

ing love between individual human beings. Thus we find that our ancestor Jacob, desiring to remove the hatred for him that was in the heart of his brother Esau and to replace it with love, ingeniously anticipated and prepared for this as much as he could. He sent Esau two hundred she-goats and twenty he-goats (Gen. 32:15), adding up to one of the friendly numbers.[94] He wanted love to be established between them whatever it may be, even if it would not be based on equality, even if it would be the love between master and servant, with Esau in the position of master and Jacob in the position of servant. That is why of his own accord he sent him the smaller of the friendly numbers, namely 220.

Let us return to our subject. We say that because of the interrelationship that occurs between the rational soul and the incorporeal intellect with the removal of the hindering matter and the evil personal traits, communion follows necessarily. This is called "the bundle of life," as in the verse, *The life of my lord will be bound up in the bundle of life* (I Sam. 25:29). Then the soul will become like an angel of God. For the difference and distinction between individual human beings and an angel lies in this life, which is the reason for the final difference incorporated into the definition of the human being: "living, speaking, dying." Thus an individual human being may say to an angel that "death separates me from you" (cf. Ruth 1:17), for that difference, which we call "dying," is what distinguishes.[95] And just as, while in earthly life, one can say "death separates me from you," so in that other, eternal life that comes after death, one can say "death joins me to you," meaning that death is the cause of the connection that occurs between us.

This communion and the delight that is its consequence are what the sages called "the world to come." And the anguish that is antithetical to it, the yearning for this communion and being prevented from attaining it, are what they called "Gehenna."[96] When the evil soul is separated from the ma-

---

94. This interpretation of the significance of the number of goats sent by Jacob is attributed in a "Yemenite manuscript" to the tenth-century Gaon of Sura, Nahshon. See Grunhut, pp. 311–12, and Kasher, *Torah Shelemah* 5:1276.

95. For this definition of the human being, see Maimonides, *Millot ha-Higayon,* 10,4 (p. 71).

96. For this purely spiritual conception of the "world to come," see Maimonides, *Commentary on the Mishnah,* introduction to chap. Ḥeleq of Sanhedrin, in Twersky, *Maimonides Reader,* pp. 411–12; cf. *Code, Teshuvah* 9,10. Maimonides' definition of "Gehenna" in the introduction to Ḥeleq (Twersky, p. 413–14) is more general than this, but it shares the notion that it refers not to a place but to the pain that comes upon the wicked. Note that in this spiritual conception, there is no positive punishment, only deprivation from the presence of God. For aggadot suggesting that there is punishment in Gehenna by physical fire, see Hillel of Verona, pp. 191–93.

terial component that strikes it with the blindness of ignorance, it yearns for the object of its desire, the quarry from which it was originally taken, yet it is prevented from communion with it, thereby enduring extreme anguish.

This is the meaning of R. Simeon ben Laqish in the first chapter of tractate Avodah Zarah (3b–4a), in a statement that is strange at first glance. It says there:

R. Simeon ben Laqish says, There is no Gehenna in the world to come, but the Holy One, blessed be He, brings the sun out of its sheath, making it fierce. The wicked are punished by it, as the prophet says, *Lo, that day is at hand, burning like an oven. All the arrogant and all the doers of evil shall be straw, and the day that is coming shall burn them* (Mal. 3:19). The righteous are healed by it, as he said, *But for you who fear My name a sun of victory shall rise with healing* (Mal. 3:20). Not only this, but they will derive pleasure from it, as he says, *You shall go forth and stamp like stall-fed calves* (Mal. 3:20)."[97]

Its meaning is as follows:

"Gehenna" is nothing other than God's removing the sun—that is, the soul, which because of its purity is called here "sun"—from its sheath—that is, the body.[98] It then says "making it fierce (*u-maqdirah*)," meaning that God adds focus and heat and ardor (26v), referring to its desire for communion with the object of that desire. You will find that in the same chapter, a little before this statement, Rashi interprets the phrase *u-maqdir 'alehem ḥamah*.[99] Consequently, "the wicked are punished by it," meaning that it follows from this that the wicked are punished. Since they yearn for communion and they are prevented from attaining it, extreme anguish for them results. "The righteous are healed by it" means that the righteous—who, while still in this life feel the pain of their flesh because of the vexation of their de-

---

97. B. AZ 3b–4a; note that this aggadah is cited by Maimonides in the context of his above-noted discussion of "Gehenna" (Twersky, *Maimonides Reader*, p. 412), but without interpretation. Hillel of Verona, pp. 204–5, argues that this must be given a figurative interpretation, although his explication of the phrase "removes the sun from its sheath" is different from that of our author. With the preacher's use of "There is no Gehenna in the world to come" in accordance with his spiritual conception, contrast the comment of R. Nissim on the parallel occurrence in B. Ned 8b, which preserves the more traditional conception: "He did not mean [that there is no Gehenna] after death, for there is certainly a Gehenna for the wicked; he was rather speaking about the world to come following the resurrection of the dead. . . ."

98. Note the allegorical interpretation of "sun" and "sheath" as referring to "soul" and "body." Unlike R. Nissim, the preacher interprets the aggadah as applying to the individual following death.

99. Rashi on B. AZ 3a, *maqdir*.

sires, *the poison of which is absorbed by their spirit* (Job 6:4), so that they have to subjugate these desires to the rule of reason—will now be healed from this pain and sickness. Following this, "not only that, but they will derive pleasure from it," meaning that the result will be not only healing, but also delight. From this communion, extreme delight results for them.

From all these acts of kindness that God has bountifully done for us—in the beginning of creation, by sustaining continued existence, by bestowing eternal life after the death of the body, by appearing to us and directing us to the path that can lead us to this eternal life[100]—it follows that anyone who does not want to be ungrateful, which is one of the greatest of sins, must strive with every ounce of his strength to serve God in manifold ways and to set up for himself religious obligations in addition to those that are commanded in our sacred Torah.[101] And one of the aspects of this task is that we accept upon ourselves vows pertaining to the service of God and fulfill them. This is what the sweet singer of Psalms meant when he said, *Make vows and pay them to the Lord your God* (Ps. 76:12).

In order to escape this grave matter of ingratitude, we are also obligated to acknowledge constantly, without interruption,[102] those acts of kindness that God has done for us. This may be done through prayer. This is the greatest of the fundamental principles of prayer: namely, the acknowledgment of the acts of kindness that flow to us from God, for in this acknowledgment are included various principles of our true faith, such as the existence of God, His unity, his Providence, and the reward and punishment that derive from God.[103]

In this regard it is said in the first chapter of tractate Berakhot, "Rabba bar Hama Saba said, Whoever does not say 'True and enduring' in the morning liturgy, and 'True and faithful' in the evening liturgy, has not fulfilled his obligation, as the Bible says, *To proclaim Your kindness at daybreak, Your faithfulness each night* (Ps. 92:3)."[104] For in these are included the acknowl-

---

100. Note the recapitulation, helping the listener to recall the points made.

101. For gratitude as the paradigm of a rational obligation of all human beings leading to the commandments of serving and thanking God, see Saadia, *Emunot ve-De'ot* 3,1 and the note by Alexander Altmann in *Three Jewish Philosophers*, part 2, p. 95, n. 5. On the obligation of service beyond the commandmants, see above, n. 16.

102. Cf. above, n. 46.

103. This passage evokes the contemporary debate over "fundamental principles," on which see Kellner, *Dogma*. The idea is that these fundamental principles are referred to in the liturgy of Jewish worship.

104. B. Ber 12a, referring to the benedictions in the morning and evening service immediately following the recitation of *Shema'* (Baer, *'Avodat Yisra'el*, pp. 84, 166).

edgments that were mentioned. The fundamental principle of prayer is not, as some people have thought, to extol and praise God by recounting his glories and praises, of which we are ignorant, as we are ignorant of God's essence.[105] It is enough that we extol Him when we acknowledge and proclaim that because of God's great exaltation, He is concealed from us.

In this way the sweet singer of Psalms praised God by saying, *I praise You, for I am in a state of awesome wonder; Your work is marvelous; I know it very well* (Ps. 139:14). For things can be praised in two ways. First is when the attributes and exalted stature of something are treated as amphibolous,[106] this being when they are known. The other is when the attributes and praises of something are not known because of its exaltation. In this case, acknowledgment will be when we admit, by articulating the words with mouths and lips, that we are ignorant of the exalted attributes of that which is to be praised, because of its exaltation. Therefore the sweet singer of Psalms said, *I praise You, for I am,* etc. (Ps. 139:14), meaning, "I will extol and praise You because I marvel at You, and Your essence is concealed from me, and a human being marvels at that which is concealed." In this, he is in the position of acknowledging things hidden from him. He then said, *Your work is marvelous, I know very well* that it is concealed. Since metaphysical matters for investigation are totally incorporeal, they are in themselves appropriate for apprehension by the intellect. We do not need to make the effort to abstract them from matter so that they may be apprehended, for they are already abstracted.[107] However, our ignorance of them comes from ourselves; we weary of apprehending that which (27r) is absolute clarity.

Therefore King David said, *Like a hind panting over the watercourses, my soul pants for You, O God* (Ps. 42:2). He meant that the hind pants for the watercourses even if they contain more than enough water to quench its thirst, for the word "courses" indicates strength and abundance of water, yet

---

105. I.e., the view of the ignorant is that the essence of prayer is praise, while the view of the learned is that its essence is grateful acknowledgment. Cf. Maimonides' attack on the "foolish persons who are extravagant in praise" in *Guide* 1,59.

106. Hebrew: *she-yesuppaq to'arei ha-devar u-ma'alotav. Shem mesuppaq* is used by Maimonides for amphibolous terms, or homonyms, that are not totally different but share a characteristic that is an accident, not an essential element, and therefore not appropriate for the attributes of God; see Maimonides, *Millot ha-Higayon,* chap. 13, pp. 95–96; Maimonides, *Guide* 1,56. Crescas, however, does use this term for attributes of God (Crescas, *Or* III,2,1,1, p. 374).

107. According to medieval epistemology, perceptions coming from the senses are abstracted when they are brought to the internal senses; see Klatzkin, 1:200 s.v. *hafshatah,* citing Abraham Bibago.

the hind does not have the strength to receive all the water it needs to quench its thirst and the ardor within it. So *my soul pants for You, O God* (Ps. 42:2), meaning that for a similar reason my soul pants when it is in a state of contemplation and deep thought about metaphysical questions. The reason it cannot apprehend these matters with the intellect is not because of their own essence. They are in themselves fully susceptible to being apprehended, for they are intellect in actuality. It is because of ourselves, for our capacity is inadequate to apprehend that which is absolute clarity. The Psalmist may have alluded to this by saying "watercourses," for the powerful flow and abundance of the water make it impossible for the hind to drink it as it can drink from water flowing slowly. Similarly here, because of the absolute clarity of the incorporeal intellects, the human intellect cannot apprehend them.

It is possible that the Psalmist said of this, figuratively, *For the Lord God is a sun and a shield* (Ps. 84:12), meaning that God is absolute brilliance and clarity, and in this respect He is a shield, that is, like a barrier between Himself and those who would apprehend Him with intellect. David also said, telling of the profundity of these metaphysical matters, *How rarefied thoughts of You* (*yaqru re'ekha*) *seem to me, O God, how powerful are their main points!* (Ps. 139:17). This means, the thoughts (the meaning of *re'ekha*) about metaphysical questions are weighty and difficult for me.[108] The meaning of *yaqru* is derived from the verse *And the word of the Lord was rare* (*yaqar*) (I Sam. 3:1). He then repeated the content by saying, *how powerful are their main points* meaning that even the "main points," which are the general principles, are difficult for me to comprehend.

He then went on to tell the reasons for this difficulty that he encounters in apprehending these things, saying *I try to count them—they are more than the grains of sand* (Ps. 139:18). He spoke precisely, saying that they are *more than the grains of sand,* not *like* the grains of sand, as in the verse, *The number of the people of Israel shall be like that of the sands of the sea* (Hos. 2:1). This is because when the intent is an immense number, it says "like the grains of sand," which is the largest quantity that has an actual correlative. That was the intent in this verse, namely, a huge number, but not an infinite number, for there was no intent to say that the people of Israel would be infinite in number. However, when the intent is an infinite number, it says *more than the grains of sand* (Ps. 139:18). It is because the divine attributes are infinite. It is not because of multiplicity in God's essence, but because of the multi-

---

108. Cf. the interpretation of this verse in Me'iri, *Tehillim,* p. 276 and Crescas, *Or* I,3,3, pp. 107–8.

plicity of things that are in relation to God.[109] This is one of the reasons for the difficulty in understanding these metaphysical questions, namely, that these attributes are infinite.

The Psalmist then told of another reason, saying *I end—but I am with You* (Ps. 139:18). This means, when I put an end to my contemplation and thought about these attributes, and I want to discover and learn what I have added to wisdom and knowledge by reason of these attributes, I find that *I am with You,* meaning that these attributes are nothing but Your essence. Just as before this I was ignorant of Your essence, so I know myself to be today as I was yesterday or the previous day, before I began investigating these attributes. And because it is possible for great damage to result from the attributes of praise and glory if they are understood as positive, for they will lead one to think of multiplicity in God's essence, those who ordained the liturgy warned us about this, saying "to acknowledge You and to proclaim Your unity."[110] This means that we may acknowledge and praise You, but only in such a manner that we affirm Your unity, so that no multiplicity in Your essence results.

In order to avoid the damages that may possibly result from acknowledgments and praises, the very best form of acknowledgment is silence. In this respect, King David said, *To You silence is praise in Zion, O God; vows are paid to You* (Ps. 65:2). The meaning of this is that in times of trouble, King David used to make a vow that if God would save him, he would go to God's altar to glorify and praise Him, coming into His presence with thanksgiving (cf. Ps. 95:2). Afterward, when he was in Zion, he found that the very best form of acknowledgment was silence, and so he remained silent. He therefore said (27v), *To You silence is as praise* (Ps. 65:2).[111] He then said, *vows are paid to You* (Ps. 65:2), meaning that the vow I made to acknowledge Your name[112] may be fulfilled for You through silence, for this is the best and the most exalted form of acknowledgment to You.

---

109. Articulating a doctrine of divine attributes that were not separate from God but also did not introduce plurality into the divine essence was one of the great challenges of medieval philosophical theology, as demonstrated in various works by Harry Wolfson. My translation "in relation to God" is based on the technical meaning of *tseruf* as "correlative": a term that makes sense only in relationship to another; cf. Maimonides, *Millot ha-Higayon,* chap. 11, pp. 79–80; Wolfson, *Crescas,* p. 497, n. 2.

110. From the benediction immediately preceding *Shema' Yisra'el* in the morning liturgy; see Baer, *'Avodat Yisra'el,* p. 81.

111. This is the interpretation of the verse given by Maimonides, *Guide* 1,59; cf. Crescas, *Or* I,3,3 p. 102 and III,2,1,1 p. 373.

112. A return to the central theme of the sermon.

Thus we do not need to utter our acknowledgments of God with our mouths and lips. We may leave these kinds of acknowledgment to God's other works and creatures, which never become quiet day or night (cf. Isa. 62:6), and without falling into silence tell the praises of the Lord.[113] It is like the statement in the verse, *All Your works shall acknowledge You, O Lord, and Your faithful ones shall bless You* (Ps. 145:10). This is because workers and artisans other than God are not praised for all of their activities. For example, if a builder constructs a royal palace, *built with turrets* (Song 4:4), it will tell his praise, for everyone who sees it will recognize that it is the work of an artist, and he will thus be extolled for what he has done. However, when he makes *houses of clay, their foundations in the dust* (Job 4:19), they do not sing the praises of the worker; perhaps they may serve to indicate his shame.

The matter is quite different with God. All of His works acknowledge and praise Him. Even the ant, the lowliest of beings, praises God. For if we really knew the anatomy of the ant, the diversity of its organs, all prepared to provide it with sustenance throughout its lifetime, and how God has given it all the perfection possible for its constitution, this would provide evidence for us to know the infinite wisdom of the Maker. That is why it says, *All Your works [shall acknowledge You]* (Ps. 145:10). The Psalmist then went on to say, *and Your faithful ones shall bless You* (Ps. 145:10). This means that Your faithful ones, who see the ingenious order of Your activities, do not need to acknowledge You; rather, they bless You, meaning that they acknowledge that the blessings flow from You. For that is the blessing said in relationship to God, namely, that we acknowledge that He makes all good things and blessings flow, that He is their source and their wellspring.[114]

Now the fundamental principle of prayer is to this end: to acknowledge these acts of kindness, the good things and the blessings that flow from God. Therefore, how precious and powerful are these activities, which the members of this society have accepted upon themselves![115] First, they have enacted public prayer. How the sages have praised this, saying that it is accepted and heard. They proved this by using the verse, *For in their multitude they were with me* (Ps. 55:19).[116] They also used the verse, *Two put ten thou-*

---

113. The final phrase is based on Isa. 43:21, but the idea seems to be linked with Ps. 19:2–3.

114. A solution to the problem of how human beings can be said to "bless" God. Cf. Me'iri, *Tehillim*, p. 286 on v. 10: "*Your faithful will bless You:* that is, those who understand the nature of existing beings will bless you, meaning they will acknowledge the patterns of all existence."

115. Here the discussion is applied to the occasion of the sermon.

116. B. Ber 8a.

sand to flight (Deut. 32:30), saying "the many who perform the commandment are not like the few who perform it."[117] This is because there is a special property in the totality that is not found in each one of the individuals
alone.[118]

In addition, there is another virtue to be found in this prayer: that it is
performed in a place where study of Torah occurs. We see this in the first
chapter of Tractate Berakhot: "Rabbi Levi [should be: R. Hiyya b. Ammi]
said in the name of Ulla, Since the day the Temple was destroyed, the Holy
One, blessed be He, has nothing [. . .] but the four cubits of Jewish law."
And there it continues, "Abaye said, At first I used to study in my house and
pray in the synagogue. Since I heard the saying of [R. Hiyya b.] Ammi in the
name of Ulla, I pray only in the place where I study."[119]

Furthermore, how very vigorous is the study of Torah with extreme precision that they engage in! For it is very desirable to be precise in this. The
sages said, "The Judaeans, who were precise in their language, retained their
learning; the Galileans, who were not precise in their language, did not retain their learning."[120] This is because every one of the letters and vowels in
our sacred Torah and the books of the Prophets was placed where it is to be
understood in a specific way. And similarly every one of the accent marks
gives reason for praise.[121] All of them teach about esoteric matters in the understanding of the verses; *the righteous may walk on them, but the sinners will
stumble on them* (Hos. 14:10).

One savant said in praise of these two activities, prayer and study of
Torah, "One who prays speaks with His God, and one who delves deeply
into the Torah, his God speaks with him."[122] See how great was his praise of
these two activities. For he compared one of them to a human being speaking with God, and the other to God speaking with a human being. Yet there
is one great advantage that differentiates them. That is why he compared

---

117. Either the preacher or the scribe was careless here. The correct verse is not Deut.
32:30 but Lev. 26:8: *Five of you shall give chase to a hundred, and a hundred of you shall give
chase to ten thousand.* On this, Rashi, based on Sifra, wrote, "the correct proportion would
have been 'and a hundred of you shall give chase to two thousand.' However, a few who observe the Torah are unlike the many who observe the Torah."

118. Cf. Moses Almosnino, in *Jewish Preaching*, pp. 227–28.

119. B. Ber 8a; cf. B. Meg 29a and MaHaRShA on "I study only in the synagogue."

120. B. 'Erub 53a.

121. A pun on *ta'amim* (accent marks, showing where the Hebrew words are to be ac-
cented and how they are to be chanted), connected with the Talmudic phrase *noten ta'am la-
shevaḥ* or *li-fgam.* "imparts an improved flavor (*ta'am*)": B. AZ 39a.

122. This statement is found in Yosippon's discussion of Daniel; see Flusser 1:27, n. 51.

prayer, which is a human invention, ordained by the men of the Great Assembly,[123] to a human being speaking with God, and he compared (28r) delving deeply into the sacred writings, which are words of the living God,[124] to God speaking with humans.

For this reason, this society is truly and honorably called *Rodfei Tsedeq*, "Seekers of Justice."[125] For since there is between the soul and the body a relentless war, strife that does not cease day or night, each one of them—and especially the body—wanting to take its share and more, we must set a ruler and judge between them, a rebuker who will exert power over both of them in accordance with justice and equity. Now it is right that each one be given what is appropriate for it, and the portion for the soul throughout this life of vanity is the time devoted to prayer and the study of Torah. Therefore these members, who give to the soul its proper portion of prayer and study of Torah, are indeed seekers of right and justice.

We may also find in these vows that the members of this society have accepted upon themselves another virtue. The verse said by King David fits them: *I will pay my vows to the Lord in the presence of all His people, in the courts of the house of the Lord, in the midst of Jerusalem, Hallelujah* (Ps. 116:18–19). For these vows are of such a nature that they cannot be fulfilled in secret, in an inner chamber; they must be fulfilled in broad daylight. To this fits the part of the verse that says, *in the presence of all His people* (Ps. 116:18). Secondly, they should be paid in the synagogue, which for us today is the *courts of the house of the Lord*, a sanctuary in miniature.[126] To this fits the second part of the verse, namely *in the courts of the house of the Lord* (Ps. 116:19). Now the sages said in Leviticus Rabbah, "Whoever makes a vow and pays it will be worthy of paying his vow in Jerusalem, as the verse says, *I will pay my vows to the Lord in the presence of all His people*. Where? *In the courts of the house of the Lord, in the midst of Jerusalem* (Ps. 116:18–19).[127]

Therefore, *be strong and resolute* (2 Sam 10:12). Let us cast our burden upon the Lord (cf. Ps. 55:23), for those who hope in Him shall not be shamed (cf. Isa. 49:23). Let us trust that by the merit of this service, God will bring near the beginning of our redemption, the time for our exodus

---

123. B. Ber 33a; B. Meg 17b; Maimonides, *Guide* 1,59.

124. Cf. B. ʿErub 13a.

125. On this society, see Assis, "Welfare and Mutual Aid," esp. p. 325. In the existing sources, this confraternity appears to be devoted primarily to charitable activities, whereas the preacher emphasizes its commitment to study and prayer, requiring a rather forced interpretation of the name.

126. Cf. B. Meg 29a.

127. Lev. Rab. 37,4 (*Midrash Rabbah* 4:471).

from the pit of our exile.[128] With skillful hands may He lead us (cf. Ps. 78:72) to the place He chose to establish His name (Deut. 12:11). In these days, at that time, the entire Jewish people will be able to say together, *I will pay my vows to the Lord in the presence of all His people, in the courts of the house of the Lord, in the midst of Jerusalem, Hallelujah* (Ps. 116:18–19).

---

128. The expression of a messianic hope is found at the end of many medieval Jewish sermons; here the emphasis is on the fullest possible service of God where Jews are at present.

נדרו ושלמו ליי אלהיכם. תלים מזמור ע״ו[1]

סבות ההתנצלות בכלל שתים, אם העלם ואם אונס. אולם ההעלם הנה הוא סבה להתנצלות עד שהוא מכל וכל מעביר ומוחה כעב הפשעים[2] אשר אין אנחנו חייבים על זדונם כרת. ואף החטאים אשר אנחנו חייבים על זדונם כרת יעביר אך אמנה עם שנחבר אליו עזר הקרבן וכמו שנראה בפרשת ויקרא[3] וכמו שאמרו במסכ׳ שבת פר׳ כלל גדול.[4] ואולם האונס הנה הוא סבה יותר חזקה ויותר עצמית להתנצלות עד שהיא תעביר זכר שם החטא, אף היא תשיב האדם הפועל דבר הפשע על דרך אונס נקי מכל חטא ומכל עונש נמשך אליו כמו שאמרו רז״ל במס׳ ע״ז פר׳ ר׳ ישמעאל, אונס רחמנא פטריה,[5] וכמו שהוכיחו מפסוק ולנערה לא תעשה דבר.[6]

ואחר שכן בעבור חושי בי[7] עון אשר חטא בהרסי לעלות[8] אל זאת המדרגה אשר אנכי בלתי ראוי אליה ר״ל לדבר בזה המעמד הנבחר כי כמה מעלות למקום הן להיותו מעון לתורתנו הקדושה ולהיותו בית תפלה, הן למעלות השומעים בחכמה בתבונה ובדעות[9] ובמעלות המדות, נסתי לעזרה[10] לשתי סבות ההתנצלות הנזכרות.

אמנם סבת ההתנצלות הראשונה אשר היא ההעלם הנה היא לי לעזר וימינה תסעדני[11] על זה האופן. וזה כי להיות ערכי בתכלית הקטן וידיעתי הלא מצער היא[12] לא יכלתי לשער קצה קטנותה, והנה זה העלם אחד. ועוד כי לגודל ערך השומעים וחכמתם כי רבה היא לא יכולתי לבא עד קצה,

---

1. תה׳ עו יב.
2. ע״פ יש׳ מד כב.
3. עי׳ ויק׳ ד כז–ה ו, ה טו–יט.
4. שבת סז ב, ע ב.
5. עבודה זרה נד א.
6. דב׳ כב כו והשוה רמב״ם, הל׳ יסודי התורה ה,ד.
7. ע״פ איוב כ ב.
8. ע״פ שמות יט כד.
9. שמות לה לא.
10. ע״פ יש׳ י ג.
11. ע״פ תה׳ יח לו.
12. ע״פ בר׳ יט כ.

והנה זה העלם שני. הן אלה קצות דרכי[13] ההעלם אשר השיאוני ויכלו לי
והביאוני לעשות הפעל הזה. כי אם לא הייתי סכל בדברים הנזכרי׳ ואמנם
הייתי (א21) משער תכלית סכלותי ותכלית מעלת השומעים לא הייתי משלח
עצמי על עשיית הפעל הזה.

ואמנם לפי שאין בסכלות וההעלם די להתנצלות עד שלפעמים נצטרך
לחבר אליו קרבן כדי להסיר כתם החטא, וכמו שנראה ביעקב אבינו ע״ה
אמ׳ אכן יש יי במקום הזה ואנכי לא ידעתי,[14] היה מפחד אולי לא עמד
בנקייות והטהרה הראויים לקדושת המקום ההוא. ועם היות נמצא אתו
אחד ממיני ההתנצלות ר״ל ההעלם כאמרו ואנכי לא ידעתי חשש שלא יספיק
אליו זה ההתנצלות ולזה נאמר אחר כן ויירא ויאמר מה נורא המקום הזה
אין זה כי אם בית אלהים.[15] אי לזאת כי יגורתי לא יספיק אלי התנצלות
ההעלם הנזכר חברתי אליו התנצלות השני ר״ל התנצלות האונס.

והוא על זה האופן כי כשבאתי במסורת הברית עם חבירי החברה
המפוארה הזאת פשטתי את כתנת[16] הבחירה אשר לי מעלי בכל עניני
החברה ונתתי את לבי ורצוני לרצון להם לפני יי. ואחר שהם הסכימו
שאעשה זה הפעל אמרתי למלאת שאלתם, כי הכריחוני באמרם שאני
מחוייב לקיים נדרי ומוצא שפתי לא אשנה,[17] וכמו שני׳ בפתיחת דברי נדרו
ושלמו.[18]

ועוד יטענו נגדי באמרם שאחר שהנדרים אשר קבלו עליהם חברי החברה
הזאת נזכרים ונעשים דבר יום ביומו בבית הכנסת הזה וחג המשמרה
הזאת[19] נעשה גם בו ומזה ימשך בלי ספק כבוד למתפללי בית הכנסת
הזה ואני ממונה מורשה לפקח בעניני הבית כנסת, הנה ראוי אלי לשום
עין ההשגחה על עניניהם בחזקת היד ופני לא אסתיר מכלמות[20] ואדברה

13. ע״פ איוב כו יד.
14. בר׳ כח טז.
15. בר׳ כח יז.
16. ע״פ שיר ה ג.
17. תה׳ פט לה.
18. תה׳ עו יב.
19. נסיבת הדרשה, וראה הערה 8 לתרגום.
20. ע״פ יש׳ נ ו.

נגד מלכים ולא אבוש[21] והם המה רבנן אקרו מלכי[22] ועם היות הייתי מתנצל
מהם באמרי כי אני מחוייב לקחת מוסר השכל מדברי קדומינו ע"ה
האומרים במס' חגיגה פ' אין דורשין,[23] במופלא ממך אל תדרוש, הנה הם
יטענו נגדי במה שנמשך אליו מן המאמר והוא אמרם במה שהורשית
התבונן, בבארם אותו שהוא ראוי אל האדם להתבונן ולשים כל מעייניו
בדבר אשר נמנה עליו מורשה.[24] ולכן נשען על ההתנצלויות הנז' ואם הם
חלושים כפי עצמת העון, ברשות וכו'.[25]

אעיין בפסוק הנז' בפתיחת דברי אשר הוא נדרו ושלמו ליי אלהיכם.[26]
ולפי שהעיון בו ימשך על סדר ראוי אחלק הדבור לארבעה חלקים. החלק
הראשון יהיה בגבול הראשון[27] שהוא נדרו ובו אבאר מהות הנדר. החלק
השני יהיה בגבול השני והוא אמרנו ושלמו ובו אבאר תשלומי הנדר. החלק
השלישי יהיה בהרכבת שני אלה הגבולים רצוני נדרו ושלמו ובו אעיין בנדר
אחר שיש לו תשלומין וביחס אשר יש לפעל כשיעשה בחיוב וקבלת נדר
עם הפעל ההוא בעצמו כשיעשה מבלי קבלת נדר. החלק הרביעי יהיה
באלה הגבולים ליי אלהיכם ובו אעיין באשר אליו יעשה הנדר ואבאר איך
ראוי לנו לקבל נדרים ולהעמיד עלינו מצות לעבודת האל ית' זולת
הכתובות בספר תורתו הקדושה. וזה לעשות זכר לנפלאותיו[28] ולהודות
חסדיו הבלתי בעלי תכלית אשר יעשה אתנו יום ליום.

אולם החלק הראשון אשר הוא בגבול הזה נדרו הנה יעדתי לבאר
מהות הנדר. ולפי שמהות הדבר לא יתבאר על מתכונתו כי אם בהנחת
גדרו[29] הנה אניח גדר הנדר כפי ההקדמות והשרשים אשר יש לנו ממנו הן

21. ע"פ תה' קיט מו.
22. עי' גטין סב א.
23. חגיגה יג א.
24. משחק מלים הקושר את המאמר („במה שהורשית") עם תפקידו של הדרשן („מורשה").
25. כאן ממשיך הדרשן ליטול רשות מנכבדי הקהל ומכלל צבור השומעים. השוה בחיי בן אשר, כד
הקמח, ערך „רשות."
26. תה' עו יב.
27. אינני מכיר במקור אחר שימוש כזה ב„גבול" במובן מלה בפסוק. כנראה שימוש זה קשור למשמעות
המונח בתורת ההגיון: חלק מחלקי ההיקש (עי' בן יהודה, מלון הלשון העברית כרך 1, דף 6750, וקלצקין,
אוצר המונחים הפילוסופיים כרך 1, דף 99).
28. תה' קיא ד.
29. השוה ספר הכוזרי ה,כה: „מהות הדבר גדרו."

מפסוקי תורתנו הקדושה הן מדברי רז״ל (ב211) ויראה שהוא זה. הנדר הוא שעבוד ביטויי לעשות דבר מה או לבלתי עשותו מורה על ענין בנפש בחיריי נחה בו ההסכמה. ועם היות הגדר אי אפשר שיתבאר במופת כפי מה שהתבאר בחכמת ההגיון האמנם בדברים ההנחיים[30] כמו זה אפשר שיתבאר וזה מכח ההקדמות אשר יש לנו מהענין.

ולכן אומר שהגבול הראשון מהגדר והוא אמרנו בו שעבוד יעמוד בגדר מדרגת הסוג.[31] ויראה התאמתותו מהנגדר רצוני מהנדר לפי שהנדר נכלל תחת מצות עשה אחת והיא האומרת מוצא שפתיך תשמור,[32] ותחת מצות לא תעשה אחת והיא האומרת לא יחל דברו.[33] ואחר שהנדר נכלל תחת אלה המצות אין ספק שהנדר ישעבד, כי כל המצות ישעבדו וזה לסבות. אם ראשונה שכל מאמר צווי מאדון לעבד ישעבד בטבע אף אם העבד לא ישתעבד בזה בפירוש, וכן הוא הענין במצות שהם צווי מאדני האדונים הוא האל ית׳ לעבדיו בני ישראל כאמרו ית׳ כי לי בני ישראל עבדים.[34] ועוד שנית נשתעבדנו בפירוש לכל המצות בכלל במאמר אחד כללי במעמד הנכבד הוא מעמד הר סיני וזה ברצון ובבחירה ממנו כמו שני׳ בסדר ואלה המשפטים כל אשר דבר יי נעשה ונשמע.[35] ויש עוד סבה שלישית והיא מיוחדת בנדר ר״ל כי דברי הנדר יכלל בהוראתם השעבוד כי מובן אמרנו אני נודר כך וכך כמובן אמרנו אני משתעבד לכך וכך. והנה זה באור החלק הראשון מהגדר.

ואולם החלק השני והוא אמרנו ביטויי הנה לפי שהחלק הראשון והוא אמרנו שעבוד יכלול כל המצות אחריו נמשך אמרנו ביטויי אשר יבדיל הנדר משאר המצות.[36] והנה יראה התאמתות זה החלק מהנגדר והוא הנדר עד שלזה אמ׳ רז״ל במס׳ שבועות פ׳ שבועות שתים בתרא,[37] אמ׳ שמואל

30. ז״א, דבר מבוסס על הנחות מקובלות, לא על המופת.

31. ז״א, היסוד הראשון של ההגדרה.

32. דב׳ כג כד.

33. במ׳ ל ג.

34. ויק׳ כה נה.

35. שמות כד ז.

36. ההגדרה האריסטוטלית כוללת סוג ומה שמבדיל את המוגדר מיתר הסוג. השוה ספר הכוזרי ד,כה:
„והגדר מחובר מסוגו והבדלו.“

37. שבועות כו ב.

גמר בלבו צריך להוציא בשפתיו בשפתיו שני מבטא שפתיך:³⁸ בשפתיך תלה רחמנא. וכן הוכיחו ג״כ רז״ל מפסוק מוצא שפתיך תשמור³⁹ ומפסוק לבטא בשפתים.⁴⁰וכן ג״כ נמצא דוד המלך ע״ה אומר אבא ביתך בעולות אשלם לך נדרי אשר פצו שפתי ודבר פי בצר לי.⁴¹

וכן ג״כ יעקב אבינו ע״ה אשר היה המתחיל בנדרים תחלה כאמרם ז״ל בב״ר⁴² אמ״ר אבהו כתי׳ אשר נשבע ליי נדר לאביר יעקב,⁴³ לאביר אברהם לאביר יצחק לא נאמר אלא לאביר יעקב: תלה הנדר במי שפתח בו תחלה. עם היות היה במראה ההיא יחידי אין איש אתו כי אם כבוד יי החונה ממולו והיה מספיק לו אז הנדר במורשי לבבו⁴⁴ כי יי יראה ללבב⁴⁵ האמנם להודיע לבני האדם הבאים אחריו דרך הנהגתם בנדרים אחר שהוא היה הפותח בהם תחלה בטא הנדר בפיו ובשפתיו כמאמר הפסוק וידר יעקב נדר לאמר,⁴⁶ אשר אי אפשר שנבאר מלת לאמר כמו שנבאר וידבר השם למשה לאמר שפירושו לאמר לבני ישראל,⁴⁷כי לא היה המאמר מזולתו אליו ולא היה ג״כ שם אתו למי יאמר זה, אבל בהכרח נאמר שהרצון באמרו לאמר שהוא בטה [צ״ל בטא] הנדר בפיו ובשפתיו לא שיעביר ענינו במחשבה לבד. והנה זה באור החלק השני מהגדר אשר הוא ראשון להבדלים.

ואולם החלק השלישי מהגדר והוא אמרנו לעשות דבר מה או לבלתי עשותו הנה הוא אע״פ שלא יושם בגדר להבדיל הנה יושם בו להודיע כי לא יחייב שכל החלקים הנמשכים בגדר אחר הסוג יושמו בו להבדיל אבל יש בהם חלקים יושמו בו להודיע לבדה כי עקר הגדר ותכליתו הוא להודיע עם היות ימשך להודעה ההבדל. ולפי שזה החלק יובן היטב אציע תחלה ואומר כי הנדרים הם שני מינים: נדרים בדבר הרשות אשר

38. במ׳ ל ז.
39. דב׳ כג כד.
40. ויק׳ ה ד.
41. תה׳ סו יג–יד.
42. בראשית רבה ע,א.
43. תה׳ קלב ב.
44. ע״פ איוב יז יא.
45. ש״א טז ז.
46. בר׳ כח כ.
47. למשל בשמות יג א, ועי׳ ו׳ עזרא שם.

הם נדרים באמת והם הנקראים נדרי בטוי ונדרים בדברי מצוה (א22)
ובעבודת האל ית' והם הנקראים נדרי הקדש ואלה הנה הם ישוו
לשבועות.⁴⁸ ולפי שיש לנו כלל גדול בנדרים אשר הם באמת נדרים והוא
שהנדר הוא מיסר חפצא הנה נמשך מזה שהנדר אינו חל בדבר שאין בו
ממש. ולזה האומר בנדר עלי שאיני ישן שאיני מדבר הנדר בטל לפי שאין
כאן חפץ יאסרהו עליו. וזה הוא אחד ההבדלים הנמצאים בין נדר
ושבועה. ולזה הרוצה לאסור עליו השינה באמצעות נדר הנה ראוי לו
שיאמר עיניו אסורים בשינה.⁴⁹

לזה נמצא דוד המלך ע"ה במזמור קל"א המתחיל זכור יי לדוד את כל
ענותו⁵⁰ ונמשך אחריו אשר נשבע ליי נדר לאביר יעקב⁵¹ ספר אחר כן שני
דברים אסר עליו האחד באמצעות שבועה והאחד באמצעות נדר. ואמ'
תחלה אם אבא באהל ביתי אם אעלה על ערש יצועי⁵² ובזה לא דקדק
כי כל הלשונות מספיקים לאסור האדם עליו הדבר באמצעות שבועה.
ואולם בדבר השני אשר אסר עליו באמצעות נדר אמר אם אתן שנה
לעיני לעפעפי תנומה,⁵³ וזה ישוב לאומרו עיניו אסורים בשינה, ואמ' כן
כדי שיהיה הנדר קיים כי זולת זה היה הנדר בטל רצוני אם אמר אם
אישן כמו שאמר אם אבא באהל ביתי.⁵⁴

עוד נמשך מזה השרש רצוני מאמרנו שהנדר מיסר חפצא שהנדר אי
אפשר שיהיה בקיום עשה ואמנם תמיד ימשך ממנו אזהרה ר"ל מצות
לא תעשה. ואמנם לא יצדק זה כי אם בנדרי הרשות ר"ל כי בנדרי הרשות
לא יחול הנדר כי אם בלא תעשה. ולזה אם נדר ואמ' בנדר עלי שאוכל
היום בנדר עלי שאוכל ככר זה אין לנדר הזה חלות.

אמנם בנדר הקדש לפי שאמירה לגבוה כמסירה להדיוט⁵⁵ נהגו בו רז"ל
חומר ורצו שיהיה קיים הן בעשה הן בלא תעשה. ולכן נאמר בגדר לעשות

48. עי' רמב"ם, הל' נדרים א,א–ב.
49. עי' רמב"ם, הל' נדרים ג,א ג,י–יא.
50. תה' קלב א.
51. תה' קלה ב.
52. תה' קלב ג.
53. תה' קלב ד.
54. תה' קלב ג.
55. ע"פ קדושין כח ב.

דבר מה או לבלתי עשותו, וזה כדי שיכלול זה הגדר כל מיני הנדרים הן
נדרי בטוי אשר הם לבד בלא תעשה הן נדרי הקדש אשר הם בעשה ולא
תעשה אשר הם כשבועה, כמו שאמ׳ חז״ל פ״ק דנדרים האומר אשנה
פרק זה או מסכתא זו נדר גדול נדר לאלהי ישראל.[56] והסכימו המפרשים
שזאת היא שבועה. ולזה אין בדעתי להבדיל בזה הגדר נדרים משבועות
אבל להניח הגדר באופן אשר יכלול שניהם.

ואמנם החלק הרביעי מהגדר והוא אמרנו מורה על ענין בנפש הנה
יראה התאמתותו מהנגדר ר״ל מהנודר עד שאם היה האדם נודר בפיו
ובשפתיו ולבו בלתי פונה למה שהוא אומר הנדר ההוא יהיה בטל. ואף אם
היה בלבו דבר מה מסוג הדבר אשר קבל עליו במאמרו אם היה ממנו
זולת מינו הנדר יהיה בטל. ולזה אמרו רז״ל במס׳ שבועות בפ׳ שבועות
שתים בתרא שאם גמר בדעתו לאסור עליו פת חטים והוציא פת שעורים
שהשבועה או הנדר בטל.[57] ויראה שזה הוא שרש גדול אצל רז״ל ר״ל
שאנחנו צריכים בהם אל הסכמת הלב.

ואפשר שבענין נדרים ושבועות יש להם על מה שיסמכו ר״ל לפסוק
האדם בשבועה.[58] וזה שצריך בהם שישתמש האדם מהכח אשר בעבורו
יקרא אדם והוא הדבור הפנימי אשר הוא השכל לא מהדבור החיצוני
לבד. ולזה פרש״י על פסוק האדם בשבועה שיהא אדם בשעת שבועה,[59]
עם היות נזכר בענין האונס.[60] והועתק זה הענין משבועות לנדרים כי
להדמות אשר ביניהם הוקשו נדרים לשבועות. והנה זה הוא באור החלק
הרביעי מהגדר והוא אמרנו מורה על ענין בנפש.

(ב22) אולם החלק החמשי מהגדר והוא אמרנו בחיריי יראה התאמתותו
מהנגדר והוא הנדר עד שלזה אמרו רז״ל במסכת נדרים נודרים לחרמין
ולהרגין ולמוכסין, עד שאמרו שהנדר הנעשה לאלה הוא בטל.[61] ועוד אמרו
על זה הענין במס׳ שבועות שרב כהנא ורב אסי היו חולקים במה ששמעו
מרב שהיה רבם וכל אחד מהם היה קפץ ונשבע הכי אמ׳ רב ואחר כך

56. נדרים ח א, והשוה רמב״ם, הל׳ שבועות א,כז.
57. שבועות כו א–ב.
58. ויק׳ ה ד.
59. עי׳ רש״י על שבועות כו א ד״ה האדם בשבועה.
60. בתלמוד שם הפסוק מובא להוציא את מקרה האונס.
61. משנה נדרים ג,ד, בבלי נדרים כז ב.

באו לפני רב ופסק כאחד מהם ואמ' האחר ואנא לשקרא אישתבעי ואמ'
ליה רב את לבך אנסך.[62] והוכיחו זה ר"ל שהשבועה או הנדר הנעשים
באונס יהיו בטלים מפסוק האדם בשבועה באמרם פרט לאנוס.[63] והנה זהו
באור החלק החמשי מהמגדר והוא אמרנו בחיריי.

ואולם החלק הששי והוא אמרנו נחה בו ההסכמה הנה יראה התאמתותו
מהמגדר והוא הנדר עד שלזה אמרו רז"ל שאף אם היו פיו ולבו שום
והוציא הנדר בפיו ובשפתיו ולבבו יבין ושב מהנדר תוך כדי דבור אשר
הוא כדי שאלת שלום תלמיד לרב הנדר בטל[64] ושהוא נדר בטעות ושבחזרה
גלה דעתו שהיה טועה. והנה זאת תקנה עשו חכמי האמת[65] הועילו חכמים
בתקנתם זאת למחשבות אדם כי המה הבל[66] ולפעמים כל רוחו יוציא[67]
מבלי עצה והסכמה קודמת ולזה רצו שתוך כדי דבור יוכל לתקן מעוותו[68]
כאות נפשו. ובכאן אשים אחרית דברי בחלק הראשון והוא בגבול הראשון
אשר הוא נדרו.

ואולם החלק השני הנה הוא בגבול השני והוא אמרנו ושלמו.[69] ואמ'
שהנדרים שני מינים האחד נדרי בטוי והם נדרי הרשות ואלה אי אפשר
שיעבור האדם עליהם כי אם בשלא יקים אותם האדם כלל. והמין השני
נדרי הקדש ואלה אפשר שיעבור האדם עליהם בשני מינים אם בשלא
יקיימם כלל ואם בשיאחר קיומם. והאיחור הנה הוא מוגבל כבר על פי
חכמי האמת כמו שנזכר במס' ר"ה שהוא שלשה רגלים כסדרן או חמשה
שלא כסדרן לפי שנכללו בהם שלשה כסדרן.[70]

ועוד נמצא מין אחר מהנדרים אנחנו מחוייבים להשלימם תכף שנדרנו
אותם, וזה כמו שאנו נודרים לצדקה כמו שנאמ' במסכת ר"ה פ"ק, אמ'
רבא וצדקה מיחייב עליה לאלתר מאי טעמא דהא קיימי עניים.[71] ואומר

62. שבועות כו א.

63. שם.

64. שבועות לב א, רמב"ם, הל' שבועות ב,יז.

65. ז"א חז"ל, ועי' הערה 40 לתרגום.

66. ע"פ תה' צד יא.

67. ע"פ משלי כט יא.

68. ע"פ קהלת א טו.

69. תה' עו יב.

70. ראש השנה ד א–ב ועי' הערה 43 לתרגום.

71. ראש השנה ו א.

שנדרי החברה המפוארה הזאת ר״ל הדברים אשר קבלו עליהם הנה הם
כמעט מזה המין. ואומר ראשונה שהתפלה אשר קבלו עליהם הנה להיותנו
מחוייבים בה שלש פעמים ביום הנה אין צריך לומר שאנחנו מחוייבים בה
לאלתה, אבל גם תמיד בלי הפסק אנחנו מחוייבים ובעת צאתנו מחיוב
התפלה האחת נכנס בחיוב האחרת הנמשכת לה:⁷²

ועוד שנית הנה הנה הדבר השני אשר קבלו עליהם והוא תלמוד תורה תמיד
כל היום האדם מחוייב בו וכל העתים והזמנים נאותים לזה. הבט נא הפסוק
האומר והגית בו יומם ולילה:⁷³ ולזה נעים זמירות באמרו ושלמו⁷⁴ הנה הוא
ידבר עם בני החברה ועם אשר בגילם⁷⁵ וזה משלשה פנים. האחד ושלמו:
קיימו נדריכם ואל תעברו עליהם, השני ושלמו: קיימו נדריכם בלי איחור,
השלישי ושלמו: אזהרה למנהיגי החברה שיכריחו שאר בני החברה לקיים
נדרם, כמו שהוכיחו רז״ל במסכ׳ ר״ה פ״ק ושם נאמר מוצא שפתיך תשמור
ועשית:⁷⁶ אזהרה לבית דין שיעשוך.⁷⁷ ומנהיגי החברה הם ב״ד לכל החברים
(א23) בכל עניני החברה. ובכאן אשים אחרית דברי בחלק השני והוא אמרנו
ושלמו.

ואולם החלק השלישי הנה הוא בהרכבת שני אלה הגבולים רצוני אמרנו
נדרו ושלמו.⁷⁸ והנה אניח פה דרוש⁷⁹ אחד והוא זה: האם הפעל הנעשה
באמצעות נדר וקבלה משובח יותר ויקנה לבעליו זכות יותר מאשר יקנה
אותו הפעל עצמו אם יעשה מבלי נדר וקבלה? או הענין בהפך? והנה יראו
בכאן פנים מן ההראות לשני חלקי הסותר⁸⁰ הן לטענות יסודתם בהרר״י⁸¹
השכל הן לטענות לקוחות מדברי הנביאים ומדברי רז״ל.

ואומר תחלה שהפעל הנעשה בלי קבלה ונדר קודם משובח ויקנה
לבעליו שעור גדול מהזכות מאשר יקנה אותו הפעל עצמו אם יעשה

72. עי׳ הערה 46 לתרגום.
73. יהושע א ח.
74. תה׳ עו יב.
75. אחרים הקרובים להם בדעתם, חברי חברות דומות. השוה רות רבה ב,ז.
76. דב׳ כג כד.
77. ראש השנה ו א, ספרי כי תצא רסה.
78. תה׳ עו יב.
79. שאלה ויכוחית נוסח תורת הסכולאסטיקה (quaestio). עי׳ הערה 17 להקדמה.
80. עי׳ הערה 50 לתרגום.
81. ע״פ תה׳ פז א.

באמצעות קבלה ונדר קודם. ונמצאו על זה הדעת חמשה טענות.

הראשונה היא זאת. אין ספק שהדבר הנעשה ברצון ובחירה הוא יותר טוב מהנעשה באונס ושעל הפעלות אשר נעשה בבחירה ימשך לנו מן השבח או הגנות לא על אשר נעשה בהכרח ואונס כמו שנראה בשלישי מהמדות.[82] והפעל הנעשה בלא קבלת נדר הוא נעשה בבחירה ורצון והפעל הנעשה באמצעות קבלת נדר נעשה בהכרח כי הנדר ישעבד ויכריח. הנה ימשך מזה שהפעל הנעשה בלי קבלת נדר הוא יותר משובח וייותר מעולה מהנעשה באמצעות קבלת נדר.

שנית היא זאת. אין ספק שהפעל אשר נוכל לעשותו מבלי שנעשה פעל אחר מגונה הוא יותר טוב מהפעל אשר אי אפשר שנעשהו מבלי שנעשה פעל אחר מגונה. וכן הוא בפעל הנעשה באמצעות נדר כי אי אפשר שנעשהו מבלי שנפשיט מעצמנו ונשליך מעלינו אותה המתנה היקרה אשר חנן אלהים אותנו והיא הבחירה והרצון, וזאת היא מהיותר מגונה שבפעלות. ואולם הדבר הנעשה מבלי קבלת נדר הנה הוא יעשה מבלתי שנעשה אותו הפעל המגונה ר״ל שנשליך ונפשיט מעלינו אותה המתנה היקרה.

שלישית היא זאת. אין ספק שהדבר הנעשה בהכרח ואונס נעשה עם צער ויגון. ואולם עבודת הש׳ ית׳ אין ראוי שתעשה ביגון ואנחה אבל בששון ובשמחה כמאמר הפסוק מזמור ק׳ עבדו את יי בשמחה.[83] ועוד שהכתוב מיעד לנו עונש אם לא נעבדהו בשמחה כמאמר הפסוק בפר׳ כי תבא תחת אשר לא עבדת את יי אלהיך בשמחה ובטוב לבב מרב כל.[84] והנה מזה ימשך שהפעל הנעשה בלי קבלת נדר אשר אפשר שיעשה בשמחה ולזה אפשר שנעבוד בו האל ית׳ יותר טוב מהפעל הנעשה באמצעות נדר אשר להעשותו באונס והכרח אי אפשר שיעשה בשמחה ולזה אי אפשר שיעבד בו האל ית׳.

הטענה הרביעית היא זאת. תכלית הנדר איננו כי אם כדי שיהיה הרצון האנושי תקוע במקום נאמן[85] באופן שיעשה האדם הפעל המעלה וייסר ממנו אפשרות עשיית הפכו. ואי אפשר שיהיה הרצון באופן יותר קיים כי

82. אריסטו, אתיקה ג,א.
83. תה׳ ק ג.
84. דב׳ כח מז.
85. ע״פ יש׳ כב כג.

אם בשיעשה העניין בפעל. הנה א״כ עשיית הפעל באמצעות נדר (ב233) איננו יותר טוב מעשייתו בלא נדר. הנה א״כ עשיית הדבר בלא נדר יותר טוב מעשייתו באמצעות נדר אחר שעשיית הנדר מותר אין תועלת בו וראוי להרחיק המותרות.

הטענה החמישית והיא לקוחה מדברי רז״ל. אמרו במס׳ [בבא] קמא פ׳ הכונס תניא ר׳ נתן אומ׳ כל הנודר כאלו בנה במה והמקיימו כאלו הקריב עליה קרבן בשעת אסור במות.[86] ראה איך גנו זה הפעל ר״ל הנדר עד שהמשילוהו לבונה במה. וזה לפי שבזה יכין עצמו לחטוא ר״ל לעבור על הנדר. ולזה אמרו רז״ל שמצוה שישאל האדם על נדרו[87] וזהו אמרו והמקיימו כאלו הקריב עליה קרבן בשעת אסור במות. וזה כי אין ראוי לאדם שיהנה עד יקיים נדרו. ואמנם ראוי לו שישאל עליו טרם יקיימהו כדי שלא יעמוד בסכנת העבירה עליו. ולזה אמרו ג״כ רז״ל בירושלמי נדרים לא דייך במה שאסרה עליך תורה אלא שאתה אוסר עליך דברים אחרים.[88] הנה מאלה הטענות יראה שיותר מעולה ויותר משובח הוא הפעל הנעשה בלא נדר מהפעל הנעשה באמצעות נדר.

ואולם הטענות על סותר זה החלק ר״ל שיותר מעלה הוא הפעל הנעשה באמצעות נדר מהפעל הנעשה בלא נדר הן ארבעה. הראשונה לקוחה מהפסוק אשר בו היתה פתיחת דברינו והיא אמרו נדרו ושלמו.[89] הנה יראה שנעים זמירות מצוה וייעץ הנדר והתשלומין.

השנית היא זאת, והיא לקוחה מדברי רז״ל. אמרו במס׳ קדושין פר׳ ראשון גדול המצוה ועושה ממי שאינו מצווה ועושה.[90] והנה העושה הדבר באמצעות נדר הוא מצווה כי תכללהו מצות עשה האומרת מוצא שפתיך תשמור[91] ומצות לא תעשה האומרת לא יחל דברו.[92] ואולם הדבר הנעשה בלא נדר אין האדם מצווה עליו כי לא יכלל תחת מצוה. הנה יראה מזה

---

86. עי׳ נדרים כב ב ורבנו נסים שם. המאמר איננו מופיע במסכת בבא קמא.
87. עי׳ רבנו נסים על נדרים כב ב ד״ה והמקיימו, רמב״ם הל׳ נדרים יג,כה.
88. ירושלמי נדרים כט א.
89. תה׳ עו יב.
90. קדושין לא א.
91. דב׳ כג כד.
92. במ׳ ל ג.

שהפעל הנעשה באמצעות נדר הוא יותר טוב וייותר משובח ויזכה יותר
לעושה אותו מהפעל הנעשה בלא נדר.

הטענה השלישית היא זאת. אמרו רז״ל נדרים פ״א, תניא, טוב אשר לא
תדור משתדור ולא תשלם.[93] טוב מזה ומזה שאינו נודר כל עקר, דברי ר׳
מאיר. ר׳ יהודה אומר טוב מזה נודר ומשלם. ונפסקה הלכה כר׳ יהודה.[94]
הנה מזה יראה שהפעל הנעשה באמצעות נדר הוא יותר מעולה מהפעל וכו׳.

הטענה הרביעית היא זאת. כי אנחנו רואים שהאבות הקדושים כמו יעקב
אבינו ודוד המלך ע״ה היו נודרים, ואם הדבר הנעשה מבלי אמצעות נדר
היה יותר משובח וייותר מזכה מהדבר הנעשה באמצעות נדר כן היו עושים
ר״ל שהיו עושים מה שהיה בדעתם לעשות בלא נדר כדי שהפעל יהיה יותר
משובח וייותר מזכה. ועוד אמרו רבי׳ ע״ה בפסוק וידר יעקב נדר לאמר[95]
דקדקו תיבת לאמר ואמרו לאמר לדורות שיהו נודרין בעת צרתן.[96] והנה
מזה יראה שהפעל הנעשה באמצעות נדר הוא יותר משובח וכו׳.

מכח אלא הטענות הנעשות לכל אחד מחלקי הסותר הנה הדרוש תלוי
ועומד ומסופק יתר מאד. והנה ראוי לנו עתה שנזכך העיון ונסיר ממנו
המבוכות. ואציע לזה חמשה הקדמות אמתיות אין מי שיכחישם.

ההקדמה הראשונה היא זאת, שהפעל הטוב והמעלה כל עוד שימשך
מרצון יותר קיים ובלתי משתנה כן יהיה יותר טוב וכן יתוסף בעלוי כמו
שהענין בהפך שהפעל הרע כל עוד שימשך מרצון (א24) יותר קיים כן יוסיף
רוע וייהיה החטא יותר גדול ואלה החטאים הם הנקראים זדונות.

ההקדמה השנית היא זאת, שאחר שהיושר שהעבד יחייב להיות סר
למשמעת האדון והנוצר ליוצר הנה ימשך מזה שאחר שיחסנו אל האל ית׳
הוא יחס העבד אל האדון והנוצר אל היוצר (שאר)[97] שאשר יהיה יותר סר
למשמעת האל ית׳ וימסור עצמו לעבודתו הנה הוא יותר מתקרב אל היושר
ועושה המוטל עליו.

93. קהלת ה ד.

94. נדרים ט א, חולין ב א, ועי׳ הערה 62 לתרגום.

95. בר׳ כח כ.

96. בראשית רבה ע,א.

97. אם אני מפענח נכון את המלה הזאת, נראה לי שהסופר טעה והתכוון למחוק את המלה ולכתוב
במקומה את המלה הבאה, שאשר.

ההקדמה השלישית היא זאת, שאשר ימסור לאל ית׳ הפעל והיכלת אשר
לו על בחירת הפעל הנה ימסור עצמו יותר לעבודת האל ית׳ מאשר ימסור
אליו הפעל לבד לא היכלת אשר לו בבחירת מה ירצה, כמו שהאיש הנותן
העץ והפרי נותן יותר מאשר נותן הפרי לבדו. וכן העניין פה ר״ל שהפעלות
הם פרי הרצון אשר לו היכלת.

ההקדמה הרביעית היא זאת, שהפעל הנעשה באמצעות נדר הוא נמשך
מרצון קיים ובלתי משתנה ואין כן העניין בפעל הנמשך [צ״ל הנעשה] מבלי
קבלת נדר.

ההקדמה החמשית היא זאת, שהנודר ומקיים נדרו מוסר לאל ית׳
הפעל והיכלת אשר לו לבחור ואולם העושה הפעל מבלי נדר הנה הוא
נותן לאל ית׳ הפעל לבד לא היכלת אשר לו.

מהההקדמות האלה אם תסודרנה כראוי ותושבנה לצורה הקשית[98]
אפשר שיצא לאור פסק דין הדרוש[99] ויראה שהוא זה שהפעל הטוב הנעשה
באמצעות נדר הוא יותר טוב ויותר משובח מהנעשה בלא נדר. וזה לפי
שהעושה הפעל באמצעות נדר הנה פעלותו זאת נמשכת מרצון קיים
ובלתי משתנה כמו שנז׳ בהקדמה רביעית ואין כן העושה הפעל בלא נדר.
והפעל הנמשך מרצון קיים ובלתי משתנה יותר מעלה מהפעל הנמשך
מרצון בלתי קיים כמו שנזכר בהקדמה הא׳. ועוד שהנודר ומקיים מוסר
לאל ית׳ פעלתו והיכלת אשר לו בבחירתו כמו שנזכר בהקדמה הה׳ והנותן
הפעל והרצון נותן יותר ומשמעת המקבל יותר מאשר יתן הפעל
לבד כמו שנזכר בהקדמה הג׳. ואשר ישתעבד יותר וסר למשמעת האל ית׳
יתקרב יותר אל היושר כמו שנזכר בהקדמה הב׳. הנה הנודר ומקיים יותר
מעלה לפי שיכניס עצמו יותר תחת עבודת האל ית׳ מהעושה הפעל בלא
קבלת נדר.

ואולם זה המשפט איננו אמתי דרך כל ובהחלט עד שכל דבר יהיה
יותר טוב עשותו באמצעות נדר מעשותו בלא נדר. ואבל ראוי להפריד[100]
כללות המשפט על זה הדרך. וזה שזה המשפט אמנם יצדק בנדרים אשר

98. עי׳ הערה 66 לתרגום.
99. ראוי לשים לב לצירוף של לשון ההלכה („פסק דין״) ולשון הפילוסופיה (ה„דרוש״).
100. עי׳ הערה 67 לתרגום.

הם בדברי מצוה כמו נדרי החברה הזאת[101] שהם תפלה ותלמוד תורה והם דברים אשר אנחנו מצווים ועומדים כבר עליהם ומאלה הנדרים ודומיהם אמרו רז"ל במס' נדרים אמ' רב גדל אמ' רב מנין שנשבעין לקיים את המצוה שנ' נשבעתי ואקיימה לשמור משפטי צדקך.[102] ונשאל בגמ' והלא מושבע ועומד מהר סיני הוא? אלא הא קמ"ל [קא משמע לן] דשרי ליה לזרוזי נפשיה.[103]

ואולם הנדרים אשר הם בדברי הרשות הנה אין ראוי שירגיל אדם עצמו בהם. ומכיוצא בהם ב[נמס'] נדרים פר' [ארבעה] נד'[104] אמ' שמואל כל הנודר ואפי' מקיים נקרא חוטא. אמ"ר אבהו מאי קראה? שנ' וכי תחדל לנדור לא יהיה בך חטא.[105] יליף חדילה חדילה: כתי' הכא תחדל וכתי' התם שם רשעים חדלו רוגז.[106] ומהם נאמר ג"כ בויקרא רבה, יש בוטה במדקרות [צ"ל כמדקרות] חרב:[107] רבן גמליאל אומ' כדאי הוא כל שמבטא בנדרים לדקרו בחרב אלא שלשון חכמים מרפא[108] לאחר שנדר מן הככר וי ליה דאכיל וי ליה דלא אכיל, אי אכיל מחייל ליה לנדריה אי לא אכיל מיית. מה יעשה ילך אצל חכם ויתיר לו נדר הה"ד [והדא הוא דכתיב] ולשון חכמים מרפא.[109] והנה (ב24) זה רצוני אמרו אי לא אכיל מיית אי אפשר שיאמר מנדרי מצוה כי לא ימשך מהם דבר רע בשום צד כי חיים הם לכל מוצאיהם.[110]

והנה נשאר עתה עלינו להשיב על הטענות אשר הובאו בתחלה על החלק הסותר האחר והם חמשה.

והנה הראשונה היא שהנדר נעשה באונס והכרח והדבר הנעשה באונס איננו משובח כדבר הנעשה ברצון. התשובה היא שהנדר התחלתו וסבתו היא הבחירה והרצון אשר הם ענין מוטבע בנפש מתחלת בריאתנו ואחר

---

101. שוב פונה הדרשן לנסיבת הדרשה וקהל השומעים.

102. תה' קיט קו.

103. נדרים ח א.

104. נדרים כב א.

105. דב' כג כג.

106. איוב ג יז.

107. ויקרא רבה לז,ג.

108. משלי יב יח.

109. שם.

110. ע"פ משלי ד כב.

שתתחלתו דבר פנימי לא דבר מחוץ הנה איננו בהכרח כי הפעל או התנועה ההכרחי הם אותם אשר סבתם דבר מחוץ.[111]

ואולם הטענה השנית הנה יסודתה הוא שבאמצעות הנדר נפשיט מעלינו מעיל הבחירה והיא המתנה היקרה אשר חנן אותנו האל ית׳. התשובה היא שהפשטת הבחירה מעלינו בשנכריע אותה לחלק המעלה מחלקי הסותר איננו דבר מגונה כמו שאיננו מגונה שנפשיט מעלינו בשנשים בפעל החלק היותר מעולה מחלקי הסותר. ועוד נאמר בזאת הטענה שבאמצעות הנדר היינו משימים עצמנו בסכנת העבירה עליו. והתשובה היא שזה לא יקנה לנדר רוע עד שבעבור זה יחוייב שירוחק כי הסכנה איננה מצד הנדר ואמנם היא מצד הרצון המשתנה מההסכמה אשר נח בה בעת עשיית הנדר.

ואולם הטענה השלישית הנה יסודתה הוא בשהדבר הנעשה באמצעות קבלת נדר הנה הוא יושפע וימשך מהכרח ואונס ושהדבר הנעשה בהכרח אי אפשר שיעשה בשמחה ובששון. הנה תשובה זאת הטענה נכללת בתשובת הטענה הראשונה וזה שהדבר הנעשה באמצעות נדר איננו מושפע מהכרח אחר שהתתחלתו היא בחירה ורצון.

ואולם הטענה הרביעית הנה יסודתה הוא בשתכלית הנדר הוא לעשות הדבר בפעל, וא״כ אחר שנעשה הדבר בפעל בלא נדר הנה הוא טוב כמו הדבר הנעשה באמצעות נדר. התשובה היא שהן אמת שהדבר הנעשה בלא נדר הנה הוא מצד עצמו טוב כמו הדבר הנעשה בקבלת נדר. ואולם הנעשה באמצעות נדר הוא יותר טוב מצד מהותו ושרשו ר״ל שהוא מושפע מרצון קיים, וכבר אמרנו שהדבר המושפע מרצון קיים הוא יותר טוב מהמושפע מרצון בלתי קיים.

ואולם הטענה החמשית הנה היא היתה לקוחה מדברי רז״ל והוא אמרם במסכת [בבא] קמא כל הנודר כאלו בנה במה, ואמרם בירושלמי נדרים לא דייך במה שאסרה עליך תורה.[112] הנה תשובת זה מבוארת וזה כי אלו המימרות לא נאמרו כי אם בנדרי איסר שהם בדברי הרשות לא בנדרי הקדש כי בנדרי הקדש ר״ל בנדרים אשר הם קבלת מצוה ראוי לאדם ומותר לעשותם וזה לזרוזי נפשיה כמו שנאמר במימרת רב גדל.[113]

111. עי׳ הערה 73 לתרגום.

112. נדרים כב א, ירושלמי נדרים כט א.

113. נדרים ח א.

ובכאן אשים קנצי למלין[114] בהפרדת זה הדרוש, והיה זה אחרית דברי בחלק השלישי אשר הוא הרכבת שני אלה הגבולים רצוני נדרו ושלמו.[115]

ואולם החלק הרביעי הנה הוא באלה הגבולים ליי אלהיכם.[116] ולפי שאלה הם החלקים האחרונים מפתיחת דברי אחבר אליהם החלקים הקודמים ואדבר מעט בכונת המאמר רצוני אמרו נדרו ושלמו ליי אלהיכם.[117] ואומר שכונת זה הפסוק היא לזרז ולעורר אישי האדם שיתחכמו בתחבולותיהם ויבקשו דרך איך יוכלו להרבות עבודות לאל ית׳,[118] כי לפי שאנחנו עם בני ישראל נשואי חסדיו ויום יום יעמס לנו[119] טובות אנחנו בלתי ראויים אליהם.

כי תחלה הנה הוא המציאנו אחר האין הגמור והאפס (א25) המוחלט. וזאת שנית יתמיד מציאותנו דבר יום ביומו כי לולי יי היו כל הנמצאות לשמה כרגע[120] שמים כעשן נמלחו והארץ כבגד תבלה יושביה כמו כן ימותון.[121] כי האל איננו כשאר הפועלים אשר אחר שהמציאו הפעול לא יצטרך אליהם להתמדת המציאות כמו הבנאי אשר ימצא הבית אשר הוא פעולו אחר העדרו ואין כן הענין בו ית׳ כי בהסתלקו יסתלקו כל הנמצאות והיו כלא היו.[122] ולזה אמרו מתקני התפלה המחדש טובו [כך] בכל יום תמיד מעשה בראשית.[123] כי אחר שהנמצאות צריכות אליו להתמדת מציאותם אפשר שיאמר בכל יום שהוא מחדש אותם כמו שעשה במעשה בראשית.

ובפרט יראו הטבתו וחסדו בהוים הנפסדים אשר יש בהם התחלה להפסדם וזה להפכיות[124] הנמצא בפשוטים אשר מהם הורכבו. ולזה נאמר

114. ע״פ איוב יח ב.

115. תה׳ עו יב.

116. שם.

117. שם.

118. עי׳ הערה 78 לתרגום.

119. תה׳ סח כ.

120. תה׳ עג יט.

121. יש׳ נא ו.

122. עו׳ טו.

123. תפלת שחרית, הברכה הראשונה לפני קריאת שמע. הגירסא המקובלת היא„ובטובו מחדש בכל יום...".

124. ז״א היסודות הפשוטים מתנגדים אחד לשני וזה גורם שינוי והפסד. עי׳ אלבו, ספר העיקרים ד, תחלת פרק נא.

טוב יי לכל ורחמיו על כל מעשיו,[125] ר"ל כי טובו מושפע על כל הנמצאות הן
בנצחים הן בהוים הנפסדים והוא סבה לקיומם והתמדתם, ואולם מעשיו
והם ההוים הנפסדים הנה הם צריכים בקיומם והתמדתם למדת רחמים
לפי שבעצמם נמצאת סבת הפסד ומהרסם ומחריבם מהם[126] ובהם.

ולזה ג"כ רמזו מתקני ברכת המזון באמרם הזן את העולם כלו בטובו
בחן בחסד וברחמים. והקדים תחלה תאר הטוב והוא אשר בו וממנו
מושפע התמדת מציאות הכל והוא הנרצה באמרו הזן כי ההזנה היא
ההתמדה. ואמ' אחר כן בחן בחסד וברחמים, ורמז באלה השלשה תארים
לשלשה חלקים נחלקו אליהם חיי האדם, ועם היות יהיו החלקים יותר
האמנם כלם נכללו באלה השלשה.

הנה הראשון הוא שהכח הטבעי הוא כל כך חזק שיספיק להביא תמורת
מה שנתך ועוד יספיק לגדול, ובזה החלק תספיק לקיום האיש והתמדתו
מדת החן. ואולם בחלק השני מהחיים הנה הכח הטבעי יספיק להביא
תמורת מה שנתך לא לגדול, ולזה החלק מהחיים יצטרך לקיום האיש
והתמדתו מדת החסד. ואולם בחלק השלישי מהחיים הנה הכח הטבעי
חלוש באופן שלא יספיק להשלים כל תמורת ההתכה ובזה החלק מהחיים
נצטרך לקיום האיש והתמדתו מדת הרחמים.

ועוד בה שלישית הגדיל האל ית' לעשות עמנו[127] וזה שיעד לנו ההצלחה
הנצחית ואחר שיוציאנו מעולם האנחות ישים אותנו בתענוג מופלג ואחר
שהיינו הוים נפסדים ישיבנו נצחיים.

ורביעית נתחסד עמנו ברחמיו וברב חסדיו והורנו הדרך ישכן אור[128]
אשר באמצעותו נשיג אלה החיים הנצחיים וזה בשנתן לנו תורתו הקדושה
אשר היא הדרך הישר להשגת אלה החיים הנצחיים, כמאמר הפסוק
תודיעני ארח חיים שובע שמחות את פניך נעימות בימינך נצח.[129] והכונה
שנצח ותמיד מאין הפסק יושפע אלינו מהאל ית' נעימות וחסדים וזה כי
את פניו והוא לעולם שכלו טוב[130] ישימנו בתענוג מופלג נגילה ונשמחה

125. תה' קמה ט.
126. ע"פ יש' מט יז.
127. ע"פ תה' קכו ג.
128. איוב לח יט.
129. תה' טז יא.
130. ע"פ קידושין לט ב.

בו.[131] וזהו הנרצה באמרו שובע שמחות.[132] ובעולם הזה יישיר אותנו אל
הדרך אשר בו נגיע אל אלה החיים הנצחיים. וכאלו זה הפסוק נחלק
לשלשה חלקים והשני חלקים הראשונים הם במדרגת ההקדמות ומהם
ימשך (ב25) החלק האחרון אשר הוא במדרגת התולדה.

ועם היות האל ית׳ אשר אין ליכלתו קצה ותכלית יוכל לתת לנו
ההצלחה הנצחית לו יחפץ מבלי שיעמס עלינו רבוי אלה המצות והעבודות
האמנם שכל כל בעל שכל יחייב שיותר טוב הוא לנו שנשיג זאת ההצלחה
ואלה החיים הנצחיים באמצעות ראיות והאותות מה קודם מאשר נשיגהו
חנם בלא האותות וראיות. וזה ההאותות הקודם הם המצות המעשיות
והשכליות המונחות בתורתנו הקדושה. ואל זה כיון ר׳ חנניה בן עקשיה
באמרו רצה המקום לזכות את ישראל לפיכך הרבה להם תורה ומצות,[133]
ר״ל כי תוספת זכות הוא להם שיקנו ההצלחה הנצחית באמצעות רבוי
מצות ועבודות מאשר יקנו אותה חנם. מצורף לזה שזאת ההצלחה הנצחית
נמשכת למצות המונחות בתורתנו הקדושה כמעט המשכות טבעי וזה
לסגולה נפלאה הטביע השי״ת בכללות המקובץ בפרטיה.

וזאת ההצלחה היא דבקות הנפש עם צור ממנו הוחצבה[134] כי אחר
שהוסר החמר אשר הוא מעיק מהדבקות כשהנפש תהיה זכה ונקייה
ממושכלות כוזבות ומתכונות רעות יגיעו מהרגל פעלות העבירות ימשך
הדבקות. וזה כי בין הנפש והשכל הנבדל אשר עמו הדבקות אהבה וחשק
להאותות והתיחסות ביניהם עד שלזה חפץ בה המלך ונקראה בשם בת
ורעיה ונקרא הוא דוד ורע כמו שנראה במגלת שיר השירים.[135]

ומדבר מזאת האהבה אמ׳ הפסוק מים רבים לא יוכלו לכבות את
האהבה ונהרות לא ישטפוה, אם יתן איש את כל הון ביתו בוז יבוזו לו.[136]
וכונת הפסוק בחלק הראשון ממנו היא שהנפש כשהיא זכה ונקייה
מהתכונות הרעות אין דבר אפשר שיעיקה מזה הדבקות והוא הנרצה
באמרו מים רבים לא יוכלו וכו׳. וכונתו בחלק השני היא להודיענו הפך

131. ע״פ תה׳ קיח כד.

132. תה׳ טז יא.

133. משנה מכות ג,טז.

134. ע״פ יש׳ נא א.

135. עי׳ הערה 87 לתרגום.

136. שיר ח ז.

זה ר״ל שהנפש כשאינה זכה בעצמותה ר״ל שלא יהיו תכונותיה תכונות שוות ומעולות אין דבר מהמעלות החיצוניות–עושר ונכסים וכבוד ונרמז אליהם באמרו הון ביתו–אשר באמצעותם יגיע אל זה הדבקות. ואמנם בוז יבוזו לאיש אשר ישער בנפשו זה כמו שיבוזו וילעיגו לאדם ידמה בנפשו לקנות אבן יקרה שוה עשרת אלפים ככר כסף בשוה פרוטה, כי זה ראוי ללעג עליו.

וזאת האהבה והחשק תפול בין הדברים להתיחסות והאותות ביניהם. ולפעמים יהיה ההתיחסות ההוא נסתר ונעלם מאד ולזה יהיה סבה לפעלות זרות בעניינו אנחנו הסכלים בהתיחסות ההוא כמו שנראה מהאבן המושכת הברזל והמושכת התבון. ויש מי שאומר שיש הנה אבן מושכת הזהב עד שנאמר שאין נמצא בעולם לא ימצא נמצא אחר בינו ובינו ההתיחסות ההוא. ואמ׳ חכם אחד שלכל נמצא מגניטאס ימשכהו.[137]

וזה ההתיחסות נמצאהו אף במספרים והם אותם אשר נקראו נאהבים. וזה כי כל אחד מאלה נכלל בחברו ונמצא בתוכו, ר״ל שהחלקים המונים כל אחד מהם יעלו בקבוצם למספר האחר. והמספרים הראשונים אשר תמצא אליהם זאת הסגלה הם קק״כ ורפ״ד.[138] ואל אלה נרמז במגלת שיר השירים באמרו סמכוני באשישות רפדוני בתפוחים כי חולת אהבה אני.[139] ופתחה החושקת וזה כי החסר ראוי שיתעורר מצד עצמו לבקש השלמות ושאלה המספר הנאהב אשר אצל חשוקה והוא רפ״ד כי הוא הגדול וראוי שיהיה מיוחס לזכר ולזה רמז הפסוק באמרו רפדוני אשר שרשו רפד אשר יעלה בגימטריא מאתים ושמנים וארבעים.

(ב26) ואחר כן בפסוק אחר נאמר לבבתיני אחותי כלה לבבתיני באחד מעיניך באחד ענק מצואריניך.[140] והנה נאמר זה בשם השכל הנבדל והוא החשוק ר״ל נקשרה נפשי בעבותות אהבתך[141] באחד מעיניך ר״ל באחד מכחותיך המשיגים כי בנפש יש כחות רבים ואין ההתיחסות וההאותות אשר בינה ובין השכל הנבדל בסבת בכחות הבלתי משיגים אבל בסבת

---

137. עי׳ הערות 89–90 לתרגום.
138. עי׳ הערה 91 לתרגום.
139. שיר ב ה.
140. שיר ד ט.
141. ע״פ הושע יא ד.

המשיגים, ומהמשיגים לא בסבת כלם כי הם הרבה ר"ל משיג בפנים בשכל ומשיג מחוץ בחושים, ואמנם ההתיחסות בסבת אחד מהם והוא הכח השכלי, ולזה כיון באמרו באחד מעיניך והוא עין השכל. ואמ' אחר כן באחד ענק ר"ל באחד מעדייך ותכשיטיך כי הכחות הם תחשיטי הנפש. ורמז באמרו ענק למספר הנאהב הקטן אשר הוא קק"כ, והוא אשר ראוי שייוחס אל הנקבה להיותה הקטן.

ולהיות אלה המספרים נאהבים יש להם סגלה בהבאת האהבה בין אישי האדם עד שלזה נמצא יעקב אבינו ע"ה, לפי שהיה חושק להסיר השנאה אשר היתה בלב עשו אחיו אצלו ולהביא תחתיה אהבה, התחכם להקדים הכנות לזה כפי כח, ולזה שלח אליו עזים מאתים ותישים עשרים[142] שהוא המספר האחד הנאהב. ולפי שהוא היה חושק שתתישב האהבה ביניהם איך שתהיה ואף עם לא תהיה על דרך השווי אבל תהיה האהבה ביניהם האהבה אשר בין האדון והעבד ויהיה עשו במדרגת האדון ויעקב במדרגת העבד, לזה שלח אליו מצדו המספר הקטון שבנאהבים שהוא קק"כ.

ונשוב לעניננו ונאמר שלהתיחסות הנופל בין הנפש המדברת והשכל הנבדל הנה כשיוסר החמר המעיק והתכונות הרעות יתחייב הדבקות. וזהו הנקרא צרור החיים כמאמר הפסוק והיתה נפש אדוני צרורה בצרור החיים.[143] ואז תשוב הנפש כמלאך יי, כי ההפרש וההתחלפות אשר בין אישי האדם והמלאך הוא באלה החיים, וזה בסבת ההבדל האחרון המונח בגדר האדם וזה הוא באמרנו חי מדבר מת,[144] עד שאפשר לאיש האדם שיאמר למלאך כי המות יפריד ביני ובינך;[145] וזה כי ההבדל ההוא והוא אמרנו מת הוא המבדיל. וכמו שאפשר אליו באלה החיים שיאמר המות יפריד ביני ובינך כן אפשר אליו שיאמר בחיים האחרונים הם הנצחיים אשר הם אחר המות, המות יחבר ביני ובינך רצוני כי המות הוא סבת החבור הנופל בינותינו.

וזה הדבקות או התענוג הנמשך אליו הוא אשר קראוהו ז"ל עולם

142. בר' לב טו.
143. ש"א כה כט.
144. רמב"ם מלות ההגיון י,ד.
145. ע"פ רות א יז.

הבא, והצער ההפכי אליו ר"ל התשוקה אל זה הדבקות וההמנע מהשגתו הוא הנקרא אצלם ז"ל גיהנם.[146] וזה כי נפש הרשע אחר הפרדה מהחמר המכה אותה בסנורי[147] הסכלות תשתוקק אל חשוקה והוא מחצבה הראשון וימנע ממנה הדבקות והנה לזה תעמוד בצער מופלג.

ואל זה כיון ר' שמעון בן לקיש במס' ע"ז פרק הראשון במאמר אחד זר בתחלת העיון. נאמר שם[148] אמ"ר שמעון, אין גיהנם לעתיד לבא אלא אלא הב"ה מוציא חמה מנרתיקה ומקדירה, רשעים נידונין בה שנ' כי הנה היום בא בוער כתנור והיו כל זדים וכל עושי רשעה קש ולהט אותם היום הבא,[149] וצדיקים מתרפאים בה שנ' וזרחה לכם יראי שמי שמש צדקה ומרפא,[150] ולא עוד אלא שמתעדנין בה שנ' ויצאתם ופשתם כעגלי מרבק.[151]

וכונתו היא זאת שגיהינם אינו דבר אחר רק שהאל ית' מוציא חמה, ר"ל הנפש אשר לזכותה נקראת פה בשם חמה, מנרתיקה, ר"ל הגוף. ואמ' אחר כן ומקדירה, ר"ל מוסיף לה דקות וחום והתלהבות (ב26) ר"ל חשק להדבק עם חשוקה, ותמצא רש"י ז"ל בפרק הנז' למעלה מזאת המימרא מעט מפרש ומקדיר עליהם חמה על זה הדרך.[152] ונמשך אחר זה רשעים נידונין בה, ר"ל שמזה ימשך שיהיו הרשעים נדונין וזה שאחר שהם ישתוקקו אל הדבקות וימנע מהם השגתו הנה מזה ימשך אליהם צער מופלג. וצדיקים מתרפאים בה, ר"ל שהצדיקים אשר בעודם באלה החיים בשרם עליהם יכאב[153] מפני עקת התאוות אשר חמתם שותה רוחם[154] והם מוכרחים להכניעם תחת ממשלת השכל הנה אז יתרפאו מזה הכאב והחולי. ונמשך אחר זה ולא עוד אלא שמתעדנין בה, וזה שלא ימשך להם מזה התרפאות לבד אבל ג"כ תענוג, וזה שמהדבקות ההוא ימשך להם תענוג מופלג.

הנה מכל אלה החסדים אשר הרבה לעשות אתנו האל ית' הן בהתחלת

146. עי' הערה 96 לתרגום.
147. ע"פ בר' יט יא.
148. עבודה זרה ג ב–ד א.
149. מלא' ג יט.
150. מלא' ג כ.
151. שם.
152. רש"י על עבודה זרה ג ב ד"ה מקדיר.
153. ע"פ איוב יד כב.
154. ע"פ איוב ו ד.

הבריאה הן בהתמדת המציאות הן בתת אלינו החיים הנצחיים אחר מות הגוף הן בהראות אלינו והיישירנו אל הדרך אשר בו נגיע אל אלה החיים הנצחיים ימשך ויחוייב למי שלא ירצה להיות כפוי טובה אשר הוא אחד מהיותר גדולים שבחטאים שישתדל בכל מאמצי כחו להרבות עבודתו לו ית׳ ולהעמיד עליו מצות מלבד אותם אשר הונחו בתורתנו הקדושה. והנה אחד מהפנים לזה הוא שנקבל עלינו נדרים בדברים יהיו לעבודתו ולקיימם ואל זה כיון נעים זמירות באמרו נדרי ושלמו ליי אלהיכם.[155]

ועוד יחוייב לנו כדי שנברח מזה העון העצום ר״ל היות האדם כפוי טובה שנודה תמיד מבלי הפסק החסדים אשר עשה אתנו האל ית׳. והנה זה יעשה בתפלה וזהו הגדול שבעיקרי התפלה רצוני הודאת החסדים המושפעים אלינו מאתו ית׳ לפי שבזאת ההודאה נכללו עקרים מה מאמונתנו האמתית כמו מציאות האל ית׳ ואחדותו והשגחתו וגמול ועונש הנמשכים מאתו.

ולזה נאמר במס׳ ברכות פ״א[156] אמ׳ רבה בר חמא סבא כל שלא אמר אמת ויציב שחרית אמת ואמונה ערבית לא יצא ידי חובתו שנ׳ להגיד בבקר חסדיך אמונתך בלילות,[157] וזה לפי שבהם יכללו ההודאות הנזכרות. לא שעיקר התפלה כמו שחשבו אנשים מה יהיה להלל ולשבח אותו ית׳ בשנספר מהלליו ושבחיו אשר אנחנו סכלים בהם כמו שאנחנו סכלים בעצמותו. והלא די לנו שנהלל אותו ונשבחהו בשנודה ונאמר שלרוב מעלתו הוא נעלם ממנו.

ובזה האופן הלל אותו נעים זמירות באמרו אודך על כי נוראות נפלאתי נפלאים מעשיך ונפשי יודעת מאד.[158] כי לפי שהדברים אפשר שיהוללו בשני פנים, האחד שיסופק תארי הדבר ומעלותיו[159] וזה בשהם נודעים, והאופן האחר הוא כשתארי הדבר ומהלליו הם בלתי נודעים לרוב מעלתו ואז הנה ההודאה תהיה בשנודה ונאמר בפינו ובשפתנו שאנחנו סכלים בתארי הדבר המעולים וזה לרוב מעלתו. ועל כן אמ׳ פה נעים זמירות אודך על כי וכו׳[160] ר״ל אהלל ואשבח אותך לפי שמאד נפלאתי ממך ועצמותך נעלם ממני והאדם יפלא מהדבר הנעלם. והנה זה יעמד במקום הודאה בדברים הנעלמים ממנו.

155. תה׳ עו יב.

156. ברכות יב א.

157. תה׳ צב ג.

158. תה׳ קלט יד.

159. עי׳ הערה 106 לתרגום.

160. תה׳ קלט יד.

ואמ' אחר כן נפלאים מעשיך ונפשי יודעת[161] שהם מאד נעלמים.

ולפי שהדרושים האלהיים ובכלל כל הנבדלים מחמר הם מוכנים מצד עצמם לשיושכלו ואין בנו צורך להטריח עצמנו בהפשטתם מחמר עד שיושכלו כי הם מעצמם מופשטים מחומר, ואמנם סכלותנו בהם הוא מצדנו אנחנו הלואים מהשכיל הדברים אשר (א27) הם בתכלית הבהירות, אמר דוד המלך ע"ה כאיל תערוג על אפיקי מים כן נפשי תערוג אליך אלהים.[162] ר"ל כי כמו שהאיל עורג על אפיקי מים עם היות שיש באפיקי המים די ויותר מדאי לרוות צמא האיל וזה כי אפיק יורה על חוזק המים ורבויים, ואמנם אין בו כח לקבל כל המים הצריכים להשקיט צמאונו וההתלהבות אשר בתוכו, כן נפשי תערוג אליך אלהים[163] ר"ל כי לכמו זאת הסבה תערוג נפשי כשהיא מתבודדת לחשוב מחשבות בדרושים האלהיים.

וזה כי הסבה בשאי אפשר שתשכילם היא איננה מצד הענינים בעצמותם כי הם מצד עצמם מוכנים לשיושכלו כי הם שכל בפעל, ואמנם היא מצדנו אנחנו אשר תשש כחנו מהשיג הדברים אשר הם בתכלית הבהירות. ואפשר שרמז ג"כ באמרו אפיקי מים[164] כי לחוזק המים ומרוצתם ורבויים אי אפשר שישתה מהם האיל כאשר ישתה מהמים ההולכים לאט, וכן ג"כ פה כי להפלגת בהירות השכלים הנבדלים אי אפשר שנשיגם השכל האנושי.

ולזה אפשר שיאמר על דרך צחות כי שמש ומגן יי',[165] ר"ל כי הוא בתכלית הזיו והבהירות ומזה הצד הוא מגן ר"ל מסך בינו ובין המשכילים. ואמ' ג"כ דוד בספרו עומק אלה הענינים האלהיים ולי מה יקרו רעיך אל מה עצמו ראשיהם[166] ר"ל רעיך והם המחשבות בדרושים האלהיים הם יקרות וקשות עלי ויהיה יקרו מענין ודבר יי היה יקר.[167] וכפל הענין ואמ' מה עצמו ראשיהם[168] ר"ל שאפי' הראשים והם הכללים קשה עלי להגבילם.

והנה אחר כן ספר סבות זה הקושי אשר ישיגהו בהשכל אלה הדברים

161. שם.
162. תה' מב ב.
163. שם.
164. שם.
165. תה' פד יב.
166. תה' קלט יז.
167. ש"א ג א.
168. תה' קלט יז.

ואמ' אספרם מחול ירבון.[169] ודקדק ואמ' מחול ירבון ולא אמר כחול כמו שאמ' והיה מספר בני ישראל כחול הים[170] וזה כי כשיכון המספר המופלג ברבוי יאמר כחול, שהוא המספר היותר גדול אשר נמצא אליו נושאים בפעל. וכן היה שם כי היה מכוין הפסוק למספר רב, לא לבלתי בעל תכלית, כי לא היה מכוין לומר שהיו בני ישראל בלתי בעלי תכלית במספר. ואולם כשיכוין למספר בלתי בעל תכלית כמו שהוא העניין פה אמ' מחול, וזה כי התארים האלהיים הם בלתי בעלי תכלית. והנה זה איננו לרבוי בעצמותו ית' אבל לרבוי הדברים אשר אליהם הצירוף.[171] והנה זאת אחת מסבות הקושי בהבנת הדרושים האלה האלהיים, רצוני היות אלה התארים האלהיים הם בלתי בעלי תכלית.

וספר אחר כן סבה אחרת ואמר הקיצותי ועודי עמך,[172] ר"ל כשהקיצותי עצמי מזה ההתבודדות המחשבי באלה התארים ורציתי להתבונן ולדעת מה הוסיף שכלי חכמה ודעת[173] בסבת אלה התארים אמצא שעדין אני עמך ר"ל שאלה התארים אינם כ"א עצמותך. וכמו שקודם זה הייתי סכל בעצמותך כן אנכי עמדי[174] היום כאשר הייתי גם מתמול גם משלשם[175] בטרם אתבונן באלה התארים. ולפי שתארי השבח והמהלל אפשר שימשך מהם נזק גדול וזה אם יובנו חיוביים כי יביאו לחשוב רבוי בעצמותו ית', הזהירונו מזה מתקני התפלה ואמרו להודות לך וליחדך,[176] ר"ל שנודה ונשבח אותך ואמנם שיהיה זה באופן שניחד אותך ולא ימשך מזה רבוי בעצמותך.

ולזה להרחיק אלו הנזקים אשר אפשר שימשכו מההודאות והשבחים היותר טובה שבהודאות הוא השתיקה. ולזה אמר' דוד המלך ע"ה לך דומיה תהלה אלהים בציון ולך ישולם נדר,[177] והרצון בזה כי דוד המלך ע"ה

---

169. תה' קלט יח.
170. הושע ב א.
171. עי' הערה 109 לתרגום.
172. תה' קלט יח.
173. ע"פ קהלת א טז.
174. ע"פ איוב ט לה.
175. ע"פ שמ' ד י.
176. ראה זליגמן בער, סדר עבודת ישראל, עמ' 81.
177. תה' סה ב.

לעתות בצרה הנה נודר שאם האל ית' יצילהו שיבא את מזבח אלהים
ויהלל וישבח אותו ויקדם פניו בתודה[178] ואחר כן בהיותו בציון היה מוצא
שהיותר טובה שבהודאות היא השתיקה והיה שותק, ולזה אמ' (27ב) לך
דומיה תהלה[179] ואמ' אחר כן ולך ישולם נדר ר"ל כי הנדר אשר נדרתי
להודות את שמך הנה ישולם לך בשתיקה כי הוא הטובה והמעולה
שבהודאות לך.

ולזה הודאותיו ית' אין אנחנו צריכים להוציאם בפינו ובשפתנו, די לנו
שנעזוב אלה ההודאות לכלל מעשיו ובריותיו אשר תמיד כל היום וכל
הלילה לא יחשו[180] ומאין דמי תהלות יי יספרו,[181] כמאמר הפסוק יודוך יי כל
מעשיך וחסידיך יברכוך.[182] וזה כי שאר הפועלים והאומנים זולתו לא
יהוללו על כל פעולותיהם, כי דרך משל הבנאי כשבנה היכל מלך בנוי
לתלפיות[183] הנה זה יספר בשבחו וזה כי כל רואיו יכירו כי הוא מעשה אמן
ויהולל על זה עושהו, ואולם כשיעשה בתי חומר אשר בעפר יסודם[184] הנה
אלה לא יספרו שבחי הפועל אבל אולי יודיעו גנותו.

ואולם הוא ית' אין העניין בו כן כי כל מעשיו יודוהו וישבחוהו ואף
הנמלה אשר היא השפלה שבנמצאות תשבחהו, וזה כי אם נדע נתוח
הנמלה והתחלפות אבריה הכליים אשר הוכנו לתת לה מחיה כל ימי צבאה
ואיך נתן לה כל השלמות האפשרי בחקה הנה זה יעידנו לדעת חכמת
הפועל הבלתי בעלת תכלית ולזה אמ', כל מעשיך. ואמ' אחר כן וחסידיך
יברכוך[185] ר"ל כי חסידיך הרואים תקון והתחכמות פעולותיך לא יצטרך
שיודוך אבל שיברכוך ר"ל שיודו שהברכות מושפעות מאתך כי זאת היא
הברכה המיוחסת לאל ית' ר"ל שנודה שהוא משפיע כל הטובות והברכות
ושהוא מקורן ומעינן.[186]

---

178. ע"פ תה' צה ב.
179. תה' סה ב, כפי פירוש הרמב"ם, מורה נבוכים א,נט.
180. ע"פ יש' סב ו.
181. ע"פ יש' מג כא והשוה תה' יט ב–ט.
182. תה' קמה י.
183. שיר ד ד.
184. איוב ד יט.
185. תה' קמה י.
186. עי' הערה 114 לתרגום.

והנה עיקר התפלה היא לזה התכלית ר"ל להודות אלה החסדים
והטובות והברכות המושפעות מאתו. ולזה מה יקרו ומה עצמו הפעלות
האלה אשר קבלו עליהם חבירי החברה הזאת, והנה תחלה פעל התפלה
בצבור: הנה כמה וכמה שבחוהו רז"ל ואמרו שהיא מקובלת ונשמעת וכמו
שהוכיחו באמרם כי ברבים היו עמדי,[187] וכמו שאמרו ג"כ בפסוק ושנים
יניסו רבבה:[188] אינו דומה מרובים העושים את המצוה למועטים העושים
אותה.[189] וזה כי יש סגלה בכללות לא תמצא בכל אחד מהפרטים לבדו.

מצורף לזה מעלה אחרת נמצאת בתפלה הזאת וזה שנעשה במקום נעשה
בו תלמוד תורה כמו שאמרו ז"ל בברכות פ"א אמ"ר לוי משמיה דעולא מיום
שחרב בית המקדש אין לו להב"ה אלא ארבע אמות של הלכה, ושם נאמ'
אמ' אביי מריש הוה גרסינא בגו ביתא ומצילנא בבי כנישתא, כיון דשמעי
להא דאמ"ר אמי משמיה דעולא לא הוה מצילנא אלא היכא דגרסינא.[190]

וכן ג"כ מה נמרץ מאד פעל התלמוד תורה עם הדיוק המופלג אשר המה
עושים אשר ראוי להקפיד עליה כמו שאמרו רז"ל בני יהודה שהקפידו
על לשונם נתקיימה תורתם בידם, בני גליל שלא הקפידו על לשונם לא
נתקיימה תורתם בידם.[191] וזה כי כל אחת ואחת מהאותיות והנקודות
אשר בתורתנו הקדושה וספרי הנביאים הוניחה שם על מכונתה[192] לכונה
מיוחדת. וכן ג"כ כל אחד מהטעמים נותן טעם לשבח.[193] וכלם יורו על דברים
נעלמים במובני הפסוקים, צדיקים ילכו בם ופשעים יכשלו בם.[194]

אמ' חכם אחד בשבחו שני אלה הפעלות ר"ל פעלת התפלה ותלמוד
תורה, המתפלל מדבר עם אלהיו והמעיין בספר תורה אלהיו מדבר עמו.[195]
ראה כמה הפליג בשבח שני אלה הפעלות כי המשיל האחת מהן לדבור

---

187. תה' נה ה יט, ברכות ח א.

188. דב' לב ל.

189. כנראה הכוונה לספרא על ויקרא כו ח, ורדפו מכם חמשה מאה ומאה מכם רבבה ירדפו: „אינו דומה
מועטין העושים את התורה למרובין העושים את התורה" (מובא ע"י רש"י שם).

190. ברכות ח א.

191. עירובין נג ג א.

192. ע"פ זכ' ה יא.

193. משחק מלים ע"פ עבודה זרה לט א.

194. הושע יד י.

195. עי' ספר יוסיפון, מהדורת פלוסר, 1:27, הערה 51.

האדם עם האלוה והאחרת כי ידבר אלהים את האדם, עם היות יש ביניהן
יתרון יתר מאד, ולזה המשילו התפלה שהיא המצאה אנושית, וזה כי אנשי
כנסת הגדולה תקנוה,[196] לדבור האדם על אלוה והמשילו (א28) העיון
בספרי הקדש, לפי שהם דברי אלהים חיים,[197] לדבור האל עם האדם.

והנה לזה באמת ובתמים החברה הזאת נקראת בשם רודפי צדק[198] כי
לפי שבין הנפש והגוף מלחמה חזקה ודברי ריבות יומם ולילה לא ישבותו[199]
וכל אחד מהם ובפרט הגוף רוצה לקחת חלקו ויתר על חלקו הנה אנחנו
צריכים לשום שר ושופט[200] ביניהם מוכיח ישית ידו על שניהם[201] על פי
הדין והשווי. ולפי שהיוישר הוא שיותן לכל אחד חקו הראוי לו וחלק הנפש
מכל ימי חיי הבלנו[202] הוא הזמן אשר ישים האדם בתפלה ובתלמוד תורה,
הנה א״כ אלה החברים הנותנים לנפש חוקה הראוי לה מתפלה ותלמוד
תורה הם רודפי יושר וצדק.

והנה נמצא לאלה הנדרים אשר קבלו עליהם אנשי החברה הזאת
מעלה אחרת עד שיצדק בם הפסוק אשר אמ׳ דוד המלך ע״ה נדרי ליי
אשלם נגדה נא לכל עמו בחצרות בית יי בתוככי ירושלם הללויה.[203] וזה כי
אלה הנדרים הם באופן שלא יקוייימו וישולמו במסתרים וחדר בחדר[204]
אבל לעיני השמש הזאת, ולזה יצדק החלק האומר נגדה נא לכל עמו. ועוד
שנית הנה הם ישולמו בבית הכנסת אשר הוא היום אצלנו חצרות בית יי
ומקדש מעט,[205] ולזה יצדק החלק השני רצוני אמרו בחצרות בית יי. והנה
רז״ל אמרו בויקרא רבה כל הנודר ומשלם זוכה שישלם נדרו בירושלם
שנאמ׳ נדרי יי אשלם נגדה נא לכל עמו, היכן? בחצרות בית יי בתוככי
ירושלם.[206]

196. השוה ברכות לג א.

197. ע״פ ערובין יג א.

198. עי׳ הערה 124 לתרגום.

199. ע״פ דב׳ יז ח ובר׳ ח כב.

200. ע״פ שמות ב יד.

201. ע״פ איוב ט לג.

202. ע״פ קהלת ט ט.

203. תה׳ קטז יח–יט.

204. ע״פ מ״א כ ל וכו׳.

205. ע״פ מגילה כט א וכו׳.

206. ויקרא רבה לג,ד על תה׳ קטז יח–יט.

ולכן חזק ונתחזק[207] ועל יי נשליך יהבנו[208] אשר לא יבושו קוויו[209] ונבטח
כי בזכות העבודה הזאת יקרב קץ גאלתנו ומועד צבאנו מבור גלותנו,[210]
ובתבונות כפיו הוא ינהגנו[211] אל המקום אשר בחר לשכן שמו שם.[212] בימים
ההמה ובעת ההיא יומר נא ישראל כאיש אחד חברים, נדרי ליי אשלם נגדה
נא לכל עמו בחצרות בית יי בתוככי ירושלם הללויה.[213]

207. ש״ב י יב.

208. ע״פ תה׳ נה כג.

209. ע״פ יש׳ מט כג.

210. מעבר להבעת תקוה משיחית, המסמנת לשומעים סוף הדרשה.

211. ע״פ תה׳ עח עב.

212. ע״פ דב׳ יב יא.

213. תה׳ קטז יח–יט.

14

A Sermon on the *'Aqedah* from the Generation of the Expulsion and Its Implications for 1391

Jewish literature through the fifteenth century has preserved few sermons on the *'Aqedah* or Binding of Isaac (Genesis 22). There is, to be sure, ample aggadic expansion of this episode in the Rabbinic texts of antiquity. But nothing in this literature can be identified as the full text of a sermon delivered by a particular rabbi on a specific occasion, comparable to the sermons and homilies of the church fathers.[1] Even in the Middle Ages, when Jews began to preserve texts of model or actual sermons, few of the works focus on the *'Aqedah*.

This is not because the passage was uninteresting to medieval Jews. On the contrary, biblical commentators and philosophical writers wrestled with its problems, while chroniclers and liturgical poets exploited to the fullest its various motifs.[2] But the earliest collections of sermon texts are organized according to the weekly Torah lessons, and the *'Aqedah*, which comes at the

---

Part of this chapter reprinted with permission from *Exile and Diaspora: Studies in the History of the Jewish People Presented to Professor Haim Beinart,* copyright 1991, by the Ben-Zvi Institute for the Study of Jewish Communities in the East.

1. Examples of patristic homilies on the Binding of Isaac include Origen, Homily 8, pp. 203-10; Caesarius, *Sermons* 2:16–19. The material in Heinemann, *Derashot* and Heinemann, *Literature* proves the point. Compared to the many thick volumes of patristic sermons, this is a slim harvest indeed. More important, the material collected in this book is obviously not transcriptions of sermons, similar to the sermons of Chrysostom or Augustine. Most of the passages are too brief to be more than the outline of a sermon. The one on the *'Aqedah* (*Derashot*, p. 40; *Literature*, p. 126) exemplifies the problem; it is less than one hundred words in Hebrew and would take less than two minutes to read. In the medieval period, this entire passage is used as a small portion of the actual sermon: see below. Jacob Elbaum has argued that the *Tanḥuma* treatment of the *'Aqedah* reflects an editorial desire to create an "aggadic literature of narrative freed from homily" (Elbaum, "Sermon to Story"). However, as is clear from the article, what is being transformed in the *Tanḥuma* literature is not an actual sermon, but a collection of discrete homiletical comments.

2. See especially Spiegel. For a review of the exegetical problems in the medieval Jewish commentators, see Schmitz.

end of *Va-Yera* [Gen. 18–22], is usually not the focal point.[3] It was indeed highlighted as the Torah lesson for the second day of Rosh Hashanah, but the Rosh Hashanah morning service, one of the longest in the year, was a less auspicious preaching occasion than were the Sabbaths before and after the New Year's holiday, which had their own lections. In any case, few texts of sermons intended for the second day of Rosh Hashanah before the sixteenth century have been preserved.

In view of its rarity, a recently discovered sermon on the *'Aqedah* dating from the generation of the Expulsion becomes therefore a significant resource for the study of Jewish preaching, and the textual and historical problems it raises deserve full elucidation.

The Text

The text of the sermon on the *'Aqedah* is found in manuscripts of two collections. The first is Shem Tov ben Joseph ibn Shem Tov's *Derashot ha-Torah* (Cambridge University MS Dd. 10.46, hereafter Shem Tov MS A, fols. 34r–36r; Cambridge Trinity College MS 140 [F12 49], hereafter Shem Tov MS B, fols. 48r–52v). Perhaps best known today for his commentary on the *Guide for the Perplexed,* Shem Tov, like his father before him, combined a broad philosophical education with a lively interest in homiletics. The collection of sermons, described in an introductory note as written versions of what he had preached publicly throughout his career, was completed in 1489. The sermons are organized by the weekly lesson (in some cases more than one per *parashah*), with some wedding sermons interspersed and a group of sermons on the theme of repentance at the end. The work was published in Salonika in 1525 (or possibly in 1530: *ha-'irah*), and in two other sixteenth-century editions.[4]

According to their respective colophons, Shem Tov MS A, written by a scribe named Isaac Zarfati, was completed in 1530, probably in Italy, and Shem Tov MS B, written by Joseph ben Isaac ha-Kohen, was completed in 1566 in Alcazarquivir (Al-Qasr al-Kabìr), Morocco.[5] These manuscripts, the

---

3. Cf. the rather superficial treatments in Anatoli, p. 18a; Anonymous (*Derashot . . . Rabbenu Yonah*), p. 40; Ibn Shu'eib, *Derashot* (1583), p. 8c, *Derashot* (1992), 1:37–38. Ibn Shu'eib also treats the *'Aqedah* briefly in his sermon for the first day of Rosh Hashanah (1583: p. 89c; 1992: 4:492).

4. On Shem Tov ibn Shem Tov, see Steinschneider, p. 120 and Saperstein, *Jewish Preaching,* pp. 180–98.

5. Shem Tov MS A, fol. 158v; the colophon to Isaac Zarfati's MS of "Derashot ha-RaN," completed about a year later, states that it was written in Venice (Cambridge MS Dd 10.46 fol. 224). Shem Tov MS B, fol. 270r.

only extant ones containing Shem Tov's sermons on Genesis, both contain material that does not appear in any of the printed editions. As I have shown elsewhere,[6] substantial sections from the manuscript sermon on *Va-Yeḥi* [Gen. 47:28–50: 26], undoubtedly authentic, were omitted without any indication in the Salonika text. Similarly, the sermon on the *'Aqedah*, which appears in both manuscripts following the sermon on *Va-Yera*, is not included in any printed edition. It is unclear whether such omissions represent an editorial decision or whether the manuscript, no longer extant, for the Salonika *Derashot* lacked the material in question.

The second sermon collection, which has never been systematically studied by scholars, is entitled "Dover Meisharim" (Oxford Christ Church MS 197, Neubauer 2447). The author's name is given simply as "Israel," and there is no basis for identifying him with any known figure. Nor does the author, in the 244 folio pages of the manuscript, mention a single date or place or contemporary person. On internal grounds, it can be shown that Neubauer's dating of the collection to the first third of the fifteenth century is incorrect: The sermons' form fits the Spanish model at the end of the century, and in many ways they are structurally similar to those of Joseph Garçon.[7] The sermons are organized according to the Torah lessons (though there is more than one cycle); our text is identified simply as a sermon on *Va-Yera* (fols. 210r–211v).

We have, therefore, essentially the same sermon in two different but more or less contemporary manuscript collections. Comparison of the three manuscripts reveals that Shem Tov MS A is clearly superior to the others, and I have used this as the basis for my transcription. There are many minor divergences in which the reading in this manuscript is obviously the correct one. In several passages it is more complete, with material having been dropped from the other versions by the scribal error of haplography. In some instances, precisely the same omissions occur in Shem Tov MS B and "Dover Meisharim"; in others, material is omitted from Shem Tov MS B that is pre-

---

6. *Jewish Preaching*, p. 187 n.15, p. 191 n. 27 end.

7. Adolf Neubauer, describing this manuscript in Catalogue of the *Hebrew Manuscripts in the Bodleian Library and in the College Libraries of Oxford*, determined that the preacher was active in the first third of the fifteenth century by his mention of Joseph Albo without the letters *z"l* ["of blessed memory"]. He failed to note that the author cites Isaac Canpanton with the letters *z"l* (fol. 231r). Canpanton died around the year 1463. For the argument that the sermons reveal a structure that is known only from the last third of the fifteenth century, see *Jewish Preaching*, pp. 66–69.

sent in "Dover Meisharim."[8] The relationship of the three manuscripts is thus not at all simple, but we may conclude that the sermon was certainly not original with the author of "Dover Meisharim." Whether it came to that author directly from a manuscript of Shem Tov's sermons or from some other source cannot as yet be determined.

There are two clear points of contact between the text in the Shem Tov manuscripts and another Shem Tov sermon. The *'Aqedah* sermon says, "The father and the son made themselves a sacrifice to God, for while the father was binding, he was [also] bound, and while Isaac was bound, he was [also] binding his father" (ll. 95–97). In his sermon for the second day of Rosh Hashanah, which appears in the printed editions of the *Derashot,* Shem Tov wrote as follows:

> Each one both bound and was bound. Abraham, who bound Isaac, was bound before his Heavenly Father. It was as if Abraham himself was an offering on the altar like his son, for there is no doubt that Abraham would have preferred his own death to the death of his son. Thus in the Binding of Isaac, Abraham was bound as well as Isaac, until God had compassion for father and son.[9]

I have not found this particular formulation—that each was *'oqed ve-ne'e-qad*—in other commentators.

Second, the *'Aqedah* sermon establishes a connection between the *'Aqedah* with its two offerings (Abraham and Isaac, as indicated above) and the requirement of two lambs for the continual burnt offering (*tamid:* Num. 28:3), concluding, "As long as the continual burnt offering was brought, these two [Abraham and Isaac] would draw near, but when the continual burnt offering was abolished, the merit of the fathers was also abolished as a defense on our behalf" (ll. 100–101). An obviously connected but considerably modified form of this astonishing assertion appears in a manuscript of the Rosh Hashanah sermon:

---

8. In my transcription, line 23 following [?] *lishḥot et beno:* 18 words ending with *lishḥot et beno* are missing from Shem Tov MS B and "Dover Meisharim." Line 38 following *le-hodi'a:* 10 words ending with *le-hodi'a* are missing from Shem Tov MS B and "Dover Meisharim." Line 30 following *ve-hineh rabbim:* 22 words ending with *ve-hineh rabbim* are missing from Shem Tov MS B but present in "Dover Meisharim." Line 65 following *yiqqare lekha zara':* 20 words ending with *yiqqare lekha zara'* are missing from from Shem Tov MS B but present in "Dover Meisharim."

9. Shem Tov, *Derashot,* p. 80c. The manuscripts of this sermon do not diverge from the printed text in any significant way.

The unblemished lambs serve as atonement for all Israel; unblemished, they allude to those who were bound on Mount Moriah, who were two. Because of the merit achieved by imitating them [i.e., offering the two lambs], God made his Presence dwell among us. But on the day when the burnt offering was abolished, all our well-being was abolished, and we were left abandoned to all the injuries of chance. But when we remember this great and awesome deed performed by father and son through the sounding of the ram's horn, which impels us to subdue our hearts to our Heavenly Father, He will accept our repentance.[10]

These two passages reveal verbal and conceptual links between the *'Aqedah* sermon and Shem Tov's sermon for Rosh Hashanah. To be sure, the common motifs are used in different ways—in the *'Aqedah* sermon they lead to the theme of martyrdom, in the Rosh Hashanah sermon to the theme of repentance—but this is to be expected in sermons intended for different occasions. While certainly not conclusive, these similarities justify a preliminary conclusion that the *'Aqedah* sermon was indeed written by Shem Tov. It should be noted, however, that despite the use of an extensive passage from Maimonides' *Guide* at the beginning, the sermon displays very little clear connection to Shem Tov's commentary on this passage.

One idiosyncracy of the Shem Tov MS A text is a long passage near the beginning (at l. 14, see n. 4 to the translation) which does not appear in either Shem Tov MS B or "Dover Meisharim." It is introduced with a personal voice in the first person: "I am ignorant and do not know. . . . I am like one who prophesies without knowing, groping like the blind for things hidden from human beings unless the light of the tradition of the wise [*qabbalat hakhamim*] has shone upon them." Although the discussion eventually returns to the *'Aqedah*, the passage comes as an interruption where it appears, for it has nothing to do with the problem of God's knowledge. Indeed, it contradicts the rest of the sermon, affirming that "certainly Isaac's merit was greater than the merit of Abraham" (l. 215), whereas the sermon emphasizes the achievements of both. I have concluded that this passage is an interpolation, possibly written by the scribe himself, Isaac Zarfati, and I have transcribed it separately at the end.

Sermon Structure

As noted above, the structure of the sermon is typical for Sephardi preaching in the late fifteenth century. The first part, which constitutes about

---

10. Shem Tov MS C, fol. 72v–73a. Shem Tov, *Derashot* (p. 80d) omits the crucial passage.

three-fourths of the sermon, exemplifies a standard form: beginning with a verse from the Torah lesson and a rabbinic dictum, it then defines the theoretical issue to be addressed (the "*derush*"), proceeds to explore the issue and resolve the problems that it raises, and eventually returns to an interpretation of the verse and of the dictum. The second part, the final fourth of the sermon, is a homily, moving verse by verse through a passage of the Bible, in this case Psalm 87. Preachers from the generation of the Expulsion were well aware that these were distinct homiletical genres, though they were sometimes combined. In the best known example of contemporary homiletical literature, Isaac Arama's *'Aqedat Yitshaq,* each "chapter" contains a "*derishah*" and a "*perishah,*" which essentially correspond to the two units here. Arama's "*perishah*" focuses on a passage from the Torah lesson, but the incorporation of exegetical sections on Psalms became quite common in sixteenth-century preaching.

The verse from the Torah lesson, known as the *nose* or theme, is actually only part of a verse: *Adonai yir'eh asher ye'amer ha-yom* (Gen. 22:14).[11] It comes as a surprise, for it violates the traditionally understood syntax reflected in the cantillation marks, which require a major pause after *yir'eh.* The very first words thus signal that a new interpretation will be given, thereby arousing expectation in the listener. The interpretation that is eventually presented (l. 86) is indeed a novel reading: in accordance with the preacher's insistence that inner intention rather than external action was paramount, the phrase is interpreted to mean "God will see what was said today"—namely, the conversation between Abraham and Isaac, which was the essence of the "test."[12] Abravanel was apparently aware of this interpretation, as he rejects this novel construction of the verse ("*ve-'ein le-faresho she-yir'eh mah she-ye'amer ha-yom*") because it is inconsistent with the cantillation marks.[13]

---

11. There is a textual problem with the "theme." Shem Tov MS A reads *Be-har H' yireh asher ye'amer ha-yom; Be-har* is actually the scribe's mistaken "correction" for an original word, *Midrash,* which is clearly out of place. Shem Tov MS B lacks the beginning of the sermon. "Dover Meisharim" reads *H' yireh asher ye'amer ha-yom be-har H' yera'eh;* however, the sermon itself shows that the preacher used only the first five words. Apparently the scribe, sensing that something was incomplete, finished the phrase.

12. Note that Azariah Figo used exactly the same five words as his theme-verse in a sermon for the second day of Rosh Hashanah. After giving an interpretation in the context of the *'Aqedah* story (very different from that of our preacher), he goes on to give a second, homiletical interpretation fitting the occasion: "God will benevolently direct the eyes of His Providence to see what all Israel says today in their prayers." Figo, nu. 5, p. 18a.

13. Abravanel, *Torah* 1:264b, question 21.

The aggadic dictum or *ma'amar*, connected with Genesis 22:1, not with the preachers' theme-verse, is an obvious selection for the *'Aqedah*. Precisely this dictum was selected by Arama in chapter 21 of *'Aqedat Yitshaq*, following the theme-verse Genesis 22:1. The passage is eventually incorporated by the preacher into his discussion of divine tests and rewards (l. 105). It is read in the context of a medieval theological problem not explicit in the original, but is otherwise treated in a predictable manner.[14]

After the introductory *nose* and *ma'amar*, the preacher defines the conceptual problem that he will address. The general subject is the "test" (*'inyan ha-nissayon*) administered by God, and this is divided into three questions. First, does not the assertion that God "tested" Abraham, culminating in the proclamation *For now I know. . .* (Gen. 22:12) imply that God's knowledge is incomplete? Second, was there a reasonable alternative to Abraham's reaction, and if not, how was he really tested? Third, since many Jews throughout the ages have given their lives as martyrs and sacrificed their children as Abraham was prepared to do, why is Abraham's behavior viewed as unique?

The first problem is resolved by direct appeal to Maimonides' discussion of the subject in 3:24 of the *Guide*. Maimonides is quoted at length, and the preacher adds nothing innovative to solve this theological problem. The passage is of interest primarily as evidence of the use of the *Guide* in preaching intended for a general Jewish audience. There appears to be nothing controversial in such citation; the preacher apparently felt that this material was a helpful solution to a theological conundrum, worthy of disseminating among all who would hear his sermon.

The second and third problems, however, generate more original fare. After indicating solutions implied by Maimonides, the preacher goes on to present his own solutions. In his reading of the story, it was not the act of sacrifice itself but rather the willingness, eagerness and joy of both Abraham and Isaac, expressed through their conversation on the mountain, that merited the reward. This brings him to the anticipated novel interpretation of the theme-verse (l. 86), and eventually to the *ma'amar*. The section concludes with a citation of Gersonides' original explanation of the nature of the "test," and a provocative passage attributed to Crescas, about the *'Aqedah* as paradigm for contemporary Jewish behavior.

Structurally and thematically, the sermon could have ended (after an appropriate final sentence) with the passage on martyrdom attributed to Crescas (l. 131). Apparently, however, the preacher did not want to conclude

---

14. This aggadah was also used in other sermons on the *'Aqedah*; see, for example, Joseph ben Moses, p. 24a.

on such a somber note, and he therefore introduced a new subject: the significance of the location where the *'Aqedah* occurred, viz., Jerusalem and the Temple Mount. This leads into a homily on Psalm 87, with interpretations of each successive verse. There is no attempt to link the Psalm with contemporary realities; indeed, some of the assertions about the uniqueness of Jerusalem seem to have no connection at all with the actual status of its Jewish community at the end of the fifteenth century. Instead, the function of the passage is to satisfy an apparently prevalent interest in exegetical material, and to direct the attention of the listeners away from the bleak subject of martyrdom to a more positive subject. This discussion culminates with a return to the theme-verse: "God will see" refers to God's special providence over the perfect inhabitants of Jerusalem and His general providence, for the sake of the Temple, over the entire world (l. 189). The sermon concludes with a messianic hope for the speedy rebuilding of the Temple.

Historical Questions

Two historical issues are raised by the sermon, both of them relating to martyrdom. The first arises in the context of questions asked about Abraham's test. What was the great merit of Abraham, the preacher rhetorically wonders.

> Why, many have been killed as martyrs, and have suffered terrible tortures during periods of violent persecution, in the service of God. . . . Many killed their children and their grandchildren, and then their wives, and afterward they killed themselves, to sanctify God's Name in public. Why is their act not considered a greater source of merit than the Binding of Isaac? Yet every Rosh Hashanah we pray, "Remember the Binding of Isaac on behalf of his descendants today." Would it not be more appropriate to pray "Remember those who were killed for the sanctification of Your Name"? (ll. 30–36).

At first reading, it seems obvious that the preacher was referring to the self-immolation of the Rhineland Jews during the First Crusade, for he aptly characterizes the behavior of many inhabitants of Mainz, Worms and Cologne in the spring of 1096. Furthermore, the comparison with the *'Aqedah* was frequently made in the wake of that disaster, and a similar rhetorical question raised: "Were there ever 1100 offerings on one day, each one of them like the sacrifice of Isaac, the son of Abraham? . . . Why did not the moon and the sun grow dark in their heavens when on one day . . . 1100 Jews were killed and slaughtered?"[15] Yet, though it is commonly assumed

---

15. Chazan, *Crusade,* p. 256.

that the martyrdom of the Rhineland Jews "influenced the thinking of the Sephardi (Spanish) Jews,"[16] the matter is not so simple and raises an interesting historiographical problem.

How much of the experience of the First Crusade, particularly the instances of communal self-destruction, was known by fifteenth-century Spanish Jews, and to what extent did it affect their thinking about martyrdom? The central historiographical texts of Spanish Jewry reveal a surprising absence of detailed information about the behavior of the Rhineland communities, even in passages where we would expect to find it.

One of the best known responses to the riots of 1391, Solomon Alami's *'Iggeret Musar*, commences with a survey of past disasters. He begins in 1148 with the Almohade persecutions and continues with other persecutions in Islamic lands during the lifetime of Maimonides. Then, "about one hundred years after these first, they were expelled from France and England and from other kingdoms. From that day on, God's people sank ever deeper (Judges 5:11). . . ; their wives and their daughters were raped, and the rest of the people apostatized."[17] Alami argues that philosophical study undermined the willingness of Jews to die as martyrs and was thereby responsible for the waves of recent apostasy. It would have helped his case to draw the contrast not only with the "martyrs" of the Book of Daniel, but with the Jews of northern Europe. The absence of any reference to the experience of the First Crusade is a strong indication that he did not know of it.

Solomon Alami may have been a man of limited general reading; the same cannot be said of Isaac Abravanel. Yet his review of Jewish suffering is similar. Referring to Leviticus 26:38, *You shall perish among the nations, and the land of your enemies will consume you,* he relies on Gersonides: the verse refers to "the murderous sorrows experienced by Israel in exile—that many Jews died of famine, sickness, and war, including the killing of holy communities, and the expulsion of the Jews from England, and especially the expulsions from all of France, in which twice the number of those who left Egypt died."[18] If Abravanel knew details about the martyrdom in the Rhineland, there is no evidence here.

The most celebrated work of Spanish historiography is Solomon ibn Verga's *Shevet Yehudah.* Ibn Verga includes some details about the expulsions from England and France (chapters 18, 20, 21), but nothing on the massacres of the First Crusade. Instead, there is a rather cryptic statement:

---

16. Ben Sasson, p. 386.

17. Alami, pp. 38–39.

18. Abravanel, *Torah* 3:262b; RaLBaG, *Torah,* p. 176b on Lev. 26:38. Cf. Abravanel, *Yeshu'ot,* p. 46a–b.

There has not remained from the seed of Israel even one out of a thousand of those Jews who left Jerusalem and the cities of Israel and came to Spain, or those who went to France and Germany, for they often were confronted with martyrdom, and thousands of them were killed. . . . The Jews of Germany and their leaders have written a scroll about their sorrows; they have composed a large work, treating many events in those lands. As these are already written, I have decided not to write about them here, especially since true details of these matters (*amitut ha-'inyanim*) have not reached us, as we are far away.[19]

The book to which the author was referring is unknown, but he clearly did not have it before him; nor was it readily accessible. It was known that German Jews had become martyrs, but the actual circumstances were apparently not common knowledge.[20] It should also be noted that there is nothing about the First Crusade in Usque's *Consolation for the Tribulations of Israel.*

All of the above leads, of course, to an argument from silence. We cannot prove that no Spanish Jews in the generation of the Expulsion knew about communal suicide in the Rhineland. However, the absence of explicit reference to these events in texts reviewing instances of persecution certainly casts doubt on the assumption that Ashkenazi martyrdom, particularly the communal self-destruction, had become part of the cultural heritage of Iberian Jews before 1492. This makes problematic the preacher's reference to the many Jews who killed their children, their wives, and themselves as martyrs. For in context, it is clear that the preacher was not divulging new information. It was the commonly known facts about Jewish martyrdom that establish the question about the *'Aqedah*; the preacher's purpose was not to teach about Jewish history, but to illuminate a problem in the biblical text.

I therefore suggest that the preacher was referring not to the period of the Crusades at all, but rather to the riots of 1391. While the most important historic legacy of that persecution was the large-scale apostasy that produced the *converso* class, there was also considerable loss of life. What is important for our purposes is not so much the actual numbers killed in comparison with the number of *conversos,* but rather the prevalent perceptions of those statistics at the time of the sermon. Ibn Verga, for example, states that in 1391 many Jews were killed as martyrs and "a few of them" apostatized.[21] To be sure, our preacher speaks about not only loss of life but the killing of family members and suicide, and this is almost exclusively associated with the First Crusade. Yet, while such immolation was certainly not the most common occurrence, there is evidence for it in 1391 as well.

19. Ibn Verga, chap. 49, p. 120.
20. Ashkenazic Jews were known in *Shevet Yehudah* for their choice of martyrdom rather than apostasy: chap. 26, p. 71.
21. Ibn Verga, chap. 27, p. 71; cf. chap. 47, p. 119.

Hasdai Crescas reports that in Barcelona "many slaughtered themselves, and some of them threw themselves from the tower." An elegy on the martyrs of Toledo tells of Rabbi Judah, a descendant of R. Asher ben Yehiel, who "sacrificed his wife and his children as an offering" (*hiqriv ishto le-'olah u-vanav*), and of a community leader who "slaughtered himself." And a letter from Juan I of Aragon, dated a few weeks after the riots, instructs his bailiffs to provide information about all Jews who died "or who slaughtered themselves so that they would not be forced to become Christians."[22] These events, much closer to home than those in the late eleventh-century Rhineland, are a more likely referent for the preacher than what had happened long before and far away.

The second historical point, linked with the first, is the passage attributed to Hasdai Crescas: through his actions, Abraham "taught us, as it were, that all those who want to be from the seed of Abraham must be prepared to offer their lives for the sanctification of God's Name when the proper time comes. Otherwise they are not from the seed of Abraham. That is why all of the righteous and virtuous Jews martyred themselves: to demonstrate that they were from the seed of Abraham and Isaac" (ll. 125–29).

But the *'Aqedah* teaches not only the willingness to give up one's own life, but also what may be even more difficult for a father: to sacrifice the life of a child. The passage concludes, "All Jews should think that, being from the seed of Abraham, they should be prepared to take the lives of their children, and the children should be prepared to be bound by their fathers and to bind them, as Abraham did to perform the will of his Heavenly Father" (ll. 129–31). Here the *'Aqedah* is presented as a contemporary paradigm, a model that every Jew worthy of the name should be prepared to imitate literally, in the present.

If indeed this passage contains the words of Crescas, the latter part has a poignant personal ring, for his only son was killed in Barcelona during the anti-Jewish riots of August, 1391. In a letter describing the riots, Crescas refers to his loss in words clearly evoking God's command to Abraham in Genesis 22:2: "Many sanctified God's Name, among them 'my only son,' a bridegroom, an innocent lamb, 'I offered him as a sacrifice.'"[23] So far as I know, this language has always been taken figuratively. The passage from his

---

22. Crescas, "Ketav," p. 129; Roth, "Elegy," stanzas 15, 22; Baer, *Juden* 1:687; cf. Baron, *SRHJ* 10:172.

23. Crescas, "Ketav," p. 129. The sentence clearly echoes two phrases in Genesis 22:2. In the phrase "innocent lamb" (*seh tamim*), *seh* picks up the question and answer in Genesis 22:7–8, and *tamim* is a word often used by the Rabbis for Isaac (e.g. Gen. Rab. 64,1, and 64,3). The phrase itself is from Exodus 12:5, implying a link between the *'Aqedah* and the paschal lamb; cf. Spiegel, pp. 57–58.

sermon, however, requires us to consider the possibility that it should be understood as an indication that Crescas, like Judah the grandson of R. Asher in Toledo, actually took his son's life.

Such a conclusion would obviously place Crescas in Barcelona during the riots. In his letter to Avignon, written in Saragossa on October 19, 1391, he says nothing of his own whereabouts during the events he describes, but he signs it with a verse from Lamentations (3:1): "*I am the man who has seen affliction by the rod of His wrath*, Hasdai Crescas," a phrase particularly appropriate for an eye-witness to the events. Furthermore, Yitzhak Baer has shown that Crescas accompanied the high-ranking diplomat Francesco d'Aranda on a "secret royal mission to Aragon" in August of 1391, and that on August 19, d'Aranda, probably along with Crescas, was recalled to Saragossa by the Queen.[24] There is nothing in these data that would make Crescas' presence in Barcelona on August 5–8, when the riots occurred, implausible.

Between August 12 and August 18, the Queen of Aragon sent at least six letters from Saragossa to Barcelona on behalf of Crescas' son, presumably in response to a personal appeal by Crescas. The most important and problematic letter, written on August 18, is addressed to Don P. de Queralt, apparently a royal official in Barcelona. In it the Queen, mentioning the important service that Crescas has rendered to the Crown, states that "the aforementioned Don Hasdai Crescas is writing to you a letter concerning the safety of his son and his household, who have remained in Barcelona, as you will see in detail in his letter," and asks that the entire household be protected and defended from harm. Unfortunately, the letter written by Crescas himself is apparently no longer extant. On August 18, Crescas' son was already dead—the violence culminated on August 8—but this was obviously not yet known in Saragossa.[25]

If Crescas was in Barcelona during the riots, presumably bearing a royal document guaranteeing his personal safety but not mentioning his son, it is

24. Crescas, "Ketav," p. 130; Baer, *History* 2:114. The confusion in the scholarly literature about Crescas' whereabouts during the riots can be seen in *EJ*. The article on "Crescas" states that he was in Saragossa, "safe from attack" (5:1080), while the article on "Barcelona" indicates that he was in Barcelona, and was one of the relatively few Jews who "escaped to the territories owned by the nobility" (4:211).

25. Baer, *Juden* 1:676–77: "Com donchs lo dit nAzday Cresques vos scriva per sa letra sobre la restauracio de son fill e de sa companya, los quals son romases en Barchinona, segons que en la sua letra veurets largament contenir, pregam vos axi affectuosament, com podem, quels dits fill seu e altra companya vullats haver per recomanats. . . ." For the other royal letters, see Baer, *Juden* 1:669, 675–67. This extraordinary flurry of letters, apparently addressed to virtually everyone in the city with any authority, reveals both the concern and the impotence of the Aragonian monarchs. On the dates of the violence in Barcelona, see Wolff, p. 11.

not difficult to imagine his sending an urgent appeal to the Queen for intervention on his son's behalf. Nor is it impossible that at the height of the violence on August 8, realizing that no royal protection would extend beyond his own person, he took his son's life, making the Queen's letter of ten days later poignantly superfluous. What is difficult to explain is why he would have written a detailed letter to a royal official in Barcelona when he was himself in the city on a royal mission. Such a letter would have made more sense had he been somewhere else in Aragon when he learned of the riots in Barcelona, and if he had written to Don P. and the Queen without knowing whether or not his son was still alive.

Whether or not Crescas played a direct role in his son's ultimate martyrdom is open to conjecture. After his son's death, however, he began to see himself as Abraham in the *'Aqedah* and glorified the role as the quintessence of Jewish identity. Apostasy, even under duress, was not a legitimate option. Drawing from the exegetical tradition that saw the behavior of the Patriarchs as models for their descendants,[26] he concluded that each Jew should be prepared not only to give his life as a martyr, but literally to sacrifice his children for God if the occasion demanded.

This was, however, a highly controversial position. An alternative stance was forcefully defended by Crescas' colleague Profiat Duran ("Ephodi"), who was himself baptized under duress in the wake of riots that reached his city of Perpignan.[27] In a letter of consolation addressed in 1393 to the son of one of the leaders of Catalonian Jewry, and thus written after his own baptism, Duran turns to the problem of the apostates. The passage merits citation at length:

> I say that this [statement in B. Men 53b] alludes to that part of the seed of Abraham who were forced publicly to deny their faith, upon whom the decree of apostasy fell in this great region. . . . Some of them have been lax with regard to repentance. . . . It is therefore thought that this group has left the category of the Jewish people, which God has chosen as His legacy. . . . The answer that comes . . . means that the salvation and redemption that we await encompass the seed of Abraham, both those upon whom the decree of apostasy has fallen, who were *broken, trapped, and taken captive*" (Isa. 8:15) and those *who subscribe by hand to the Lord, and are called by the name of Israel* (Isa. 44:5).

26. *Ma'aseh avot siman le-vanim,* implied by Crescas' statement that Abraham taught us by his conduct how we should act. On this exegetical principle, see above, chap. 3, with references to the research of Amos Funkenstein.

27. See Emery. The conclusion of the letter cited below states in what seems to me an unequivocal manner that it was written while the author was living as a Christian, though his loyalty to Judaism and the Jewish people is obvious.

This matter in the present exile is just like that in previous ones. In the Egyptian exile, the people stumbled in idolatry, willingly . . . , yet this did not remove them from the category of the seed of Abraham. In the Babylonian exile, all of them stumbled in idolatry under duress except for a few individuals such as Hananiah and his companions, yet this did not remove them from the category of the seed of Abraham; no, in love and compassion God redeemed them. So it should be in this great exile of the present: if a part of the people has stumbled in a similar manner under absolute duress,[28] because of fear for their lives, this has not removed them from the category of God's people and the seed of Abraham who loved him [cf. Isa. 41:8], for God knows the secrets of their hearts, and He will redeem them with the rest of their brothers.[29]

This is obviously a polemical passage; the repetition of "this did not remove them from the category of the seed of Abraham" bears all the marks of a rebuttal speech. Juxtaposition with the statement by Crescas, in which the phrase "seed of Abraham" appears four times in a few lines, makes it look like Duran might well have been responding to this specific text. If so, then Crescas must have written or spoken it between August 1391 and the autumn of 1393, when Duran's letter was written. Crescas' passage has a clearly homiletical character: as it appears in no known work of his, it may have been part of a sermon that became famous enough to be frequently cited.[30]

The controversy over Crescas' position continued into the generation of the Expulsion. By citing the passage without reservation, the preacher endorsed the claim that Abraham's willingness to sacrifice his son should be viewed as an actual model for contemporary Jews. Other Jewish thinkers of the same generation were troubled by this view and carefully distanced themselves from it. One detects this approach in the commentary of Isaac

28. This phrase, in Hebrew *ha-ones ha-gamur,* would appear to reflect the canon law term "absolute compulsion" (*coactio absoluta*), which invalidates baptism. According to canon law, however, baptism accepted because of fear and threats of violence would not be in this category, which applies only to those who are baptized against their will and despite their ongoing protests. See Innocent III in Grayzel, *Church and Jews,* p. 103; Raymond of Penaforte and Alexander of Hales in Chazan, *Church, State and Jews,* pp. 38, 49.

29. Duran, p. 195. Cf. the discussion in Ben-Sasson, "Golei Sefarad," p. 35; Baer, *History* 2:157–58; Netanyahu, p. 92.

30. Reports of the content of sermons delivered by Crescas in various synagogues, apparently in the wake of the 1391 riots, were circulated widely enough to come to the attention of Joshua Halorki (Hieronymus de Sancta Fide), who cited them in the Disputation of Tortosa: Baer, *History* 2:161–62.

Abravanel. In his reading, the purpose of the *'Aqedah* was to teach Isaac that the body and its powers are ultimately of little import, and that the intellect, which alone is eternal, must prevail. Once Isaac learned this, no purpose was to be served in his actual slaughter. Since the spiritual triumph over the body, not the act of martyrdom, is paramount, we learn from Abraham and imitate him not by actually sacrificing our children, but "by serving God with all our heart and all our soul as Abraham did."[31] This spiritualization of the *'Aqedah* defuses its potential for inspiring real acts of violence in the present.

More explicit in his repudiation of the *'Aqedah* as a model for actual imitation is Isaac Arama.

> One should not think, "If God were to command me to bind this son of mine before Him, I would do so just as Abraham did." . . . It is as the prophet Micah said, *With what shall I approach the Lord? . . . Shall I give my firstborn for my transgression? . . . He has told you, O man, what is good, and what the Lord requires of you: Only to do justice, and to love goodness, and to walk humbly with your God* (Mic. 6:6–8). This means that the binding and slaughtering of children is not wanted by God, only submission and subjection.[32]

Read in isolation, this interpretation of the story seems eminently sensible. Our sermon shows that it was intended as part of a powerful internal polemic.

What cannot be determined is the most important historical question of all: in what specific context was the sermon first written and delivered? There is obviously a great difference between an abstract discussion of martyrdom in relatively quiet times and an appeal to Jews actually faced with the choice to be prepared to give up their own lives and take the lives of their children as martyrs. But at this point, any link with a concrete situation facing a community of Spanish Jews in, let us say, the 1480s (Shem Tov's work was completed in 1489) can be no more than speculation. As with so many sermons of the age, the underlying purpose of the preacher and the resonance of the words in the hearts of the original listeners can only be surmised.[33]

---

31. Abravanel, *Torah* 1:267b.

32. Arama, *'Aqedat,* chap. 21, p. 121b.

33. The same is true of Abraham ha-Levi's powerful glorification of martyrdom in "Megillat Amraphel"; see below, p. 300, n. 21. The historical value of this poignant statement would be even greater if it could be located in a concrete setting, intended for a specific audience. It is noteworthy that the theme of the *'Aqedah,* the paradigm of martyrdom for Crescas and our preacher, is completely absent from this text.

A SERMON ON THE BINDING [OF ISAAC] AND ON THE TEST

The Lord will see as it is said today (Gen. 22:14).[1]

What is written? *You have given to them that fear You a banner to be displayed* (Ps. 60:6). Test after test, exaltation after exaltation, in order to test them in the world, in order to exalt them in the world, like a ship's banner. And for what reason? *Because of the truth, selah* (Ps. 60:6). In order that God's justice may be established as truth in the world. For if a person should say, "Whomever He wants He makes rich, whomever He wants He makes into a king," you can respond by saying, "Can you do what Abraham did?" And say to him, "At age 100 he circumcised, yet after all this suffering God said to him *Take your son, your only son* (Gen. 22:2), and he did not hesitate." This is what the verse means, *You have given to them that fear You a banner to be displayed* (Ps. 60:6).[2]

The matter of the test is something that reason finds difficult. For it would appear to mean that the test is a way for God to determine and thereby know the faith of a person or of a particular nation, or the capacity of their service. But this meaning is problematic, as Maimonides has explained.[3] Even more problematic is the binding of Isaac, known by no one except for God and the two of them, namely Abraham and Isaac. Yet it is said to Abraham, *For now I know that you fear God* (Gen. 22:12).[4]

This is highly problematic. For if God did not know what was going to be until after this experiment, then God's knowledge would contain something new, and it would be just like our knowledge, which is false, and a lie. Yet the problem is apparent, for it says *now I know*, implying something He did not know before. He also said, *That He might test you by hardships to*

---

1. See p. 256, n. 11 above. The manuscripts have varying readings for this opening citation; the preacher's citation and interpretation of the verse (see n. 22) show that the correct reading is *Adonai yir'eh asher ye'amer ha-yom.*

2. Gen. Rab. 55,1. The text cited contains the deviant reading "At age 100 he circumcised" (see Theodor-Albeck, *Bereshit Rabbah*, Jerusalem, 1965, p. 585). This is the same as the text cited by Arama at the beginning of chap. 21 of *'Aqedat Yitshaq* (Arama, 1:331). Apparently the phrase means that Abraham circumcised Isaac at age 100 (Gen. 21:4–5), but see below, n. 31.

3. Maimonides, *Guide* 3,24, beginning; this and the following sentence are virtually a direct citation.

4. At this point, Shem Tov MS A (but not Shem Tov MS B or "Dover Meisharim") contains a passage of some 25 lines that appears to be an interruption. I have argued that it is an interpolation (see p. 255 above), and I have therefore included it after the conclusion of the sermon. The following passage is an explication of the problem stated more succinctly in the *Guide.* Cf. Shem Tov's commentary *ad loc.* (there is no verbal link) and Abravanel's commentary on Genesis 22, Question 16 (Abravanel, *Torah* 1:264a).

learn what was in your hearts (Deut. 8:2), indicating that God tests human beings to learn what is in their hearts as if He Himself were a human being. This is the major problem in the matter of the test.

There is also another problem no less difficult than this one. That is, why was it considered such a great achievement for Abraham to do something that had never been done before and would never be done again? After all, what else could Abraham have done when God told him to slaughter his son? If he had not slaughtered him, God would have killed [Isaac] and also killed Abraham! Therefore it was better for him to have slaughtered his son than to have left him, for *Inasmuch as the king's command is authoritative, and none can say to him "What are you doing?"* then *one who obeys orders will not suffer from the dangerous situation* (Eccl. 8:4–5). By following God's command, it was possible that God might relent and have compassion upon him. What else was he to do?[5]

Thirdly, we may raise the problem that this should not be considered [so great] for Abraham. After all, if one of us should come to believe that God had spoken to him, telling him to take his son quickly for His service, without delay he would take that son and make him a burnt offering. Why, many have been killed as martyrs, and have suffered many terrible tortures during periods of violent persecution, all in the service of God. How could Abraham not have slaughtered his son, even though Isaac was his only son, in God's service? Why, many killed their children and their grandchildren, and then their wives, and afterward they killed themselves, to sanctify God's Name in public. Why is their act not considered a greater source of merit than the binding of Isaac? Yet every Rosh Hashanah we pray, "Remember the binding of Isaac on behalf of his descendants today." Would it not be more appropriate to pray, "Remember those who were killed for the sanctification of Your Name"?[6]

---

5. The second problem, about the unique greatness of Abraham's behavior, is not so common in contemporary commentaries, particularly in the form that it is raised here: "What else could Abraham have done?" Essentially, the preacher is applying a kind of rudimentary "Game theory" analysis to Abraham's decision; cf. Brams, pp. 36–45.

6. In antiquity, Gentiles raised a similar question, pointing to many examples of human sacrifice for idealistic purposes attested in ancient literature. See Philo, *On Abraham*, pp. 89–91; Spiegel, pp. 9–12. Here the comparison is with the sacrifices made with other Jews; cf. Albo 3:333: "This is the reason also why in our prayers we always mention the sacrifice of Isaac by Abraham and do not mention the sacrifice of all the pious and holy men who offered their lives to sanctify the name of God, like Rabbi Akiba and his associates and all the holy men in every generation." After referring to cases of traditional martyrdom in which Jews were tortured and killed, the preacher invokes the more unusual instance of mass communal suicide, which is phenomenologically closer to the *'Aqedah*. See Introduction. For the liturgical passage, see Baer, *'Avodat Yisra'el*, p. 402; Spiegel, p. 89.

Now as for the first problem, Maimonides has already responded and given a perfect explanation. The matter of the test is to inform *others* of the intensity of faith that a person or nation has in God. The binding of Isaac was to inform us of the extent of Abraham's love and fear of God.[7] God commanded something that is not equalled by any surrender of property or by any other sacrifice of life, something that is rather the most extreme act possible, for it cannot be imagined that there could be any natural human tendency toward it. Think of a man who had been without child, had been longing intensively for a child, was extremely rich, and was chosen and given to expect that a nation from his seed would long endure. Then, after having despaired, a son was born to him. How great must have been his delight in him, how great his love for him! Yet because he revered God and loved to do what God commanded, he thought little of that beloved child and set aside all his hopes, and agreed to slaughter him after a journey of three days.

For if God had wanted him to do it immediately, as soon as God's word came to him, it would not have seemed that this was done with forethought and consideration. But he did it after three days, with careful examination of what is due to the Divine command and the love and fear of God. There is no need to look for any other idea or anything that might have affected his emotions. Our ancestor Abraham did not hasten because he was afraid that God would kill him or make him poor; he hastened out of love and reverence for God, without hope of reward, without fear of punishment.

The angel said to him *For now I know that you fear God* (Gen. 22:12): you will be called a truly God-fearing man, for this act will make it public knowledge among human beings[8] that our ancestor Abraham did not serve God in any way out of hope for reward or because of being afraid, but because of the love and fear of God. This fear is not akin to being afraid—that is contemptible in God's sight. It is rather fear inspired by the grandeur of God, as Maimonides wrote in the Laws of the Foundations of the Torah.[9]

Now if a person is worthy of understanding all that Maimonides said, all the problems will be resolved. For all those who were killed during periods of persecution gave their lives out of terror of punishment in Gehinnom, or in order to receive the reward of life in the World to Come. But Abraham had delight in God's commandments, not in their reward. He was the

---

7. From this point on, the entire answer is taken almost word for word from *Guide* 3,24. For two interesting textual details, see nn. 19–20 to the Hebrew text below.

8. This too is based on *Guide* 3,24, though no longer cited word for word. It reflects Maimonides' interpretation of *yada'ti* in Gen. 22:12 as "made known."

9. See Maimonides, *Code, Yesodei ha-Torah* 2,2 and 4,12, on the fear of God arising from an awareness of God's grandeur and the individual's lowliness.

beloved of God, something no prophet or sage or righteous person was ever called except for him alone.[10] All that he did, he did out of love. In this way all the difficulties vanish.

We may further say[11] that what Abraham did was indeed an act that had never been done before and would never be done again. God had said to him, *It is through Isaac that offspring shall be continued for you* (Gen. 21:12). When God later said *Take your son, your only son* (Gen. 22:2), he might appropriately have replied, "Yesterday You said to me *It is through Isaac that offspring shall be continued for you* (Gen. 21:12), and now You say *Offer him to Me as a burnt offering* (cf. Gen. 22:2)?!"[12] Or Abraham might appropriately have prayed to God, saying, "O Lord, do not command this thing."[13] But he got up early in the morning to do it with great enthusiasm, as if he were going to his son's wedding.[14] This was a great achievement for Abraham, a uniquely great act.

Furthermore, he requested that there be no obstacles. Before he came to the mountain, he took the wood for the burnt offering.[15] Moreover, he said to his young servants, *You stay here with the ass* (Gen. 22:5), so that they would not prevent him from performing this act.[16] Even after the angel said to him *Do not raise your hand against the boy, or do anything to him* (Gen. 22:12), paramount in his mind was what he could offer as a burnt offering on that altar. The Bible says, *Abraham looked up, and he saw a ram* (Gen. 22:13), as if he did not intend to take his son down without knowing what he could use for a burnt offering instead.[17]

---

10. See Isa. 41:8. The unique love of Abraham for God expressed in this biblical phrase and in Maimonides' answer to the first problem also resolves the second and third problems: Abraham's response was not a rational calculation of self-interest; it was motivated differently from the behavior of other Jewish martyrs.

11. After giving the answers stated and implied by Maimonides, the preacher goes on to give his own solutions to the second and third problems.

12. Gen. Rab. 56,10 and parallels; cf. Spiegel, pp. 90–91. In this version, the text of the biblical verse is altered to make God say "offer him to Me [*li*, rather than *sham*] as a burnt offering."

13. Thus, in response to the second problem, there were alternative responses that might have led to a more favorable outcome. Abraham could have appealed to God's prior promise, and he could have prayed that God reconsider the command.

14. On this motif in late Midrashim and in the post-Crusade poetry of Ashkenaz, see Spiegel, p. 135.

15. In order to make sure that there would be wood meeting ritual specifications. For this explanation, see Nahmanides and Bahya ben Asher ad loc.

16. This explanation of Abraham's instructions to the youths is given by Bahya ben Asher.

17. The preacher interprets Gen. 22:13 to mean that Abraham looked around for an alternative sacrifice, without which he would have been reluctant to remove his son from the altar. See the beginning of Abravanel's comment ad loc. (Abravanel, *Torah* 1:275a).

Now God said to Abraham that because he had done this great deed and not beseeched God with prayer, nor questioned God's ways as we have said,[18] therefore Abraham would be blessed in a manner different from the other blessings. For he had been blessed with multitude of offspring like the stars of the heavens and the sand on the seashore. He was blessed that because of this his offspring would prevail over their enemies and inherit their land. And he was given a third blessing: that all the nations of the earth would bless themselves by his descendants. Before this God said that the nations would bless themselves by Abraham, now by his descendants.[19]

Now Abraham said that he actually had not done anything, for he had not offered his son as a burnt offering.[20] But God saw the things that had passed between father and son. When Isaac said, *Here are the firestone and the wood, but where is the lamb for the burnt offering?* (Gen. 22:7), Abraham replied that the lamb would be be Isaac. This is the meaning of his statement, *God will see to the lamb for the burnt offering, my son* (Gen. 22:8), meaning, "my son" will be the burnt offering. Nevertheless, *the two of them walked together* (Gen. 22:8),[21] and Isaac agreed to be bound upon the altar. Thus God said to Abraham, "Don't say that you have done nothing." Rather, *God will see what was said today,*[22] for God will see in every generation what you have done today. This is the meaning of *God will see . . . because you have done this thing* (Gen. 22:14,16).

Now Abraham performed everything he did with great enthusiasm and

---

18. An interpretative paraphrase of Gen. 22:16, based on what the preacher has just explained.

19. An interpretative paraphrase of Gen. 22:17–18, comparing 22:18 with Gen. 12:3 and Gen. 18:18.

20. In this reading, Abraham modestly protests that, after all, he did not actually do anything. This is apparently triggered by Gen. 22:16, *because you have done this thing.*

21. The interpretation of Gen. 22:8 is that Abraham's answer is intended to communicate gently to Isaac that he would be the sacrificial lamb. "My son" is read not as a vocative but as an appositive: "God will provide a lamb for the sacrifice: my son." With this awful knowledge divulged, Isaac now knows the purpose of their climb, yet still *the two of them walked together.* This interpretation follows David Kimhi and Bahya ben Asher.

22. The preacher here returns to the verse fragment cited at the beginning of the sermon, and his novel interpretation is given: *Adonai yir'eh asher ye'amer ha-yom* means "God will see (in every future generation) what was said today." In this reading, the conversation in verses 22:7–8 is the essence of Abraham's achievement and the justification of his reward. Abravanel cites the underlying idea with approval: "Commentators have written that since Abraham did not actually do what he had intended, he gave that place a name in accordance with his intention. . . . He called it *Adonai yir'eh,* meaning, God sees what I would have planned in my heart to do had not the angel prevent me" (Abravanel, *Torah* 1:275b). This passage seems to have been quoted almost directly from Arama's *'Aqedat Yitsḥaq* (Arama, 1:242).

with joy. If this act had been done in sadness, prophecy would not have come to him in a waking state.[23] Therefore, he received this great reward because of the enthusiasm and the joy.[24] Father and son made themselves a sacrifice to God, for while the father was binding, he was [also] bound, and while Isaac was bound, he was [also] binding his father.[25] Abraham subdued his compassion, in order to do the will of his Creator with perfect heart,[26] and so did Isaac. And because in this sacrifice there were two sheep—Abraham and Isaac, for both of them were made into a burnt offering—God commanded that Israel bring two regular offerings as provided by law.[27] So long as the regular offering was in effect, these two would draw near. But when the regular offering was annulled, so was the merit of the ancestors annulled from protecting us.[28]

The conclusion to be drawn is that the test was to make known Abraham's love for God and the love of his son Isaac. This is what is said in tractate Avot, "With ten trials was our ancestor Abraham tested [. . .] in order to make known how great was the love of our ancestor Abraham before God."[29] Many of the commentators have said that the term *God tested* (*nissah*) *Abraham* (Gen. 22:1) is etymologically connected with *nes,* banner, meaning that it was to exalt Abraham, not to examine him.[30] So it says in the aggadic statement at the beginning of our sermon that God "tests" righteous men in order to exalt them, so that no one will say that whomever He wants God makes into a king of flesh and blood, for Abraham was given great blessings without any previous account of his deserving such blessings.[31]

---

23. Cf. B. Shab 30a.

24. With this idea that the inner state of joy becomes the reason for God's reward, compare the disputed question in Ravitzky, "Zehuto," p. 163.

25. Cf. Shem Tov, *Derashot,* Sermon for the second day of Rosh Hashanah, p. 80c, bottom, cited in the Hebrew text, n. 52.

26. The language is taken from Gen. Rab. 56:10.

27. Num. 28:3. The link between the binding of Isaac and the two lambs of the *tamid* offering was made by the Zohar 3:242a. Cf. also Crescas, *Or* II,2,6, p. 174.

28. Note the striking theory that the merit of the fathers acquired by the 'Aqedah was efficacious only while the *tamid* was offered in the Temple. For a more moderate formulation allowing for the efficacy of repentance, see Shem Tov's Rosh Hashanah sermon, cited in the Hebrew text, n. 55.

29. M. Avot 5,3.

30. Cf. Abravanel, *Torah* 1:267a, near bottom: *Ve-ha-Elohim nissah et Avraham hu mi-gezerat nes.* The opposite view, that *nissah* means to confront or oppose, is maintained by RaSHBaM ad loc. This explanation of *nissah* leads the preacher to the rabbinic *aggadah* cited at the beginning of the sermon.

31. The preacher reads the *aggadah* as refuting the philosophical-theological position that everything is determined by God's arbitrary will, which is totally independent of ethical standards.

We should indeed respond to the heretics. If they say that everything follows upon God's arbitrary will, the answer should be that Abraham deserved all the blessings and dignities that we mentioned for two reasons. First, because he circumcised himself after he was 100 years old, making of his soul and his blood a sacrifice.[32] And after this, he made his son a sacrifice, something no other man has ever done. That is why God wanted to make him into a banner and to exalt him in the sight of all the nations on earth, as the Bible says, *All the nations of the earth shall bless themselves by you.*[33]

The savant Rabbenu Levi ben Gershom said that the test was that God said to him, *And offer him as a burnt offering (ve-haʾalehu le-ʾolah) on one of the mountains* (Gen. 22:2). This can actually be understood in two ways. It can be understood to mean that he should sacrifice him and make him into an offering, or that he should take him up (*yaʾalehu*) there to an offering (*le-ʾolah*) in order to educate Isaac in the service of God.[34] God's test of Abraham was whether what God commanded him would be so difficult to do that this would cause him to understand the statement in a different way, namely, that he would understand it to mean that he should offer up a different offering, not that he should sacrifice his son.

The rabbi R. Hasdai said that this act was accredited to Abraham[35] because in sacrificing his son upon the altar he sacrificed all the generations that would come from him. For it had already been said that *It is through Isaac that offspring shall be continued for you* (Gen. 21:12). Therefore it is as if he had sacrificed all Jews who would come to be in the future.[36] And it is as if he taught us also that all those who want to be from the seed of Abra-

---

32. This passage makes it clear that the preacher understood the phrase *ben meʾah shanah mal* in his version of the midrash to mean that Abraham circumcised *himself* at age 100, even though this contradicts Gen. 17:24. With this description of circumcision as a sacrifice, compare Crescas, *Or* II,2,6, p. 173: ". . . as if they [the Israelites] had sacrificed from their own blood and their own flesh."

33. A mingling of Gen. 12:3 and 18:18.

34. Gersonides noted that God's instruction to Abraham could be understood to mean "take him up the mountain to a burnt offering." This is a plausible, though not the obvious, meaning of the words. If Abraham had seized on this as a technicality allowing him to bypass God's command, he would have failed the test. The passage quotes directly from Gersonides' commentary (RaLBaG, *Torah*, p. 31a).

35. The question addressed here is why Abraham was given all the credit for the *ʾAqedah*, rather than Isaac. The passage that follows is not to be found in the extant writings of Crescas; the preacher seems to be reporting a tradition of oral communication ("R. Hasdai said . . . "). See above, p. 264, n. 30.

36. Cf. Crescas, *Or* II,2,6, p. 174: "As if he had sacrificed to God Isaac and all those who would emerge from his loins."

ham must be prepared to offer their lives for the sanctification of God's Name when the proper time comes. Otherwise they are not from the seed of Abraham. That is why all of the righteous and virtuous Jews martyred themselves: to demonstrate that they were from the seed of Abraham and Isaac. And all Jews should think that, being from the seed of Abraham, they should be prepared to take the lives of their children, and the children should be prepared to be bound by their fathers and to bind them, as Abraham did to perform the will of his Heavenly Father.[37]

This sacrifice was performed on Mount Moriah. As the Midrash ha-Gadol said, it was from the place where the first man was created, and it was appropriate that this be said, for man was created from the place of his atonement.[38] In the same place, Adam offered his sacrifice, and so did Cain and Abel and Noah.[39] Abraham said *In the mountain of the Lord there is vision* (Gen. 22:14), meaning that he called the name of that site "God will see," for God would watch providentially over this place more than any other. Even though all places are His, as we see in the verse *The earth is the Lord's and its fullness* (Ps. 24:1), nevertheless, *Who may ascend the mountain of the Lord, who may stand in His holy place?* (Ps. 24:3), for this is better prepared.[40]

Now the entire world was created only for this place. The sages said, one who dwells outside the land [of Israel] should pray in the direction of the land, one who dwells in the land should pray in the direction of Jerusalem, one who prays in Jerusalem should face [the Temple, and one who prays in the Temple should face] the Holy of Holies,[41] for this place is better prepared than any other, and from it providence extends to all other places, in accor-

---

37. Thus the *'Aqedah* is defined as paradigmatic and exemplary. See Introduction. At this point the preacher moves on to a new subject: the location of the *'Aqedah*.

38. I understand the Hebrew initials *mem-heh* to stand for *Midrash ha-Gadol*; see *Midrash ha-Gadol* 1:78 (on Gen. 2:7), identifying the place of Adam's creation as Mt. Moriah, and the many parallels noted by the editor, including Gen. Rab. 14,8, the source of the statement that man was created from the place of his atonement.

39. *Pirqei de-R. Eliezer*, chap. 31, cited by Nahmanides and Bahya ben Asher in this context.

40. *Be-har Adonai yera'eh* is interpreted to mean not that God will be seen on the mountain, but that God extends special providence to the Temple Mount. Cf. Crescas, *Or* II,2,6, p. 176: "Although the One who watches providentially has the same relationship with various places, if that which is watched over does not have the same relationship with these places, there will necessarily be a difference in providence. But it is clear that this is so, because different places have different degrees of the necessary preparations for God's service." On this passage in Crescas, see Harvey, "Crescas."

41. Cf. *Sifre* Deut. 29; B. Ber 30a; the passage is paraphrased and with an ellipsis.

dance with the verse, *For from Zion shall go forth Torah, and the word of the Lord from Jerusalem* (Isa. 2:3).

Abraham called that place *Yir'eh* (Gen. 22:14) and Melchizedek called it *Shalem* (Gen. 14:18). What did the Holy One do? He made a compromise between these two righteous men and called it *Yerushalem,* Jerusalem,[42] meaning that perfection (*shelemut*) would be seen (*yera'eh*) in this place. It is as God said, *And none who lives there shall say, "I am sick"; it shall be inhabited by folk whose sin has been forgiven* (Isa. 33:24). This verse asserts that among the people who dwell in Jerusalem there will be no sickness or blemish; they will be whole, without any defect, because the entire people dwelling in it is forgiven of sin. There will be in it no sinner or transgressor, but all will be God-fearing. Or if there should be among them a sinner and transgressor, the morning sacrifice atones for sins of the night and the night sacrifice atones for sins of the day, and therefore perfection is apparent in this city.[43] Also the true perfection, which is wisdom and knowledge, will be found in Jerusalem more than in any other land, as the sages said, "The air of the land of Israel makes wise."[44]

Now the perfect were many, as the poet said, *I mention Rahab and Babylon* (Ps. 87:4), for this Psalm begins, *Of the Korathites. A psalm. A song. [. . .] Its foundation is on the holy mountains* (Ps. 87:1–2). This means that the main point of this Psalm, its foundation, is about the holy mountains, namely Zion.[45] The Psalmist brought support for this, saying that Mount Zion is holy because God loves it and makes His presence dwell there more than any other place. He therefore said, *The Lord loves the gates of Zion [. . .] more than all the dwellings of Jacob* (Ps. 87:2), from which we see that it is exalted in holiness above all other dwellings of Jacob.

After this he said, *Glorious things are spoken of you, O city of God, Selah* (Ps. 87:3), meaning that people attribute holiness and stature to this mountain and say that it is distinguished because it is the city of God. And this applies permanently. If God dwelled in Gibeon or in Shiloh, that was only temporary, but Zion is the dwelling place of God, the God of Jacob, forever.[46] Or it could mean, it is said of Zion that there are in it people of wealth, stature, and distinction, and at the same time there are in it people of wisdom and

---

42. Gen. Rab. 56,10.

43. Pesiqta de-Rav Kahana 5,17.

44. B. BB 158a. This statement is cited by Me'iri in the introduction to his comment on Psalm 87, to which the preacher now turns (Me'iri, *Tehillim,* p. 169).

45. Following Rashi, RaDaK, Me'iri.

46. *Selah* means permanence: cf. Me'iri.

understanding, God-fearing, people of truth. Therefore the Psalm says, "city of God in truth," for *selah* is like "true."[47]

Now this city and this mountain are different from all other places even though they may be great and distinguished. In all other places, an outstanding person, someone truly wise, may be born at one time or another, but in Zion many wise men are born each generation. This is the meaning of, *I mention Rahab, and Babylon . . . each was born there* (Ps. 87:4), but *It shall be said of Zion "Man after man was born there"* (Ps. 87:5).[48] It then says, *May He, the Most High, preserve it* (Ps. 87:6), for the prophet was praying that it would be so, lasting forever, and no evil eye would affect it, nor *murderous, treacherous men* (Ps. 55:24). Or it means that the reason why there are so many wise and well-known people in Jerusalem is God's permanent providence over it, as is widely known.[49]

He then said, *The Lord will inscribe in the register of peoples that each was born there* (Ps. 87:6). This means that no human being can count the number of wise people found in Zion, for they are too many to count, but God is able to count them as He counts and inscribes the other nations.[50] Or it means that God, who inscribes the languages and peoples, will say that one person born in Zion is equivalent to an entire people. The phrase *each was born there* implies that the one who was born in Zion is equal to an entire people. *Singers and dancers, all my springs are in You* (Ps. 87:7). This means that there will be singers and dancers who will not cease, like springs of water.[51] Or it means that in this city nothing will be lacking, for in it are singers and dancers who will not cease, like springs of water. In Zion there will be all the springs: the spring of wisdom, the spring of righteousness, the spring of stature and wealth and honor, the spring of pleasure, for human beings need pleasures. This is a musical instrument, an instrument of song.[52] These especially will be in the city, and it will be praised when all the perfections are found in it. For when a person takes pleasure that has no moral loftiness, it is of an animal nature. Thus is explained the superiority of Zion over all other places.

That is why we said at the beginning of our sermon that Abraham called the name of that place *God will see* (Gen. 22:14), for in this place God watches providentially over the perfect, and because of it He watches provi-

---

47. *Selah* means truth: cf. Ibn Ezra.
48. Following Ibn Ezra, RaDaK, Me'iri.
49. Both interpretations are in RaDaK (in the reverse order).
50. Ibn Ezra; cited by RaDaK after his own interpretation.
51. Following Ibn Ezra.
52. Cf. RaSHBaM, cited *Otsar Tehillot,* 10:343.

dentially over the entire world. May it be the will of the God of heaven that it be rebuilt and established, soon and in our days. Amen, so may it be God's will! Blessed is the Merciful One who helps us.

[Interpolation; see above, p. 266, n. 4]

I am ignorant and do not know,[53] but I have seen that all the savants who have written about the binding of Isaac are chirpers and moaners,[54] inventing no end of absurdities. I am like one who prophesies without knowing, groping like the blind[55] for things hidden from human sight, unless the light of the tradition of the wise has shined upon them.[56]

I would say that the sins of the Prophets are concealed from us, just as the real meanings of their prophecy are hidden from us. Also hidden from us is the sin of the first man, and the sin of Moses at the waters of Meribah.[57] But what I think is that because of Adam's sin, the root has been changed. It is like the branch of a vine that has been cut off and galingale[58] introduced into it. Then many stalks of it are planted, and all the wine that results has thrice the power of frankincense.[59]

So it is with the first man, who is like the branch, in all the fruits of which

---

53. Based on Ps. 73:22.

54. Based on Isa. 8:19.

55. Based on Isa. 59:10.

56. The author does not claim to have access to this esoteric tradition and therefore affects modesty in presenting his view.

57. The precise nature of Moses' sin at the waters of Meribah (Num. 20:1–13) and Adam's sin in eating the fruit of the tree of knowledge of good and evil remain matters of controversy. The same is true of sins committed by the Prophets, in which category the author undoubtedly includes the Patriarchs; see, e.g., RaMBaN on Gen. 12:10, Rashi on Gen. 15:8 and Isa. 43:27.

58. This word (in the Hebrew text *gariqo*) obviously comes from one of the European vernacular languages. My best guess is that it is a transcription of the variant form "garingal" (English "galingale"), the aromatic root of an Oriental plant that was considered in the Middle Ages to have medicinal properties. See *Dictionnaire de la langue Française du seizième siècle* (Paris, 1950), 4:256; *Trésor de la langue Française (Paris, 1981), 9:101; Diccionario critico etimológico Castellano e Hispanico* (Madrid, 1984) 4:26; cf. *OED* (1933) 4:19. The idea seems to be that the spice from the galingale root is introduced into the vine stalk in such a way that it is absorbed and penetrates to the grapes.

59. I cannot confidently explain three of the Hebrew words in the text underlying this sentence. From context, it appears that parts of the stalk (*kera'ayim?*) are planted so as to produce contaminated wine. The mixture of garingal with wine is attested in the first citation of the previous note, although there it has a medicinal quality. The author seems to associate the garingal with the grain of frankincense (*levonah*) mixed with wine to induce a state of stupor in one who is being led to execution (B. Sanh 43a). My translation is conjectural, based on the possible reading as *meshullash ha-levonah.*

the influence of galingale is present. In this way, death is necessary for all human beings not because of their deeds but because of the nature imprinted in their stock, which is like a fatal drug. Adam was the progenitor of all human bodies, and a fatal drug was instilled in him, imprinted in him and in all his offshoots.[60] And Moses was the progenitor of the Message,[61] which endures, and he sinned by water, which stands for Torah, thereby introducing a fatal drug into our Torah.[62] This was the reason for the controversies found in the Mishnah.[63] Thus one man was the reason for the separation of (?)[64] from each other.

Perhaps this is the meaning of the Prophet's statement, *Your earliest ancestor sinned* (Isa. 43:27), referring to the first man, *and your spokesmen transgressed against Me* (Isa. 43:27), referring to Moses and Aaron.[65] For Aaron also had a role in the receiving of the Torah, as we have found occasional

---

60. Thus the author believes that Adam's sin made death a natural phenomenon inherent in the nature of the human body, necessary whether or not any individual human being chooses to sin. Cf. the Talmudic dispute, B. Shab 55a–b. This passage suggests similarities with the Christian doctrine of "original sin." Clearly, our author is not suggesting that a permanent spiritual corruption has been transmitted to the souls of all human beings as a result of Adam's sin. Like some other Jews, however, he does believe that a decay-inducing admixture that affected Adam is transmitted to his descendants (cf. Rembaum, pp. 369–70 on Abraham Farissol). Through his botanical analogy, he is more specific on the mechanism of this transmission than other writers I have seen. Cf., however, Bahya ben Asher's *Kad ha-Qemah*, p. 41: "It is known through nature that when the root is defective and damaged, the branches will also acquire their portion of the damage. . . . So with the matter of this death: it is the way everyone, for they are branches of the root and descendants of Adam." For discussion of the medieval Jewish positions, see Rembaum; Lasker, "Ha-Ḥeit"; Schechterman. For a bibliography on earlier Jewish views on "original sin," see Lasker, "Ha-Ḥeit," p. 130, n. 16.

61. *Avi ha-te'udah,* a medieval characterization of Moses (see Davidson, *Thesaurus* 1:10). *Te'udah* is associated with Torah, as in Isa. 8:16, 20.

62. Moses' sin through "water" (Num. 20) is transferred, through the rabbinic identification of "water" with Torah (Song Rab. 1:2:3), to the Torah itself. Just as Adam's sin made all human beings mortal, so Moses' sin made Torah susceptible to misunderstanding and controversy.

63. The Hebrew text appears to have the word *le-vilti* here; if this is correct, something is missing from the manuscript.

64. I am unable to decipher the first part of the word following "separation"; the assertion completes the parallel between Adam and Moses. On Adam's sin as effecting "separation," cf. Zohar 1:35b, 36a, and Bahya ben Asher *Kad ha-Qemah,* p. 41: "The death of Adam is the separation of the soul from the body, and the punishment was on the model of the sin that separated the fruit from the tree. This is what the sages meant in their statement 'he cut down the shoots' [B. Hag 14b], for he sinned by separating things in deed and in thought."

65. Cf. RaDaK on Isa. 43:27; I have not found either in Rabbinic literature or in medieval commentators the interpretation of both parts of the verse as given here.

mention of him. Even though the sin of the first man was greater than that of Moses and Aaron, "transgression" is written of them, as something in nature, and "sin" is attributed to the first man, as in the verse *May sinners disappear* (Ps. 104).[66]

Just as we do not know the sins of the Prophets, so we do not know the nature of their worship and their observance of the commandments of their Creator. But I think that just as Adam instilled a fatal drug in his descendants, so Abraham and Isaac instilled some life-giving drug in theirs. And just as Adam made natural death necessary for his offspring, so Abraham and Isaac instilled natural life for the souls of their offspring after them.[67] Perhaps Abraham's fear of God became known in the world through the binding of Isaac, but this binding was significant in its own right. That is why it says *and you have not withheld* (Gen. 22:12), rather than saying "because you have not withheld."[68]

Certainly the merit of Isaac was greater than that of Abraham, for he handed himself over to be killed without having been addressed by God.[69] But the reality of the binding and its life-giving powers for their offspring are attributed to Abraham because he was the first, just as the first man was first for the fatal drug. Concealed from us is the matter of the reward for the binding,[70] just as it is concealed from us that because [Adam] sinned, all who enter the world will die regardless of any wrong they may have done. This is why [Isaac] was bound in the place where the first man was created, from the

---

66. Ordinarily *pasha'* (transgress) would be more serious than *ḥata* (sin) (cf. B. Yoma 36b), but this does not apply to Isa. 43:27. The precise point of the end of the sentence and the reference to Ps. 104:35 are unclear to me.

67. The usual rabbinic model makes the Torah itself the antidote to the contamination (*zuhama*) instilled in human nature through the sin of Adam and Eve (e.g., B. Shab 146a, Yeb 103b, AZ 22b). Crescas finds the antidote already in circumcision (see Crescas, *Or* II,2,6, p. 173, Lasker, "Ha-Ḥeit," p. 127). Our author interprets the *zuhama* of the Talmudic statement not as lust, or the evil inclination, but as mortality imprinted in the physical body, and his antidote—of eternal life—comes through the *Aqedah*. Cf. the continuation of the discussion by Crescas (pp. 173–74), passage cited by Sirat, p. 165.

68. I.e., the binding of Isaac was an act that had merit of its own, in addition to demonstrating Abraham's fear of God; that is why Gen. 22:12 speaks of two distinct things: "I know that you are God-fearing *and* you have not withheld your son from Me."

69. This affirmation that Isaac's merit was greater than that of Abraham is inconsistent with the sermon, which indicates a mutuality and equality of father and son in their sacrifice. The question whose merit was greater was debated by commentators; cf. Bahya ben Asher on Gen. 22:7, where the reason attributed to those who argue for Isaac's greater merit is the same as that given here.

70. I.e., the reward of the potential for eternal life, not the rewards promised in Gen. 22:17-18.

same dust.[71] It is also possible that by this act he bound up the attribute of judgment forever,[72] which is why we say, "[The Lord our God has remembered for us] the covenant . . . and the binding . . . ," specifying two things.[73]

This is highly problematic . . . .[74]

---

71. Cf. above, n. 38.
72. Cf. Zohar 1:119b; Saba, Genesis, p. 24a.
73. Cf. above, p. 267, n. 6 end.
74. The manuscript continues here with the material following n. 4 on p. 266, above.

דרש לעקדה ולנסיון

(בהר) ה' יראה אשר יאמר היום.[1]

מאי דכתיב נתת ליראיך נס להתנוסס[2]? נסיון אחר [נסיון] גדלון אחר גדלון בשביל לנסותם בעולם בשביל לגדלם בעולם כנס (והנס שהוא ספינה).[3] וכל כך למה? מפני קשט סלה[4] בשביל שתתקשט מדת הדין בעולם. שאם יאמר לך אדם למי שהוא רוצה מעשיר למי שהוא רוצה עושה מלך יכול אתה להשיבו ולומר, יכול אתה לעשות כמו שעשה אברהם? והוא אומ' לך מה עשה אברהם? ואתה אומר לו בן מאה שנה מל ואחר כל הצער הזה א"ל קח נא את בנך את יחידך[5] ולא עיכב. הוי אומר נתת ליראיך נס להתנוסס.[6]

ענין הנסיון דבר קשה אצל השכל, כי יראה מעניינו כי הנסיון הוא בחינה אשר ידע השם אמונת האיש או האומה ההיא או יכולת עבודתו, וזה הענין הוא הספק כמו שביאר הרב המורה.[7] וכ"ש ענין העקידה אשר לא ידעה בלתי השם והם שניהם ר"ל אברהם ויצחק, ונאמר לו עתה ידעתי כי ירא אלהים אתה.[8] זהו הספק הגדול, כי אם השם לא ידע מה שעתיד להיות אלא אחר הבחינה יהיה לו ידיעה מחודשת ויהיה ידיעתו כידיעתנו וזהו שוא ודבר כזב.[9] והנה יראה ספק כי אמר עתה ידעתי[10] מה שלא היה יודע קודם. וג"כ אמר למען ענותך לנסותך לדעת את אשר בלבבך וכו'[11] כי הוא מנסה לבני אדם לדעת את אשר בלבם כאלו הוא בן אדם. זהו הספק הגדול אשר יש בענין הנסיון.

5

10

15

20

1. בר' כב יז, ועי' הערה 1 לתרגום.
2. תה' ס ו.
3. צ"ל, בהתאם לכ"י דובר מישרים, "כנס אשר הוא בספינה."
4. תה' ס ו.
5. בר' כב ב.
6. תה' ס ו. המאמר הוא מבראשית רבה נה,א.
7. רמב"ם, מורה נבוכים ג,כד.
8. בר' כב יב. עי' הערה 4 לתרגום, והקטע בסוף הדרשה (שורה 191 ואילך).
9. ע"פ משלי ל ח.
10. בר' כב יב.
11. דב' ח ב.

ויש ספק אחר אינו למטה מזה בקושי והוא כי למה נחשב זה
לאברהם למעלה גדולה כשעשה פועל אשר לא קדם לו ולא נתאחר,
כי מה יכול אברהם לעשות אם השם א״ל לשחוט את בנו, כי אם לא
ישחטנו היה הש״י הורגו והיה הורג את אברהם, ובעבור זה יותר
ראוי לשחוט את בנו יותר מלעזוב אותו, כי כאשר דבר מלך שלטון
25 ומי יאמר לו מה תעשה?[12] והנה שומר מצוה לא ידע דבר רע[13] ובעשות
מצות השם אולי ישוב יי וירחם עליו[14] ומה לו לעשות?

ג׳ יש לספק כי זאת לא יחשב לאברהם, כי אם אחד ממנו יהיה
מאמין שהש״י דבר עמו ושיקח את בנו לעבודתו במהרה בלי איחור
30 יקח את בנו ויעשהו עולה. והנה רבים נהרגו לקדושת השם וסבלו
יסורין רבים ורעים בשמדות לעבודת הש״י, ואיך לא ישחוט את בנו
אפילו שיהיה יחידו לעבודת השם? והנה רבים הרגו את בניהם ואת
בני בניהם ואח״כ את נשיהם ואח״כ הרגו את עצמם לקדוש השם
ברבים ואיך לא נחשב להם לצדקה[15] גדולה יותר מעקידת יצחק אשר
35 אנו מתפללים בכל (תפלותינו וצרותינו כמ״ש)[16] ״ועקידת יצחק היום
[לזרעו תזכור]״, כי ראוי יותר ״וההרוגים על קדושת שמך תזכור״[17]

והנה לספק האחד כבר השיב הרב המורה[18] וביאר בתכלית הביאור
כי ענין הנסיון הוא להודיע לאחרים שיעור האמנת האיש או האומה
בש״י, והנה העקידה להודיע אותנו גדול אהבת הש״י ויראתו עד היכן
40 הוא מגיע, וצוה בזה הענין אשר לא ידומה לא נתינת ממון ולא נתינת
נפש אבל הוא המופלג מה שאיפשר שיבוא במציאות ממה שלא
ידומה שטבע האדם יטה אליו, והוא שיהיה איש עקר בתכלית הכוסף
לולד ובעל עושר גדול ואיש נבחר ובוחר שישאר לזרעו אומה, ומה
שנולד בן אחר היאוש איך יהיה חשקו בו ואהבתו אותו, אבל ליראה

12. קהלת ח ד.
13. קהלת ח ה.
14. ע״פ מיכה ז יט.
15. ע״פ בר׳ טו ו.
16. ראה זליגמן בער, סדר עבודת ישראל, עמ׳ 402.
17. על ענין זה עי׳ הערה 6 לתרגום והדיון במבוא.
18. עי׳ רמב״ם, מורה נבוכים ג,כד.

את השם ולאהבתו ולקיים מצותו יבז[19] הולד האהוב והניח כל מה 45
שקווה והסכים לשחוט אותו אחר מהלך כמה ימים, כי אלו היה
רוצה לעשות לשעתו בבוא דבר יי אליו לא היה נראה[20] שהיה זה נעשה
במחשבה ובהשתכלות, אבל אחר ג' ימים עשאו בבחינת חק מצותו
ואהבתו ויראתו ושאין צריך להשגיח על ענין אחר ולא להפעלות כלל
כי אברהם אבינו לא מיהר לפחד מהשם שיהרגהו או ירוששהו אבל 50
לאהבת הש"י ויראתו לא לתקות גמול ולא לפחד עונש.

וא"ל המלאך כי עתה ידעתי כי ירא אלהים אתה,[21] תקרא ירא
אלהים גמור כי התפרסם לבני אדם זה הפועל,[22] כי אברהם אבינו לא
היה עובד את השם לשום עבודה לא לתקות גמול ולא לפחד אלא
בעבור אהבת הש"י וליראתו, לא יראת פחד כי זאת היראה היה 55
נמאס לפניו, אבל היראה שהיה כפי גודל השם ומעלתו כמ"ש הרב
בהלכות יסודי התורה.[23]

והנה כשיזכה האדם להבין כל מה שאמר הרב יותרו כל הספקות,
כי כל הנהרגים בשמדות הוא לאימת עונש גיהנם או לקבל שכר
העה"ב, אבל אברהם היה חפץ במצות השם לא בשכרן והוא היה 60
אוהבו של הקב"ה[24] מה שלא נקרא נביא ולא חכם ולא צדיק אלא
הוא לבדו, כי כל מה שהיה עושה היה עושה מאהבה. ובזה יסולקו כל
הספקות.

ונוסיף ונאמר כי מה שעשה אברהם הוא פועל שלא קדם כמותו
ולא נתאחר כי אחר שא"ל השם כי ביצחק יקרא לך זרע[25] היה ראוי 65
שיאמר כשאמר לו השם קח נא את בנך את יחידך,[26] אתמול אמרת לי

19. יש להעדיף נוסח זה על המלה „בו" המופיעה בתרגום ו' תבון הנדפס. השוה מהדורת
פרידלנדה, כרך ג, עמ' 116, הערה 1.
20. נוסח זה, שהוא שונה מנוסח ו' תבון, כמעט זהה עם הניסוח שבפירוש שם טוב שם.
21. בר' כב יב.
22. גם קטע זה מבוסס על מורה נבוכים, שם. במקום לצטט מילולית, מסכם הדרשן את תכן
עמדתו של הרמב"ם, המפרש את המלה „ידעתי" כאלו היא „הודעתי".
23. עי' הל' יסודי התורה ב,ב וד,יב.
24. עי' יש' מא ח.
25. בר' כא יב.
26. בר' כב ב.

כי ביצחק יקרא לך זרע ועכשו אתה אומר והעלהו לי לעולה.[27] או היה
ראוי שהתפלל אברהם לשם ולומר לו, בי אדוני אל תצוה את הדבר
הזה. אבל השכים בבקר[28] לעשות זה בזריזות גדולה כמו שהיה הולך
70　לחופת בנו,[29] וזה היה מעלה גדולה לאברהם ופועל גדול אשר א״א
כמותו, וגם כי בקש שלא יהיו לו מונעים כי לקח קודם שיבוא אל
ההר את עצי העולה[30] וגם שאמר לנעריו שבו לכם פה עם החמור[31]
כדי שלא יעכבוהו מלעשות זה הפועל[32] וגם כי אחר שא״ל המלאך
אל תשלח ידך אל הנער ואל תעש לו מאומה[33] לתכלית כוונתו היה
75　מה יעלה לעולה בזה המזבח ואמר וישא אברהם את עיניו וירא את
האיל[34] כאלו לא היה כוונתו להוריד את בנו מעל המזבח אבל מה
יעשה לעולה.[35]

והנה אמר הש״י לאברהם כי יען אשר עשה זה המעשה[36] הגדול
ולא בקש תפלה ממנו או לא הרהר אחר מעשי הש״י כמ״ש[37] ובעבור
80　זה נתברך אברהם מה שלא נתברך בברכות אחרות, והנה נתברך
ברבוי הזרע ככוכבי השמים וכחול אשר על שפת הים[38] ונתברך
שבעבור זה יתגברו על האויבים וירשו את ארצם[39] ונתברך בברכה ג׳
שיתברכו בזרעו כל גויי הארץ[40] שעד כאן אמר שיתברכו באברהם[41]
אבל כאן בזרעו.

---

27. ע״פ בר׳ כב ב (והעלהו שם לעולה). הקטע מבוסס על בראשית רבה נו,י ומקבילות.

28. ע״פ בר׳ כב ג.

29. על מוטיב זה עי׳ שלום שפיגל, The Last Trial, עמ׳ 135.

30. עי׳ בר׳ כב ג ופירושי רמב״ן ובחיי בן אשר שם.

31. בר׳ כב ה.

32. עי׳ פירוש בחיי בן אשר שם.

33. בר׳ כב יב.

34. בר׳ כב יג.

35. יתכן שנפל כאן שבוש בטקסט, והכוונה שאברהם לא רצה להוריד את יצחק מעל המזבח
בלי למצוא מה יעשה לעולה במקומו.

36. ע״פ בר׳ כב טז.

37. „כמו שבארנו״ בקטע הקודם.

38. בר׳ כב יז.

39. הרחבה פרשנית של סוף בר׳ כב יז.

40. ע״פ בר׳ כב יח.

41. עי׳ בר׳ יב ג ובר׳ יח יח.

והנה אמר אברהם שאף לא נעשה בזה שום דבר[42] כי לא עלה (כך) 85
את בנו עולה, אבל הש״י יראה[43] הדברים שעברו בין האב לבנו כשאמר
לו הנה האש והעצים ואיה השה לעולה[44] ומה שהשיב לו ואמר לו כי
השה הוא יהיה יצחק, וזהו אומרו אלהים יראה לו השה לעולה בני[45]
הרצון לפניו שיהיה בני לעולה, ועכ״ז הלכו שניהם יחדיו[46] וקבל יצחק
ליעקד ע״ג המזבח. והשם א״ל אל תאמר שלא עשית דבר אלא כי יי 90
יראה אשר יאמר היום[47] כי השם יראה בכל דור ודור מה עשית היום,
וז״א[48] אלהים יראה יען אשר עשית את הדבר הזה.[49]

והנה אברהם עשה כל מה שעשה בזריזות גדולה ובשמחה כי אם
היה זה הפועל נעשה בעצב לא היה זה הנבואה בהקיץ[50] לכן קבל זה
השכר הגדול בעבור הזריזות והשמחה.[51] והאב והבן עשו עצמן קרבן 95
לש״י כי האב אם היה עוקד היה נעקד ואם יצחק היה נעקד היה
עוקד לאביו[52] כי אברהם כבש רחמיו לעשות רצון בוראו בלבב שלם[53]
וכן יצחק. ובעבור שהיה בזה הקרבן ב׳ כבשים והם אברהם ויצחק כי
שניהם נעשו עולה צוה השם ית׳ שיקריבו ישראל שני תמידין כהלכתן[54]
ובכל זמן שהתמיד היה קרב היו נקרבין אלו הב׳ ובזמן שבוטל בתמיד 100
בוטל זכות אבות מהגן בעדנו.[55]

---

42. כנראה, תגובת אברהם למאמר „יען אשר עשית את הדבר הזה.״

43. ע״פ בר׳ כב יד.

44. בר׳ כב ז.

45. בר׳ כב ח.

46. ע״פ בר׳ כב ח, ועי׳ הערה 21 לתרגום על פירוש זה לפסוק.

47. בר׳ כב יד, ועי׳ הערה 22 לתרגום על פירוש זה לחלק הפסוק.

48. וזה אומרו.

49. ע״פ בר׳ כב יד וטז.

50. עי׳ שבת ל א.

51. עי׳ הערה 24 לתרגום.

52. השוה שם טוב ן׳ שם טוב, דרשות התורה, עמ׳ פ ג: „והנה כ״א היה עוקד ונעקד כי אברהם
אשר היה עוקד את יצחק היה נעקד לפני אביו שבשמים וכאלו אברהם היה עולה ע״ג המזבח כמו
בנו כי אין ספק כי יותר היה רוצה אברהם במיתתו ממיתת בנו ולכן בעקידת יצחק נעקד אברהם
ויצחק, עד שחמל הב״ה על אב ועל בן והראה להם האיל.״

53. ע״פ בראשית רבה נו,י.

54. במ׳ כח ג, ועי׳ זהר ג,רמב א, וקרשקש, אור ה׳, ב,ב,ו.

55. השוה הניסוח המתון בדרשת ראש השנה לשם טוב ן׳ שם טוב, כ״י בית המדרש לרבנים שבניו
יורק R 212, עמ׳ עב ב–עג א: „ולמה שהאב והבן נעקדו יחד ע״ג המזבח צוה הש״י לעשות בכל יום ב׳

והכלל העולה כי הנסיון היה להודיע חבת אברהם לש״י וחבת בנו
יצחק וז״ש במסכת אבות י׳ נסיונות נתנסה אברהם אבינו להודיע
כמה היתה חבתו של אברהם אבינו לפני השם.[56] ורבים מהמפרשין
אמרו כי לשון נסה את אברהם[57] כי הוא מלשון נס, כי היה להגדילו
לא להבחינו.[58] וז״ש בהגדה בתחלת דרושינו כי הש״י מנסה לצדיקים
כדי להגדילם, כדי שלא יאמרו למי שהוא רוצה יעשה מלך בשר ודם,
שהרי אברהם נתברך בברכות גדולות מבלתי שקדם ספור היות
אברהם זוכה לברכות הללו. ולכן ראוי להשיב למינים אם יאמרו
שהכל הולך אחר הרצון הפשוט[59] שישיבו להם שאברהם היה ראוי
לכל ברכות ומעלות אשר אמרנו בעבור ב׳ דברים אחד בעבור שמל
את עצמו אחר מאה שנה ועשה קרבן מנפשו ומדמו[60] ואחר כן עשה
קרבן מבנו מה שלא עשה שום אדם. לכן רצה הש״י לעשות לו נס
ולהגדילו בעיני כל גויי הארץ כמ״ש ונברכו בך כל גויי הארץ.[61]

והחכם רבינו לוי בן גרשום אמר כי הנסיון הוא שאמ״ל והעלהו
[שם] לעולה על אחד ההרים[62] וזה סובל ב׳ פירושים: יתכן שיובן
שיזבח אותו ויעשהו עולה או שיעלהו שם לעולה כדי שיתחנך יצחק
בעבודת הש״י.[63] ונסהו השם אם יקשה בעיניו לעשות שום דבר שיצוה
השם עליו עד שיהיה זה סבה אל שיבין מזה המאמר זולת מה שיובן
ממנו מזה הענין, רצונו שיבין ממנו שיעלה שם עולה אחרת לא
שיזבח בנו.

כבשים בני שנה תמימים והם באים לכפרה על כל ישראל והם תמימים כי הם רמז לנעקדים בהר
המוריה כי היו שנים ובזכות עשות עשות דמותם השרה שכינתו ביניגו. וביום שבוטל התמיד בוטל כל
טובינו ונשארנו מוכנים לכל מקרה ופגע ובעבור זכירת המעשה הגדול והנורא שעשה האב והבן
בתקוע השופר של איל כדי שנכני׳ לבנו לפני אבי׳ שבשמים יקבל תשובתנו.״

56. אבות ה,ג.

57. בר׳ כב א.

58. עי׳ הערה 30 לתרגום.

59. של האלהים, המנהיג עולמו באופן שרירותי.

60. עי׳ הערה 32 לתרגום.

61. בכל כתבי היד נמצא צירוף זה של בר׳ יב ג ובר׳ יח יח, במקום בר׳ כב יח.

62. בר׳ כב ב.

63. עי׳ רלב״ג, פירוש על התורה, עמ׳ לא א: אפשר להבין את ההוראה ״,והעלהו שם לעולה״ כאלו
הכוונה היא ״,שיראה יצחק שם הקרבת העולה.״

והנה הרב ר' חסדאי אמר כי נחשב זה הפועל לאברהם[64] כי
בהקריבו בנו ע"ג המזבח הקריב כל הדורות הבאים ממנו כי כבר
נאמר כי ביצחק יקרא לך זרע[65] ולכן היה זה כאלו הקריב כל ישראל
125   העתידין להיות[66] וכאלו הורה לנו ג"כ כי כל הרוצה להיות מזרע
אברהם ראוי שיפרד נפשו[67] לתתה על ידי קדושת הש"י כשיבוא עת
וזמן ואם לא יהיה כן לא יהיה מזרע אברהם. ולכן כל הצדיקים ואנשי
המעלה נתנו עצמם ע"י קדושת הש"י להורות כי הם מזרע אברהם
ויצחק. וראוי לכל איש מבני ישראל שיחשוב כי אחר שהוא מזרע
130   אברהם שיכין האב להרוג את הבן והבן יהיה נעקד ועוקד את אביו
כמו שעשה אברהם לעשות רצון אביו שבשמים.

והנה זה הקרבן נעשה בהר המוריה והיה כמו שאמר במ"ה[68]
ממקום שנברא אדם הראשון והיה ראוי שיאמר כי אדם ממקום
כפרתו נברא[69] ובזה המקום הקריב אדם הראשון קרבן וקין והבל
135   ונח[70] ואמר אברהם בהר יי יראה[71] אשר הרצון בו כי קרא שם המקום
ההוא יי יראה כי יי ישגיח בזה המקום יותר ממקום אחר[72] כי אם כל
המקומות הם שלו כמש"ה כי ליי הארץ ומלואה[73] עכ"ז מי יעלה בהר
יי ומי יקום במקום קדשו וכו'[74] כי זה יותר מוכן. והנה כל העולם לא
נברא אלא בעבור זה המקום כמשחז"ל היושב בחוצה לארץ יתפלל
140   כנגד הארץ והיושב בארץ יתפלל כנגד ירושלים והמתפלל בירושלים
כנגד בית קדשי הקדשים;[75] כי זה המקום הוא יותר מוכן משאר
המקומות וממנו יושגחו כל המקומות כמ"ש כי מציון תצא תורה

64. עי' הערה 34 לתרגום.

65. בר' כא יב.

66. השוה קרשקש, אור ה', ב,ב,ו: „כאלו כבר הקריב לשם יצחק וכל יוצאי ירכו."

67. כנראה הכוונה בבטוי זה היא לעשות נפשו כמו שכל נפרד מחמר.

68. במדרש הגדול, ועי' שם א, עח על בר' ב ז ומקבילות.

69. בראשית רבה יד,ח ומקבילות.

70. עי' פרקי דרבי אליעזר, פרק לא, מובא ע"י רמב"ן ובחיי בן אשר בהקשר זה.

71. בר' כב יד.

72. עי' הערה 40 לתרגום.

73. תה' כד א.

74. תה' כד ג.

75. ספרי דברים כט, ברכות ל א.

ודבר ה׳ מירושלים.[76] והנה אברהם קרא המקום ההוא יראה[77] ומלכי
צדק קראו שלם,[78] מה עשה הקב״ה? עשה פשרה בין ב׳ צדיקים וקראו
145   ירושלם,[79] אשר הרצון בזה שהשלמות יראה במקום הזה כמו שאמר
ובל יאמר שכן חליתי העם היושב בה נשוא עון.[80] אה״כ[81] כי העם
היושב בירושלים לא ימצא בהם שום חולי ולא מום והם שלמים מכל
פגע בעבור שכל העם שיושבים בה נשוא עון אשר לא היה בה חוטא
ופושע אבל כולם היו יראים אל הש״י. או אף שימצא בהם חוטא
150   ופושע, קרבן של בקר היה מכפר על עונות שבלילה וקרבן שבלילה
מכפר על עונות שביום[82] ולכן היה השלמות נראית בזה העיר. וגם
השלמות האמיתי שהוא החכמה והדעת היה נמצאת בירושלם יותר
מכל הארצות כמשאז״ל אוירא דארעה דישראל מחכים:[83]

והנה השלמים היו רבים כמ״ש[84] המשורר אזכיר רהב ובבל וכו׳[85]
155   כי זה תחלת המזמור אמר לבני קרח מזמור שיר יסודתו בהררי קדש.[86]
אה״כ בזה שעקר זה המזמור ויסודתו הוא אל הררי קדש שהוא ציון.[87]
והביא טענה ע״ז ואמר כי הר ציון הוא קדוש למה שהש״י אהב אותו
ושכן שכינתו בו יותר מכל שאר המקומות. ולכ״א[88] אוהב יי שערי ציון
מכל משכנות יעקב[89] אשר ממנו יראה שהוא נתעלה בקדש על כל שאר
160   משכנות יעקב. ואחז״א[90] נכבדות מדובר בך עיר האלהים סלה,[91] אה״כ

76. יש׳ ב ג.

77. בר׳ כב יד.

78. בר׳ יד יח.

79. ע״פ בראשית רבה נו,י.

80. יש׳ לג כד.

81. אמר הכתוב.

82. פסיקתא דרב כהנא ה,יז.

83. בבא בתרא קנח א. עי׳ הערה 44 לתרגום.

84. כמו שאמר.

85. תה׳ פז ד.

86. תה׳ פז א–ב.

87. ע״פ רש״י, רד״ק, מאירי.

88. ולכן אמר.

89. תה׳ פז ב.

90. ואחר זה אמר.

91. תה׳ פז ג.

כי נותנים לזה ההר קדושה ומעלה ואומרים עליו שהוא נכבד מצד
שהוא עיר האלהים, וזה בתמידות, כי אם השם שכן בגבעון ובשלה
לא היה אלא לפי שעה[92] אבל ציון היה משכן אלהים אלהי יעקב
לעולם.[93] או ירצה שאומ' מציון שיש בו אנשי עושר ומעלה וכבוד ועם

165   זה ימצאו בהם אנשים חכמים ונבונים יראי אלהים אנשי אמת ולכן
היה עיר האלהים באמת, כי סלה הוא כמו אמתי.[94]

והנה נבדלה זאת העיר וזה ההר מכל שאר המקומות אעפ"י שיהיו
גדולים ונכבדות מצד שבכל המקומות יולד איש מעולה או חכם בזמן
מהזמנים אבל בציון יולדו אנשים רבים חכמים בכל דור ודור, וז"א

170   אזכיר רהב ובבל וכו' זה יולד שם[95] אבל לציון יאמר איש ואיש יולד
וכו'.[96] ואומר והוא יכוננה עליון,[97] וזה כי הנביא היה מתפלל ושיהיה
כן ושיתמיד לעולם ולא ישיגה עין הרע ולא יהיו הדרים בה אנשי
דמים ומרמה.[98] או יאמר כי הסבה בהיות בציון רבים חכמים וידועים
מצד שהש"י משגיח בה תמיד והיא ידועה.[99]

175   ואומר יי יספור בכתוב עמים זה יולד שם,[100] ירצה כי לא יוכל[101]
לספור מנין כל האנשים החכמים הנמצאים בציון כי רבו מלספור
אבל השם הוא[102] לספור אותם כשיספור ויכתוב שאר העמים.[103] או
יאמר כי השם שיכתוב הלשונות והעמים יאמר כי איש אחד הנולד
בציון הוא שקול כנגד עם אחד. ואומר זה יולד שם[104] ר"ל זה הנולד

180   בציון שוה במעלה לעם א'. שרים כחוללים כל מעיני בך,[105] ירצה כי

92. השוה תה' עח ס.
93. ז"א „סלה" פירושו בתמידות, לנצח והשוה מאירי שם.
94. ע"פ ן' עזרא, רד"ק, מאירי.
95. תה' פז ד.
96. תה' פז ה.
97. תה' פז ה.
98. ע"פ תה' נה כד.
99. שני הפירושים ברד"ק, בסדר הפוך.
100. תה' פז ו.
101. בכ"י דובר מישרים, „לא יוכל איש לספור."
102. בכ"י דובר מישרים, „השם הוא שיוכל לספור."
103. ן' עזרא שם, מובא ע"י רד"ק אחר פירושו שלו.
104. תה' פז ו.
105. תה' פז ז.

שם ימצאו שרים וחוללים שלא יפסיקו כמו מעייני מים.[106] ובציון
ימצאו כל מעיינים: מעיין החכמה מעיין הצדקה מעיין המעלה ועושר
וכבוד ומעיין תענוג, כי צריך אדם אל התענוגים והוא כלי זמר וכלי
שיר[107] ובפרט אלו ימצאו במדינה ויהללו אותה כשימצאו כל שאר
185 השלמיות כי להתענג האדם בלי מעלה הוא דבר בהמי. הרי התבאר
מעלת ציון על כל שאר המקומות.

ולכן אמרנו בתחלת דרושינו כי שם המקום ההוא קראו אברהם
ה׳ יראה[108] כי בזה המקום הוא משגיח על שלמים ובעבורו ישגיח
אל כל העולם. יהי רצון מלפני אלהי השמים שתבנה ותכונן[109] אמן
190 במהרה בימינו, וכן יהיה רצון. בריך רחמנא דסייען.

ואני[110] בער ולא ידעתי[111] אך ראיתי כי כל אותם החכמים אשר
דברו בענין העקדה הלא הם מצפצפים ומהגים[112] בודים דברים
והתולים אין קץ. ואני כמתנבא ואיני יודע מגשש כעורים[113] דברים
שנעלמו מבני אדם אלא א״כ זרח עליהם אור קבלת חכמים. ואומ׳
195 כי עונות הנביאים נעלמו ממנו כאשר נעלמו ממנו מציאות נבואתם
מהן, ונעלם ממנו עון אדם הראשיון גם עון משה במי מריבה.[114] רק
מה שאני חושב הוא שבסבת חטא אדם הראשיון נשתנה שרשה כמו
זמורת הגפן שיחתכוה ויתנו בה קצת גאריקו[115] ויטעוה ממנה כרעים
רבים וכל היין היוצא מהן הוא משלש הלבנה.[116] כן נעשה אדם
200 הראשון שהוא כמו הזמורה שענין הגאריקו ימצא בכל הפרי, כן

106. ע״פ ן׳ עזרא שם.
107. השוה רשב״ם, באוצר תהלות ישראל, כרך י, עמ׳ 343.
108. בר׳ כב יד.
109. ע״פ במ׳ כא כז.
110. קטע זה מופיע רק בשם טוב כתב יד א׳ ואיננו שייך לדרשה המקורית. עי׳ לעיל הערה 8.
הערה 4 לתרגום והמבוא.
111. ע״פ תה׳ עג כב.
112. ע״פ יש׳ ח יט.
113. יש׳ נט י.
114. עי׳ הערה 57 לתרגום.
115. עי׳ הערה 58 לתרגום.
116. פיענוח שלוש המלים „כרעים,״ „משלש,״ ו„הלבנה״ איננה בטוחה ומשמעותן המדוייקת
בהקשר איננה ברורה לי. השוה הערה 59 לתרגום.

המיתה מחייבת לכל בני אדם לא מצד מעשיהם אלא מצד הטבע
שהוטבע בו ובכל נטיעותיו.[117] ומשה היה אבי התעודה[118] אשר היא
קיום וגם חטא במים שהם התורה ונתן סם מות בתורתנו.[119] וזה היה
סבת המחלוקות שנמצאו במשנה לבלתי[120] וכן היה אדם א' סיבת
205   הפרדת (?)תה[121] זה מזה. ואולי זהו שא' הנביא אביך הראשון חטא[122]
זה אדם הראשון, מליציך פשעו בי[123] זה משה ואהרן,[124] שגם אהרן יש
לו חלק בקבלת התורה כמו שמצינו כמה זכרון לאהרן. ואע"פ שעון
אדם הראשיון היה גדול מעון משה ואהרן כתוב בהן פשיעה כמו
נת(ן?) בטבע הוא ובאדם הראשון חטא כמו יתמו חטאים וכו'.[125]

210   וכמו שלא ידענו עונות הנביאים כן לא ידענו ענין עבודתם וקיום
מצות בוראם, רק שאני חושב כי כמו שהטיל אדם אחד סם המות
בתולדותיו כן אברהם ויצחק הטילו איזה סם חיים בתולדות, וכמו
שחייב אדם מיתה טבעית בזרעו כן הטילו אברהם ויצחק חיים
טבעיים לנפשות זרעם אחריהם.[126] ושמא יראת אברהם לש"י נודע
215   בעולם בסבת העקדה אבל העקדה ענין בפני עצמו. וזהו ולא חשכת[127]
ואינו אומר „כי לא חשכת."[128] ובודאי זכות יצחק יותר גדול מזכות
אברהם שהיה מוסר עצמו להריגה בלא דיבור השם אליו,[129] אבל
מציאות העקדה ועניינות החיים בזרעם יתואר לאברהם כי הוא

---

117. עי' הערה 60 לתרגום.

118. כינוי למשה בספרות ימי הביניים. "תעודה" (למשל ביש' ח יז) היא תורה.

119. עי' הערה 62 לתרגום.

120. אם מלה זו נכונה חסר משהו מהטקסט.

121. לא הצלחתי לפענח האותיות הראשונות במלה. על חטא אדם הראשון כגורם להפרדה, עי'
הערה 64 לתרגום.

122. יש' מג כז.

123. שם.

124. השוה רד"ק שם.לא מצאתי בספרות חז"ל או בפרשנות ימי הביניים פירוש לשני חלקי הפסוק
המופיע כאן.

125. תה' קד לה. עי' הערה 66 לתרגום.

126. עי' הערה 67 לתרגום.

127. בר' כב יב.

128. ז"א עקדת יצחק והפגנת יראתו לש"י הם שני עניינים נפרדים, כל אחד בעל זכות משלו.

129. עי' הערה 69 לתרגום.

הראשון כמו שהיה אדם הראשון ראשון לסם המות. ונעלם ממנו

220 ענין שכר העקדה[130] כמו שנעלם ממנו כי בשביל שחטא[131] ימותו כל
באי עולם על לא חמס עשו.[132] וע״כ נעקד במקום שנברא אדם הראשון
מאותו עפר.[133] אפשר ג״כ שעקד באותו מעשה מדת הדין לעולמי עד,[134]
ולכן אנו אומרי׳ ״[וזכר לנו יי אלהינו] את הברית וכו׳ ואת העקדה,״[135]
שהן ב׳ דברים.

225   וזהו הספק הגדול....[136]

130. השכר בעולם הבא, לא מה שהוזכר בבר׳ כב יז–יח.

131. אדם הראשון.

132. ע״פ יש׳ נג ט.

133. עי׳ לעיל, הערה 68.

134. השוה זהר א, קיט ב, אברהם סבע, צרור המור, בראשית, עמ׳ כד א.

135. עי׳ לעיל, הערה 16.

136. הטקסט ממשיך אחרי הערה 5 לעיל.

15

A Spanish Rabbi on Repentance: Isaac Aboab's Manuscript Sermon for *Shabbat Shuvah*

Rabbi Isaac Aboab (1433–1493) was known in the sixteenth century as one of the outstanding Talmudists in the final generation of Jewish life in Spain. Head of a celebrated academy in Guadalajara, his commentaries on at least part of the great Spanish code *Arba'ah Turim, novellae* on Talmudic tractates, and voluminous responsa (almost all of which have been lost) established his reputation as one of "the greatest of his generation."[1] His work of biblical exegesis, a supercommentary on Nahmanides, was esteemed enough to have been printed at Istanbul in 1525.

Nehar Pishon, the book containing records of Aboab's sermons, was first published in 1538 and reprinted in 1806.[2] While never systematically studied, it has been used by historians for the past generation.[3] Not so the Oxford Bodleian manuscript entitled "Qetsat Parashiyot me-ha-RR"Y Aboab" (Some Scriptural Lections by Rabbi Isaac Aboab).[4] Containing material totally different from the sermons in the printed text, it has not yet to my knowledge been studied at all. The following sermon for the Sabbath of Repentance, by far the longest in the manuscript, is an important representative of Jewish homiletical art and a significant document of Jewish intellectual history in the last years of Jewish life preceding the Expulsion.

---

1. Levi ibn Habib, *Responsa,* 2:24d nu. 122 end. Joseph Karo's *maggid* singles out Aboab's yeshivah as preeminent in the recent past, promising Karo that "your academy will be even greater than that of My chosen one, Isaac Aboab." See *Maggid Meisharim,* p. 2b, cited in Jacobs, *Testimonies,* p. 113.

2. Venice? 1538, Zolkiew, 1806. For the relationship between these two editions and London MS Or. 10701, see above, p. 80, n. 18.

3. See especially the use (or misuse) of the parable of the man and his son looking for a cemetery as a sign that they are approaching a city: Saperstein, *Jewish Preaching,* p.84 n.9.

4. Oxford Bodleian MS 952, Huntingdon 342.

Before analyzing the structure and content of the sermon, it is necessary to say something about the manuscript. Although written in a clear hand, it is filled with all kinds of scribal malfeasance: substitution of one word for another, omission of words, combining two words into one, butchering simple phrases from the Talmud, and more. It seems clear that the scribe was copying a text that he did not always understand, even though the content of the sermon is not especially technical or difficult. In many cases, we can confidently reconstruct what the original text must have been; in others such certainty is impossible.[5]

By contrast, the text itself appears to be a fairly faithful account of a sermon actually delivered. It seems to have been intended for a particular situation and audience. Its length, while excessive by modern standards, does not seem to be inappropriate for a Shabbat Shuvah sermon in premodern times.[6] Although the sermon was undoubtedly delivered in the vernacular and the Hebrew text therefore represents a reworking, there does not seem to be anything in its present form that could not have been delivered in the original. While certainly not a paradigm of Jewish homiletical art at its best, it provides us with a good indication of the kind of preaching that could be expected from a leading Spanish Talmudic scholar of the late fifteenth century, and the kind of sermon a Jewish audience of the time could expect to hear.

A firm dating of the sermon would help considerably in evaluating its historical significance. Unfortunately, no external information is provided. Unlike the manuscript of the sermons of Joseph Garçon, which contains details about the dates, locations, and occasions of delivery,[7] this manuscript informs us only that the sermon was intended for the Sabbath between Rosh Hashanah and Yom Kippur. A sermon in *Nehar Pishon* refers to this one,[8] so it cannot be from the very end of Aboab's career. A reference in the text to a problem especially acute "in my place" suggests that Aboab was not preaching in his home community of Toledo or Guadalajara, and several phrases imply that this may have been a particularly distinguished audience. But there are no references to clearly recognizable historical circumstances, except for a statement that he was preaching at a time of great "dearth," when

5. Scribal errors will be noted in the annotation to the Hebrew text. For the sake of the translation, obvious emendations have been rendered in intelligible English; indication of the underlying textual problem will appear only for more serious difficulties.

6. See *Jewish Preaching*, p. 32.

7. On Garçon, see ibid., pp. 199–200 and references to the studies by Benayahu and Hacker there.

8. See nn.33 and 52 to the text.

impoverished Jews were suffering.[9] Any resonance with the burning issues of Jewish life in Spain during its final generation can only be surmised.

Structure

The sermon is divided into two unequal parts, a lengthy introduction, which takes up about one third of the total text (indicated by I), and the body of the sermon (indicated by II). Introductions like this were not part of the standard weekly sermon; they were used on more important, ceremonial occasions, when one of its standard rhetorical themes was a justification of the preacher's enterprise. This frequently took the form of elaborating the reasons why he should have remained silent, and then providing the reasons why he nevertheless decided to speak.[10] In the present instance, the groundwork for the reasons pointing toward silence is laid through a discussion of

---

9. I will suggest several possibilities for dating this reference. Earl J. Hamilton, writing about Aragon, notes that the "calamitous scarcity of all four of the grains [wheat, barley, oats, rye] forced prices upward 95.4 percent in 1470; and owing to the continuation of the famine, about two-thirds of the rise was retained the following year." A contemporary document refers to it as "the greatest scarcity of wheat within memory" (Hamilton, pp. 103, 198–99, cf. p. 125). In a more recent study of Castile, Angus MacKay does not include prices on grains, but cites Henry IV claiming in 1469 that the poor were suffering from a scarcity of small coins that made their transaction functions difficult. MacKay shows a significant decrease in the value of the maravedi between 1469 and 1470 (MacKay, p. 12 n. 22; pp. 149, 161; cf. p. 76). The sermon might therefore be dated in the fall of 1470 or 1471.

In a Hebrew chronicle written by a Castilian Jew, Joseph ben Zaddik, covering events until 1487, we are told of a "great famine" in the year 1478, dramatically raising the price of wheat and barley. This could place the sermon in the fall of 1478; by the fall of 1479, our chronicler reports that "great abundance" had returned. He also describes a nine-month drought beginning in January 1487 (David, *Shetei Kroniqot*, pp. 17–18; cf. Roth, *Conversos*, pp. 281–82).

Finally, William Prescott, speaking of the early part of 1489, refers to "the fearful pest that had desolated the country during the past year, and the extreme scarcity of grain, owing to the inundations caused by excessive rains in the fruitful provinces of the south." His note states, "Such was the scarcity of grain that the prices in 1489, quoted by Bernaldez, are double those of the preceding year" (Prescott, 2:50). This would require us to date the sermon in the fall of 1489 or 1490 (as the later sermon that refers to this does not seem likely to have been delivered during the first Days of Awe following the Expulsion, and Aboab died in February of 1493).

Of these possibilities, I tend to favor the earlier ones as more probable. But this, of course, would mean that the reference to martyrdom (below, n. 21) could have nothing to do with the Inquisition.

10. See *Jewish Preaching*, pp. 76–77 and the example in Joseph Garçon's sermon, pp. 202–6. Cf. also the use of this motif in chap. 13, above.

several characteristics of public speaking, derived from a homiletical exposition of the first two verses of the weekly scriptural lesson, *Ha'azinu.* These are: 1) a speech should be pleasant while it is being heard and retain its power to please and benefit the listener even after it is finished; 2) a speech should be addressed to listeners in accordance with their level; and 3) a speaker's words should be "limited in quantity and great in quality."

Having established these criteria for effective preaching, Aboab asks whether a sermon on repentance can fulfill the first requirement of pleasing and benefiting the listeners, "for a discussion of repentance must be so obvious to everyone that the listeners will find nothing new to remain with them." But this reason for silence is balanced by an argument that speech is not superfluous even to those who know the content of what is being said. This argument is supported by an extensive discussion of the psychological impact of hearing a message, with evidence taken from "experience, reason, and the Bible." The introduction builds to a justification of the universal custom of preaching about repentance on this Sabbath, and indeed at any time of the year; the last point is grounded in a rather stunning new interpretation of the familiar verse, *It is time to act for the Lord; they have violated Your teaching* (Ps. 119:126). The formal asking of "permission" (*reshut*),[11] indicated in the text only by the word "etc.," would have signaled to the listeners that the introduction was drawing to a close.

The body of the sermon is organized around its central theme: repentance. It begins with a preliminary discussion of the status of repentance within Judaism (II.A): Is it one of the "roots" of the Torah, or a "branch" like the other commandments?[12] The topic is addressed in the form of a "disputed question," one of the characteristic structural modes of Scholastic discourse and increasingly popular in fifteenth-century Spanish Jewish preaching.[13] The form requires presentation of arguments for one position and then arguments for the opposite position, after which the apparent contradiction is resolved. If one of the positions is repudiated, then the arguments supporting it must be refuted or at least explained away. The discussion of the status of repentance, which includes an important digression of ethical rebuke (see below), takes up about one fourth of the body of the sermon.

The second question (II.B) relates to the nature of repentance itself. In which category of commandments does it fall: the rational or the traditional? Is the efficacy of repentance compatible with reason, or is divine forgiveness

11. See n. 56 to the text.
12. The attempt to discover the "roots" or "fundamental principles" of Judaism was one of the central intellectual issues in fifteenth-century Jewish thought. See n. 57 to the text.
13. See above, chaps. 7 and 13.

a result of God's arbitrary and incomprehensible grace and love? The treatment of this issue, lasting about as long as the first, involves a discussion of several well-known rabbinic statements and the incorporation of Kabbalistic material. Aboab's fundamental argument, consistent with that of other fifteenth-century Jews, is that the process by which repentance atones for sin is not a logical one, although he qualifies this in several ways. First, atonement is not a totally irrational process: there are requirements, and it is incorrect to conclude that "since it flows from divine grace, anything one does will suffice." And second, it does not follow that the efficacy is absolute, that any sin can be immediately obliterated in God's sight. Following the rabbinic tradition, Aboab reminds his listeners that some sins require physical suffering, or even death, in addition to repentance, for full atonement.

Two additional issues (II.C) relate to the status of repentance as a commandment. First, all the commandments must be fulfilled in joy, yet an integral part of repentance is the profound sorrow for the sin that has been committed. After reporting the solution of Crescas to this paradox, Aboab suggests his own answer, including a tantalizing illustrative reference to the psychology of suffering by the martyr (see below). Second, why is repentance subsumed under the commandment of confession, rather than commanded explicitly in the Torah? This is linked with a somewhat eccentric consideration of the repentance performed by Adam and Cain.

The remainder of the sermon (II.D) raises several related questions. Why is repentance especially appropriate during the Days of Awe? Why do we pray for life, when the sages informed us that the reward for the observance of the commandments is not in the realm of this world? If a person's destiny for the coming year is inscribed and sealed on the Days of Awe, what use are prayer and medicine in the following months? The sermon does not build to a climactic peroration or end with a messianic prayer, but with the prosaic statement, "Thus all these problems have been resolved, and they could be given different solutions, but it is not appropriate for me to speak any longer." It is possible that a prayer for redemption or forgiveness followed that was not included in the text because it was considered standard.

Clearly, the structure of the sermon was determined not primarily by aesthetic but rather by intellectual considerations. The preacher conceived of his challenge as articulating interesting problems and resolving them;[14] his

---

14. This technique of raising problems and then resolving them is well-known from biblical commentaries of the period, especially those of Abravanel. For the use of this technique in sermons, which probably preceded its use in commentaries, see *Jewish Preaching*, pp. 74–75 and n. 28. Whether these "problems" or "doubts" (*sefeqot*, from the Latin *dubitationes*) represent questions already troubling Jewish audiences, or whether the writer or preacher thought it important to raise questions even where none existed is an important issue not yet adequately addressed.

sermon was constructed in accordance with the issues that in his judgment most deserved to be explored within the constraints of the time allotted. Significant for the listener, however, the questions are not given at the start, but rather are formulated when the previous ones are resolved. Thus there is no way for the listener to grasp the sermon's structure or to sense how much content remains to be delivered. There is no internal indication that the end is near until the preacher announces it.

Content

Aboab's sermon contains several kinds of material. Let us begin with what is not included. Totally absent is the technical discussion of detailed Talmudic law. It would be impossible to prove from this text that the preacher was one of the most highly respected Talmudists and halakhic authorities in all of Spain. Nor is this absence of technical halakhic material to be explained simply by the genre of the sermon for the Sabbath of Repentance. We need only compare this text with the sermons preached by Ezekiel Landau in Yampol from 1747 to 1751, collected in *Doresh le-Tsiyon,* to see how a rabbi who wanted to demonstrate his Talmudic mastery from the pulpit on the Sabbath of Repentance could do so. At the same time, Aboab's sermon has none of the most popular kind of material—illustrative parables or narratives, or analogies to everyday life—that some of his other sermons contain. Neither highly technical nor overly popular, its style is appropriate for a fairly well educated and intellectually curious audience.

Philosophy. Some of Aboab's sermons contain philosophical material of a most unexpectedly technical nature, showing familiarity not only with the Greek philosophers and their Arabic commentators but with Thomas Aquinas.[15] There is nothing of that sort here. Aboab cites some of the leading figures of the Spanish tradition—Hasdai Crescas and Joseph Albo—but summarizes their positions in ways that would make them intelligible to listeners who did not know the original passages intimately. And although he uses some of the fundamental distinctions of philosophical thought—rational versus traditional commandments, essence versus attribute—these concepts were by this time part of the general discourse of Spanish Jews.

Philosophy reveals its import on this sermon primarily in two ways. The first is formal: the use of the disputed questions structure to investigate the central subject in the body of the sermon. The second is in the subject it-

---

15. See above, p. 79, nn. 15–17.

self—not, of course, in the choice of repentance as a topic for the sermon on this Sabbath, but rather in the exploration of the problematics of repentance. The sermons of this generation provide ample evidence that the doctrine of repentance was being subjected to philosophical critique, and that Jewish preachers believed it required a sophisticated philosophical defense.[16]

Kabbalah. More surprising than the philosophical influence is the use of Kabbalistic material. Aboab is not known as a Kabbalist. Furthermore, it is sometimes assumed by scholars that with the exception of Joshua ibn Shu'eib, Jewish preachers before the second half of the sixteenth century did not incorporate Kabbalistic doctrines into their sermons.[17] This text provides important evidence to the contrary. It is not just the quotations from the Zohar, which could be cited simply as a work of rabbinic midrash without any sense of disclosing esoteric doctrine.[18] Two passages in the sermon are of a different nature: Aboab, referring explicitly to the *sefirot,* uses Kabbalistic doctrine to explain the elevated status of repentance and to justify the law that the New Moon is not mentioned on Rosh Hashanah. He does not identify himself personally with this trend, but gives every indication that he sees nothing inappropriate about using it in the pulpit.[19]

Social Criticism. The sermon contains one powerful attack on the behavior of contemporary Jews: Aboab laments and denounces the refusal of some to lend money to Jews in desperate need. (The Law prohibits the charging of interest on such loans. There is no such restriction on loans to a Gentile.) This criticism is particularly significant. While most of the attacks by moralists on wealthy Jews of the period accused them of neglecting the commandments, here the problem is that their observance of the commandment prohibiting interest caused severe hardship for the poor. To be sure, there are many instances of rabbis in subsequent generations chastising Jewish businessmen for arrangements that violated the prohibition of interest,[20] but

---

16. For indications of the philosophical critique of repentance, see *Jewish Preaching,* p. 397, and above, pp. 85–86.

17. See Horowitz, *Jewish Sermon,* pp. 30, 159; Bonfil, *Rabbis,* p. 312; Bonfil, *Jewish Life,* p. 170.

18. See, for example, the sermon of Joseph Garçon, *Jewish Preaching,* pp. 201–2, n. 3 and 216, n. 57.

19. This is not to say that there was no opposition to the use of Kabbalah in sermons at the time. See the anonymous text "For the Guidance of Preachers," above, p. 169, n. 29, and, later, the protest by Leon Modena, in *Jewish Preaching,* pp. 406–7. The point is that we still do not have enough sermon literature from the fourteenth and fifteenth centuries to judge whether or not Aboab's use of Kabbalah was unusual and would have raised eyebrows in the audience.

20. See above, pp. 101 and 138–39.

here the emphasis is on the human cost of technical adherance to the Law. Aboab's statement, "I am tempted to say that it should be considered a greater sin for someone to refuse to make the loan than it is for someone to make the loan and take interest, for in the first case there is danger [to life] and in the second there is not" is a dramatic expression of a Talmudic authority's willingness to broaden the category of *piqquaḥ nefesh* (saving of life) to include not only individual cases but also general circumstances of communal need in a period of economic hardship.

Contemporary Resonance. In every discussion of repentance from the generation of the Expulsion, the issue of the *conversos* looms in the background. To what extent did the congregation, listening to a discussion of the efficacy of repentance, think of those who had left the Jewish people and were living as Christians? It is not a question that can be readily answered on the basis of this text. What can be said is that there does not seem to be any clear allusion to the *conversos'* situation, or anything that could not have been intended for an internal Jewish context.

The one passage that may have had some contemporary resonance is the discussion of martyrdom. It is introduced as an illustration of a rather abstract point about the relationship between joy and anguish in the performance of the commandment of repentance. Aboab goes on to say,

> It is similar to a person who accepts death as a martyr. It is beyond doubt that he feels pain at the moment when death comes, for the corporeal faculties react to this. Yet insofar as the person imagines that by this act he attains true communion [with God], the mind rejoices.

This appears to be a critique of the tradition that the true martyr does not feel the pain of torture.[21] It is tempting to interpret this as a response to the sight of men and women being burned at the stake and obviously suffering pain. But without further details about the date and circumstances of the sermon's delivery,[22] such a reading must remain on the level merely of the possible, and not of the proven.

---

21. Known in this generation from the text called "Megillat Amraphel." See Scholem, "Ḥaqirot," p. 153; Baer, *History,* 2:430–31, and 508 n. 4. However, it was attributed to Rabbi Meir of Rothenburg (see Spiegel, p. 136, n. 51) and may have originated in a Christian context. In a different sermon (*Nehar Pishon,* p. 23c), Aboab appears to endorse the idea that the martyr feels no pain. That passage may be earlier, and our present passage may have been intended to clarify his position. For a discussion of this theme in the context of sermons from the Warsaw Ghetto, see Polen, *Holy Fire,* pp. 67–68, 154.

22. See the discussion above, n. 9.

SERMON FOR THE SABBATH BETWEEN
ROSH HASHANAH AND YOM KIPPUR[1]

[From] the lesson *Ha'azinu* [Deut. 32:1–52]: *May my discourse come down as the rain* (Deut. 32:2).

I. It is well known[2] that artificial acts can be divided into two categories based on their ultimate purpose. First, there are those for which the purpose exists after the act; this applies to the builder or the carpenter, the purpose of whose activity is attained after the action itself. Second, there are those for which the purpose is bound up with the act, so that it exists while the act is occurring, but ceases when the act ceases. Examples of this are the art of playing a musical instrument or singing; in these the purpose is attained only while the art is being practiced.

Now in our sacred Torah, both of these categories are bound together. A purpose is achieved while its acts are being performed, and a purpose is achieved afterward. This was Moses' intent in this verse with which I began, saying that even though he is speaking in the form of a poetic song, the characteristic of a song—that its purpose is achieved only while it is being sung, not afterward—does not apply to it. Rather, this is something which will have a purpose even afterward, just like the rain.

When the rain falls to the earth, its purpose is attained not during the rainfall itself. On the contrary, sometimes "the day of rainfall is as difficult as the day of judgment, and even if there was a drought like that of Elijah's time, and rain fell on the eve of the Sabbath, it is not a sign of blessing,"[3] for people would be unable to prepare for the Sabbath.[4] Rather, the purpose from the rains is attained later, at the time of the harvest. It is as in the Psalm, *Though he goes along weeping, (12v)* [*carrying the seed-bag, he shall come back with songs of joy, carrying his sheaves*] (Ps. 126:6). This means, even though the act of sowing is great toil, the sower imagines what will come later,

---

1. In Hebrew, *shabbat beintayim,* the "intermediate" Sabbath. Cf. Saba, Exodus, p. 24a: "That is why it is called *shabbat beintayim,* for it is between Rosh Hashanah and Yom Kippur, standing between the judgment of Rosh Hashanah and the mercy of Yom Kippur." Cf. also Gross, *Iberian Jewry,* p. 45.

2. A characteristic opening for the sermons of Aboab, and also of his contemporary Shem Tov ben Joseph ibn Shem Tov; see pp. 80–81, above. After a verse from the Torah lesson or a rabbinic statement, the preachers begin with a generally accepted proposition and build upon it.

3. B. Ta'an 8b; in the source: ". . . is nothing but a sign of curse."

4. Following the comments of Rabbenu Gershom and Rashi on this passage.

namely, the act of reaping, and he sows for this purpose. That is why Moses said *May my discourse come down as the rain* (Deut. 32:2), meaning that the people will receive from him something for which the purpose will remain after they have learned it.

It is also similar to the dew,[5] which is pleasant to people at the very time it is descending. So with the Torah. When a perfected person hears words of Torah, they are as pleasant to him as the honeycomb's flow. At the time they are performed, they are also pleasant. Even with something that entails no deed, a person perceives the pleasantness at the time of study, and afterward it will be even more pleasant.

Moses then said, *Like droplets [on young growth, like showers on the grass]* (Deut. 32:2). He meant by this that these kinds of pleasantness will not be at the same level for everyone, but rather they will be different to various people depending on their level of comprehension. Those at the beginning of their intellectual development will find the words of Torah like the light rain that falls upon the grass when it begins to sprout. This is called in Hebrew *se'irim,* derived from the word *se'ar,* "hair," for it is as fine as hair.[6] Those who are advanced in their intellectual development will find the words of Torah like the showers, the heavy rain that falls upon the mature grass. Thus we learn from this that those who speak words of Torah, even when they begin like a song, should combine these two qualities.[7]

We also learn from the simile comparing speech to rain and dew that the public speaker should make his words little in quantity and much in quality. For rain is greater in quality than dew, yet he said that the purpose to be attained from his speech is like the rain when his speech is as little as the dew.

Furthermore, we learn from the beginning of his speech a third quality. He said *Give ear, O heavens, let me speak* (Deut. 32:1). He did not say, "Give ear, O Heavens [and earth],[8] let me speak," as he did on previous occasions, saying *I call heaven and earth to witness* (Deut. 30:19), always mentioning heaven and earth together. Yet here he divides them, for one should not address the heaven and the earth on the same level, but rather each one according to its respective dignity. Therefore he said to the heavens, separately, that they should give ear and let him speak. He showed them honor by not

---

5. The verse (Deut. 32:2) continues, *[May] my speech distill as the dew.*

6. Abraham ibn Ezra cites this etymology in his comment on the verse.

7. Thus Aboab applies the verse to all who speak words of Torah in public, including especially the preacher.

8. The words in square brackets do not appear in the manuscript but are required by the context. There are many scribal errors in the manuscript, most of which will not be identified in notes to this translation.

saying *hear the words that I utter* (Deut. 32:1) as he said to the earth. He said *give ear,* speaking as if to teach that they will hear nothing new, but that it would be nice for them to remain silent while he speaks to the earth.[9] They should make no movement, as this would cause confusion for the earth, making it difficult for its inhabitants to receive what he will say. For the heavens produce a sound with their movement. He therefore said, *let the earth hear the words that I utter* (Deut. 32:1), indicating that the purpose of his speech is for the earth to understand it.

This seems to be (13r) the view of the sages in their statement,[10] "Moses said *Give ear* because he was close to the heavens, and Isaiah, because he was distant, said *Hear, O heavens* (Isa. 1:2)." The distinction they were making is that one who says *Give ear* implies that he hears the sounds made by the heavens in their movement because he was close to them, and he therefore said *Give ear* so that they would not make a sound, like a person who whispers into the ear of his friend. But Isaiah, because he was distant and did not hear the sound, did not say *Give ear* but rather *Hear,* he was like a person speaking at a distance. But because he was close to the earth and heard the movement of those who walk upon it, he spoke of "giving ear" to the earth.

Whatever may be the difference between "giving ear" and "hearing," it is clear that the reason why Moses did not say that he would address "the words I utter" to the heaven was that he was showing deference to them, saying that he would speak with others, and asking that they of their own accord remain silent. But Isaiah did not speak with this kind of deference, even though he made a distinction and addressed each one separately. For although he would speak with the earth, he was not worthy to speak in this manner that the earth would hear the words he uttered; his stature was not great enough to speak with the earth this way. He therefore said *for the Lord has spoken* (Isa. 1:2), meaning, what I say to you is not of my own accord but rather from the glory of the Lord.

Now I have seen in the Midrash Zohar[11] that when Isaiah said these things the heavenly family came to beat him. He therefore said to them, "Do not consider it a sin that I asked those of great stature to hear my voice. This is not of my own accord, but rather *because the Lord has spoken* (Isa. 1:2)." But Moses was of such great status that he said *the words I utter* (Deut. 32:1), namely that he himself would speak thus, and that they should listen to him. In that other Midrash, there is no distinction made between Isaiah and

---

9. Aboab apparently interprets the word *ha'azinu* ("give ear") not as a synonym for *shim'u* ("hear"), but as implying silence. See the following paragraph.

10. *Tanḥuma Ha'azinu,* chap. 2. Cf. Aboab, *Nehar Pishon,* pp. 30c, 52d.

11. Cf. Zohar 3:286b. Aboab does not cite literally but summarizes the content in his own words.

Moses in that Moses addressed the heavens and the earth with the definite article, while Isaiah spoke merely of heavens and earth. For these heavens are the supernal heavens, the Name of the Holy One,[12] which the sages said were composed of fire and water,[13] meaning the attribute of justice (called fire) and the attribute of kindness (called water).[14] And *the* earth here is "the earth of the living."[15]

According (13v) to this, "the earth" is at an extremely lofty level, higher than the heavens. Therefore it would be the opposite [of what we said before]: Moses showed greater deference to the earth than to the heavens. To the heavens he said *give ear,* meaning it should lend an ear to what he was saying, showing that he was very close to them. But of the earth he said that it should *hear the words I utter,* as if he was speaking with one who was far away. And with the earth he used the word "utter," which refers more explicitly to verbal communication than does the word "speak," as we see in the verse *Thus shall you utter to the house of Jacob* (Exod. 19:3).[16] *May my discourse come down as the rain* (Deut. 32:2), as RaMBaN explained.[17] Whatever the case, the third requirement that I said is that one who speaks should address the great people in one way and address the ordinary people in another, a lesson derived from this verse.

According to the simple meaning, the heavens are of greater distinction, and according to the Midrash Zohar the earth is greater. Now if the view of the sages[18] agrees with the statement of the Zohar,[19] we would have to say that their statement that Moses used the phrase "give ear" because he was closer means what I explained: that Moses, who was closer to the lower heavens, used the word "hear" [for the supernal earth]. The earth that Isaiah addressed was the physical earth, which is why he said "give ear" to it, while

---

12. See Zohar 3:286b.

13. Gen. Rab. 4,7 and elsewhere.

14. Zohar 3:137b and elsewhere.

15. I.e., the world to come. Cf. Be-Midbar Rab. 19,18; *Tanḥuma Buber Metsora,* chap. 4; Zohar 1:1b, and elsewhere.

16. It is not clear to me why he proposes this particular verse to establish his interpretation of the word.

17. It is not clear to me how Nahmanides' commentary on these words in Deut. 32:2 relate to the matter at hand. Cf. his commentary on Deut. 5:5: "Moses ascended to the mountain and heard God's words; then he descended and uttered them to the people, until God spoke with them face to face. This refers to all that is mentioned [in Exodus 19] from *Thus shall you utter to the house of Jacob* (Exod. 19:3) until *The Lord said to him, 'Go down'* (Exod. 19:24)."

18. I.e., that Moses showed greater deference to the heavens.

19. Intepreted by Aboab to mean that the earth is on a higher level than the heavens.

the earth that Moses addressed is "the earth of the living." Thus "heaven" and "earth" are understood here to be amphibolous terms.[20]

Thus the three requirements are made clear.[21] First, that appropriate deference should be shown to each one that is addressed. Second, that one should plan for his speech to have two purposes: one should remain after it is over, but those who hear it should also derive enjoyment from it while it is occurring; this is the intent of the simile of rain and dew. Third, that the words should be limited in quantity and great in quality, as I explained. The speech that does not fulfill these requirements is thus shown to be an imperfect speech.

Now based on this, it appears that the present speech[22] is imperfect in that it fails to fulfill two of the requirements. First, there will not be a purpose that remains after it is over. For a discussion of repentance is so obvious to everyone that there can be nothing new for the listeners that will remain with them. This purpose is too well known. There is not here a single person who does not know how one makes repentance. Therefore, there can be no enjoyment in hearing it,[23] and on the contrary, there will be discomfort in hearing about one's failings and sins.[24] Moreover, the sages said[25] that one who transgresses intentionally, knowing that he sins, should no longer be warned: "Just as it is a commandment to say something that will be heeded, so it is a commandment not to say something that will not be heeded."[26] Based on this consideration, silence would be appropriate for an audience such as this, where everyone knows what should be done.[27]

---

20. Or homonyms, words that are spelled and pronounced the same but have different meanings (e.g. *ha-arets* referring to the physical earth and the supernal "land" of the world to come). On this important concept in medieval Jewish philosophy, see Maimonides, *Guide* 1,8; ibn Tibbon, "Millot Zarot," s.v. *shem meshuttaf*; cf. Harry Wolfson, "The Amphibolous Terms in Aristotle, Arabic Philosophy, and Maimonides," in Wolfson, *Studies*, 1:455–77.

21. After a rather complicated passage, which may well have lost some of the listeners, the preacher returns and summarizes his conclusions for their benefit. Cf. the introduction to Joel ibn Shu'eib's *'Olat Shabbat*, translated in *Jewish Preaching*, pp. 394–95.

22. I.e., the preacher's sermon about repentance.

23. Cf. Aboab, *Nehar Pishon*, p. 18c: "Speech about repentance appears to be superfluous, for everyone knows the ways of repentance. Solomon said, *But idle chatter is pure loss* (Prov. 14:23), meaning, one of the things that keeps 'chatter' from being idle is that the listener be in need of what is said. But since the ways of repentance are known by all, speech is in a sense superfluous."

24. Here the preacher subtly warns that there will be an element of ethical rebuke in the body of the sermon.

25. Cf. B. Shab 144b.

26. B. Yeb 65b.

27. On the topos of silence in the homiletics of the period, see *Jewish Preaching*, pp. 76–77, 205.

Yet another consideration suggests the necessity of speaking.[28] Indeed, the speech is more appropriate for those who know than for those who do not know. Even though a person may not be motivated by his own intiative to do what is good and right, he nevertheless may be motivated by another when there is. . . .[29] The reason for this is that speech is to the soul as clapping of the hands is to the body for impelling to action. We see that one who hears a pleasant voice feels pleasure naturally, and one who hears the sound of a sigh feels impelled to sigh. If we truly knew the essence of the soul and . . . ,[30] we would know the reason for this. But just as its essence is not known, so it is not known how these things affect it.[31] We must nevertheless admit that when the soul hears a sound that seems to it a source of strength, it becomes stronger because it derives help from this sound. That is why people cheer on runners, shouting encouragement to one who falls down, (14r) or is engaged in other such acts.

Thus the soul finds strength when we say "Go and do it" which it cannot find by itself. For the separate intellects are similar to God. Just as He created everything through speech,[32] so they act upon those beneath them through words. In this manner a person rebukes one who is beneath him in a certain respect, so that the other will be motivated because of the rebuker's superior status.[33] Because of this [the sages said], "I would be surprised if

28. According to this topos, after the reasons that justify the silence, the preacher continues to give the reasons that justify his speech.

29. There appears to be a lacuna in the Hebrew text.

30. I cannot render the next four Hebrew words (*Ve-ha-yosher she-yesh ba-hen le-hekhalah*) so as to make sense in this context.

31. This agnostic position regarding the essence of the soul may be compared with Arama, chap. 6, 1:41b:

The rational soul . . . would that we knew what it is . . . for confusion and uncertainty abound in the speculation of those scholars who have delved deeply into such matters. One holds one view and another a view quite different, and all that has been preserved of their opinions has not led us to escape perplexity, but rather has deepend it. . . . Thus the essence of the soul remains without solid grounding.

For a review of ancient ideas about the soul, see Shem Tov Falaquera, "Sefer ha-Nefesh," chap. 19, in Jospe, pp. 315–17.

32. Cf. M. Avot 5,1.

33. With this passage, cf. Aboab, *Nehar Pishon*, p. 18d:

When the soul hears a voice from another soul, the first soul is strengthened by this hearing, for a voice is to the soul as clapping is to the body, and it is enabled to add to its perfection in contending with material constraints. In this regard, when a person falls to the ground, [cheering] voices will help him, and the soul of the one who has fallen will be strengthened; even if his soul is not on a lower level, it seems that it can be helped. *Although I have written in another sermon that this [capacity to be helped]*

there is anyone in this generation who accepts rebuke, for if one says to him, 'Remove the chip from between your teeth,' he answers, 'Remove the beam from between your eyes!' "[34] They taught here that the moral rebuke may be accepted because the rebuker is of superior status, and it is natural then for the person criticized to be motivated. But if the rebuker is inferior, then his rebuke will not be accepted.

Regarding this, I found written in another book—it seems to me that it is a statement by RABaD[35] —who wrote that the rabbinic interpretation [of *be-hibbaram*, Gen. 2:4) "He created them with [the letter] *heh*"[36] means that the *heh* has no place where it can be uttered by a moving part of the mouth, such as the throat, the palate, or the tongue.[37] Thus when the rabbis said that God created the heavens with a *heh*, it means without toil, as one who says *heh*. Thus the sages said that those who pounded the incense would say "hit hard, hard hit" (*hetev hadeq hadeq hetev*), because the sound of the voice is beneficial to spices.[38] They meant by this that the sound of the *heh* enunciated when they said "hit hard, hard hit" helps those who pound the spices very much, for it enables those who labor strenuously to relax and rest.[39]

The conclusion that emerges from all this is what we said: just as the soul makes the body act inasmuch as intellect can act upon inert matter, so the soul, when it is perfected, can affect one that is beneath it in its level of perfection,[40] which can accept the verbal message and increase its perfection with every spoken communication, just as it would receive perfection if God

---

applies when the soul [*of the person in need*] is on a lower level, we may say that even if it is not on a lower level, it will necessarily be helped. *There I also wrote another reason, and cited relevant biblical verses.* Whatever the truth may be, the difficulty I mentioned—that speech would not benefit those who know its content—is resolved (my emphasis).

It is clear that the sermon in *Nehar Pishon* is referring to the passage in our own text.

34. B. Arak 16b.

35. R. Abraham ben David of Posquières; the reference may possibly be to a commentary on the tractate Keritot that has not been preserved. RABaD's innovation appears to have been the linking of the midrash "He created them with a *heh*" and the passage in tractate Keritot.

36. Gen. Rab. 12,9 and parallels.

37. Cf. Bahya ben Asher's first interpretation ("according to the simple meaning") of the statement "He created them with a *heh*" in his comment on Gen. 2:4.

38. B. Ker 6b; Y. Yoma 23a. The text of Aboab's paraphrase at first seems to indicate that the workers themselves are speaking, but it then becomes clear that he understands the passage as Rashi does: the foreman is speaking to those who pound the incense.

39. The interpretation rationalizes the statement, "The sound of the voice is beneficial to the spices," by showing that it helps not the spices but the workers. All of this is in accordance with the preacher's topic: the influence of speech upon the others.

40. Cf. the passage from *Nehar Pishon* cited above, n. 33.

spoke with it. For it is obvious that so long as the soul is in communication with God it attains a level of perfection that it did not have before. This is what the sages meant when they said that God did not speak to Abraham all at once but on many occasions—for example, *on one of the mountains that I will divulge to you,* and similarly *take your son, your favored one* (Gen. 22:2), and so in other places, in order to give him a reward for each spoken communication.[41] And truly *his reward is with him, his recompense is before him* (Isa. 40:10), for each spoken communication brought him a level of perfection that he did not have before.

Thus there is a third aspect in addition to what we said about the soul's capacity for essential action, and this is action in an incidental manner. For one soul does not affect another soul essentially. Rather it works incidentally, as it acts upon the matter pertaining to the second soul, bringing improvement to that which is deficient. That is to say, if this matter is corrupted in one of the ways in which matter is deficient, the first soul will correct it, diminishing its desire with respect to this deficiency.(14v) Thus this soul can through its own stature correct what the other soul cannot correct by itself, being subjugated to this matter to which it is bound up.[42]

We have already seen that King Solomon said that hearing a rebuke is a major factor in bringing a person toward perfection. Here is the quote: *What brightens the eye gladdens the heart; a good report broadens the bones. One whose ear heeds the discipline of life lodges among the wise* (Prov. 15:30–31). He meant by this that hearing is better than seeing, for seeing only gladdens the heart, but something good that is heard broadens even the bone, which has no sense of its own.[43] In this way he affirmed that since speech brings perfection to the soul as we have said, one who hears something good will rejoice and exult in it, for it may produce what the Prophet referred to when

---

41. Gen. Rab. 39,9 and 55,7. The idea is that God could have divulged to Abraham immediately the location of the sacrifice, and He could have specified Isaac immediately instead of saying "Your son, your favored one. . . ." Instead, God expanded the opportunities for communication with Abraham in order to raise him to a higher level.

42. Although this paragraph, couched in the technical language of medieval philosophy, is expressed with less than optimal clarity, the idea seems to be that the words of a speaker affect the soul of the listener only indirectly. Their influence is felt upon the physical substratum (brain, heart, liver, etc.) with which the soul of the living human being is inextricably connected.

43. Cf. Gerundi, *Sha'arei Teshuvah,* part 2, chap. 12 on these verses: "The eye is a distinguished organ, for with it we see the lights that gladden the heart, but the ear is more distinguished, for with it we hear the good report that broadens the bone, which is insensate." The word *shemu'ah* in Prov. 15:30, translated "report," can also mean "something that is heard," a meaning that fits the preacher's purpose better.

he said, *He will satisfy your soul in drought, and give strength to your bones* (Isa. 58:11), referring to the true perfection that he attains.[44] But if it is a matter of seeing alone, the joy pertains only to the heart. Now this is different in two ways. First, seeing does not "broaden," meaning to bring perfection through the genuine good that flows upon it, but only removes the sadness. Second, it does this only to the heart, without making the joy on such a high plane that all the faculties of the body will rejoice in it. But a good report produces a flow of true superabundance, such that even the dry bones (cf. Ezek. 37:4) will attain perfection through it.

After this he said, *One whose ear heeds* [*the discipline of life lodges among the wise*] (Prov. 15:31). This teaches something more about the perfection of the ear. It is not only that through the ear one attains perfection during the moment of hearing, but that great benefit is derived for the future.[45] Because the *ear heeds the discipline of life* and finds pleasure in it, the result is that it moves in the midst of those who are wise, or as the verse says, *lodges among the wise* .

Now I have seen in the "Midrash ha-Ne'elam"[46] an interpretation of the verse *For the ear tests words as the palate tastes food* (Job 34:3). The ear is made with certain curvatures because before a sound enters it, it cannot distinguish whether this sound is worthy of entering it or not. If it were straight, the sound would by nature enter. Therefore the verse says *the ear tests words,* for the ear by its nature distinguishes, as it is made in such a way that we can distinguish between good and evil. Thus the rabbis commonly use phrases like: "the word enters," "let my words enter yours ears," "we have heard with our ears,"[47] meaning that the sound passes through all the curvatures, but the evil word remains at the entrance and does not pass. In the same sense it says, *the palate tastes food* (Job 34:3). God created the palate enabling it to discern that certain food is good and fit (15r) to be eaten, and if not, it does not [allow it to be swallowed]. For the sages said, "If deaf, he gives him the entire price,"[48] for deafness is the absence of all, as the deaf person cannot hear a rebuke. See how the sages emphasized the importance of hearing good words!

Thus we have here proofs from sense experience, from reason, and from the Bible, that hearing things is an important gateway to perfection, even if

44. By linking the two verses pertaining to "bones," Aboab asserts that hearing brings about true perfection.

45. Here the preacher returns to the distinction made at the very beginning of his sermon.

46. See Zohar 3:294b ("Idra Zuta").

47. Gen. Rab. 56,22; *Tanḥuma Buber, Va-Yiggash* 6; B. Shab 89a.

48. B. BQ 85b. Gerundi, *Sha'arei Teshuvah,* also cites this statement in the same context.

we know them already.[49] That is why the custom exists everywhere that on this Sabbath, every congregation of Jews gathers to hear words related to repentance, and the custom of the Jewish people has the status of Torah.[50] Nevertheless, there is room to question why our master Moses, who ordained that we preach about the laws of Pesach on Pesach, the laws of [Shemini] Atzeret on Atzeret, the laws of Sukkot on Sukkot,[51] did not ordain that we preach on this Sabbath or the Sabbath preceding Rosh Hashanah about laws relating to repentance, which is a great fundamental principle?[52]

The answer to this is that when our master Moses ordained the sacrifices for the Israelites, he did not have to ordain anything else [for atonement]. For with the sacrifices, he ensured that any sinner, whether sinning against God or another human being, would have a way to rectify the sin, as the Torah says, [*When a person sins*] *and commits a trespass against the Lord and deals deceitfully with his fellow* (Lev. 5:21). He also provided a confession for each one. Thus he ordained for each Jew what it was possible to do. And those transgressions for which the sacrifices of the rest of the year do not make atonement are atoned for by the sacrifices of Yom Kippur. There was thus no need to specify any other means of rectification; such rectification was the responsibility of the priest. The sages said, "Seven days before Yom Kippur they would separate the High Priest,"[53] so that he could prepare and know fully the laws of the sacrificial cult. Thus while the Temple stood, there was no need for any other means of rectification for Israel. This may be what the sages meant when they said, "Moses ordained for Israel *in their time* ."

---

49. A summation of the preacher's argument that hearing a speech is beneficial even though the listeners know the subject matter (in this case, repentance). The proof "from experience" is the example of the fallen runner responding to applause; "from reason" is the discussion of the influence of a superior soul on one beneath its level, based on the analogy with divine communication; "from the Bible" is the interpretation of the verses from Proverbs.

50. Solomon ibn Adret, *Torat ha-Bayit ha-Arokh*, cited in *Tur, Oraḥ Ḥayyim*, 591. Cf. Tosafot B. Men 20b: "The custom of our ancestors has the status of Torah," and Sperber, 1:235–37. The point here is that unlike the sermons on other occasions that the preacher goes on to specify, the sermon for the Sabbath of Repentance is not mandated in rabbinic literature, and therefore is in the category of "custom."

51. B. Meg. 32a.

52. Cf. Aboab, *Nehar Pishon*, p. 19a: "Why did Moses ordain for Israel that they preach about the laws of Pesach on Pesach, but he did not ordain that they would preach about the laws of repentance at this time? I have already explained a reason for this. . . ." Aboab proceeds to summarize the reason he goes on to give in our text. Note that by characterizing repentance as a "great fundamental principle" (*'iqar vi-ysod gadol*), he anticipates the discussion he will soon begin in the body of his sermon.

53. M. Yoma 1,1.

Thus he ordained only for those times. But in our age we need a different means of rectification for different times, for now the responsibility is placed upon us, not on anyone else.[54]

I would also say that the sermon on repentance is necessary all the time, at every moment, for it is always an obligation to preach about the laws of repentance. That is why there was no need to set a fixed time for it. It is as the Psalmist said, *It is time to act for the Lord, for they have violated Your teaching* (Ps. 119: 126). This means, whoever seeks a nice time for serving God and says, "This is a good time, but this is not so good," has *violated Your teaching* in this,[55] for Your teaching says *You shall meditate upon it day and night* (Josh. 1:8). Whatever the reason may be, the custom of the Jewish people should be followed, etc.[56]

II. A. We must now investigate the matter of repentance. But before (15v) we begin to explain it, we must determine whether it is a root, like the other root principles of the Torah,[57] or whether it is a branch, like the other commandments. On this issue there are arguments making it seem that it is a root of the entire Torah and arguments making it seem just the opposite.[58]

Now it seems that reason would lead us to conclude that repentance is a foundation of the Torah, for if there were no repentance, there could be no Torah. If it were true that whoever sins can find no atonement for this sin,

---

54. Cf. B. Meg. 32a. Immediately before the statement, "Moses ordained for Israel that they ask and preach about subject matter pertaining to the day . . . ," comes the statement, "It is the commandment [of the festivals] that each one be proclaimed *in its time*."

55. A fine homiletical twist on the well known verse, as if it were punctuated, "'It is time to act for the Lord': they [those who say this] have violated Your teaching." Cf. "Iggeret Shemuel" of Samuel Uçeda, cited in *Sefer Tehillim Meluvveh Sefer Miqdash Shelomoh* (Beligrod? 1937), p. 752a.

56. Here ends the introductory unit of the sermon. It is probable that the preacher proceeded to offer a brief *reshut* (formal asking of "permission" to preach: see *Jewish Preaching*, pp. 77, 206 n. 18), which was usually not written out in full.

57. On the disputes regarding the fundamental principles of the Torah in the fifteenth century, see Kellner, *Dogma*. Aboab uses the term "root" (*shoresh*) as a synonym for "foundation" (*yesod*); cf. Kellner, *Principles*, pp. 30, 80–81. Most Jewish thinkers of the fifteenth century did not include repentance in this category.

58. This indicates that the preacher is about to introduce a "disputed question," used by Jewish preachers from at least the late fourteenth century. See *Jewish Preaching*, pp. 395–97; above, pp. 84–86; and the fine example in chap. 13. Cf. Aboab, *Nehar Pishon*, p. 56b: "We must investigate whether repentance is a foundation of our sacred Torah or a branch. We may say that there are aspects pointing in both directions." The discussion there is much more abbreviated than here.

then the Torah would be a misfortune,[59] its purpose subverted by the antithesis of that purpose. For every human being sins all the time, and innu-
merable sins occur every moment. The more commandments, the more
transgressions. We Jews have been given many commandments and believe
that they were given to to benefit us,[60] as the prophet said, *The Lord, desiring His* [*servant's*] *vindication, makes his Torah great and glorious* (Isa. 42:21).
Yet the opposite would occur, for we would necessarily sin regarding most of
them, or all of them. If then there were no cure for our illness, our punishment would be infinite, and we would be totally destroyed.[61] The necessary
conclusion is that there must be repentance to serve as a cure.

There is another kind of argument leading to the necessary conclusion
that repentance is a foundation of the world. The sages said, "Seven things
preceded the [creation of the] world," one of which was repentance,[62]
thereby teaching that repentance is a foundation of the world. They also said
that Adam made repentance, and that this was the reason why he did not die
on the day he ate [the forbidden fruit].[63] If he had not made repentance, we
would not be here today.[64]

Yet there are other indications that repentance is not a foundation. First, we
have not found any of those who have enumerated the roots who counted it
as a foundation. Rather, they have counted it among the other positive commandments.[65] Moreover, the punishment stated for it is like the punishment
for the transgression of one of the positive commandments, nothing more. [If
it were a fundamental principle], there should indeed be a greater punishment.
Furthermore, how can repentance even be a commandment? If it were, then
the fulfillment of a commandment would result from a transgression.[66] The

---

59. As the Christians claim, beginning with Paul. Note that in the following sentences,
Aboab appears to follow Paul's assumption that the commandments of the Torah will inevitably result in sin, although of course he repudiates Paul's conclusion.

60. Cf. M. Makkot 3,16.

61. The argument is a kind of *reductio ad absurdum*: the assumption that repentance can
be dispensed with and is not a foundation of the Torah leads to an absurd conclusion. This is
thus an argument "from reason."

62. *Tanḥuma Buber, Naso* 19. This is, of course, an argument not from reason but from
the authority of the sages.

63. Cf. *Pirqei de-R. Eliezer,* chap. 20. That Adam did *teshuvah* ("repentance" or "returning") immediately after his son is not a widespread view of the sages. See below.

64. I.e., without repentance, Adam would have died without having had children, and
there would be no human beings in the world.

65. E.g. Maimonides, *Mitzvot,* Positive 73 and Code, introduction to *Teshuvah.*

66. In opposition to the well-known statement that performing a commandment brings
about the opportunity for another, and a sin brings about another sin (M. Avot 4,2; Deut.
Rab. 6,4, etc.).

reason why one repents is that he has sinned. If repentance were a commandment, then repentance might result whenever a sin occurs. But this cannot be,
for just as fulfillment of a commandment cannot bring about a transgression,
so transgression cannot bring about the fulfillment of a commandment. Indeed, we see that the Bible cries out against those who make the fulfillment of
a commandment the cause of a transgression.

Here is what it says regarding the sabbatical year: *Beware lest you harbor
the base thought,* (*16r*) *"The seventh year, the year of remission is approaching,"*
[*so that you are mean to your needy kinsman and give him nothing.*] *He will cry
out because of you to the Lord, and you will incur guilt* (Deut. 15:9). This
teaches that there are people who make something entirely good a basis for
something entirely bad. For since the sabbatical year approaches, and God
commanded that on it they remit the debt owed them, they behave in a way
that reflects their unwillingness to lend money to the poor at all. This is the
opposite of the Bible's intention, which is to benefit the poor. Yet the opposite occurs, and what was intended to improve the situation makes it
worse.[67] Therefore the verse says *He will cry out because of you,* meaning that
he will lodge a complaint against God who commanded this,[68] and *you will
incur guilt,* for you have perverted the purpose.

This has occurred many times, particularly where I come from,[69] with regard to loans. Since the Bible prohibits interest, when one Jew comes to another for a loan, he does not want to lend to him. Because the impoverished
Jew may not pay interest as a Christian may, he cannot find funds, and he dies
of hunger. Thus the commandment turns into a transgression in this case. I
would almost say that it should be considered a greater transgression for a Jew
to refuse to give a loan than to give a loan on interest, for in the first case there
is a danger [to life and health], and in the second there is none.[70]

Now the Torah already expressed concern about this, saying *If you lend
money* (Exod. 22:24), speaking in a conditional mode, as if to say, "If you are
worthy of lending money *to My people, to the poor among you, do not act to-*

---

67. For the phrase, see Maimonides, *Code, Megillah* 1,8, and elsewhere. Cf. Karo, *Toledot
Yitshaq,* p. 103b: "The commandment of the Sabbatical year will turn into a sin, as it is a
cause of sin."

68. Aboab apparently interprets the phrase *el ha-Shem* in the verse to mean "*about* or
against God," implying a profaning of the divine name. For an example of the preposition *el*
understood to mean "against," see the last phrase in Genesis 4:8 (*va-yaqom Qayin el Hevel*),
which is paraphrased in the Midrash (Gen. Rab. 22,7) and by commentators (Gersonides,
Saba, and others) *'al Hevel.*

69. If the reference is to Aboab's home in Guadalajara, this would indicate that the sermon was delivered not in his own community but to a special audience elsewhere.

70. On this interesting passage, see the introduction.

ward them as a creditor; exact no interest from them (Exod. 22:24). This teaches
that someone gives a loan to another because he wants the borrower to be in
bondage to him, as the Bible states: *The borrower is a slave to the lender* (Prov.
22:7), or because of the benefit he will attain by receiving interest. Yet here
the Torah says, *If you lend money to My people . . . do not act toward them as
a creditor,* pertaining to one who lends his money because of the prestige, and
also *exact no interest from them,* for the loan should be effected by mutual
agreement of lender and borrower.[71] Or the warning may be for the lender,
the borrower, and the witnesses, as the sages said;[72] indeed it is true. I have
dwelt at length upon this because I see impoverished Jews crying out and not
being heard at this time of prevalent dearth, the result of our sins.

Let us return to our topic. It is clear that from good nothing but good can
emerge, and from evil nothing but evil. Yet according to this, transgression
results from a commandment, something that reason cannot allow.[73]

Now I would say that repentance has some of the qualities of a root principle, but is not one. A root principle must be something the absence of
which, if it could be imagined, would bring down the entire Torah.[74] But in
this case, the Torah would not collapse. For if we were to say that repentance
does not benefit the sinner, but that all will be judged according to their individual sins, this would not be so destructive.(16v) Indeed, there is a basis
for something good in it for those who think about it. They would conclude
that for a human being who appreciates God's greatness, there should be no
atonement for sinning merely by a verbal confession. Rather, the sinner
should be disciplined according to the sin. Societies based on conventional
rules set fines and punishments to discipline those who do evil; they do not
allow a kind of justice in which the sinner may perform repentance by saying that he won't do anything wrong again. In our case, one should think
that it is all the more true.[75]

---

71. There follow three words (*ve-'alav yashuv la-kesef*) which are unclear to me in this
context.

72. Cf. B. BM 75b.

73. Thus, following the argument from authority ("those who have enumerated the
roots"), an argument from reason has apparently led to the conclusion that *teshuvah* cannot
be a fundamental principle, and may not even be a commandment. After the arguments on
both sides, the preacher proceeds to propose a solution to the problem.

74. With this "axiomatic" definition of "root" cf. Crescas, *Or,* introduction to Treatise 2,
p. 123, and Albo, I,10, 1:97; see also Kellner, *Principles,* pp. 24–26. Maimonides suggests a
similar conception in *Code, Teshuvah* 5,3–4 regarding freedom of choice.

75. I.e., if human society can be built upon the principle of pure justice— every transgression is punished without the possibility of clemency for the offender who shows remorse—then the system of divine commandments, which are so much more important than
human laws, can also be built on such a foundation without clemency for those who repent.

If you should say that we may not draw a legal analogy between something possible and something that is impossible[76]—for in our case, sinning is inevitable, while it is possible [not to break the laws of society], the answer to this is clear. God does not command something that is impossible.[77] God commanded us to observe the entire Torah. If this were in the category of the impossible, how could He have commanded this? Indeed we have seen righteous, pious people who never tasted sin, and died through "the sin of the serpent."[78]

Furthermore, look at the wording of the Torah in this matter: *If the anointed priest should sin* (Lev. 4:3). It also says, *If the whole community of Israel should err* (Lev. 4:13). But regarding the individual sinner, it says *A person who sins* (Lev. 4:2), and regarding a ruler, *When a ruler sins* (Lev. 4:22). Note the difference in wording. For one who may indeed not sin, it uses a conditional mode: *If the anointed priest should sin* (Lev. 4:3), meaning, if there should occur an occasion whereby this individual should sin in a manner that is not befitting. And similarly for the people as a whole: *If the whole community of Israel should err* (Lev. 4:13), for reason tells us that it is quite unlikely that the entire community would err through oversight.

Of the individual, it used a formulation that might not improbably be taken to imply either that he will inevitably sin, or that he will not sin. But of the ruler it says, *When a ruler sins* (Lev. 4:22), indicating by this formulation that he will inevitably sin. This verse was interpreted in "Midrash ha-Ne'elam" to mean that it is inevitable for a ruler to sin, because power corrupts, but this is not the case for an individual.[79] They also said that this is why *the rulers brought lapis lazuli and other stones for setting* (Exod. 35:27). Because they saw that they were more disposed to sin than other people, they brought precious stones set upon the heart, for their hearts impel them to do improper things.[80]

If this is so, repentance would not be a fundamental principle if people were to behave properly, but it is a fundamental principle insofar as people are drawn toward avarice. This is as King Solomon said, *God made human*

---

76. Cf. B. Suk 60b and elsewhere.

77. Cf. Maimonides, *Guide* 3,32: "God refrained from prescribing what the people by their natural disposition would be incapable of obeying." This is an important Jewish response to the argument of Paul.

78. "We have seen" introduces an argument from empirical experience. These models of holiness died as a result of Adam's sin, which made all human beings mortal; cf. *Sifrei* Deut. 323. Here Aboab seems to refer to individuals who have never sinned, a position quite different from the one he outlined above.

79. Zohar 3:23a; cf. Tishby, *Wisdom*, pp. 1343–44.

80. Cf. Zohar there.

beings upright, but they have engaged in many calculations (Eccles. 7:29). In this way we can understand why the sages counted repentance among the things that preceded the world.[81] God, foreseeing that the world would not be set right without repentance because of the evil of human actions, made it precede the world.[82] However, regarding choice, the human being has free choice and is capable of turning toward the good. No one is compelled (17r) to behave in a particular way.[83]

What about Rabbi Ilai's statement in the Gemara, "If a person sees that his impulses are overpowering him, let him put on black clothes, and cover himself in black, and go to a place where he is not known, and do what his heart impels him to do, but let not God's name be publicly profaned"?[84] This has been explained to mean, if a person's impulses are totally powerful, he should subdue them totally, so that he will not be able to sin. This is the meaning of "let him put on black clothes and cover himself." Then if he does what his heart impels him to do, meaning if they allow him to do whatever his heart prompts, he will do only good.[85]

Thus according to this analysis repentance is a commandment like the other specific commandments. As for the problem we raised that it is not right for it to be considered a commandment since it results from a transgression, it results not essentially but incidentally. The commandment of repentance is not an essential component of the sin, as it would be for a person who said "I will sin and then make repentance, or I will sin and Yom Kippur will atone."[86] For in this case, the repentance has no effect. The sages said that such considerations block repentance.[87] But repentance for someone whose impulses are too strong and sinned against his will—for such a person things can be set right by making repentance for his sin. It therefore comes as a positive commandment, so that the sinner will not despair but will make repentance, even though it would seem to be of no avail. That is

---

81. *Tanḥuma Buber,* Naso 19.

82. The following words, *kemo she-qara' le-adam ha-rishon* ("as He called to Adam") are not clear to me in context, and some phrase may be missing from the text before the word *kemo.* The idea would appear to be that Adam needed to do *teshuvah,* and it was therefore good that it was already prepared for him.

83. Cf. Maimonides, *Code, Teshuvah* 5,1–2.

84. B. MQ 17a and elsewhere.

85. Cf. Hai Gaon cited by Rashi there, and Tosafot Hag 16a, *Ve-ya'aseh.* According to this interpretation, the gemara does not give permission to sin but rather indicates a way to refrain from sinning.

86. Cf. B. Yoma 85b.

87. Ibid.

why it came in the form of a commandment, rather than merely saying that if one does it, it will be accepted.

B. In this way we have solved another relevant problem, namely, whether repentance is a rational commandment or merely traditional, that is to say that reason would not require it if we were not so commanded.[88] What we have said already provides the solution. This is that it appears that repentance should by law be of no avail.[89] For what is the use of repentance made with the mouth for one who has denied God through his deeds? Furthermore, who can annul the reality of things that have already occurred? Who can set right what they have perverted? Thus we find in a statement of the sages:

> Wisdom was asked, "What is the punishment of the sinner?" It replied, *Misfortune follows sinners* (Prov. 13:21). [The Holy Spirit] was asked, ["What is the punishment of the sinner?" It replied], *May sinners disappear from the earth* (Ps. 104:35). Prophecy was asked, "What is the punishment of the sinner?" It replied, *The person who sins shall die* (Ezek. 18:4). The Torah was asked, "What is the punishment of the sinner?" It replied, "Let him bring a sacrifice and it will atone." The Holy blessed One was asked. He replied, "Let him make repentance, and it will atone."[90]

The sages taught in this statement that according to reason and strict justice, this sinner should not be able to achieve atonement through a verbal utterance. That is why they said, "Wisdom was asked" about what reason would require, and the "Holy Spirit," which represents an even greater degree of apprehension. Then Prophecy, which is of higher status: they asked it according to strict justice what reason would require for a sinner. They also asked the Torah what reason would require according to strict justice. All (17v) replied that according to the requirement of reason, no person may achieve atonement without punishment. Now even though you will find much about repentance in the Torah and the Prophets, this follows what God says through His gracious goodness, not following strict justice. That is what the sages meant in saying "The Holy blessed One was asked."

---

88. This distinction between two categories of commandments is prevalent in medieval Jewish philosophical thought from the time of Saadia Gaon; see his *Emunot ve-De'ot*, 3,1, and Heinemann, *Ta'amei ha-Mitsvot*, pp. 49–52.

89. I.e., the efficacy of repentance does not appear to be rational.

90. Y. Mak 2,6 and parallels. For this version of the text with five questions, attested only in medieval citations, see Lieberman, p. 76. Compare the commentary on this passage published in Saperstein, "Bedersi's Commentary," pp. 439–40.

Now in this they taught that the plane of the Torah is beneath the plane that they call "The Holy blessed One." And this is the truth for those who know.[91] For they have said that repentance reaches from below up to the *sefirah* of the name YHVH pronounced "Elohim,"[92] while Torah is in the *sefirah yesod*.[93] This is what the prophet meant when he said, *Return, O Israel, unto YHVH* (Hos. 14:2), namely, that Israel should not return to the quality of strict justice,[94] which is of a lower level, for if the returning was to that it would not be accepted, for this is the quality that judges exclusively according to justice. But the quality above it[95] is not essentially justice but mercy, except that it has an aspect of justice from the emanation that it produces.[96]

Similarly, God said, *If you return, O Israel, declares YHVH, to Me you shall return* (Jer. 4:1). This means that if Israel makes repentance, the complete repentance they perform will be of no avail unless it is done to the name YHVH,[97] which acts by will, desiring to benefit whomever it wants, even though the person does not deserve it. So the sages said on the verse, *I will grant the grace that I will grant* (Exod. 33:19): even if the person does not deserve it.[98] Thus repentance rises ever higher, as is hinted in the statement "Repentance reaches the very throne of glory."[99] This makes sense of the rab-

---

91. A common epithet for medieval Kabbalists.

92. The passage is not entirely clear in the Hebrew, and the scribe may not have understood what he was writing. *Teshuvah* is associated with the *sefirah Binah* (e.g. Zohar 3:215a), which is represented by the Tetragrammaton *YHVH* vocalized with the vowels for *Elohim* (e.g. Zohar 3:65a).

93. In general, Torah is associated with the *sefirah Malkhut* or *Tiferet*, not with *Yesod*.

94. I.e., the "returning" must be above the *sefirah Gevurah*, which is called *din* ("judgment", or "strict justice").

95. The *sefirah Ḥesed*.

96. Because the *sefirah Gevurah* is emanated from the *sefirah Binah*, *Binah* must have within it a potential element of strict justice, which is represented by the the Name *YHVH* pronounced *Elohim*. Cf. Zohar 3:65a (in the translation of Tishby, *Wisdom*, p. 345): "Since they call her 'mother,' female, *Gevurah* and Judgment emerge from her. She is called 'Mercy' in her own right, but Judgments are aroused from her side, and so [the name *YHVH*] is written as Mercy, but vocalized as Judgment: the consonants indicate Mercy but Judgment is at her side." Cf. also Gikatilla, *Sha'arei Orah*, 2:43 (beginning of the chap. 8; cf. Gikatilla, *Gates of Light*, p. 283): "The Name written *YHVH* and pronounced *Elohim* is the mystery of *Binah*. From this name, the beginning of the quality of Judgment is drawn into the *sefirot*. But it is not absolute Judgment, for it is ensconced in the realm of Mercy." Aboab interprets Hosea 14:2 to mean that the returning unto *YHVH Elohekha* means returning unto the name *YHVH* pronounced *Elohim*.

97. Representing the quality of Mercy.

98. B. Ber 7a.

99. B. Yoma 86a.

binic statement, "In the place where the penitent stand, the totally righteous cannot stand."[100] For truly, the penitent rise above the level of the righteous. The righteous are judged by the court below, while the penitent rise ever higher. This is also the idea of the statement, "Children, length of life, and sustenance depend not upon a person's merit, but upon the star."[101] This means that these things depend upon God's will: even though by strict justice one may be guilty, according to the "star" that God has, the person may be saved.[102] The Prophet referred to this when he said, *For the Lord* (*YHVH*) *is our judge* (Isa. 33:22), meaning that He is judge, scribe, and king, and *He shall save us* (ibid.), for no one *can say to Him, "What are You doing?"* (Job 9:12). And this is what the sages said on the verse *Show us Your favor that we may be saved* (Ps. 80:4): "There is nothing for us except His favor,"[103] meaning His will, for no one can compel Him [to do otherwise].

Now even though it is true that repentance is a matter of grace, which is confirmed forever,[104] we must nevertheless explain why it becomes effective through confession and remorse and the other requirements for repentance,[105] not through something else, such as beating of the body.[106] For if repentance is a matter of grace, then anything at all should suffice. An answer is (18r) that when we make repentance, we thereby kill the one who

---

100. B. Ber. 34a. This rabbinic statement was one of the most challenging for Jewish thinkers throughout the Middle Ages and was discussed in many sermons on repentance. Cf. Shem Tov, *Derashot*, p. 81d.

101. B. MQ 28a. On this much-discussed statement in medieval Jewish literature, see Horowitz, *Jewish Sermon*, p. 149 with appertaining notes. The preacher will return to this statement at the end of his sermon.

102. Aboab interprets "star" here not in its astrological, deterministic sense but as a symbol of divine mercy. This may reflect the Kabbalistic tradition: see Horowitz, *Jewish Sermon*, at n. 66; Gikatilla, *Sha'arei Orah*, 1:163 n. 28.

103. Midrash Tehillim on Ps. 80:4.

104. For the formulation, cf. Ps. 89:3. By arguing that the efficacy of repentance was not rational or just but rather a matter of divine *ḥesed* or "grace," Aboab is following an established Spanish tradition: cf. Nissim ben Reuben, *Derashot*, pp. 97–98; Crescas, *Or* III,ii,2,1, pp. 377–78; Joseph ibn Shem Tov, in Regev, "Teshuvah," p. 191; Karo, *Toledot Yitsḥaq*, p. 103b. For the opposing view, see Saba, Deuteronomy, p. 27b–c.

105. On the necessary components of repentance, cf. Sa'adia Gaon, *Emunot ve-De'ot* 5,5 ("*inyenei ha-teshuvah*"); Bahya ibn Paquda, *Hovot ha-Levavot* 7,5 ("*gidrei ha-teshuvah*"); Maimonides, *Code*, Teshuvah 2,2; Gerundi, *Sha'arei Teshuvah* 1,9 ("*yesodot ha-teshuvah*").

106. This may be a reference to the movement of Flagellants, which flourished in European Christianity in the middle of the fourteenth century and appeared again in Spain at the beginning of the fifteenth under the influence of the famous preacher of penitence, the Dominican San Vicente Ferrer. However, the preacher may have been referring to an internal Jewish matter: the custom of scourging on the day preceding Yom Kippur.

sinned, namely the impulse toward evil.[107] This deserves to be killed. But the intellect, which did not sin, should not be punished, as we find in "Sefer ha-Orah" on the verse, *Will you destroy the innocent along with the guilty?* (Gen. 18:23), interpreting it to mean that the human being has a part which is innocent, which should not be wiped out unless it has sinned with the other part.[108] Now by making repentance, we kill the impulse toward evil, which is considered as if dead, as the sages said, "David rose up against it and killed it. With what did he kill it? With sackcloth and fasting."[109] Thus we see that *God's judgments are true* (Ps. 19:10), for He does not want anything except for that which sinned to be punished.

The definition of repentance is that if the occasion for sin recurs—in the same situation, the same place, the same woman—and the sinner refrains from it, then he is truly penitent,[110] for he thereby shows that the source of harm has died and disappeared. Perhaps this is the meaning of the verse in Ezekiel, *When a wicked man turns back from his wickedness and does what is just and right, [it is he who shall live by virtue of these things.] And you will say, "The way of the Lord is unfair"* (Ezek. 33:19–20). In this he taught that there were Jews who attacked him because he said that the wicked person would escape by making repentance. They said that it could not be, according to reason, for how was it possible that through making repentance a person could be saved from the punishment already due him for an evil act. Therefore they said, *The way of the Lord is unfair,* namely, this is unacceptable rationally; reason requires that this person should die if he is guilty, nothing else. But God responded, *It is your ways that are unfair* (Ezek. 18:25). This means, what I do is just and proper, for I kill only the source of harm, while you act differently, killing "innocent along with guilty" when a person transgresses in a matter of law.

---

107. In general, Jewish authorities tend to speak about "conquering" the impulse toward evil (*kevishat ha-yetser*), while the "killing" of the impulse is usually limited to an eschatological context. Cf., however, Lev. Rab. 9,1: "*He who sacrifices a thank offering honors Me* (Ps. 50:23): This is Achan, who sacrificed his impulse by means of a thank offering." See also below, n. 109.

108. See Gikatilla, *Sha'arei Orah,* 2:14; *Gates of Light,* p. 255. The work was referred to by the title *Sefer ha-Orah* by contemporaries in the generation of the expulsion: see Abraham Shalom, *Neveh Shalom* 5,5 pp. 66b–67a, cited in Davidson, *Bibago,* p. 15; Joseph Garçon, in Benayahu, "Garçon," p. 57. The interpretation cited here removes the biblical verse totally from its simple meaning and applies it to the inner life of human psychology; it is actually closer to philosophical than to Kabbalistic exegesis.

109. While this is presented as a direct quote from rabbinic literature, I have not been able to find its verbatim source. Cf. Y. Sot 5,5 ("Abraham made the impulse toward evil good . . . but David could not do so, so he killed it in his heart"), B. Sot 25a, B. Ber 67b.

110. B. Yoma 86b; cf. Maimonides *Code, Teshuvah* 2,1.

The authorities of previous generations also had other explanations why repentance was efficacious through the remorse that a person feels over what he has done. When a person [feels remorse] for having done something, it is as if the act were not done through choice. The remorse shows that it was an act performed by mistake. There is a lengthy discussion of this reason in *Sefer ha-Iqqarim*.[111] This may be true, but in any case it seems that the reason I gave is more satisfying.

Now according to the first reason [killing the impulse toward evil], there is a sensible explanation for the rabbinic assertion that the willful sins of the penitent become for him as merits when he repents out of love, and when he repents out of fear they become for him as unintentional sins.[112] The reason for this is that when the penitent feels remorse for his sin, he feels great pain in the intellectual portion of his personality, which sinned against its will. It is therefore fitting that this pain that he experiences because of its [unwilling] participation be counted toward his merit. (18v) He therefore said[113] that if he repents out of fear, which is not on such a high plane, his [willful sins][114] are counted for him as unintentional sins, while if he returns out of love, which is the highest plane, his willful sins will be counted as merits, because of the pain he felt as a result of his love. But according to the second explanation,[115] these statements cannot be as sensibly explained. For why should the remorse felt by the sinner then have the effect of making willful sins into merits? It is enough that God will not consider what he transgressed to be a sin. But for willful sins to become merits—that is something reason cannot accept.

Now according to the first explanation, you see that the reason for the verdict of a death penalty given by human beings against each other for capital crimes is that human beings cannot kill only the source of harm. How could they remove the impulse toward evil and kill it alone? Even though at that moment the person who is sentenced to death appears to be absolutely remorseful, what human being can know [enough to be certain] whether this

111. Albo, 4,27, 4:257–64. The question raised is, "Once a transgression has actually been committed, what is the efficacy of repentance done through remorse and confession?" At the end of the discussion, Albo concludes, "Repentance is efficacious for the sinner in this respect: it makes the sin as if it had not actually been committed, as if it were something done by mistake, without awareness."

112. Cf. B. Yoma 86b. This too was an extremely problematic statement for medieval Jewish thinkers; cf. Shem Tov, *Derashot,* p. 81d.

113. There follows the Hebrew word *ez'aq,* which makes no sense to me in the context. There is apparently a problem in the text.

114. The Hebrew text says "merits," but the context obviously requires "willful sins."

115. That of Albo. He discusses this statement in chap. 25, 4:232–35, and his interpretation is not as convincing as that of Aboab.

is genuine repentance that arises because he sees the danger to his soul. For the man is going to be killed. If he is saved from this, he may return to his perversity.[116] Repentance can enter into the decision only of God, *who probes the mind and conscience* (Ps. 7:10). When a person sins against God and is remorseful, God knows whether the repentance is genuine or not.

Perhaps this is part of the reason why the sages said[117] that one whom the court deems innocent, even though they later see that by law he deserves the death penalty, is not rejudged, as we said on the verse, *Do not bring death upon those who are innocent and in the right* (Exod. 23:7).[118] The reason for this is that since God sits with them in judgment,[119] when this person was deemed innocent it can be seen as a divine act. God placed this decision in their hearts because He saw that although the person had sinned, he felt genuine remorse and would never again return to his foolishness. Because of this, they should pardon him. This is consistent with the continuation of the verse, *for I will not acquit the wrongdoer* (Exod. 23:7).[120] It means that God is with them in their judgments, and if God sees that this person is wicked and will return to his perversity, He will not acquit him. But since we see that he has already been declared innocent, it appears that God looks into the future and knows that this man will be righteous.

Now even though there is a basis for arguing that [the efficacy of] repentance is compatible with reason, nevertheless we must explain why we said that repentance is a matter of divine grace.[121] For strictly speaking, when this person sinned, he should not have been a sinner;[122] his inclination was toward the good: why then did he choose evil? But it seems that reason does have some initial relationship to the performance (19r) of evil,[123] and therefore it deserves to be punished, were it not for divine grace that watches over

116. The discussion of the death punishment administered by the state in capital crimes explains why the principle of repentance cannot serve as a foundation for a system of human justice.

117. B. Sanh 33b. Aboab provides a rational explanation for the halakhah.

118. Aboab is apparently referring to another sermon or written work of his. This interpretation does not appear in his supercommentary on RaMBaN.

119. Cf. *Sifrei* Deut. 190 on Deut. 19:17; B. Sanh 19a; Exod. Rab. 5,12.

120. I.e., God promises that He will not allow the judges to acquit a person who is indeed evil. This is totally different from the interpretation of Rashi, who wrote, "If he emerges innocent from your jurisdiction, I have many ways of killing him."

121. See above, n. 104.

122. If there is no error in the text, the meaning would appear to be that there is no rational reason for a person to sin. A person chooses to sin against his natural inclination toward the good.

123. Aboab may mean here that reason can furnish arguments that appear to justify sin.

us with compassion and sees that we are dust (Ps. 103:14), and that the act was not done with absolute free choice. God therefore ordained that we kill the source of harm, as I said, and by doing this we will fulfill our obligation.

Now even though it is divine grace, God did not give us repentance as an absolute. There are some things for which there can be no repentance until the day of death; there are some that suffering is required to cleanse;[124] there are impediments to repentance:[125] all this [according to] the greatness of the transgression. Regarding the transgression of profaning God's name, which entails causing others to sin, atonement should not be made for this until the day of death,[126] for then the source of harm will be entirely killed. Even a sin that is not so great should be judged through suffering because this too kills the source of harm and subdues the impulse toward evil. It may also be a transgression that by its nature prevents a person from returning in full repentance, because it seems so trivial to a person, such as [those included in] the 24 impediments to repentance.[127] Transgressions of this category include partaking of a meal that is insufficient for the host. Because this transgression seems trivial to the offender, he will not make repentance, inasmuch as he does not consider it to be a sin, as Maimonides explained in the Laws [of Repentance from the Book] of Knowledge.[128]

There are also transgressions among these 24 that are difficult to desist from because one is so accustomed to doing them, and others because even if a person wants to make repentance he cannot. An example is one who robs the public, and therefore does not know to whom restitution should be made.[129] Of such and similar matters, the sages said that these are impediments to repentance,[130] meaning that even if the person wants to make repentance, he may be unable to do so. Now in this there is no deficiency in the divine grace that God works for us—namely that God accepts us in repentance, but He does not accept us in these matters. The deficiency is on our side: that we do not make genuine repentance. Similarly with what the

---

124. B. Yoma 86a; Maimonides, *Code, Teshuvah* 1,4.

125. See below, n. 127.

126. Maimonides, *Code, Teshuvah,* end of chap. 1. Maimonides does not define there "profaning of God's name" as "causing others to sin."

127. See Maimonides, *Code, Teshuvah* 4,1.

128. Ibid. 4,4.

129. Cf. Ibid. 4,3: "The sinner does not know to whom he has to make restitution." Maimonides' examples are "one who curses a multitude" and "one who shares with a thief." A better source is Tosafot BB 88b, "*hatam*": "A robber . . . who has stolen from the public does not know to whom he must make restitution."

130. No such statement appears in the rabbinic literature. See Maimonides, *Responsa,* 1,216–17 with the editor's notes. With this whole passage, cf. Crescas, *Or* III,ii,2,2, p. 379.

sages said about one who says I will sin and then repent: that he will not be able to make repentance.[131] The reason is already explained: since this person planned to do evil, thereby perverting God's intention, his repentance should not be accepted, for a transgression cannot bring about the fulfillment of a commandment, as we explained.

C. Now concerning our prior assertion that repentance is a commandment, don't be troubled by the question how can that be, for part of the definition of a commandment entails joy in its performance. Granted that insofar as repentance transforms willful sins into merits[132] as we wrote, beyond doubt there is great joy. Yet from another perspective it seems that there can be no (19v) joy in it. For repentance by definition entails sorrow and anguish over what was done in violation of religious law; how then can joy and delight be associated with it?[133] It is impossible to maintain that while a person is engaged in repentance he must feel sorrow, but that after he has completed it he must feel joy because he has performed a commandment. This is impossible, for we are commanded that even at the moment we perform the commandment we should feel joy.[134] Furthermore, if this were so, then the joy would necessarily exceed the sorrow, for the final cause is more important than any other. Thus with the joy that comes at the end, the sorrow and anguish would be annulled.

Now this question was already raised by Rabbi Hasdai of blessed memory,[135] and his answer was that we have here part sorrow, part joy. There is joy because of the communion attained through the performance of repentance, as the person rises to a higher plane even than the completely righteous. And there is sorrow because of the time that has already elapsed during which the person did not cleave to the service of God. For now he realizes that it should be considered a grievous fault that he transgressed and made his holy spirit rebel. The higher his level now, the more he recognizes his deficiency of previous days when he did not cleave to the service that was required. This is the view of the Rabbi mentioned, his answer to the question.

---

131. B. Yoma 85b.

132. B. Yoma 86b.

133. I.e., sorrow and anguish are an integral part of repentance, and joy is an integral part of any commandment; how then can repentance be a commandment? Cf. Aquinas, *Summa Theologica* Pt. III, Q. 84, Art. 9, Objection 2, p. 2437a, citing Aristotle (*Ethics* 9,4): "Man cannot rejoice and grieve at the same time."

134. Cf. Bahya ben Asher, *Kad ha-Qemaḥ*, s.v. *simḥah*, p. 273.

135. See Crescas, *Or* III,ii,2,2, p. 379. Aboab's summary in the following lines does not represent precisely what is written there.

However, we can answer this in a different way. Those commandments bound up with sadness—for example, mourning over the destruction of Jerusalem or grieving over the dead—are not associated with joy either at the moment when they are performed or afterward. This is true even if we have performed a great commandment, from which great benefit is derived, as the sages said, "Whoever mourns over Jerusalem will be worthy of seeing her rejoicing."[136] Similarly when a person weeps over a decent man that God has laid to rest in His storehouse.[137] These statements teach that such commandments have great dignity.

Now we should look into this. How can joy be associated here, whether in the moment the commandment is performed—for there is none in sorrow and anguish—or after it is done: for then the destruction of Jerusalem would be a reason to bring us joy, which should not be the case. Rather it seems that in these commandments there are two aspects, one of pain and one of joy. Consider, for example, a person who weeps over the loss of a close relative. There is no doubt that when a person weeps, he lightens the anguish. Even though he feels great pain, it would be even more intense if he were not crying. Similarly in our case as well: in the experiencing of pain that is part of a commandment we necessarily feel sadness in our corporeal organs, all of which are sad, yet we feel joy in our mind as the body experiences this pain, (20r) for the mind knows that it is a divine commandment that sadness come to us in sorrow and anguish. Thus joy and anguish come in alternate aspects: the intellect decrees that we should accept this pain with joy, and it is only the physical faculties that feel the pain.

In this sense it is also possible that repentance can encompass both sorrow and joy. The joy is from intellect that feels pleasure in the remorse and sorrow of the corporeal organs when they receive this pain. It is similar to a person who accepts death as a martyr. It is beyond doubt that he feels pain at the moment when death comes, for the corporeal faculties react to this.[138] Yet insofar as the person imagines that by this act he attains true communion [with God], the mind rejoices.

There is another basis for refuting the thesis of the Rabbi [Hasdai Crescas]. We may say that the repenting sinner should feel pain because he does not know that he is truly a penitent until the day of his death. "Do not trust in yourself until the day of your death."[139] Who knows if he will return

---

136. B. BB 60b.

137. B. Shab 105b.

138. Here Aboab seems to reject the tradition that the martyr feels no pain. See p. 300, above.

139. B. Ber 29a.

to his original perversion. Even though the opportunity to sin arises and he escapes it, if he should continue to sin in the future his punishment will be severe. Therefore he should feel anguish throughout his life, lest he return to his perversion, not having reached the end of the process of repentance that allows him to rejoice because his willful sins have become like merits. Enough about this problem.

D. Do not be perturbed that you will not find in the entire Torah that repentance is explicitly in the form of a commandment. The only form in which we find repentance is in the phrase *you shall confess* (Lev. 5:5). This is the basis on which those who enumerated the commandments considered repentance to be a commandment, namely, that confession is a commandment.[140] This is not a real problem, for it is obvious that this confession requires remorse. If the heart does not correspond to what is proclaimed by the mouth, what use is it? Thus there must necessarily be remorse. Therefore, the Torah must have abbreviated its explanation of the elements of repentance, for when it said that they shall confess, it is obvious that in such a matter, words that are merely of the mouth have no status.[141]

In addition, the reason why the Torah abbreviated in this matter was that remorse is something required by reason. If a person has reverence for the divine, he will necessarily feel remorse. Therefore the Torah said, *When you are in distress because all these things have befallen you and, in the end, return* (Deut. 4:30), it is as if it said, "I know you: when these sorrows have befallen you, you will return to the Lord your God." Similarly it said in the lesson *Nitzavim: When all these things befall you, the blessing and the curse . . . and you take them to heart amidst the various nations* (Deut. 30:1). Here too it says that the person will be impelled to return by his intellect, upon seeing how grave is his calamity.

It goes on to say, *For this commandment . . .* is not too baffling for you in an intellectual sense,[142] *nor is it beyond reach* (Deut. 30:11), such that you might say that you need to do things that are extremely difficult. It is not so, for *it is not beyond reach. It is not in the heavens* (Deut. 30:12), (20v) indicat-

---

140. E.g. Maimonides, n. 65 above; *Sefer ha-Ḥinukh,* commandment 363, pp. 458–61; cf. Nissim ben Reuben, *Derashot,* p. 108.

141. A play on the statement in B. Qid 49b: "Words [that remain] in the heart [and are not spoken] have no status."

142. This interpretation of the biblical phrase, "*not too baffling for you,*" does not fit well with Aboab's previous statement that repentance is not a rational commandment. A similar interpretation of the phrase as indicating the rationality of repentance is given by Saba, Deuteronomy, p. 27b–c.

ing, you should not say that with regard to repentance you have no free choice, for you were compelled in the choice of evil, and if you do not receive a cure from heaven, changing your nature, you are unable to do it.[143] Now it went on at length, stating, *that you should say, "Who among us can go up to the heavens and get it for us?"* (Deut. 30:12), explaining that even though in a certain sense heaven plays a role, as the sages said, "When one wants to become pure, they help him [from heaven],"[144] this does not affect the essence of repentance so as to justify the statement that it is in the heavens.

It also said, *Neither is it beyond the sea, that you should say* (Deut. 30:13). This means, you should not say that location is decisive, as many people who claim that a certain location makes repentance impossible, but not a different location,[145] and that you therefore need to go to a place to learn in what manner the people behave so that you can do likewise. Such is not the truth. The truth is, rather, that *the thing is very close to you,* for the Torah is *in your mouth*[146] and you may feel remorse *in your heart that you may do* repentance (Deut. 30:14). Thus it is clear that remorse is a foundation of repentance, and every person who has reverance for the divine will make repentance; that is why it is not explicit in the Torah.[147]

It is perhaps for this reason that the repentance of Adam is never mentioned explicitly in the Torah, even though in truth he made repentance, and this was the reason why the decree that pertained to him—*for on the day you eat of it, you shall die* (Gen. 2:17)—was annulled, as the sages said.[148] For the repentance of Adam was not verbal. Because repentance is not compatible

---

143. An argument denying the possibility of repentance because of a repudiation of freedom of choice. Cf. Abravanel's commentary on this verse: "Don't think that repentance is dependent upon a planet or constellation" (Abravanel, *Torah* 3:284b), and Karo, *Toledot Yitsḥaq,* p. 111a.

144. B. Shab 104a and elsewhere.

145. The idea that geographical locations and climates influence or determine human behavior was common in the Middle Ages. See, e.g., Gruner, pp. 199, 205–9; Melamed, "Erets Yisra'el."

146. Translating the text as written: *she-ha-Torah be-fikha.* The content and structure of the sentence suggest that the original reading may have been *she-titvadeh* or *she-todeh be-fikha,* "that you may confess, or admit, with your mouth." Cf. Saba, Deuteronomy, p. 28a: *she-yodeh pesha'av be-fiv ve-yitḥaret mehem ve-ya'aseh teshuvah.*

147. Aboab's claim is that even though it is not rational that repentance should make atonement for sin, since God has promised the efficacy of repentance, no rational person will refrain from it, and there was thus no need to state it explicitly in the Torah.

148. The prevalent view among the sages does not agree with this formulation. For example, in Gen. Rab. 21,6 and parallels, we find that God opens before Adam an "opening of repentance," but that Adam refuses. The alternative position is suggested by B. 'Erub 18b, which speaks of ascetic penances rather than actual repentance. A position close to that of Aboab is found in *Zohar Ḥadash,* p. 19b; cf. Tishby, *Wisdom* 3:1504.

with reason, Adam did not do it verbally, thinking that it would be of no avail. But in his heart he felt genuine remorse. And God saw that the remorse of his heart was total and accepted it, bestowing upon him extra years.[149] When Adam saw this, he knew that it was the result of the repentance he had made, and he later taught his children the way of remorse. That is why [Cain] made repentance,[150] for he saw that it had helped his father, saving him by annulling the decree of death, and it [i.e. the repentance of Cain?] was written in the Torah. Or we may say that God said to Adam, "*You did well that it was in your heart* (2 Chron. 6:8), and therefore the decree that pertains to you will be annulled," and Adam taught it to his son.

Now the repentance of Cain was efficacious, as is written in the "Midrash ha-Ne'elam." Regarding the curse against Cain, *A quaker and wanderer [you shall be upon the earth]* (Gen. 4:12), they said that only one of these was fulfilled, as the Bible tells us, *He settled in the land of Nod, east of Eden* (Gen. 4:16).[151] The rabbinic interpretation of *quaker and wanderer* is that he must wander from city to city, and in every place where he stayed the earth would quake beneath him,[152] but one component of this was annulled. Thus we have a full explanation why repentance is not made explicit in our Torah.

E. After the solution to these problems, we must consider some others relating to the subject of repentance. The first (21r) pertains to the time. Now there is a reason why these times—Rosh Hashanah and Yom Kippur—were specifically designated for repentance. Indeed, Rabbenu Nissim[153] wrote that there are two reasons: first, that because the world was created at this time of year, and Adam was judged at this time, God determined that his descendants would also be judged at this time, as we find in the Midrash;[154] and second, because this is the period of the constellation Libra,[155] a time

---

149. *Hirviah lo*; cf. Gen. Rab. 19,8, which provides a textual basis for the "extra years," not, however, linking this with any repentance by Adam.

150. The addition of "Cain" is required by context. The Midrash states the opposite: that Adam learned the efficacy of repentance by observing his son Cain; see Lev. Rab. 10,5.

151. See *Zohar Hadash*, p. 19d; cf. Lev. Rab. 10,5.

152. Cf. *Tanhuma, Bereshit* 9.

153. See Nissim Gerundi on Alfasi to B. RH 16a, "be-rosh" (Nissim ben Reuben, *Hiddushim*, p. 23b).

154. E.g. *Pesiqta de-Rav Kahana*, 23,1. It is interesting that this midrash does not mention any repentance by Adam, but in Aboab, *Menorat ha-Ma'or*, p. 619 (by the first Isaac Aboab) we find "On the day when Adam was created he sinned and made repentance and found atonement, and that is why this day is appropriate for judgment, repentance, and atonement."

155. Cf. *Pesiqta Rabbati*, chap. 40,7; Nahmanides, "Derashah le-Rosh Hashanah," in RaMBaN 1:221; Me'iri, *Teshuvah*, p. 238.

appropriate for judgment, because the entire world hangs upon the scales. Whatever the reason may be, we must ask why these ten days between [the beginning of] Rosh Hashanah and [the end of] Yom Kippur[156] are set apart, the first day being holy and the last the most holy, but the intermediate days being ordinary days. Reason would seem to indicate that the intermediate days should be as sacred as the first day, or even more so, for "in matters of holiness we increase and do not decrease."[157] At the very least, they should have the status ordained by the rabbis for the intermediate days of a festival.

According to the way of the Kabbalists,[158] the answer to this is that Rosh Hashanah is the *sefirah malkhut*. Now on it we pray that it be complete, for then it dwells in Judgment.[159] That is why we do not mention the new moon on Rosh Hashanah,[160] for the new moon teaches of the effluence that *malkhut* receives from the *sefirot* above it,[161] and then we do not know what will be. Therefore we do not mention it, and therefore the sages said, "Which is the month [holiday] on which the moon is hidden? Rosh Hashanah."[162] Now when this divine hypostasis *malkhut* is perfected, all the others are as well, but when this last one is not full, the others remain in their proper fullness. That is why we make holy only the first and the last, for if we made the intermediate days holy, it would teach that there is within them some schism, God forbid![163]

Now as for reasons that apply to ordinary human behavior, we might say that no holiness was determined to apply to these intermediate days because on them people need to do what is necessary for repentance, trying their utmost to go to the various places where they sinned in order to rectify these

---

156. This somewhat unusual expression is commonly used in Jewish discourse; see Y. RH 7a. Cf. Crescas, *Or* II,2,6, p. 177 on the special character of these days.

157. B. Ber 28a.

158. *Ḥakhmei ha-emet,* literally "the sages of truth," a common epithet for experts in Kabbalah.

159. See Zohar 3:231a and the comment of Tishby, *Wisdom,* 3:1299 n. 193: "The New Year, the Day of Judgment, represents *Gevurah,* the attribute of strict Judgment. . . . Because the world could not withstand the application of strict Judgment a second day is added, representing *Malkhut,* in order to temper Judgment with Mercy, for *Malkhut* is the attribute of lenient Judgment, being linked to *Tiferet,* the attribute of Mercy."

160. On this matter, see B. Erub 40a and Tosafot, "Zikhru"; *Tur Oraḥ Ḥayyim,* 591; Abraham ben David, *Derashah,* pp. 18, 49 and notes; Me'iri, *Teshuvah,* p. 380; *Siddur ha-Geonim* 12:326–28. I have not found a Kabbalistic explanation for this practice.

161. The first day of the month is linked with the moon, which receives its light from another, just as the *sefirah Malkhut* receives effluence from the *sefirot* above it.

162. B. RH 8b, 34b.

163. Note the Kabbalistic explanation for the halakhah as contrasted with the rational, philosophical explanations given elsewhere (above, n. 117) and in the following sentence.

sins. It was therefore appropriate for these days not to have the status of holiness, so that people could do whatever was possible to rectify their sins.[164] Thus we have an explanation for the division of time regarding repentance.

Now there are other problems pertaining to repentance. First, according to the view that maintains that the reward for performing the commandments is not in this world, as the sages said in tractate Qiddushin[165] (and the Psalmist also apparently held this view when he said, *Until I entered God's sanctuary* (Ps. 73:17), teaching that the wicked (21v) remain in peace and quiet in this world),[166] how can we say in our prayer, "Remember us for life"?[167] This indicates that when we return in repentance and are in a state of communion we will attain longer life. But it is not so. While we are in a state of communion, we are not assured of attaining this kind of life,[168] as the reward for performing the commandments is not in this world but in the world to come. Hence repentance is not an instrument to attain longer life, but rather an instrument to attain preparation [for eternal life]. It is no answer to claim that when we say "Remember us for life" we are referring not to corporeal life but rather to the true life, as is written in "Sefer ha-Orah."[169] For everyone who says "Remember us for life" is thinking about this life [in the here and now]. When we are thinking about this life, who knows anything about the mysteries [of the world to come]?

There is another problem, arising from the rabbinic statement, "Children, length of life, and sustenance depend not upon a person's merit, but upon the star."[170] This means that when we ask for life as a result of repen-

---

164. As repentance and the Day of Atonement atone for interpersonal transgressions only after the offended party has been appeased (B. Yoma 85b), there is need for an opportunity during the intermediate days for such appeasement and for a rectification of wrongs that have been done, including monetary matters that could not be rectified on a holiday. For behavior appropriate during the intermediate period, see Gerundi, *Sha'arei Teshuvah,* 2,14.

165. B. Qid 39a, B. Hul 142a; the quote is mangled in the manuscript text.

166. Interpreting the phrase "God's sanctuary" as a reference to the reward in life after death.

167. In the *Avot* benediction of the *Tefillah* for the High Holy Days (Baer, *'Avodat Yisra'el,* p. 383).

168. This may be a repudiation of the controversial Maimonidean doctrine of divine providence as explained in *Guide* 3,51 ("The cause of our being exposed to choice, and abandoned to destruction like cattle, is to be found in our separation from God. Those who have their God dwelling in their hearts are not touched by any evil whatever"). Note how this doctrine is modified by Ephodi in his commentary ad loc.

169. Cf. above, n. 108. This interpretation appears in Gikatilla, *Sha'arei Orah,* 2:65; *Gates of Light,* p. 306. Cf. Tosafot RH 17b, *ve-nehtamim.*

170. B. MQ 28a; see above, n. 101.

tance, we do not ask for life that would not be devoted to God's service; our intention is rather that we attain life in which we are good, for the wicked are called dead even while they are alive.[171] That is why we say "Inscribe for a good life."[172] Thus we see that all the righteous desire this life not for its own sake but for the end derived from it, which is the goal. When the sages said "depend not upon a person's merit, but upon the star," they meant that if the horoscope of a pious person is unfavorable, God does not change it, because this person does not want God to change his horoscope, for that would diminish his stock of merits, as happened to R. Hanina ben Dosa.[173] And if the person's horoscope is favorable, then these two things act together—the horoscope and the piety—producing greater good than could be attained by a person who had only a favorable horoscope. According to this, our prayer for life entails the hope that we might be in such a state of communion that we would reach the plane of the totally righteous, who have the power to change a horoscope from unfavorable to favorable, as our father Abraham did.[174]

Or we may say that we pray for life because the horoscope does not absolutely cause the loss of life; it only affects probability, and we seek to maximize our probability. That is why we pray for (22r) all good things. You might say, if the horoscope does not absolutely cause something bad, then consequently it causes something good, for there is no middle ground between these, and therefore we do not need to pray for the good, as it will come of its own accord.[175] The answer to this is that the horoscope does not absolutely cause a specific detail; it causes things in general, as the sages said, "This one who is born under Mars will be a shedder of blood." But a person born under Mars [could be a surgeon, a thief, a slaughterer, or a circumciser, while] another person might kill by inflicting judicial punishment.[176] This teaches that the horoscope does not teach about specifics; it teaches about things in general. If merit prevails, there will be general good, and if not, there will be evil. Thus merit has the power to change the general disposition from evil to good,

---

171. Gen. Rab. 39,7 and parallels.

172. In the Modim benediction of the *Tefillah* for the High Holy Days; cf. the comment in Baer, *'Avodat Yisra'el,* p. 389.

173. See B. Ta'an 25a.

174. Cf. B. Shab 156a. On this conception, cf. Nissim ben Reuben, *Derashot,* p. 138, and Ravitzky, "Miracles."

175. The general problem here is the purpose of a prayer of petition for material things. For a treatment of a different aspect of this problem, see Saperstein, "Bedersi's Commentary," pp. 426, 433–35.

176. Cf. B. Shab 156a.

as R. Abraham ibn Ezra wrote about this.[177] Accordingly, even if the horoscope is malevolent, prayer can help, for the horoscope affects things in general, a realm in which there is the capacity to change for the better.

However, following our own interpretation of the statement about "children, length of life, and sustenance," it would seem that according to this position the horoscope does determine specific things. Accordingly, the proper interpretation of the phrase is that these matters are determined not only by merit, but also by the star, for one who has an appropriate star can achieve these things as well as one who has merit. Therefore there is room for our prayer that we reach the pinnacle of communion and achieve long life and good things. Or we might say that even if the horoscope determines that good will come, we pray that God will sustain this and not annul it. In this we have the solution to these problems.

Now there are the following additional problems that I have found written by Rabbenu Nissim.[178] First, if a person is judged on Rosh Hashanah and his decree is sealed on Yom Kippur, of what avail are his prayers and the medicines he takes during the ensuing year? But the sages have said that even if a sharp sword is resting on a person's neck, he should not refrain from hoping for mercy.[179] Second, since the sages said that the world is judged on the basis of the majority, and since an individual's judgment will be based on the majority of the world,[180] of what avail is his merit to him? Even if he is upright, it will not help him. Third, we see that in ordinary times, in a population of ten thousand about a hundred or two hundred will die, while in a year of plague three or four thousand might die.[181] How is it possible that

177. See the sources cited in Nissim ben Reuben, *Derashot,* p. 138, n. 126; Twersky, *Rabad,* pp. 281–82; Heinemann, *Ta'amei ha-Mitsvot,* pp. 68–69; *The Beginning of Wisdom: An Astrological Treatise by Abraham ibn Ezra,* ed. Raphael Levy and Francisco Cantera (Baltimore, London, Paris, 1939).

178. These questions do not appear in the work by Rabbenu Nissim cited above, n. 153.

179. B. Ber 10a.

180. Cf. B. Qid 40b: "The world is judged by the majority, and the individual is judged by the majority [of his deeds]." Aboab cites the first part of the statement, "The world is judged by the majority," and raises the question, if the world (or the state) is judged to deserve destruction because the majority of its inhabitants are sinners, even the individual who is in the minority of good people will perish. What then is the advantage of his goodness?

181. For example, during the Black Death, when a third of the population of many regions in Europe perished; this would indeed fit the time of R. Nissim. This sentence (and a similar one at the end of the sermon) is interesting in giving an estimate of the mortality rate in normal years as between one and two percent. Modern demography suggests a percentage slightly higher for the Christian population in this period; see Braudel, *Mediterranean,* 1:413: "The rates of birth and death, wherever they are known, [are] approximately 40 per thousand."

the amount of their evil changed so drastically that so many died in a particular year, in comparison with the previous one. Fourth, we see that sometimes medicine helps, as does prayer, or constitutional fortitude. What is the cause of this?

I would say that it works this way. If a certain person is decreed for death, there is no law or judge[182] that can annul the decree. Similarly, if his horoscope is absolutely bad, he will necessarily die unless he is like our father Abraham, who had the capacity to change the horoscope. However, if his judicial decision is for life, the following possibilities exist.[183] If a person comes to a place upon which one of the forms of judicial execution is decreed and the horoscope is predominantly a bad one, this person will die, because there is both decree and astral influence, and in this matter he is judged[184] in accordance with the majority of factors. Neither constitutional fortitude nor medicine nor prayer will help him, because of the decree. That is why we find that in the case of most of those who die in a plague, medicine does not help, for if it did, then human ingenuity would annul a divine decree. Even though a decree was annulled when the Israelites went out from Egypt, since the land was desolate of inhabitants, it can be said that the decree was partially fulfilled.[185]

If the horoscope is neutral, then in this case the constitution of the sick person and medicine and prayer may help, since a good fate was decreed, and the various factors balance each other, so that the result will be determined by his physical strength or weakness, the ability of his physician or the righteousness of his prayer. If the horoscope is predominantly for the good, such people will not become sick, or if they do they will recover even without a physician or natural strength or prayer. Now you may ask, how can you

---

182. Cf. Lev. Rab. 28,1 and parallels.

183. Here the preacher attempts to explain the relationship among four factors—God's decree during the Days of Awe, the astrological horoscope, the fortitude of the body and talent of the physician, and the power of prayer—in determining the destiny of a person for life or death during a particular year.

184. By the heavenly court.

185. This passage seems to reflect the well-known crux that God told Abraham that his descendants would be afflicted in a land not theirs for 400 years (Gen. 15:13), yet no chronology places the Israelites in Egypt for such a long time. One (minority) solution is that God counted the time double, thus in a sense annulling the decree, because of the merit of the Patriarchs (*Pirqei de-R. Eliezer*, chap. 48); Gersonides also holds that "the Israelites left Egypt before the designated end" (RaLBaG, *Torah*, pp. 54c–d, 55b, 63a), a position described by Abravanel, Gen. 15, question 17 (Abravanel, *Torah* 1:204b), as "strange." The alternative position begins the count of 400 years while the Patriarchs were still living in the land of Canaan, which the preacher seems to justify by describing it as "desolate of its inhabitants."

maintain that a decree for the bad will not change but a decree for the good may; is not the capacity for good greater than the capacity for punishment?[186] The answer is that God declares the great majority of people innocent in their judgment, even though half or even most of them are wicked. For it does not make sense that in a city of ten thousand people, during normal times when no more than a hundred will die, there are no more than a hundred wicked people.

In this way all the difficulties are resolved. They can also be resolved in a different way, but this is not the place to prolong the discussion.

---

186. Cf. B. Shab 100b.

דרש לשבת בנתים[1]

פרשת האזינו. יערוף כמטר לקחי[2]

ידוע הוא[3] כי הפעולות המלאכיות יסלק[4] בתכליותם אל ב׳
פנים: הא׳ הוא שימצא התכלית אחר הפועל כמו שיקרה לבנאי
ולנגר שהתכלית בא אחר הפעולה, והב׳ הוא שימצא התכלית
מחובר אל הפועל שבעוד שהפועל נמצא ימצא התכלית וכשהפועל   5
נפסק נפסק התכלית כמו מלאכת הנגון והשיר שבאלו אינו נמצא
התכלית אלא בהמצא הוא. והנה בתורתינו הקדושה ימצאו אלו
הב׳ דברים מחוברים שימצא בהם תכלית בשעת עשייתם ותכלית
לאחר כך ולזה כיוון משה אדוננו ע״ה בזה הפסוק שהתחלתי[5]
שאמר שאעפ״י שהוא מדבר דרך שיר לא יקרה לו מקרה שיר שלא   10
ימצא לו תכלית אלא בעת עשייתו אבל לא אחר כך אבל הוא דבר
שימצא לו התכלית אחר כך כמו שיקרה לגשם שהגשם כשהוא בא
לארץ אין התכלית מושג בעת הביאה אבל אדרבה הוא בהפך
שקשה יומא דמיטרא כיומא דדינא ואפי׳ שיהיו שנים כשני אליהו
ובאו גשמים בע״ש אינו סימן ברכה[6] שלא יוכלו לתקן צורכי שבת[7]   15
והנה התכלית המבוקש מהם הוא באחרונה בשעת הקצירה כמו
שאמר הלך ילך ובכה (12ב) כו׳[8] אמר בכאן שעם היות שפועל
הזריעה הוא עמל גדול, מצד היותו משער מה שיהיה אחר כך
שהוא פועל הזריעה עושה אותו לזה התכלית. ולזה אמר יערוף
כמטר לקחי[9] שר״ל שמה שיקבלו ממנו יהיה שימצאו בו תכלית   20
אחר שילמדוהו.

---

1. השבת שבין ראש השנה ליום הכפורים.
2. דב׳ לב ב.
3. עי׳ הערה 2 לתרגום.
4. כך בכתב היד, וכנראה צ״ל „יחלק״ המלה הקודמת פירושה מלאכת האדם.
5. דב׳ לב ב.
6. תענית ח ב, ובמקור „אינן אלא סימן קללה״.
7. ע״פ רבינו גרשום ורש״י על המקום.
8. תה׳ קכו ו.
9. דב׳ לב ב.

והנה ג"כ הוא דומה לטל[10] שבאותה שעה יהיה להם ג"כ בו
עריבות וזה מבואר היותו ג"כ שהרי מי שהוא שלם כשישמע
הדברים התורניים יערבו לו כנופת צופים[11] ובשעת עשייתם ג"כ הם
עריבים ואפי' שיהיה בדבר שאין בו מעשה הנה ישיג העריבות
בשעת הלימוד ואחר כך יהיה לו עריבות יותר.

והנה אמר אח"כ כשעירים וכו'[12] רצה בזה שאלו הערביות לא יהיו
במדרגה אחת לכל אבל לכל אחד יתחלק כפי השגתו ולזה אמר
שלמי שהם מתחילים בעיון יהיה להם זה כמו הגשם הדק שיבא על
הדשאים בתחלת הצמיחה שהרי שעירים הוא נגזר מלשון שער לפי
שהוא דק כמו השער[13] ולמי שהם גדולים בעיון יהיה להם זה כמו
הרביבים[14] שהוא הגשם הגס שיבוא על העשבים כשהם גדולים. הרי
למדנו מכאן שהמדבר בדברי תורה אפי' שיתחיל דרך שיר ראוי
שיתחברו אליו אלו הב' תנאים.

ועוד למדנו מהדמיון שדמה אותו לגשם והטל שהמדבר ברבים
צריך שיהיו דבריו מעטי הכמות ורבי האיכות שהרי הגשם הוא רב
האיכות מהטל ואמר שהנה התכלית שישיגו מדיבורו הוא כמו
הגשם עם היות שהדיבור יהיה קטן כמו הטל.

והנה למדנו עוד מהתחלת דיבורו תנאי שלישי במ"ש האזינו
השמים ואדברה[15] וכו' שלא אמר האזינו השמים ואדברה[16] כמו
שהיה אומר עד הנה העידותי בכם היום את השמים ואת הארץ[17]:
לעולם הוא לוקח אותם מחוברים וכאן חלקם לפי שאין ראוי
שידבר עם השמים והארץ במדרגה אחת אבל לכל אחד ידבר כפי
כבודו ולפי' אמר לשמים בפני עצמן שיאזינו ושידבר שהנה בכאן

10. באותו הפסוק.
11. ע"פ תה' יט יא.
12. עלי דשא, דב' לב ב.
13. עי' ראב"ע על הפסוק: "דקים...וי"א כי שעירים מגזרת שער."
14. "וכרביבים עלי עשב" באותו הפסוק.
15. דב' לב א.
16. לפי ההמשך, מסתבר שהגירסא הנכונה כאן היא "שלא אמר האזינו השמים והארץ ואדברה."
17. דב' ל יט.

חלק להם כבוד כשלא אמר תשמעו אמרי פי כמו שאמר בארץ אבל 45
אמר להם שהם יאזינו והוא ידבר כאלו הורה[18] בזה שהם לא יקבלו
בזה שום חדוש מצד עצמם אבל נאה להם השתיקה מצד שהוא
מדבר עם הארץ ואין ראוי להם שיעשו להם תנועה בעבור שיהיה בזה מן
הבלבול לארץ שלא יקבלו[19] הדברים שהוא אומר לה מצד שהשמים
נותנים קולות בתנועתם ולכן אמר ותשמע הארץ אמרי פי[20] שבכאן 50
הורה שתכלית הדיבור יהיה לה להבינה.[21]

וזה נראה (13א) סברת חז"ל כמה שאמרו[22] משה אמר האזינו מצד
שהיה קרוב אל השמים וישעיה בעבור שהיה רחוק אמר שמעו
שמים[23] שהנה נר' שהבדילו בזה שכשאומר האזינו נר' שהיה שומע
הקולות שהם נותנים בתנועתם מצד שהיה קרוב להם ולפי' אמר 55
האזינו שלא יתנו קולות כמו שאומר האדם לחבירו שהוא נותן קול
האוזן[24] אבל ישעיה בעבור שהיה רחוק ולא היה שומע הקול לא היה
אומר האזינו אבל היה או' שמעו שהוא כמו המדבר למרחוק אבל
הארץ שהיה קרוב לו והיה שומע תנועות ההולכים בה אמ' האזנה.
יהיה מה שיהיה ההבדל שיש בין האזנה לשמיעה מבואר הוא 60
שהסבה שלא אמר שלא ידבר[25] עמהם אמרי פי הוא מצד שחלק
כבוד להם שהוא מדבר עם אחרים והם מצדם ראוי שיתקן.[26] והנה
ישעיהו לא דבר בזה הדרך מהכבוד כל כך עם היות שהבדילם כל
אחד בפני עצמו מצד שאפי' שידבר עם הארץ אינו ראוי שידבר
עמה בזה האופן שתשמע אמרי פיו שאינו כ"כ גדול המעלה שידבר 65
עמה בזה הדרך ובעבור זה אמר כי השם דבר[27] כלו' זה שאני אומר
לכם אינו מצדי אבל מצד כבוד יי.

18. בכ"י לפני מלה זו, "אמר להם" מחוק.
19. תושבי הארץ.
20. ז"א כדי שהארץ תשמע אמרי פי.
21. ז"א לארץ, לאפשר לה להבין.
22. תנחומא האזינו פ"ב.
23. יש' א ב.
24. אולי צ"ל באוזן.
25. אולי צ"ל שלא אמר שידבר.
26. אולי צ"ל שישתקו.
27. יש' א ב.

וכבר ראיתי במדרש הזוהר[28] שכשישעיה אמר אלה הדברים יצאו
לקראתו פמליא של מעלה להכות אותו ולכן אמר להם אל תשימו בי
70 עון אשר חטא במה שדברתי לגדולי המעלה שישמעו קולי שאין זה
מצדי אלא מצד כי י דבר אבל משה שהיה גדול הערך כ"כ לא אמר
אלא אמרי פי כלו׳ שהוא מעצמו אומר כן וראוי להם שישמעו קולי.
אבל אין במדרש הנז׳[29] הבדל שיש בין ישעיהו ומשה במה שאמר
כאן[30] השמים בה"א הידיעה והארץ ג"כ ולשם[31] אמר שמים וארץ
75 שהנה אלו השמים הם השמים העליונים שהם שמו של הב"ה[32]
שבהם אמרו שהם אש ומים[33] כלו׳ שהם מדת הדין המכונה באש
ומדת החסד המכונה במים[34] והארץ כאן היא ארץ החיים[35] והנה לפי
זה הארץ היא כמדרגה גדולה שהיא למעלה מן השמים ולפי זה נאמר
בהפך[36] שיותר כבוד חלק לה מן שחלק לשמים שבשמים אמר מלת
80 האזינו שר"ל שיטה אוזן למה שהוא או׳ ובזה יראה שהוא קרוב
אצלם מאד ובארץ אמר שישמע אמרי פי כאלו הוא מדבר עם מי
שהוא רחוק ואמר לשון אמירה שהוא מורה שהוא דבור בפה יותר
מלשון דבור כמו כה תאמר לבית יעקב[37] ויערוף כמטר לקחי כמו שפי׳
הרמב"ן.[38] מכל מקום התנאי הג׳ שאמרתי שראוי למדבר שידבר עם
85 הגדולים באופן אחד ושידבר עם הקטנים באופן אחר הוא מדוקדק
מזה הפסוק.

ולפי (13 ב) הפשט השמים הם יותר גדולי הערך ולפי מדרש הזוהר

---

28. השוה זוהר ג, רפו ב. אבוהב איננו מצטט מילולית אלא מסכם את התכן במלים שלו.
29. לכאורה הכוונה למדרש הזוהר, אולם הקטע שם מדגיש בהמשך את ההבדל שאבוהב מזכיר
כאן. לכן מסתבר שהכוונה למדרש תנחומא.
30. דב׳ לב א.
31. יש׳ א ב.
32. עי׳ זוהר ג, רפו ב.
33. בראשית רבה דה,ז וכו׳.
34. זוהר ג, קלו ב וכו׳.
35. ז"א עולם הבא, השוה במדבר רבה יט,יח, תנחומא בובר מצורע ד, זוהר א, א ב ועוד.
36. הפך הפירוש הראשון, לפיו חלק משה כבוד יותר לשמים.
37. שמות יט ג. לא ברור לי למה הוא מציע דוגמה זו.
38. דב׳ לב ב. לא ברור לי איך מתיחס פירושו של הרמב"ן למלים אלה ("ואמר יערף כמטר
לקחי כי מה שלקח מן השמים ואמרתו על הארץ יערף על ישראל") לענין הדרש.

הארץ היא יותר גדולה והנה אם יסכים דעת רז״ל[39] עם מאמר
הזוהר[40] נאמר שמה שאמרו[41] במשה מצד שהיה קרוב אמר האזינו
שרצו בזה מה שפירשתי שמשה מצד שהיה קרוב אפי׳ לשמים 90
התחתונים אמר לשון שמיעה.[42] והארץ שישעיה אומר היא הארץ
היסודית ומצד זה אמר בה האזינו,[43] והארץ שמרע״ה או׳ היא ארץ
החיים, והנה לקחו בכאן שמים וארץ בשיתוף השם.[44]

הרי מבוארים הג׳ תנאים: הראשון דרך כבוד שידבר עם כל אחד
מהם הב׳ שיכוין שיהיה בדיבורו ב׳ תכליות תכלית שישאר ממנו 95
ההויה אחר כך ובעוד נעשה שישיגו ג״כ ממנו עריבות שזהו הנרצה
בדמיון גשם וטל ועוד תנאי ג׳ שיהיו דבריו מעטי הכמות ורבי האיכות
כמו שפירשתי. והנה הדבור שלא יהיה באלה התנאים הנה יראה
שהוא דבור חסר.

ולפי הנראה בדיבור שלפנינו[45] יר׳ שיחסר לו הב׳ תנאים הא׳ שלא 100
יהיה בכאן תכלית נשאר שהרי הדיבור בתשובה הוא כ״כ מבואר
לכל שלא יהיה שום חדוש לשומעים במה שישאר בידם שהרי זה
התכלית ידוע הוא לפי שאין בכאן שום אדם שלא ידע באיזה דרך
יעשה תשובה ולפי זה אין בכאן שום עריבות[46] אבל אדרבה יהיה
בכאן להם מן הצער בשמעם פשעיהם ועונותם וכל שכן ממה שאמרו 105
ז״ל[47] שמי שהוא עובר על הדברים במזיד שהוא יודע שחוטא אין
להזהירו יותר כמו שאמר כמו שמצוה על האדם לומר דבר הנשמע
כך חובה[48] עליו שלא לומר דבר שאינו נשמע.[49] והנה מזה הצד היה

---

39. האומרת שמשה חלק יותר כבוד לשמים.
40. האומר, לפי פירושו של אבוהב, שהארץ היא במדרגה יותר גבוהה מהשמים.
41. רז״ל.
42. בנוגע לארץ החיים הרחוקים מעל השמים.
43. צ״ל האזיני.
44. עי׳ הערה 20 לתרגום.
45. ז״א הדבור על התשובה.
46. עי׳ הערה 23 לתרגום.
47. השוה שבת קמח ב.
48. צ״ל מצוה.
49. יבמות סה ב.

ראוי השתיקה[50] בעם כזה שכלם יודעים דבר הראוי לעשות.

אבל מצד אחר יש הכרח לדיבור שראוי הדיבור ליודעי׳ יותר מי
שאינם[51] יודעים שהרי אע״פ שהוא לא יתפעל מעצמו לעשות הטוב
והישר עם כל זה יתפעל מאחר כשיש[52] והסבה בזה כי הדיבור לנפש
הוא כמו ההכאה לגוף לעשות דבר מה וכמו שאנו רואים שמי
שישמע קול ערב יתעדן בטבע כן מי שישמע קול אנחה יהיה לו
אנחה ואם היינו יודעים מהות הנפש והיושר שיש בהן להיכלה[53]
היינו יודעים הסבה לזה אבל כמו שלא נודע מהותה כך לא נודע
היאך אלו הדברים פועלים בה[54] אבל נודה בהכרח שכשהנפש תשמע
קול הדומה לה להחזיק לו הרי היא מתחזקת בזה מצד מה שיש לה
עוזרת ולזה הצד ישמיעו קולות למי שרצו[55] לעזור אותו כשנופל לארץ
וכשהוא (14א) עושה דבר מה.

והנה מצד אחר שהנפש תתחזק כשיאמרו לה קום עשה מה שלא
תתחזק מצד עצמה וזה מצד שהשכלים הנבדלים הם דומות לש״י
שכמו שהוא ברא כל הדברי׳ במאמר[56] כך הרי פועלים בדברים
שלמטה מהם. ומזה הצד מוכיח האדם למה שהוא למטה ממנו בזה
הדבר שהרי הוא מתפעל ממנו מצד שהוא גדול המעלה ממנו.[57]
ובעבור זה[58] ז״ל תמהתי אם יש בדור הזה מי שראוי להוכיח שאם
יאמרו לו טול קיסם מבין שיניך יאמרו לו טול קורה מבין עיניך,[59]
שהורו בזה שמה שהתוכחת ראוי לקבל הוא מצד שזה גדול במעלה
ובטבע הוא שיתפעל האחר מצדיו אבל אם למטה אז אין תוכחתו
מקובלת וכדומה.

50. טופוס רווח בדרשנות התקופה. עי׳ הערה 27 לתרגום ודוגמאות נוספות בקובץ זה.

51. צ״ל משאינם.

52. כנראה חסר כאן משהו בטקסט.

53. משמעות המלים האלה בהקשר אינננה ברורה לי.

54. עי׳ הערה 31 לתרגום.

55. ז״א לרצים במרוצה.

56. השוה אבות ה,א, אוצר המדרשים תעד,יב.

57. עי׳ הערה 33 לתרגום.

58. כנראה צריך להוסיף כאן „אמרו.״

59. ערכין טז ב.

לזה מצאתי כתוב בספר אחר וכמדומה לי שהוא מאמר הראב"ד⁶⁰
שכתב שמה שאמרו ז"ל בה"א בראם⁶¹ הוא מצד שהה"א אין לה
מקום שיאמר בכלי התנועה כמו הגרון והחיך והלשון. ומזה הצד
שאמרו שהשי"ת ברא השמים בה"א כלומ' בלי עמל אלא כמי
שאומר ה"א⁶² ומזה הצד אמרו ז"ל⁶³ ששוחקי' היו אומרים היטב   135
הדק הדק היטב מפני שהקול יפה לבשמים רצו בזה שקול הה"א
שהיה אומר כשהיה אומר היטב הדק הדק היטב הוא מסייע הרבה
לאלו שוחקי הבשמים שבזה ינוח כחם וינוחו בזה יגיעי כח.

והנה העולה מכל זה מה שאמרנו שכמו שהנפש יפעל הגוף מצד
מה שהשכל פועל בחומר כן זה הנפש שהיא שלימה יפעל במה   140
שלמטה ממנה במדרגה ויקבל מאמרה ויוסיף בה שלימות בכל
דבור ודבור כמו שהיתה מקבלת שלימות אם היה השם מדבר עמה
שפשיטא שבכל שעה שהיא מדברת עמו⁶⁴ היא משגת מן השלימות
מה שלא היה לה קודם לכן. ולזה כיוונו רז"ל במה שאמרו באברהם
שהשם לא היה אומר לו הדבר מיד אלא בפעמים רבים כמו על   145
אחד ההרים אשר אומר, וכן קח נא את בנך את יחידך,⁶⁵ וכן
במקומות אחרים, כדי ליתן לו שכר על כל דבור ודבור⁶⁶ והאמת הנה
שכרו אתו ופעולתו לפניו⁶⁷ שכל דבור היה משיג שלימות מה שלא
היה משיג קודם.

לכן עוד יש בחינה ג' מצד מה שנאמר מה יכולה לפעול בעצמה וזה   150
במקרה מצד שזה הנפש אינה פועלת בעצם בנפש האחרת אבל היא
פועלת במקרה מצד מה שפועלת בחומרה שהיא פועלת בה שלימות
במה שהיה לו חסרון וזה שאם זה החומר היה נפסד באחת מן

60. עי' הערה 35 לתרגום.
61. מנחות כט ב, בראשית רבה יב,ט, תנחומא בובר בראשית טז.
62. השוה רבנו בחיי על בר' ב ד, פרושו הראשון („ע"ד הפשט") למאמר „בה"א בראם."
63. כריתות ו ב, „הדיבור יפה לבשמים." מאמר זה מתאים לכוונת הדרשן להדגיש את השפעת
הדיבור על התחום החומרי.
64. ז"א שהנפש מדברת עם ה'.
65. שני הציטוטות מבר' כב ב.
66. בראשית רבה לט,ט, נה,ז.
67. ע"פ יש' מ י.

הדרכים שהוא לו חסרון זה הנפש יתקנהו ויגרע תאותו באותו הדבר

155 שהיה לו חסרון (14 ב) והנה זה הנפש יכול לתקן בקומה מה שלא יתקן הוא מצד שהיא כבר משועבדת לזה החומר מצד שהיא דבקה עמו.

וכבר מצינו שלמה המלך שאמר זה ששמיעת התוכחה היא דבר גדול להביא האדם אל השלימות וזה אמר מאור עינים ישמח לב ושמועה טובה תדשן עצם אזן שומעת וכו' תוכחות חיים בקרב

160 חכמים תלין.[68] הנה רצה בזה שהשמיעה היא טובה מהראייה מצד שהראייה אינה אלא שישמח לב אבל השמועה טובה היא תדשן אפי' העצם שאינו נופל בו הרגש וכן בזה הצד הצד[69] שמי שישמע דבר טוב מצד שזה הדיבור מביא שלימות לנפש כמו שאמרנו כשישמע דבר טוב ישמח ויגיל בו ואם ישיג למה שאמר הנביא והשביע

165 בצחצחות נפשיך ועצמותיך יחלוץ[70] שזהו שלימות אמיתי שהוא משיג אבל אם הוא דבר של ראיה בלבד אין בכאן שמחה אלא ללב.[71] והנה הוא נבדל בב' דברים הא' מצד שאינו מדשן רצוני שמביא שלימות במה שיושפע עליו טוב אמיתי אבל הוא עושה שמסיר הדאגה והב' שאפי' בזה אינו עושה אלא ללב בלבד אבל אינו עושה השמחה

170 במדרגה גדולה כ"כ שכל הכוחות ישמחו בה אבל השמועה טובה היא משפעת שפע אמיתי ואפי' העצמות היבשות[72] משיגות בה שלמות והנה אמ' אח"כ אזן שומעת וכו'[73] שהורה בזה יותר שלימות האוזן שרצה בזה שהאוזן לא די לה השלימות שמשגת בשעת השמיעה אבל נמשך לה מזה תועלת גדול למה שיבוא וזה שמצד שזה האוזן שמעה

175 תוכחת חיים ויתעדן בהם נמשך לה מזה שהיא הולכת בין החכמים וזהו שנא' בקרב חכמים תלין.[74]

---

68. משלי טו ל–לא, ועי' הערה 43 לתרגום.

69. כך בכ"י, ואולי צ"ל „העיד."

70. יש' נח יא. אבוהב מקשר בין „ושמועה טובה תדשן עצם" ו„ועצמותיך יחלוץ" כדי לטעון שהשמיעה מביאה לידי השלימות האמיתית.

71. ע"פ הפסוק במשלי.

72. ע"פ יח' לז ד.

73. משלי טו לא.

74. שם.

והנה ראיתי במדרש הנעלם[75] בפסוק כי אזן מלים תבחן וחיך
יטעם לאכול[76] שהכוונה בזה שהאוזן היא נעשית באלו העקמימיות
בעבור שקודם שיכנס הקול לא יבחין בזה הקול אם הוא ראוי
ליכנס אם לאו או שאם היה פשוטה מיד היה נכנס בעצם וזהו מה
שאמר כי אזן מלים תבחן שהאוזן בעצמ' היא מבחנת בזה מצד
שהיא נעשית בזה הסדר שנבחן בין הטוב והרע וזהו הלשון הנהוג
שאמרו חז"ל הדבר נכנס, וכן יכנסו דברי באזניך, באזנינו שמענו,[77]
שר"ל שעוברת כל אלו העקמימיות ועובר אבל הדבר הרע נשאר
בפתח ולא עבר. וכן בזה האופן אמ' וחיך אוכל יטעם לו,[78] שהחיך
בראו הש"י מצד שאם יראה שזה המזון נאות וראוי (15א) שיאכלהו
ואם לאו לא. והרי אמרו חז"ל[79] שאם חרשו נותן לו דמו כולו מצד
שהחרשות היא העדר הכל שהרי אינו ראוי לקבל תוכחת. ראה במה
הפליגו בשמיעת הדברים הטובים.

הרי בכאן ראיות מצד החוש ומצד השכל ומצד הכתוב שמבוא
גדול בשלימות שמיעת הדברים אפי' שכבר נדעם ובעבור זה נמשך
המנהג בכל מקום שבזה השבת כל קהל וקהל נקבצים לשמוע דברי
תשובה, ומנהגן של ישראל תורה,[80] עם שיש לשואל שישאל ויאמר
מפני מה משה אדונינו כמו שתקן לישראל שיהו דורשין הלכות
פסח בפסח הלכות עצרת בעצרת הלכות חג בחג[81] לא תקן שיהו
דורשים בזה השבת או בשבת שקודם ר"ה בהלכות תשובה שזה
עיקר ויסוד גדול?[82] והנה יש להשיב בזה שמשה אדונינו כשתיקן
להם לישראל הקרבנות לא היה צריך לתקן להם תיקון אחר שהרי
בענין הקרבנות תקן להם כל מי שהוא חוטא בין שהוא חוטא

---

75. עי' זוהר ג, רצד ב (אידרא זוטא).
76. איוב לד ג.
77. למשל, בראשית רבה סה,כב, תנחומא בובר ויגש ו, שבת פט א.
78. איוב יב יא.
79. בבא קמא פה ב.
80. רשב"א, תורת הבית הארוך, ברלין, תקכ"ב, עמ' לד א, מובא בטור א"ח תקצ"א. השוה
תוספות מנחות כ ב, "מנהג אבותינו תורה היא."
81. מגילה לב א.
82. עי' הערה 52 לתרגום.

לשמים בין שהוא חוטא לחבירו התיקון שיעשה כמו שכתוב ומעלה 200
מעל ביי וכחש בעמיתו[83] וג"כ כתב בכל אחד הוידוי: הרי תקן להם
לישראל מה שהיה איפשר להם לעשות והנה העוונת אחריו שאין
הקרבן שבתוך השנה מכפר הנה הוא מכופר בקרבנות של י"ה ובזה
אין צריך לומר להם התיקון אבל התיקון הוא לכהן, וכבר אמרו ז'
ימים קודם יום הכפורים היו מפרישין לכהן גדול[84] כדי שיתכונן 205
וידע בהלכות עבודה. הרי מבואר שאין צריך תקון לישראל בזמן
שבית המקדש קיים. ואולי כוונו בזה במה שאמרו משה תיקן להם
לישראל בזמנם[85] ובעבור זה לא תקן אלא באלו הזמנים אבל בזמנינו
צריך תיקון אחר בזמנים אחרים שהרי בזה הזמן התיקון מוטל
עלינו ולא על אחר[86]. 210

ועוד יש לומר שהדרשה בתשובה היא צריכה בכל עת ובכל שעה
שהרי בכל עת ובכל שעה אינו מחויב[87] לדרוש בהלכות תשובה ומפני
זה אין ראוי לקבוע לה זמן ויהיה זה כמו שאמר דוד עת לעשות ליי
הפרו תורתך,[88] שרצה בזה שמי שהוא מבקש עת נאות לעבודת ה'
ואומר זה העת ראוי וזה בלתי ראוי הנה בזה הפרו תורתך[89] 215
שהתורה אומרת והגית בו יומם ולילה.[90] יהיה מה שיהיה מנהגם של
ישראל ראוי להחזק בידו וכו'.[91]

הנה יש לעיין בענין התשובה (ב 15) קודם שנתחיל בביאורה וזה
שצריך לידע זאת התשובה אם היא שורש כמו אחת משרשי
התורה[92] או אם היא ענף כמו אחת משאר המצות. והנה בזה יש 220

83. ויק' ה כא.
84. משנה יומא א א.
85. השוה מגלה לב א.
86. ז"א, לא על הכהן הגדול.
87. כך הוא בכ"י, ולפי התוכן צ"ל „הוא מחויב".
88. תה' קיט קכו.
89. חידוש דרשני יפה לפסוק, ועי' הערה 55 לתרגום.
90. יהו' א ח.
91. כאן מסתיימת ההקדמה לדרשה, ומסתבר שבא „רשות" עי' הערה 15 לתרגום הדרשה שבפרק 13.
92. עי' הערה 57 לתרגום.

צדדין⁹³ שיראה מהן שהיא שורש לכל התורה כולה וצדדין יראה
מהן ההפך וזה שאם⁹⁴ שהנה יראה מצד השכל שהתשובה יסוד מוסד
לתורה שאם לא יהיה בכאן תשובה אי איפשר שיהיה בכאן תורה
וזה שאם היה האמת שכל מי שיחטא לא יתכפר לו עונו אשר חטא
הנה לפי זה התורה היא תקלה והתכלית המכוון בה תפסד בהפך
וזה שכל אדם חוטא בכל עת ובכל שעה חטאים אין קץ ולפי מנין
המצות יהיה מנין העבירות שהרי מי שהוא מרובה במצות כמו
אנחנו כת המאמינים שהתורה נתנה לנו ברבוי מצותיה לזכותינו⁹⁵
כמו שאמר הנביא ה׳ חפץ למען צדקו יגדיל תורה ויאדיר⁹⁶ הנה
נמשך מזה ההפך שבהכרח הוא שנחטא ברובם או בכולם ואם לא
יהיה רפואה למחלתינו אין קץ לענשינו ואז נהיה בתכלית ההפסד⁹⁷
ולפיכך יתחייב שיהיה בכאן תשובה שיתרפא זה.

ועוד יתחייב מצד אחר שהתשובה היא יסוד לעולם במה שאמרו⁹⁸
ז׳ דברים קדמו לעולם וא׳ מהם תשובה הנה הורו שהתשובה היא
יסוד לעולם וכן אמרו ג״כ⁹⁹ שאדם הראשון עשה תשובה וזו היתה
סבה שלא מת ביום שאכל הרי שאם לא היתה בכאן תשובה אנו לא
באנו לעולם.

ומפנים אחרים יראה שאין התשובה יסוד. הא׳ שלא ראינו לא׳
שמנו השרשיים שמנו אותה כמו יסוד אבל מנו אותה כמו אחת
מצות עשה.¹⁰⁰ ועוד שהרי אין העונש מבואר בה אלא כמו מי שעובר
על א׳ ממצות עשה לא יותר ולפי האמת ראוי הוא שיהיה יותר. ועוד
היאך איפשר שיהיה התשובה מצוה? א״כ עבירה גוררת מצוה¹⁰¹ וזה

---

93. „צדדים" (כמו „חלקי הסותר") הוא מונח טכני בשאלה הויכוחית המופיע הדרשות יהודיות
החל מסוף המאה הי״ד. עי׳ הערה 58 לתרגום.
94. כך בכ״י, וכנראה חסר משהו בטקסט או המלה „שאם" מיותרת.
95. השוה משנה מכות ג,טז.
96. יש׳ מב כא.
97. עי׳ הערות 59 ו‎611 לתרגום, והשוה מנחם המאירי ,חבור התשובה, ניו יורק תש״י, עמ׳ 23.
98. תנחומא בובר נשא יט.
99. השוה פרקי דרבי אליעזר פרק כ, וזהר חדש בראשית דף יט ב. שאדם הראשון עשה תשובה
מיד אחרי חטאו איננה דעה נפוצה בין חז״ל. ראה למטה, ועי׳ הערה 148 לתרגום.
100. למשל רמב״ם, ספר המצות, עשה עג והלכות תשובה הקדמה.
101. בנגוד למאמר הידוע, מצוה גוררת מצוה ועבירה גוררת עברה (אבות ד,ב,דברים רבה ו,ד ועוד).

ששב בתשובה הוא מחמת שחטא ואם התשובה מצוה א״כ בכל עת
שהוא חוטא יתגלגל תשובה וזה אי אפשר שכמו שמצוה אינה גוררת
245 עבירה עבירה אינה גוררת מצוה. שהרי ראינו הכתוב צווח על זה
במי שהיה עושה שהמצוה יהיה סבה לעבירה במה שאמר בענין
השמיטה השמר לך פן יהיה דבר עם לבבך בליעל לאמר (16א) קרבה
וכו׳[102] והנה אמר וקרא אליך ה׳ והיה בך חטא;[103] שהורה בזה שהנה
זה האיש עושה תכלית הטוב הצעה לתכלית הרע שמצד שקרבה
250 שנת השמיטה והשם צוה שישמוט חובו הוא עושה מצד שאינו רוצה
להלוות לעני כלל וזה הפך כוונת הבת[104] שבמה שרצה להיות חונן
העני זה שב הפך והנה תקנתו קלקלתו[105] ולפי׳ אמר וקרא עליך
שר״ל שיקרא תגר נגד השם[106] שכך צוה, וזה יהיה בך חטא[107] שאתה
מחטיא הכוונה.

255 וכבר יקרה זה הרבה פעמים ובפרט במקומי[108] בענין ההלואה
שמאחר שהכתו׳ אוסר הריבית כשיבוא ההלואה לישראל אינו רוצה
להלוות לו והנה העני מצד שאינו יכול ליתן ברבית כמו הגוי אינו
מוצא מעותיו והוא מת ברעב והנה שב לו המצוה עבירה וכמעט אם
אומר שיותר תחשב לו לעבירה למי שאינו רוצה להלוות יותר ממי
260 שילוה ברבית שבזה יש סכנה ובזה אין סכנה.[109] וכבר יראה שהתורה
חששה לזה במה שאמר אם כסף תלוה[110] שהנה דברה תורה בלשון
מסתפק לו[111] אם תזכה שכסף תלוה את עמי את העני עמך ואמר

102. דב׳ טו ט.

103. שם.

104. כך בכי״י, וכנראה צ״ל הב״ה או הכת׳.

105. השוה רמב״ם, הלכות מגילה א ח ועוד.

106. כנראה מפרש „וקרא עליך אל יהוה״ במובן וקרא בגללך על יהוה, שיש כאן ענין של חילול
השם. עי׳ הערה 68 לתרגום.

107. דב׳ טו ט.

108. כנראה הכוונה לGuadalajara, ואם כן יש סימן כאן שאבוהב דורש לא בעיר שלו אלא
במקום אחר לקהל מיוחד.

109. על קטע מעניין זה ראה במבוא.

110. שמות כב כד.

111. לומר.

לא תהיה לו כנושא לא תשימון עליו נשך[112] שהורה בזה שהמלוה
ילוה לאחר מצד מה שהוא רוצה שיהיה לו משועבד כמו שאמר
הכתו' עבד לוה לאיש מלוה[113] או מצד התועלת שיהיה לו רבית והנה
אומר בכאן הכתו' אם כסף תלוה את עמי לא תהיה לו כנושה שהוא
מי שמלוה מעותיו מפני הכבוד וג"כ לא תשימון עליו נשך שהנה זה
יעשה בהסכמת שניהם המלוה ולוה ועליו ישוב לכסף[114] או יהיה
אזהרה למלוה וללוה ולעדים כמו שאמרו רז"ל[115] והוא האמת. והנה
הארכתי בזה בעבור שאני רואה היהודים האמללים צועקים ואינם
נענים בזמן הזה שהיוקר מצוי בעוונותינו.[116]

ונחזור לעניינו שדבר מבואר הוא שמהטוב לא יצא אלא טוב
ומהרע לא יבוא אלא רע והנה לפי זה שיתגלגל ממצוה עבירה זה
דבר שהשכל לא יחייבהו.[117]

הנה יש לומר שהתשובה היא כבר מהשרש ואינה שרש שהרי
אינה שרש שהשרש הוא שאם תדומה הפסידו תפיל התורה
בכללה[118] אבל בכאן לא תפול התורה שהרי אם נאמר שאינו מועיל
התשובה למי שחטא אבל כל א' וא' לפי חטאו יהיה נידון אין בזה
הריסה (16ב) אבל כבר יש לה מבוא בטוב למי שיחשוב בזה ויאמר
שהאדם בהיותו מעריך גודל הש"י ראוי הוא לו שאם יחטא לא
יהיה לו כפרה בוידוי פיו כי אם שיהיה נוסר כפי חטאו שהרי
הדתות הנימוסיות מניחות קנסות ועונשין ליסר כל עושי רשעה
ואינן מניחות המשפט מצד מה שיחזור החוטא בתשובה לומר שלא
יעשה עול ובכאן ראוי שיחשוב זה מק"ו.[119]

112. שמות כב כד, וצ"ל כנושה.
113. משלי כב ז.
114. כוונת שלוש המלים האחרונות אינה ברורה לי.
115. השוה בבא מציעא עה ב.
116. עי' הדיון במבוא.
117. ז"א שהשכל לא יקבל אותו. אחרי הטענות לשני הצדדים, מציע הדרשן בהמשך פתרון לבעיה.
118. עי' הערה 74 לתרגום.
119. מקל וחומר.

285 ואם תאמר אין דנין אפשר משאי אפשר[120] שבכאן בהכרח הוא
שיחטא ולשם היה איפשר, התשובה בזה מבוארת הוא שהשם לא יצוה
על הנמנע שהרי השם צוה לנו שתשמור התורה בכללה ואם זה בחק
הנמנע היאך יצוה על זה?[121] והרי ראינו כמה חכמים וחסידים שלא
טעמו טעם חטא ומתו בחטא של נחש.[122] והרי אתה רואה לשון התורה

290 מזה שאמר אם הכהן המשיח יחטא[123] ואמר ג״כ ואם כל עדת ישראל
ישגו[124] ואמר ביחיד החוטא נפש כי תחטא[125] ואמר בנשיא אשר נשיא
יחטא[126] הנה אתה רואה בכאן בהבדל הלשון שמי שאינו ראוי שיחטא
אמר הלשון כמסתפק אם הכהן המשיח יחטא כלומר אם יקרה מקרה
כזה שיחטא מה שלא היה ראוי שיחטא וכן ג״כ אמר בקהל אם אמר כל

295 עדת ישראל ישגו שהוא דבר לפי השכל רחוק מציאותו שכל העדה
יהיו שוגגין וביחיד אמר לשון שאינו רחוק כ״כ שיש בו במשמע
שיחטא בהכרח או לא יחטא ובנשיא אמר אשר נשיא יחטא שזה
הלשון מורה בהכרח שיחטא. וכבר פירשו זה הפסוק כן במדרש
הנעלם[127] שמי שהוא נשיא בהכרח הוא שיחטא שמצד השררה יבוא

300 לידי חטא אבל ביחיד לא יבוא לידי כך וכבר אמרו לשם ג״כ שמצד זה
הנשיאים הביאו את אבני השהם ואת אבני המילואים[128] מצד מה שראו
שהם מוכנים לחטא יותר מכל אדם בעבור זה הביאו האבנים שהם
נתונים על הלב מצד שלבם לוקחם לעשות מה שאינו ראוי.[129]

 א״כ אין התשובה יסוד אם האנשים ינהגו על האמת אבל היא

305 יסוד למה שנטו אחרי הבצע וזה אמר ש״ה ע״ה עשה [אלהים] את
האדם ישר והמה בקשו חשבונות רבים.[130] והנה בזה יתיישב מה שמנו

120. השוה סוכה נ ב ועוד.

121. עי׳ הערה 77 לתרגום.

122. השוה ספרי דברים שכג.

123. ויק׳ ד ג.

124. ויק׳ ד יג.

125. ויק׳ ד ב.

126. ויק׳ ד כב.

127. זוהר ג כג א, ועי׳ ישעיה תשבי, משנת הזוהר, ירושלים תשמ״ב, עמ׳ תקצג–תקצד.

128. שמות לה כז.

129. השוה המקור בזוהר: ,,נשיאים דלבייהו גס בהו.״

130. קהלת ז כט.

אותה חז״ל עם הדברים שקדמו לעולם[131] שמצד שראה הש״י שהעולם
לא יתיישב אלא בתשובה מצד רוע מעלליהם קדמה לעולם כמו
שקרא לאדם הראשון[132] אבל מצד הבחירה הנה בעל בחירה הוא

310 והיה לו מקום להטות את הטוב שהרי אין שום אדם מוכרח (17א)
במעשיו[133] שמה שאמר בגמ' בשם ר' אלעאי, אם רואה אדם שיצרו
גובר עליו ילבש שחורים ויתכסה שחורים וילך למקום שאין מכירין
אותו ויעשה מה שלבו חפץ ואל יתחלל שם שמים בגלוי,[134] כבר פרשו
בזה המאמר שכוונתו היה שמי שתקפו יצרו בתכלית יעשה לו הכנעה

315 בתכלית שאז אי אפשר שיחטא וע״ז אמר שילבש שחורים ויתכסה
ואם יעשה מה שלבו חפץ כלו' אם נותנים לו רשות שיעשה מה שלבו
חפץ שבודאי לא יעשה אלא טוב,[135] והנה לפי זה תשאר זאת המצוה
כמו מצוה פרטית אחרת.

ומה שהקשינו שהוא אינו נאה שימנה מצוה מצד שהיא נמשכת
320 מעבירה הנה אינה נמשכת ממנה בעצם אבל במקרה ר״ל שאין מצות
התשובה נמשכת לחוטא בעצם ואומר אחטא ואשוב או אחטא ויום
הכפורים מכפר[136] שהרי לזה אינו מועיל התשובה שהרי אמרו חז״ל
שאלו הדברים מעכבין את התשובה[137] אבל התשובה למי שתקפו יצרו
וחטא על כרחו לזה בא התיקון שיעשה תשובה וישוב מחטאו ובא
325 אליו במצות עשה בעבור שלא יתיאש אך יעשה תשובה שהרי לפי
ה(?)[138] אינו מועיל. לכן בא הצווי במצות עשה שיעשה ולא הספיק
באמרו שאם יעשנה תהיה מקובלת.

והנה בזה תרצנו ספק אחר[139] שהיה בכאן וזה אם התשובה היא

---

131. תנחומא בובר נשא יט.

132. לא ברורה לי כוונת המלים כאן, ואפשר שחסר משהו לפני המלה „כמו." כנראה הוא מתיחס
לרעיון שאדם הראשון היה זקוק לתשובה ולכן טוב היה שהיא כבר היתה מוכנה בשבילו.

133. השוה רמב״ם הלכות תשובה ה,א–ב.

134. מועד קטן יז א ועוד.

135. עי' האי גאון מצוטט ע״י רש״י שם, ותוס' חגיגה טז א ד״ה ויעשה.

136. השוה יומא פה ב.

137. שם.

138. המלה מחוקה בכ״י ואיננה קריאה. אולי יש לגרוס „הנראה."

139. על יסוד המסקנה שהתשובה היא מצוה מתעוררת השאלה מאיזה סוג של מצוה היא
ואומר הדרשן שהפתרון לבעיה זו נובע ממה שהוא כבר אמר.

מצוה שכלית או מקובלת לבד[140] ר״ל שהשכל לא יחייבה אם לא היינו

330 מצווים בה. והנה בזה כבר היא מתורצת, וזה שהתשובה לפי הנר׳ לא
מן הדין שתועיל[141] כי מה תועיל התשובה בפה למי שכפר במעשיו ועוד
הדברים שעברו שעליהם מי יוכל לבטל מציאות שהיה להם כבר ומי יוכל לתקן
את אשר עוותו? וכן מצינו במה שאמרו,[142] שאלו לחכמה חוטא מה
עונשו? אמ׳ לו חטאים תרדף רעה[143] שאלו יתמו חטאים מן הארץ.[144]

335 שאלו לנבואה חוטא מה עונשו? אמר הנפש החוטאת היא תמות.[145]
שאלו לתורה חוטא מה עונשו? יביא קרבן ויכפר. שאלו להקב״ה,[146]
יעשה תשובה ויכפר. הנה הורו במאמרם זה שמצד שמחייב השכל
והדין לא היה ראוי שיכפר זה האיש במאמר פיו ולזה אמר שאלו
לחכמה במה שיתחייב שכלה ואח״כ לרוח הקדש שהיא השגה יותר

340 ואח״כ לנבואה שהיא למעלה ממנו והיו שואלים לה מצד הדין מה
יתחייב שכלה באיש החוטא והנה ג״כ שאלו לתורה היאך יתחייב
השכל כפי הדין והנה כולם (17 ב) השיבו שלפי מה ששכלם מחייב אין
האיש מכופר אלא בעונש. והנה אע״פ שתמצא בתורה ובנבואה
תשובה הרבה הנה זהו מצד מה שהיה הב״ה אומר הב״ה מצד טובו וחסדו

345 לא מצד הדין. וזהו מה שאמרו חז״ל שאלו להב״ה.[147]
והנה בזה הורו שמדרגת התורה הוא למטה מהמדרגה שהם
קורים הב״ה וכך הוא האמת ליודעים[148] שהרי אמרו שהתשובה
היא מגעת לספירה מלמטה למעלה של שם מדתייעם קראת אל[149]
ומדרגת התורה היא ביסוד[150] ולזה כיון הנביא באמרו שובה ישראל עד

---

140. על הבחנה זו בין שני סוגי המצוות, עי׳ הערה 88 לתרגום.

141. ז״א שלא מתקבל לשכל שהתשובה מועילה.

142. ירושלמי מכות ב ו ומקבילות, ועי׳ הערה 90 לתרגום.

143. משלי יג כא.

144. תה׳ קד לה. לפי המשך הדיון, צריך לגרוס „שאלו לרוח הקדש חוטא מה עונשו אמר יתמו וכו׳. אינני מכיר מקור בספרות חז״ל הכולל שאלה ותשובה זו.

145. יח׳ יח ד.

146. להקדוש ברוך הוא. צריך להוסיף „חוטא מה עונשו? אמר" וכו׳.

147. לקדוש ברוך הוא.

148. הכוונה למקובלים.

149. עי׳ הערה 92 לתרגום.

150. בדרך כלל, התורה קשורה לספירת מלכות או תפארת, לא ליסוד.

350 יי¹⁵¹ שרצה בזה שלא ישוב למדת הדין¹⁵² שהוא למטה שהרי אם ישוב
לה התשובה לא תהיה מקובלת שזאת המדה אינה דנה אלא כפי הדין
אבל המדה שלמעלה ממנה¹⁵³ אינה דין בעצם אלא רחמים לולי שיש לה
צד הדין מצד ההשפעה שהיא מושפעת.¹⁵⁴ וכן אמר ג״כ אם תשוב ישראל
נאם יי אלי תשוב¹⁵⁵ שרצה בזה שאם ישראל יעשו תשובה התשובה

355 הגמורה שיעשו לא יועיל אם לא יעשו לשם יי¹⁵⁶ שהוא יעשה הדבר
ברצון שהוא רוצה להטיב למי שירצה אע״פ שאינו ראוי כמו שאמרו
ז״ל¹⁵⁷ על וחנותי את אשר אחון¹⁵⁸ אע״פ שאינו ראוי. הרי שהתשובה
עולה עד למעלה וזה רמוז שהתשובה מגעת עד כסא הכבוד.¹⁵⁹

ובזה יתישב מה שאמרו ז״ל במקום שבעלי תשובה עומדי׳ אין
360 צדיקים גמורים יכולין לעמוד¹⁶⁰ שהרי לפי האמת בעלי תשובה הם
עולים למעלה מן הצדיקים שהצדיקים הם נדונים בב״ד של מטה
ובעלי תשובה עולים עד למעלה. וזהו שאמרו ג״כ בני חיי ומזוני לאו
בזכותא תליא מילתא אלא במזלא¹⁶¹ שרצו בזה שאלו הדברים תלוין
כפי הרצון שאע״פ שמן הדין יהיה חייב כפי המזל שיש לו לשם הוא

365 ניצול.¹⁶² ולזה כיון הנביא באמרו כי ה׳ שופטינו,¹⁶³ שרצה בזה שהוא
השופט והוא הסופר והוא המלך והוא יושיענו¹⁶⁴ שאין מי יאמר לו מה

151. הושע יד ב.
152. ז״א, התשובה צריכה לעלות מעל ספירת גבורה, הנקראת גם ״דין.״
153. ספירת חסד.
154. עי׳ הערה 96 לתרגום.
155. יר׳ ד א.
156. למדת הרחמים.
157. ברכות ז א.
158. שמות לג יט.
159. יומא פו א.
160. ברכות לד ב, אחד המאמרים הקשים להוגי ישראל בימי ביניים.
161. מועד קטן כ א.
162. על פירוש זה למלה ״המזל,״ עי׳ הערה 102 לתרגום. בספר שערי אורה כתוב, ״הוא המזל העליון הידוע בכתר...ונקרא מזל, כי ממנו נוזלים הכוחות ובכל הספירות ובכל בני העולם....והטעם, לפי שכל הרוצה להשיג שלושה דברים הללו [ז״א בני חיי ומזוני] אינו יכול להשיג אותם בעולם הזה על פי הדין הנקרא זכות...ראוי להעלות כוונתו למעלה, לפנים מן העולם הבא, עד מקום הכתר.״
163. יש׳ לג כב.
164. שם.

תעשה.[165] וזהו מה שאמרו ז"ל על והאר פניך ונושעה[166] אם אין לו
אלא הארת פניך,[167] שרצו לרצונו שאין מי שיכריחנו.

והנה אע"פ שהאמת הוא כך שהתשובה היא מצד החסד ועולם
החסד יבנה,[168] עכ"ז יש לתת טעם לתשובה היאך הוא מועילה בוידוי
וחרטה ושאר תנאי התשובה[169] ולא יועיל בענין אחר שאם שיעשה
הכאות בגופו[170] או דבר אחר, שמאחר שהיא מצד החסד איזה דבר
שיעשה היה די. אבל יש לומ' (18א) שכשאנו עושים תשובה אנו
הורגים בכאן למי שחטא החוטא בכאן היצר הרע.[171] הנה לזה ראוי
להורגו, השכל שלא חטא אין ראוי שיהיה הוא נענש כמו שכתוב
בספר האורה[172] על פסוק האף תספה צדיק עם רשע,[173] שהנה נתכוון
בזה שאם יש באדם חלק שהוא צדיק אם לא חטא שאין ראוי
שיכרת אם לא חטא עם האחר. והנה בעשיית התשובה אנו הורגים
ליצר הרע שהרי הוא נחשב כמת כמו שאמרו ז"ל[174] דוד קם עליו
והרגו במאי הרגו בשק ותענית. הרי בזה יראה שמשפטי השם אמת[175]
שאינו רוצה שיענש אלא מי שחטא.

והרי גדר התשובה שאם בא דבר עבירה לידו באותו פרק באותו
מקום באותה אשה[176] ונבל[177] ממנה הוא בעל תשובה שהנה הורה
בזה שכבר מת המזיק והלך לו. ואולי זהו פירוש הכתוב שאמר

165. ע"פ איוב ט יב.

166. תה' פ ד.

167. מדרש תהלים על הפסוק, וצ"ל אין ל נ ו.

168. ע"פ תה' פט ג, ועי' הערה 104 לתרגום.

169. על יסודות התשובה, עי' הערה 105 לתרגום.

170. עי' הערה 106 לתרגום.

171. בדרך כלל מדובר על כבישת היצר, והריגת יצר הרע מוגבלת להקשר אסכטולוגי. אבל ראה
ויקרא רבה ט,א"זובח תודה יכבדנני, זה עכן שזבח את יצרו בתודה," וגם המקור בהערה 174 למטה.

172. עי' הערה 108 לתרגום.

173. בר' יח בג.

174. השוה ירושלמי סוטה ה, ה: "אברהם עשה יצר הרע טוב...אבל דוד לא היה יכול בו והרגו
בלבו." והשוה אברהם סבע, צרור המור, כי תשא (שמות, עמ' כד א–ב),"העושה מהריגת גלית ע"י דוד
משל להריגת יצר הרע.

175. ע"פ תה' יט י.

176. יומא פו ב, השוה הלכות תשובה ה א.

177. כך בכ"י, וכנראה צ"ל ונבדל או וניצל.

יחזקאל, ובשוב רשע מרשעתו ועשה משפט וצדקה ואמרתם לא
יתכן דרך ה׳,[178] שהנה הורה בזה שישראל היו משיגים אותו על שהוא
אומר שהרשע ימלט בעשיית תשובה והיו אומרים שזה דבר לא
יתכן מצד השכל שהיאך איפשר שבעשיית התשובה יהיה ניצול
מהעונש שכבר קדם לו בעשיית הרע ולזה היו אומרים לא יתכן דרך
ה׳ כלו׳ אין זה דבר שהשכל יחייבהו אבל השכל יחייב שזה האיש
ימות אם הוא חייב לא בענין אחר ובעבור זה אמר הלא דרכיכם לא
יתכן[179] כלו׳ מה שאני עושה הוא בדין ובשורה שאני הורג למחזיק
לבד לא כמו שאתם עושים שאתם הורגים צדיק עם רשע כשיחטא
איש בדבר המשפט.

וכבר יש בכאן טעמים אחרים לראשונים במה שאמרו שהתשובה
היא מועילה מצד שאדם עושה חרטה על מה שעשה והדבר שאדם
על עשייתה[180] הרי הוא כאילו לא נעשה בבחירה אבל יורה שהוא
פועל שנעשה בתכלית[181] וכמו שהאריכו בזה הטעם בספר העיקרים[182]
ואיפשר זה אבל מכל מקום יראה שהטעם שאמרתי הוא יותר
מספיק.

והנה לפי הטעם הראשון יתישב מאמר רז״ל שאמרו[183] בעל
תשובה זדונות נעשו לו כזכיות כשהוא שב מאהבה וכשהוא שב
מיראה נעשו לו כשגגות. הסבה בזה שמצד שבעל התשובה כשהוא
יתחרט על עונו הוא מצטער הרבה בחלק השכלי שזה חטא על כרחו
ומפני זה ראוי שתחשב לו לצדקה[184] (18 ב) זה הצער שהוא עובר מצד
השיתוף לזה אמר אזעק[185] שאם הוא שב מיראה שאינה מדרגה כל

178. יח׳ לג יט-כ.

179. יח׳ יח כה, כט.

180. כנראה יש לגרוס „והדבר שאדם [מתחרט] על עשייתה״.

181. לפי הקשר ולפי הדיון בספר העיקרים (ראה למטה), המלה הנכונה כאן צריכה להיות „בטעות״.

182. יוסף אלבו, ספר העיקרים, מאמר ד פרק כז: „וגמר בלבו שהפעל שעשה בראשונה היה בטעות״. עי׳ הערה 111 לתרגום.

183. יומא פו ב. גם הוא מאמר בעייתי ביותר במחשבת ישראל של ימי הביניים, והשוה שם טוב ן׳ שם טוב, דרשות התורה, עמ׳ פא ד.

184. ע״פ תה׳ קו לא, „לצדקה״ במובן לזכותו.

185. נראה שנפלה טעות כאן בטקסט, ולא ברורה לי גירסא מתקבלת על הדעת.

כך זכיות נחשבים לו כשגגות ואם שב הוא מחמת אהבה שהוא

מדרגה גמורה הנה בזה יהיו זדונות נחשבים כזכיות מחמת הצער

שקיבל מצד האהבה ולפי הטעם השני[186] לא יתייישב יפה פירוש אלו

410   המאמרים שהרי כשזה האיש יעשה חרטה למה יועיל חרטתו שיעשו

זדונותיו זכיות? די לו במה שעבר שלא יחשב יי לו עון לשיהיו

זדונותיו זכיות אין השכל מחייב זה.

והנה לפי הטעם הראשון תמצא שהמשפט שעושי׳ האנשים

באנשים שהורגים אותם על עון אשר בידם הסבה בזה היא לפי

415   שאינן יכולין להרוג למזיק שהיאך יוציאו היצר הרע ויהרגו אותו

ואע״פ שבאותה שעה שהוא בן מות הוא מתחרט חרטה

גמורה לפי הנר׳ מי יודע בני אדם אם זה תשובה גמורה מצד שהוא

רואה את נפשו ברע שהרי הוא יוצא להריגה וכשינצל מזה ישוב

לקלקולו. הנה אין מקום בזה אלא להשם שהוא בוחן לב וכליות[187]

420   וכשאדם יחטא אליו והוא מתחרט הוא יודע אם התשובה גמורה

היא או לא. ואולי יהיה זה קצת סבה למה שאמרו ז״ל[188] שמי שיצא

מבית דין זכאי אע״פ שראו בו אחר כך מן הדין שהוא חייב מיתה

שלא ידונו לו כמו שאמרנו על ונקי וצדיק אל תהרוג,[189] שהיה הסבה

בזה שמאחר שהש״י יושב עמהם בדבר המשפט[190] וזה האיש באותה

425   הגזרה יצא זכאי יראה שהוא פועל אלהי ששם בלבבם זה מצד שראה

שזה האיש אע״פ שחטא הנה הוא בחרטה גמורה ולא ישוב עוד

לכסלו ובעבור זה ראוי שיעבירו לו וזה מה שאמר כי לא אצדיק

רשע,[191] שרצה בזה שהש״י היה עמהם בדבר המשפט ואם הוא היה

רואה שזה האיש הוא רשע יחזור לקלקולו לא היה מצדיק אותו

430   אבל מאחר שאנו רואים שכבר יצא צדיק[192] כבר יראה שהשם צופה

בעתידות וידע שזה האיש יהיה צדיק.

186. זה של בעל ספר העיקרים, הדן במאמר זה במאמר ד פרק כה.

187. ע״פ תה׳ ז י.

188. סנהדרין לג ב.

189. שמות כג ז.

190. השוה ספרי דברים קץ על דב׳ יט יז, סנהדרין יט א, שמות רבה ה,יב.

191. שמות כג ז. עי׳ הערה 120 לתרגום.

192. ואולי יש לגרוס כאן „זכאי״

והנה אעפ״כ שיש טעם לתשובה שהיא מחייבת מצד השכל עם
כל זה מחוייבים אנו להורות למה שאמרנו שהתשובה היא מצד
החסד שהרי היה מן הדין שזה האיש כשחטא לא יהא חוטא והנה
האיש שיטה לדרך הטובה למה בחר ברעה? אבל יראה שהשכל יש
לו צד מבוא בעשיית (19א) הרע ולפי׳ היה ראוי שיהיה נענש לולי
חסד אלהי שהשגיח עלינו בעין החמלה וראה כי עפר אנחנו[193] כשזה
הדבר לא נעשה בבחירה גמורה ולפי׳ תקן עלינו שנהרג למזיק כמו
שאמרתי ובזה נוציא ידי חובותינו.

והנה אע״פ שהיה חסד אלהי לא נתן לנו התשובה בהחלט
שהרי יש דברים שאין להם תשובה עד יום המיתה ויש דברים
שיסורין ממרקין[194] ויש דברים שמעכבים את התשובה[195] כל זה גודל
העבירה[196] שאם יש בעבירה חלול השם שזהו מי שיחטיא לאחרים
הנה אין ראוי שיכופר לו עד יום מותו[197] שאז יהיה המזיק נהרג
לגמרי. ואף העבירה אינה כל כך גדולה ראוי שיהיה נדון ביסורין
בעבור שאלו ג׳כ הורגים מזיק ומכניעין ליצר הרע. ואם הוא עבירה
שמטבעה היא שלא יחזור בתשובה גמורה על זה ומצד קלותה
שהיא קלה בעיניו כמו כ״ד דברים שמעכבין את התשובה[198] עבירות
מזה המין כמו האוכל בסעודה שאינה מספקת לבעליה שזאת
העבירה מצד שהיא קלה בעיניו לא יחזור ממנה שאינו רואה עון
אשר חטא כמו שכתב׳ הרמב״ם בהלכות מדע.[199]

ויש ג״כ עבירות באלו הכ״ד שמחמת ההתמדה יהיה קשה
מהסרתם או מחמת שאע״פ שירצה לעשות תשובה אינו יכול כמו
הגוזל את הרבים שאינו יודע למי ישוב הגזלה אשר גזל[200] הנה

193. ע״פ תה׳ קג יד.
194. יומא פו א, רמב״ס, הלכות תשובה א,ד.
195. ראה הרי״ף סוף מסכת יומא, רמב״ס הלכות תשובה פרק ד, המאירי חבור התשובה, עמ׳
112–72. וע׳ בהמשך.
196. כנראה צריך לגרוס ״כל זה [לפי] גודל העבירה.״
197. השוה רמב״ס, הלכות תשובה סוף פרק א.
198. עי׳ הלכות תשובה ד א.
199. שם ד ד.
200. עי׳ שם ד ג, והערה 129 לתרגום.

455 בדברים אלו ודומים לאלו אמרו רז"ל שאלו הדברים מעכבים את
התשובה[201] ר"ל שאע"פ שירצה לחזור בתשובה לא יוכל. והנה אין
בזה קוצר בחסד האלהי שהוא עושה עמנו שהוא מקבל אותנו
בתשובה שלא קבל אותנו באלו הדברים מאחר שהחסרון היה
מצדנו שאין אנו עושים תשובה גמורה. וכן ג"כ מה שאמרו שמי
460 שאומר אחטא ואשוב אין מספיקי' בידו לעשות תשובה[202] הנה
הסבה כבר נתבארה שמאחר שזה האיש שם הדבר עשיית הרע
והוא מחטיא בזה הכונה האלהית הנה אין ראוי שיקובל בתשובה
שלא יהיה עבירה גוררת מצוה כמו שביארנו.

והנה לא יהיה קשה עליך על מה שכתבנו למעלה שהתשובה היא
מצוה היאך איפשר שיהיה מצוה, שהרי גדר המצוה היא שישמח
465 בעשייתה שהרי בזו[203] שזדונות נעשו לו כזכיות[204] כמו שכתבנו הנה
אין ספק שיהיה בזה שמחה גדולה והנה מצד אחר יראה שאי אפשר
(19ב) שיהיה בזה שמחה שהרי גדר התשובה היא יגון ואנחה על מה
שלא כדין וכהלכה והנה לפי זה היאך יתחברו ששון ושמחה?[205]
שהרי אי אפשר שנאמר שבעוד שהוא מתעסק בתשובה הוא מחוייב
470 שיהיה לו יגון ואחר שעשאה הוא מחויב שיהיה לו שמחה מצד
עשה מצוה הנה זה אי אפשר שהרי אנו מצוים שאפילו בשעת
המצוה יהיה לנו שמחה[206] ועוד שאפי' יהיה הדבר כן הנה בהכרח
יהיה השמחה יתירה על היגון שהרי הסבה התכליתית יהיה יותר
חשובה מאחר שבאחרית יהיה לנו שמחה ויהיה בטל היגון ואנחה.

הנה זה הספק כבר נסתפק בו הרב ר' חסדאי ז"ל[207] ומה שהשיב
475 בזה הוא שהנה בכאן יהיה לנו יגון מקצת שמחה מקצת. יהיה לו

---

201. עי' הערה 130 לתרגום.

202. יומא פה ב.

203. אולי צ"ל „והרי בזו": במצוה זו של תשובה.

204. יומא פו ב.

205. עי' הערה 133 לתרגום.

206. השוה בחיי בן אשר, כד הקמח, ערך „שמחה": „השמחה על מעשה המצוה בדרך הבינוני
הוא שנצטוה אדם עליה, ועל זה הזכיר דוד בכאן: עבדו את ה' בשמחה, ביאר: כי השמחה שלמות
העבודה".

207. עי' חסדאי קרשקש, ס' אור ה', מאמר ג, חלק ב, כלל ב, פרק ב.

שמחה מצד הדבקות שהשיג בעשיית התשובה שעלה למדרגה
העליונה יותר מצדיק גמור ויהיה לו אנחה מצד הזמן שכבר עבר
שלא היה דבק בעבודת האלהות שהרי הוא מכיר עכשיו שהיה ראוי
שיחשב לו לאשמה גדולה היאך עבר והמרה את רוח קדשו וכל עוד   480
שיהיה יותר במעלה עכשיו יכיר החסרון מן הימים שעברו שלא היה
דבק בעבודה המחוייבת. זה דעת הרב הנזכר בזה הספק תשובתו.
והנה יש להשיב בזה בדרך אחרת והוא שהמצוות התלויות בעצבון,
כמו שאנו מצווים להתאבל על חרבן ירושלם ולעשות הספד על
המתים, הנה בכאן לא יתחבר השמחה בשעת העשיה ולא אחר כך   485
אע״פ שעשינו מצוה גדולה וימשך לנו מזה תועלת גדולה כמו שאמרו
ז״ל המתאבל על ירושלם זוכה ורואה בשמחתה?[208] ג״כ על מי שמוריד
דמעות על אדם כשר שהב״ה מניחם בבית גנזיו וכו׳?[209] הנה בזה יורו
שיש לאלו המצוות שלימות גדול.

והנה לפי זה ראוי להביט איך יתחבר בכאן שמחה לא בשעת   490
עשיית המצוה שהרי אין ביגון ואנחה ולא אחר שיעשנה שהנה לפי
זה חרבן ירושלם יהיה לנו סבה להביא שמחה וזה דבר שאינו ראוי.
אבל יראה שבאלו המצוות יש ב׳ בחינות לדאגה ולשמחה כמו מי
שבוכה על מתו שהרי אין ספק שכשמוריד דמעות הוא מקל באנחה
אע״פ שיש לו דאגה גדולה יותר היה לו אם לא היה בוכה הנה מזה   495
הצד ג״כ בעשיית הדאגה שהיא של מצוה הנה בהכרח הוא שיהיה
לנו עצבון בכלים הגופניים שכלם עצבים[210] ויהיה לנו שמחה מצד
השכל כשהם יקבלו מזה הדאגה (20א) מצד שהשכל ישער שזה
מצוה אלהית שיהיה לנו עצבון ביגון ואנחה. והנה יהיה שמחה
ואנחה בבחינות מתחלפות השכל גזר שראוי שיקבלו זאת הדאגה   500
בשמחה והנה אין בו משום דאגה אבל הכחות החמריות הם באנחה
ודאגה. ומזה הצד איפשר ג״כ בתשובה שיהיה יגון ושמחה שמחה
מצד השכל שהוא מתעדן בחרטה ויגון בכלים הגופניים שאם[211]

208. בבא בתרא ס ב ועוד.
209. שבת קה ב.
210. אולי צ״ל עצובים.
211. אולי צ״ל שהם.

יקבלו הדאגה. והרי זה כמו שמקבל המיתה על קדשת השם שאין
ספק שיהיה לו בכאן דאגה בשעה שהוא מקבל המיתה שהכחות 505
הגופניות הם מתפעלות בזה[212] אבל מצד מה שהוא משער שבזה הוא
משיג דבקות אמיתי השכל הוא שמח בזה.

ועוד יש להכחיש הקדמת הרב[213] ונאמר שזה האיש ראוי לו
הדאגה מצד שאינו יודע שהוא בעל תשובה עד יום מותו. אל תאמן
בעצמך עד יום מותך.[214] ומי יודע אם ישוב לקלקולו הראשון. אע"פ 510
שבא דבר עבירה לידו וניצל ממנה הנה אם יוסיף לחטוא בה עונשו
מרובה ולפי' ראוי לו שיאנח כל ימיו שמא ישוב לקלקולו ועדיין לא
הגיע לסוף התשובה כדי שישמח שהזדונות נעשו לו כזכיות. הנה די
בזה לזה הספק.

והנה ג"כ לא יקשה בעיניך למה שלא תמצא בכל התורה מזאת 515
התשובה מבוארת שיהיה מצוה. לא מצינו תשובה אלא בלשון
והתודה,[215] ומזה הצד מנו מוני המצות שהתשובה מצוה מצד שהוידוי
מצוה.[216] אין זה ממה שיקשה שפשיטא שהרי הוידוי הוא צריך הוא
לחרטה שאם לא יהיה בלב כמו שהוא אומר בפה מה יועיל זה אבל
בהכרח שיהיה בכאן חרטה ולפי' קצרה התורה בביאור דברי 520
התשובה כי כשיאמר שיתודו שפשיטא שבענין כזה דברים שבפה
אינם דברים.[217] ועוד יש לומר שהתורה קצרה בזה היתה בשביל
שהחרטה הוא דבר שהשכל יחייבה שהרי כשאדם אם הוא ירא
שמים בהכרח הוא שיתחרט ולפי' אמרו בתורה בצר לך ומצאוך
[...] ושבת,[218] שהרי הוא כאומר אני יודע בך שכשיהיו לך אלו הצרות 525
תשוב עד [יהוה אלהיך]. וכן אמר בפרשת אתם נצבים והיה כי יבואו
עליך כל הדברים האלה הברכה והקללה [...] והשבות אל לבבך

212. כאן דוחה אבוהב את המסורת האומרת כי המת על קדוש השם אינו מרגיש את כאב
העינוים. עי' במבוא.
213. פתרון הרב קרשקש שסוכם לעיל.
214. ברכות כט א.
215. ויק' ה ה (והתודה), במ' ה ו (והתודו).
216. למשל רמב"ם, ראה לעיל הערה 100, ס' החינוך, מצוה שסג.
217. משחק על המאמר שבקידושין מט ב, "דברים שבלב אינם דברים."
218. דב' ד ל.

בכל הגוים,[219] הנה אמר בכאן שישוב מצד שכלו בראותו גודל צערו.

ואמ׳ כי המצוה הזאת לא נפלאת היא ממך[220] מצד השכל[221] ולא

530   רחוקה היא,[222] (20ב) כשתאמר שאתה צריך לעשותה דברים שהם

קשה המציאות אין הדבר כן שלא רחוקה היא. ואמר אח״כ לא

בשמים היא,[223] כאומר לא תאמר שהתשובה אינך בה בעל בחירה

שהרי אתה בבחירת הרע מוכרח ואם מן השמים לא יביאו לך

רפואה שישנו את טבעך אינך יכול לעשותה[224] והנה האריך במה

535   שאמר לאמר מי יעלה לנו השמימה ויקחה לנו;[225] לבאר שאע״פ שהיא

מן השמים בצד מה כמו שאמרו ז״ל בא לטהר מסייעין אותו,[226]

אינה בעצם לשם אמר[227] שהיא בשמים. וג״כ אמר ולא מעבר לים

היא לאמר[228] כאומר לא תאמר שהמקומות גורמים כמו שאומרים

רבים שמקום אחד יתחייב שלא יעשה תשובה מה שלא יהיה כן

540   באחר[229] ולפי זה היית צריך ללכת שם ללומדי[230] באי זה דרך הם

מונהגים שתעשה אתה כן. אין באמת ככה שהאמת קרוב אליך

הדבר מאד שהתורה בפיך ותעשה חרטה בלבבך לעשות התשובה.[231]

הרי נתבאר שהחרטה היא יסוד התשובה שכל אדם ירא שמים

יעשה אותה ולפי׳ לא בא בתורה בפי׳.[232]

545   ואולי לזאת הסבה לא נתבארה בתורה תשובת אדם הראשון עם

219. דב׳ ל א.

220. דב׳ ל יא.

221. עי׳ הערה 142 לתרגום.

222. דב׳ שם.

223. דב׳ ל יב.

224. עי׳ הערה 143 לתרגום.

225. דב׳ ל יב.

226. שבת קד א ועוד.

227. אולי צ״ל ״לאמר.״

228. דב׳ ל יג.

229. עי׳ הערה 145 לתרגום.

230. כך בכ״י וכנראה צ״ל ״ללמוד.״

231. ע״פ דב׳ ל יד. בכ״י כתוב ״שהתורה בפיך,״ אבל לפי ההקשר יותר מתקבל לגרוס ״שתתודה בפיך״ או ״שתתודה בפיך.״ השוה אברהם סבע, צרור המור, דברים עמ׳ כח א:״שיודה פשעיו בפיו ויתחרט מהם ויעשה תשובה.״

232. בפירוש.

היות שלפי האמת עשה תשובה וזאת היתה הסבה שנתבטלה
הגזירה שנגזרה עליו כי ביום אכלך ממנו מות תמות[233] כמו שאמרו
חז״ל[234] לפי שתשובת אדם הראשון לא היה דבר בפה לפי שהתשובה
לא היתה דבר שהשכל יחייבה ולפי׳ אדם הראשון לא עשאה בפה
מצד שהיה חושב שלא יועיל אבל בלבו היה לו חרטה גמורה והנה
השי״י ראה חרטת לבו שהיה נעשה בתכלית[235] וקבלה ואז הרויח לו.[236]
אדם הראשון ראה זה וידע שמפני התשובה שעשה בא לו זה ולמד
לבניו אחריו דרך החרטה ומפני זה עשה תשובה[237] שראה שאביו
הועיל לו להצילו לבטל גזירתו ונכתבה בתורה. או נאמר שהשם אמר
לו לאדם הראשון הטיבות כי היה עם לבבך[238] ולפי׳ יתבטל גזירתך
והוא למד זה לבנו.

והנה תשובת בנו הועילה כמו שכתו׳ במדרש הנעלם[239] במה
שאמרו שמקללת נע ונד[240] שנתקלל לא נתקיים בו אלא א׳ מהם
והוא שיהיה נד כמו שאמר וישב בארץ נד קדמת עדן[241] שנע ונד
פירוש כדברי רז״ל שהוא היה הולך מעיר לעיר ובכל מקום שהיה
יושב הארץ מתרגזת תחתיו[242] והנה מזה נתבטל הא׳. הרי נתבאר
הסבה שלא נתפרש בתורתינו ענין התשובה בהחלט.

והנה אחר תירוץ אלו יש לספק בעניינים אחרים מעניין התשובה
הראשון (21א) מצד הזמן שעם היות שיש סבה[243] למה נתיחדו אלו
הזמנים ר״ה ויום הכפורים לתשובה כמו שכתב הר״ן בזה יש ב׳

550

555

560

565

---

233. בר׳ ב יז.

234. עי׳ הערה 148 לתרגום.

235. השוה לעיל (והערה 181). אמנם כאן המלה „בתכלית" נכונה ופירושה „בשלמות."

236. במובן הוספת שנים. ראה בראשית רבה יט,ח, הדורש „לרוח היום (בר׳ ג יח): הריני מחיה
לו את היום."

237. צריך לגרוס „עשה [וקין] תשובה." ועי׳ הערה 150 לתרגום.

238. ע״פ דבה״ב, ו ח.

239. זוהר חדש, יט ד, והשוה ויקרא רבה יה,ה.

240. בר׳ ד טב.

241. בר׳ ד טז.

242. השוה תנחומא בראשית ט.

243. לתשובה.

סבות[244] הא׳ מצד שהעולם נברא עכשיו ואדם הראשון היה נידון
בזה הזמן קבעו לבניו אחריו שיהיו נדונים בזה הזמן כמו שאמרו
במד׳,[245] והב׳ מצד שבזה הזמן שולט מזל מאזנים[246] ואז היא ראויה
לדין הואיל והעולם תלוי במאזנים. יהיה הסבה מה שיהיה הנה יש
לשאול למה אלו הי׳ ימים שבין ר״ה ליום כפור[247] הם נבדלים
שהראשון קדש והאחרון קדש קדשי׳ והאמצעיים חול וראוי היה
לפי השכל שיהיה האמצעי שלם כמו הראשון או יותר ממנו שמעלים
בקדש ואין מורידים[248] או לפחות יהיה כמו חול המועד ויתקנוהו
רבנן.[249]

570

והתשובה בזה על דרך חכמי האמת[250] שהנה ראש השנה היא
הספירה שהיא מלכות והנה אז אנו מתפללים שתהיה היא שלימה
לפי שאז היא יושבת בדין[251] ולפיכך אין אנו מזכירים בראש השנה
ראש חדש[252] לפי שראש חדש הוא מורה על השפעה שמקבלת מדת
מלכות מהספירות שלמעלה ממנו[253] ואז אין אנו יודעים מה יהיה.
לפיכך אין אנו מזכירים אותו ולפיכך אמרו ז״ל אי זהו חדש
שהלבנה מתכסה בו הוא ראש השנה,[254] והנה כשיהיה שלמה זאת
המדה[255] כל המדות כולם בשלימותם וכשהיא לא תהיה מליאה
האחרו׳ נשארו במלואם ובתקונם ולפי׳ אין אנו עושים קדש אלא

575

580

244. ראה ר׳ נסים גירונדי על הרי״ף לראש השנה טז א, ד״ה בראש, וחדושי הר״ן על מסכת
ראש השנה, ירושלים תשל״ב, עמ׳ כג ב.

245. במדרש, למשל פסיקתא דרב כהנא פסקא כג, ועי׳ הערה 154 לתרגום.

246. השוה פסיקתא רבתי פיסקא מ ט ומקורות אחרים בהערה 155 לתרגום.

247. עי׳ הערה 156 לתרגום.

248. ברכות כח א ומקבילות.

249. לא ברור לי, ואולי הכוונה היא שלפי תקנות חז״ל יש בחול המועד הגבלות במלאכה, מה
שאין כן בימים שבין ר״ה ליוה״כ.

250. ז״א המומחים בקבלה.

251. ראה זהר ג, רלא א, ועי׳ הערה 159 לתרגום.

252. עי׳ המקורות בהערה 160 לתרגום.

253. ראש חדש קשור ללבנה, המקבלת את אורו ממאור אחר, כמו שספירת מלכות מקבלת
השפעה מספירות שמעליה.

254. ראש השנה ח ב, לד ב (במקור: „איזהו חג שהחודש מתכסה בו״).

255. ספירת מלכות.

הראשונה והאחרונ׳ שאם היינו עושים קדש הימים האמצעיים היה
585 מורה שיש בהם פירוד חלילה וחס.[256] והנה לפי טעמי בני אדם[257]
שהם נוהגים לתת לדברים מהותם י״ל שלא קבעו שום קדושה
באלו הימים לפי שהאדם צריך לעשות בהם תשובה וללכת ולהשתדל
בכל עוז אל איזה מקום שעשה שום עבירה לתקנה[258] ולפי׳ ראוי שלא
יהיה בהם שום קדושה כדי שיוכל לעשות כל התיקונים שאפשר לו
590 שחטא. הרי בכאן תרוץ לענין חלוק הזמן בתשובה.

והנה בענין התשובה יש ספקות אחרות והם אלו: ספק א׳ שכפי
הסברא שאומ׳ שכר מצות בריא בעלמא ליכא[259] כמו שאמרו ז״ל
במסכת קדושין[260] והמשורר ג״כ יראה שהיה לו זאת הסברא כשאמר
עד אבוא אל מקדשי אל,[261] שהנה הורה בזה שהרשעים (221ב) הם
595 בשלוה ובהשקט בזה העולם[262] א״כ אין[263] אנו מתפללים ואומרים
זכרנו לחיים[264] שהנה הורה בזה שכשנחזור בתשובה ונהיה דבקים
נשיג חיים. והרי אין הדבר ככה, שכל עוד שנהיה דבקים לא נשיג
אלו החיים, ששכר המצוה ליתיה בזה העולם אבל בעולם הבא וא״כ
התשובה לא יהיה כלי להשיג חיים[265] אבל יהיה כלי להשיג הכנה.[266]
600 והנה אין להשיב ולומר שכשאנו אומרים זכרנו לחיים אין אנו
מכוונין לאלו החיים הגשמיים אבל אנו מכוונים לחיים אמתיים
כמו שכתב בספר האורה,[267] שהרי לפי כונת כל העולם כשאומרים

---

256. ברור כי עשרת ימי התשובה רומזים לעשר הספירות (ראה רמב״ן, "דרשה לראש השנה;"
בכתבי רמב״ן, א רכא, ופירוש התורה על ויקרא כג כד בסוף), והנהגת הימים שבין ר״ה ליוה״כ
כימי חול מוצדקת בכך שהיא מבטיחה את ההתאחדות עולם הספירות. אבל הדרשן אינו מסביר
איך ייחוס קדושה לימים האמצעיים יביא לידי פירוד בעולם הספירות.

257. בניגוד לטעם חכמי הקבלה. כאן בא טעם המתקבל על הדעת בלי חכמה נסתרת.

258. עי׳ הערה 164 לתרגום.

259. כך בכ״י, וברור שהסופר לא הבין מה שהוא כותב וצ״ל "בהאי עלמא."

260. קדושין לט א ("שכר מצוה") וחולין קמב א ("שכר מצוות").

261. תה׳ עג יז.

262. "מקדשי אל" מובן כבינוי לעולם הבא.

263. כך בכ״י, וכנראה צ״ל "איך."

264. בברכת אבות של תפילת ימים הנוראים.

265. עי׳ הערה 168 לתרגום.

266. לחיים נצחיים בעולם הבא.

267. עי׳ הערה 169 לתרגום. דעת מאוחרת של יעב״ץ היא "שכל כונתו בקשתנו היום על החחים

זכרנו לחיים אין כוונתם אלא אל אלו החיים כי מי יודע הנסתרות כשיתכוין אל אלו החיים?

ועוד יש להקשות ממאמר ז"ל שאמרו ובני חיי ומזוני לאו בזכותא [268] תליא מלתא אלא במזלא,[268] ר"ל שמה שאנו שואלים חיים מחמת התשובה אין אנו שואלים חיים שלאיהיו בעבודת השם אבל כוונתינו היא שנזכה לחיים שנהיה טובים שרשעים אפי' בחייהם קרויים מתים,[269] ולפיכך אנו אומרים וכתוב לחיים טובים.[270] והרי אנו רואים כל הצדיקים שהם חפצים באלו החיים לא למענם אלא מצד התכלית הנמשך בהם שהוא המטרה שאמרו ז"ל לאו בזכותא תליא מילתא אלא במזלא ירצו בזה שכשיהיה האדם חסיד אם המערכת הוא רע אין השם משנה מערכה שלו מצד שזה האיש אינו רוצה שישנה השם המערכה בשבילו כדי שיחסר לו מזכיותיו כמו שאירע לר' חנינא בן דוסא.[271] ואם המערכה שלו היא לטובה מתחברים אליו שני דברים המערכת והחסידות ומשיג טובות יותר ויותר ממה שמשיג מי שאין לו אלא מערכה והנה לפי זה אנו מתפללים לחיים שיזכנו השם שנהיה דבקים כל כך שנשוב במדרגת הצדיקים הגמורים שיש בהם כח לשנות את מערכתם מרעה לטובה כמו שעשה אברהם אבינו.[272]

או נאמר שאנו מתפללים על החיים לפי שהמערכה לא יתחייב העדר חיים לגמרי אלא על צד המעט ואנו מחזיקים עצמינו מרובא דרובא[273] לפיכך אנו מתפללים על (22א) כל הטובות. תאמר אם המערכה לא יחייב הרע יחייב הטוב שאין בין זה לזה אמצעי ולפי זה אין אנו צריכים להתפלל על הטוב שמאליו הוא יבא?[274] יש לומר שהמערכה לא יחייב דבר פרט אבל יחייב דבר כללי כמו שאמרו ז"ל האי מאן דיהא במאדים יהא גברא אשיד דם ומר נמי במאדים הואי מר נמי עניש

605

610

615

620

625

הידועים המוחלטים בשם חיים הם חיי העה"ב" (מצוטט בסדר עבודת ישראל, עמ' 383).

268. מועד קטן כח א.

269. בראשית רבה לט,ז ומקבילות.

270. בברכת מודים של ימים הנוראים, ועי' ההערה בסדר עבודת ישראל, עמ' 389.

271. עי' תענית כה א.

272. עי' שבת קנו א, והערה 174 לתרגום.

273. כוונת המלים איננה ברורה לי לגמרי. פירוש אפשרי נמצא בתרגום.

274. עי' הערה 175 לתרגום.

וקטיל.[275] הנה הורו בזה שמערכה לא יורה על דבר פרט אבל יורה על
דבר כללי שאם תגבר הזכות יהיה זה הכללי לטובה ואם לאו יהיה
לרעה ובזה ישכח[276] לזכות לשנות זה הכללי מרעה לטובה וכמו שכתב
ראב"ע בזה.[277] והנה לפי זה אפי' המערכת הרעה יועיל התפלה שהרי
המערכת הוא כללי ובכללי ישכח[278] לשנותו לטובה. אבל לפי מה
שפירשנו בבני חיי ומזוני[279] יראה שמערכת לפי זאת הסברא יחייב
בדבר פרט ולפי זה פי' הלשון הוא כך לאו בזכותא לבד תליא מילתא
שאף במזלא ג"כ תליא מלתא שמי שיש לו מזל יכול להשיגו[280] כמו מי
שיש לו זכות. ולפי זה יש מקום לתפלתי' שאנו מתפללים שנהיה
דבקים בתכלית הדבקות ונשיג החיים והטובות. או נאמר שאפי'
שהמערכת יתחייב שיבוא בטוב מתפללים אנו שהשם יקימוהו ולא
יבטלוהו.[281] הנה זהו היתר אלו הספקות.

והנה יש בכאן ספקות אחרות שמצאתי כתובים להר"ן[282] והם אלו:
אם האדם נידון בר"ה וגזר דינו נחתם ביום הכפורים מה יועיל אחר
כך בימות השנה תפלות ורפואות? והרי רז"ל אמרו אפי' חרב פשוטה
מונחת על צוארו של אדם לא ימנע עצמו מן הרחמים.[283] ב' מה
שאמרו רז"ל שהעולם נדון אחר רובו והיחיד נדון אחר רוב
העולם[284] מה יועיל לו זכותו אפי' שיהיה הוא ישר אינו מועיל לו. ג'
שאנו רואים שבמקום שיש עשרת אלפים בני אדם בשנים כתקנן
מתים מאה או מאתים על הרוב ובשנת הדבר מתים ג' אלפים או ד'
אלפים[285] והיאך איפשר זה שנשתנה כל כך רעתם שימותו כל כך בזה
השנה שלא מתו קודם לכן? ד' שאנו רואים לפעמים שהרפואה

630

635

640

645

275. השוה שבת קנו א, ועי' דרשות הר"ן, עמ' קלו.

276. כך בכ"י וברבור שצ"ל „יש כח."

277. למשל בפירוש לשמות ו,ג ול,ג, כא, ועי' הערה 177 לתרגום.

278. גם כאן צ"ל „יש כח."

279. מועד קטן כח א.

280. ז"א להשיג את החיים הארוכים.

281. כך בכ"י, וכנראה צ"ל „יקימנו ולא יבטלנו."

282. לא מצאתי ספקות אלה בחדושי הר"ן למסכת ראש השנה ולא בדרשות הר"ן.

283. ברכות י א.

284. השוה קידושין מ ב:„העולם נידון אחר רובו והיחיד נידון אחר רובו," ועי' הערה 180 לתרגום.

285. עי' הערה 181 לתרגום.

מועלת ותפלה וגבורה[286] מה היא הסבה אשר תחייב זה?

650 י"ל שכך הוא המידה אם זה האיש יגזר למיתה לית דין ולית דיין[287]
שיוכל לבטלה וכן ג"כ אם המערכת שלו רע בהחלט בהכרח הוא
שימות לולי אם לא יהיה כאברהם אבינו שיהיה כח בו לשנות המערכת.
אך אם הוא נידון לחיים בזה הוא כל חלוקים:[288] שאם זה האיש נתחבר
למקום שנגזור (22ב) עליו מיתת בית דין[289] ורוב מערכת לרעה ימות זה
655 האיש מאחר שיש בכאן הגזרה והמערכה ובזה הוא נדון אחר רובו
ולא יועיל לו לא הגבורה ולא הרפואה ולא התעלה[290] מאחר שיש בכאן
גזרה ולכן נמצא ברוב המתים בחולי הדבריי שלא תועיל להם הרפואה
שאם היה מועיל להם נמצא שהתחכמות האדם מבטל הגזירה
האלהית. אע"פ שכשיצאו ישראל מארץ מצרים נתבטל הגזירה[291] יש
665 לשאול[292] שמאחר שהארץ חריבה מיושביה תתקיים הגזירה במקצת.

ואם המערכת מחצה על מחצה בזה תועיל טבע האיש בעל החולי
והרפואה והתפלה לפי שגזר דינו לטובה ויעמוד אחר נגד אחר והנה
יכריח בזה החזיק או החולשה או טוב הרופא או רוע הרופא או צדק
התפלה. ואם מיעוט המערכת רע ורובו טוב האנשים האלה לא יקרה
670 להם חולי ואם יחלו יבראו[293] בלי רופא בלי חוזק הטבע בלי תפלה.
ואם תאמר היאך אמרנו שגזר דין לרעה לא תשתנה וגזר דין לטובה
תשתנה והלא מידה טובה מרובה ממדת פורענות,[294] י"ל לפי שהשם
יזכה בדינם קרוב לכל האנשים ואע"פ שחציים רשעים או רובם לפי
שאינו נר' עיר שיש בה עשרת אלפים בשנים כתקנן לא ימותו יותר
675 ממאה א"כ לא יהיה רשעים רק אחד ממאה.

ובזה יתורצו כל הקושיות ואפשר לתרץ באלו הקושיות תירוץ אחר
אבל אין לי מקום להאריך.

286. בריאות וחזק הגוף.
287. ע"פ ויקרא רבה כח א ועוד.
288. הרבה אפשרויות. עי' הערה 183 לתרגום.
289. של מעלה.
290. כך בכ"י, וכנראה צ"ל התפלה.
291. עי' הערה 185 לתרגום.
292. כנראה צ"ל להשיב.
293. צ"ל יבראו.
294. שבת ק ב.

16

The *Hesped* as Historical Record and Art-Form: Saul Levi Morteira's Eulogies for Dr. David Farar

No genre of Jewish preaching is more extensively discussed and fully documented in the ancient sources than the eulogy. While there is ample evidence for regular preaching in synagogues throughout the rabbinic period, the weekly sermon itself has no clear halakhic status. The proper structure and appropriate content, the place within the worship service and the qualifications of the preacher—all are undefined in the Talmudic halakhah. Our knowledge of Jewish preaching in antiquity is based almost entirely on the aggadic literature, with its hortatory statements about the importance of the sermon, its narrative accounts of individual preachers, and its reworking of sermonic material in new literary forms.[1]

The eulogy, by contrast, is an integral part of the halakhah governing the proper treatment of the dead. The legal ramifications of the eulogy are discussed in the classical rabbinic texts, and they are incorporated into the great codes *Arba'ah Turim* and *Shulḥan 'Arukh*.[2] No other homiletical form is given as extensive treatment in the classics of medieval Hebrew ethical literature.[3] There can be little doubt that eulogies were delivered over the dead, partic-

---

1. For general surveys of preaching during the Talmudic period, see Zunz; Heinemann, *Derashot* (with bibliography, p. 29); Heinemann, *Literature*, pp. 107–99 (with bibliography, p. 199); Bregman, pp. 3, 19, 36; Melamed, *Parashiyot*, pp. 20–26. For evidence of Jewish preaching derived from Christian writings, see Wills.

2. *Yoreh De'ah* 344a; cf. *The Tractate "Mourning,"* p. 19 and index s.v. "Eulogy"; *Entsiqlopediyah ha-Talmudit* 9:606–19; Nahmanides, *Torat ha-Adam*, in RaMBaN, 2:80–94; Math, p. 116c–d; Greenwald, 1:96–104. The ambiguity of the word *hesped*, which can mean "formal manifestation of mourning" as well as "eulogy," must be kept in mind in evaluating texts relevant to the history of the homiletical genre.

3. For example, the discussion in Bahya ben Asher, comment on Gen. 50:10–11, in *Torah*, 1:397; Bahya ben Asher, *Kad ha-Qemaḥ*, pp. 50–52; Me'iri, *Teshuvah*, pp. 618–22; Aboab, *Menorat ha-Ma'or*, pp. 440–51. In later ethical literature, the sermon of rebuke became the paramount genre of Jewish Preaching: see Saperstein, *Jewish Preaching*, pp. 412–27.

ularly for esteemed scholars and other important leaders, throughout the Middle Ages.[4]

It is therefore somewhat surprising to note that no examples of the prose eulogy have been preserved before a relatively late date. The Talmud contains a number of pithy, epigrammatic statements attributed to eulogists,[5] but these could hardly have been all that they said. Medieval Hebrew writers cultivated the poetic elegy (*qinah*) to a high level of sophistication,[6] but of the eulogy no records are extant. Even when, in the thirteenth century, Jewish preachers began to write collections of model sermons, the eulogy was not at first represented. For several centuries, the collections were organized according to the weekly Torah lessons, sometimes with holiday sermons added. Some of these sermons may have been used in connection with weddings or circumcisions, but there is no evidence of their use at a funeral service.

The texts of eulogies begin to appear in conjunction with the major transformation in the nature of the written sermon—from a model for future use to a record of something said in the past—for which abundant evidence exists in the middle of the fifteenth century.[7] As the record of the earliest Jewish eulogies has never been properly discussed, it is worth a brief assessment at this point.

As far as I can discover, the earliest extant Jewish eulogies are three that are preserved in St. Petersburg MS (see above, pp. 179–80). None of them provides the name of the deceased; the texts refer to "this distinguished *ḥasid*," "this distinguished rabbi who is before us," "our master, the rabbi, a great man." Furthermore, the descriptions of the men being eulogized are quite general, without reference to a single biographical fact that would help in identifying them. Nevertheless, these are clearly texts of specific eulogies rather than models, alluding to circumstances such as the place of delivery (the cemetery), the age of the deceased, and the preacher's decision to depart from some of the conventions of the genre. The second of the three shows

4. See, for example, Goitein, *Mediterranean Society*, 2:216 and 567 n. 27, 5:164–65; Samuel ben Hofni, *Torah*, comment on Gen. 50:10, pp. 396–97; Me'iri, *Teshuvah*, p. 622; Abrahams, *Ethical Wills*, 2:217.

5. E.g. B. MQ 25b. On the preaching of eulogies in the rabbinic period, see Zunz, p. 165, and the source material cited there; Carmi, pp. 191–92.

6. See Levin; Pagis, *Ḥiddush u-Masoret*, pp. 162–63; Immanuel of Rome, *Maḥberot*, 2:383–95. The distinction between poetic elegy and eulogy is not always absolute; Samuel ben Hofni (*Torah*, pp. 394–97) speaks of eulogies in rhyme and meter; cf. Salo W. Baron, *SRHJ*, 7:98–99.

7. In *Jewish Preaching* (pp. 18–20), I located this change in the middle of the fifteenth century. I would now push this change earlier, to the beginning of that century, as the "Anonymous, St. Petersburg" manuscript contains sermons reflecting the new conception. See the example translated above, chap. 13.

considerable artistry and power, with the theme-verse *this mound is a witness* (Gen. 31:48) recurring as a leitmotif that both reinforces the preacher's message and provides structural coherence to the eulogy as a whole.[8]

A generation later, we have eulogies by Ephraim ben Gerson of Veroia, known as Ephraim ha-Darshan, who left a manuscript of sermons delivered in Ottoman Turkey during the third quarter of the fifteenth century. Among these are eulogies, some described only as "a sermon on the passing of a scholar," or "a sermon over a dead person," but others identified more explicitly as follows: "This sermon I . . . delivered upon the death of the physician R. Emanuel at the time of his decease in the city Agrippa"; "This sermon I delivered at the time that the daughter of R. Elijah Ha-Levi passed away"; "This sermon I preached when the sister of the physician R. Samuel passed away."[9] Some of these contain material that is quite personal, referring to the grief felt by the friends, mother, and sister of the departed. They were obviously composed for a specific occasion of mourning.

With the exception of the eulogy for Crescas, the earliest eulogies for known historical figures would appear to be those delivered by Joseph Garçon, a refugee from Portugal who arrived in Salonika in 1500, whose sermon texts begin from that date. Some twenty-one of the sixty-six sermons in Garçon's manuscript are eulogies, some of them on such well-known figures as Jacob ibn Habib, Abraham Zacut, Samuel Abravanel, and Joseph Hamon, and others on lesser known individuals.[10] Whether the more widespread preservation of eulogy texts at this time is bound up with a consciousness of mortality uniquely characteristic of the generation of the Expulsion remains open to further investigation.[11]

From the sixteenth century on, eulogies become an increasingly significant component of the legacy of extant Jewish sermons. Their importance as evidence for the image contemporaries held of Jewish notables is obvious: a eulogy for Isaac Luria, the AR"I, has been preserved,[12] and one would give a great deal to find a comparable text delivered at the death of Israel Baal

---

8. "Anonymous, St. Petersburg," fols. 28v–39r. See n. 5 to chap. 13, above.

9. Ephraim ben Gerson, fols. 181v, 250v, 186v, 236v, 238v, 192v. On Ephraim, see *Jewish Preaching*, pp. 18–19, 33, 42.

10. Hacker, "Li-Demutam," pp. 66–67, 69.

11. For the evidence pointing to this consciousness of mortality, see Hacker, "Ga'on ve-Dika'on," pp. 541–86. From the same period, the manuscript of sermons entitled "Dover Meisharim" contains eulogies, some of them quite moving, although none are of known historical figures. See also "Anonymous, 'Bibago,'" fol. 332m and Aboab, *Nehar Pishon,* p. 8a: "Ma'amar le-Met," and p. 37d.

12. See Pachter, "Demuto."

Shem Tov. In many cases eulogies provide otherwise unknown or important corroborative biographical evidence. Even for more ordinary figures, including close relatives of the preachers, they supply significant material: beliefs and superstitions about suffering, death, divine justice, and the afterlife; and expressions revealing the texture of emotional attachments to family members, friends, teachers, or students.[13]

In addition to its value as a historical document, the eulogy can also be studied as a genre of Hebrew literature with its own conventions and rules—one that presented the preacher with special rhetorical challenges. Indeed, it is worth distinguishing among its various subcategories: the eulogy delivered in the cemetery at the time of burial was different in length and tone from that delivered at the conclusion of the seven or thirty day period of mourning; and both were different from the eulogy delivered after hearing about the death of a Jewish scholar in a distant land. In all these situations, the content of the eulogy sometimes included illustrative or narrative material of striking originality.[14]

Many of these generalizations are illustrated by the eulogies in the manuscript sermons of Saul Levi Morteira, rabbi and regular preacher of the Beth Jacob congregation of Amsterdam from about 1619 until his death in 1660. During most of his career he was recognized as the leading rabbi of that city's Portuguese community. The manuscripts, which Morteira himself wrote week after week, contain more than ten times the volume of material published in his *Giv'at Sha'ul* (Amsterdam 1645), some 550 different sermons in all. They thus represent the largest known extant repository of sermons by any Jewish preacher before the nineteenth century.[15]

Our focus here is on two previously unknown Morteira eulogies for one of the early leaders of the Portuguese community, Dr. David Farar.[16]

---

13. See Benayahu, "Hespedo," for an example of a eulogy on the preacher's father; *Jewish Preaching*, pp. 301–26, for an example of a eulogy expressing important popular conceptions about death.

14. See Saperstein, "Stories," and *Jewish Preaching*, pp. 99–100, 317–26.

15. Dr. Yosef Kaplan of the Hebrew University first called my attention to the existence of this manuscript in the fall of 1988. See also below, chap. 17, and Saperstein "Treatise." I did not know of the existence of this manuscript when I wrote about Morteira in "Art Form" (above, chap. 9).

16. I have used this spelling although there seems to be no standard form in the secondary literature or even in the primary sources, so that one finds also Farrar, Farer, Pharrar, etc. The name is spelled Farar and Farrar in the same Spanish document (Melnick, p. 57); Morteira, writing in Hebrew, spells the name *Peh-Resh-Resh* at the end of the first eulogy and *Peh-Yod-Resh-Resh* at the end of the second.

Research by Joao Manuel A. S. de Carvalho in the archives of the University of Coimbro has revealed that Farar, born in Lisbon ca. 1570, graduated as a Bachelor in Arts from the University of Evora and registered as a medical student at the University of Coimbra. He then went to the University of Salamanca, where he passed his first and second *Tentativas* in medicine. He was incorporated in Coimbra and graduated from that University with two Bachelor's degrees in May, 1596. These degrees would have permitted him to practice medicine anywhere.[17] The circumstances in which he affirmed his Jewish identity are not yet known. According to evidence later submitted to a Venetian rabbinic court, he was "among the first in that city (Amsterdam), the founders of the synagogue." His name appears in various archival documents with regard to his commercial enterprises and his work on behalf of the Beth Jacob congregation.[18]

Literary sources present Farar in two different contexts. The first relates to his disputes as a representative of Judaism with the Puritan controversialist Hugh Broughton. Mercilessly satirized by Ben Jonson in *The Alchemist* (II,3; IV,5), Broughton was actually a Hebraist and biblical scholar of considerable learning. The frequent references to Farar in his writings provide information about Farar's background. For example, Broughton writes of "A Jew of Amsterdam, named Rabbi David Farar, a revolted Christian, as of late I have been informed, and as it seemeth, for he is ready in our Latine School-men, and a great searcher of advantages, by our over-sights" (366).[19]

Farar challenged Broughton to public debate, apparently around the year 1608: "Farar the Jew, that openly in a Colledge [sic] Hall at Amsterdam, as

---

17. I am grateful to Prof. H. P. Salomon for sending me a copy of communications to him from Dr. Carvalho, and to Dr. Carvalho for permitting me to use this information. The period of study in Salamanca may explain Morteira's reference to Spain (l. 143), although it is unlikely that Farar could have openly identified himself as a Jew at the University of Salamanca.

18. See Pieterse, *Bet Haim,* pp. 186–87; Kaplan, *Ha-Qehillah,* pp. 162–63; Salomon, *Tratado,* pp. xlv–xlviii. Farar's Christian name, which he, like others in the community, used in commercial transactions, was Francisco Lopes Henriques.

19. Page references below are to the collected works of Broughton, edited by John Lightfoot, entitled "The Works of the Great Albionean Divine, renowned in many Nations for Rare Skill in Salems and Athens Tongues, and Familiar Acquaintance with all Rabbinical Learning, Mr. Hugh Broughton" (London, 1662). (I was unable to gain access to a copy of Broughton's book *Our Lordes Famile Opened Against a Jew, Rabbi David Farar* [Amsterdam, 1608]). Broughton served as preacher to the English congregation at Middleburg from about 1604 until his final return to England in 1611. For a full account of his life and the controversies in which he was embroiled, see *Dictionary of National Biography,* 63 vols. (London, 1885–1901) 6:459–62; cf. also Baron, *SRHJ* 15:26–27, 390–91.

I told, disputed upon Daniel to disgrace Christians" (370: cf. 367). The argument from Daniel pertained to the identity of the "fourth kingdom," and Farar's reasoning, a kind of reversal of the Christian arguments based on Genesis 49:10, put Broughton on the defensive.

> Thus reasoned D. Farar: If the fourth Kingdom, which must be dust in the image before God of Heaven his Kingdom is set up, if this Kingdom be the Romans, ye mistake the true Christ. But the fourth Kingdom is the Romans. Therefore the true Christ is not yet come (367).

Referring to contemporary Christian scholarship in England and on the continent, Farar also attacked the reliability of the New Testament text:

> Your New Testament is corrupted in Text. And that your Preachers grant; and some Amsterdamean Jews have dwelt in London, and read English condemnation of the text, and Beza in Latine often amendeth the text. Now you will grant it is not of God, if it be corrupted" (373).

Additional arguments against the veracity of Christian faith are also recorded (617–18).

At one point in Broughton's account of the dispute, Farar is quoted as saying, "I will write a book in Latin, that answer you in print." Farar apparently did compose this work, as the eminent biblical scholar John Lightfoot attests in his introduction to Broughton's collected works:

> Let this be added more, than what he [Broughton] relateth, That the same Rabbin [Farar] wrote a Tract in Latine to have confuted Mr. B.'s opinion, if he could, about the fourth Monarchy, (the Original under the Rabbin's own Hand hath been long in the hands of the Penner of this Preface) but it doth not appear that Mr. B. ever set himself to answer it.[20]

All of this fits a pattern: a "New Christian," well educated in traditional Christian literature, discovers his Jewish identity and with the zeal of the convert uses his knowledge to attack the religion into which he had been born.[21] Particularly striking is the aggressiveness of Farar's attack, as well as the fact that he was permitted to voice it publicly in an academic setting. In Broughton's writings, Farar's knowledge of Christian literature appears far

20. H. P. Salomon has surmised that the Latin text was present with the rest of Lightfoot's books in the Harvard College Library, where it was destroyed in the fire of 1764. See Salomon, "Excommunication," p. 189, n. 3.

21. For accounts of others who fit a similar pattern, see Cooperman; Salomon, *Portrait*; Yerushalmi, *Spanish Court*; Kaplan, *From Christianity*.

more pronounced than his knowledge of Jewish texts, although he is regularly identified as "Rabbi." It may have been in connection with his public polemical role that Farar addressed nine questions to Leon Modena and received a response, published by Isaiah Sonne, in which the Venetian rabbi speaks to the Amsterdam physician with friendship and respect.[22]

The second context is an inner Jewish dispute in which Farar became embroiled around the year 1618. Among his opponents were Rabbi Joseph Pardo, then the Hakham of the Beth Jacob congregation. Although some of the relevant documents have been lost, the basic events and the central issues can be reconstructed from two extant sources. Farar was accused of mocking the words of the sages and denying the validity of the Oral Law, serious charges during the period when Uriel da Costa was first getting into trouble on similar grounds. The case was submitted to rabbinic authorities in Venice and Salonika. The Venetian court examined the evidence—written documents submitted by both sides, including Farar himself—and exonerated the accused, finding no basis for the heresy charge.

About six months later, a formal letter condemning Farar, signed by some of the rabbis of Salonika, arrived in Venice. Leon Modena's response to this letter is our major source for the events. Expressing surprise at the inappropriate involvement of the Salonika sages, Modena argued that the specific infractions with which Farar had been charged—giving figurative interpretations of problematic rabbinic passages and diverging from Rashi in the reading of the Bible—were not at all heretical, but in fact common practice among contemporary authors and preachers. Another accusation, that Farar denied the efficacy of practical Kabbalah, is dismissed almost contemptuously as constituting no sin. And the other charges are said to have no more merit.

Beyond this, Modena defended Farar's orthodoxy and piety in ringing terms: the evidence established that he

> put on phylacteries and wore a fringed garment almost every day; he did not drink any impure wine since his coming to take refuge in God, but strictly fulfilled the sages' decrees, which many of those circumcised from birth, and even teachers of the Torah in our provinces, take lightly and observe in a permissive manner.

As for the motivation of Farar's opponents, Modena states simply that "the greater the man, the more numerous will be those who hate him."[23]

---

22. This suggestion was made by Sonne, "Modena," pp. 15–17.

23. Modena, *Ziqnei*, nu. 33; cf. Kaplan, "Ha-Qehillah," p. 162. On this controversy, see Sonne, pp. 14–15; d'Ancona, pp. 229–39; and more recently, Adelman, pp. 558–63; Idel, "Conceptions," pp. 142–52; Bodian, pp. 54–57.

According to recently published archival documents, the conflict was re-solved with a compromise. Hakham Rabbi Pardo was deemed not to be in error for attacking Farar, but neither was Señor Doctor David Farar in error for holding the opinions he held; neither is to be dishonored, both "remain as equals." Furthermore, in order to put an end to the controversy that "oth-ers still join even today," the leaders of the Beth Jacob congregation resolve, under sanction of a solemn ban of excommunication, that "henceforth no one is to join in this dispute, and the earlier [disputes] are not to be men-tioned."[24]

This conflict (and others that succeeded it) have led some historians to view Farar as a representative of the so-called "Marrano skepticism" that rocked the Amsterdam community, something of a free-thinker who fol-lowed a course similar to that of da Costa but narrowly escaped the censure da Costa suffered. Or, at least, one of the leaders of the "rationalistic" faction within the Sephardic community—a group powerful enough to drive the conservatives out of Beth Jacob.[25]

As noted above, however, Modena's powerful defense and the archival sources picture Farar rather differently, as a pillar of the congregation. In 1610 he signed a contract providing properly slaughtered meat for the com-munity, and in the following years held various other positions of leadership and responsibility in the synagogue and its eleemosynary associations. Morteira's eulogies confirm Farar's substantial contributions to the Por-tuguese community of Amsterdam from its earliest days until his death in the fall of 1624.

---

24. The text, described as a literal translation into Spanish of the Hebrew original (appar-ently lost), affirms that Farar "is not in error for his statements concerning the Scriptures and the words of our [sages]" (*S Doctor no yerro en sus declaraciones sobre las Scripturas y palabros de nuestros [sabios]*). See Salomon, "Excommunication," pp. 182–83; Melnick, pp. 57–59.

25. See Sonne, pp. 12–13, 17–18; d'Ancona, pp. 230, 239–40; Revah, p. 17. There re-mains considerable confusion in the scholarly literature about the relationship between this and the dispute recorded in a responsum of Joel Sirkes, a full text of which with translation is given in Schochet, pp. 248–53. Sirkes refers to a "doctor" in Amsterdam (without giving the name) who challenged the rabbinical leadership by appointing an ignorant ritual slaugh-terer and refusing to back down; he is also accused of mocking the aggadah and rejecting rab-binical tradition. This dispute is generally assumed to have been instrumental in the breakup of Beth Jacob and the formation of the new Beth Israel congregation. Some scholars main-tain that the doctor involved here was Abraham Farar the Elder, who died December 14, 1618; see Kayserling, p. 276; Gebhardt, pp. xxiv, xxv, 244–45; Roth, "Lopez Rosa," p. 491; Bodian, pp. 52–53. Others consider this to be the same conflict described in the Modena re-sponsum, involving David Farar; see d'Ancona, p. 229; Revah, pp. 16–17; Salomon, "Ex-communication, p. 183; Adelman, p. 559; Idel, pp. 142–43.

The two eulogies, bound in different volumes,[26] were delivered a month apart. The first is identified at the end as "the sermon I delivered in the cemetery, over the coffin of the consummate Hakham, the outstanding physician, Rabbi David Farar, may his soul be bound up in the bonds of eternal life, my dear and pleasant friend, on Tuesday, the second day of Ḥeshvan, 5385 [October 15, 1624]. His soul is for life in the world to come." The second is similarly identified at the end: "The sermon I delivered at the conclusion of the thirty day period following the decease of my dear and pleasant friend, the outstanding physician, the consummate Hakham Rabbi David Ferrar (*sic*), may the memory of the righteous and saintly be for blessing. It was on the second day of the month of Kislev, 5385 [November 13, 1624]." Of all the eulogies in the manuscript, these are the only ones in which the deceased is characterized by the preacher as "my friend."

Before reviewing the substance of these eulogies and the information they contain about Farar, some attention should be devoted to their literary structure. As we have already seen,[27] Morteira was a master at organizing his material to facilitate both comprehension and recollection. These eulogies are no exception; even in the first, unusual for its brevity and bearing the marks of emotional turmoil and little time for preparation, the component building blocks are readily discernible.

The section following the opening verse (*nose*) and rabbinic dictum (*ma'a-mar*) is introductory, though unlike the formal introduction of Morteira's Sabbath sermons. Instead, he follows an established convention of medieval Jewish homiletics by indicating the reasons why he will speak despite the powerful arguments for refraining.[28] He recounts the traditional functions of the eulogy, indicating that none of them apply in this case: it is premature to attempt comfort before the burial has taken place; there is no need to inform anyone of the death, to arouse the heart to tears, or to recount the praises of the deceased. Tears already flow, and Farar's praises are well-known and too many to rehearse. Instead, Morteira claims to fulfill a personal obligation, repaying a small part of the debt he owes to Farar in every realm:

---

26. The pages of the manuscript are not numbered, which makes citation awkward. The first eulogy, in vol. 3, is the second sermon on the lesson *Noaḥ* in the second cycle of sermons. If the pages were numbered consecutively, it would be fol. 91r. The second eulogy, in vol. 5, is the eighth sermon on the lesson *Toledot*. If the pages were numbered consecutively, it would be fol. 27r–v. All references in the following discussion are to lines in the printed Hebrew text which ensues.

27. On the structure of Morteira's sermons, see chap. 9, above.

28. On this convention, see *Jewish Preaching*, pp. 76–77 and chaps 13 and 15, above.

Physical, for he was so diligent regarding my recuperation and the healing of
those in my household without taking payment. . . . Financial, inasmuch as
he is the reason why I am in the situation I am in today. Spiritual, for from
his deeds I learned to serve God properly (ll. 15–18).

Furthermore, the preacher claims to be following the advice of the sages that
pain in the heart may be alleviated by expressing it to others. The personal
voice, revealing details of Morteira's private life and conveying a deep emotion that can be sensed even without hearing the actual delivery, is extremely
unusual in the texts of Morteira's sermons.

After the brief introduction, the eulogy is given its structure by an unexpected reference to Hebrew grammatical writing. The grammarians—and
here Morteira may be referring specifically to an early work, *Safah Berurah,*
by his younger contemporary Menasseh ben Israel—distinguish among four
categories of nouns: proper, adjectival, relational, and numerical.[29] When
applied to the deceased, all four of these categories demonstrate his goodness. The final category, in which Morteira mentions Farar's childlessness,
leads into the concluding, homiletical portion of the eulogy, bearing the
message that Farar's many good deeds were his true children. This is linked
with a midrashic reading of the opening verse from the Torah lesson: *These
are the offspring of Noah: Noah's being a righteous and whole-hearted man in
his age* (cf. Gen. 6:9). The eulogy ends with a traditional plea: "May God
have mercy upon us, for we have lost the crown from our heads. *Woe to us,
for we have sinned* (Lam. 5:16), *for the righteous is gathered because of evil* (Isa.
57:1). May it be God's will to put an end to our sorrows, *to tell the angel of
destruction, 'Stay your hand'* (cf. I Chron. 21:15). But our duty is to accept
this judgment, and to say 'Blessed is the Judge of Truth.'"

The second eulogy, considerably longer and more elaborate, reveals a
more leisurely preparation, and its calmer tone reflects the passage of time.
The introduction, dealing with the importance of the eulogy, is an exegesis
of a striking rabbinic hyperbole: "Whoever is slothful regarding the eulogy
of a decent man deserves to be buried alive" (b. Shab 105a). Morteira's novel
intepretation is that the statement applies not to the person who delivers the

---

29. Menasseh ben Israel wrote that he had completed this work, which then circulated in
manuscript, at age 17, i.e., in 1621: see Roth, *Menasseh,* pp. 27, 86, 320. A copy of the manuscript is in the *Ets Haim* collection, 47 D 7. The second chapter, dealing with nouns, speaks
of seven categories. Among these are the *nome sustantivo* (proper nouns of people or places),
nome do agnome ou titulo (adjectival nouns and epithets or titles; examples are ḥakham, tsaddiq, gibbor), *nome da familia ou da terra* (gentilic nouns, such as *Sefardi, Yehudi*), and *nome
do numero* (numbers) (fol. 13r–14v). These clearly correspond to Morteira's *shem ha-'etsem,
shem ha-to'ar, shem ha-yaḥas,* and *shem ha-mispar.* Cf. Klijnsmit, especially p. 147.

eulogy but to the listeners: those who hear the praises of a good man who has died, and fail to draw the appropriate lesson that they themselves are in need of repentance, are beyond hope.

The body of the sermon is divided into three parts, based on the *ma'amar,* the well-known rabbinic lament: "If the cedars have caught fire, what hope is there for the moss on the wall? If Leviathan has been hauled in by a fish-hook, what hope is there for the minnows? If the hook has fallen into the mighty river, what hope is there for the waterholes?" (b. MQ 25b). These three metaphors express the relationship between the great man and the masses, and Morteira explores the implications of each in turn. But each section has its own homiletical twist. The first, based on a Sabbath sermon he had delivered previously,[30] explicates six qualities that the cedar shares with the human soul, and with the deceased. The second explores four different meanings of the Hebrew root in the word *Leviathan,* and the third uses five different meanings of the root *nḥl* ("river"), each of which is applied to the qualities of Farar. In every case, the *a fortiori* lesson is reiterated for the listeners: if death can overtake a giant like Farar, what can we the living expect for ourselves?

The concluding section moves from the end of the *ma'amar,* "Weep for the losers, not for the lost," to the verse from the Torah lesson which, as in the previous eulogy, is introduced only at the very end. Jacob's dwelling *in tents* (Gen. 25:27) is taken as an emblem for Farar's success in both realms, of this world and the world to come, and the preacher moves quickly to his peroration, based on Psalm 15.

The eulogies confirm what is known about David Farar from archival sources, presenting a fuller picture of the man and in some cases providing previously unknown information. His precise relationship to Abraham Farar the Elder (d. 1618) and Abraham Farar the Younger (d. 1664) has never been clearly established by historians. Pieterse, who has worked extensively in the Amsterdam archives, makes the younger Abraham the son of the elder and the cousin of David; Cecil Roth similarly makes David the nephew of the elder Abraham.[31] The second eulogy clarifies this beyond question: David was the "son of the esteemed R. Abraham Ferrar the Elder, of blessed memory" (ll. 201–202). Furthermore, we are told that David was "of distinguished ancestral lineage, connected with the chosen tribe of Levi [like Morteira himself] on his mother's side." Morteira had preached eulogies for both the father and mother of David, who died within a few weeks of each

30. See the annotation to the second eulogy, n. 13.
31. Pieterse, *Bet Haim,* p. 186; Roth, "Lopez Rosa." D'Ancona correctly makes David the son of Abraham the Elder (d'Ancona, pp. 212, 229).

other in December of 1618.[32] The passages in question not only clarify the relationships in one of the most important early families of the Portuguese community, but also confirm the importance some New Christian families attributed to traditions of levitical lineage.

Morteira's eulogies do not give a full biography of David Farar, and we are left ignorant of details of his early life and the circumstances of his decision to leave the Iberian peninsula and join the Jewish community of Amsterdam. Nevertheless, we are given some clues. The first eulogy affirms that Farar "loved God to the point of endangering his body" (ll. 28–29) and speaks of the pride he took in his Jewish identity:

> His relational name was "Jew." What respect he had for that name, as he spread the fame of God's Law and the honor of this people! Where now will go the Gentiles who would come to seek out the word of God? Gone is the man who, before the great councillors of the land, would proclaim that God's Law is perfect and eternal. Gone is the man who brought to the right path a number of the descendants of our people (ll. 39–43).

This passage indicates that, perhaps because of the reputation acquired in his public debate with Broughton, Farar was sought by Christian savants who wanted to learn more about Judaism. The reference to the dangers he faced, here little more than a tantalizing hint, is clarified somewhat in the second eulogy.

> Wherever he went, God's name was invoked upon him. During the first years in this land, when people used to conceal their [Jewish] names, he would proclaim his in public, as occasions frequently presented themselves. Therefore many Gentiles came from far away to seek him out. Even in Spain [Iberia, including Portugal?], in a place of danger, he did not conceal it, but identified himself as a "Jew," a word in which the name of God is contained (ll. 140–44).

Here too a measure of greater specificity would have been welcome. Is the reference to the period before Farar and his family left the Iberian peninsula for their new life in Amsterdam? If so, the proclamation of Jewish identity would have constituted an open challenge to the Inquisition and required the family to flee for their lives. Or does it refer to a temporary return to Spanish soil after Farar's arrival in Amsterdam in order to attend to business or family affairs, or perhaps even to propagandize among the New Christians (cf. l. 42)?

---

32. The eulogies, placed in vol. 4 of the manuscript, were both delivered at the end of the thirty-day mourning period. The first contains the information that Abraham the Elder died at age seventy, making his year of birth 1548.

(More than a few Portuguese Jews did return to the "lands of idolatry,"[33] and Morteira criticized this practice vehemently in a later sermon.) It would have been suicidal for a New Christian to proclaim his Jewishness under such circumstances, unless he had been granted a special protection by the Spanish crown. Presumably, the actual circumstances of Farar's self-endangerment would have been known to the listeners. In either case, the respective passages in the two eulogies point not only to a deep pride in the appellation "Jew" but also to a defiant bravado consistent with Farar's public challenge of Broughton.

The references to Farar's earlier life and his first years in Amsterdam apply to a period before Morteira knew him. Most of the material in the eulogy, however, reflects personal knowledge in a context of friendship and admiration. We hear of Farar's noble physical appearance, much admired among the Sefardi Jews: he was "handsome, looking like royalty, like an angel of God" (ll. 171–72). Indeed, it was his robust health and the suddenness of his death after a relatively minor illness that made the loss so shattering (l. 21, 112, 173). We are also told of Farar's personal integrity: "He would speak what was in his heart, not saying one thing and thinking another" (ll. 152–53). Indeed, Morteira presents the deceased as a kind of *uomo universale*: "In him were all the qualities that combine as yet another fine quality to make beautiful music: wisdom, reverence, beauty, decency, love, justice, strength, eloquence, healing" (ll. 211–13).

According to the eulogy, these personality traits were successfully woven into the fabric of traditional Jewish life. Farar was beloved by God "because of his observance of the commandments, his zeal to be first in all matters of holiness" (l. 27–28, cf. l. 130); this description recalls Modena's characterization of Farar in his 1618 responsum. The communal positions he held are carefully enumerated. Most important was *parnas u-memmuneh*,[34] an office he occupied in the year of his death (l. 121, cf. l. 36). He was also the "physician of the Society for Visiting the Sick" (ll. 33–34), perhaps the single most important voluntary society of the congregation.[35] We are told that he had the honor of standing to the right of the cantor on the Days of Awe, and that he delivered sermons in the synagogue on regular occasions (ll. 37–38). This

---

33. On this phenomenon, see Yerushalmi, "Professing Jews"; Kaplan, "Travels"; Israel, "Pereira," p. 109.

34. This was a common designation for the governing elders of the community: see Baron, *SRHJ* 15:39 and, for Venice, Salomon, "Excommunication," p. 197.

35. On the *Ḥevrat Biqqur Ḥolim,* founded in December 1609, see Pieterse, *Barrios,* and Kaplan, *From Christianity,* pp. 189–92. For extensive background information on this type of society in Italy, see Rivlin, pp. 87–100; in Spain, see Assis, "Welfare and Mutual Aid," pp. 327–30. The installation of new officers for the Society in Amsterdam occurred each year on the Sabbath during Hanukkah, and many of Morteira's manuscript sermons on the lesson *Mi-Qets* [Gen. 41:1–44:17] end with a list of the outgoing and incoming officers. They are therefore an additional resource for the history of this Society.

last detail illuminates one aspect of the dispute in which he was embroiled. Modena's responsum does not indicate in what context the controversial interpretations of biblical verses and rabbinic statements were expressed. It now becomes plausible that the protest was over Farar's sermons, and Modena's defense—that this kind of interpretation was common among contemporary preachers—responds directly to the attack.

Against the background of that dispute, it is interesting to note Morteira's repeated emphasis on Farar's role as a peacemaker within the community (lines 31, 123, 218–19). Also prominent is his concern for the poor: as leader of the *ḥevrat biqqur ḥolim,* he "healed the poor cheerfully, going up to their houses, and giving them charity." In the second eulogy, this theme is developed further, linking Farar's generosity and charitableness with his business investments:[36] "When his ships arrived [in port], the poor, the orphan and the widow would rejoice when they went forth from his house. People entered and left carrying many gifts" (ll. 196–97). At one point in the second eulogy, the list of the eleemosynary and public activities in which Farar excelled seems almost endless:

> Judging so as to make peace, gathering charitable funds to redeem the captive and marry off the orphan, passing ordinances for a voluntary society, establishing an academy, suppressing transgression, involving himself in the needs of the community, speaking before Gentile scholars (ll. 130–32).

Many of these activities can be corroborated from the manuscripts of Morteira's sermons or in the archives of the community.

It need not be emphasized that eulogies cannot be taken at face value as historical evidence. The occasion inspires charity on the part of the eulogist; the genre invites exaggeration. Obviously Farar was not beloved by all; Morteira's failure even to allude to the controversy of 1618 may have resulted from his desire to conform strictly with the proclamation prohibiting any further mention of it, but its memory would no doubt have lingered six years after its conclusion.

Nevertheless, these texts transcend the conventions of praise and retain their power to convince and impress. Comparison with the other eulogies in the Morteira manuscripts, and in the extant sermon literature as a whole, reveals that these are unusual in the amount of personal material they contain and the depth of emotion they reflect. Morteira apparently thought of Farar as a giant as well as a friend. "From his deeds I learned to serve God prop-

36. For a list of archival records mentioning Farar's business transactions, see Kaplan, "Ha-Qehillah," p. 163, n. 6.

erly" (ll. 17–18) is not something that a rabbi proclaims casually in public, and Morteira was anything but self-effacing. In addition to what the eulogies tell us about Dr. David Farar himself, they reveal perhaps the second most inspiring personage in Morteira's life: like the better known Dr. Elijah Montalto (whom Morteira described in at least one manuscript sermon as his mentor), a New Christian physician who became a proud and sophisticated spokesman for Judaism.

SAUL LEVI MORTEIRA
FIRST EULOGY FOR DR. DAVID FARAR

These are the offspring of Noah. Noah was a righteous blameless man in his generations; Noah walked with God (Gen. 6:9).

Genesis Rabbah [30,6]: So the Bible says, [*The fruit of the righteous is a tree*][1] *of life* (Prov. 11:30). What are the fruits of the righteous? Commandments performed and good deeds.

The goals of the preacher delivering a eulogy are various: to arouse weeping,[2] [   ] in justice, to comfort the mourners,[3] to honor the dead by recounting his praises.[4] I have not come here[5] [to proclaim] this bitter loss, for it is of itself openly known,[6] and furthermore, I do not have the heart [   ] or cite biblical texts,[7] for the sword threatens the very life! (Jer. 4:10). Nor have I came to comfort the mourners, for the sages commanded us [not to comfort a person] while his deceased is lying unburied

---

1. The upper left corner of the page on which Morteira wrote this eulogy is missing, the result of a jagged tear. The maximum width of the paper lost is 3.3 centimeters from the left margin, entailing a lacuna of about 10–12 letters at the end of the first and the third through seventh lines of the manuscript, and progressively fewer letters in subsequent lines. I have indicated the lacunae with square brackets, filling in only where conjecture seems secure. The original manuscript in Budapest reveals at the end of many lines an additional letter or two that are not legible on the microfilm.

2. Cf. *Tur Yoreh De'ah* 344a: "To say over him words that break the heart in order to produce intense weeping."

3. See Almosnino, p. 218b: "The comfort that is also part of the eulogy done for all the dead."

4. Cf. *Tur Yoreh De'ah* 344a: "And to make mention of the praises [of the deceased]." According to Leon Modena, this is the quintessential task of the *hesped* for the righteous; see Modena, *Midbar,* pp. 59b, 62b.

5. The preacher claims that he is not fulfilling any of the traditional functions of the eulogy, i.e., that he is not delivering an actual eulogy. It is a rhetorical topos to say "I do not intend to give a speech," and then to go and give one.

6. Assuming the correctness of my reconstruction *le-hakhriz,* Morteira would be making homiletical use of the halakhic obligation to make public proclamation of a lost article, perhaps reflecting the view of R. Meir that one is obliged to proclaim it "until his neighbors may know of it" (M. BM 2,6).

7. A possible reconstruction would be [*lomar ḥiddushim*]: "[to give novel interpretations] and cite biblical verses"; this would make sense of the rather strange word *u-feshatim* immediately following the lacuna. Here too, he proceeds to do what he says he cannot.

before him.[8] Nor to arouse weaping, for our eyes are flowing of their own accord [   ] a scholar without peer who is lost.[9] Nor to recount his praises, for they are openly known, and furthermore [   ] for they are extremely numerous.

Nevertheless, my great indebtedness has impelled me to lament and to eulogize this righteous man [in order to fulfill] my responsibility toward him, so as not to be ungrateful at this final parting.[10] My indebtedness to him pertains to all the good things we can acquire: physical, spiritual, and financial. Physical, for he was so diligent regarding my recuperation and the healing of those in my household without taking any payment; on the contrary, with outstanding [   ]. Financially, inasmuch as he is the reason why I am in the situation I am in today.[11] Spiritually, for from his deeds I learned to serve God properly.[12] Therefore, to let a little stand for a lot,[13] following the rabbinic statement, "*If there is anxiety in a person's heart let him quash it* (Prov. 12:25) means, let him talk about it to others,"[14] I have decided to lament bitterly two things, even though my remarks will not be well structured because of [   ] given us, and because of the suddenness of this bitter and precipitous tragedy.[15]

So as to follow some kind of order, I will say that grammarians divide the nouns of the sacred tongue into four categories: proper, descriptive, relational, and numerical.[16] From these, various things can be known about that

---

8. Cf. M. Avot 4,18. Morteira alludes here to the circumstances of his delivery: in the cemetery, before the open grave—circumstances mentioned in his written remark at the end of the text.

9. Cf. B. Hor 13a.

10. Thus the preacher claims that he is unable to benefit either the deceased or the listeners, but only to fulfill his personal obligation to the deceased. This is the topos of modesty, but he goes on to convince the audience that his debt to the deceased is indeed great.

11. Perhaps he alludes to his position as rabbi of the Beth Jacob congregation: David Farar may well have had a hand in the negotiations between the congregation and Morteira. It is also possible that Morteira earned profits from investing in commercial transactions of Farar (cf. l. 30, and the second eulogy, l. 196).

12. A striking assertion from the rabbi of the congregation; we do not know to what precisely he is referring.

13. Based on Gen. Rab. 5,7.

14. B. Yoma 75a.

15. Based on Hab. 1:6. From the reference to the "suddenness of the . . . tragedy," we learn that Farar died without a prolonged illness, and that the preacher did not have much time to prepare his eulogy. Cf. the second eulogy, lines 112, 173. Here the preacher concludes the introduction and passes to the body of the eulogy.

16. It is likely that Morteira is referring here to the small book called "Safah Berurah" by Menasseh ben Israel, which was circulating in manuscript at this time. See n. 29 to the introduction.

which is specified. If we apply them to this *tsaddiq* who has departed, we find that they all point toward the good.

His proper name was David, which in Hebrew expresses love, as in the word *dodim.* Who does not know all this: how he was beloved on high and beloved by human beings?[17] On high, because of his observance of the commandments, his zeal to be first in all matters of holiness,[18] loving those beloved by God.[19] He loved God to the point where he actually endangered himself.[20] And he loved his fellow creatures. Let those who love him now say so; let the poor say so, let the widows whom he graced with his generosity, making their resources flourish,[21] say so (and the reconciliations he effected between different people)[22]—all this is in accordance with his proper name. He was David, and his acts were *dodim,* acts of love.

The descriptive name applied to him was "Doctor."[23] See how many years he was a physician for the *Biqqur Ḥolim* Society, gladly healing the poor, going up to their houses and giving them charity.[24] He also had another such title: *parnas* and *memmuneh* of the Beth Jacob Congregation.[25] Let all weep for him because of this title. Where is your leader? Where is your officer? The glory has departed from Jacob![26] No more will he stand at the cantor's right hand on the Days of Awe. No more will he preach on those special Sabbaths.[27] Happy is the man described by such titles.

Now his relational name was "Jew." What respect he had for this name,[28]

---

17. Cf. B. Ber 17a ("beloved on high and pleasing below") and B. Qid 40a ("good to heaven and to human beings").

18. Based on B. Git 59b. Cf. the second eulogy, l. 130.

19. Following the manuscript reading *ohev ahuvav.* This may be an error for *ohev ohavav,* as in Num. Rab. 8,4 ("Who is a God like this, who loves those who love Him?"). Because Morteira is talking here about Farar's relationship with God, he would have meant "loving those who loved Him (i.e. God)."

20. See the second eulogy, ll. 143–44.

21. See above, n. 11.

22. The words in parentheses are written between the lines as an addition by the author. We may assume that in the actual delivery he expanded a bit upon this topic.

23. In the documents of the community, Farar appears consistently with his title as "*o doutor* David Farar." See, e.g., Pieterse, *Bet Haim,* pp. 14, 33, 111, etc.

24. On the *Biqqur Holim* Society, see n. 35 to the introduction.

25. Farar served in these positions in the year of his death (second eulogy, ll. 120–21). For the terminology, see n. 34 to the introduction.

26. Based on I Sam. 4:21, *The glory has departed from Israel,* here with an allusion to the name of the congregation.

27. It was not previously known that Farar preached in the synagogue. It is possible that his sermons occasioned the controversy over his interpretations of the Bible and the sages: see the introduction.

28. See the more detailed description in the second eulogy, ll. 140–44.

as he spread the fame of God's Law and the honor of this people. Where now will go the Gentiles who would come to seek out the word of God?[29] Gone is the man who, before the great councilors of the land, would proclaim[30] that God's Law is perfect and eternal.[31] Gone is the man who brought back to the right path a number of the descendants of our people.[32] All this is in accordance with his relational name.

Now the numerical noun applied to him is "one," for he left no son.[33] He was unique in his generation, like Joshua, God's servant, who also had no son, for the Bible recounts the genealogy of his family and stops with Joshua.[34] What does the good-hearted man deduce from this? The immortality of his soul, which derives joy in Eden[35] from the many deeds whose reward God will not withhold,[36] for they are his true offspring.

This is as we began,[37] *These are the offspring of Noah: Noah's being a righteous blameless man.*[38] *In his generations* he was considered righteous, for the spirit of his fellow human beings was pleased with him, and therefore the spirit of the Omnipresent was pleased with him,[39] and *Noah walked with*

---

29. Apparently evidence that Christian scholars turned to Farar with questions about Jewish matters. Later on, Christians turned to Morteira himself, as his students report in their introduction to *Giv'at Sha'ul*. Cf. Katchen, pp. 107–11.

30. The letters *heh-zayin* can be deciphered as the beginning of the last word on the line. The correct reading may be *hizhir*, in the sense of "teach" (Exod. 18:20), or *hiz'iq*, in the sense of "proclaim" (Jon. 3:7). The meaning is that Farar was not afraid to proclaim the truth of the fundamental beliefs of Judaism even in the presence of powerful Christians.

31. The eternity of the Torah was one of Morteira's favorite subjects, to which he devoted long discussions in his sermons and a treatise in Portuguese (see Salomon, *Tratado*).

32. I.e., Farar convinced "New Christians" to return to Judaism. Cf. the second eulogy, l. 66.

33. The manuscript contains a sermon delivered by Morteira on 28 Shevat 5480 (February 2, 1620) "in the house of the Doctor David Farar," in which the preacher expresses the wish that God will give children to Farar.

34. I Chron. 7:26; B. Meg 14b; cf. Ginzberg 6:95 n. 526, 143 n. 847.

35. I.e., the fact that a righteous man such as Farar dies childless is presented not as a punishment (as in the conception of the Kabbalists: see Hacker, "Ga'on ve-Dika'on," p. 581), but rather as proof of the eternity of his soul and his reward in the world to come. Morteira employs here the unusual form *she'erut ha-nefesh*, the title of a book he wrote on the subject; see Saperstein, "Treatise," pp. 132–34.

36. Based on Tanḥuma, Va-Yera 3 and parallels.

37. The *nose* from the Torah lesson, which the preacher read at the beginning of the eulogy.

38. The novel homiletical interpretation is that "*toledot Noaḥ*" in the verse refers not to Shem, Ham, and Japheth, mentioned in the following verse, but to Noah's righteousness and blamelessness and his good deeds, which are his "true offspring." In this way, the preacher links the *nose* and the rabbinic *ma'amar* to the situation of the deceased. The interpretation is based on *Tanḥuma, Noaḥ* 2.

39. Based on M. Avot 3,10.

God (Gen. 6:9), resting [*la-nuaḥ*] in quiet resting places.[40] So it is written, *they shall have rest on their couches* (Isa. 57:2), as it was said of Enoch: *Enoch walked with God, then he was no more, for God took him* (Gen. 5:24).

May God have mercy upon us, for we have lost the crown of our heads. *Woe to us that, we have sinned* (cf. Lam. 5:16) *for the righteous is taken away because of evil* (Isa. 57:1). May it be God's will to put an end to our sorrows, *to tell the angel of destruction "Stay your hand"* (cf. I Chron. 21:15). But our duty is to accept this judgment, and to say "Blessed is the Judge of Truth."[41]

The sermon I delivered in the cemetery[42] over the coffin of the consummate Hakham, the outstanding physician, Rabbi David Farar, may his soul be bound up in the bonds of eternal life, my dear and pleasant friend, on Tuesday, the second day of Heshvan, 5385 [October 15, 1624].[43] His soul is for life in the world to come.

---

40. Based on on Isa. 32:18. The novel homiletical interpretation of the second half of the *nose* is that *Noaḥ* is not a repetition of the name but an adverb; he walked with God *be-noaḥ*: serenely or restfully. Here too the *nose* is linked with the present situation of the deceased.

41. This sentence appears at the end of every eulogy in Morteira's manuscript. It also concludes his Portuguese eulogy for Moses Mercade (printed in 1552): "e a nos toca justificar os juizos Divinos, dizendo, Bendito o Juis de Verdade."

42. On the custom of delivering eulogies in the cemetery, see *Jewish Preaching*, p. 37 n. 30.

43. Cf. Pieterse, *Bet Haim*, pp. 111, 187.

An innocent man, dwelling in tents (Gen. 25:27).

Mo'ed Qatan, the chapter [beginning] "These may shave" [p. 25b]: When the soul of Rav Ashi departed, a certain eulogizer began to speak of him as follows: "If the cedars have caught fire, what hope is there for the moss on the wall? If Leviathan has been hauled in by a fish-hook, what hope is there for the minnows? If the hook has fallen into the mighty river, what hope is there for the waterholes?" Bar Abbin said to him, "God forbid that I should talk of 'hook' or 'flame' in connection with the righteous. Rather, 'Weep for the losers, not for the lost, for he is at rest, while we are in distress.'"[2]

The sages spoke hyperbolically about the obligation of eulogizing a decent man, saying "Whoever is slothful regarding the eulogy of a decent man deserves to be buried alive."[3] Now they revealed the reason for their hyperbole in the formulation of their statement. They did not say "whoever does not eulogize a decent man," but "whoever is slothful regarding the eulogy, etc." This teaches us the great benefit that comes to us from the eulogy, for in it the qualities of the deceased are made public and recalled to memory. Furthermore, the listener will fear for his own judgment and strive to emulate the *tsaddiq* who has died. Thus, whether one strives to emulate those fine qualities, or whether one thinks "If this happens to the *tsaddiq,* how much worse will it be for the wicked," he will be impelled to return to God, who will have compassion upon him, and thereby become invigorated to perform God's commandments.[4]

Now the statement "Whoever is slothful regarding the eulogy of a decent man" does not mean "whoever is slothful in *delivering* the eulogy; it means whoever is slothful regarding the commandments at the eulogy of a decent

---

1. Isa. 57:1. By giving a title to this (almost always a biblical phrase), as he does for all his sermons but not for the eulogy in the cemetery at Farar's burial, Morteira indicates that this will be an "official," formal sermon.

2. This *ma'amar* will provide the structural basis for the eulogy.

3. B. Shab 105a.

4. Thus one of the functions of this genre, in addition to those mentioned at the beginning of the first eulogy, is to inspire the listeners to repentance. Cf. Katzellenbogen, sermon 3 (a eulogy for Judah Moscato), p. 19a–b. The idea was probably a commonplace.

man. When one hears the eulogy given for a decent man, when one hears about those fine qualities, and yet remains slothful, there is no more hope for him, for he has not arisen or budged from his sloth even in the face of such a great stimulus as the death of the *tsaddiq*.[5] That is why "he deserves to be buried alive," for he must indeed be totally wicked, his heart made of stone, incapable of melting. Now the evil are called "dead" even when alive,[6] and the dead are to be buried. Therefore such a person is like a wicked man; he deserves to be buried alive. That is why they said "whoever is slothful," rather than saying "whoever does not deliver a eulogy, etc."

Both of these beneficial lessons were derived by that eulogist with whose words we began from the eulogy for Rav Ashi.[7] He recounted the praises of the deceased, and he taught the listeners a lesson: that they should apply the message *a fortiori* to themselves. He thereby brought benefit both to the listeners and to the deceased:[8] to the listeners, because they will return from their evil way, and to the deceased, because this will be a source of great merit for him in facing his Maker, since even in his death he remains God's servant as he was during his life, bringing his people back to the right path.[9]

The eulogist divided his words into three, providing three metaphors[10] for the *tsaddiq*, calling him a cedar, Leviathan, and a mighty river. These are intended to express the perfection of the deceased in each of the three areas of human behavior: governing of oneself, of a state, and of a house-

---

5. The interpretation is that the phrase "whoever is slothful regarding the eulogy of a decent man" refers not to the eulogist but to those who hear the eulogy, as if to say, "Whoever is slothful in deriving benefit from the eulogy of a decent man." Thus the exegetical problem of the hyperbole in the statement is resolved. This appears to be a novel interpretation, but Moses Albelda shows that he understands the statement in a similar way (Albelda, p. 93b), so that it may not have been entirely original. Compare the quite different treatment in Katzenellenbogen, sermon 5 (a eulogy for Isaac Foa), pp. 27b–29b.

6. B. Ber 18b.

7. In the *ma'amar* read at the beginning of the eulogy. Here the preacher begins the transition from the introduction to the body of the sermon.

8. I.e., the eulogy is beneficial to the listeners and to the deceased. The *a fortiori* argument implied by the Talmudic dirge will serve as a refrain throughout the oration, signalling the end of each of its sections. Such an argument from the fate of the righteous to that of the ordinary sinner was used in contemporary Christian preaching. For example, "If the righteous man will be saved by the skin of his teeth, what will become of the sinner?" (cited by Delumeau, p. 330). As for the second kind of benefit, Morteira claimed that it was indeed possible to benefit a person even after that person had died (a matter of dispute among medieval Jewish thinkers), and he refers to this idea in several of his manuscript sermons.

9. Cf. the first eulogy, l. 42. This concludes the introduction.

10. *Meshalim*, meaning here not "parables" but metaphors expressing comparison.

hold.[11] From these he derived an *a fortiori* lesson: if this is what happened to one who was perfect in all areas, what hope is there for those who are imperfect in all?

(He began by saying, "If the cedars have caught fire, what hope is there for the moss on the wall?") He began by saying, "If the cedars have caught fire."[12] He compared him to a cedar, in which alone there are a number of fine qualities similar to the human soul, as I explained at length in my sermon for the lesson *Ḥuqqat* on the verse *The priest shall take cedar wood* (Num. 19:6).[13]

First, the cedar is the most distinguished of all trees, as in the message sent by the king of Israel to the king of Judea: "The moss on the wall sent to the cedar in Lebanon,"[14] meaning the most distinguished to the lowly. This is a unique quality of the human soul among everything created on the six days of creation. Of it alone the Bible says *Let us make* [*man*] (Gen. 1:26); into it life was exhaled by God,[15] and consultation was required. All this clearly shows its eternality, as we have explained many times.[16]

---

11. This is the Aristotelian division of practical philosophy into ethics, economics, and politics. Cf. ibn Daud, beginning of Ma'amar 3. It apparently became a topos in Italian preaching of the sixteenth and seventeenth century: see "Miqnat Kesef" (a collection of sermons purchased by Leon Modena in 1595), fol. 10b, Figo, sermon 13, p. 47a–b and sermon 75 (a eulogy for Abraham Aboab), p. 122c–d. Morteira returns to this at the end of the first section (l. 167), but in the continuation it is all but forgotten.

12. Apparently dittography: the author forgot to cross out the first citation of the statement, which contains words he did not need in the present context.

13. The sermon is entitled "When a Man Dies"; see the description in Morteira 1645, p. 104a. The full text of the sermon has been preserved in the third volume of the manuscript. In the notes below, I shall identify the material Morteira drew from his earlier sermon.

14. Cf. 2 Kings 14:9 (apparently cited from memory). In the sermon "When a Man Dies":

> First, we know that the cedar is by nature superior to all other trees, as the biblical verse says, *From the cedar in Lebanon to the moss upon the wall* (I Kings 5:13), meaning, from the greatest tree of all to the least of them all, for the cedar is always taken as the greatest of the trees. So the king of Israel sent to the king of Judah, "The moss sent to the cedar in Lebanon" (cf. 2 Kings 14:9).

15. I.e., Gen. 1:26 and Gen. 2:7 indicate the uniqueness of the human soul.

16. The eternality of the soul is the subject of one of the earliest books written by Morteira; see Saperstein, "Treatise." Cf. the first eulogy, ll. 46–47. In "When a Man Dies":

> Also from here we may derive the eternality of the soul. For if we assume the opposite, how would this human being be greater than the lights that were created on the fourth day? As these were such a marvelous act, God did not precede their creation with the word "Let us make," which indicates consultation and the greatness of the act performed afterward.

The interpretation of "let us make" as implying that God sought consultation (either with His own heart or with other heavenly beings) is based on the Midrash (e.g. Gen. Rab. 8,3–4).

How fitting, then, in this respect is the metaphor of the cedar for this *tsaddiq* who has departed,[17] for he was designated as outstanding in this congregation, the first among the founders of Judaism,[18] established as a pillar of iron to this day.[19] He did not hesitate in his labor and toil until it was established in its proper place. Therefore it is fitting to call him an outstanding cedar.[20]

Now what can be said "if the cedars have caught fire"? Not that the flame can prevail over the righteous![21] We may deduce *a fortiori* from the golden altar[22] and from Hananiah, Mishael and Azariah,[23] over whom fire did not prevail—that is, over their bodies—that the flame does not prevail over a *tsaddiq*. No, we speak of fire to express the quickness of his passing.[24] If the designated cedars, the pillars of the diaspora, have caught fire, what hope is there for the lowly moss generated upon the wall, when the wall is devastated and destroyed by their behavior?[25] What will become of them in their punishment, what will become of them when their protecting wall has been removed?

---

17. Here the preacher passes from a general comparison between the cedar and the human soul, drawn from his sermon on *Ḥuqqat,* to the special character of the deceased.

18. I.e, David Farar was one of the founders of the Jewish community in Amsterdam. Cf. Modena, *Ziqnei,* nu. 33. Morteira wrote *hyhvd'* as an abbreviation, apparently for *ha-yehudut,* an unusual form that Morteira uses elsewhere in his sermons. Cf. Ben Yehudah, 4:1084b. The reason for the use of this form may be explained below (l. 144) : "Jew, a word in which the name of God is contained," (i.e., unlike in the form *Yahadut,* in this form the divine name YHV is included). See below, nn. 37 and 39.

19. The metaphor expressing strength and obstinate determination is based on Jer. 1:18. Elsewhere in his sermons, Morteira says, "Like this pillar which stands erect, not moving for anything" (vol. 2, fol. 161r), and "It was made as strong as this iron, which is not susceptible to destruction" (vol. 5, fol. 104r).

20. Having shown that "cedar" fits the deceased in this one respect, the preacher applies the statement of the Talmudic eulogist to the congregation of listeners. This will be the pattern throughout the rest of the eulogy.

21. Morteira does not want to concede that "the cedars have (actually) caught fire," i.e., that fire can overcome the righteous man, perhaps because of the resonance with the *auto da fé* of the Inquisition. There was an old tradition among Iberian Jews that one who is killed as a martyr does not feel pain even when being burned. See above, chap. 15, intro., n. 21).

22. According to the Midrash, Moses was amazed that the fire of the continual offering would not burn the bronze or the wood of the altar (but there is no reference in this context to the altar of gold): *Tanḥuma Terumah* 10–11, cf. Ginzberg, 3:162. If the fire does not prevail over the inanimate elements, it will certainly not prevail over the *tsaddiq*.

23. See Dan. 3:19–27.

24. Cf. the first eulogy, l. 21.

25. I.e., the protecting wall is destroyed through the behavior of inferior beings ("the moss"), who are left without protection.

The cedar also serves as an example of height, for example in the verse *whose stature was like the cedar's* (Amos 2:9). Similar to this is the human soul in that its source is lofty, elevated above all other created beings, for it was exhaled by God. The sages said, "Whoever exhales exhales something of his own essence."[26] In this respect too we may say and apply the word "cedar" to this *tsaddiq,* thinking of his stature during the year when he walked with God.[27] This too God showed us as a sign of his love, for he was leader, officer, *parnas* and *memmuneh,*[28] elevated above all others. When one rises to greatness, all his sins are pardoned.[29] If the cedars have caught fire—one who could lead the congregation and unify it—what hope is there for the moss of the wall, those who in their lowliness cause divisiveness and remove from the congregation good leadership?[30]

The cedar was also taken for the building of things pertaining to the divine, as we see in the verse, *The cedar of the interior of the house . . . was all cedar, no stone was exposed; . . . he overlaid its cedar altar* (1 Kings 6:18,20). This is a particular quality of the human soul, which alone can serve to apprehend spiritual things, not the body from which they are in a different category.[31] That is why the prophets used figurative language in apprehending

26. On this epigram, see Halamish (I am grateful to Moshe Idel for this reference). Morteira's formulation is identical with that of Moses Cordovero, *Pardes Rimonim* 1,5. Almost all the sources cited by Halamish belong to the Kabbalistic tradition and attribute the epigram either to the Zohar or to RaMBaN, even though it does not appear in either one. It is noteworthy that Morteira cites it as a rabbinic statement. In the sermon "When a Man Dies," he wrote, "*He blew into his nostrils the breath of life* (Gen. 2:7): the sages taught about the essence of the act in their statement, 'Whoever exhales exhales something of his own essence.'"

Halamish does not discuss the fascinating history of this statement in Christian sources. It was apparently used by Gnostics in conjunction with Genesis 2:7 to prove that the human soul was part of the actual substance of God. See Augustine, *Literal Meaning,* 2:4, and *De Genesis,* p. 202. Thomas Aquinas cites it as an accepted principle: "Sed ille qui spirat aliquid a se emittit" (Summa Theologiae Ia 90:1), but argues against the conclusion that seems to flow from it. The interrelations between the Christian and Jewish sources need to be investigated.

27. This allusion to Genesis 6:9 recalls the ending of the first eulogy.

28. Cf. the first eulogy, l. 35.

29. Cf. B. Sanh 14a.

30. Morteira emphasizes the role of Farar as a force for unity, contrasting this with other forces for divisiveness in the congregation. It is likely that he is alluding to events that the listeners would remember well. Cf. ll. 218–19.

31. In the sermon "When a Man Dies," he writes, "So the knowledge of metaphysical matters rests upon the human soul, for this comes not from any power of the physical body but from the special quality of the divine soul."

spiritual things.[32] In this too, our righteous departed may be compared to the cedar, for he served all things of a spiritual nature, and was first for everything pertaining to holiness:[33] judging in peace, gathering charitable funds to redeem the captive and marry off the orphan,[34] passing ordinances for a voluntary society, establishing an academy, annulling transgressions, involving himself in communal necessities, speaking before Gentile scholars.[35] In short, he was like a cedar, serving in all matters pertaining to God. If the divine cedars have caught fire, what hope is there for the moss on the wall, those whose social life is represented by a wall: material things, food and drink, prostitutes, swearing, and all other sins?

The cedar is always associated with the name of God, as in the verses, *the cedars of God by its boughs* (Ps. 80:11), [*The trees of the Lord drink their fill,*] *the cedars of Lebanon, His own planting* (Ps. 104:16). This quality also is to be found in the human soul, which is called the spirit of God,[36] *the soul of Shaddai* (Job 32:8), *the lamp of the Eternal* (Prov. 20:27), and many similar expressions. How fitting too is this quality for the *tsaddiq* who was called by God's name wherever he went. During the first years in this land, when people used to conceal their [Jewish] names, he would proclaim his in public, as events occurred every day.[37] That is why many Gentiles from the ends of the earth came to seek him out.[38] Even in Spain, in a place of danger, he did not

---

32. Although the manuscript clearly reads *yeradmu*, this is substantively problematic, as no Jewish thinker holds that prophetic apprehension comes only while the prophet sleeps. The following parallel passage from the sermon "When a Man Dies" indicates the word intended by Morteira was undoubtedly *yedammu* (i.e., "use figurative language")—the same Hebrew letters except for the *resh*: "Here we see how the prophets envisioned the divine and apprehended incorporeal matters by expressing them through corporeal forms, even though those forms did not actually exist. They could not communicate the reality to which they alluded because of the exalted nature of the subject and the lack of appropriate words."

33. Cf. the first eulogy, l. 28.

34. A reference to Farar's involvement in the *Santa Companha de dotar orphas e donzellas* (see Pieterse, *Bet Haim*, p. 186). Presumably, listeners would have been able to recall Farar's deeds in all of the various contexts enumerated.

35. See the discussion of Farar's public disputation with Hugh Broughton in the introduction.

36. It is unclear which of the many occurrences of this phrase in the Bible Morteira understands as a reference to the human soul (as opposed to divine inspiration). The sermon "When a Man Dies" gives Gen. 6:3 as an illustration.

37. During the earliest period of Jewish settlement in Amsterdam, there was no official permission for Jews to live openly as Jews. See the review of this period in Baron, *SRHJ* 15:22–25, with bibliography in the relevant notes, and for a more recent analysis of the later texts on the origins of the community, see Salomon, "Myth."

38. Cf. the first eulogy, ll. 40–41. *Qetsot ha-'arets* may allude to England (Angle-terre), from which Broughton, Farar's antagonist, hailed; cf. Roth, *Menasseh*, p. 207.

conceal it; he identified himself as a Jew, a word in which the name of God is contained.[39] If the cedars have caught fire, what hope is there for the moss on the wall which, because of excessive fear and insufficient trust, spurned it and denied it and voluntarily went to a place where they had to hope not to be recognized, lying to God by denying His name.[40]

The cedar is a simile for the *tsaddiq,* as we see in the verse, *The righteous* (*tsaddiq*) *flourish like a date-palm, they thrive like a cedar in Lebanon* (Ps. 92:13). This is indeed a quality of the soul, which finds no true serenity or joy except in justice, honesty, and truth. It rejoices not in physical pleasures, but rather in the disciplines of wisdom and the apprehension of truth.[41] So with this *tsaddiq*: we know that he flourished like a date-palm, straightforward, without deviousness, never diverting himself to left or right as he walked. And his truthfulness:[42] speaking what was in his heart, not saying one thing and thinking another. How he rejoiced in truth and justice, how distant he was from falsehood![43] If the cedars have caught fire, what hope is there for the moss on the wall, which has no roots? Sometimes they will be there and sometimes not, and truth is absent from their lips.

The cedar is also a tree into which no worm can enter, which does not decay, a quality indeed present in the human soul, which does not decay and is not destroyed.[44] So it is that this *tsaddiq* was like a cedar which did not decay. We see this in the verses, *we will panel it with cedar* (Song 8:9), *for the name of the righteous* (*tsaddiq*) *is invoked in blessing, but the fame of the wicked*

---

39. I.e., the three different letters of the tetragrammaton are in the word *Yehudi;* cf. n. 18 above. The reference to "Spain" may clarify the assertion in the first eulogy, l. 29, but it is not itself fully clear; see the introduction.

40. A reference to the return of Jews to the Iberian peninsula for various purposes: see n. 31 to the introduction. Former New Christians on Spanish or Portuguese soil would have had to conceal their reclaimed Jewish identity.

41. In the sermon "When a Man Dies," he writes, "So the soul rejoices only in justice, and nothing but probity can rest comfortably upon it, for we have observed all this ourselves: that all the good things and successes that chance upon the body, bringing it benefit and pleasure, do not bring it happiness, as the well-being of the body is not what makes happy the soul."

42. I am uncertain how to render intelligibly in this context the following word, *va-amito.* The proposed rendering seems to express Morteira's thought, but the Hebrew syntax is wrenched, and the word may be out of place or the beginning of a thought that was then formulated differently.

43. The emphasis placed by Morteira on these qualities of truthfulness and forthrightness might indicate that others saw in Farar an intolerance for ambiguities, a lack of discretion, or an inability to refrain from saying what was on his mind, qualities that could well have left bruised feelings. It is the eulogist's task not to falsify, but to present things in the best possible light.

44. In the sermon "When a Man Dies," he writes, "Just as the cedar is the one tree that does not decay, into which the worm cannot enter, so the soul is eternal and is not annihilated."

rots (Prov. 10:7). His memory is for the world to come;[45] it will not rot or be destroyed throughout the generations. This is a clear indication of his perfect rest, for all those with whom the spirit of their fellow human beings are pleased, the spirit of the Omnipresent is pleased with.[46] His memory will always be blessed, *the tsaddiq will be remembered forevermore* (Ps. 112:6). If the cedars have caught fire, what hope is there for the moss on the wall—the ordinary people who have no memorial, who have never performed an act to be mentioned with blessing—after their death. Such acts are extremely beneficial, as we see in the verse, *the name of the righteous is invoked in blessing, but the fame of the wicked rots* (Prov. 10:7). What blessing and rotting can be meant here, except for reward and punishment?[47] Thus in the first part of the metaphorical statement, using the cedar, we see explained some of the qualities of the *tsaddiq* pertaining to personal conduct.[48]

Secondly, he said, "If Leviathan has been hauled in by a fish-hook, what hope is there for the minnows?" This statement too applies essentially to this *tsaddiq*. For "Leviathan" has four meanings. The first is the name of a great fish, as in the verses, *Leviathan that You formed to sport with* (Ps. 104:26), *Leviathan the elusive serpent* (Isa. 27:1), and so forth. Now it is said, if Leviathan—a healthy man, handsome, looking like royalty, like an angel of God (cf. Jud. 8:18, 13:6),[49] *whose eyes were undimmed and his vigor unabated* (Deut. 34:7), who never had pain in his head[50] and was healthy—was "hauled in by a fish-hook"—by such a minor illness,[51] "what hope is there for the minnows"— the elderly, the weak, frail in body and emaciated? How easily *the wind shall carry them off, the whirlwind shall scatter them* (Isa. 41:16), unless they *look to their ways* (Ps. 119:15).

A second meaning for "Leviathan" is derived from the word *yelalah,* "wailing." The Aramaic translation of the word in the verse *those prepared to rouse up Leviathan* (Job 3:8) is "wailing."[52] Thus the meaning of "If Leviathan . . . " is, if one who causes wailing and grief for the entire people[53] at his illness, as

45. Based on B. Qid 31b.

46. M. Avot 3,10; cf. the first eulogy, ll. 49–50.

47. I.e., the proper interpretation of Proverbs 10:7 is in relation to the reward and punishment of the deceased.

48. Cf. above, n. 11. The preacher summarizes and brings to an end the first part of the eulogy, based on the metaphor of the cedar.

49. A reference to Farar's handsome appearance. Morteira referred not infrequently in his sermons to the noble bearing of the Sephardic Jews.

50. Based on B. 'Erub 54a. Not only were there no signs of aging, but there was no serious illness, as he goes on to emphasize.

51. Cf. the first eulogy, l. 21, and the second, l. 112.

52. Cf. Jastrow, p. 49, s.v. *'ilavyuta,* Ben Yehudah, 2642–43, s.v. *leviyatan* (b).

53. I am unable to render intelligibly in this context the following word *MQTsH.*

all of them prayed to God to cure him,[54] and at his death the entire household of Israel wept—an unambiguous indication of his righteousness[55]—"what hope is there for the minnows," at whose death people will rejoice because of their lowliness and wickedness? We see this in the verse, *When the wicked perish there are shouts of joy* (Prov. 11:10).

A third meaning for "Leviathan" is derived from the word *livvuy*, "accompaniment." Thus he said, "If Leviathan," who was *a graceful wreath (leviyyat ḥen) upon our head, a necklace upon our throat* (cf. Prov. 1:9), he who used to honor us by his accompaniment,[56] who was at the head of the funeral procession, the voluntary society, the academy[57]—if he "has been hauled in by a fish-hook, what hope is there for the minnows," from whom people keep their distance because of their stench.

A fourth meaning is derived from "Levite."[58] He said, "If such a great man, of distinguished ancestral lineage, linked with the chosen tribe of Levi on his mother's side,[59] for that is why he was not redeemed although he was a first-born[60]—if Leviathan reaching such a level of perfection has been hauled in by a fish-hook, what hope is there for the minnows" of ordinary families, having no merit from their ancestors?

He concluded by saying, "If the hook has fallen into the mighty river (*naḥal*), what hope is there for the waterholes?" This too can be interpreted in five ways, each one of them proclaiming the kinds of excellence in character and mind found together in this *tsaddiq*. First, *naḥal* has the meaning "river," for his excellence was like a river flowing continuously day and night, never ceasing to do the will of his heavenly Father.[61] Who has not seen him on many days? When his ships arrived,[62] the poor, the orphan and the

---

54. Thus Farar's illness lasted long enough for communal prayers to be offered for his recovery.

55. Cf. B. Shab 153a and MaHaRaL of Prague, *Ḥiddushei Aggadot* ad loc. (MaHaRaL, 9:87).

56. Perhaps by his participation in funeral services in his role as a leader of the *Biqqur Ḥolim* Society.

57. Cf. l. 131 above.

58. The Levitical office was especially important to Morteira because of his own identity as a Levite.

59. The reading *mi-tsad immo* is not certain; if correct it would mean that Farar was not a Levite himself, but his mother was the daughter of a Levite. In any case, the passage is striking confirmation of the penchant among certain New Christian families to preserve the traditions of family lineage. Cf. Roth, *Marranos,* pp. 192–93.

60. Alluding to the biblical obligation of redeeming the first-born (Exod. 13:13 and elsewhere) but not the son of a Levite woman (Maimonides, *Code, Bikkurim,* 11,10).

61. Cf. Gen. 8:22 and M. Avot 5,20.

62. On Farar's commercial activity, see n. 36 to the introduction.

widow would rejoice when they went forth from his house.[63] People entered and left carrying many gifts, such that *his food was given* [away], *his drink was assured* (Isa. 33:16), always consistently, like a flowing river. "If the hook has fallen into the mighty river, what hope is there for the waterholes," which are not of benefit to all others?

The word can also be derived from *nahalah,* inheritance, for he was a lion whose father was a lion, a good man whose father was good, a priest whose father was a priest.[64] His goodness was a legacy from his ancestors. He was the son of the esteemed R. Abraham Farar the Elder, of blessed memory,[65] a model of goodness, such that there was a constantly flowing inheritance (*nahalah*). If even into this "the hook has fallen, what hope is there for the waterholes," that have no origins to speak of?

In addition, *nahal* can be derived from *holi,* "sickness," as we see in the biblical phrase *my wound is grievous* (*nahlah makati*) (Jer. 10:19). He therefore says, "If in the mighty *nahal*"—if one whose passing has caused a general sickness (*holi*), a universal weeping, *for every head is ailing* (*le-holi*) *and every heart is sick* (Isa. 1:5), for our heads and our hearts have been wounded—despite it all "the hook has fallen, what hope is there for the waterholes," at whose passing no one will pay any attention?

Furthermore, *nahal* is etymologically linked with music, as in the biblical phrase *For the leader, on the nehilot* (Ps. 5:1). Thus the eulogist spoke of continuous, harmonious music—for this *tsaddiq* was composed of all the qualities that combine as yet another fine quality to make beautiful music: wisdom, reverence, beauty, decency, love, justice, strength, eloquence, healing. All the sounds of this music were played continuously with a sweetness that brought joy to God and man.[66] If with such a man "the hook has fallen, what hope is there for the waterholes," that lack any element of perfection?

Finally, *nahal* can be derived from the Talmudic phrase for a swarm (*nahil*) of bees.[67] He therefore said, if this mighty *nahal,* the entire congregation—for he was the one who unified it, in him alone the entire congregation was represented, he perfected it, he brought it together, he was the

---

63. Cf. the first eulogy, l. 30.

64. Cf. Y. Ber 7d, B. Ber 28a.

65. On Abraham Farar the Elder, see Pieterse, *Bet Haim,* p. 186, and the introduction. In his eulogy delivered thirty days after the death of Abraham the Elder, Morteira pointed to the fine son of the deceased as a factor that had enabled him to face death with equanimity.

66. The various personal qualities are compared to the strings of a string instrument (*nimei ha-niggun*), which produce a series of harmonious chords. In other sermons as well, Morteira occasionally reveals a love of music, possibly acquired during his youth in Venice.

67. As in, e.g., M. BQ 10,2.

source of its joy[68]—if here too "the hook has fallen, what hope is there for the waterholes," who fail to manifest even their own individual potential? In short, whoever can think of all these things and not fear for his soul, but remains slothful in the fear of God during the eulogy for a decent man, such a person deserves to be buried alive.[69]

Young children have no thought or concern about the provisions they need for survival so long as their father, at whose table they eat, remains alive, for they rely upon him. But when he dies, they must necessarily begin to fear and make an effort to find provisions for themselves. So at the loss of a shelter like this, a protecting father for all,[70] about whom we once said, *in his shade we live among the nations* (cf. Lam 4:20), the people as a whole must begin to think that now he is missing, each person needs to face the burdens of individual work. This is the meaning of the statement, "Weep for the losers, not for the lost, for he is at rest—about to receive the reward for his actions—while we are in distress."[71] Instead of being protected by his merit, we are now left in distress, each one to be helped by his own efforts. That is why we say, "They have departed for their resting places, leaving us to our sighs."[72] For he is certainly at rest, at perfect rest. Even though "not every man is worthy of two tables,"[73] through the beauty and decency of his deeds he earned both. He had success in this world, and it will be good for him in the next.

This is as we began in our theme verse, *An innocent man* (*tam*) (Gen. 25:27), meaning a complete man (*tamim*), perfect in everything, *dwelling in tents* (Gen. 25:27),[74] dwelling peacefully in two tents, this world and the world to come, for both of them are called "tents."[75] This world, in the verse, *stretched them out like a tent to dwell in* (Isa. 40:22). The world to come, in the verse, *Lord, who may sojourn in Your tent, who may dwell on Your holy mountain? He who lives without blame, who does what is right, and in his heart acknowledges the truth, whose tongue is not given to evil, who has never done*

68. Again the emphasis on Farar as a force for unity in the congregation, making it like a hive of bees; cf. l. 123.

69. By returning to the statement discussed in the introduction, Morteira signals the end of the body of the sermon and the transition to the coda.

70. Cf. above, ll. 113–15.

71. The conclusion of the *ma'amar* (with the preacher's interpolation of a phrase about the reward awaiting the deceased).

72. *Seliḥot*, p. 166.

73. See B. Ber 5b and Tosafot s.v. *lo'*.

74. As in the first eulogy, Morteira reaches the *nose* from the weekly lesson (*Toledot*) only at the end, as part of his conclusion.

75. The plural "tents" is interpreted as a reference to the two realms (before and after death), the two "tables" in the Talmudic statement.

harm to his fellow, or borne reproach for his neighbor; for whom a contemptible man is abhorrent, but who honors those who fear the Lord; who stands by his oath even to his hurt; who has never lent money at interest, or accepted a bribe against the innocent (Ps. 15:1–5): all qualities openly manifest and recognized in this *tsaddiq*. He will therefore receive their reward with the conclusion of the Psalm: *He who acts thus shall never be shaken* (Ps. 15:5). May God remember his merit on our behalf and put an end to our sorrows. But our duty is to accept this judgment, and to say "Blessed is the Judge of Truth."[76]

The sermon I delivered at the conclusion of the thirty day period following the decease of my dear and pleasant friend, the outstanding physician, the consummate Hakham, Rabbi David Ferrar (*sic*), may the memory of the righteous and saintly be for blessing. It was on the second day of the month of Kislev, 5385 [November 13, 1624].[77]

---

76. See n. 41 to the first eulogy.
77. The thirtieth day counting the day of the funeral.

שאול לוי מורטירה
ההספדים על ד"ר דוד פרר

.1

אלה תולדות נח נח איש צדיק תמים היה בדורותיו את האלהים
התהלך נח[1] ב"ר הה"ד [פרי צדיק עץ][2] חיים. צדיק מה פירותיו?
מצוות ומעשים טובים.[3]

בהיות כי מגמת הספדנין בהספד היא דברים רבים לעורר
הלבבות לבכי[4] [   ] בדין לנחם האבלים[5] לכבד את המת בסיפור   5
תושבחותיו[6] אני לא באתי כאן [להכריז] על האבידה המרה הזאת
הן כי ממנה נודעת וממנה נגלית[7] והן כי לבי בל עמי [   ][8]
ופשטים כי נגעה חרב עד הנפש.[9] ולא באתי לנחם האבלים כי כן
צוו חכמים [ולא לנחם אדם] בשעה שמתו מוטל לפניו[10] ולא לעורר
הלבבות לבכי כי מאליהם תזלנה העינים [   ] חכם שאבד אין לך   10
כיוצא בו.[11] ולא לספר תושבחותיו הן כי נודעות וגלויות והן כי
יו [   ] בהיותם הם רבי המספר.

אכן רוב חובתי הכריחני לקונן ולהספיד על הצדיק הזו[ה לסלק]
חובותי אליו ושלא להיות כפוי בפירוד האחרון הזה. וחובותי אליו
הם בכל הטובות הנק[נות] גוף ונפש וממון: בגוף בהיותו כל כך   15
זריז בתרופתי ורפואת אנשי ביתי בלי שכר ואדרבה ב[   ] מעולות,
בממון בהיותי בעבורו במצב אשר אני נמצא היום, בנפש כי

1. בר' ו ט.
2. משלי יא ל.
3. בראשית רבה ל,ו.
4. עי' טוב, יורה דעה, שמד,א: "לומר עליו דברים המשברים את הלב כדי להרבות בבכיה."
5. עי' משה אלמוסנינו, מאמץ כח, עמ' ריח ב: "הנחמה אשר היא גם היא חלק מההספד
הנעשה על כל המתים."
6. עי' טוב, שם: "ולהזכיר שבחו [של הנפטר]."
7. כנראה ע"פ משנה בבא מציעא ב,ו: "ועד מתי חיב להכריז [על האבידה]? עד כדי שידעו בו
שכניו."
8. אולי יש לגרוס "[לומר חידושים] ופשטים."
9. יר' ד י.
10. עי' משנה אבות ד,יח.
11. ע"פ הוריות יג א.

ממעשיו למד[תי] לעבוד את ה' כראוי. אם כן כדי להחזיק מעט את

המרובה,[12] ולעשות כמאמרם ז"ל דאגה [בלב] איש ישחנה: ישיחנה

20 לאחרים,[13] בחרתי לקונן בקול מר שני דברים הגם כי בלתי סדר כפי

אן] נתן לנו ומן פתאומיות הרע המר והנמהר הזה.[14]

וכדי לילך בסדר אומר כי שמות לשון הקדׁ[נש] יחלקום

המדקדקים לד' מינים והם שם העצם יחס תואר מספר[15] ומתוכם

יודע כמה ענ[י]נ[ים] בדבר הנקרא. ואם נייחסם בצדיק הזה הנפטר

25 נמצאם כולם לטובה.

כי שם העצם שלו הוא דוד שמורה אהבה ודודים מי לא ידע כל

אלה כמה היה אהוב לשמים ואהוב לברי[ו]ת[16] לשמים במצוותיו

בקנאתו ראשון לכל דבר שבקדושה[17] אוהב אהוביו[18] אוהב ה' עד

שמסתכן גופו אוהב את הבריות יאמרו נא אוהביו יאמרו נא

30 העניים יאמרו נא האלמנות אשר ביד רחבה יחנם ויפרה ממונם

[והשלומות אשר שם תמיד בין אדם לחבירו)[19] וכל זה כפי שמו

העצם דוד הוא ודודים מעשיו.

והנה שם התואר שלו הוא רופא ראו כמה שנים היה רופא חברת

בקור חולים רופא העניים בשמחה ועולה לבתיהם ונותן להם

35 צדקה. ועוד יש לו שם תואר אחר פרנס וממונה של ק"ק בית יעקב

בכו כולם עליו על תואר זה איה ראשכם איה פרנסכם גלה כבוד

מיעקב[20] לא יעמוד לימין החזן בימים נוראים לא ידרוש עוד

בשבתות הידועים אשרי איש מתואר בתוארים אלה.

והנה שם היחס שלו הוא יהודי כמה היה מכבד השם הזה

40 בפרסמו תורת ה' כבוד העם הזה אנה ילכו עתה הגוים אשר יבואו

12. ע"פ בראשית רבה ה,ז ועוד.

13. ע"פ יומא עה א, פירוש של משלי יב כה.

14. ע"פ חב"י א ו.

15. עי' הערה 29 למבוא על "שפה ברורה" של מנשה בן ישראל.

16. ע"פ ברכות יז א ("אהוב למעלה ונחמד למטה") וקדושין מ א ("טוב לשמים לבריות").

17. ע"פ גטין נט ב.

18. ע"פ במדבר רבה ח,ד.

19. עי' הערה 22 לתרגום.

20. ע"פ ש"א ד כא ("גלה כבוד מישראל"), כאן בהתיחסות לשם הקהילה (בית יעקב).

לבקש את דבר ה' פנה האיש אשר לפני גדולים וייעצי ארץ הזן]²¹[
כי תורת ה' תמימה²² ונצחית, פנה אשר החזיר למוטב כמה מבני
עמנו וכל זה כפי היחס שלו.

והנה] שם המספר הנה לו אחד כי לא הניח בן והנו א' בדורו
45 כיהושוע עבד ה' שלא היה לו בן כי ספר הכתוב תולדות אבותיו עד
יהושוע ולא יותר.²³ ומה יוציא מכאן האיש הנלבב כי אם שארו]ות[
נפשו אשר תעדן בעדן במעשים הרבים אשר לא יקפח ה' שכרם²⁴
כי הם בניו באמת כמו שהתנ]חלנו[אלה תולדות נח:²⁵ היות נח איש
צדיק תמים²⁶ היה בדורותיו כצדיק כי רוח הבריות נוחה הימינו וכן
50 רוח המקום נוחה הימינו²⁷ ואת האלהים התהלך נח לנוח במנוחה
שאננה²⁸ כדכתיב ינוחו על משכבותם²⁹ כענין שני בחנוך ויתהלך
חנוך את האלהים ואיננו כי לקח אותו אלהים.³⁰

ואותנו יחמול ה' כי אנחנו אבדנו עטרת ראשנו ואוי נא לנו כי
חטאנו³¹ כי מפני הרעה נאסף הצדיק.³² יהי רצון מלפ]ניו[שיאמר
55 לצרותינו די, למלאך המשחית הרף ידך.³³ ועלינו להצדיק את הדין
ולומר ברוך דיין האמת.³⁴

דרוש שדרשתי בבית החיים על ארון החכם השלם הרופא
המובהק כמה"ר דוד פרר תנצב"ה אהובי היקר והנעים ביום ג'
ב' לחדש חשון משנת השפ"ה לפ"ק נשמתו לחיי העולם הבא.

21. אפשר לגרוס „הזהיר" (במובן הוראה, עי' שמ' יח כ) או „הזעיק" (במובן הכרזה, עי' יונה ג,ז).

22. תה' יט ח.

23. עי' דבה"א ז ז, מגילה יד ב.

24. ע"פ תנחומא, וירא ג, ועוד.

25. בר' ו ט, נושא הדרשה.

26. השוה תנחומא, נח פרק ב, ועי' הערה 38 לתרגום.

27. ע"פ משנה אבות ג,י.

28. ע"פ יש' לב יח. הדרשן מפרש „נח" בסוף בר' ו ט כשם פעולה: התהלך במנוחה.

29. יש' נז ב.

30. בר' ה כד.

31. ע"פ איכה ה טז.

32. יש' נז א.

33. השוה דבה"א כא טו.

34. סיום קבוע לכל ההספדים של מורטירה.

"הצדיק אבד"[1]

.2

60 איש תם יושב אהלים.[2]

מועד קטן פרק אלו מגלחין, כי נח נפשי דרב אשי פתח עליה
ההוא ספדנא אם בארזים נפלה שלהבת מה יעשו אזובי קיר אם
לויתן בחכה הועלה מה יעשו דגי הרקק אם בנחל שוטף נפלה חכה
מה יעשו גבים. א"ל בר אבין ח"ו בחכה ושלהבת אמינא בצדיקי
65 אלא בכו לאובדים ולא לאבידה שהיא מנוחה ואנו לאנחה עכ"ל.[3]

מאד הפליגו רז"ל בחובת ההספד על אדם כשר עד אשר אמרו כל
1 המתעצל בהספדו של אדם כשר ראוי לקוברו בחייו.[4] והנה הראו
סיבת הפלגתם בענין באופן דבורם כי לא אמרו כל שאינו מספיד
אדם כשר אלא אמרו כל המתעצל בהספדו וכו' להורות כי תועלת
70 גדולה תגיע לנו מן ההספד והוא כי בה יתפרסמו ויוזכרו מעלות
הנפטר וגם יפחד האדם מן הדין ויבקש להדמות לצדיק ההוא
באופן כי או במה שיבקש להדמות אל המדות ההמה או במה
שיעשה ק"ו בעצמו אם בצידיקים כן ברשעים עאכ"ו ובזה ישוב אל
ה' וירחמהו ויהא זריז במצוות האל ית'.
75 ועתה יאמר כל המתעצל בהספדו של אדם כשר לא שיתעצל
בהספדת ההספד אלא כל המתעצל מן המצוות בהספדו של אדם
כשר בשומעו ההספד שעושים על אדם כשר ושומע מעלותיו
ומתעצל שוב אין לו תקנה הואיל ולא קם ולא זע מעצלותו בענין
גדול כזה כאשר הוא מיתתם של צדיקים. ולכן ראוי לקוברו בחייו
80 כי בודאי זה רשע גמור ולבו לב האבן לא ימס, ורשעים בחייהם
קרוים מתים[5] והמתים קוברים אותם, ולכן זה כרשע ראוי לקוברו
בחייו. ועל כן אמרו כל המתעצל ולא אמרו כל מי שאינו עושה
הספד וכו'.

1. יש' נז א.
2. בר' כה כז, נושא הדרשה.
3. מועד קטן כה ב. המאמר ישמש כיסוד מבנה ההספד.
4. שבת קה א.
5. ברכות יח ב.

התעלות האלו שניהם היה מוציא מהספד רב אשי ההוא ספדנא
שהתחלנו דבריו[6] שהיה מספר תושבחות הנפטר ומלמד מהם מוסר
אל השומעים לעשות מהם ק״ו בעצמם ובזה היה מהנה לשומעים
ולנפטר, לשומעים כי ישובו מדרכם הרעה ולנפטר להיות לו לזכות
גדול לפני בוראו הואיל ואף במיתתו עבד האל כבחייו להחזיר
למוטב בני עמו.[7]

והנה חלק דבריו לג׳ חלקים ונתן בצדיק ג׳ משלים וקראו ארז
לויתן נחל שוטף. והנה הנם להורות שלמותו בכל שלשת ההנהגות
אשר בהם יתנהג האדם והם הנהגת עצמו הנהגת המדינה והנהגת
הבית והוציא מהם ק״ו אם לשלם בכולם קרה כך מה יעשו
החסרים בכולם. והתחיל ואמר אם בארזים נפלה שלהבת מה יעשו
אזובי קיר.

והתחיל ואמר אם בארזים נפלה שלהבת,[8] ודמהו לארז אשר בו
לבדו כמה מעלות טובות מתדמות לנפש האדם כמו שבארתי באורך
בדרושי לפרשת חוקה על פסוק ולקח הכהן עץ ארז,[9] כי תחלה הארז
הוא המעולה שבאלנות כמו ששלח מלך ישראל למלך יהודה, האזוב
אשר בקיר אל הארז אשר בלבנון[10] ר״ל המעולה אל הפחות. מעלה
פרטית אל נשמת האדם בין כל נבראי ששת ימי בראשית כי בה
לבדה נאמר נעשה ונופחה מה״,[11] והוצרכה להמלכה מה שיורה
בבירור נצחיות הכאשר בארנו פעמים רבות.

ועל כן כמה יאות כפי הבחינה הזאת התאר הזה של ארז אל
הצדיק הזה הנפטר כי היה המסומן והמעולה שבקהלה הזאת
להיות הראשון ממייסדי היהוד[12] ואשר כעמוד ברזל העמידוהו[13] עד

---

6. במאמר שנקרא בתחלת ההספד. כאן מתחיל הדרשן מעבר מההקדמה לגוף הדרשה.
7. עי׳ בהספד הראשון. כאן סיום ההקדמה.
8. כנראה שכח המחבר למחוק את המשפט הקודם. הניסוח השני הוא נכון, כיון שהדרשן
   ישתמש כאן רק בארבע המלים הראשונות של המאמר.
9. במ׳ יט ו. על הדרשה „אדם כי ימות״ עי׳ הערה 13 לתרגום והערות בהמשך.
10. השוה מ״ב יד ט. הציטוט אינו מדויק.
11. ז״א הפסוקים בר׳ א כו ובר׳ ב ז מצביעים על יחידותה של הנשמה האנושית.
12. דוד פרר היה אחד ממייסדי הקהלה היהודית באמסטרדם. כנראה התשמש מורטירה
    במלה „היהודות,״ עי׳ הערה 18 לתרגום והערה 29 למטה.
13. ע״פ יר׳ א יח.

היום הזה ולא חשש לעמל וטורח עד אשר העמידהו על עמדו[14]
באופן כי ארז מעולה ראוי להקראות.

ועתה מה יאמר אומר אם בארזים נפלה שלהבת ולא ח״ו
שישלוט שלהבת בצדיק דק״ו ממזבח הזהב[15] ומחנניה מישאל
ועזריה[16] שלא שלט בהם האש ר״ל בגופם כי לא ישלוט בצדיק
שלהבת אלא אמרנו שלהבת על מהירות פטירתו ואם בארזים
המסומנים עמודי הגולה נפלה שלהבת מה יעשה אזובי קיר שפלים
אשר יולדו בקיר לאבדונו ולהרסו בפעולותיהם מה יהיה מהם
כעונשם ומה יהיה מהם כי לוקח חומתם ומגינם.

הארז גם כן ילקח למשל הגובה כמו שני אשר כגובה הארזים
גובהו[17] ונדמה אליו נשמת האדם בזה כי מקורה גבוה מכל
הנבראים בבריאה כי נופחה מה׳ ואז״ל כל הנופח מעצמותו הוא
נופח[18] והנה אף בבחינה זו נאמר ונייחס שם ארז לצדיק הזה
בחשבנו במדרגתו בשנה אשר הלך את האלהים כי גם זו הראה לנו
ה׳ סימן אהבתו כי היה לנו לראש ולקצין ופרנס וממונה וגבוה על
הכל כי העולה לגדולה מוחלין לו על כל עונותיו[19] ואם בארזים נפלה
שלהבת במי שהיה מנהיג את הקהל ומאגדו, מה יעשו אזובי קיר
אשר בשפלותם מפרידים אותו ומסירים ממנו כל הנהגה טובה.

ולקח הארז לבנין העניינים האלקים שני וארז אל הבית פנימה
כולו ארז אין אבן נראה ויצף מזבח הארז[20] מעלה פרטית לנשמת
האדם שהיא לבדה תשמש להשיג העניינים הרוחניים ולא הגוף
שאינם ממינו. ולכן ירדמו[21] הנביאים בהשגתם. ואף גם זאת
ידמה היטיב הצדיק הזה אל הארז כי הוא היה משמש לכל העניינים

---

14. ע״פ דבה״ב לד לא.

15. השוה תנחומא, תרומה 10–11, והערות 22–21 לתרגום.

16. עי׳ דנ׳ ג יט-כז.

17. עמוס ב ט.

18. על פתגם זה, עי׳ הערה 26 לתרגום.

19. השוה סנהדרין יד א.

20. ע״פ מ״א ו יח ומ״א ו כ.

21. כך בכ״י, אבל לפי התוכן והקטע המקביל בדרשת „אדם כי ימות״, נראה שהמלה הנכונה
היא „ידמו״, שפרושה להביע עניינים מופשטים ע״י דימויים חומריים. עי׳ הערה 32 לתרגום.

130 הרוחניים ולכל דבר שבקדושה הוא היה ראשון[22] לשפוט לשלום
לקבץ צדקה לפדות שבוי להשיא יתומה לתקן חברה לעשות ישיבה
לבטל עבירה לעסוק בצרכי ציבור לדבר לפני חכמי העמים[23] סוף
דבר כארז היה משמש בכל העניינים האלקיים אם בארזים
האלקיים נפלה שלהבת מה יעשו אזובי קיר אותם האנשים אשר
135 אין חברתם אלא הקיר ואל החומר אל המאכל ואל המשתה ואל
הזונות ואל השבועות ואל כל עון.

נקרא הארז תמיד בשם ה' כמו שני' וענפיה ארזי אל,[24] ארזי לבנון
אשר נטע.[25] מעלה אשר נמצאת גם כן בנפש האדם שנקראת רוח
אלק',[26] נשמת שדי[27] נר ה'[28] וכאלה רבים. וכמה גם כן יאותה מעלה
140 הזאת בצדיק אשר שם ה' נקרא עליו בכל מקום שהיה הולך
ובזמנים הראשונים בארץ הזאת אשר היו מעלימים את שמם הנה
הוא בראש חוצות יודיעהו כאשר קרהו מעשים בכל יום ועל כן
יבואו גוים רבים מקצות הארץ לבקש את פניו ואף בספרד במקום
הסכנה לא יעלימהו ויקרא בשם יהודי אשר שם ה' כלול בתוכו.[29]
145 אם בארזים נפלה שלהבת מה יעשו אזובי קיר אשר מרוב פחדם
ומיעוט בטחונם יבזוהו ויכחישוהו וילכו ברצונם למקום אשר
יתנכרו וישקרו אל ה' בכחש את שמו.

נמשל הארז אל הצדיק שני' צדיק כתמר יפרח כארז בלבנון
ישגא[30] מעלת הנשמה ממש אשר לא תשקוט ותשמח כי אם בצדק
150 וביושר ואמת כי לא תשמח בעדוני הגוף אלא בחכמות והשגת
האמת. כמו כן הצדיק הזה ידענו ממנו כי היה כתמר בפרחו ישר

22. ע"פ גטין נט ב, והשוה ההספד הראשון.
23. עי' הדיון בויכוחו של פרר עם היו בראוטון במבוא.
24. תה' פ יא.
25. תה' קד טז.
26. בדרשת ,,אדם כי ימות" מורטירה מצטט בר' ו ג להדגיש כינוי זה לנפש.
27. איוב לב ח, לג ד.
28. משלי כ כז.
29. ז"א שלוש האותיות השונות שבשם הויה מופיעות במלים ,,יהודי" ו,,יהודות" (עי' לעיל, הערה 12).
30. תה' צב יג.

בלי עקום ולא יפנה ימין ושמאל בלכתו ואמתו[31] וידבר מה שבלבו
ולא א׳ בפה וא׳ בלב וכמה ישמח באמת ובצדק ויהיה השקר מרוחק
ממנו. אם בארזים נפלה שלהבת מה יעשו אזובי קיר אשר אין להם
155 שרש ופעם יהיו פעם לא יהיו ואין אמת בפיהם.

האָרז כמו כן עץ אשר לא יכנס בו התולעת ולא יעופש, ענין ממש
נמצא בנפש האדם אשר לא תתעפ׳ ותכלה. כמו כן הצדיק הזה הוא
כארז שלא יתעפש שנ׳ נצור עליה לוח ארז,[32] כי זכר צדיק לברכה ושם
רשעים ירקב,[33] וזכרונו לחיי העולם הבא[34] ולא ירקב ולא יכלה בכל
160 הדורות סימן גמור לשלומו ומנוחתו כי כל שרוח הבריות נוחה הימנו
רוח המקום נוחה הימנו[35] ותמיד יבורך זכרו ולזכר עולם יהיה
צדיק[36] ואט בארזים נפלה שלהבת מה יעשו אזובי קיר האנשים
השפלים אשר אין להם זכרון ולא עשו מעולם פעולה אשר יבורכו
עליה אחרי מיתתם אשר יועיל מאד כדכתיב זכר צדיק לברכה ושם
165 רשעים ירקב[37] שאם אינו לשכר ועונש מה בברכה וברקבון? והנה כי
בחלק המשל הזה הראשון מן הארז נתבארו קצת ממדות הצדיק
בהנהגת עצמו.[38]

והנה אמר שנית לויתן בחכה הועלה מה יעשו דגי הרקק, מאמר
אשר יתייחס בעצם אל הצדיק הזה כי לויתן יש לו ד׳ כונות הא׳ הוא
170 שם לדג גדול כדכתיב לויתן זה יצרת לשחק בו[39] וכתיב לויתן נחש
בריח[40] וכו׳ והנה נאמר אם לויתן איש בריא ויפה תוארו כתואר בני
המלך מראהו כמראה מלאך האלקים[41] לא כהתה עינו ולא נס

31. אינני מבין משמעות מלה זו כאן, ואולי חסר משהו.
32. שיר ח ט.
33. משלי י ז.
34. ע״פ קדושין לא ב.
35. משנה אבות ג,י והשוה ההספד הראשון, הערה 27.
36. תה׳ קיב ו.
37. משלי י ז.
38. עי׳ הערוה 11 לתרגום. כאן מסיים הדרשן החלק הראשון של ההספד, המבוסס על
המטפורה של הארז.
39. תה׳ קד כו.
40. יש׳ כז א.
41. השוה שו׳ ח יח ושו׳ יג ו.

ליחה[42] ולא חש בראשו[43] ובריא אולם בחכה הועלה בחולי כל כך קל
מה יעשו דגי הרקק מה יהיה מהזקנים החלשים דקי הבשר
והכחושות הלא ודאי יותר בנקל סערה יזרם ורוח תשאם[44] אם לא
יביטו אורחותם.[45]

הכוונה השנית היא לויתן מלשון יללה כדכתיב העתידים עורר
לויתן דמתרגמינן יללה[46] ותהיה הכוונה אם לויתן מי שסיבב יללה
והספד לכל העם מקצה בחוליו בהתפללם כולם אל ה' ירפאהו
ובמותו בכו אותו כל בית ישראל[47] סימן גמור על צדקותיו[48] מה יעשו
דגי הרקק אשר לשפלותם ורשעותם באבדם ירננו כדכתיב באבוד
רשעים רינה.[49]

והכונה השלישית היא לויתן מלשון ליווי ויאמר אם לויתן מי
שהיה לוית חן לראשנו וענקים לגרגרותינו[50] מי שהיה מכבדנו
בלויתו מי שהיה ראש לויה וחברה וישיבה בחכה הועלה מה יעשו
דגי הרקק אשר לסרחונם יתרחקו מהם בני אדם.

והכונה הרביעית היא מלשון לויה ויאמר אם איש גדול ומיוחס
מצד אבותיו כי היה נוגע בשבט הנבחר שבט לוי מצד אמו[51] כי על כן
בהיותו בכור לא נפדה[52] אם לויתן בהיותו שלם אף כזו בחכה הועלה
מה יעשו דגי הרקק ממשפחות בזוויות אשר אין להם זכות אבות.

סיים דבריו ואמר אם בנחל שוטף נפלה חכה מה יעשו גבים
קטנים. ואף אותו יתפרש על ה' דרכים כולם מכריזים מעלות
המידות והמושכלות אשר נמצאות יחד בצדיק הנזכר. ותחלה יהיה
נחל מלשון נהר כי כן היו מעלותיו כנחל שוטף בהמשך רב יומם

42. דב' לד ז.
43. ע"פ עירובין נד א.
44. ע"פ יש' מא טז.
45. ע"פ תה' קיט טו.
46. איוב ג ח, וע"י הערה 52 לתרגום.
47. ע"פ במ' כ כט.
48. השוה שבת קנג א ורש"י שם ד"ה „אם בן עוה"ב הוא."
49. משלי יא י.
50. ע"פ משלי א ט.
51. עי' הערה 59 לתרגום.
52. מצוות פדיון הבכור (שמ' יג יג) איננה חלה על בן לוייה (רמב"ם, הל' בכורים יא י).

195 ולילה לא ישבות[53] מעשות רצון אביו שבשמים.[54] מי לא ראה ימים
רבים בבוא אליו ספינותיו ישמח העני היתום והאלמנה בהמשך
יוצאי ביתו נכנסים ויוצאים נושאי מתנות רבות באופן כי לחמו נתן
מימיו נאמנים[55] בתמידות תדיר כנחל שוטף ואם בנחל שוטף נפלה
חכה מה יעשו גבים קטנים אשר לא יועילו לכל.

200 ויהיה גם כן מלשון נחלה כי היה ארי בן ארי טוב בן טוב מזה בן
מזה[56] והיתה לו הטוביות ירושה לו מאבותיו בנו של הזקן הנכבד ר'
אברהם פירר זצוק"ל דפוס הטוביות באופן כי היתה נחלה שוטפת
ותמידית, ואם בו נפלה חכה מה יעשו גבים קטנים אשר אין להם
שום התחלה.

205 ויהיה גם כן נחל מלשון חולי כענין שכתוב נחלה מכתי[57] ויאמר
אם בנחל שוטף אם במי שבפרידתו מסבב חולי כללי ובכי כולל כי
כל ראש לחלי וכל לבב דוי[58] הואיל והיתה המכה בראשנו ובלבנו,
עם כל זה נפלה בו חכה מה יעשו גבים קטנים אשר לא יקפיד אדם
על פרידתם.

210 ויהי גם כן נחל מלשון נגון כמו למנצח על הנחילות[59] ואמר אם
בניגון מתמיד ומסודר כאשר הוא הצדיק הזה כלול מכל המידות
אשר כמידה הגונה בניהם יחברו ניגון יפה, בו חכמה בו יראה בו
יופי בו דרך ארץ בו אהבה בו צדקה בו עצה בו הלצה בו רפואה וכל
נימי הניגון הזה היו מנגנין בתמידות בנועם המשמח אלקים
215 ואנשים, ואם באיש כזה נפלה חכה מה יעשו גבים קטנים נעדרי כל
שלמות.

ויהיה נחל מלשון נחיל של דבורים[60] ויאמר אם בנחל שוטף שהוא
העדה כולה כי הוא היה מאגדה ובו לבדו נמצאת כל העדה הוא

53. ע"פ בר' ח כב.
54. ע"פ משנה אבות ה,כ.
55. יש' לג טז.
56. השוה ברכות כח א וירושלמי ברכות ז ד.
57. יר' י יט.
58. יש' א ה.
59. תה' ה א.
60. כמו, למשל, במשנה בבא קמא י,ב.

משלימה הוא מאגדה הוא משמחה, אם בו נפלה חכה מה יעשו גבים
220   קטנים אשר אפילו עצמותם לא יתראה בהם. סוף דבר מי יחשוב
בכל אלו ולא יירא לנפשו ויתעצל מיראת ה׳ בהספדו של אדם כשר
ראוי לקוברו בחייו.[61]

כי כמו שבנים קטנים בהיות אביהם חי וסומכים על שולחנו הנה
לא היה לכם (צ״ל להם) מחשבה ודאג׳ לבקש מחייתם כי עליו היו
225   סומכים הנה במותו בהכרח יראו וישתדלו למצוא להם טרף, כן
ראוי לכל העם לחשוב במות חומה כזאת אב כללי ומגן כי מתחלה
אמרנו בצלו נחיה בגוים[62] כי עתה אשר חסר כל א׳ צריך לטרוח
ביגיע כפיו. וזהו בכו לאובדים ולא לאבידה שהיא למנוחה ולקבל
שכר פעולותיה ואנו אנחה,[63] כי במקום שזכותו היה מגין עלינו עתה
230   אנחנו באנח׳ להעזר כל א׳ בזרועו. וזהו מה שאנו אומרים סעו המה
למנוחות עזבו אותנו לאנחות,[64] כי הוא ודאי למנוחה ולמנוחה גמורה
כי בהיות שאין כל אדם זוכה לשתי שולחנות[65] הנה מיופי פעולותיו
והכשרם זכה לשניהם ורוח לו בעה״ז וטוב לו לעולם הבא.

והוא כמו שהתחלנו בפסוק נושאנו[66] איש תם ר״ל איש תמים
235   שלם בכל יושב אהלים יושב בשלוה בשני אהלים בעה״ז ובעה״ב כי
שניהם נקראים אהל, העה״ז שני וימתחם כאהל לשבת,[67] והעה״ב
שני ה׳ מי יגור באהלך מי ישכון בהר קדשך הולך תמים ופועל צדק
ודובר אמת בלבבו לא רגל על לשונו לא עשה לרעהו רעה וחרפה לא
נשא על קרובו נבזה בעיניו נמאס ואת יראי ה׳ יכבד נשבע להרע
240   ולא ימיר כספו לא נתן בנשך ושחד על נקי לא לקח:[68] מידות ניכרים
גלוים וידועים בצדיק הזה, ולכן יקבל שכרם בתשלום המזמור:

---

61. בחזרתו למאמר חז״ל שבו דן הדרשן המבוא, הוא מסמן את סוף גוף ההספד ומעבר לחלק
המסיים.
62. ע״פ איכה ד כ.
63. סיום המאמר ממועד קטן כה ב, בצירוף ביטוי המזכיר את השכר המוכן לצדיק הנפטר.
64. עי׳ סליחות לאשמורות הבקר כפי מנהג ק״ק ספרדים, עמ׳ 166.
65. עי׳ ברכות ה ב ותוספות שם ד״ה לא.
66. בר׳ כה כז. כמו בהספד הראשון, הדרשן מגיע לנושא רק בסוף דרשתו.
67. יש׳ מ כב.
68. תה׳ טו א–ה.

עושה אלה לא ימוט לעולם. ויזכור לנו ה׳ זכותו ויאמר לצרותינו די ועלינו להצדיק את הדין ולומר ברוך דיין האמת.[69]

דרוש שדרשתי ביום תשלום שלשים לפטירת אהובי היקר
והנעים הרופ׳ המובהק החכם השלם כמהר״ר דוד פירר זצוק״ל 245
והיה זה ביום ב׳ לחדש כסליו משנת השפ״ה.

69. עי׳ הערה 34 להספד הראשון.

17

"Their Words Are Their Memorial"
Saul Levi Morteira's Eulogy
for Menasseh ben Israel

In September of 1655, Menasseh ben Israel, prayerful yet exhuberant, set out from Holland for London on a widely publicized mission to reverse the Expulsion of 1290. Two years later, he departed from England, devastated by a series of setbacks and personal tragedies. Though Oliver Cromwell appeared sympathetic to his appeal, adverse public opinion impelled the Lord Protector to refrain from a formal announcement that the Jews would be readmitted. Despite his best efforts, Menasseh's mission seemed to have ended in failure. Further, he had run out of funds; and although his requests for a stipend from Cromwell received a favorable response, no money was forthcoming from the Treasury. Most heartbreaking, his only surviving son, Samuel Soeiro, lay mortally ill in London. On his death bed, Samuel implored his father to have him buried in his native land.[1]

His financial and emotional resources drained, Menasseh returned to Holland to arrange for Samuel's burial. Though only fifty-three years old, Menasseh's own health was precarious. Whether because he was too weak to travel or because he no longer felt comfortable in the city where he had spent most of his life, he decided not to return to Amsterdam, and settled in Middleburg. He died in mid-November 1657, some ten weeks after his son, less then two months after his return from England. His body was brought to

---

Part of this chapter reprinted with permission from *Traditional Quest: Essays in Honour of Louis Jacobs,* edited by Dan Cohn-Sherbok, copyright 1991, by Sheffield Academic Press.

1. Roth, *Menasseh,* pp. 268–72. Menasseh's older son, Joseph, died suddenly on a business venture to Poland in the late 1640s (ibid., p. 68). Menasseh's emotional state is undoubtedly reflected in the following passage from *Nishmat Ḥayyim,* published in 1651: "It is as we see at the deaths of beloved children. The parents are overcome by trembling in the cemetery; they cannot bear to leave their children, to turn away from them. With unceasing lament and distress, they go to the graves even during the seven day period of mourning; they want nothing more than to be there in the company of their children. Afterward, the powerful love and affection abate gradually with time" (Menasseh, *Nishmat* 2, 18, p. 41a).

Amsterdam and buried in the cemetery of the Portuguese community at Ouderkerk.[2]

Among the final tributes was a eulogy delivered by his senior colleague, the leading rabbi of the Portuguese community in Amsterdam, Saul Levi Morteira. I discovered the text of this eulogy among the voluminous manuscripts of Morteira's sermons.[3] The eulogy tells us nothing about Menasseh's biography that was not previously known, but it is important evidence for his contemporary reputation following the greatest failure of his career, and yet another impressive example of Morteira's homiletical art.

Detailed information about the relations between these two rabbis is not abundant in published sources. Morteira was probably one of Menasseh's teachers, and he may well have ordained the brilliant young scholar.[4] Menasseh mentions his older colleague only once in his voluminous works, in the introduction to his *Thesouro dos Dinim* (he had consulted with "*o dotissimo e clarissimo Senhor Hacham Saul Levi Mortera*");[5] Morteira wrote an approbation for that book, but I have not found any reference to Menasseh in Morteira's own writings, with the exception of this eulogy.[6] With the merger of the three Portuguese synagogues in 1639, Menasseh became third in the rabbinical hierarchy; his perennial rival, Isaac Aboab da Fonseca, was Morteira's senior assistant. Menasseh was to preach once a month while Morteira would preach three times, and his salary was considerably lower than that of either colleague. Feelings of hurt and slight undoubtedly rankled.[7]

---

2. Roth, *Menasseh*, pp. 272–73; on the actual date of Menasseh's death, see below, n. 14. I do not know the basis for the assertion by Aaron Katchen (in Katchen, pp. 127 and 313 n. 70), that Menasseh was first buried in Middleburg and later reinterred in Ouderkerk; the present eulogy makes it clear that his remains were immediately brought to Amsterdam.

3. The manuscript (Morteira, "Giv'at Sha'ul") includes five large volumes of sermons, each written by Morteira himself in Hebrew before the delivery, which was undoubtedly in Portuguese. The Menasseh ben Israel eulogy is in vol.3; the pages are not numbered, but if they were numbered consecutively, the original sermon would be on folios 169r–v and 172r, the addition for the eulogy is 171r–v (it is placed backward in the volume); 170r–v is blank.

4. Roth, *Menasseh*, p. 33.

5. Salomon, *Tratado*, p. lxxx. Menasseh's *Nishmat Ḥayyim* appeared six years after Morteira's *Giv'at Sha'ul*, which contains an extensive discussion of the judgment of the soul in the sermon on *Va-Yelekh* [Deut. 31:1–30], but Menasseh does not refer to it, nor have I found reference to Morteira in Menasseh's work of biblical exegesis, *Conciliador*: see "Bibliographical Notices" in Menasseh, *Conciliator*, pp. xvii–xxxii.

6. Morteira appears to use a youthful unpublished work by Menasseh on grammar, without citing the author's name, in one of his eulogies for David Farar delivered in 1624; see above, p. 376.

7. Roth, *Menasseh*, pp. 49–51; Salomon, *Tratado*, p. lxv; A. Wiznitzer, pp. 117–18.

On the other hand, Menasseh was chosen to deliver the welcoming oration at the visit to the synagogue on May 22, 1642 by Queen Henrietta Maria of England and the Prince of Orange.[8] Morteira, not the easiest man to get along with, may have been jealous at Menasseh's growing reputation in the Christian world. Tension between the two rabbis impelled the lay leaders of the Ma'amad to intervene in June of 1642—less than two weeks after Menasseh's triumphant oration[9]—and again, more vigorously, a decade later. Four documents recently published by H. P. Salomon reveal a conflict that became something of a public scandal.

The first, dated the nineteenth of Adar I, 5413 [February 16, 1653] refers to a dispute of unspecified cause, resulting in the temporary suspension of both rabbis from preaching or teaching Jewish law. The second, from the following month, calls for a reconciliation between the two rabbis and warns them not to offend or contradict each other in their sermons. A year later, on March 21, 1654, a new problem has arisen: both rabbis are suspended without pay for a period of two months, and Menasseh is fined twenty florins, to be given to charity, for "having raised his voice in the synagogue and violated the agreement." The document ends with a threat that any further such incident will lead to their "exclusion from the service of this congregation." The final document, dated some three weeks later, attempts to establish a mechanism for the resolution of disputes over the teaching and preaching of the law.[10] David Franco Mendes, writing in 1788, concluded that "the wardens of the community made peace between them, but from that day on, Menasseh decided to leave Amsterdam."[11] It was not long after that he departed for London; Morteira never again saw Menasseh alive.

Morteira was thus faced with rhetorical challenges that transcended the poignance of eulogizing a former student and younger colleague. He had to express well-deserved respect for the deceased despite the known tensions be-

---

8. Franco Mendes, pp. 51–52; Roth, *Menasseh,* pp. 66–67; Méchoulan, "Visite," p. 82–86, including a French translation of the oration, which is not in the form of a sermon. The text was immediately published in Portuguese, Dutch and Latin (Roth, *Menasseh,* pp. 67, 300–301); David Franco Mendes wrote in *Ha-Me'assef* 4 (1788):168 that Menasseh delivered the oration *be-lashon Sefaradi.*

9. Salomon, *Tratado,* p. lxxiv.

10. Salomon, *Tratado,* p. xcii, documents published pp. cxli–cxlii; the date at the beginning of the first document should be corrected to 16 February. Menasseh's raising of his voice in the synagogue violated the regulations of the Talmud Torah Congregation; see Wiznitzer, p. 125. For an analogous case in Mantua, 1671, where the community stopped paying the salaries of both quarreling rabbis until they made peace with each other, see Simonsohn, p. 579.

11. *Ha-Me'assef* 4 (1788):168.

tween them. And he had to give due praise to the successes of a spectacular career despite the notorious failure of Menasseh's final endeavors.[12] In addition, he decided to use the occasion of Menasseh's burial in Ouderkerk to reiterate his position on an issue that apparently aroused strong feelings within the community: the practice of some of the wealthier members to erect lavishly ornate tombstones for their families. The plain simple tombstones of both Menasseh and Morteira indicate that opposition to ostentatious and elaborate monuments was a point on which the two rabbis agreed.[13]

For his eulogy, Morteira took an older sermon that he had delivered many years before and adapted it to the purpose at hand. It was not at all unusual for Morteira to reuse sermons after sufficient time had elapsed, and he routinely recorded these subsequent occasions, either beneath the final line of the text or on the back of the sheet (sometimes in a different color ink): "I preached it a second time in the year . . . ;" "I preached it a third time in the year . . . , and I added . . . ." That is what we have here. The original sermon was on the lesson *Ḥayyei Sarah* [Gen. 23:1–25:18]; the theme-verse (*nose*) was Genesis 23:17. On the back of the second page, we find, "I preached it a second time in the year 5401 [1640]." Then a new page bears the heading, "And I preached it again in the year 5418 [1657] at the conclusion of seven days from the burial of the Hakham Rabbi Menasseh ben Israel, may the memory of the righteous be for a blessing. He passed away in Middleburg, on his way from London. This was on the second day of the week, the twentieth of the month of Kislev [Monday, November 26].[14] And I added what follows." The text on this single page, front and back, contains just the "ad-

---

12. On Menasseh's sense of disillusion and failure upon his return from England, see Israel, "Menasseh," pp. 152–53.

13. On ornate sculptured gravestones, with figures of humans and angels, see Henriques de Castro, plates 9–12; Vega, p. 22. Contrast the plain stones of Menasseh ben Israel and Morteira, shown in Vega, p. 19. Cf. Yovel, 2:54–57.

14. This raises anew the question of the date of Menasseh's death. Morteira's statement is, unfortunately, ambiguous, as the word "this," associated with the date, could syntactically refer to Menasseh's death, to his burial, or to the delivery of the eulogy. According to the Portuguese inscription on Menasseh's tombstone, he died (*faleceo*) on 14 Kislev = Tuesday, November 20. If he had been buried in Amsterdam the same day, then Morteira's date of 20 Kislev = Monday, November 26 would fit perfectly for the seventh day, on which the eulogy was delivered. However, since it would have taken several days for Menasseh's remains to be brought from Middleburg to Amsterdam, his burial could not possibly have been on the day of his death. If, then, Morteira's date refers to the burial, then the eulogy would have been delivered on 26 Kislev = Sunday, December 2. But the eulogy uses the pericope *Va-Yeshev*, read on Saturday, December 1, and Morteira is not likely to have used the previous week's lesson. It may therefore be necessary to look again at the date for Menasseh's death recorded by hand in a copy of the 1652 edition of *Nishmat Ḥayyim*: November 15, 1657; see Kaplan, "Ta'arikhei," pp. 611–13. Kaplan concluded that this date was simply wrong, but it is con-

ditions" to the original sermon; in some cases, these passages replaced sections of the original.

Although it is not possible to reconstruct with certainty precisely how the new material fit together with the old, there is little question about the structure and content of what was said. Neither the theme-verse from *Ḥayyei Sarah* nor the rabbinic dictum, Genesis Rabbah 58,8, which plays on the name "Machpelah" in that verse, played an integral role in the original sermon, and they could be readily replaced. The new theme-verse was from the current Torah lesson, *Va-Yeshev* [Gen. 37:1–40:23]: *Afterward his brother exited, by his hand the crimson thread; he was named Zeraḥ* (Gen. 38:30).[15] The new dictum, Genesis Rabbah 82,10, which had been discussed in the body of the original sermon, deals with the burial not of Sarah but of Rachel.

Like most contemporary eulogies, a large portion is of a general homiletical nature, without direct reference to the deceased. The introductory section of the original sermon was apparently reused without change; it is worth citing at length.

> What is the meaning of the verse, *Bless the Lord, O my soul and all that is within me bless His holy name* (Ps. 103:1)? He replied, Come and observe how the capacity of human beings falls short of the capacity of the Holy One blessed be He. It is in the capacity of a human being to draw a figure on the wall, but he cannot invest it with breath and spirit, entrails and viscera. But the Holy One blessed be He is not so; He shapes one form in the midst of another, and invests it with breath and spirit, entrails and viscera. That is what Hannah said: *There is no one holy like the Lord, for there is none beside You, there is no tsur* [rock] *like our God* (I Sam. 2:2). What is the meaning of There is no *tsur* like our God? There is no artist [*tsayyar*] like our God (B. Ber 10a).
>
> From this we see that the difference between the forms made by human beings and the forms made by the Creator is that the former have only external, superficial significance, while the latter have inner content and substance. This same difference applies within the category of forms that God has made. The "drawing made upon the wall" may indeed be beautiful to behold, pleasing in its colors, adorned with fine clothing and ornaments, a great delight to the eyes, yet it has no breath or spirit; a person who reaches out to touch it

---

sistent with Morteira's date if the burial was on November 20 and the eulogy delivered on November 26. This, of course, requires a conclusion that the tombstone erroneously gives the date of burial as the date of death (it might have been taken from the community register of burials by the engraver, who assumed that, as was usually the case in Amsterdam, the date of death was the same). None of these solutions is completely satisfying.

15. I have translated *yatsa* as "exited" and *'al yado* as "by his hand" in order to preserve the ambiguity used by the preacher in the homiletical application of the verse to Menasseh at the end of the sermon: see below.

grasps nothing at all.[16] Even so there are some forms not "drawn upon the wall," but rather made from the mold of the first human being, yet all their aspirations are for external ornaments. These people may be quite beautiful to behold—fashionable, bedecked in jewels, lacking none of the accoutrements of glory and prestige. But there are no "breath and spirit, entrails and viscera" within them, for they have no real substance. Inside they are nothing but intrigue and deceit, and every vile blemish.[17]

Indeed, such people are worse than those pictures, for the pictures have no inner content at all, while the people are filled with violence and corruption. . . . Thus we must make it our goal to achieve perfection in those inner qualities that truly make us human, and not aspire to gain perfection in external things, which we share in common with a painted portrait. And if this is so while we are alive, how much more is it so at the time of death, after which we will be rendering account for all.

The midrashic passage, expressing the well-known topos of God as artist (*Deus pictor*),[18] had an obvious appeal for Jews living in an environment where portrait painting was highly valued. Leon Modena used it at the beginning of the opening sermon in his *Midbar Yehudah*— the first sermon he delivered in the Great Synagogue of Venice—and this was a book Morteira must certainly have owned.[19] Even more than his older Venetian colleague, Morteira reveals an aesthetic appreciation of the achievements of contemporary painters, and we may assume that most of those in his audience could envision some of the crowning examples of Dutch portraiture as he spoke.[20] Yet it is clear that the aesthetic dimension of human artifice is not a supreme value and will have to be transcended in favor of some religious ideal. Painting serves here not primarily to highlight the glories of God's handiwork, but to introduce the sermon's central motif: the contrast between external appearance and inner qualities not readily observable to the eye.

---

16. Cf. the argument used by Savonarola, that "there is a certain living quality in natural things which art cannot express"; no matter how beautiful painted grapes may appear, birds will never fly to them. See Clements, pp. 148–49.

17. Savonarola made a similar point: without the beauty of the soul, the body must necessarily lose its beauty. Ibid., p. 6.

18. Cf. Curtius, p. 562; Clements, pp. 81, 145. Note that the God as painter topos is ordinarily used to exalt painting as a kind of *imitatio dei,* while the midrash uses the topos to denigrate painting.

19. Modena, *Midbar,* p. 5a; cf. Saperstein, *Jewish Preaching,* p. 409 (the citation of the midrash is omitted).

20. Possibly in their homes. According to Salomon, *Tratado,* p. lxi, n. 19, there is a Portuguese responsum by Morteira in manuscript in which he permits Jews to have paintings and sculptures in their homes. The codex is identified as Biblioteca Nacional de Madrid 18292, fols. 132–35.

This contrast undergirds the preacher's criticism of those whose lives were excessively oriented toward the trappings of wealth and prestige, such as ostentatious clothing and jewelry. This was not the first time Morteira forcefully addressed the problem, which was an important theme in the sermons of contemporary Dutch Calvinist preachers as well.[21] For the purpose of the eulogy, however, the emphasis would eventually have to be not on rebuke but on praise. Everyone knew that Menasseh ben Israel could not be included in the category of those concerned only with externals. During most of his life he was beset by financial problems and lacked the resources for ostentatious comportment. The introduction to the eulogy therefore establishes the basis for emphasizing the inner qualities of the man—his intellectual prowess and his spiritual fortitude—and for the climactic pronouncement that though his mission failed in external terms, he was assured an ultimate reward by God.

The introductory section in all of Morteira's sermons ends with a succinct statement of the central subject to be addressed and an invocation of God's help in the delivery. The body of the sermon often begins on a somewhat different tack; in this case the fundamental dichotomy is immediately reinforced by a quote from the great oration in Isaiah 58:5–6 denouncing the outward forms of religious observance devoid of genuine concern for the underprivileged. It might seem that the Prophet himself substitutes another set of actions—to unlock the fetters of wickedness, to untie the cords of the yoke—but Morteira seizes on precisely the terms that underline his emphasis on inwardness: *if you remove* from within you *the yoke . . . and extend* your soul *to the hungry* (Isa. 58:9,10).[22] "These are things the artist cannot paint, for they are specific characteristics of the divine form, in which inner perfections may be found."

The same point, he continues, is made by the ethical instruction of the sages: "It is not the position that honors the man, but it is the man who honors the position," one of the two most important rabbinic statements in the eulogy.[23] For the present purpose, Morteira rewrites the discussion in the

---

21. Cf. Morteira's sermon in *Jewish Preaching*, pp. 272–85. For contemporary Dutch preaching denouncing the display of costly ornaments, see Schama, p. 331.

22. This interpretation of the phrases as speaking of inwardness may have been influenced by Abravanel's commentary on Isa. 58:9 and 10 (Abravanel, *Prophets* 2:270a); Abravanel points to the rabbinic interpretation of Isa. 58:10 in B. BB 9b as a source.

23. B. Ta'an 21b. In rendering the Hebrew word *maqom*, the word "office" would probably best reflect what the preacher is discussing. I have used the word "position" to convey some of the ambiguous connotation of both geographical place and occupational status. I assume that the preacher translated the rabbinic text by the Portuguese word *cargo*, used for the Rabbi's position in the documents of the community (see Salomon, *Tratado*, p. cxlii: "ese tal sera excluido de seu cargo").

original sermon, sharpening its focus. "We should not understand this assertion simplistically to mean that the position bestows absolutely no honor upon the man. Several biblical verses indicate otherwise . . . [Prov. 4:8, 22:29, 25:7]. Rather, the meaning is that a truly distinguished man does not need to be honored by his position; his own distinction brings honor to the position even if it has no distinction of its own. But if the position is one of honor, it adds to the honor of the one who holds it."

This reformulation of the original statement is illustrated through an analysis of the examples given in the Talmud. Mt. Sinai and the various locations in the wilderness where the Tent of Meeting stood had absolutely no distinction of their own. They were sanctified only by the presence of God; as soon as the Divine Presence departed, the places remained devoid of any special holiness. By contrast, the Temple Mount, and Jerusalem as a whole, retain their sanctity even after the destruction of the Temple because they had special distinction prior to the Temple. The holiness of Jerusalem was not merely the result of God's presence during the time the Temple stood. Unlike the wilderness of Sinai, even pre-Israelite Jerusalem was a source of honor to God, and God responded by honoring it even more. Thus it exemplifies the conclusion that while "a man honors his position, if his position itself is distinguished, each brings honor to the other."

As will become apparent, Morteira's rewriting, which moves away from the original statement by emphasizing the capacity for mutual honor between person and position (a point made only incidentally at the end of the section in the original) is by no means accidental. As soon as he cited the rabbinic statement, it was obvious to the attentive listener that he would eventually apply it to Menasseh. Yet Morteira did not want to imply that Menasseh's position—as rabbi in Amsterdam—was like the wilderness of Sinai, with no intrinsic distinction of its own, honored only because Menasseh filled it. That would be demeaning to the incumbents of the position, and to the listeners themselves. It is Jerusalem, rather than Sinai, that would serve as the model for the Amsterdam rabbinate.

We recall that at the end of the sermon's introductory section, Morteira concluded that the aspiration to perfection in inner qualities rather than externals applies both to a person's life and to his death. Having discussed the problem in the context of the lifetime by means of the first rabbinic statement, about the honor of a position, Morteira turns to the subject of externals in the context of death, citing another statement that is crucial for the eulogy:

The same idea is taught by the statement in the Yerushalmi, Tractate Sheqalim, chapter 2: "With what is left from the funeral expenses one builds a monument over the grave. Rabban Simeon ben Gamaliel said, We do not build a monument for the righteous; their words are their memorial." Maimonides incorporated this as a halakhah in the fourth chapter of "The Laws of the Mourner." The reason for this is that people want to honor the deceased through "the honor of position" [i.e., a monument that will distinguish the place of burial], and this implies that the deceased have no other source of honor. But the righteous do not need this [external honor], for their words are their memorial. However, this principle seems to be contradicted by Jacob's erecting of a tombstone for Rachel, as the Bible tells us: *Rachel died. She was buried on the road to Ephrath, now Bethlehem. Over her grave Jacob set up a pillar; it is the pillar at Rachel's grave to this day* (Gen. 35:19–20). If this is improper, how did Jacob do it? And the same with other righteous people as well. This truly needs to be answered.

I would say that the general purpose in building a tombstone and a monument over the grave is so that the name of the deceased will not be forgotten by his relatives and neighbors. When people pass by the grave and see his name, they will remember him as if he were alive.[24] This has led some individuals to extremes, making such monuments exceedingly prominent so as to attract the attention of passersby, in order that the deceased will thereby be remembered more. . . . The Psalmist referred to this explicitly in Psalm 49 (vv. 11–12): *One sees that the wise die, the fool and the ignorant both perish, leaving their wealth to others. They think to themselves that their houses will endure forever, their dwelling-places to all generations, proclaiming their names far and wide.* This refers to those whose sole ambition is to have built for themselves a magnificent grave and a costly sarcophagus, so that these edifices in which they will dwell forever will cause their name to be remembered throughout the land.[25] Yet they have forgotten that the essential thing is to clear the space and prepare what is necessary to enter into the splendor of the King, for without this, all the glory of their graves is futile.

Beginning with a conceptual problem—the Talmudic statement codified as halakhah by Maimonides that does not fit the reality either of biblical times (Rachel's monument) or of the present (monuments that are indeed used for Jews considered righteous)[26]—Morteira returns to the preaching of

24. On the link between the tombstone and memory, see Ganzfried, chap. 199, para. 17; cf. Ariès, *Death*, pp. 202–3, 229–30.

25. The interpretation of Ps. 49:12 as a reference to tombstones is based on a long tradition, reflected in the Targum, which reads *qirbam* as an inversion of *qibram*; cf. Ibn Ezra and David Kimhi ad loc. Morteira develops the criticism of elaborate tombstones implicit in Ibn Ezra, as Hatam Sofer would later do; see *Otsar Tehillot*, 6:322–25.

26. For a discussion of the contrast between the Talmudic statement codified by Maimonides (though not by later codifiers) and the contemporary practice of building elaborate memorials even for *tsaddiqim*, see Aaron ben Moses, 5:40, p. 224a; Kluger, p. 2a.

rebuke. The matter of ostentatiously elaborate tombstones is not raised by the literary sources he is discussing. It arises rather from the practice of his own community, as can be seen to this day in the monuments built for wealthy members of the Portuguese congregation dating from the mid-seventeenth century in the Ouderkerk cemetery.[27] Knowing that Menasseh would have a plain stone bearing only his epitaph, he used the opportunity to work his criticism of the new practice into the general theme of externals versus inner qualities, applying it to death as well as to life, and thereby coming closer to the actual occasion of the address.

He is not yet finished, however, with the conceptual problem; he still needs to explain Jacob's erection of a monument at Rachel's grave. After his discussion of the general purpose of tombstones, cited above, he continues, "However, the monuments and tombstones placed at the graves of the righteous, such as Rachel, serve a different purpose." For this he turns to the rabbinic dictum read at the beginning immediately following the theme-verse. It is a midrash (Gen. Rab. 82,10) on Genesis 35:20, which gives two explanations for Jacob's behavior: to teach us that "Israel is known by Rebecca's name," and because Jacob, foreseeing that his descendants would pass into exile by that site, wanted Rachel to be in position to pray on their behalf. This midrash is discussed extensively in the original sermon, and it is unclear how much of this discussion was incorporated into the eulogy. In the additional material, Morteira writes simply that both explanations show that "the honor of the place publicized the honor of the *tsaddiq*."

At this point, with all the main themes of the sermon introduced, it is time for the preacher to apply them to the deceased. The first explicit mention of Menasseh brings together two central rabbinic statements already discussed, both of which relate to the contrast between externals and inner qualities in the context of life and of death. As in this case of Rachel,

> this *tsaddiq* does not need an imposing monument or sarcophagus to honor him for the sake of his position. "His words are his memorial:" the words in the books he wrote will preserve his memory. Indeed, the truth is that he did have an honored position; his position honored him and he it. His position honored him, for he was a teacher and a mentor from his youth in this distinguished place, in the greatest congregations of the region. And he honored his position through his distinguished achievements, which earned him constant praise and glory and honor. Thus his position was fitting for him, and he for it.

---

27. See above, n. 13.

Having emphasized Menasseh's tenure in Amsterdam, Morteira begins to address the final mission that would take him away from that city for the remainder of his life. He introduces the subject through an analogy with a midrash on Joseph, appropriate to the lesson for the week when the eulogy was delivered.

> He recognized the glory of his place, for the same thing that happened to the righteous Joseph happened to him. The sages gave a parable of thieves who entered a cellar and stole a barrel of wine. The owner said to them, "You have drunk the wine, now return the barrel to its place."[28] Even so the Bible tells us, *The bones of Joseph, which the children of Israel brought up from Egypt, were buried at Shechem* (Josh. 24:32). So it was with this *tsaddiq*: his lofty ideas stole him from his place (for thoughts are called "friends" and "brothers," as in the verse, *How precious to me are Your friends, O God* [Ps. 139:17]), and brought him to England in his desire to establish there a community that would call upon the name of God in that country.[29]

The analogy between Menasseh and Joseph works on several levels: a man removed from his home by a kind of *force majeure*—in Menasseh's case a compelling idea—never to return alive; by implication, a man playing a role in a providential plan which may not be clear to superficial observers.

Here Morteira confronts directly the painful subject of the apparently total failure of Menasseh's mission. "His effort is well known; and even if he did not succeed in completing all that he intended, nevertheless the reward is his, and his recompense precedes him." This assertion is buttressed by a Talmudic statement (B. Ber 6a), analyzed in the classic homiletical style:

> *It shall be written in a book of remembrance before Him concerning those who revere the Lord and think of His name* (Mal. 3:16). What is the significance of "who think of His name"? Rab Ashi said, Whoever thinks of doing a mitsvah and, for reasons beyond his control, is unable to do it, is considered in this verse as if he had indeed performed it. Now it may well be asked, how is this

---

28. Gen. Rab. 85:3. Morteira must have assumed his listeners would not remember the statement at the beginning of this midrash, which would have been highly inapproprate in the present context: "Whoever begins with a mitsvah and does not finish it buries his wife and his sons."

29. The original Portuguese may have echoed the conclusion of Menasseh's Portuguese broadside, sent to various Jewish communities on September 2, 1655 to explain his mission to England as he set out upon it. He asks his fellow Jews to pray that Cromwell "may give us liberty in his land, where we may similarly pray to the most high God for his prosperity" (*para que nos dem em suas terras liberdade, donde possamos tembém orar ao Altissimo Senhor por sua prosperidade*). Roth, *Menasseh,* p. 227; Portuguese text in Salomon, *Tratado,* p. cxliii.

interpretation related to the beginning of the verse, about which the rabbis said, "How do we know that when two sit together and study Torah, the Divine Presence is with them? From the verse, *Then those who revere the Lord converse with each other; God listens, and notes, and it shall be written* (Mal. 3:16)."

A close analysis reveals that the two points are beautifully interconnected. For when two sit and study Torah in depth, one may conclude that something is forbidden while the other concludes that it is permitted. Now certainly one of them is not saying what is true. But since his intention was to clarify the truth, it is considered as if he had actually hit upon the truth.[30] So those who revere the Lord, who tremble at His word in fear of sin, do not actually perform any act. All these qualities pertain to intention and thought. That is why they are written in the book in a separate category, inscribed together with those who think of His name. Hence, "Whoever thinks of doing a *mitsvah* and, for reasons beyond his control, is unable to do it, is considered in this verse as if he had performed it," and it is written in the book. So it is with this *tsaddiq. His reward is his, and his recompense precedes him* (Isa. 40:10).

This kind of passage raises the danger that the preacher will become so entangled in the exegetical problem and its solution that the listener will be distracted from the main point. Morteira deftly avoids this pitfall. The digression is brief and succinct; the fundamental assertion—that Menasseh will be rewarded by God as if he had succeeded in his mission—is linked with the underlying thesis of the sermon—that inner qualities are more important than externals, in life and in death—and firmly rooted in traditional texts.

Having dealt with the unsuccessful mission, Morteira returns to the present. Some may have been puzzled that Menasseh lingered in Middleburg rather than returning to Amsterdam; the preacher defuses this by emphasizing the significance of Menasseh's return to Holland, and the half-consolation that his grave would not be on foreign soil, in a country without Jews. "God has granted him the reward about which the righteous of old felt so strongly, for which they made such great exertion: to be buried in the graves of their ancestors. Both Jacob and Joseph acted accordingly, exacting a stringent oath, for they considered the matter extremely serious, of utmost con-

---

30. It is not unlikely that in this passage, Morteira is alluding to the apparently bitter disputes between himself and Menasseh that marred their last years together in Amsterdam, as recounted above. Certainly some of the listeners may have made this association. It is, however, difficult to determine whether the message would have been, "It makes no difference which one of us was right when we disagreed," or "It makes no difference that Menasseh was wrong when we disagreed."

sequence.[31] They therefore called it a matter of *true kindness* (Gen. 47:29). Miraculously, he has arrived here, for *God will not deprive the soul of the righteous* (Prov. 10:3). He has come to his place, which he loved so much, thereby revealing his own merit, and giving us the merit that comes from burying him and from mourning him in a manner appropriate to our master and teacher." Part of the reward promised for the intention of the unsuccessful mission is already manifest in Menasseh's burial near the graves of his father and his teacher.

Through an ingenious application of the theme-verse, the conclusion of the eulogy links Menasseh's death with the recent loss of another rabbinic colleague.

> This new pain of our sorrow is especially great, for only eight months ago the pious scholar Rabbi David Pardo departed from us (may the memory of the sacred pious be for blessing).[32] And *afterward, his brother* [i.e., Menasseh] *exited,* as we said at the beginning in our theme-verse, *by his hand the crimson thread* (Gen. 38:30). To understand this, recall that crimson is a metaphor for splendor of speech and eloquence, as in the verse, *Your lips are like a crimson thread, your speech is lovely* (Song 4:3). And his beautiful eloquence, his delightful words, were not in his mouth alone, but also *by his hand,* in his books, which he wrote in such an elegant style. *Therefore he was named Zerah* (Gen. 38:30), "shining," for his radiance has shined throughout the world.

This peroration leaves the listeners with the thought not of the failure that embittered Menasseh's final months, but of his widespread reputation and his vaunted mastery of language. The motif of eloquence, unexpectedly read into the theme-verse, gives special substance to the rabbinic assertion, "Their words are their memorial." The eulogy ends in Morteira's accustomed manner; returning to Isaiah 58, he contrasts the reward of the deceased with the painful obligations of the living: "*May God shine upon him, and fill his soul with splendor* (Isa. 58:11). But our duty is to affirm the decree, and to say, 'Blessed is the Judge of Truth.' "

---

31. Cf. Gen. Rab. 96,5. The midrashic passage assumes that the desire of Jacob and Joseph was to be buried in the Land of Israel; Morteira applies this to burial in the cemetery of the Jewish community of Amsterdam. For Menasseh's view on the importance of being buried next to compatible people, see Menasseh, *Nishmat,* 2, 26, p. 38d.

32. David Pardo, son of Joseph Pardo, the first rabbi of the Beth Jacob congregation, and father of Josiah Pardo, Morteira's son-in-law, died on March 19, 1657. Cf. Kaplan, "Ta'arikhei," p. 612.

[Additions: fol. 171v]

And I preached it again in the year 5418 [1657] at the conclusion of seven days from the burial of the Hakham Rabbi Menasseh ben Israel, may the memory of the righteous be for a blessing. He passed away in Middleburg, on his way from London. This was on the second day of the week, the 20th of the month of Kislev [Monday, November 26].[1] And I added what follows.

A. *Afterward his brother exited, by his hand the crimson thread; he was named Zerah* (Gen. 38:30).[2]

["The Pillar at Rachel's Grave," fol. 169v]

Over her grave Jacob set up a pillar; it is the pillar at Rachel's grave to this day (Gen. 35:19–20). Rabban Simeon ben Gamaliel said, We do not build a monument for the righteous; their words are their memorial." He taught us that Israel is known by Rachel's name, in accordance with the verse, *Rachel weeps over her children* (Jer. 31:15).[3] Another interpretation: *Rachel died; she was buried on the road to Ephrath* (Gen. 35:19). Why did our ancestor Jacob decide to bury her on the road to Ephrath? Our ancestor Jacob envisioned the exiles that would befall there, and that is why he buried her at that spot: so that she could beseech mercy on their behalf.[4]

["The Pillar at Rachel's Grave," fol. 169r]

In tractate Berakhot, chapter 1: What is the meaning of the verse, *Bless the Lord, O my soul, and all that is within me bless His holy name* (Ps 103:1)? He replied, Come and observe how the capacity of hman beings falls short of the capacity of the Holy One, blessed be He. It is in the capacity of a human being to draw a figure on the wall, but he cannot invest it with breath and

---

1. For a discussion of the problematics of this date, see introduction, n. 14.

2. Morteira chose this as a new theme (undoubtedly from the lesson of the week) for the eulogy.

3. In the original context, the meaning seems to be that as Jeremiah asserted that Rachel wept for *all* of the tribes, not just Ephraim, Menasseh, and Benjamin (her direct descendants), all Israel was known as her children.

4. Gen. Rab. 82,10. This was cited and discussed at length in the middle of the original sermon. However, the additions indicate that Morteira used this as his *ma'amar qodem* (see below, n. 25), and I have accordingly added it. The preacher begins the introduction to his original sermon and eulogy with yet another rabbinic quotation.

spirit, entrails and viscera. But the Holy One, blessed be He, is not so; He shapes one form in the midst of another, and invests it with breath and spirit, entrails and viscera. That is what Hannah said, *There is no one holy like the lord, for there is none beside You, there is no rock* [tsur] *like our God* (1 Sam. 2:2). What is the meaning of *there is no rock* [tsur] *like our God?* There is no artist [*tsayyar*] like our God.[5]

From this we see that the difference between the forms made by human beings and the forms made by the Creator is that the former have only external, superficial significance, while the latter have inner content and substance. This same difference applies within the category of forms that God has made. The "drawing made upon the wall" may indeed be beautiful to behold, pleasing in its colors, adorned with fine clothing and ornaments, a great delight to the eyes,[6] yet it has no breath or spirit; a person who reaches out to touch it grasps nothing at all.[7] Even so there are some forms not "drawn upon the wall," but rather made from the mold of the first human being,[8] yet all their aspirations are for external ornaments. These people may be quite beautiful to behold— fashionable, bedecked in jewels, lacking none of the accoutrements of glory and prestige. But there are no "breath and spirit, entrails and viscera" within them, for they have no real substance. Inside they are nothing but intrigue and deceit,[9] and every vile blemish.

Indeed, such people are worse than those pictures, for the pictures have no inner content at all, while the people are filled with violence and corruption. . . . Thus man must make it his goal to achieve perfection in those inner qualities that truly make him human, and not aspire to gain perfection in external things, which he shares in common with a painted portrait. And if this is so while he is alive, how much more is it so at the time of his death, after which he will be rendering account.[10] . . .

Of special relevance to our topic is what the Prophet Isaiah said in chapter 58 concerning the fast. He proclaimed, *Is such the fast I desire, a day for people to starve their bodies? Is it bowing the head like a bulrush and lying in sackcloth and ashes? Do you call that a fast, a day when the Lord is favorable?* (Isa 58:5). By this he meant that all these things could be painted by an artist with perfection as a "drawing made upon a wall"—a work of surpassing quality—for all these things pertain to externals. *No, this is the fast I desire:*

---

5. B. Ber 10a. Cf. introduction.
6. Cf. Gen. 3:6.
7. Cf. Prov. 30:4.
8. Cf. M. Sanh. 4,5.
9. Cf. Ps. 55:12.
10. Based on Avot 3,1.

to unlock the fetters of wickedness, and untie the cords of the yoke, to let the op-pressed go free, and to break every yoke (Isa. 58:6) . . . *If you remove from within you the yoke* (Isa. 58:9) . . . *and extend your soul to the hungry* (Isa. 58:10). For these things the artist cannot paint. They are the specific characteristics and details of the divine form, which contain the inner perfections of spirit and soul, "entrails and viscera." These are the basis of the ultimate distinction, namely between living people and imaginary forms, like the fundamental distinction between being and nothingness.

This very same idea is the focal point of the lesson taught to us by the sages in the third chapter of Ta'anit[11]: "R. Yose taught, It is not the position that honors the man, but it is the man who honors the position, for so we find that so long as the Divine Presence was upon Mt. Sinai, the Torah said *nei-ther shall the flocks and the herds graze at the foot of the mountain* (Exod. 34:3), but when the Divine Presence departed, the Torah said, *When the ram's horn sounds a long blast, they may go up on the mountain* (Exod. 19:13). And simi-larly with the Tent of Meeting in the wilderness: as long as it was pitched, the Torah said, *They shall remove from the camp anyone with an eruption or a dis-charge;* as soon as the curtains were rolled up,[12] those with an eruption or dis-charge were permitted to enter."

[Additions, fol. 171v]:
B. We should not understand this assertion simplistically to mean that the position bestows absolutely no honor to a man. Several biblical verses indi-cate otherwise. For example, *Hug her to you and she will exalt you* (Prov. 4:8), and similarly *See a man skilled at his work—he shall attend upon kings* (Prov. 22:29), and *It is better to be told "Step up here"* (Prov. 25:7).[13] Rather, the meaning is that a truly distinguished man does not need to be honored by his position; his own distinction brings honor to the position even if it has no distinction of its own. But if the position is one of honor, it adds to the honor

---

11. B. Ta'an 21b. Cf. introduction, n. 23.

12. At the time when the Israelites were traveling (Rashi).

13. Prov. 4:8 is interpreted to mean that the person who cherishes wisdom or Torah will be honored because of this. Cf. B. Ber 48a: King Yannai seats Simeon ben Shetah between himself and his wife, and the sage says, "It is not you who have done me honor, but Torah that has done me honor, as it is written, *Hug her to you and she will exalt you.*" But this as-sumes that sitting next to a king is a place of honor. Similarly, Prov. 22:29 and 25:6–7 indi-cate that being in the presence of kings is a position that has some distinction in itself, to which a worthy person may aspire. It is difficult to imagine that the mere citation of these verses would have been meaningful to any listener, and the preacher may well have elaborated the point in his delivery.

of the one who holds it. The proof brought was from God and Mt. Sinai, which had no distinction of its own, being the most lowly of mountains. Indeed, that is why God chose it.[14] Its honor lasted only so long as the Divine Presence rested upon it, not afterward, in order to teach that its honor was dependent upon the Divine Presence. Similarly with the wilderness: it had no distinction of its own, being a place through which people did not pass, but so long as the Tent of Meeting was pitched, the honor was within it.

Not so the case with Mount Zion, for that was already a place of distinction, and the Divine Presence honored it more. Therefore, even after the Divine Presence departed, the honor remains in it. The Bible says, *I will make desolate your sanctuaries* (Lev. 26:31), interpreted to mean that even after their destruction they retain their sanctity.[15] Similarly with Jerusalem, for its first sanctification hallowed it both temporarily and for all time to come.[16] Why was this? Because these places were distinguished in themselves, as the poet said, *He built His sanctuary like the heavens, like the earth that He established forever* (Ps. 78:69). *He built like the heavens,* for the sages said that the earthly Temple is set against the heavenly Temple.[17] *The earth he established forever* refers to Jerusalem. For at first its kings were called "kings of of justice,"[18] and in those places people honored God and God honored them.

The mutual relationship was like in the verses, *You have affirmed God* (Deut. 26:17) and *God has affirmed you* (Deut. 26:18). Corresponding to Sinai and the Tent of Meeting, these were truly a place of Torah and of prophecy. Similarly, *For instruction shall come forth from Zion, the word of the Lord from Jerusalem* (Isa. 2:3). That is why Jerusalem was called the "valley of vision," for every prophet whose city of origin was not named hailed from Jerusalem, as the sages said.[19] Thus the meaning is that there is no need for a person to be honored by his position. Rather, the position honors the person. However, if the position is itself one of distinction, then each brings honor to the other.

C. The same idea is taught by the statement in the Yerushalmi, Tractate Sheqalim, chapter 2: "With what is left from the funeral expenses one builds a monument over the grave. Rabban Simeon ben Gamaliel said, We do not

14. Cf. Num. Rab. 13,3.
15. B. Meg 28a.
16. Maimonides, *Code, Beit ha-Beḥirah,* 6,14.
17. Midrash Tehillim 30,1.
18. Cf. Nahmanides on Gen. 14:18.
19. Lam. Rab., Proem 24.

build a monument for the righteous; their words are their memorial." Maimonides incorporated this as a halakhah in the fourth chapter of "The Laws
of the Mourner."[20] The reason for this is that people want to honor the deceased through "the honor of position,"[21] and this implies that the deceased
have no other source of honor. But the righteous do not need this [external
honor], for their words are their memorial.

However, this principle seems to be contradicted by Jacob's erecting of a
tombstone for Rachel, as the Bible tells us:

["The Pillar at Rachel's Grave," fol. 169b] *Rachel died. She was buried on the
road to Ephrath, now Bethlehem. Over her grave Jacob set up a pillar; it is the
pillar at Rachel's grave to this day* (Gen. 35:19–20). If this is improper, how
did Jacob do it? And the same with other righteous peiople as well. This truly
needs to be answered.

I would say that the general purpose in building a tombstone and a monument over the grave is so that the name of the deceased will not be forgotten by his relatives and neighbors.[22] When people pass by the grave and see
his name, they will remember him as if he were alive. This has led some individuals to extremes, making such monuments exceedingly prominent so
as to attract the attention of passersby, in order that the deceased will
thereby be remembered more. This is sheer vanity, unworthy of the righteous, who have no need for this, for their deeds and their words are their
memorial.

The Psalmist referred to this explicitly in Psalm 49: *One sees that the wise
die, the fool and the ignorant both perish, leaving their wealth to others. They
think to themselves that their houses will endure forever, their dwelling-places to
all generations, proclaiming their names far and wide* (Ps. 49:11–12). This
refers to those whose sole ambition is to have built for themselves a magnificent grave and a costly sarcophagus, so that these edifices in which they will
dwell forever will cause their name to be remembered far and wide.[23] Yet
they have forgotten that the essential thing is to clear themselves some space
and prepare what is necessary[24] to enter into the splendor of the King, for
without this, all the glory of their graves is vanity.

---

20. Maimonides, *Code, Evel* 4,4.
21. I.e., a monument that will distinguish the place of burial.
22. Hebrew based on Ruth 4:10.
23. For the background of this interpretation of the verses, see introduction, n. 27.
24. The first phrase would appear to be based on Rashi's comment on Genesis 46:28, the
second on Joshua 1:11.

[Additions: fol. 171v]

D. However, it would seem that our original rabbinic statement[25] serves to solve all aspects of this problem as required, in each of its explanations. The sages wanted to teach that the honor of the place publicizes the honor of the righteous person, whether because by this pillar it would be seen that Israel is known by Rebecca's name, or whether it was so that she would pray on their behalf.[26]

["The Pillar at Rachel's Grave," fol. 169v]

Now this statement is extremely difficult for two reasons. First, the assertion "He taught us that Israel is known by Rachel's name": yet we can see for ourselves that in all that was said previously, such a lesson never emerged for us. Second, the statement, "Another interpretation: Why did our ancestor Jacob decide . . . ?" It would seem that this second explanation and the reason it contains should be analogous to what was said above, just like all the other instances of "another interpretation" found in rabbinic literature. But apparently these two matters are not at all equivalent, or pertaining to the same subject.[27]

It seems to me that the intent of the sages in this place was to raise our question: If R. Simeon ben Gamaliel said, "We do not build a monument for the righteous," providing an immediate explanation: "Their words are their memorial," how did Jacob make a monument and a tombstone for the burial of Rachel, as we read, *Jacob set up a pillar* (Gen. 35:20)? The answer is "He taught us that Israel is known by Rachel's name." We must read *limmedanu*, with a *ḥiriq* under the *lamed,* meaning "he taught us," not *lamadnu*, with a *pataḥ* under the *lamed,*[28] meaning "we have learned."

---

25. This is the technical term for the rabbinic statement always cited immediately after the verse from the Scriptural lesson (*nose*) at the beginning of each sermon; see above, chap. 9. The statement, from Gen. Rab. 82,10, was not the *ma'amar* of the original sermon, but it was cited and explained at length in that sermon.

26. Morteira undoubtedly incorporated more material from the original here not indicated in his "additions," explaining how this statement solves the problem he has raised. The continuation of the "additions," on the top of a new page, introduced by "similarly," indicates that it follows a discussion of Rachel. I have therefore included this passage from the original sermon here, stopping where I believe the transition could be made to the continuation of the "additions."

27. I.e., the first statement addresses the matter of the tombstone, the second the location; they are therefore not two parallel interpretations of the same subject as is usually the case with *davar aḥer.*

28. Morteira's pen slipped here: the correct vowel for the form he is rejecting should, of course, be *qamats.*

The sense is that by this act he taught us that Israel is known by Rachel's name, and this pillar is not a reminder of renown and splendor and glory, as those who seek to have their name proclaimed far and wide would hope it to be. Rather, it teaches something very specific: that Israel is known by Rachel's name. Thus this pillar that our ancestor Jacob set up at her grave is like other pillars set up as a sign and indication of something specific. For example, *This mound is a witness* (Gen. 31:48), and *this pillar shall be witness* (Gen. 31:52). Thus this pillar [at Rachel's grave] is to teach that Israel is known by Rachel's name, in the manner that we shall now explain.

Let us begin by asking, Why is it that after God called Abram "Abraham" he was never again referred to by his original name, whereas even though the Holy One called Jacob "Israel," he is later referred to as "Jacob"?[29] Now we may say that the name Abram was changed in its essence, so that nothing of it remained. Think of a person who alters an old piece of clothing: it is no longer possible to wear the old piece as it was. Different is the person who buys a new garment and leaves the old one unchanged, for he can wear it again. Yet the question remains unanswered. For if the name "Israel" was fundamental and the name "Jacob" was secondary,[30] why, after the angel changed his name, was he not called "Israel"? Only where the Torah is telling what would be in future generations does it say *That is why the children of Israel do not eat* [*the thigh muscle*] (Gen. 32:33). Similarly, he calls the altar El-Elohei-Yisrael (Gen. 33:20). However, there is no reference to him by the name of "Israel" until God confirmed the words of the angel.[31]

But if the reason is that he was not referred to by the name "Israel" until God used this name, as soon as God did use it he should immediately have been called "Israel," even though he might still [occasionally] be known [also] as "Jacob." Yet we find that immediately afterward he is called "Jacob" two or three times: *God appeared again to Jacob . . . . God said to him, you whose name is Jacob . . . . Israel shall be your name. . . . God said to him, I am El Shaddai . . . . The land that I assigned . . . . God parted from him . . .* (Gen. 35:9–13). [But then] *Jacob set up a pillar . . . . Jacob named the place . . .* (Gen. 35:14–15).

Granted, we may resolve this by claiming that these names mention what he did while his name was still Jacob, not having been changed to Israel. The meaning of the verses would then be, *God parted from him at the spot where*

---

29. Cf. Abravanel, *Torah* 1:220 (question 8).

30. Cf. B. Ber 13a, Gen. Rab. 46,8. The illustration through the contrast between altering a garment and buying a new one would seem to be Morteira's own.

31. In Genesis 35, as will be seen.

He had spoken to him and Jacob set up a pillar (Gen. 35:13–14), i.e., "at the spot where Jacob had already set up an altar, and offered a libation, and called the place Beit El," the entire matter being the vision of one who dreamed. Yet the problem still remains unresolved. For what can we say afterward, concerning the death of Rachel, about the verse *Jacob set up a pillar over her grave* (Gen. 35:20). This certainly cannot be applied to the past. Yet he is still not called "Israel," even after God used this name. However, after the erection of this pillar, he is immediately called (172r) "Israel" three times, one after the other. *Israel journeyed on* from there . . . . *While Israel stayed in that land* . . . . *Israel heard* . . . (Gen. 35:21–22).[32]

The reason for this is that he was not called "Israel" until the birth of Benjamin, at the time when Rachel died. If he had been called "Israel" [before Benjamin was born], then it would be possible for the tribe of Benjamin to be wiped out, God forbid, and "we have it by tradition that no tribe will become extinct,"[33] for there is no "Israel" without the twelve tribes. Thus the Torah says, *Israel heard. Now the sons of Jacob were twelve* (Gen. 35:22), meaning the sons he had while his name was still "Jacob" were twelve, and after this he was called "Israel." Until he had twelve sons, he was not called "Israel," for if he had, one could have said that it was possible for Israel to exist without Benjamin. Therefore, after Rachel died, Jacob set up a pillar over her grave as testimony that she was the *rock of Israel* (Gen. 49:24), which *became the chief cornerstone* (Ps. 118:22), completing the number, and making him worthy of being called "Israel." [This was the function of][34] the pillar; it was not for self-glorification.

That is what the sages responded to Rabban Simeon ben Gamaliel's problem pertaining to Rachel: "It taught us—namely, the pillar taught—that Israel is known by Rachel's name, in accordance with the verse, *Rachel weeps over her children* (Jer. 31:15)." For the divine task is attributed to the one who completes it,[35] and if Rachel completed the number, and [   ][36] the use of the name "Israel," then it was appropriate that Israel be known by her name.

Similarly, it said "Another interpretation," meaning another explanation

---

32. Cf. Saba, Genesis, p. 49b–c, who gives a different explanation for the sudden shift from that which Morteira will give.

33. B. BB 115b. If Jacob could have been known as "Israel" before the birth of Benjamin, that means that "Israel" is conceivable without one of its tribes, and Benjamin could theoretically be destroyed. However, this is contradicted by a Talmudic tradition.

34. A reconstruction from context of a Hebrew word or abbreviation I cannot decipher.

35. Cf. Gen. Rab. 85,3 and Deut. Rab. 8,4; the continuation of this passage will be used when the preacher turns to Menasseh (see n. 37).

36. I cannot confidently decipher two Hebrew words here.

why Jacob set up a pillar over her grave even though we do not build a monument upon the graves of the righteous. This was not for glory or honor, for that is inappropriate, as their deeds and their words are their memorial. Rather, it is for the benefit of the living, to enhance their reputation or for some similar purpose. This was the consideration that applied to Rachel . . . .

(Additions: fol. 171r)

Similarly this *tsaddiq* does not need an imposing monument or sarcophagus to honor him for the sake of his position. "His words are his memorial": the words in the books he wrote will preserve his memory. Indeed, the truth is that he did have an honored position; his position honored him and he it. His position honored him, for he was a teacher and a mentor from his youth in this distinguished place, in the greatest congregations of the region. And he honored his position through his distinguished achievements, which earned him constant praise and glory and honor. Thus his position was fitting for him, and he for it.

He recognized the glory of his place, for the same thing that happened to the *tsaddiq* Joseph happened to him. The sages gave a parable of thieves who entered a cellar and stole a barrel of wine. The owner said to them, "You have drunk the wine, now return the barrel to its place." Even so the Bible tells us, *The bones of Joseph, which the children of Israel brought up from Egypt, were buried at Shechem* (Josh. 24:32). In Shechem they sold him, to Shechem they restored him.[37] So it was with this *tsaddiq*: his lofty ideas stole him from his place (for thoughts are called "friends" and "brothers" as in the verse *How precious to me are Your friends, O God* [Ps. 139:17][38]), and brought him to England in his desire to establish there a community that would call upon the name of God in that country.[39] His efforts were great, as is well known. If he was unable to complete all he had planned, *His reward is his, and his recompense precedes him* (Isa. 40:10).

This fits the rabbinic statement in the first chapter of Berakhot: "*It shall be written in a book of remembrance before Him concerning those who revered the Lord and think of His name* (Mal. 3:16). What is the significance of "who think of His name"? Rab Ashi said, Whoever thinks of doing a *mitsvah* and, for reasons beyond his control, is unable to do it, is considered in this verse as if he had indeed performed it."[40]

---

37. Gen. Rab. 85,3, Exod. Rab. end of chap. 20, Deut. Rab. 8,4. See introduction, n. 28.
38. Following the interpretation of Abraham ibn Ezra on this verse.
39. See introduction, n. 29.
40. B. Ber 6a.

Now it may well be asked, how is this interpretation related to the beginning of the verse, about which the rabbis said, "How do we know that when two sit together and study Torah, the Divine Presence is with them? From the verse *Then those who revere the Lord converse with each other; God listens, and notes, and it shall be written* (Mal 3:16).

A close analysis reveals that the two points are beautifully interconnected. For when two sit and study Torah in depth, one may conclude that something is forbidden while the other concludes that it is permitted. Now certainly one of them is not saying what is true. But since his intention was to clarify the truth, it is considered as if he had actually hit upon the truth. So those who revere the Lord, who tremble at His word[41] in fear of sin, do not actually perform any act. All these qualities pertain to intention and thought. That is why they are written in the book in a separate category, inscribed together with those who think of His name. Hence, "Whoever thinks of doing a *mitsvah* and, for reasons beyond his control, is unable to do it, is considered in this verse as if he had indeed performed it," and it is written in the book. So it is with this *tsaddiq*. Therefore, *his reward is his, and his recompense precedes him* (Isa. 40:10).

God has granted him the reward about which the righteous of old felt so strongly, for which they made such great exertion: to be buried in the graves of their ancestors. Both Jacob and Joseph acted accordingly, exacting a stringent oath, for they considered the matter extremely serious, of utmost consequence.[42] They therefore called it a matter of *true kindness* (Gen. 47:29). Miraculously, he has arrived here, for *God will not deprive the soul of the righteous* (Prov. 10:3). He has come to his place, which he loved so much, thereby revealing his own merit, and giving us the merit that comes from burying him and from mourning him in a manner appropriate to our master and teacher.

This new pain of our sorrow is especially great, for only eight months ago the pious scholar Rabbi David Pardo departed from us (may the memory of the sacred pious be for blessing).[43] And *afterward, his brother*[44] *exited*, as we said at the beginning in our theme-verse, *by his hand the crimson thread* (Gen. 38:30). To understand this, recall that crimson is a metaphor for splendor of speech and eloquence, as in the verse, *Your lips are like a crimson*

---

41. Cf. Isa. 66:5.
42. Cf. Gen. Rab. 96,5, and introduction, n. 31.
43. On Pardo, see introduction, n. 32.
44. I.e., Menasseh. The preacher turns to the *nose* at the very end of his eulogy, as he did in the two eulogies for David Farar.

thread, your speech is lovely (Song 4:3). And his beautiful eloquence, his delightful words, were not in his mouth alone, but also *by his hand,* in his books, which he wrote in such an elegant style. *Therefore he was named Zeraḥ* (Gen. 38:30), which means shining, for his radiance has shone throughout the world. *May God shine upon him, and fill his soul with splendor* (Isa. 58:11). But our duty is to affirm the decree, and to say, "Blessed is the Judge of Truth."[45]

---

45. See above, p. 386, n. 41 to the first eulogy for David Farar.

שאול לוי מורטירה
הספד על ר' מנשה בן ישראל

(הוספות השייכות להספד, 171 ב)

ודרשתי אותו עוד בשנת התי"ח בתשלום שבעה ימים לקבורת החכם כמהר"ר[1] מנשה בן ישראל זצ"ל נפטר במידילבורג בבואו מלונדריס והיה זה ביום ב' כ' לחדש כסליו והוספתי הנמשך.[2]

א. ואחר יצא אחיו אשר על ידו השני ויקרא שמו זרח.[3]

(מצבת קבורת רחל, 169 ב)

ויצב יעקב מצבה על קבורתה היא מצבת קבורת רחל עד היום.[4] תני ר' שמעון בן גמליאל אומר אין עושין נפשות לצדיקים, דבריהם הן זכרוניהם. למדנו שנקראו ישראל על שם רחל שנ' רחל מבכה על בניה.[5] ד"א[6] ותמת רחל ותקבר בדרך אפרת.[7] מה ראה אבינו יעקב לקבור את רחל בדרך אפרת אלא צפה אבינו יעקב שהגליות עתידות לעבור שם לפיכך קברה שם כדי שתהא מבקשת עליהם רחמים.[8]

(מצבת קבורת רחל, 169 א)

בברכות פרק ראשון,[9] א"ל מאי דכתיב ברכי נפשי את ה' וכל קרבי את שם קדשו.[10] א"ל בו וראה שלא כמידת הקב"ה מדת ב"ו.[11] מדת ב"ו צר צורה על גבי הכתל ואין יכול להטיל בה רוח ונשמה קרבים ובני מעים והקב"ה אינו כן צר צורה בתוך צורה ומטיל בה רוח ונשמה קרבים ובני

1. כבוד מורנו הרב רבי.
2. על בעית התאריך, עי' הערה 14 למבוא.
3. בר' לח ל, פסוק הנושא של ההספד.
4. בר' לה יט-כ.
5. יר' לא טו.
6. דבר אחר.
7. בר' לה יט.
8. בראשית רבה פב,י המופיע באמצע הדרשה המקורית. ההוספות מראות שמורטירה השתמש בה כמאמר הקודם של ההספד. עי' למטה, הערה 56.
9. ברכות י א.
10. תה' קג א.
11. בשר ודם.

מעים, והיינו דאמרה הנה אין קדוש כה' כי אין בלתך אין צור כאלהינו,[12] מאי אין צור כאלהינו? אין צייר כאלהינו ע"כ.[13]

מזה ראינו כי הפרש צורות הנעשות ע"י אדם לנעשות ע"י הבורא ית' הוא כי אלו אין בהם אלא חיצוניות וההוראה השטחיית ואלו יש בהם תוך וממש. ההפרש הזה עצמו נ"ל שיש בין הצורות עצמם הנעשות על ידו ית', כי כמו שהצורה הנעשית ע"ג הכותל הנה היא יפה מראה ונאה בצבעיה מקושטת בבגדיה ובתכשיטיה ותאוה היא מאד לעינים[14] אולם רוח וממשות אין בה ואם ישלח איש את ידו יאסוף רוח בחפניו,[15] כן יש כמה מן הצורות בלתי נעשות על גבי הכותל והם נעשות בחותמו של אדם הראשון[16] אולם שמגמת שלמותם בתכשיטים החיצונים והנם יפים למראה מתוקנים ומקושטים עד מאד ולא יבצרו מהם כל[17] עניני הכבוד וההדר, אולם אין בהם רוח ונשמה קרבים ובני מעים כי אין בהם ממש וכל תוכם מלא תוך ומרמה[18] וכל מדה רעה. הלא אלה הם פחותים מן הצורות האלה כי הצורות אין להם תוך ואלו מלאי חמס ועול...ולכן צריך שישים האדם את כל מגמתו למלא חדריו הפנימים[19] במה שהוא בהם איש ולא ישים תקותו להשתלם בחצונותיו באשר הוא בהם צורה מצויירת. ואם בחייו כך הנה במיתתו אשר אחריה הוא עתיד ליתן דין וחשבון עאכ"ו...[20]

ענין מיוחד אל הנושא אשר אנו עליו הוא מה שאמר הנביא ישעיהו סי' נ"ח בענין הצום. אמר, הכזה יהיה צום אבחרהו יום ענות אדם נפשו הלכוף כאגמון ראשו ושק ואפר יציע הלזה תקרא צום ויום רצון לה'?![21] ר"ל הלא כל אלה יוכל מצייר לצייר נשלם כצורה שבפנים כצורה ע"ג הכותל

12. ש"א ב ב.
13. עד כאן (לשון מאמר התלמוד).
14. ע"פ בר' ג ו.
15. משלי ל ד.
16. ע"פ משנה סנהדרין ד,ה.
17. ע"פ בר' יא ו.
18. משחק מלים ע"פ תה' נה יב.
19. ע"פ דבהי"א כח א (כאן במשמעות מטפורית).
20. על אחת כמה וכמה. השוה משנה אבות ג,א.
21. יש' נח ה.

מעולה מאד מאד ממה שהם עושים כי כל אלה ענינים חצוניים הם. הלא
זה צום אבחרהו פתח חרצובות רשע התר אגודות מוטה ושלח רצוצים
חפשים וכל מוטה תנתקו וכו'[22] אם תסיר מתוכך מוטה וכו'[23] ותפק לרעב
נפשך;[24] כי כל אלה לא יוכל המצייר לצייר כי המה תנאי ופרטי הצורה
האלקית אשר בהם השלמיות הפנימיים רוח ונשמה קרבים ובני מעים
ובהם יבדלו בתכלית ההבדל, רצוני להיותם אנשים חיים או צורות
מדומות, כהבדל ממש אשר בין היש ובין האין.

על הכוונה הזאת עצמה יסוב המוסר אשר למדונו ז"ל בפ"ג דתענית,[25]
תניא ר' יוסי אומר לא מקומו של אדם מכבדו אלא אדם מכבד את
מקומו, שכן מצינו בהר סיני שכל זמן שהשכינה עליו אמר תורה גם
הצאן והבקר אל ירעו אל מול ההר ההוא,[26] נסתלקה השכינה ממנה
אמרה תורה במשך היובל המה יעלו בהר,[27] וכן מצינו באהל מועד
שבמדבר שכל זמן שהוא נטוי אמרה תורה וישלחו מן המחנה כל צרוע,[28]
הוגללו הפרוכות[29] הותרו זבין ומצורעין ליכנס שם.

(הוספות השייכות להספד, 171 ב)

ב. ואין להבין הכלל הזה כפשוטו שאין המקום מכבד את האדם מכל
וכל שהרי כמה כתובים מורים ההפך כגון סלסלה ותרוממך[30] וכן חזית
איש מהיר במלאכתו לפני מלכים יתיצב,[31] כי טוב אמר לך עלה הנה[32]
וכו'. אלא הכוונה היא שאין צורך לאדם נכבד יכבדהו מקומו אלא די
כבודו לכבד את מקומו אעפ"י שמאליו המקום אינו נכבד, אבל אם
המקום נכבד יוסיף כבוד לכבוד. והביא ראיה מהי"ת[33] מהר סיני כי לא

---

22. יש' נח ו.
23. יש' נח ח.
24. יש' נח י.
25. תענית כא ב.
26. שמ' לד ג.
27. שמ' יט יג.
28. במ' ה ב.
29. בשעת נסיעתם של בני ישראל (רש"י).
30. משלי ד ח.
31. משלי כב כט.
32. משלי כה ז. על השמוש בשלשת הפסוקים האלה, עי' הערה 13 לתרגום.
33. מהשם יתברך.

היה נכבד מאליו כי הוא שפל שבהרים כי לכך בחרו ה'[34] והיה כבודו בעוד השכינה עליו ולא אחרי כן להורות כי כל כבודו תלוי בשכינה. וכן המדבר לא היה נכבד מאליו בהיותו ארץ אשר לא עבר בה איש[35] ובעוד אהל מעד נטוי היה בו כבוד.

לא כן הר ציון כי היה המקום נכבד והשכינה מכבדו ולכן אחרי הסתלקות השכינה נשאר בו הכבוד שני והשימותי את מקדשיכם,[36] אפי' אחר חרבן הם בקדושתם.[37] וכמו כן ירושלים כי קדושה ראשונה קדשה לשעתה וקדשה לעתיד לבא.[38] וכל כך למה? כי היו המקומות האלו נכבדים מאליהם כמו שאמר המשורר ויבן כמו רמים מקדשו כארץ יסדה לעולם.[39] ויבן כמו רמים שאז"ל בית המקדש של מטה מכוון כנגד בית המקדש של מעלה.[40] כארץ יסדה לעולם זו ירושלים כי מתחילה נקראו מלכיה מלכי צדק[41] ובמקומות האלו כבדו את ה' וה' כבדם על דרך את ה' האמרת[42] וה' האמירך[43] והם ממש כנגד סיני ואהל מועד מקום התורה והנבואה. כמו כן כי מציון תצא תורה ודבר ה' מירושלים[44] כי על כן נקראת ירושלים גיא חזיון שכל נביא שלא נזכר שם עירו הוא מירושלים כמו שאז"ל.[45] הרי כי הכונה היא אין צורך לאדם שיכבדהו מקומו אלא הוא מכבד את מקומו אולם אם מקומו הוא נכבד זה מכבד לזה וזה מכבד לזה.

ג. הכונה הזאת ילמדנה מה שאמרה הירושלמי דשקלים פ"ב על הא דתנן מותר המת בונין לו נפש על קברו תני רבן שמעון בן גמליאל הצדיקים

34. עי' במדבר רבה יג,ג.
35. יר' ב ו.
36. ויק' כו לא.
37. מגילה כח א.
38. עי' רמב"ם, הלכות בית הבחירה ו,טז.
39. תה' עח סט.
40. מדרש תהלים ל,א.
41. עי' פירושו של הרמב"ן לבר' יד,יח.
42. דב' כו יז.
43. דב' כו יח.
44. יש' ב ג.
45. איכה רבתי פתיחה כד.

אין בונין להם נפש וכו׳ דבריהם הם זכרוניהם.[46] וכן פסק הרמב״ם ז״ל
להלכה בפ״ד מה׳ אבל,[47] מפני שרוצין לכבד הנקבר בכבודו של מקום
ונר׳ שאין להם כבוד אחר והצדיקים אין להם צורך בזה כי דבריהם הם
זכרוניהם. אולם ק׳[48] נגד זה מה שעשה יעקב במצבת רחל כמו שכתוב

(מצבת קבורת רחל, 169 ב)

ותמת רחל ותקבר בדרך אפרתה היא בית לחם ויצב יעקב מצבה על
קבורתה היא מצבת קבורת רחל עד היום.[49] ואם הדבר אינו הגון איך
עשאו יעקב אע״ה?[50] וכמו כן בצדיקים אחרים? באמת הדבר צריך תשובה.

והנה נר׳ לומר כי התכלית הכללי בבנין הציון והנפש על הקבר הוא
כדי שלא ימחה שם המת מאת אחיו ומשער מקומו[51] וכי יעברו על הקבר
ויראו את שמו יזכרוהו ויעלה על לב[52] בתוך החיים. ומזה ימשך שכמה מן
האנשים יפליגו ציונים אלה להיותם מעולים מאד לבעבור יהיו יותר
ממשיכים להם הראות וההבטה ומתוך כך יזכר יותר האיש הנקבר שם.
וזה הבל ואינו ראוי לצדיקים כי אינם צריכים לזה כי מעשיהם ודבריהם
הם זכרונם. וכבר דבר המשורר הזה על זה בבירור בס׳ מט׳[53] אמר, כי
יראה חכמים ימותו יחד כסיל ובער יאבדו ועזבו לאחרים חילם קרבם
בתימו לעולם משכנותם לדור ודור קראו בשמותם עלי אדמות, ר״ל שמו
כל מגמתם לבנות להם קברות מפוארים ובנינים יקרים להיות הבתים
אשר בקרבם ישכבו לעולם סיבה להזכר שמם עלי אדמות ולא זכרו מן
העיקר להשתדל לפנות להם מקום[54] ולהכין להם צידה[55] ליכנס ביקר
המלך, ומבלעדי זה כל כבוד קבריהם הבל.

46. ירושלמי שקלים מז א.
47. רמב״ם, הלכות אבל ד,ד.
48. קשה, או קושיא.
49. בר׳ לה יט-כ.
50. אבינו עליו השלום.
51. ע״פ דב׳ כה ו ורות ד י.
52. ע״פ יר׳ ג טז.
53. בסימן מט (תהלים מט יא-יב).
54. עי׳ פירושו של רש״י לבר׳ מו כח.
55. ע״פ יהושע א יא.

(הוספות השייכות להספד)

ד. אולם נר' כי מאמרנו הקודם[56] בא לתרץ הענין הזה הכל כבדרוש בכל א' משני הפירושים כי באו להורות כי כבוד המקום היה מפרסם כבוד הצדיק, אם שבמצבה היה נראה שישראל נקראו על שם רחל ואם כדי שתתפלל בעדם.

(מצבת קבורת רחל, 169 ב)

והנה המאמר הזה ק' מאד משני ענינים. הא' במה שאמר למדנו שנקראו ישראל על שם רחל, ועינינו רואות כי בכל הנאמר לעיל לא יצא לנו הלמוד כזה. והב' דאמר דבר אחר מה ראה יעקב אבינו וכו' דנר' כי הפירוש הזה השני והטעם אשר בו הוא מעין מה שנא' לעיל, כענין כל „דבר אחר" הבא בדבריהם ז"ל. ולכאורה נר' שאין הענינים שום בנושא א'[57] ונ"ל כי כונתם ז"ל במקום הזה היא לומר אם אמר ר' שמעון בן גמליאל אין עושין נפשות לצדיקים, ונימוקו עמו דדבריהן הם זכרונן,[58] איך עשה יעקב נפש וציון לקבורת רחל כדכתי' ויצב יעקב מצבה וכו'?![59] ותירץ למדנו שנקראו ישראל על שם רחל. וצריך לקרות לימדנו בלמד חיריק ולא למדנו בלמד פתח[60] ר"ל בפעולה הזאת לימדנו שישראל נקראו על שם רחל ואין המצבה הזאת לזכירת שם ולתפארת ולכבוד כתכלית אותם אשר בקשו לקראת אם שמם עלי ארצות[61] אלא להורות ענין פרטי ומיוחד והוא שישראל נקראו על שם רחל ותהיה אם כן המצבה הזאת אשר הקים יעקב אבינו על קבורתה כענין שאר המצבות אשר הוקמו להורת ואות ענין פרטי, כמו שנ' עד הגל הזה ועדה המצבה וכו'[62] ותהיה המצבה להורות כי נקראו ישראל על שם רחל, ויהיה זה על האופן אשר נבאר.

והוא שנשאל מה טעם אחרי אשר קרא השי"ת את אברם אברהם לא

56. מאמר חז"ל המצוטט מיד אחרי פסוק הנושא מפרשת השבוע (כאן בראשית רבה פב,י). עי' לעיל, הערה 8 והערות 25 ו־261 לתרגום.

57. עי' הערה 27 לתרגום.

58. בירושלמי שקלים מז א (ולעיל הערה 46).

59. בר' לה כ.

60. כמובן צ"ל „בלמד קמץ."

61. ע"פ תה' מט יב.

62. בר' לא נב.

נזכר עוד אחרי כן בשמו הראשון, ויעקב אעפ״י שקרא הקב״ה שמו
ישראל נקרא אחר כך בשם יעקב? ואעפ״י שנאמר ששם אברהם נשנה
בעצמותה ולא נשאר ממנו כלום ולכן אי אפשר לחזור בקריאתו מה
שאין כן בשם ישראל כי נתחדש ושם יעקב נשאר ולכן אפשר זכירתו,
כאדם המתקן את בגדו הישן שאי אפשר לו ללבוש עוד הישן כאשר היה,
לא כן הקונה בגד חדש ומניח הישן כמות שהוא שאפשר ללבשו עוד, הנה
עוד השאלה במקומה עומדת כי בהיות שם ישראל עקרו ושם יעקב טפל
למה אחרי ששנה המלאך את שמו לא קראוהו בשם ישראל אלא התורה
במספרת מה שיהיה בדודות הבאות אמר על כן לא יאכלו בני ישראל[63]
וכן הוא קרא למזבח אל אלקי ישראל[64] אולם שיזכרהו בשם ישראל לא
נמצא עד אשר הסכים ה׳ על דברי המלאך.[65]

ואם היתה הסיבה כי לא נקרא בשם ישראל עד אשר נקרא כן שמו
השי״ת הנה היה ראוי שמיד שקראו ה׳ יקרא בשם ישראל אעפ״י שיקרא
בשם יעקב, ואנו מצאנו שנקרא מיד בשם יעקב פעמים שלש שני ירא
אלקים אל יעקב וכו׳ ויאמר לו אלקים שמך יעקב וכו׳ ויקרא שמו ישראל
וכו׳ ויאמר לו אלקים אני אל שדי וכו׳ ואת הארץ אשר נתתי וכו׳ ויעל
מעליו אלקים וכו׳ ויצב יעקב מצבה וכו׳ ויקרא יעקב את שם המקום
וכו׳,[66] ולא קראו ישראל. ואעפ״י שיש לתרץ כי השמות האלו הם כמזכירים
מה שעשה בעוד שמו יעקב ועדיין לא נקרא שמו ישראל ויהיה פירוש
הכתוב כך ויעל מעליו אלקים במקום אשר דבר אתו ויצב יעקב מצבה[67]
ר״ל במקום אשר כבר הציב מצבה ונסך עליה נסך וקרא את שם המקום
בית אל[68] והוא ענין מראה החלום, הנה עוד הקושיא במקומה עומדת כי
מה נאמר אחרי כן במיתת רחל שני ויצב יעקב מצבה על קבורתה,[69] שאין
לפרשו על העבה, ועדיין לא נקרא בשם ישראל אחרי שקראו השי״ת כן.
אולם אחרי הקמת המצבה הזאת נקרא מיד ישראל ג׳ פעמים זה אחר

63. בר׳ לב לג.

64. בר׳ לג כ.

65. בבר׳ פרק לה, כפי שיבאר.

66. בר׳ לה ט–טו.

67. בר׳ לה יג–יד.

68. ע״פ בר׳ לה יד–טו.

69. בר׳ לה כ.

זה, ויסע משם ישראל וכו' ויהי בשכון ישראל בארץ ההיא וכו' וישמע ישראל.[70]

וטעם הדבר הוא כי לא נקרא ישראל עד לידת בנימין כי אז מתה רחל, שאילו היה נקרא בשם ישראל הנה ח"ו היה אפשר להכרת שבט וגמירי דלא כליא שבטא,[71] כי אין ישראל אלא בי"ב שבטים. וכן כתיב שם וישמע ישראל ויהיו בני יעקב שנים עשר,[72] ר"ל הבנים אשר היו לו בעוד נקרא בשם יעקב היו שנים עשר ואחר כן נקרא שמו ישראל, ועד אשר לא היו לו י"ב בנים לא נקרא ישראל שאילו נקרא היה אפשר לומר כי בזולת בנימין אפשר להיות ישראל. ולכן אחרי אשר מתה רחל הציב יעקב מצבה על קבורתה לעדות כי היא אבן ישראל[73] והיא היתה לראש פינה[74] והשלימה המנין וזכתה להקרא ישראל, [?!][75] היא המצבה לא להתפארות.

זה הוא שהשיבו רז"ל באשר הקשו לרשב"ג[76] מענין רחל לימדנו ר"ל המצבה הזאת כי ישראל נקראו על שם רחל דכתיב רחל מבכה על בניה.[77] כי אין המצוה נקראת אלא על מי שגומרה[78] ואם רחל גמרה המנין [? ה?][79] קריאת שם ישראל הנה ראוי להקרא שם ישראל על שמה.

וכפי זה אמר ד"א ר"ל פירוש אחר למה הציב יעקב מצבה על קבורתה אחרי אשר אין בונין נפש על קברות הצדיקים והוא לא לכבודה ולהתפאר שהוא הבלתי ראוי כי מעשיהן ודבריהן הם זכרונן אלא לתועלת החיים לשום להם שם או ענין אחר כיוצא, וזה היה ברחל...

(הוספות השייכות להספד, 171א)

כמו כן הצדיק הזה אין צורך לנפש ובנין גדול לכבדו בשביל מקומו כי דבריו הם זכרונו בספריו אשר חבר אשר הם יזכרהו.

70. בר' לה כא–כב.
71. בבא בתרא קטו ב.
72. בר' לה כב.
73. ע"פ בר' מט כד.
74. ע"פ תה' קיח כב.
75. לא הצלחתי לפענח שלוש אותיות הנראות כמו ראשי תיבות.
76. לרבי שמעון בן גמליאל.
77. בראשית רבה פב,י המצטט יר' לא טו.
78. השוה בראשית רבה פה,ג ודברים רבה ח,ד.
79. לא הצלחתי לפענח שתי מלים כאן.

אולם האמת הוא כי היה לו מקום נכבד ומקומו כבדו והוא כבד את
מקומו. מקומו כבדו בהיותו מורה הוראה ומלמד מנעריו במקום נכבד כזה
בקהילות הגדולות אשר בארץ. והוא כבד את מקומו בפעולותיו הנכבדות
ובהיותו תמיד מהודר ומסולסל ונכבד באופן כי מקומו היה נאה לו והוא
נאה אל מקומו.

והוא ז״ל הכיר כ״כ יקר מקומו כי קרה לו כאשר קרה ליוסף הצדיק
כאשר אז״ל מלה״ד[80] ללסטים שנכנסו למרתף וגנבו חבית של יין א״ל בעל
הבית שתיתם היין החזירו החבית למקומו. זהו שני ואת עצמות יוסף אשר
העלו בני ישראל ממצרים קברו בשכם,[81] בשכם מכרוהו לשכם החזירוהו.[82] כך
הצדיק הזה עשתונותיו הרמות גנבוהו ממקומו (כי המחשבות נקראו רעים
ואחים כמו ולי מה יקרו רעיך אל[83]) ויוליכוהו לאינגלטירה בתשוקתו ליסד
שם קהל לקרוא בשם ה׳ שמה והשתדל כידוע ואם לא יכול לגמור את כל
אשר זמם הנה שכרו אתו ופעולתו לפניו[84] כאמור במאמרנו בברכות פ״א[85]
ויכתב בספר זכרון לפניו ליראי ה׳ ולחושבי שמו.[86] מאי ולחושבי שמו? אמר
רב אשי חשב מצוה ונאנס ולא עשתה מעלה עליו הכתוב כאילו עשאו ע״כ.

וצריך לשאול איך יקשר הפירוש הזה עם ראש הפסוק כי שם אמרו
מנין לשנים שיושבים ועוסקים בתורה ששכינה עמהם שנ׳ אז נדברו יראי
ה׳ איש אל רעהו ויקשב ה׳ וישמע ויכתב.[87] אולם בטוב ההתבוננות הנה
הוא יעלה יפה יפה כי שנים שיושבים ומתבוננים בתורה זה אומר אסור
וזה אומר מותר ודאי א׳ אינו אומר אמת, ובהיות כונתו לברר האמת הנה
יחשב לו כאילו קלע אל האמת. וכן [?][88] ה׳ החרדים על דברו[89] ויראים מן
החטא הנה לא יפעלו שום פעולה, הנה כל אלה זכותם בכונה ובמחשבה,
ולכן נכתבים בספר בפני עצמם ונכתבים ביחד עם חושבי שמו, וזהו חשב

80. משל: למה דבר דומה?
81. יהושע כד לב.
82. ע״פ שמות רבה סוף פרק כ.
83. תה׳ קלט יז ע״פ פירושו של אברהם ו׳ עזרא. המלים בסוגריים נכתבו בין השורות.
84. יש׳ מ י.
85. ברכות ו א.
86. מלאכי ג טז.
87. מלאכי שם.
88. לא הצלחתי לפענח את המלה הזאת.
89. ע״פ יש׳ סו ה.

מצוה ונאנס ולא עשאו מעלה עליו הכתוב כאילו עשאו ונכתב בספר. ככה היה הצדיק הזה ולכן שכרו אתו ופעולתו לפניו.[90]

ונתן לו ה׳ השכר אשר עליו נתרגשו הצדיקים ונתחבטו בו מאד: להקבר בקברות אבותיהם.[91] ככה עשה יעקב ככה עשה יוסף בשבועה חמורה כי הדבר חמור מאד והיה נוגע לנפשם והיו קורי׳ אותה חסד ואמת[92] ולכן בדרך נס הגיע הנה כי לא ירעיב ה׳ נפש צדיק[93] ובא אל מקומו אשר חבב כל כך וזכה וזיכה אותנו בקבלתנו אותו לספוד אותו כחובתנו למורנו ורבינו. ובפרט בהתחדש היגון בצערנו כי זה כח׳ חדשים יצא ממנו כמהר״ר[94] דוד פארדו זצוק״ל,[95] ואחר יצא אחיו, כאשר התחלנו בפסוק נושאנו,[96] אשר על ידו השני, הרצון כי השני הוא כינוי אל תפארת הדיבור וההלצה כמו שכתוב כחוט השני שפתותיך ומדברך נאה,[97] ולא בפיו לבד היה בהלצתו היפה ודבריו הנעימים אלא על ידו, בספריו אשר כתב ביופי הלשון, כי בזה נקרא שמו זרח אשר זרח אורו בכל העולם. כן יזרח עליו ה׳ וישביע בצחצחות נפשו.[98] ועלינו להצדיק את הדין ולומר ברוך דיין האמת.[99]

---

90. יש׳ מ י.
91. השוה בראשית רבה צו,ה.
92. בר׳ מז כט.
93. משלי י ג.
94. עי׳ הערה 1 לעיל.
95. זכר צדיק וקדוש לברכה. עי׳ 32 לתרגום.
96. בר׳ לח ל.
97. שיר ד ג.
98. יש׳ נח יא.
99. עי׳ הערה 34 להספד הראשון על דוד פרה.

18

In Praise of an Anti-Jewish Empress:
Ezekiel Landau's Eulogy
for Maria Theresa

Ezekiel Landau's reputation as one of the foremost rabbinic scholars of his age is universally recognized. It is often overlooked, however, that he was also widely esteemed by contemporaries as a powerful and stirring preacher. The sermons recorded in *Derushei ha-Tselaḥ* and *Ahavat Tsiyon* contain not only homiletical and exegetical insights, but powerful social and religious criticism. Those who heard Landau preach were deeply impressed by his manner of delivery, his bearing, and his deep resonant voice.[1]

The announcement that Landau, as Chief Rabbi of Prague, recognized by the government as supreme rabbinical authority for Bohemian Jewry, would deliver a eulogy for the Empress Maria Theresa in the Meisl Synagogue on December 10, 1780, was therefore bound to generate considerable excitement. According to the contemporary description, the gathering included the entire leadership of the Jewish community: The Primator Israel Fränkel and his associates, the members of the supreme rabbinical court, and all other judges and appointed officials. In addition, we are told, a number of Christian notables from both the Government and the Army were present.[2] Landau was obviously expected to display the rhetorical and homiletical skill appropriate for such an occasion.

A Hebrew text of the eulogy was apparently published within three weeks of its delivery, as it bears a publication date of 1780. Not long after, two German versions appeared, one in German type, the other in Hebrew letters. The "translator" was Leopold Tirsch, a Christian scholar who had written several volumes on the Hebrew and Yiddish languages.[3] As official "Transla-

---

Part of this chapter reprinted with permission from *Shofar* 6(1987):20–25, copyright 1987, by Purdue Research Foundation.

1. Klemperer, p. 58.
2. Landau, *Derush Hesped*, p. 1a.
3. See, for example, Muneles, p. 84, nu. 286.

tor and Censor of Hebrew writings," he had given his approval for the original Hebrew publication. While based on the Hebrew text (not on the actual delivery), the German version is actually a reworking, eliminating some of the more technical discussions based on details of biblical or rabbinic language, rearranging the order of the praises, and expanding some of the passages in the spirit of the original.

The German version written in Hebrew letters concludes with the following statement by Landau: "The printers here asked me to print the sermon which I preached as a eulogy for our lady . . . the Empress, of blessed memory. I gave them permission to print it. However, they had already made extensive preparation to print it also in the German language, that is in Jewish writing but in the vernacular. I said, since they have already incurred so much expense for this, they may have permission to print it, too." What we have, therefore is a fine specimen of ephemera: a sermon that aroused considerable interest in both Jewish and non-Jewish communities when it was delivered, but one that was of minimal importance ten or twenty years later. Never incorporated into the later collections of Landau's sermons, extremely few exemplars remain.[4]

In some ways, the written text of the sermon may be disappointing to the modern reader. Much of it is conventional. The first two-thirds is devoted to an explanation of the eight-day delay between the arrival of the news of the Empress's death and the eulogistic response. This is based on the commonplace of Jewish occasional preaching, which can be traced back at least to the fifteenth century, of presenting reasons why one should have remained silent, offset by the reasons one nevertheless felt constrained to speak.[5] All of these are embellished by homiletical exegesis of biblical and aggadic material.

In addition to the conventional material, however, there is a substantial section bearing upon the image of the Empress. This is obviously the crux of the text. Modern historians agree that Maria Theresa was perhaps the most anti-Jewish monarch of her day. Robert Kann, historian of the Habsburg Empire, writes that regarding the Jews, "the empress had inherited all existing prejudices and acquired some additional ones;" her "bigotry was, indeed, a highly personal feature, somewhat out of step with the mores of the times."

---

4. I used copies of the Hebrew *Derush Hesped* from the British Library and the National Library in Jerusalem. Microfilms of the two German editions were provided by the Hebrew Union College Library in Cincinnati (see the HUC Klau Library Catalogue, 15:113).

5. On this convention, see Saperstein, *Jewish Preaching*, index, s.v. "Reasons" for silence and preaching, and above, chap. 13, introduction, at n. 11; chap. 15, introduction, at n. 10; and chap. 16, introduction, at n. 28.

Her most recent biographer, Edward Crankshaw, was more succinct: "Maria Theresa detested Jews."[6]

This personal antipathy, the product of a deep traditional piety, was no secret in her time. It was manifest in policies that created considerable hardship for the Jews in her realm. She was responsible for the expulsion of the Jews from Prague in 1744. Her government imposed extremely high taxes on Jewish subjects, and at one point toyed with the idea of an unprecedented levy on the *etrogim* necessary for the observance of Sukkot. When fiscal pressures compelled her to meet with the Jewish financier Diego d'Aguilar, she insisted on being separated by a screen, refusing to sit in the same room as a Jew. As late as 1777, she reaffirmed her opposition to a Jewish community in the imperial capital of Vienna, stating, "I know of no greater plague than this race, which on account of its deceit, usury and avarice is driving my subjects to beggary. Therefore as far as possible, the Jews are to be kept away and avoided."[7] Yet Landau's eulogy is filled with expressions of deep grief and effusively emotional praise.

To be sure, the preacher was operating under obvious constraints. Maria Theresa was a popular ruler. The eulogy was delivered only after a license had been issued by governmental authorities.[8] As official representative of the Jewish community, speaking at a public gathering with Christian notables in the audience, Landau could not very well have launched into a diatribe even if he had been so inclined. Nevertheless, there are rhetorical techniques available to the speaker who wants to communicate a message at variance with the apparent surface meaning. Some of these would be bound up with the manner of delivery and therefore no longer accessible to us, but others, including the use of veiled biblical allusions, irony, and "faint praise," should be evident in the written text, particularly in the Hebrew version intended only for Jewish readers. A proper assessment of the historical significance of the eulogy therefore depends on a careful literary reading.

My reading of the text convinces me that Landau was sincere in his praise for the deceased monarch and that he genuinely felt the admiration and the grief he professes. This does not mean that he was out of contact with reality or unaware of the Empress's anti-Jewish policies. He does not falsify the record, never claiming that she loved the Jewish people (although he does note that Jews always found refuge in the realms of the Habsburg mon-

---

6. Kann, pp. 189–90; Crankshaw, p. 313.

7. On the Expulsion, see most recently Mevorakh, "Ma'asei Hishtadlut;" for earlier bibliography see there, pp. 125–26, nn. 1 and 2.

8. Landau, *Derush Hesped,* p. 6b.

archs). Rather, he praises her for qualities that other non-Jewish contemporaries recognized as worthy of adulation and deep respect.

Landau marvels at her abilities as a ruler.

> It is indeed amazing that one woman could rule over so many great states with such goodness and integrity, appointing worthy and qualified judges, promulgating edicts throughout her realms, all with wondrous wisdom. It is almost beyond belief that all this could have been done by this woman for 41 years.[9]

He praises her courage as a leader in war, and her capacity to inspire the dedication and sacrifice of her soldiers.

> At the very beginning of her reign, several kings and rulers gathered against her with forces like the sands of the sea. But she *was not dismayed by their shouts, not cowed by their numbers* (Isa. 31:4). This fearlessness enabled her to drive them away from her lands with heroic power. Truly it is amazing that a woman should array herself in the adornments of a man, wearing the spirit of heroism.[10]

And further,

> in times of war, we saw that all her subjects actually risked their lives for her. Those in the army, from the highest officers to the lowly privates, stood their ground and fought her battle with all their might. Nobles and officials responsible for purveying supplies, whether for war or for other imperial needs, together with the rest of those associated with the affairs of state, both non-Jews and Jews—all of us eagerly awaited the opportunity of serving our Queen with all our strength, not because of any expectation of reward, but because of genuine love.[11]

Landau reminds his listeners of the Empress's social welfare programs, which expressed the commitment of the sovereign to education and the care of the disadvantaged. "Look at all the orphanages, called *Waisenhäuser*, look at all the poorhouses, called *Armenhäuser*, look at the money she contributed to this. May God remember her for good."[12]

---

9. Ibid., p. 4b. The dates of Maria Theresa's reign were October 20, 1740 to November 29, 1780.

10. Ibid., pp. 4b–5a; reference is to the Silesian Wars of the early 1740s against the armies of France, Prussia and Bavaria, on which see Pick.

11. Ibid., p. 5a–b. On the army's devotion to the Empress, see Roider, *Maria Theresa*, pp. 22, 103.

12. Landau, op. cit., pp. 5a, 5b. On schools opened during the reign of Maria Theresa, see Roider, *Maria Theresa*, pp. 57–60, and Kerner, pp. 347–48.

He even mentions her piety—not her devotion to the Christian faith, but her ascetic lifestyle, for which she was widely known, especially after the death of her husband in 1765.

> She was modest and withdrawn, separating herself from all physical desires and lusts. For many years, she did not participate in games or listen to music, either vocal or instrumental; she did not attend the comedy or the operas. Has such a thing ever been heard or seen—that a Queen as powerful as she was, raised from birth in royal luxury, should totally spurn all temporal pleasures?[13]

To devotees of high culture this may not seem like much praise, but Landau, who had used the pulpit to criticize his own people for attending comedy and opera,[14] could find much to admire in this royal repudiation of the worldly "vanities."

Finally, he praises her for her son Joseph II. While some of this is couched in familiar eulogistic motifs—one who has a righteous son is not really dead—other passages are far from conventional. Indeed, the last part of the eulogy is devoted to an encomium for the new Emperor based on a stunning use of Isaiah 11, perhaps the most blatantly messianic passage of the entire Bible.[15] The tensions between Joseph and Maria, and their fundamental differences in policy, especially with regard to the Jews, are totally overlooked.

Except for this messianic language, everything mentioned to this point might have been included in a eulogy of the monarch by a contemporary Christian preacher.[16] Of course, Landau could not entirely ignore the question of the Empress's attitude toward the Jews. Perhaps his listeners remembered how he had treated the issue of taxes in earlier sermons. There was no denying that the taxes imposed upon the Jews of Bohemia were extremely

---

13. Landau, *Derush Hesped,* p. 5b. On Maria Theresa's attitude toward music and theater, see Groll; also, Crankshaw, pp. 169–84; on her avoidance of public events toward the end of her life, see Roider, *Maria Theresa,* p. 131.

14. Landau, *Derushei,* p. 36a; cf. p. 131, above.

15. Ibid., p. 6a.

16. For actual examples of Christian eulogies from France and Belgium, especially a sermon by the bishop of Blois delivered at Notre Dame of Paris in May, 1781, see Michaud; an impressive list of such funeral orations can be found on pp. 698–700. Themes emphasized similar to those in the Landau eulogy include Maria Theresa's strength, or "manliness" (pp. 676–77), her military campaigns (pp. 677–80), her concern for the poor, widows and orphans (pp. 686–87), her support for the institutions of health care and education (pp. 691–93), her resisting of the negative influences of philosophy and Enlightenment (p. 689), and her Christian piety (pp. 675, 685, 693). For reference to her attitude toward non-Catholics, see p. 695.

high, perhaps unparalleled anywhere else in the Diaspora. "Yet our Queen, may she live a long life, is not cruel by nature; she is indeed gracious and compassionate, and her outstanding qualities are widely known. Rather, God placed in her heart the idea of increasing the burden of our taxes as chastisement for our sins."[17]

In the eulogy, there is no mention of taxes. There is, however, a reminder of a more positive point of contact between the Empress and the Jews of Bohemia.

> We saw with our own eyes during the years of dearth and famine [1771] the extent of her devotion. Indeed, she found no pleasure in eating or drinking herself until, with vigorous and decisive action, she brought food to these realms from afar. She did not rest throughout the period of famine, nor did she desist from sending wheat and foodstuffs time after time. Remember her, O God, and reward her in the world of reward, that the verse may be fulfilled, *You offer your compassion to the hungry, and satisfy the famished creature, therefore shall your light shine in the darkness, and your gloom shall be like noonday* (Isa. 58:10). . . . Also for us, the Jews, there was an edict from the Queen to provide food in accordance with their needs.[18]

This recollection is confirmed in a Hebrew chronicle recounting the history of the Jewish community of Prague during the years 1767-1791: "We found favor in the eyes of our Lady the Empress and her son. For she gave the order to distribute to us from her own silos provisions of food that were intended for the soldiers. . . . She assured us that we had no need to fear because of the famine, for she would provide enough for all the poor until the new harvest."[19] Modern research based on imperial records corroborates this picture of decisive and compassionate action by Maria and Joseph during a time of emergency.[20]

How are we to explain the positive image of the Empress in this text? To some extent, it should be seen as yet another chapter in the history of medieval Jewry's infatuation with the various monarchs under whom they lived, an infatuation that led to a whitewashing of kings such as Ferdinand of Aragon and Manuel of Portugal, as shown by Yosef Yerushalmi in his study of the Lisbon Massacre of 1506.[21] Ezekiel Landau clearly stands in this tra-

---

17. Landau, *Derushei*, p. 16a, cf. p. 50d; on p. 29c–d, Landau speaks of "haters of Israel" who slander the Jews before the gracious and powerful Queen and her ministers.

18. Landau, *Derush Hesped*, p. 5a.

19. Sadek, p. 63. The image of the Empress is thus corroborated in a purely internal Jewish source, which cannot possibly be dismissed as a concession to public relations needs.

20. See Weinzierl-Fischer.

21. Yerushalmi, *Lisbon Massacre*, esp. pp. 37–66.

dition, viewing the strong monarch as a source of stability and ultimately protection, and any challenge to the monarch as a threat.

This attitude toward royal authority can be seen in another sermon, delivered by Landau on the Sabbath preceding Pesach, 1775, in which he discusses the revolt of the Bohemian serfs that erupted the previous January. The rebels, whose cause was not without justification, had swept through the land toward Prague, attacking the castles of the overlords who had humiliated them. It took forty thousand troops, reinforced by four regiments of cavalry, to suppress the uprising.[22]

Landau, preaching at the holiday of liberation perhaps just at the time when the serfs were being defeated, showed little sympathy for the aspirations of those who had felt themselves to be enslaved. He explains the rebellion as divine punishment of the Jews for the heresy of free-thinking so rampant in his generation: "They say that the world follows a fixed pattern, and there is no sovereign ruler who watches providentially, but all is according to the law of nature; therefore God set against us the serfs in Bohemia, who similarly say 'we have no sovereign ruler; let everyone do as he sees fit.'"

What follows powerfully evokes the Jewish leader's horror at the potential anarchy of a popular uprising, which he perceives to be more devastating than conventional warfare. The contrast he draws is particularly poignant for an inhabitant of Prague, which had been ravaged by battles between major powers for decades.

> We were in great distress. Indeed, it was worse than the upheaval of war. For when some enemy army comes to fight, there is a king and officers above them. Individual soldiers are not free to decide what to do. And even the king is the subject of providence from above, for he has a supernal prince, so that he is not entirely free to choose, but *as streams of water is the heart of the king in the power of the Lord.* (Prov. 21:1) But this was different: when the serfs rose up against us, each one was free to choose what he wished.[23]

Clearly any sovereign, no matter what the royal policy toward Jews, is preferable to this chaos. Not surprisingly, Landau is a royalist, not a democrat, in his political sympathies.

But in addition to the medieval attitude, this loyalty may be seen as evidence of a new way of thinking. Both in this sermon and in other sources, Landau reveals a bond of emotional identification with the Empress and her realm that I do not find, for example, in the literature of Iberian Jewry. It

---

22. On this uprising, see Wright, pp. 48–49, and Trebitsch, paragraph 42 on the year 5535 [1774–1775].

23. Landau, *Derushei,* p. 55d.

certainly did not begin with this eulogy. As we have seen above (chapter 11), at the outbreak of the Seven Years' War in 1756, Landau read a public proclamation in the Alt-Neu Synagogue, threatening with excommunication any Jews who would spy for the Prussian enemy and invoking God's blessing upon the imperial house, the functionaries of the state, and the armies of Austria. During the Prussian siege of Prague in 1757, Landau apparently put himself in a position of considerable danger because of loyalty to the Empress, a fact he recalls in this eulogy.

Another public prayer, this time of thanksgiving, was offered in the Alt-Neu-Shul on June 29, 1757, when the siege was broken. Not long after Joseph II acceded to the position of co-regent with his mother, Landau devoted part of his Shabbat ha-Gadol sermon to recounting the praises of the new ruler. When Maria Theresa fell ill in 1767, Landau composed a public prayer for her recovery. Eight years after our eulogy, Landau preached a sermon of thanksgiving for the victory of Joseph II in the battle of Belgrade (1789), the first major battle in which Jewish soldiers, subjected to the draft in the previous year, had fought. He offered yet another public prayer at the Coronation of Leopold II (1791).[24] All of this shows a considerable concern on the part of the *Oberrabiner* for the affairs of state, particularly the fortunes of its political leaders and its armies. This cannot be dismissed as a government functionary merely going through the motions. I would suggest that it reflects what might be termed the emotions of incipient patriotism, which he felt it important to share with his fellow Jews and to demonstrate to his Christian neighbors.[25]

Nor is Landau unique in this. Other Jews as well seem to have been taken by the figure of Maria Theresa. We have at least one other Jewish eulogy, delivered in Trieste by Elia Morpurgo. It includes lavish praises based on the *eshet ḥayil* passage in Proverbs 31, as well as a collection of memorial poems published in Prague.[26]

24. Most of these public prayers were published, like our sermon, as ephemera. See chap. 11, above, nn. 16, 17, 19, On Landau's behavior during the siege of 1757, to which allusion is made in *Derush Hesped,* p. 5b, cf. Kemelhar, p. 36, which gives no documentation. Landau refers to his sermon on the accession of Joseph II (apparently not extant) in *Derush Hesped,* p. 4a. For his Thanksgiving sermon after the victory at Belgrade, published as *Derush ha-Shevah,* in which he defends the justice of the Emperor against the charge of aggression, see chap. 11 above, nn. 28 and 29.

25. Baron uses the term "patriotic allegiance" to characterize the feelings of Landau: Baron, *Community* 3:183, n. 2.

26. Morporgo; I am grateful to Lois Dubin for directing my attention to this text. The collection of memorial poems is entitled *Maria Theresia, Klaglied eines Prager Juden über ihren Tod* (Muneles, p. 90 nu, 306).

We have already noted that beginning in the second half of the eighteenth century, events such as the death or coronation of a monarch, the outbreak or end of a war, the victory or defeat of the nation's armies in a critical battle, in short, any national triumph or danger, became occasions for Jewish preaching in cities such as Berlin and London as well as in Prague. On such occasions, Jews gathered in their synagogues while Christians gathered in their churches, and the sentiments articulated by the Jewish and Christian preachers were not noticeably different. Jewish leaders in "enemy" countries, however, were often expressing quite different perspectives of the same events.[27]

My thesis, developed in chapter 11, is that we have here indications of a psychological transformation within major Jewish communities of central and western Europe, manifest in feelings of closeness and even identification with the rulers of their countries and a sense that they and their Christian neighbors were part of the same enterprise, a transformation that precedes the Emancipation and the external pressures upon Jews to redefine themselves as Frenchmen or Germans. The full dynamics of this transformation remain to be studied, but occasional sermons such as this eulogy by Ezekiel Landau represent a kind of evidence that should not be overlooked.

---

27. One such occasional sermon, delivered in London near the beginning of the Seven Years' War, is included in *Jewish Preaching*, pp. 247–58. See also above, chap. 11.

EZEKIEL LANDAU
EULOGY FOR EMPRESS MARIA THERESA

(The Eulogy delivered by . . . [a series of honorifics] Rabbi Ezekiel Segal Landau, chief justice of the court and head of the rabbinic academy of our community on Sunday, the twelfth of Kislev, 5541 [December 10, 1780] here in Prague in the Meisl Synagogue[1] at a great public gathering in that synagogue. At the head of the congregation was the Primator,[2] R. Israel Frankel[3] with his distinguished colleagues.[4] Also gathered there was the supreme court with its judges[5] and all the others who held communal appointments, and all the other Jewish dignitaries of the city. There with us as well in the synagogue were many nobles and dignitaries, and distinguished representatives of the military.

This sermon has two parts. First, words that break the heart,[6] intended to inspire wailing and weeping over the death of our pious, most serene sovereign, Queen and Empress Maria Theresa, may her memory be for goodness. Second, praise and thanksgiving for bountiful favor bestowed by God upon the queen and empress in enabling her to see during her lifetime her distinguished son, perfect in every way, our sovereign—noble, pious, well-born, heroic and wise—the Emperor Joseph II, may His Majesty be exalted, sitting upon the imperial throne. Now he fills his mother's place; on his head rest all the crowns and the dignities of his mother the empress. Also included are blessings for our sovereign the emperor, may His Majesty be exalted, and prayers on his behalf that his realm and his governance be supremely successful. This sermon also contains but a tiny measure of the praises of this great dynasty, the House of Austria, from the day when its radiant majesty began to shine until the present.)

---

1. The Meisl Synagogue was named after the sixteenth-century merchant and benefactor Mordecai Meisl, on whom see Baron, SRHJ, 14:164–66 and appertaining notes; David, *Hebrew Chronicle*, pp. 92–93. On the synagogue, see Seibt, p. 103.

2. Fully, *der Primator der Prager Judenstadt,* mayor of the Prague Jewish municipality. See Kestenberg-Gladstein, 1:24, 338.

3. Israel Fränkel (1712–1791) was the most disintinguished lay leader of Prague Jewry at the time (Kestenberg-Gladstein, 1:141).

4. Three to five *parnesei ḥodesh,* who together with the Primator constituted the "Elders," the highest body of lay leadership: Kestenberg-Gladstein, 1:23–24. The Yiddish version of the sermon uses the term *Eltesten* here.

5. Composed of the Chief Rabbi and five *Oberjuristen:* Kestenberg-Gladstein, 1:26.

6. Cf. *Tur Yoreh De'ah* 344a: "To say over the departed words that break the heart, in order to produce intense weeping"; cf. above, chap. 16, first eulogy at n. 2.

It is written in the Bible, *And you, O mortal, sigh; with tottering limbs and bitter grief, sigh before their eyes. When they ask you, "Why do you sigh?" answer, "Because of the tidings that come." Every heart sinks and all hands hang limp; every spirit grows faint and all knees turn to water. It has indeed come to pass, declares the Lord God* (Ezek. 21:11-13).

Today is the eighth day since the evil tidings came that the crown has fallen from our head (Lam. 5:16).[7] It was my obligation to see that we should immediately have arranged a great memorial service, following the biblical text, *In every square there shall be lamenting, in every street cries of "Ah, woe!" The farm hand shall be called to mourn, and those skilled in wailing to lament* (Amos 5:16). We should have fulfilled the verse, *I was bowed with gloom, like one mourning for his mother* (Ps. 35:14). For the mother of the realm[8] has fallen, our sovereign, pious, humble and righteous, the Queen and Empress Maria Theresa, may her soul rest in the Garden of Eden. She was indeed the mother of the realm; from her loins royalty has gone forth (cf. Gen. 35:11).

However, I delayed until now, not out of laziness, God forbid, but because of several reasons.[9] First, because of the intense grief that overwhelmed me when I heard the news, I had no strength to speak, and I knew not what to say. In me was fulfilled the verse that applies to the friends of Job: *They sat with him on the ground seven days and seven nights. None spoke a word to him for they saw how very great was the suffering* (Job 2:13). So with me: so great was the pain of my grief that I could not collect my thoughts to speak coherently for seven days, until today. That is one reason.

The second reason is that nothing confounds a physician who comes to attend a sick man more than discovering two opposite conditions, such that whatever diminishes one intensifies the other. He is hard pressed to know what to do without making things worse. That is our situation today. Now Kohelet spoke of twenty-eight different times, saying, *A season is set for everything, a time for every experience under heaven: a time to give birth and a time to die . . . a time to weep and a time to laugh, a time of mourning and a time*

---

7. Maria Theresa died in Vienna during the evening of November 29. According to Landau's statement, the news would have arrived in Prague on December 2 or 3.

8. *Ima shel malkhut*: This and similar phrases used throughout the eulogy render the German *Mutter des Königsreiches* or *Landesmutter,* commonly used of an empress or queen. In the German version of the eulogy, the term used here is "Mother of our beloved country" (*Mutter unsers geliebsten Vaterlandes*). Cf. Kestenberg-Gladstein 1:91, n. 94.

9. Landau is reverting to an established tradition of Jewish occasional preaching: explaining the reasons why he should remain silent (here why he did remain silent), and then going on to explain why he nevertheless decided to speak. See introduction, n. 5.

of dancing (Eccles. 3:1-2, 4). He specified twenty-eight times, fourteen good and fourteen bad. In all he used the infinitive: to be born, to die, to plant, to uproot. But with mourning and dancing he did not use the infinitive, saying *a time of mourning and a time of dancing.*

I interpret this to suggest[10] . . . that it is as if the time itself is mourning, and the same with its opposite, dancing. This means, if not everyone realizes how much is lost in the death of a certain person, someone must stand up in public and inform the others about the significance of the loss and the mourning that is appropriate. However, at the loss of a great individual, highly esteemed and unique, whose great and glorious splendor is obvious to everyone, all will feel the loss spontaneously. It is as if the sun were to set at noontime: darkness would cover the earth, and all would recognize the absence of the sun's light.

This is our situation today. It is a *time of mourning:* no one needs to stand and preach and inspire, for the sun of our monarch the Empress Maria Theresa shined brilliantly; the power of her fine personality, the fairness of her heart, the abundance of her graciousness were known throughout the world. Now her sun has set, her radiance has been extinguished. Will not all grow faint, and each one of us say, *Oh that my head were water, my eyes a fount of tears; then would I weep day and night* (Jer. 8:23), for the mother of the nation has died, the queen who was as a mother to all the nations. That is why it is a *time of mourning.*

Yet, by contrast, it is also a *time of dancing,* for in us has been fulfilled the verse, *The sun rises, and the sun sets* (Eccles. 1:5), which the sages interpreted to mean: when the sun of one righteous person sets, the sun of another rises; when David's sun set, Solomon's began to shine.[11] So it is now: when the sun of our mighty and gracious sovereign the empress set, there shines that of her son, the great and mighty, wise and pious, more precious than gold and gems, the Emperor Joseph, may His splendid Majesty be exalted. In him is fulfilled the verse, *His throne as the sun before Me* (Ps. 89:37). Just as the radiant sun is seen throughout the world, all welcoming its light, so the fame of our emperor is known throughout the world, his praises sung in every kingdom, near and far. Happy are we, how goodly is our lot that we have

---

10. I have eliminated a technical discussion of the nature of the infinitive that is not entirely clear to me in the Hebrew text. It was dropped from the German version of the eulogy, with a note describing the passage as "grammatical sophistries." My translation follows the German here.

11. Cf. Gen. Rab. 58,2, where the reference to David and Solomon is not to be found.

been deemed worthy of a such a fine and noble king. May our eyes behold the king in his beauty (Isa. 33:17), the king who sustains the land through his justice (Prov. 29:4), the king who reigns in righteousness (Isa. 32:1).

Now *in the light of the king's face there is life* (Prov. 16:15) for the subjects of his realms. This is "dancing" out of abundant joy. Thus at present, two opposing and mutually incompatible times have come together: a time of mourning for the great sorrow, of anguished grief and weeping over the death of Her Majesty the Empress, and a time of joyous and delightful celebration over the accession to her throne of our gracious sovereign the Emperor. For this reason I did not know how to direct my mood; I was uncertain how to act. That is why Solomon did not say "A time to mourn and a time to dance," for a person cannot perform two contradictory actions simultaneously, but the time can combine them both. What impelled me now to summon this memorial assembly I shall divulge a bit later.

The third consideration that led me to silence until now is that I thought it unbefitting the glory of our gracious Majesty the Empress to eulogize her. One does not give a eulogy for the living, only for the dead. And I say that we should not attribute death to our gracious Majesty. Let me explain by citing a passage from the Talmud (B. Ta'anit 5b):

> Rabbi Johanan said, Our ancestor Jacob did not die. R. Nahman replied, Was it for nothing that the wailers wailed and the embalmers embalmed and the buriers buried? He answered, I am interpreting a biblical verse: *Have no fear, My servant Jacob declares the Lord, Be not dismayed, O Israel! I will deliver you from far away, your descendants from their land of captivity* (Jer. 30:10). This verse establishes an analogy between Jacob and his descendants: just as his descendants are living, so he is living.

All the commentators have worn themselves out trying to explain this passage: why this message is derived from the verse, and how it answers the question, Was it for nothing that the wailers wailed, and they embalmed and buried him?

It seems to me that the meaning is to be found in another Talmudic passage (B. BB 115a):

> Rabbi Phinehas ben Hama interpreted the verse, *Hadad heard in Egypt that David had ben laid to rest with his fathers and that Joab the army commander was dead* (I Kings 11:21). Why does it say that David was laid to rest, and that Joab was dead? David, who left a son like him, is said to have been laid to rest, whereas Joab, who did not leave a son like him is said to be dead.

Thus one who leaves a son like him is not said to be dead. I would give a philosophical explanation for this. We know that a living human being is composed of matter and form, namely, the body, which is matter, and the soul, which is its form.[12] Death applies primarily to matter, while the soul returns to God who gave it (cf. Eccles. 12:7). Even during the period of human life, life is applied primarily to the form. We must therefore try to understand how death can pertain to the soul, if even after death it returns to its origin, the root of all life.

The answer is that the soul comes into this world in order to cleave to this matter so that it may become worthy of acquiring a level of perfection. The more a person attains this perfection, the higher is the level to which the soul ascends. This is how we should understand the rabbinic statement that the righteous human being is superior to the angel.[13] Truly, Gentile scholars have repudiated this statement as altogether bizarre, and indeed, basic principles of philosophy make it seem surprising.[14] The explanation is that the angel is pure form without any material component, and it therefore has no capacity for any kind of sin, for every sin and transgression originates in matter following its own tendency. The angel, pure form, has no evil inclination;[15] it always remains at the same level, never ascending or descending from the moment of its creation.

By contrast, the righteous person who serves God and overcomes the material component ascends from one level to the next, and in this respect is superior to the angel. The righteous person is described as moving, the angel as standing, for the righteous person moves from level to level. That is his true life, and that is why he was created. All this applies throughout a lifetime. However, at death, when the form (which is the soul) is separated from the matter (which is the body) and the body is buried in a grave while the spirit returns to God, then the soul has no evil inclination, and it can no longer ascend to any level higher than that which it attained at the time of its separation from matter. That is why we speak of death with regard to the form, for it has died from the status of being able to ascend higher.

Now a father can bestow merit upon his son; the righteousness of the

---

12. Despite his ambivalence about the study of philosophy (see Saperstein, *Jewish Preaching*, pp. 367–69), Landau here follows the Aristotelian tradition in defining the soul as the form of the body.

13. B. Sanh 93a.

14. This was a controversial issue not only between Gentiles and Jews but within Jewish thought. See Abraham ibn Ezra's commentary on Exodus 23:20; Ibn Gabbai, part 3, chaps. 3–4, p. 60a–c.

15. B. Shab 89a, Gen. Rab. 48,11.

blameless one can smooth the way of his child. Father and mother are always looking out for their children from the day they have a mind of their own, guiding them in the right path and teaching them to be ethical. Thus every good deed of the child follows the principles learned from the parents. Whatever good the child does throughout life is counted toward the merit of the parents, as if they themselves had done it. In this sense, even after their death, they can still ascend to a higher status.

In this regard, I offer an interpretation of the following verses:

> *He further showed me Joshua, the high priest, standing before the angel of the Lord. . . . Now Joshua was clothed in filthy garments when he stood before the angel. The latter spoke up and said to his attendants, "Take the filthy garments off him!" And he said to him, "See I have removed your guilt from you, and you shall be clothed in [priestly] robes." Then he gave the order, "Let a pure diadem be placed on his head." . . . And the angel of the Lord charged Joshua as follows: "Thus said the Lord of Hosts, If you walk in My paths and keep My charge, you in turn will rule My House and guard My courts, and I will permit you to move about among these attendants"* (Zech. 3:1-7).

The Aramaic translation of Jonathan renders the phrase "filthy garments" as referring to the sons of the priest who were married to women disqualified from the priesthood. The phrase "You shall be clothed in [priestly] robes" means that they should put aside their improper wives and take proper ones. Thus God announced to the Prophet in a prophetic vision that Joshua should rebuke his sons and make them repent, taking proper wives in place of the improper ones. He certainly hinted that through Joshua's act of rebuking his sons, they would so act. That is why he said "You [Joshua] shall be clothed in [priestly] robes." If his sons would repent of their own accord, he would have no [priestly] robes, which allude to merit, as Jonathan's Aramaic translation of the verse shows.

This interpretation fits the end of the passage, *I will permit you to move about among these attendants.* The righteous person is called a "mover," for he is always moving from one level to the next, as I already indicated. The angel is called an attendant, one who stands in place. At the death of the righteous one, as his spirit ascends to the place of the angels, then his soul too remains stationary among the attendants. But if he has children whom he guided to be themselves righteous, then even after this he may "move about" to a higher level. So long as Joshua failed to inspire his sons to repent, even though he was fully righteous, a priest of the most high God, moving ever upward throughout his life, his upward movement ceased with his death, and he was stationary. But once he acted to bring about the repentance of his sons, the promise was *I will permit you to move about among these attendants,* namely the angels: even after death I will allow you to move.

Therefore, the homiletical interpretation of R. Phinehas in Baba Batra is appropriate: "David, who left a son like him, is not said to be dead," except in relation to his material component, his body, which was buried in the earth. But as for his formal component, the soul, he is not said to be dead, for he commanded his son Solomon before his death to walk in God's ways. The Bible says, *When David's life was drawing to a close, he instructed his son Solomon as follows: I am going the way of all the earth; be strong and show yourself a man. Keep the charge of the Lord your God, walking in His ways and following His laws, His commandments, His rules, and His admonitions . . .* (I Kings 2:1-3). Therefore all of Solomon's additional achievements redounded to the credit of his father, and even after his death he ascended higher. That is why he was not said to be dead.

Now let us return to the statement of R. Johanan in tractate Ta'anit that our ancestor Jacob did not die. R. Nahman replied, Was it for nothing that they wailed and embalmed and buried? He answered, I am interpreting a biblical verse . . . which establishes an analogy between Jacob and his descendants: just as his descendants are living, so he is living. Now Jacob left a son like him. Even though all twelve sons were equal in goodness, nevertheless there was one most blessed, whom he himself toiled to teach all he had learned from his own masters, to transmit to him all his wisdom: his most beloved son, *the fruitful vine* (Gen. 49:22), Joseph. This how the sages interpreted the verses, *These are the generations of Jacob: Joseph* (Gen. 37:2) and *He was the child of his old age* (Gen. 37:3).

Thus so long as Joseph was alive—and by "alive" I mean ascending from one level to the next, all because of the influence of Jacob who guided him properly—Jacob continued to ascend, even after his death, and was called "alive." Therefore R. Johanan replied, "I am interpreting a biblical verse." The meaning is, indeed the wailers and the embalmers and the buriers performed their tasks, but so long as his offspring is alive, he thereby remains alive.

Let us now look at our gracious sovereign the Empress Maria Theresa, may she be remembered for good. She was worthy of leaving a son like this: our sovereign, who excels in all virtues and achievements, the Emperor Joseph, may His Majesty be exalted. It was his mother who guided him from his youth in every fine virtue. She therefore should not be called dead, for even though she has departed from us, her subjects, her splendor and majesty have not departed. They are her son, this esteemed emperor. He is her splendor, he is her majesty, about him it is fitting to say, *in the light of the king's face there is life* (Prov. 16:15), for in the light of his face is the life of his gracious mother after her death.

All of this I thought about, and I was inwardly torn, whether to deliver a eulogy or to remain silent. What made me decide to deliver a public eulogy was the verse with which I began. Let us examine it in detail. It says, *And you, O mortal, sigh; with tottering limbs and bitter grief, sigh before their eyes. When they ask you, "Why do you sigh?" answer, "Because of the tidings that come." Every heart sinks and all hands hang limp; every spirit grows faint and all knees turn to water. It has indeed come to pass, declares the Lord God* (Ezek. 21:11-13).

This passage certainly requires explication. The statement, *When they ask you, "Why do you sigh?"* implies that if someone else had been sighing no one would have asked; it is a particular individual who is asked "Why do you sigh?" This is highlighted by a redundancy in the wording: *When they ask you, "Why do you sigh?"* when it would have been enough to say, "When they ask, 'Why do you sigh?'" Since it says, *When they ask you,* it indicates that the question is directed specifically to you. This requires an explanation.

Furthermore, if the tidings had been about an unknown disaster, then the Prophet would have had to sigh in order to bring it to the attention of the asker and to communicate the seriousness of the calamity. But the disaster was to be perceptible, even obvious to all, as it says, *Because of the tidings that come. Every heart sinks and all hands hang limp.* Thus everyone would recognize it by themselves. Why then did the Prophet need to sigh in their presence? If it was simply to mourn about the disaster, he could have mourned privately, by himself.

Furthermore, what is the function of the question, *Why do you sigh?* After all, the disaster is obvious to all, for we are told, *every heart sinks . . . ."* Note that the Masoretes were sensitive, indicating by the position of the cantillation mark that the word *ba'ah* is in the present tense, not the past, indicating it was not something that already occurred. This resolves a problem in the verse. I once gave a sermon interpreting the phrase *Why do you sigh?* in its own context. However, on this occasion, we shall interpret it as applying to us.

I am the man about whom it is said. My name is Ezekiel. *And you, O mortal, sigh!* You must certainly remember that sixteen years have passed since a certain *Shabbat ha-Gadol*—it was the year 5524 [1764]—when God bestowed strength to our king, the Emperor Joseph, may His Majesty be exalted, and elevated him while his father, the gracious Emperor Francis, was still alive, may he be remembered for good. Our sovereign the Emperor

Joseph was then given the royal crown in Frankfurt am Main and made *Römischerkönig.*[16] This was on the first day of Nisan in 5524 [April 3, 1764].[17] Soon after that, on *Shabbat ha-Gadol,* I delivered a public sermon, proclaiming the praises of this tower of strength, our sovereign the Emperor, who was then king, for his praises were known from his youth.[18]

I gave praise and thanks to God for having established such an excellent, good king. And I said that heaven had given a sign that he was a fine and decent king, for the rabbis said in tractate Rosh Hashanah that good, ethical kings count their reign from the month of Nisan.[19] An example is Cyrus, about whom the Prophet said, *Thus said the Lord to Cyrus, His anointed one, whose right hand He grasped* (Isa. 45:1). Now if the Prophet called him God's anointed, he was certainly an ethical king. And they counted his reign from the month of Nisan, as is demonstrated in tractate Rosh Hashanah.[20] Since it was an act of heaven that this Emperor was anointed and the royal crown set upon his head in the month of Nisan, it is certainly a sign from heaven that all who see him will recognize that he is recognized from heaven as a fine and decent king, and that God would grasp his right hand and exalt him. I then proclaimed publicly some of his praises, for they are too numerous to complete.

But now I feel pain deep inside me over the death of our sovereign, the Empress. *I sigh with tottering limbs and bitter grief* (Ezek. 21:11) before the entire congregation. *When they ask you, "Why do you sigh?,"* that is, why do you in particular sigh? They ask me, as it were, "If it is because of the death of the queen, why you yourself proclaimed publicly the praise of our sovereign the Emperor who has arisen now in place of his mother. It is therefore as if the queen is still here."

The answer is, *Because of the tidings that come. Every heart sinks* (Ezek 21:12). The human being is a microcosm, the organs are like people within a society. The heart is compared to the royal sovereign, for it rules over all the other organs. We find this in the Kuzari, Part IV, section 25, where it

---

16. *Römischerkönig*: King of the Romans. One who held this position would automatically become emperor upon the death of the incumbent, thereby avoiding an interregnum. See Beales, 1:110.

17. April 3, 1764: This was the precise date of Joseph's coronation, held in Frankfurt am Main (where imperial coronations regularly took place); it was vividly described by Goethe in his autobiography, *Dichtung und Wahrheit.* See Beales, 1:111–13.

18. The text of this sermon is apparently no longer extant; all that we know of it is from the summary Landau goes on to give.

19. B. RH 2b.

20. B. RH 3a.

says, "The heart is not mentioned, because it is sovereign." Now we have heard the tidings that our sovereign the Emperor, may His Majesty be exalted, has himself been overcome with grief over the death of his mother the Empress.[21] Now he certainly knows his own outstanding valor and strength; he knows his consummate wisdom; he knows that he is the equal of his ancestors and his mother in every good trait. Nevertheless, the love for his mother and her immense glory were overpowering for him, to the point that he is engaged in profound mourning and lament.

What then should we do? Should we not mourn for this glorious mother, who was the mother of her realms, who reigned for so many years? Since the heart sinks, alluding to the king, the mighty Emperor, who has been overcome and has sunk into grief at the death of the queen, all the organs that depend upon the heart, all the subjects of the realms, should also engage in profound mourning and lament. For *all hands hang limp, every spirit grows faint, all knees turn to water.* Therefore, when I heard of the extensive mourning in Vienna, involving everyone, led by the Emperor himself, I was inspired to stand before the congregation and offer a eulogy. However, I was seized with fear and trembling at the thought that I, an insignificant creature, would utter words in praise of our gracious sovereign, the Empress, until the government graciously granted me permission to do so.

Now my dear friends, our sages debated whether the eulogy is an honor for the living or an honor for the dead.[22] In the category of "honor for the dead" is included two things: celebration of the glory of the person being eulogized, and also celebration of the glory of that person's ancestors according to their respective merits.

How shall I begin? Time does not suffice to express even a minute portion of praise that is due. Well known is the splendor of this great dynasty, the House of Austria, from the day when its radiant majesty began to shine. How many Emperors reigned, one after the other, each one exalted, each one a gracious monarch who dealt beneficently with all. We Jews as well have always found refuge in their realms.[23] May God reward the goodness and graciousness of each one in the world of truth. Thus for the honor of the dead we should indulge in deep lamenting and grief.

---

21. On Joseph's apparently overwhelming grief for his mother, see Gooch, p. 116.

22. B. Sanh. 46b.

23. Landau does not speak here as a historian, overlooking blatant examples of persecution by earlier Habsburg monarchs (for example in 1421: see Grunwald, pp. 32–38) and in the mid-sixteenth century (Baron, *SRHJ* 14:150–51), as well as Maria Theresa's own expulsion (introduction, n. 6).

Also in the category of "honor for the dead" is the glory of her highness, the Empress, may she be remembered for good in her own right because of her outstanding personal qualities. Alas for the splendor that has been lost to this generation! How shall we begin to tell her praises? Her conduct as a reigning monarch? It is indeed amazing that one woman could rule over so many great states with such goodness and integrity, appointing worthy and qualified judges, promulgating edicts throughout her realms, all with wondrous wisdom. It is almost beyond belief that all this could have been done by this woman for forty-one years![24] In this regard, she was indeed *a woman of valor* (Prov. 31:10), the crowning glory of all the realms.

There was also her eloquence, the logical manner of her speech with nobles and officials of the various realms, always with intelligence, insight, and knowledge. *Her mouth was full of wisdom, her tongue with kindness* (Prov. 31:26). She did not speak in fury, rage, or anger. All was in good taste and refinement.[25] *Her mouth produced wisdom, her lips knew what is pleasing* (cf. Prov. 10:31-32). Maria Theresa, Maria Theresa! I apply to you the verse, *You are more beautiful than all men, your speech is endowed with grace, rightly has God given you an eternal blessing* (Ps. 45:3). Eternal, because even after your death, your good name is like fine oil (cf. Song 1:3), your name will not be forgotten, your good reputation will endure for all time.

And her heroic counsel in military matters. How strong she showed herself to be! Her resolute heroism is indeed well known. At the very beginning of her reign, several kings and rulers gathered against her with forces like the sands of the sea. But she *was not dismayed by their shouts, not cowed by their numbers* (Isa. 31:4). This fearlessness enabled her to drive them away from her lands with heroic power. Truly it is amazing that a woman should array herself in the adornments of a man, wearing the spirit of heroism![26] She should be praised for having confidence in the righteousness of her cause. Cowardice is a great flaw, especially for sovereigns. We find that the Torah warns against cowardice and fear in battle: *You are about to join battle with your enemy. Let not your courage falter, do not fear or panic* (Deut. 20:3). This is how the Queen then clothed herself in fortitude. Her star strode forth, her scepter rose and smashed the brow of all her enemies (cf. Num. 24:17).

As for her kindness and compassion over all her subjects, this is so well known it needs no demonstration. Never have we heard that she became full

---

24. See introduction, n. 8.

25. On Maria Theresa's eloquence, including her capacity to sway an audience in a Latin address, see Mahan, pp. 116, 121, 123–24.

26. See introduction, n. 9.

of vengeful spite to punish sinners with cruelty. To the contrary, she was quite ready to forgive and deal graciously with the guilty.

Her concern for all the states of her empire, especially in times of suffering? We saw with our own eyes during the year of dearth and famine [1771] the extent of her devotion. Indeed, she found no pleasure in eating or drinking herself until, with vigorous and decisive action, she brought food to these realms from afar. She did not rest throughout the period of famine, nor did she desist from sending wheat and foodstuffs time after time. Remember her, O God, and reward her in the world of reward, in fulfillment of the verse, *You offer your compassion to the hungry, and satisfy the famished creature, therefore shall your light shine in the darkness and your gloom shall be like noonday* (Isa. 58:10). Let also the name of our sovereign, Emperor Joseph II, be remembered for good in this context. He acted energetically at the time of dearth, opening the warehouses like the biblical Joseph. May God prolong his days and make his years pleasant for having saved many lives. Also for us, the Jews, there was an edict from the Queen to provide food in accordance with their needs.[27]

Her commitment to the welfare of the realms? Look at how she spread learning throughout the land; look how many schools she established.[28] Surely this deserves the praise, *Many women have done well, but you surpass them all* (Prov. 31:29).

As for the Queen's conduct of her own palace and court, the nobles and the attendants: with all her servants it is known that she never made their burden too harsh. She spoke to them with calm respect and never humiliated a single one, male or female.

In addition to the splendor of royalty, bestowed upon her from heaven, she had the adulation of all the inhabitants of her realms, near and far. They served her with devotion, not out of fear but out of love. In times of war we saw that all her subjects actually risked their lives for her. Those in the army, from the highest nobles to the lowly privates, stood their ground and fought her battle with all their might. Nobles and officials responsible for purveying supplies, whether for war or for other imperial needs, together with the rest of those associated with the affairs of state, both non-Jews and Jews— all of us eagerly awaited the opportunity of serving our Queen with all our strength, not because of any expectation of reward, but because of genuine love.[29] This is how we all acted during the siege of the year 1757. I myself

27. See introduction, nn. 16–18.
28. See introduction, n. 11.
29. See introduction, n. 10.

labored then with all my might; indeed, I placed my life in grave danger, as was well known then, all because of love.[30] This is nothing but the gift of God, who graciously implanted the love of the Queen in the hearts of all her subjects.

Her personal qualities? She was modest and withdrawn, abstaining from all physical desires and lusts. For many years, she did not participate in games or listen to music, either vocal or instrumental; she did not attend the comedy or the operas. Has such a thing ever been heard or seen: that a queen as powerful as she was, raised from birth in royal luxury, should totally spurn all temporal pleasures?[31] She was humble in a position of greatness. In her humility she would listen to the great and the small alike and receive their petition.

Her beneficent acts? She supported many charitable causes while denying herself, as is known from the regular allotment of food she provided for so many. Look at all the orphanages, called *Waisenhäuser,* look at all the poor houses, called *Armenhäuser,* look at the money she contributed to this! May God remember her for good.

Every aspect of her departure from this world (was blessed). She died with a good name, with a mind clear to the final hour, speaking sensibly before her death, giving instructions that testify to her consummate perfection.[32] For a woman with all these qualities, we may weep day and night for many days, indulging in deep mourning and lament, yet we will not fulfill even a small part of our obligation. Never has there been such a degree of royal splendor as we see in her death: the daughter of an emperor, the wife of an emperor, the mother of an emperor. Yet she took no pride in any of these. Not only her subjects but also this entire generation throughout the whole world cannot imagine what we have lost in the death of our noble Queen, our sovereign, Empress Maria Theresa, may her memory be for good.

Alas! I cry out bitterly, not knowing how to find solace, citing the words of the lamenter, *What can I take as witness or liken to you . . . what can I match with you to console you?* (Lam. 2:13). The commentators explain that when sorrow befalls a person, those who try to console often say, "A similar tragedy befell so and so, and he accepted consolation; so you should do the same."[33]

---

30. The details of the events to which Landau is alluding are no longer known, although he assumed they would be to members of his congregation. The German edition of the sermon omits the reference to the siege of 1757 and Landau's personal involvement. Cf. above, chap. 11, at n. 16.

31. See introduction, n. 12.

32. This description is confirmed by contemporary sources: see Beales, p. 481.

33. Cf. Rashi on this verse.

But if a tragedy befell someone that had never occurred to anyone else, the comforters would have no basis for consolation. So I say, if we were able to find a woman of comparable stature, even several generations ago, whose memory was preserved in the history books of bygone ages—a woman comparable in greatness, lineage, achievements, personal qualities, humility and abstinence—and had she died before reaching the age of seventy, and her contemporaries been consoled, then we too might have listened to words of consolation. But if we search and are unable to find her peer, I know not how we can be comforted.

Up to this point we have spoken in our eulogy about honor to the deceased. As for honor to the living: see how her immense praiseworthiness is obvious from her offspring. All of her children are blessed, monarchs have issued from her loins (cf. Gen. 35:11). There is a maxim that states, "If one cannot see the tree, let him look at its fruits."[34] One who has never seen a particular field but sees only its produce and praises the fruits and vegetables knows that the tree must be flourishing and the field blessed by God. Happy is the one who bore and raised such children, monarchs of various peoples, spread through states far and near, primed for sovereignty or for high positions in the governments of great nations. Supreme over them all is *the fruitful vine, Joseph* (Gen. 49:22), our noble monarch, consummate in every character trait, the Emperor, may his majestic splendor be exalted. Now all these, her offspring, suffer the sorrow and distress of mourning for the Queen. We must share in their sorrow, to feel pain for the pearl without price that has been lost to us. Alas for those who are lost but not forgotten.[35]

And so, every consideration requires us to deepen our mourning. There is no comforter at hand except for the Lord of Hosts, who brings healing even before the affliction.[36] God exalted the Emperor during his mother's lifetime, and we have recognized his enormous merit, seen that he is a great and noble king. This is the source of our consolation: that there has come forth a shoot from the stump of Queen Maria Theresa, a twig has sprouted from her stock (cf. Isa. 11:1). From her has blossomed a radiant flower, producing glorious fruit. He will be for us and for all the states of his empire a source of consolation, for nothing of all the fine qualities found in his gracious mother, of blessed memory, are lacking in him. God has bestowed

---

34. This is presented as a direct quote; the German edition of the sermon paraphrases the idea and attributes it to "our sages." I have not found it in rabbinic literature; cf. Davidson, *Meshalim*, p. 4.

35. B. Sanh 111a.

36. Cf. B. Meg 13b.

upon him *the spirit of wisdom and insight, the spirit of counsel and valor* (Isa. 11:2). He shall *judge the poor with equity and decide with justice for the lowly of the land* (Isa. 11:4).[37] He will be a source of refuge for every one of his realms, the great eagle under whose wings all will find shelter and live securely. For he is a valiant king, a man who wages war with both strength and wisdom so as to prevail against his enemies, exulting in the shouts of victory. He will succeed in every enterprise to which he turns.

And now, my brothers and friends, Jews and indeed everyone who hears these words, whether Jews or non-Jews: is this not the fruit of all the good that has come to us, to repay our sovereign, the gracious Queen Maria Theresa, for all the good things she did throughout her life by serving wholeheartedly her son, our noble sovereign the Emperor, with all our heart and with all our soul (cf. Deut. 6:5), with abundant love as we served his mother the queen, the Empress? It is incumbent upon us to pray to the King of Kings, whose throne is in the heavens above and who bestows sovereignty to kings, that He will give strength to our king the Emperor, and exalt his reign on high.

May God make his throne greater than that of any other emperor. May He set his hand upon the sea, his right hand upon the rivers (cf. Ps. 89:26). O God, let the king rejoice in Your strength and exult in Your victory (cf. Ps. 21:2). Give him what his heart desires, do not deny him the request of his lips (cf. Ps. 21:3). Proffer him blessing of good things, set upon his head a crown of fine gold (cf. Ps. 21:4). Increase his glory, endow him with splendor and majesty; make him blessed forever, gladden him with joy (cf. Ps. 21:6-7). Let him accept with good cheer comfort for the loss of his mother, and let him sit upon his throne in happiness. May power leap before him (Job 41:14), may the king rejoice in God. Add days to the days of our king (cf. Ps. 61:7), the noble Emperor, long years to his life, O God, that he may judge Your people righteously. Make us worthy of his compassion that he may favor us, watch over us in mercy, and act toward us with kindness. And we shall bless our gracious sovereign, the Emperor, as all of us say together (and the entire congregation responded and said), "Long live our sovereign, Emperor Joseph the Second! Amen."

This eulogy was delivered by the aforementioned rabbi in the aforementioned synagogue with the permission of the authorities.

---

37. Note the blatantly messianic language in this passage.

דרוש הספד

מה שדרש ה״ה אדמו״ר[1] תפארת ישראל ראש גולת אריאל הרב המאור הגדול המפורסם רבו של כל בני הגולה נ״י ע״ה פ״ה[2] כבוד מוהר״ר[3] יחזקאל סג״ל לאנדי נר״ו[4] אב בית דין ור״מ[5] דקהילתנו יע״א[6]

ביום א׳ י״ב כסליו תקמ״א לפ״ק[7] פה פראג בבה״כ[8] מייזל באסיפה גדולה בבה״כ ההיא ובראשם הפרימוס הראש והקצין ר׳ ישראל פרענקלש עם חביריו רו״ט יצ״ו[9] ונאספו שמה הב״ד הגדול ב״ד מו״ש[10] וכל הדיינים וכל שאר התמניו׳ שבעיר על פני הקהילה וכל חשובי העיר והיו שם אתנו בבה״כ ההיא גם שרים רבים ונכבדים וגם מאנשי הצבא חשובים ונכבדי׳ ודרוש זה כולל שתים, א׳ דברי׳ המשברי׳ הלב[11] לעורר המספד והבכי על מיתת אדונתינו החסודה האדירה המלכה הקיסרית **מאריא טרעזיא** יזכר זכרונה לטובה, ב׳ שבח והודיה על הטובה הגדולה שעשה הקב״ה[12] עם המלכה הקיסרית שזכתה עוד בחייי׳ לראות בנה הגדול המושלם בכל השלימות הוא אדונינו האדיר החסיד המיוחס גבור וחכם הקיסר **יאזעפוס השני** ירום הודו יושב על כסא הקיסרות ועתה הוא ממלא מקום אמו ויונחו על ראשו כל הכתרים וכל החשיבו׳ שהי׳ לאמו הקיסרת. וגם כולל ברכות לראש אדונינו הקיסר האדיר יר״ה[13] ותפלה עבורו שירום הודו ותתנשא מלכותו וממשלתו ונכלל בדרוש הזה אפס קצה משבח הבית הגדול בית איסטרייך מיום אשר צמח קרן הודם עד היום הזה:

1. הנשר הגדול אדוננו מורנו ורבנו.
2. נר ישראל עמוד הימיני פטיש החזק (ע״פ ברכות כח ב).
3. מורנו הרב רבי.
4. נטריה רחמנא וברכיה (הרחמן ישמרהו ויברכהו).
5. וריש מתיבתא.
6. יגן עליה אלהים.
7. לפרט קטן.
8. בבית הכנסת.
9. ראשים וטובים ישמרם צורנו ויחיים.
10. הבית דין הגדול בית דין מורים וטובים.
11. ע״פ טור ושלחן ערוך יורה דעה שמ״ד.
12. הקדוש ברוך הוא.
13. ירום הודו.

(1b) כתיב (יחזקאל כא יא) ואתה בן אדם האנח בשברון מתנים ובמרירות תאנח לעיניהם והיה כי יאמרו אליך על מה אתה נאנח ואמרת אל שמועה כי באה ונמס כל לב ורפו כל ידים וכהת׳ כל רוח וכל ברכים תלכנה מים הנה באה ונהיתה נאם ד׳י.[14] הנה זה היום יו׳ השמיני אשר באה השמועה הרעה כי נפלה עטרת ראשנו.[15] וכפי החיוב המוטל עלי הי׳ ראוי תכף לעשות מספד רב וכמו״ש[16] (עמוס ה ט״ז) בכל רחבות מספד ובכל חוצות יאמרו הו הו וקראו אכר אל אבל ומספד אל יודעי נהי. ולקיים כאבל אם קודר שחותי[17] כי נפלה אמה של מלכות[18] היא אדונתינו החסודה הענוה והצדקנית המלכה הקיסרית **מאָרי׳ טרעזיא** תנוח נפשה בג׳ע[19] והיא אמא של מלכות ומלכים מחלצי׳ יצאו.[20] אמנם ח״ו[21] לא מפני עצלות איחרתי עד כה אבל כמה טעמים יש בדבר. הא׳ כי מרוב חרדה ויגון שהי׳ לי פתאום בבוא השמועה לא הי׳ בי כח לדבר וגם לא ידעתי מה לדבר ונתקיים בי כמו שהי׳ לחבירי איוב שנאמר (איוב ב׳ י״ג) וישבו אתו לארץ ז׳ ימים וז׳ לילות ואין דובר אליו דבר כי ראו כי גדול הכאב מאוד. כן אני מרוב גודל הכאב ויגון לא יכולתי לישב דעתי מה לדבר כל ז׳ ימים עד היום הא חדא.[22]

השנית כי אין לך דבר שיבלבל דעת רופא בבואו אצל החולה יותר ממה שיבלבל אותו בהמצאו שני דברים נגדיים דקשה להאי מעלי להאי[23] כי לא יוכל לתת עצות בנפשו מה לעשו׳ שלא יהי׳ דבר המתנגד. כן אנחנו היו׳ הזה. והנה קהלת בחשבו כ״ח עיתים אמר (קהלת ג׳ א׳) לכל זמן ועת לכל חפץ תחת השמים עת ללדת ועת למות ועת לבכות ועת לשחוק עת ספוד ועת רקוד וגומ׳.[24] הנה חישב שם כ״ח עיתים י״ד לטובה וי״ד

14. יח׳ כא יא–יג.

15. ע״פ איכה ה טז.

16. וכמו שכתוב.

17. תה׳ לה יד.

18. עי׳ הערה 8 לתרגום.

19. בגן עדן.

20. ע״פ בר׳ לה יא.

21. חס ושלום.

22. הרי זה הסיבה הראשונה.

23. זה שמזיק לדבר אחד מחזק את הדבר השני (ע״פ פסחים מב ב).

24. קהלת ג א–ב, ד.

לרעה ובכלם אמר עם שימש למ"ד בתחלה ללדת למות לטעת לעקור
ובספוד ורקוד אמר בלא למ"ד המשמשת ואמר עת ספוד ועת רקוד והנ'
יי"ל[25] בזה כי עם שימש הלמד הוא על הפועל שהפועל יפעול לעורר לב
לעשות דבר זה או שעוש' דבר זה כמו ללדת שהאשה יולדת או שהמילדת
היא מילדת האשה. וכן לבכות שמצוה לבכות[26] וכן לשחוק ובזה נכון
ג"כ דעת מלחמה עת שלום[27] אמר ג"כ בלא למד המשמשת משום דלא
משכחת[28] שיהיה מצוה ללחום ואם אחד דעשה שלא כהוגן וראוי ללחום
עמו אבל לא שייך מלחמה כ"א[29] שני הצדדי' נלחמו זה נגד זה וממ"נ[30] א'
עושה שלא כהוגן אבל ספוד ורקוד הוא בלי פועל כאלו העת ספוד וכן
להיפך רקוד והכונה כי אם אין הכל מרגישי' במיתת אדם כמה העדר יש
במיתתו צריך אדם לעמוד ברבים ולהודיע להם מעלת הנעדר ומה
ההפסד יש בהעדרו. אבל בהעדר אדם רב ויקר הערך יחיד בדור אשר
הכל הכירו גדלו ותפארתו ובהוד זיו יקרו היה (2a) מאיר לכל, הנה
בהעדרו הכל מרגישי' מעצמם. והוא כמשל אם פתאום יבא השמש[31]
בצהרי' הלא החושך יכסה ארץ[32] והכל יכירו גודל חסרון אור השמש כן
אנחנו היום הזה עת ספוד כל א' מעצמו ואין צריך שאדם יעמוד לדרוש
ולעורר כי הלא אור המלכה הקיסרית **מאריא טרעזיא** היה מאיר ומבריק
ועוצם מדותי' הטובי' יושר לבבה ורוב חסדה היה מפורסם בכל העולם
ועתה באה שמשה ונאסף נגהה הלא ע"ז[33] ידוו כל הדוים וכל אחד יאמר
מי יתן ראשי מים ועיני מקור דמעה ואבכה יומם ולילה[34] כי מתה אם
המדינת[35] המלכה שהיתה כאם לכל המדינות ולכן עת ספוד.

אבל נגד זה יש ג"כ עת רקוד כי הלא נתקיים בנו וזרח השמש ובא

25. והנה יש לומר.
26. השוה מועד קטן כז ב, רבינו בחיי על בר' כג ב, רלב"ג, פרשת חיי שרה, התועלת הא'.
27. נכון גם כן בפסוק „עת מלחמה ועת שלום".
28. שלא נמצא.
29. כי אם.
30. וממה נפשך, מכל מקום.
31. אם שקעה השמש (ע"פ בר' כח יא).
32. ע"פ יש' ס ב.
33. על זה.
34. יר' ח כג.
35. כך בדפוס.

השמש[36] ודרשו רבותינו עד שלא שקעה שמשו של צדיק זה זרח שמשו של צדיק אחר ועד שלא שקעה שמשו של ד"ה[37] זרחה של שלמה המלך בנו. כן עתה עד שלא שקעה שמשו של אדונתנו האדיר' החסודה המלכ' הקיסרית זרח' שמשו של בנה הגדול האדיר החכם החסיד יקר מפז ומכל אבני סגולה הקיסר **יאזעף** ירום הודו ותתנשא מלכותו אשר בו נתקיים (תהילים פ"ט ל"ז) כסאו כשמש נגדי כמו שהשמש נראה זיו בכל העולם והכל יאותו לאורו[38] כן יצא שמו של הקיסר בכל העולם ונודע שבחו בכל המדינות הקרובים והרחוקי' ואשרינו מה טוב חלקינו[39] שזכינו למלך יקר הערך ואדיר כזה מלך ביפיו תחזינה עינינו[40] מלך במשפט יעמיד ארץ[41] הן לצדק ימלוך מלך:[42] והנה באור פני מלך חיים[43] לכל בני המדינות שלו והוא רקוד מרוב שמחה באופן שכעת נקבצו יחד שני עתות הפכיים ומתנגד' זה לזה עת ספוד על גודל צער ויגון ואבל ובכי על מיתת המלכה הקיסרית ועת חדוה וש`ון ושמחה על ישיבת אדונינו החסיד הקיסר על כסא מלכותה. ולכן לא ידעתי לתת עצות בנפשי[44] איך ומה להתנהג ולכן לא אמר שלמה עת לספוד ועת לרקוד כי הפועל אינו יכול לפעול שני הפכיים בפועל יחד אבל העת מזדמן כאחד. ומה שהביאני כעת לקרוא למספד נגיד אחר כך.

השלישי' אשר הביאני לשתוק ע"ע[45] כי אמרתי בלבי אין זה כבודה של אדונתינו החסודה הקיסרית לדבר עלי' מילי דהספידה כי הלא לא שייך להספיד את החי כי אם את המת ואני אומר הלא אדונתינו החסודה המלכה לא נאמר בה מיתה ואקדים דברי רבותינו (במס' תענית פ"א דף ה ע"ב). אר"י[46] יעקב אבינו לא מת א"ל וכי בכדי ספדי ספדניא וחנטו

---

36. קהלת א ה.

37. דוד המלך. השוה בראשית רבה נח,ב.

38. ע"פ ברכות נא ב.

39. ע"פ נוסח ברכות השחר.

40. ע"פ יש' לג יז.

41. ע"פ משלי כט ד.

42. ע"פ יש' לב א.

43. משלי טז טו.

44. ע"פ תה' יג ג.

45. עד עכשו.

46. אמר רבי יוחנן.

חנטייא וקברו קברייא[47] א"ל מקרא אני דורש ואתה אל תירא עבדי יעקב ואל תחת ישראל כי הנני מושיעך מרחוק ואת זרעך וגומ'[48] מקיש הוא לזרעו מה זרעו בחיים אף הוא בחיים. והנה כל מפרשי' נלאו לעמוד על שורש כוונת הגמ'[49] ומה בכך שדורש זה מן המקרא ואכתי מה תשובה יש בזה להקושי' (2b) וכי בכדי ספדו ספדניא וחנטו וקברו. ולי נראה הכוונה בזה ע"פ מה שאמרו (במס' ב"ב פ"ח[50] דף קי"ו ע"א) דרש ר' פנחס בן חמא מה דכתיב והדד שמע במצרים כי שכב דוד עם אבותיו וכי מת יואב שר הצבא (מלכי' א' י"א).[51] מפני מה בדוד נאמר בו שכיבה וביואב נאמרה בו מיתה? דוד שהניח בן כמותו נאמרה בו שכיבה יואב שלא הניח בן כמותו נאמרה בו מיתה. הרי שהמניח בן כמותו לא נאמרה בו מיתה.

ואני אמרתי ליתן טעם לדבר ולהסביר הענין ע"פ השכל והוא כי ידוע שהאדם בחייו הוא מחובר מחומר וצורה והוא הגוף עם הנשמה הגוף הוא החומר והנשמה הוא הצורה ועקר המיתה הוא מצד החומר אבל הנשמה היא שבה לאלקי' אשר נתנה[52] וגם בחיי האדם עקר החיים מיוחס לצורה. וצריך להבין איך שייך מיתה בנשמה והלא גם אחר מיתה היא שבה אל מקורה ושם עקר החיים. ואמנם טעם ביאת הנשמה לעוה"ז[53] ולהדבק בחומר הזה הוא כדי שתזכה לקנות שלימות וכל מה שהאדם מוסיף שלימות עולה הנשמה ממדרגה למדרגה יותר גבוה. ובזה יש להבין דברי רבותינו בעלי התלמוד שאמרו שהצדיק הוא עדיף מהמלאך[54] ובאמת כל חכמי האומות רחקו סברה זו בתכלית הזרות. הנה לפי המושכל ראשון הוא דבר תמוה[55] אבל אחר הייישוב דבר גדול דברו כי המלאך הוא צור' לבד בלי חומר ואין למלאך מבוא לחטוא בשום דבר כי כל חטא ועוון ופשע הוא מצד החומר שנוטה אחר שרשו אבל המלאך שהוא צורה אין

---

47. וכי לשוא הספידו הספדנים וחנטו החונטים וקברו הקברנים?

48. "...מארץ שבים" יר' ל י.

49. הגמרא.

50. במסכת בבא בתרא פרק ח.

51. מ"א יא כא.

52. ע"פ קהלת יב ז.

53. לעולם הזה.

54. סנהדרין צג א.

55. עי' הערה 14 לתרגום.

לו יצר הרע כלל[56] ותמיד עומד במדרגה אחת כפי תחילת בריאתו לא
ירד ולא יעלה אבל הצדיק שעובד את ד' ומתגבר על החומר הוא עולה
ממדרגה למדרגה ובדבר זה הוא עדיף מהמלאך ונקרא הצדיק מהלך
והמלאך נקרא עומד כי הצדיק מהלך ממדרגה למדרגה וזה הוא החיים
שלו כי לכך נברא וכל זה כל ימי חייו אבל במיתתו שנפרדה הצורה שהיא
הנשמה מהחומר שהוא הגוף והגוף נקבר בקבר והרוח תשוב אל אלקי'
ואז גם הנשמה אין לה יצר הרע ושוב אינה יכולה לעלות למדרגה יותר
גבוה מהמדרגה שכבר היתה בעת הפרדה מן החומר ולכן בדבר זה
אנו אומרים מיתה גם אצל הצורה שמתה ממדרגת העלי' לעלות עוד
יותר. והנה האב מזכה את בנו וצדקת תמי' תייׁשר דרכו[57] של בנו ותמיד
משגיחי' האב והאם על בנם מיום שהתחיל להגיע להיות בו דעת להדריכו
בדרך טוב וללמדו חוקים ומשפטים[58] צדיקים. ונמצא כל מעשה הטוב של
הבן הזה הכל הולך אחר השורש והעקר שהדריכוהו אביו ואמו. וכל הטוב
אשר יעשה הבן כל הימים הוא ג״כ נחשב זכות לאביו ואמו כאלו המה
עושים ונמצא גם אחר מותם המה עולים ממעלה למעלה יותר גבוה.

ובזה אמרתי פרוש הפסוקי' (זכרי' ג') ויראני את יהושע הכהן הגדול
עומד לפני (3a) מלאך ד'. ויהושע היה לבוש בגדים צואים ועומד לפני
המלאך ויען ויאמר אל העומדים לפניו לאמר הסירו הבגדים הצואים
מעליו ויאמר אליו ראה העברתי מעליך עונך והלבש אותך מחלצות
ויאמר ישימו צניף טהור על ראשו וגו' ויעד מלאך ד' ביהושע לאמר כה
אמר ד' צבאו' אם בדרכי תלך ואם את משמרתי תשמור וגם אתה תדין
את ביתי וגם תשמור את חצרי ונתתי לך מהלכי' בין העומדי' האל'.[59]
ויונתן תרגם בגדי הצואי' שהיו בניו נשואי' לנשי' הפסולת לכהונה ומה
שכתוב אח״כ והלבש אותך מחלצות[60] היינו שיגרשו הפסולת ויקחו נשים
כשרות. הנה בשר הקב״ה להנביא במראה הנבואה שיהושע יוכיח את
בניו ויפעול שישובו בתשובה ויגרשו הפסולת ויקחו כשרות ובודאי רומז

---

56. שבת פט א, בראשית רבה מח,יא.

57. ע״פ משלי יא ה.

58. ע״פ דב' ד ה.

59. זכ' ג א–ז.

60. זכ' ג ד.

לו שע״י פעולת של יהושע שהוא יוכיח את בניו שיעשו כן ולכן נאמר
והלבש אותך מחלצות ואם בניו מצד עצמם יעשו תשובה אין לו בגדי
מחלצות שהוא רומז לזכות כמו שתרגם יונתן על פסוק זה. ובזה הפירוש
ניחא סוף המקרא ונתת לך מהלכי׳ בין העומדי׳ האלה[61] כי הצדיק נקרא
מהלך ע״ש שהולך תמיד ממעלה למעלה כנזכר למעלה והמלאך נקרא
עומד ובמיתת הצדיק ורוחו עולה למעלה במקום המלאכים אז גם הנשמה
עומדת בין העומדים אבל אם יש לו בנים שהדריך אותם להיות צדיקי׳
אז גם אח״כ הוא מהלך גם למעלה. וכל זמן שלא פעל יהושע שיעשו בניו
תשובה אף שהוא הי׳ צדיק גמור וכהן לאל עליון[62] וכל ימי חייו היה מהלך
ממעלה למעל׳ אבל במותו כבר היה פוסק מלהלך והיה עומד אבל עתה
שהוא פעל שישובו בניו בתשובה בישרו ונתתי לך מהלכי׳ אפי׳ בשעה
שתהיה בין העומדים האלה שהם המלאכים דהיינו אחר מיתה ג״כ אתן
לך מהלכי׳.

וא״כ יפה דרש ר״פ במס׳ ב״ב[63] דוד שהניח בן במותו לא נאמרה בו
מיתה לפי שגם אחר מותו לא שייך בו מיתה רק בחומרו שהוא הגוף
הנקבר בארץ אבל מצד צורתו שהיא הנשמה לא נאמר׳ בו מיתה לפי
שהוא צוה את שלמה בנו קודם מותו ללכת בדרכי ה׳ כמ״ש (מלכי׳ א׳ ב׳)
ויקרבו ימי דוד למות ויצו את שלמה בנו לאמר אנכי הולך בדרך כל הארץ
וחזקת והיית לאיש ושמרת את משמרת ה׳ אלקיך ללכת בדרכיו לשמור
חקתיו מצותיו ומשפטיו ועדותיו וגומ׳[64] וא״כ כל מה שהוסיף שלמה
שלימות נחשב לדוד אביו לזכות וא״כ גם אחר מותו עלה ממעלה למעלה
לכן לא נאמרה בו מיתה. ועתה נשוב לדברי ר״י[65] במס׳ תענית שאמר יעקב
אבינו לא מת והשיב ר״נ[66] וכי בכדי ספדו וחנטו וקברו והשיב לו ר״י מקרא
אני דורש וכו׳ מקיש הוא לזרעו מה זרעו בחיים אף הוא בחיים. והנה
יעקב הניח בן כמותו כי אם כל י״ב שבטים כולם שווים לטובה ואמנם
זרעו הכרוך (3b) אחריו ביותר והוא בעצמו יגע בו ללמדו כל מה שקיבל

61. זכ׳ ג ז.

62. ע״פ בר׳ יד יח.

63. רבי פנחס במסכת בבא בתרא (קטו א).

64. מ״א ב א–ג.

65. רבי יוחנן.

66. רבי נחמן.

מרבותיו ולמסור לו כל חכמתו הוא בנו האהוב לו ביותר בן פורת יוסף[67]
וכמו שדרשו רבותינו ז״ל בפסוק אלה תולדות יעקב יוסף ובפסוק כי בן
זקונים הוא לו.[68] וא״כ כל זמן שיוסף חי והכוונה באומרו חי היינו העלי׳
ממדרגה למדרגה וכל זה הי׳ בסבת יעקב שהוא הדריכו בדרך הטוב
ההוא גם יעקב אחר מותו עולה למעלה ונקרא חי וזה שהשיב ר״י מקרא
אני דורש והכוונה כי בודאי חונטו חנטי׳ וספדו ספדי׳ וקברו קברי׳ אבל
מה זרעו בחיים ועל ידי זה הוא בחיים.

ומעתה נחזי אנן אדונתינו החסודה הקיסרית **מארי׳ טרעזי׳** על הטוב
יזכר זכרונה שהיא זכתה להניח בן כזה הוא אדונינו האדיר השלם
במעלות ומדות הקיסר **יאזעף** ירום הודו והיא אמו שהדריכתו מילדותו
בכל מדות טובות ומעלות א״כ לא שייך בה מיתה כי אף שנפרדה מאתנו
בני מדינותי׳ אעפ״כ[69] לא פנה זיוה והודה מאתנו כי הוא בנה הגדול
הקיסר המהולל הזה הוא זיוה והוא הודה ועליו ראוי לומר (משלי ט״ז)
באור פני מלך חיים[70] כי באור פניו הוא חיים חיים לאמו החסודה אחר מותה.
את כל אלה נתתי אל לבי והיו מחשבותי וסעיפי נלחמים בקרבי אם
להספיד או לשתוק:

ואמנם אשר העירני להכריע לצד זה להספיד בקרב קהל ועדה הוא
הפסוק אשר התחלתי בו והנה נדקדק בו איזה דקדוקי׳. הנה הפסוק
אומר ואתה בן אדם האנח בשברון מתני׳ ובמרירות תאנח לעיניהם והי׳
כי יאמרו אליך על מה אתה נאנח ואמרת אל שמועה כי באה ונמס כל
לב ורפו כל ידים וכהתה כל רוח וכל ברכים תלכנה מים הנה באה
ונהייתה נאם ה׳.[71] מקרא זה אומר דרשוני באמרו והי׳ כי יאמרו אליך על
מה אתה נאנח משמעות הדבר שאם היה היה אחר נאנח לא היו שואלים
ודוקא אותו שואלים על מה אתה נאנח וזה מדוקדק מכפל המלות אליך
ואתה והי׳ די באמרו והי׳ כי יאמרו על מה אתה נאנח ומדכתיב כי יאמרו
אליך משמע דוקא אליך יאמרו כן והדבר צריך טעם. ועוד בשלמא אם

---

67. בר׳ מט כב.

68. בר׳ לז ב וג, ועי׳ בראשית רבה פד ח.

69. אף על פי כן.

70. משלי טז טו.

71. יח׳ כא יא–יג.

הי' השמועה על צרה נסתרת הי' צריך הנביא להיות נאנח כדי שיתנו לב
לשאול ויודיע להם גודל הצרה אבל כיון שהוא צרה גלוי' ונראית ונרגשת
לעיני הכל כמ"ש[72] אל שמועה כי באה ונמס כל לב ורפו כל ידים וגומ'
א"כ הרי הכל יכירו מעצמם ומה צורך שיאנח לעיניהם ואם הוא רוצה
להתאבל על הצרה יתאבל לעצמו ואבל יחידי יעשה לו.[73] ועוד איך שייך
כלל שאלה על מה אתה נאנח והרי הצרה גלוי' ומפורסמת שהרי נמס כל
לב וגומ' וראיתי שבעל הטעמים הרגיש בזה ולכן נתן הטעם במלת באה
מלרע שפירושו (4a) הוה לא לשון עבר שכבר באה. ובזה כבר נתיישב
המקרא וגם על אמרו על מה אתה נאנח כבר דרשתי פעם אחר ליישב
המקרא לפי ענינו ואמנם אנן כעת נפרש הפסוקי' עלינו.

ואני הגבר אשר עלי נאמר ששמי יחזקאל בן אדם האנח וכו' והנה
בודאי אתם זוכרי' שזה שש עשרה שנה כבר עבר בשבת הגדול העבר
שהוא שנת תקכד"ל ואז נתן ה' עוז למלכנו הקיסר **יאזעף** יר"ה והרים
קרנו בעוד אביו הקיסר החסיד **פראנצישקוס** יזכר לטובה הי' חי ונכתר
אדונינו הקיסר **יאזעף** בפפ"ד[74] בכתר מלוכה ונעשה רעמשיר קעניג[75] וזה
הי' בר"ח ניסן תקכ"דל ותכף אחר זה בשבת הגדול דרשתי ברבים
ופרסמתי שבחו שבח מגדול עוז של אדונינו הקיסר שהי' אז מלך כי
מילדותו ניכר שבחו ונתתי שבח והודאה למקום שהעמיד מלך חשוב
וטוב ושלם בכל מדות כזה ואמרתי סימנא מילתא[76] היא שמן השמים
הכירוהו שהוא מלך כשר וישר ע"פי מה שאמרו במס' ר"ה שהמלכים
הכשרים והטובי' מונין להם מניסן[77] כמו מלך כורש שהנביא אמר עליו
(ישעי' מ"ה) כה אמר ה' למשיחו לכורש אשר החזקתי בימינו,[78] וא"כ
שהנביא קראו משיח ה' ודאי שכשר הי' ומנו לו מלכותו מניסן כמו
שהוכיחו שם במס' ר"ה.[79] וכיון שהי' מן השמים שהקיסר הזה נמשח

72. כמו שכתוב.
73. ע"פ יר' ו כו.
74. בפרנקפורט דמיין.
75. מלך הרומיים, ועי' הערות 16 ו171 לתרגום.
76. סימן לדבר, ע"פ הוריות יב א.
77. ראש השנה ב ב.
78. יש' מה א.
79. ראש השנה ג א.

והושם כתר מלכותו בראשו[80] אז בחדש ניסן ודאי הוא אות מן השמים שכל רואיו יכירו כי הוא מן השמים ניכר למלך כשר וישר וה' יחזיק בימינו וירם קרנו ופרסמתי אז ברבים מקצת שבחיו הטובי' כי אי אפשר לסיימנהו לכולהו שבחא דמרן.[81]

והנה עתה המו מעי עלי[82] על מיתת המלכה הקיסרית ואני נאנח בשברון מתני' ובמרירות[83] לעיני כל העדה. והי' כי יאמרו אליך על מה אתה נאנח אתה דייקא שאלי יאמרו על מה אני נאנח אם בשביל מיתת המלכה הלא אתה בעצמך פרסמת שבחו של אדונינו הקיסר שהוא קם עתה תחת אמו וא"כ הרי כאלו המלכה קיימת. והתשובה ע"ז ואמרת אליה' אל שמועה כי באה ונמס כל לב:[84] הנה האדם הוא עולם קטן והאיברים שבו הם כמו האישים שבעולם והלב נמשל למלך על כל האיברים כי הוא המנהיג המושל בכל אברי הגוף וכן מבואר בכוזרי במאמר רביעי סימ' כ"ה וז"ל[85] ולא יזכר הלב מפני שהוא המלך. והנה שמועה שמענו שאדונינו הקיסר יר"ה בעצמו נתעורר מאד באבל ובכי על מיתת אמו הקיסרית ואם הוא בעצמו שמכיר עצמו ויודע עוצם גבורתו וכל מעשה תקפו ושלימתו וחכמתו שהוא ממלא מקום אבותיו ומקום אמו בכל המעלות ועם כל זה גברה אהבת האם וכבודה הרב והעצום עד שהוא מרבה בהספד ובאבל, אנו מה נעשה? והלא ראוי לנו להתאבל על האם הנכבדת שהיית' אם המדיניות ומלכה משך א"ס[86] שנים? (4b) ואחרי אשר נמס כל לב שהוא רומז להמלך[87] הוא הקיסר האדיר נתעורר ונמס למיתת המלכה ראוי שיהי' כל האברי' נמשכי' אחר אבר הראש וכל בני המדיניות ירבו באבל ומספד להיות רפו כל ידי' וכהתה כל רוח וכל ברכים תלכנה מים.[88] ולכן בשמעי גודל המספד שבוינא מגדול ועד קטן

---

80. ע"פ אסתר ו ח.

81. ע"פ ברכות לג ב.

82. ע"פ יר' לא יט.

83. יח' כא יא.

84. יח' כא יב.

85. וזה לשונו.

86. אין סוף (כמובן, דרך גוזמא).

87. זאת אומרת, ה„לב" (בפסוק יח' כא יב) רומז למלך יוסף (ע"פ המאמר שבכוזרי).

88. יח' כא יב.

וההתחלה על הכל הוא הקיסר בעצמו נתעוררתי לעמוד בקהל ועדה לדבר
מילי להספידא אמנם אחזני חיל ורעדה מי אנכי ברי׳ קלה אשא על שפתי
את אדונתינו הקיסרית החסוד׳ עד שבחסדי השררה אשר הרשני לדבר
מילין ולהזכיר שבח הקיסרית החסוד׳. והנה אחיי ורעיי רבותינו פלפלו
אם הספידא יקרא דחיי׳ או יקרא דשכבי׳[90] והנה יקרא דשכבי כולל שתים
יקר תפארת המת הנספד אשר אותו מספידין וגם נכלל בכלל יקרא דשכבי
יקר תפארת אבותיו של המת מדורי דורות כל א׳ לפי גודלו:

והנה במה שנתחיל לא יספיק הזמן להגיד אפס קצת השבח. הלא נודע
תפארת עטרת הבית הגדול הזה בית אייסטרייך מיום אשר צמח קרן הוד
הבית הזה כמה קיסרי׳ זה אחר זה בתכלית הרוממות וכלם מלכי חסד היו
הרבו להטיב עם הכל וגם אנחנו היהודי׳ תמיד אנחנו חוסים בצל
מדינותי׳[91] השם יתברך ישלם בעלמא דקשוט[92] לכל א׳ את טובו וחסדו
וא״כ ליקרא דשכבי ראוי לנו להרבות הבכי וההספד מאד. ואם משום יקרא
דשכבי יקר תפארת הוד המלכה הקיסרית זכרונה לטובה בעצמה לגודל
מעלותיה ומדותי׳ הטובים הוי ואבוי על האי שופרא דאתעלים מההוא
דרא[93] ובמה נתחיל בשבחה? אם מצד הנהגותי׳ בעסק המלוכה הלא הוא
דבר נפלא שאשה אחת תנהוג כמה מדינות גדולות כאלו בהנהגה טובה
ובמישור ולהעמיד שופטי׳ הראוים וטובי׳ ולתקן כמה תקנות במדינותי׳
הכל בחכמה הנפלאה לא יאומן כי יסופר[94] שיהי׳ כ״ז[95] נעשה ע״י אשה זה
אחד וארבעים שנה על זאת ראוי לומר אשת חיל עטרת תפארת[96] כל
המדינות:

ואם בנועם מליצותי׳ וסידור דברי׳ עם שרי וסגני מדינותי׳ הכל בהשכל
ומועצת ודעת פי׳ פתחה בחכמה וחסד על לשונה[97] לא בקול רעם ובחרי אף

89. ע״פ דה״ב לד ל.
90. אם ההספד הוא לכבוד קרובי הנפטר החיים או לכבוד הנפטר (סנהדרין מו ב).
91. עי׳ הערה 23 לתרגום.
92. בעולם האמת, דהיינו בעולם הבא.
93. על תפארת זאת שנעלמה מהדור הזה. השוה ר״ן על נדרים נ ב.
94. ע״פ חב׳ א ה.
95. כל זה.
96. ע״פ משלי יב ז, טז לא, לא י, ושים לב לשמוש בפסוקים מפרשת„אשת חיל" (משלי לא י–לא) בקטעים הבאים.
97. משלי לא כו.

וזעם. רק הכל בדברי טעם ובאמרי נועם פי' ינוב חכמה ושפתותי' ידעו רצון.
(משלי י"ד)[98] **מארי' טרעזיא מארי' טרעזי'** אומר אני שעליך ראוי לומר
(תהלים מ"ה ג') יפיפית מבני אדם הוצק חן בשפתותיך ע"כ ברכך אלקי'
לעולם. לעולם דייקא שגם אחר מותך שמך הטוב שמן תורק[99] שמך לא
ישכח זכרך הטוב יזכר לדור אחרון. ואם בעצה וגבורה למלחמה[100] חגרה
בעוז מתני' ותאמץ זרועותיה[101] הלא נודע מעשה תקפה וגבורתה ופרשת
גדולתה תכף בתחלת מלכותה נקבצו יחד (5a) עלי' כמה מלכי' ושלטוני' עד
חיל כחול הים והיא מקולם לא תחת וממהונם לא פחדה[102] והיא אשר עלתה
לה שגירשה אותם מארצות הללו בכח וגבורה ובאמת אשה תתלבש בעדי
איש ללבוש רוח גבורה הוא דבר נפלא וע"ז ראוי לשבחה שבטח לבה
ביושרה ובצדקה והמורך הוא חסרון גדול וביחוד למלכי' ומצינו שהתורה
הזהירה על המורך ועל הפחד במלחמה (דברים כ' ג') אתם קרבים היום
למלחמה על אויביכם אל ירך לבבכם אל תראו וגומ'. ולכן לבשה המלכה
אז רוח גבורה דרך כוכבה וקם שבטה וקרקרה כל בני שונאי'.[103]

ואם מפאת חסד ורחמים על בני המדיניות המפורסמת א"צ[104] ראי' כי
מעולם לא שמענו שלבשה בגדי נקם[105] לשלם לחוטאים לה כגמולם בעונש
אכזרי אבל היתה מרבה לסלוח ונתנה חסד לחייבים. ואם בהשגחתה על כל
מדינותי' ולעמוד עליהם בעת צרותיהם הלא בעינינו ראינו בשנת היוקר
והרעבון כמה התעוררת התעוררה המלכה וממש לא ערב לה אכל ושתות
עד הרביתה פעולות גדולות וזריזות להביא ממרחק לחם[106] למדינות הללו
לא נחה ולא שקטה כל ימי הרעב בשילוח בר ומזון פעם אחר פעם זכור לה
אתה ד' גמולה הטוב בעולם הגמול ולקיים לה מקרא שכתוב (ישעי' נ"ח יוד)
ותפק רעב נפשך ונפש נענה תשביע וזרח בחשך אורך ואפילתך בצהרים.

---

98. כך בדפוס, והשוה משלי י לא–לב.

99. ע"פ שיר א ג.

100. מ"ב יח כ.

101. משלי לא יז.

102. ע"פ יש' לא ד.

103. ע"פ במ' כד יז.

104. אינו צריך.

105. ע"פ יש' נט יז.

106. ע"פ משלי לא יד.

ועל הטוב יזכר שם אדונינו הקיסר **יאזעף** השני שהוא נזדרז בזה מאד
בימי היוקר ועשה כמעשה יוסף לפתח אוצרו' בר בשפע גדול השם יאריך
ימיו ושנותיו בנעימי'[107] שהחי' נפשות רבות. וגם לנו היהודי' היתה פקודה
מהמלכה לתת להם בר ומזון לפי צרכם. ואם בתיקון המדינות כמה חכמות
הרביתה במדינה וכמה שוהלין[108] תקנה וראוי לומר עלי' רבות בנות עשו
חיל ואת עלית על כלנה.[109] ואם בהנהגת המלכה בביתה ובחצרה עם השרים
ושרות המשרתים אותה ועם כל עבדי' הלא נודע שלא הכבידה עול עליהם
כלל וכל דברי' עמהם בנחת ובכבוד לא הכלימה לשום א' או אחת כלל:

ואם מצד הוד מלכות שניתן עלי' מן השמים ותהי נושאת חן בעיני כל
יושבי מדינותי' הרחוקי' והקרובי' כלם עבדו אותה בכל לב ולא מצד יראה
כ"א מאהבה גמורה וכאשר ראינו בעתות מלחמה שכל באי המדינות ממש
מסרו נפש עבורה אם החיל אנשי הצבא למגדול ועד קטן[110] עמדו על
משמרתם ונלחמו מלחמותי' בכל כחם ואם השרים והסגנים לפקח בכל
צרכי'הן לצרכי המלחמה והן לשאר צרכי המלכות והן שאר אישי המדינות
הן אינם יהודי' והן יהודים היינו מחכים ומצפים מתי יביא לידינו לעבוד
עבודת המלכה בכל כחנו והכל לא למען תשלום גמול כלל רק (5b) מאהבה
גמורה. וכמו שעשינו כלנו בימי המצור בשנת תקט"ו וגם אנכי בכל כחי
עבדתי אז וממש מסרתי נפשי בסכנות גדולות כמו שהי' מפורסם בעת
ההיא[111] והכל מאהבה אין זה כ"א[112] מתת אלהי' אשר ברוב חסדו על המלכה
נטע אהבתה בלב כל בני מדינותי':

ואם מצד מדותי' הטובי' צנועה ופרושה היתה ופירשה עצמה מכל
חמודת ותאוות הגופנית זה שנים רבות לא ישבה בסוד משחקים ולא
שמעה קול שירים ומיני זמר ולא באה בקאמדייע ובאפרוש[113] הנשמע או
הנראה שמלכה אדירה כזו אשר נתגדלה תפנוקי מלכי' מיום לידתה
תמאוס בכל תענוגי העולם לגמרי? ואם מצד ענוותנותה במקום גדולתה

107. ע"פ איוב לו יא.
108. בתי ספר.
109. משלי לא כט.
110. ע"פ אסתר א ה.
111. עי' הערה 30 לתרגום.
112. כי אם.
113. קומדיה ואופרה.

הי' ענוותנותה כקטן כגדול תשמע דבריו ותקבל דברי בקשתו. ואם מצד
מעשי' הטובי' והנעימי' גודל צדקתה להרבות צדקות וגודל ווותרנותה
כנודע מצד ארחת תמיד שעשתה לרוב מאד וכמה בתי יתומי' שקורין
וואזן הייזר וכמו כן כמה בתי עניים שקורין ארים הייזר[114] וכמה ממון
נדבה לזה זכרה לה אלהי' לטובה. ועל הכל אות ומופת פטירתה מעו"הז[115]
בשם טוב ובשכל צח ובשכל צח עד שעה אחרונה ובטעם סידור דברי' קודם מותה
וצואה שעשתה הכל יעיד על גודל שלימותה. ואשה אשר אלה לה כל
המעלות הנזכרים אם נבכה יומם ולילה ימי' הרבה ונרבה בדברי הספד
וקול יללה לא יספיק לצאת י"ח אפס קצה מהראוי לפי כבודה. הנשמע
או הנראה בחשיבות וביקר תפארת מלוכה כמותה בת קיסר ואשת קיסר
ואם הקיסר ובכל אלה לא תתגאה כלל אשר ע"כ לא נוכל לשער לא
אנחנו בני מדינות לבד כ"א ממש כל הדור כלו בכללו בכל כדור הארץ
מה שאבדנו במיתת מלכי' אדירה ומושלמת בכל המעלות ומדות היא
אדונתינו הקיסרית **מארי' טרעזיא** זכרונה לטובה. הוי הוי אזעק בקול מר
כי לא אדע במה להנחם וקורא אני מאמר המקונן (איכה ב' י"ג) מה
אעידך מה אדמה לך מה אשוה לך ואנחמך ופירשו המפרשים[116] שאם
אירע לאדם צרה המנחמים דרכם לנחמו ולומר גם לפלוני אירע צרה כזו
וקבל תנחומין אף אתה תקבל תנחומין אבל אם אירע לאדם צרה שלא
אירע כמותה לא ימצאו המנחמי' במה לפתוח פה לנחמו. אף אני אומר אם
היינו מוצאים אשה גדולה כמותה אף מכמה דורות שיעלה לזכרון או
ימצא בדברי הימים אף עשרה דורות שנמצא כמותה גדולה ביחוס
ובגדולה ובמעלות ובמדות ובצניעות ופרישו' כמותה ומתה קודם מלאות
לה שבעים שנה ובני דורה קבלו תנחומי' הי' מקום לפתוח גם לנו דברי
תנחומי' אבל אם נחפשנה לא נמצא כמותה לא אדע למצוא תנחומין. עד
עתה דברנו בהספד מצד יקרא דשכבי.

‏(6a) ‏ומצד יקרא דחיי הנה מתולדותיה ניכר שבחה הרב והעצום להיות
כל תולדותי' זרע בירך ומלכי' מחלציה יצאו[117] מתלא אמרין מאן דלא חזי

114. כך בדפוס, וצריך להיות ארמן הייזר (Armenhäuser).
115. מעולם הזה.
116. השוה רש"י על איכה ב יג.
117. ע"פ בר' לה יא.

אילנא יחזי איבי׳[118] ומי שלא ראה השדה יראה תבואותי׳ ומשבח הפירות
והתבואות ניכר כי העץ הוא עץ רענן והשדה היא שדה אשר ברכו ה׳.
אשרי׳ שאלו ילדה ואשרי׳ שאלו גדלה מלכי עמים ממנה קמו ומאלה
נפוצו בכל המדינות הרחוקי׳ והקרובי׳ אלה למלכי׳ הוכנו ואלה לסגני
ארץ מושלי מדינות גדולות והעולה על כולם בן פורת **יאזעף**[119] הוא אדונינו
האדיר המושלם בכל המעלות ומדות הקיסר האדיר ירום הודו ותתנשא
מלכותו. הנה כל אלה עתה הם בצער וטרודי׳ בהספד המלכה ובצערם
חייבים אנחנו להשתתף ולהצטער על מרגניתא דלית בה טימא[120] שנאבדה
מאתנו חבל על דאבדין ולא משתכחין.[121]

ומעתה מכל צדי צדדי׳ ראוי להגדיל ההספד כי רחוק ממנו מנחם[122]
לולי ה׳ צבאות הקדי׳ רפואה למכה[123] והרים קרן הקיסר יר״ה[124] בחיי אמו
והכרנו שבחו הרב והעצום כי מלך גדול ואדיר הוא ובזה יש לנו להנחם כי
יצא חוטר מגזע המלכה **מארי׳ טרעזי׳** ונצר משרשיו פרה[125] וצמח ממנה
צמח לצבי ולכבוד[126] ופרי לגאון ולתפארת הוא יהי׳ לנו ולכל מדינותיו
לנחמה כי לא חסר ממנו שום שלימות מכל השלימות שנמצא באמו
החסודה זכרונה לברכה הריחו ברוח חכמה ודעת רוח עצמה וגבורה[127]
הוא ישפוט בצדק דלים ויוכיח במישור לענוי ארץ[128] הוא יהי׳ מחסה לכל
מדינותיו הוא הנשר הגדול אשר כלם תחת כנפיו יחסיון[129] וישבו לבטח כי
הוא מלך גבור חיל ואיש מלחמה בכח ובחכמה על אויביו יתגבר יריע אף
יצריח[130] ובכל אשר יפנה יצליח.[131] ומעתה אחי ורעיי היהודי׳ כלם וכמו כן

118. אומרים משל: „מי שלא ראה את העץ ישתכל בפריו.‟
119. בר׳ מט כב.
120. עי׳ ירושלמי ברכות סב ב ותוספות בבלי ברכות יב א ד״ה אמת.
121. סנהדרין קיא א.
122. איכה א טז.
123. ע״פ מגילה יג ב.
124. ירום הודו.
125. ע״פ יש׳ יא א.
126. ע״פ יש׳ ד ב.
127. יש׳ יא ב.
128. יש׳ יא ד.
129. ע״פ תה׳ לו ח.
130. ע״פ יש׳ מב יג.
131. ע״פ תה׳ א ג ומשלי יז ח.

כל מי שמגיע לאזניו הדברי׳ האלה יהי׳ יהודי או א״י[132] הלא זה פרי כל טוב
אשר עלינו לשלם לאדונותינו המלכה החסוד׳ **מארי׳ טרעזי׳** על כל הטובות
שעשתה בכל ימי חיי׳ לעבוד בכל לב את בנה אדונינו האדיר הקיסר בכל לב
ובכל נפש[133] באהבה רבה כמו שעבדנו לאמו המלכה הקיסרי׳ ז״ל[134] ועלינו
להתפלל למלך מלכי המלכי׳ אשר כסא כבודו ממעל והוא הממליך
מלכי׳ שיתן עוז למלכנו הקיסר יר״ה וירם קרנו בתכלית הרוממות ויגדל
כסאו מכסא כל הקסרי׳ וישים בים ידו ובנהרות ימינו[135] ה׳ בעז ישמח מלך
ובישועתך יגיל מאד[136] תאות לבו תן לו וארשת שפתיו בל תמנע[137] תקדמנו
ברכת טוב תשית לראשו עטרת פז[138] תגדיל כבודו הוד והדר תשוה עליו
תשיתיהו ברכות לעד תחדהו בשמחה[139] ובטוב לב יקבל תנחומין על אמו
וייטב לבו וישב על כסאו בשמחה לפניו תדוץ דאבה[140] המלך ישמח באלהי׳
וימים על ימי מלכנו (6b) הקיסר האדיר תוסיף[141] אורך ימים ושנות חיים
תוסיף לו[142] ידין עמך בצדק ותתן אותנו לרחמים לפניו להטיב עמנו
ולהשגיח עלינו בעין חמלה ולעשות עמנו חסד ואנחנו נברך את אדונינו
החסיד הקיסר ונאמר כלנו יחד
(וענו ואמרו כל הקהל) **יחי אדונינו**
הקיסר **יאזעפוס השני**
לעולם אמן
סליק
דרוש הזה דרש הרב הנ״ל בבה״כ הנ״ל[143] על פי רשיון **מהשררה** יר״ה

132. אינו יהודי.
133. ע״פ דב׳ ו ה.
134. זכרונה לברכה.
135. ע״פ תה׳ פט כו.
136. ע״פ תה׳ כא ב.
137. ע״פ תה׳ כא ג.
138. ע״פ תה׳ כא ד.
139. ע״פ תה׳ כא ו–ז.
140. איוב מא יד.
141. ע״פ תה׳ סא ז.
142. ע״פ משלי ג ב.
143. בבית הכנסת הנזכר למעלה.

Bibliography

MANUSCRIPTS:

Aboab, "Nehar Pishon." Isaac Aboab, "Nehar Pishon." London MS Or. 10701 (Gaster, 1398).

Aboab, "Qetsat Parashiyot." Isaac Aboab, "Qetsat Parashiyot me-ha-RR"Y Aboab." Oxford-Bodleian MS 952.

Alkabetz. Solomon Alkabetz, "Derashot." British Library MS Or. 6361.

Anatoli, MS. Jacob Anatoli, "Malmad ha-Talmidim." British Library MS Add. 26,898.

Anonymous, "Bibago." Sassoon MS 702.

Anonymous, Harvard. Harvard Houghton Hebrew MS 61.

Anonymous, "Disciple of R. Asher." "Sefer Midrashim." British Library MS Add. 27,292.

Anonymous, Moscow. Moscow Guenzberg Hebrew MS 926.

Anonymous, St. Petersburg. St. Petersburg Hebrew MS Firkovitch, First Series 507.

Balbo. Michael ben Shabbetai ha-Kohen Balbo, "Derashot" and other writings. Vatican Hebrew MS 105.

Cambridge University MS Add. 1022.

Cantarini. Isaac Hayyim Cantarini, Italian Sermons. Budapest Kaufmann MS 314- 319.

Dato, "Derashot." Mordecai Dato, "Derashot." British Library MS Add. 27,050.

"Dover Meisharim." Israel(?), "Dover Meisharim." Oxford Christ Church MS 197 (Neubauer 2447).

"'Ein ha-Qore." Joseph ibn Shem Tov, " 'Ein ha-Qore." British Library MS Or. 10550.

Ephraim ben Gerson. Ephraim ben Gerson ("Ha-Darshan") of Veroia, "Tsintsinet ha- Man." British Library MS Or. 1307.

Foa. Eliezer Nahman Foa, "Goren Ornan." Mantua MS 59.

Ibn Basa. Moses ben Samuel ibn Basa, "Tena'ei ha-Darshan." Columbia University MS X893 J151 Q.

Jacob ben Hananel. Jacob ben Hananel Sikili (of Sicily), "Torat ha-Minḥah." Vienna Hebrew MS 37.

Joseph ben Hayyim, "Derashot." Joseph ben Hayyim of Benevento, "Derashot." Parma Hebrew MS 2627 (De' Rossi, 1398).

Levin, "Derashot." Hirschel Levin, "Derashot." Jewish Theological Seminary of America MS R79.

"Miqnat Kesef." Jewish Theological Seminary of America MS 172.

Morteira, "Giv'at Sha'ul." Saul Levi Morteira, "Giv'at Sha'ul," 5 vols. Rabbinical Seminary, Budapest, MS 12.

Portaleone, MS. Samuel ben Elisha Portaleone, "Derashot." British Library MS Add. 27,123.

Segal. Jacob ben Kalonymos Segal, "Qol Ya'aqov." Columbia University MS X893 J151 Q.

Shem Tov, MS A. Shem Tov ibn Shem Tov, "Derashot ha-Torah." Cambridge University MS. Dd. 10.46.

Shem Tov, MS B. Shem Tov ibn Shem Tov, "Derashot ha-Torah." Cambridge Trinity College MS 140 [F 12.49].

Shem Tov, MS C. Shem Tov ibn Shem Tov, "Derashot." Jewish Theological Seminary of America MS Rab. 212 (Adler 2506).

Yizhari. Mattathias Yizhari, "Parashiyyot." Parma Hebrew MS 2365 (De' Rossi 1417).

PRINTED WORKS:

Aaron ben Moses. Aaron ben Moses of Modena, *Ma'avar Yaboq*. Reprint edition, Jerusalem, 1989.

Abelard. Peter Abelard, *A Dialogue of a Philosopher, a Jew, and a Christian,* trans. Pierre Payer. Toronto, 1979.

Aboab, *Menorat ha-Ma'or.* Isaac Aboab I, *Menorat ha-Ma'or,* ed. Judah Horeb. Jerusalem, 1961.

Aboab, *Nehar Pishon.* Isaac Aboab II, *Nehar Pishon.* Zolkiew, 1806.

Abraham ben David, *Derashah.* Abraham ben David, *Derashah le-Rosh Hashanah le-RABaD mi-Posquières,* ed. Abraham Halevi. London, 1955.

Abraham ben Nathan. Abraham ben Nathan ha-Yarhi, *Perush Masekhet Kalah Rabbati.* Tiberias, 1906.

Abrahams, *Ethical Wills.* Israel Abrahams, ed., *Hebrew Ethical Wills.* 2 vols. Philadelphia, 1926.

Abrahams, *Studies.* Israel Abrahams, *Studies in Pharisaism and the Gospels.* 2 vols. Cambridge, Eng., 1917–24.

Abravanel, *Torah.* Isaac Abravanel, *Perush ha-Torah.* 3 vols., reprint edition, Jerusalem, 1964.

Abravanel, *Prophets.* Isaac Abravanel, *Nevi'im Rishonim ve-Aharonim.* 3 vols., reprint edition, Jerusalem, 1949–60.

Abravanel, *Zevah Pesah.* Isaac Abravanel, *Zevah Pesah,* in *Otsar Perushim ve-Tsiyyurim 'al Haggadah shel Pesah,* ed. J. D. Eisenstein. New York, 1920.

Ackerman. Ari Ackerman, "Zerahia Halevi's Sermon on Genesis 22:14." MA Thesis, Hebrew University of Jerusalem, 1993.

Adelman. Howard Adelman, "Success and Failure in the Seventeenth Century Ghetto of Venice." Ph.D. dissertation, Brandeis University, 1985.

Adret. Solomon ibn Adret, *She'elot u-Teshuvot ha-RaShBA.* 7 vols. in 4. Benei Beraq, 1958.

Agnon, *Heart.* S. Y. Agnon, *In the Heart of the Seas.* New York, 1947.

Alami. Solomon Alami, *Iggeret Musar.* St. Petersburg, 1912; reprinted Jerusalem, 1965.

Alba. Jacob di Alba, *Toledot Ya'aqov.* Venice, 1609.

Albelda. Moses Albelda, *Darash Mosheh.* Venice, 1603.

Albo. Joseph Albo, *Sefer ha-'Iqqarim,* ed. I. Husik. 5 vols, Philadelphia, 1930.

Almog. Shmuel Almog, ed., *Antisemitism Through the Ages.* Oxford, 1988.

Almosnino. Moses Almosnino, *Me'ammets Koah.* Venice, 1588.

Alsheikh, *Mar'ot.* Moses Alsheikh, *Mar'ot ha-Tsov'ot.* Fiorda, 1865.

Alsheikh, *Romemut El.* Moses Alsheikh, *Romemut El.* Warsaw, 1875.

Altmann, "Ars Rhetorica." Alexander Altmann, "Ars Rhetorica as Reflected in Some Jewish Figures of the Italian Renaissance," in *Jewish Thought in the Sixteenth Century,* ed. Bernard Cooperman. Cambridge, MA, 1983.

Altmann, "Eternality." Alexander Altmann, "Eternality of Punishment: A Theological Controversy within the Amsterdam Rabbinate in the Thirties of the Seventeenth Century," *PAAJR* 40 (1973):1–40.

Altmann, *Mendelssohn.* Alexander Altmann, *Moses Mendelssohn: A Biographical Study.* University, AL, 1973.

Anatoli. Jacob Anatoli, *Malmad ha-Talmidim.* Lyck, 1866.

Ancona. Clemento Ancona, "L'inventario dei beni di Leon da Modena," *Bolletino dell'istituto distoria della societa e dello stato veneziano* 10 (1967):256–67.

Anonymous (*Derashot . . . Rabbenu Yonah*). *Derashot u-Ferushei Rabbenu Yonah Gerundi 'al ha-Torah,* ed. Samuel Yerushalmi. Jerusalem, 1980.

Aquinas, Metaphysics. Thomas Aquinas, *Commentary on the Metaphysics of Aristotle,* 2 vols., trans. John Rowan. Chicago, 1961.

Aquinas, *Summa Theologica.* Thomas Aquinas, *Summa Theologica.* 3 vols. New York, Boston, Cincinnati, Chicago, San Francisco, 1947.

Arama, *'Aqedat.* Isaac Arama, *'Aqedat Yitshaq.* 3 vols., Warsaw, 1883.

Arama, *Hazut.* Isaac Arama, *Hazut Qashah.* Warsaw, 1884.

Ariès, *Childhood.* Philippe Ariès, *Centuries of Childhood: A Social History of Family Life.* New York, 1962; from the French edition of 1960.

Ariès, *Death.* Philippe Ariès, *The Hour of Our Death.* New York, 1982, from the French edition of 1977.

Asprey. Robert Asprey, *Frederick the Great.* New York, 1986.

Assaf. Simha Assaf, *Meqorot le-Toledot ha-Hinukh be-Yisra'el.* 4 vols. Tel Aviv, 1930–54.

Assis, "Welfare and Mutual Aid." Yom Tov Assis, "Welfare and Mutual Aid in the Spanish Jewish Communities," in *Moreshet Sepharad: The Sephardi Legacy,* ed. Haim Beinart. Jerusalem, 1992, pp. 318–45.

Augustine, *De Genesis.* St. Augustine, *De Genesis contra Manichaeos.* Migne, *PL,* vol. 34.

Augustine, *Literal Meaning.* St. Augustine, *The Literal Meaning of Genesis,* trans. and annot. John Taylor. 2 vols. New York, 1982.

Baer, *'Avodat Yisra'el.* Seligman Baer, *Seder 'Avodat Yisra'el.* Redelheim, 1868.

Baer, "Ha-Megamah." Yitzhak Baer, "Ha-Megamah ha-Datit ha-Hevratit shel 'Sefer Hasidim,'" Zion 3 (1938):1–50.

Baer, "Ha-Reqa'." Yitzhak Baer, "Ha-Reqa' ha-Histori shel ha-Ra'ya Mehemna," Zion 5 (1940):1–44.

Baer, *History.* Yitzhak Baer, *A History of the Jews in Christian Spain.* 2 vols. Philadelphia, 1961–66; from the Hebrew edition of 1959.

Baer, *Juden.* Yitzhak Baer, *Die Juden im christlichen Spanien.* 2 vols. Berlin 1929.

Bahya ben Asher, *Encyclopedia. Encyclopedia of Torah Thoughts,* trans. and ed. Hayyim Chavel. New York, 1980.

Bahya ben Asher, *Kad ha-Qemah. Kitvei Rabbenu Bahya,* ed. Hayyim Chavel. Jerusalem, 1970.

Bahya ben Asher, *Torah. Rabbenu Bahya 'al ha-Torah,* ed. Charles Chavel. 3 vols. Jerusalem, 1966.

Baldwin. John Baldwin, *Masters, Princes and Merchants; The Social Views of Peter the Chanter and His Circle.* 2 vols. Princeton, 1970.

Bamberger. Bernard Bamberger, *Fallen Angels.* Philadelphia, 1952.

Baron, *Community.* S. W. Baron, *The Jewish Community.* 3 vols. Philadelphia, 1942.

Baron, *History.* S. W. Baron, *History and Jewish Historians.* Philadelphia, 1964.

Baron, *SRHJ.* S. W. Baron, *A Social and Religious History of the Jews.* 18 vols. Philadelphia and New York, 1952–83.

Barzilay. Isaac Barzilay, *Between Reason and Faith.* The Hague and Paris, 1967.

Beales. Derek Beales, *Joseph II.* Cambridge, Eng., 1987.

Benayahu, "Garçon." Meir Benayahu, "Derushav she-le-Rabbi Yosef ben Meir Garçon," *Mikhael* 7 (1982):42–205.

Benayahu, "Hespedo." Meir Benayahu, "Hespedo shel Rabbi Shemu'el Yafeh Ashkenazi 'al Aviv Rabbi Yitshaq Yafeh," *Qovets 'al Yad* 8 (18) (1976):435–49.

Benjamin ben Elhanan. Benjamin Meir ben Elhanan, *Kerem Binyamin.* Vilna, 1885.

Benjamin of Tudela. *The Itinerary of Benjamin of Tudela,* trans. Marcus Nathan Adler. London, 1907; reprinted New York, 1960 and Malibu, CA, 1983.

Ben-Sasson, "Golei Sefarad." Haim Hillel Ben-Sasson, "Dor Golei Sefarad 'al 'Atsmo," *Zion* 26 (1961):23–64.

Ben-Sasson, *Hagut.* Ben Sasson, *Hagut ve-Hanhagah.* Jerusalem, 1959.

Ben-Sasson, *History.* Haim Hillel Ben-Sasson, *A History of the Jewish People.* Cambridge, MA, 1976.

Ben-Shalom. Ram Ben-Shalom, "Vikkuaḥ Tortosa, Vicente Ferrer, u-Va'ayat ha-Anusim 'al Pi 'Eduto shel Yitsḥaq Natan," *Zion* 66 (1991):21–45.

Ben Yehudah. Eliezer Ben Yehudah, *Millon ha-Lashon ha-Ivrit.* 8 vols. New York and London, 1960.

Berger, "Abulafia." Abraham Berger, "The Messianic Self-Consciousness of Abraham Abulafia," in *Essays on Jewish Life and Thought Presented in Honor of Salo Wittmayer Baron,* pp. 55–61. New York, 1959.

Berger, *Jewish-Christian Debate.* David Berger, *The Jewish-Christian Debate in the High Middle Ages.* Philadelphia, 1979.

Bernardino, *Prediche.* Bernardino da Siena, *Prediche volgari sul Campo di Siena 1427,* ed. Carlo Delcorno. 2 vols. Milan, 1989.

Berthold von Regensburg. Berthold von Regensburg, *Vollständige Ausgabe seiner Predigten,* ed. Franz Pfeiffer. 2 vols. Berlin, 1862–80, reprinted Berlin, 1965.

Bettan. Israel Bettan, *Studies in Jewish Preaching.* Cincinnati, 1939.

Bibago, "Zeh Yenaḥamenu." Abraham Bibago, "Zeh Yenaḥamenu." Salonika 1522(?).

Blasco-Martinez. A. Blasco-Martinez, "Instituciones socioreligiosas judias de Zaragoza (siglosa XIV-XV)—Sinagogas, cofradias, hospitales." *Sefarad* 50 (1990):3–46, 265–88.

Bloch. Issachar Baer Bloch, *Binat Yissachar.* Prague, 1785.

Bodian. Miriam Bodian, "Amsterdam, Venice, and the Marrano Diaspora in the Seventeenth Century," *Dutch Jewish History* 2 (1989):47–65.

Bonfil, "Dato." Robert Bonfil, "Aḥat mi-Derashotav shel R. Mordekai Dato," Italia 1 (1976):1–32.

Bonfil, *Jewish Life.* Robert Bonfil, *Jewish Life in Renaissance Italy.* Berkeley, Los Angeles, London, 1994.

Bonfil, *Rabbis.* Robert Bonfil, *Rabbis and Jewish Communities in Renaissance* Italy. London, 1990.

Bonfil, "Iggerot." Robert Bonfil, "Shteim-'Esrei Iggerot me-et R. Elyahu b"R. Shelomoh Raphael ha-Levi (de Veali)," *Sinai* 71 (1972):163–90.

Bossuet. *Oeuvres de Bossuet.* 4 vols. Paris, 1862.

Boswell, *Kindness.* John Boswell, *The Kindness of Strangers.* New York, 1988.

Brams. Steven J. Brams, *Biblical Games: A Strategic Analysis of Stories in the Old Testament.* Cambridge, MA, 1985.

Brant, *Narrenschiff.* Sebastian Brant, *Das Narrenschiff.* Tubingen, 1962.

Brant, *Ship of Fools.* Sebastian Brant, *The Ship of Fools,* trans. Edwin H. Zeydel. New York, 1944.

Braudel, *Mediterranean.* Fernand Braudel, *The Mediterranean and the Mediterranean World in the Ages of Philip II.* 2 vols. New York, 1972.

Bregman. Marc Bregman, "The Darshan: Preacher and Teacher of Talmudic Times." *The Melton Journal,* Spring, 1982.

Brett-James. Antony Brett-James, *Europe Against Napoleon: The Leipzig Campaign,* 1813. London, 1970.

Brinton. *The Sermons of Thomas Brinton, Bishop of Rochester (1373–1389),* ed. Mary Devlin. 2 vols. London, 1954.

Bromyard. John Bromyard, *Summa praedicantium.* Venice, 1586.

Brundage. James Brundage, *Law, Sex, and Christian Society in Medieval Europe.* Chicago, 1987.

Bynum, *Holy Feast.* Carolyn Bynum, *Holy Feast and Holy Fast.* Berkeley and Los Angeles, 1987.

Caesarius, *Sermons.* Caesarius of Arles, Sermons, trans. M. M. Mueller. 2 vols. Vols. 31 and 47 of The Fathers of the Church. Washington D.C. 1956, 1964.

Caplan. Harry Caplan, *Of Eloquence: Studies in Ancient and Mediaeval Rhetoric.* Ithaca, 1970.

Carlebach. Elisheva Carlebach, *The Pursuit of Heresy: Rabbi Moses Hagiz and the Sabbatian Controversies.* New York, 1990.

Carmi. T. Carmi, *The Penguin Book of Hebrew Verse.* Philadelphia, 1981.

Cassuto, *Firenze.* Umberto Cassuto, *Gli ebrei a Firenze nell'eta del Rinascimento.* Florence, 1918.

Cassuto, "Rabbino." Umberto Cassuto, "Un rabbino fiorentino del secolo XV," *Rivista Israelitica* 3 (1906):116–28, 224–28; 4 (1907):33–37, 156–61, 225–49.

Charland. Th.-M. Charland, *Artes Praedicandi.* Ottowa, 1936.

Chazan, Crusade. Robert Chazan, *European Jewry and the First Crusade.* Berkeley and Los Angeles, 1987.

Chazan, *Church, State, and Jews.* Robert Chazan, *Church, State, and Jews in the Middle Ages.* New York, 1980.

Chenu. M. D. Chenu, *Toward Understanding St. Thomas.* Chicago, 1964.

Chrysostom, *Discourses.* John Chrysostom, *Discourses Against Judaizing Christians,* trans. Paul W. Harkins. Washington, D. C., 1979.

Chrysostom, *Homilies.* John Chrysostom, *Homilies on the Epistles of Paul to the Corinthians.* Vol. 12 of *A Select Library of the Nicene and Post-Nicene Fathers.* 14 vols. Grand Rapids, MI, 1956.

Clements. Robert J. Clements, *Michelangelo's Theory of Art.* New York, 1961.

Cohen, "*Be Fertile*". Jeremy Cohen, "*Be Fertile and Increase.*" Ithaca, 1989.

Cohen, Friars. Jeremy Cohen, *The Friars and the Jews: The Evolution of Medieval Anti-Judaism.* Ithaca, 1983.

Cohn. Norman Cohn, *The Pursuit of the Millennium.* Oxford, 1970.

Cooperman. Bernard Cooperman, "Eliahu Montalto's 'Suitable and Incontrovertible Propositions': A Seventeenth-Century Anti-Christian Polemic," in *Jewish Thought in the Seventeenth Century,* ed. Bernard Septimus and Isadore Twersky, pp. 469–97. Cambridge, MA, 1987.

Crane. Th. Frederick Crane, *The Exempla of Jacques de Vitry.* London, 1890.

Crankshaw. Edward Crankshaw, *Maria Theresa.* London, 1983.

Crescas, "Ketav." Hasdai Crescas, "Ketav . . . el Qehillot Avignon," in Solomon ibn Verga, *Shevet Yehudah,* ed. M. Wiener, Hebrew section, pp. 128–30. Hanover, 1924.

Crescas, Or. Hasdai Crescas, *Or ha-Shem.* Jerusalem, 1990.

Croatto. J. Severino Croatto, *Exodus: A Hermeneutics of Freedom.* Maryknoll, NY 1981.

Curtius. Ernst Robert Curtius, *European Literature and the Latin Middle Ages.* Princeton, 1953.

Dan, "Goralah." Joseph Dan, "Goralah ha-Histori shel Torat ha-Sod shel Ḥasidei Ashkenaz," in *Studies in Mysticism and Religion Presented to Gershom G. Scholem*, ed. Chaim Wirszubski, R. J. Z. Werblowsky, E. E. Urbach, pp. 87–99. Jerusalem, 1967.

Dan, "Sifrut ha-Derush." Joseph Dan, "'Iyyun ba-Sifrut ha-Derush ha-'Ivrit bi-Tequfat ha-Renesans be-Italyah," *Proceedings of the Sixth World Congress of Jewish Studies*, Division 3, pp. 105–10. Jerusalem, 1977.

Dan, *Sifrut ha-Musar.* Joseph Dan, *Sifrut ha-Musar ve-ha-Derush.* Jerusalem, 1975.

Dan, *Sippur.* Joseph Dan, *Ha-Sippur ha-Ivri bi-Ymei ha-Beinayim.* Jerusalem, 1974.

Dan, "Tefillah ve-Dim'ah." Joseph Dan, "Derush 'Tefillah ve-Dim'ah' le-Rabbi Yehudah Moscato," *Sinai* 76 (1975):209–32.

Dan, *Torat ha-Sod.* Joseph Dan, *Torat ha-Sod shel Hasidut Ashkenaz.* Jerusalem, 1968.

d'Ancona. J. d'Ancona, "Komst der Marranen in Noord Nederland de Portugese Gemeenten te Amsterdam Tor de Vereinigung (1639)," in *Geschiedenis der Joden in Nederland*, ed. H. Brugmans and A. Frank. 2 vols. Amsterdam, 1940. 1:201–69.

Daniélou, *Shadow.* Jean Daniélou, *From Shadow to Reality: Studies in the Biblical Typology of the Fathers.* London, 1960.

Daniélou, "Typologie d'Isaac." Jean Daniélou, "La Typologie d'Isaac dans le christianisme primitif," *Biblica* 28 (1947):363–93.

David, *Hebrew Chronicle.* Abraham David, ed., *A Hebrew Chronicle from Prague, c. 1615.* Tuscaloosa and London, 1993.

David, *Shetei Kroniqot.* Avraham David, *Shetei Kroniqot Ivriyot mi-Dor Gerush Sefarad.* Jerusalem, 1979.

David ha-Nagid. *Midrash David ha-Nagid: Genesis,* ed. Abraham Katsch. Jerusalem, 1964.

Davidson, *Bibago.* Herbert Davidson, *The Philosophy of Abraham Bibago.* Berkeley and Los Angeles, 1964.

Davidson, *Meshalim.* Israel Davidson, *Otsar ha-Meshalim.* Jerusalem, 1979.

Davidson, *Thesaurus.* Israel Davidson, *Thesaurus of Mediaeval Hebrew Poetry,* 4 vols. New York, 1924.

Delbrueck. Hans Delbrueck, *History of the Art of War.* 4 vols. Westport, CT, 1985.

Delcorno. Carlo Delcorno, *Exemplum e letteratura: Tra Medioevo e Rinascimento.* Bologna, 1989.

Delumeau. Jean Delumeau, *Sin and Fear.* New York, 1990; from the French edition of 1983.

Deyermond. Alan Deyermond, "The Sermon and its Uses in Medieval Castilian Literature", *La Coronica,* 8 (1980):127–45.

Dictionnaire de Theologie. Dictionnaire de Theologie Catholique. 15 vols. Paris, 1908–50.

Diego de Estella. Fray Diego de Estella, *Modo de predicar y Modus concionandi,* ed. Pio Sagues Azcona. 2 vols. Madrid, 1951.

Dinur, *Mifneh.* Ben-Zion Dinur, *Ba-Mifneh ha-Dorot.* Jerusalem, 1955.

Dubnow, *Russia and Poland.* Simon Dubnow, *A History of the Jews in Russia and Poland.* 3 vols. Philadelphia, 1916–20.

Duby, *Knight.* Georges Duby, *The Knight, the Lady, and the Priest: The Making of Modern Marriage in Medieval France.* New York, 1983; from the French edition of 1981.

Duran. Profiat Duran, *Ma'aseh Efod.* Vienna, 1865.

Duschinsky. Charles Duschinsky, *The Rabbinate of the Great Synagogue.* London, 1921.

Eidlitz. Zerah Eidlitz, *Or la-Yesharim.* Prague, 1785.

Eiximenis. Francisco Echimenis' *Ars praedicandi populo,* in P. Marti de Barcelona, "'L'Ars Praedicandi' de Francesc Eiximenis," *Analecta Sacra Tarraconensia* 12 (1936):301–40.

EJ. Encyclopedia Judaica. 16 vols. Jerusalem, 1971–72.

Elbaum, *Petiḥut.* Jacob Elbaum, *Petiḥut ve-Histagrut: Ha-Yetsirah ha-Ruḥanit ha-Sifrutit be-Polin u-ve-Artsot Ashkenaz be-Shalhei ha-Me'ah ha-Shesh-'Esreh.* Jerusalem, 1990.

Elbaum, "Sermon to Story." Jacob Elbaum, "From Sermon to Story: The Transformation of the Akedah," *Prooftexts* 6 (1986): 97–116.

Elbaum, "Shalosh Derashot." Jacob Elbaum, "Shalosh Derashot Ashkenaziyot Qedumot mi-Q[etav] Y[ad] Beit ha-Sefarim," *Kiryat Sefer* 48 (1973): 340–47.

Eleh Divrei ha-Berit. Sefer Eleh Divrei ha-Berit: Qovets ha-Ḥaramot u-Fisqei ha-Halakhah Neged Rishonei ha-Reformim be-Hamburg. Altona, 1819; reprinted Jerusalem, 1970.

Eliach. Yaffa Eliah, *Hasidic Tales of the Holocaust.* New York, 1983.

Elijah ben Moses. Elijah ben Moses Gerson, *Hadrat Eliyahu.* Prague, 1785.

Elijah ha-Kohen, *Midrash Eliyahu.* Elijah ha-Kohen of Izmir, *Midrash Eliyahu.* Izmir, 1759.

Elijah ha-Kohen, *Shevet.* Elijah ha-Kohen of Izmir, *Shevet Musar.* Jerusalem, 1978.

Emery. Richard Emery, "New Light on Profayt Duran 'The Efodi,'" *JQR* 58 (1967–68): 328–37.

Entsiqlopedyah Talmudit. Entsiqlopedyah Talmudit, 4th ed. 21 vols. Jerusalem, 1955–93.

Epstein. Isidore Epstein, *Studies in the Communal Life of the Jews of Spain.* 2 vols. in 1. New York, 1968.

Erb. Peter C. Erb, "Vernacular Material for Preaching in MS Cambridge University Library I. III. 8," *Mediaeval Studies* 33 (1971): 63–84.

Eybeschuetz. Jonathan Eybeschuetz, *Ya'arot Devash.* Jerusalem, 1965.

Feierberg. M. Z. Feierberg, *Whither? And Other Stories.* Philadelphia, 1973.

Feldman, "Determinism." Seymour Feldman, "A Debate Concerning Determinism in Late Medieval Jewish Philosophy," *PAAJR* 51 (1984): 15–54.

Figo. Azariah Figo, *Binah le-'Ittim.* Warsaw, 1866; first published Venice, 1648.

Fleckeles, *'Olat.* Eliezer Fleckeles, *'Olat Ḥodesh.* Prague, 1785.

Fleckeles, *Sheni.* Eliezer Fleckeles, *'Olat Ḥodesh Sheni.* Munkacs, 1907.

Flusser. David Flusser, *Sefer Josippon.* 2 vols. Jerusalem, 1978–80.

Flynn. Maureen Flynn, *Sacred Charity: Confraternities and Social Welfare in Spain. 1400–1700.* Ithaca, NY: 1989.

Foster. Kenelm Foster, "Appendix 2: Satan," in Thomas Aquinas, *Summa theologiae.* 60 vols. New York and London, 1964–76, 9:306–21.

Fox, *Interpreting Maimonides.* Marvin Fox, *Interpreting Maimonides.* Chicago and London, 1990.

Franco Mendes. David Franco Mendes, *Memorias do Estabelecimento e progresso dos judeos pro-tuguezes e espanhoes nesta famosa cidade de Amsterdam,* ed. L. Fuks and R. G. Fuks Mansfeld. Amsterdam, 1975.

Funkenstein, "Nahmanides." Amos Funkenstein, "Nahmanides' Symbolical Reading of History," in *Studies in Jewish Mysticism,* ed. Joseph Dan and Frank Talmage, pp. 129–50. Cambridge, MA, 1982.

Funkenstein, "Parshanuto." Amos Funkenstein, "Parshanuto ha-Tippologit shel ha-RaMBaN," *Zion* 45 (1979–80): 35–49.

Funkenstein, *Perceptions.* Amos Funkenstein, *Perceptions of Jewish History.* Berkeley and Los Angeles, 1993.

Ganzfried. Solomon Ganzfried, *Qitsur Shulḥan Arukh,* trans. Hyman Goldin. New York, 1927.

Gebhardt. Carl Gebhardt, *Die Schriften des Uriel da Costa.* Amsterdam, 1922.

Gelman. Arye Gelman, *Ha-Noda' bi-Yhudah u-Mishnato.* Jerusalem, 1962.

Gerundi, *Sha'arei Teshuvah.* Jonah Gerundi, *Sha'arei Teshuvah.* Jerusalem, 1968.

Gikatilla, *Gates of Light.* Joseph Gikatilla, *Gates of Light,* trans. Ari Weinstein. San Francisco and London, 1994.

Gikatilla, *Sha'arei Orah.* Joseph Gikatilla, *Sha'arei Orah,* ed. Joseph Ben Shelomo. 2 vols. Jerusalem, 1970.

Gilbert. Martin Gilbert, *The Holocaust.* New York, 1985.

Ginzberg. Louis Ginzberg, *Legends of the Jews.* 7 vols. Philadelphia, 1912.

Goetschel. Roland Goetschel, "Torat ha-Nevu'ah shel R. Yosef Giqatillah ve-R. Mosheh de Leon," *Jerusalem Studies in Jewish Thought* 8 (1989): 217–37.

Goitein, *Mediterranean Society.* S. D. Goitein, *A Mediterranean Society.* 5 vols. Berkeley, Los Angeles, London, 1967–88.

Gooch. G. P. Gooch, *Maria Theresa and Other Studies.* London and New York, 1951.

Grasso. Domenico Grasso, *Proclaiming God's Message.* Notre Dame, 1965.

Grayzel, *Church and Jews.* Solomon Grayzel, *The Church and the Jews in the XIIIth Century.* New York, 1933.

Green. Arthur Green, *Tormented Master: A Life of Rabbi Nahman of Bratslav.* University, AL, 1979.

Greenberg. Moshe Greenberg, "Atem Qeruyim Adam," *Shedemot* 76 (1980):67–76.

Greenwald. Leopold Greenwald, *Kol Bo 'al Avelut.* 3 vols. Jerusalem and New York, 1973.

Gregory VII. *The Correspondence of Pope Gregory VII,* trans. Ephraim Emerton. New York, 1960.

Groll. Gerhard Groll, "Anmerkungen zu Musik, Theater, und Muskiern in Wien zur Zeit Maria Theresias und Josephs II," *Österreich im Europa der Aufklärung,* 2 vols., 2:663–72. Vienna, 1985.

Gross, *Iberian Jewry. Iberian Jewry From Twilight to Dawn: The World of Rabbi Abraham Saba.* Leiden, 1995.

Gross, "Pulmus." Avraham Gross, "Pulmus al Shitat ha-'Shemirah,' *AJS Review* 18 (1993): Hebrew section 1–20.

Gruner. O. C. Gruner, *A Treatise on the Canon of Medicine of Avicenna.* London, 1930.

Grunhut. L. Grunhut, "L'exégèse biblique de Nahschon Gaon," *REJ* 39 (1899):310–13.

Grunwald. Max Grunwald, *Vienna.* Philadelphia, 1936.

Guedemann. Moritz Guedemann, *Geschichte des Erziehungswesens und der Cultur des Abend-laendischen Juden.* 3 vols. Vienna, 1880–88.

Guttmann. Alexander Guttman, *The Struggle over Reform in Rabbinic Literature.* New York, 1977.

Hacker, "Ga'on ve-Dika'on." Joseph Hacker, "Ga'on ve-Dika'on: Qotavim bi-Havvayatam ha-Ruhanit ve-ha-Hevratit shel Yots'ei Sefarad u-Fortugal be-Imperiyah ha-Otomanit," in *Tarbut ve-Hevrah be-Toledot Yisra'el bi-Ymei ha-Beinayim: Qovets Ma'amarim le-Zikhro shel Hayyim Hillel Ben-Sasson,* ed. Robert Bonfil, Menahem Ben-Sasson, and Joseph Hacker, pp. 541–86. Jerusalem, 1989.

Hacker, "Li-Demutam." Joseph Hacker, "Li-Demutam ha-Ruhanit shel Yehudei Sefarad be-Sof ha-Me'ah ha-Hamesh-'Esreh," *Sefunot* 2 (17) (1983):21–95.

Hacker, "Yisra'el ba-Goyim." Joseph Hacker, "Yisra'el ba-Goyim be-Te'uro shel R. Shelomoh le-Veit ha-Levi," *Zion* 34 (1969):43–89.

Halamish. Moshe Halamish, "Le-Meqoro shel Pitgam ba-Sifrut ha-Qabbalah: Kol ha-Nofeaḥ mi-Tokho hu Nofeaḥ," *Sefer Bar Ilan* 13 (1976):211–23.

Hamilton. Earl J. Hamilton, *Money, Prices, and Wages in Valencia, Aragon, and Navarre, 1351–1500.* Cambridge, MA, 1936.

Harris. Monford Harris, "Marriage as Metaphysics," *HUCA* 33 (1962):197–220.

Harvey, "Averroes." Steven Harvey, "Averroes on the Principles of Nature: The Middle Commentary of Aristotle's Physics I–II." Ph.D. dissertation, Harvard 1977.

Harvey, "Crescas." Ze'ev (Warren) Harvey, "R. Hasdai Crescas 'al Yiḥudah shel Erets Yisra'el," in *Erets Yisra'el ba-Hagut ha-Yehudit bi-Ymei ha-Beinayim,* ed. Moshe Halamish and Aviezer Ravitzky, pp. 151–65. Jerusalem, 1991.

Heath. Thomas Heath, *A History of Greek Mathematics.* 2 vols. Oxford, 1921.

Heinemann, *Derashot.* Joseph Heinemann, *Derashot be-Tsibbur bi-Tequfat ha-Talmud.* Jerusalem, 1970.

Heinemann, *Literature.* Joseph Heinemann with Jakob Petuchowski, *The Literature of the Synagogue.* New York, 1975.

Heinemann, *Maggid.* Benno Heinemann, *The Maggid of Dubno and His Parables.* New York, 1967.

Heinemann, *Ta'amei ha-Mitsvot.* Isaac Heinemann, *Ta'amei ha-Mitsvot be-Sifrut Yisra'el.* Jerusalem, 1966.

Heller-Wilensky. Sarah Heller-Wilensky, *R. Yitsḥaq Arama u-Fe'ulato ha-Sifrutit.* Jerusalem and Tel Aviv, 1956.

Henriques de Castro. David Henriques de Castro, *Keur van Grafsteenen op de Nederl. Port. Isral. Begraffplaats te Ouderkerk a/d Amstel.* Leiden, 1883.

Hillel of Verona. Hillel ben Samuel of Verona, *Tagmulei ha-Nefesh,* ed. Joseph Sermoneta. Jerusalem, 1981.

Horner. Patrick J. Horner, "A Sermon on the Anniversary of the Death of Thomas Beauchamp, Earl of Warwick," *Traditio* 34 (1978):381–401.

Horowitz, *Jewish Sermon.* Carmi Horowitz, *The Jewish Sermon in 14th Century Spain.* Cambridge, MA, 1989.

Horowitz, "Image of God." Maryanne Cline Horowitz, "The Image of God in Man—Is Woman Included?" *Harvard Theological Review* 72:3–4 (1979):175–206. Horowitz, "Speaking of the Dead." Elliot Horowitz, "Speaking of the Dead: The Emergence of the Eulogy among Italian Jewry of the Sixteenth Century," in *Preachers of the Italian Ghetto,* ed. David Ruderman, pp. 129–62. Berkeley and Los Angeles, 1992.

Hsia. R. Po-chia Hsia, *The Myth of Ritual Murder.* New Haven, 1988.

Hughes. Diane Hughes, "Distinguishing Signs: Ear-Rings, Jews and Franciscan Rhetoric in the Italian Renaissance City," *Past and Present* 112 (1986):3–59.

Humbert of Romans. "Humbert of Romans' Treatise on the Formation of Preachers," in *Early Dominicans,* ed. by Simon Tugwell, pp. 181–370. New York, 1982.

Hurvitz, "RABaD." Elazar Hurvitz, "Seridim mi-Derashat ha-Pesah le-ha-RABaD [R. Abraham ben David of Posquières]. *Ha-Darom* 35 (1972):34–73.

Hurvitz, "Torat ha-Minhah." Elazar Hurvitz, "'Torat ha-Minḥah' le-Rabbi Ya'aqov ha-Siqili ve-'Midrash David' le-Rabbi David ha-Nagid." *Sinai* 59 (1966):29–38.

Husik. Isaac Husik, *A History of Mediaeval Jewish Philosophy.* New York, 1966.

Iannucci. Remo Iannucci, *The Treatment of the Capital Sins and Their Corresponding Vices in the German Sermons of Berthold von Regensburg.* New York, 1942.

Ibn 'Aqnin. Joseph ibn 'Aqnin, *Hitgalut ha-Sodot ve-Hofa'at ha-Me'orot: Perush Shir ha-Shirim,* ed. A. S. Halkin. Jerusalem, 1964.

Ibn Daud. Abraham ibn Daud, *Ha-Emunah ha-Ramah,* ed. Simson Weil. Frankfurt-am-Main, 1852.

Ibn Gabbai. Meir ibn Gabbai, *'Avodat ha-Qodesh.* Reprint edition, Jerusalem, 1973.

Ibn Musa. Hayyim ibn Musa, "Letter to his Son," ed. by David Kaufmann, in *Beit ha-Talmud* 2 (1842):110–25; reprinted with "Sefer Magen ve-Romah." Jerusalem, 1970.

Ibn Nahmias. Joseph ibn Nahmias, *Perush 'al Sefer Mishlei,* ed. by. M. L. Bamberger. Berlin, 1911.

Ibn Shu'eib, *Derashot* (1583). Joshua ibn Shu'eib, *Derashot 'al ha-Torah.* Cracow, 1583, reprinted Jerusalem, 1969.

Ibn Shu'eib, *Derashot* (1992). Joshua ibn Shu'eib, *Derashot R"Y ibn Shu'eib 'al ha-Torah u-Mo'adei ha-Shanah,* ed. Zeev Metzger. 2 vols. Jerusalem, 1992.

Ibn Shu'eib, *'Olat Shabbat.* Joel ibn Shu'eib, *'Olat Shabbat.* Venice, 1577.

Ibn Tibbon, "Millot Zarot." Samuel ibn Tibbon, "Perush me-ha-Millot Zarot," in *Moreh Nevukhim.* Reprint edition, Jerusalem, 1970.

Ibn Verga. Solomon ibn Verga, *Shevet Yehudah.* Jerusalem, 1947.

Idel, "Conceptions." Moshe Idel, "Differing Conceptions of the Kabbalah in the Early 17th Century," in *Jewish Thought in the Seventeenth Century,* ed. Bernard Septimus and Isadore Twersky, pp. 137–200. Cambridge, MA, 1987.

Idel, *Kabbalah.* Moshe Idel, *Kabbalah: New Perspectives.* New Haven, 1988.

Idel, "Moscato." Moshe Idel, "Judah Moscato: A Late Renaissance Jewish Preacher," in *Preachers of the Italian Ghetto,* ed. David Ruderman, pp. 41–66. Berkeley and Los Angeles, 1992.

Idel, *Mystical Experience.* Moshe Idel, *The Mystical Experience in Abraham Abulafia.* Albany, 1988.

Immanuel, *Maḥberot.* Immanuel of Rome, *Maḥberot,* ed. Dov Yarden. 2 vols. Jerusalem, 1957.

Irwin. T. Irwin, *Aristotle's First Principles.* Oxford, 1988.

Isaac min ha-Leviyim. Isaac min ha-Leviyim, *Sefer Medabber Tahapukhot,* ed. Daniel Carpi. Jerusalem, 1985.

Israel, "Menasseh." Jonathan Israel, "Menasseh ben Israel and the Dutch Sephardic Colonization Movement of the Mid-Seventeenth Century," in *Menasseh ben Israel and His World,* ed. Yosef Kaplan, Henri Méchoulan, and Richard Popkin, pp. 139–63. Leiden, 1989.

Israel, "Pereira." Jonathan Israel, "Manuel Lopez Pereira of Amsterdam, Antwerp and Madrid," *Studia Rosenthaliana* 19 (1985):109–26.

Izbicki. Thomas Izbicki, "Pyres of Vanities: Mendicant Preaching on the Vanity of Women and Its Lay Audience," in *De Ore Domini: The Preacher and Word in the Middle Ages,* ed. Thomas Amos, Eugene Green, Beverly Kienzle, pp. 211–34. Kalamazoo, 1989.

Jacobs, *Testimonies.* Louis Jacobs, *Jewish Mystical Testimonies.* New York, 1977.

Jastrow. Marcus Jastrow, *A Dictionary of the Targumim, the Talmud Babli and Yerushalmi, and the Midrashic Literature.* 2 vols. New York, 1950.

Jessurun. Rehuel Jessurun, *Dialogo dos Montes,* ed. and trans. Philip Polack. London, 1975.

Johnston. Mark D. Johnston, "The Rhetoric nova of Ramon Llull," in *De Ore Domini: The Preacher and Word in the Middle Ages,* ed. Thomas Amos, Eugene Green, Beverly Kienzle, pp. 119–45. Kalamazoo, 1989.

Joseph ben Moses. Joseph ben Moses of Trani, *Tsofnat Pa'aneah.* Jerusalem, 1977.

Joseph ben Solomon. Joseph ben Solomon Darshan of Posen, *Yesod Yosef.* Reprint edition, Jerusalem. 1967.

Jospe. Raphael Jospe, *Torah and Sophia: The Life and Thought of Shem Tov ibn Falaquera.* Cincinnati, 1988.

Kanarfogel. Ephraim Kanarfogel, *Jewish Education and Society in the High Middle Ages.* Detroit, 1992.

Kann. Robert Kann, *A History of the Habsburg Empire 1526–1918.* Berkeley and Los Angeles, 1974.

Kaplan, *From Christianity.* Yosef Kaplan, *From Christianity to Judaism: The Story of Isaac Orobio de Castro.* Oxford, 1989.

Kaplan, "Ha-Qehillah." Yosef Kaplan, "Ha-Qehillah ha-Portugalit be-Amsterdam ba-Me'ah ha-Yod-Zayin: Bein Masoret le-Shinnui," *Divrei ha-Aqademiyah ha-Le'umit ha-Yisra'elit la-Mada'im* 7 (1984-88):161–81.

Kaplan, "Morteira." Yosef Kaplan, "R. Sha'ul Levi Morteira ve-Ḥibburo 'Ta'anot ve-Hasagot Neged ha-Dat ha-Notsrit," *Meḥqarim 'al Toledot Yahadut Holand* 1 (1975):9–31.

Kaplan, "Ta'arikhei." Yosef Kaplan, "Le-Berur Ta'arikhei Petiratam shel Benei Mishpahat Nunes Henriques u-Sheloshah mi-Gedolei Rabbaneha shel Amsterdam." *Kiryat Sefer* 54 (1979):611–13.

Kaplan, "Travels." Yosef Kaplan, "The Travels of Portuguese Jews from Amsterdam to the 'Lands of Idolatry,'" in *Jews and Conversos,* ed. Yosef Kaplan, pp. 197–224. Jerusalem, 1985.

Karo, *Toledot Yitsḥaq.* Isaac Karo, *Toledot Yitsḥaq.* Riva di Trento, 1558.

Kasher, "Musag ha-Zeman." Menahem Kasher, "Musag ha-Zeman be-Sifrei Ḥazal ve-ha-Rishonim," *Talpiyot* 5:3–4 (1952): 799–827.

Kasher, *Torah Shelemah.* Menahem Kasher, *Torah Shelemah.* 43 vols. Jerusalem, 1949—.

Katchen. Aaron Katchen, *Christian Hebraists and Dutch Rabbis.* Cambridge, MA, 1984.

Katz, *Exclusiveness.* Jacob Katz, *Exclusiveness and Tolerance.* New York, 1962.

Katz, *Ghetto.* Jacob Katz, *Out of the Ghetto.* Cambridge, MA, 1973.

Katz, "Halakhah." Jacob Katz, "'Al Halakhah u-Derush ki-Meqor Histori," in *Halakhah ve-Qabbalah,* pp. 333–39. Jerusalem, 1984.

Katz, "Nissu'im." Jacob Katz, "Nissu'im br-Hayyei Ishut be-Mots'ei Yemei ba-Beinayim," *Zion* 10 (1945):21–54.

Katz, "Shabbes Goy". Jacob Katz, *The "Shabbes Goy": A Study in Halakhic Flexibility.* Philadelphia and New York, 1989; from the Hebrew edition of 1984.

Katz, *Tradition.* Jacob Katz, *Tradition and Crisis: Jewish Society at the End of the Middle Ages,* trans. Bernard Cooperman. New York, 1993; from the Hebrew edition of 1958.

Katzenellenbogen. Samuel Judah Katzenellenbogen, *Shneim 'Asar Derushim.* Jerusalem, 1959, reprint of Warsaw, 1876; first published Venice 1594.

Kaufmann. David Kaufmann, "The Dispute about the Sermons of David del Bene of Mantua," *JQR* 8 (1895–96):513–27.

Kayserling. Meyer Kayserling, "Un conflit dans la communauté hispano-portugaise d'Amsterdam -ses consequences," *REJ* 92 (1901):275–76.

Kellner, *Dogma.* Menachem Kellner, *Dogma in Medieval Jewish Thought.* Oxford, 1986.

Kellner, "Gersonides' Commentary." Menachem Kellner, "Gersonides' Commentary on Song of Songs: For Whom Was it Written and Why?" in *Gersonide en son temps,* ed. Gilbert Dahan, pp.81–97. Louvain and Paris, 1991.

Kellner, *Principles.* Menachem Kellner, *Principles of Faith (Rosh Amanah).* London and Toronto, 1982.

Kellner, "Torah." Menachem Kellner, "The Torah as Deductive Science," *REJ* 146 (1987):265–79.

Kemelhar. Yekuthiel Kemelhar, *Mofet ha-Dor.* Pietrokov, 1934.

Kendrick. Laura Kendrick, *The Game of Love.* Berkeley and Los Angeles, 1988.

Kermode. Frank Kermode, *The Genesis of Secrecy: On the Interpretation of Narrative.* Cambridge, MA, 1979.

Kerner. Robert Kerner, *Bohemia in the Eighteenth Century.* Orono, ME, 1969.

Kestenberg-Gladstein. Ruth Kestenberg-Gladstein, *Neuere Geschichte der Juden in den böhmischen Ländern. Erster Teil: Das Zeitalter der Aufklärung 1780–1830.* Tübingen, 1969.

Kimhi, *Covenant.* Joseph Kimhi, *The Book of the Covenant,* trans. Frank Talmage. Toronto, 1972.

Kimhi, *Sefer ha-Berit.* Joseph Kimhi, *Sefer ha-Berit u-Vikkuḥei RaDaQ 'im ha-Notsrim,* ed. Frank Talmage. Jerusalem, 1974.

Klatzkin. Jacob Klatzkin, *Otsar ha-Munaḥim ha-Pilosofiyim.* 4 vols. in 2. New York, 1968.

Klein-Breslavy. Sarah Klein-Breslavy, "Metsi'ut ha-Zeman ve-ha-Yamim ha-Rishonim la-Beri'ah ba-Pilosofiah ha-Yehudit shel Yemei ha-Beinayim," *Tarbiz* 45 (1975–76): 106–27.

Klemperer. Gutmann Klemperer, "The Rabbis of Prague," *Historia Judaica* 12 (1950): 33–66, 143–52; 13 (1951): 55–82.

Klijnsmit. Anthony Klijnsmit, "Amsterdam Sephardim and Hebrew Grammar in the Seventeenth Century," *Studia Rosenthaliana* 22 (1988):144–64.

Kluger. Solomon Kluger, *'Ein Dim'ah.* Zolkiew, 1834.

Kretzmann and Stump. *Logic and the Philosophy of Language.* Vol. 1 of *The Cambridge Translations of Medieval Philosophical Texts,* ed. Norman Kretzmann and Eleonore Stump. Cambridge, Eng., 1988.

Ladurie, Montaillou. Emmanuel Le Roy Ladurie, *Montaillou: Cathars and Catholics in a French Village, 1294–1324.* New York, 1980; from the French edition of 1978.

Landau, Ahavat Tsiyon. Ezekiel and Samuel Landau, *Ahavat Tsiyon.* Jerusalem, 1966.

Landau, *Derushei.* Ezekiel Landau, *Derushei ha-Tselah.* Warsaw, 1899; reprint edition Jerusalem, 1966.

Landau, *Derush ha-Shevaḥ.* Ezekiel Landau, *Derush ha-Shevaḥ ve-ha-Hoda'ah 'al Hatslaḥot Adonenu ha-Qaisar Yosef ha-Sheni be-Lakhdo 'Ir ha-Betsurah Belgrad 'al Yedei Sar Tsava' Ha-Mefursam Baron Landau.* Prague, 1790.

Landau, *Derush Hesped.* Ezekiel Landau, *Derush Hesped . . . 'al Mitat ha-Qaisarit Maria Theresa.* Prague, 1780.

Landau, *Noda'.* Ezekiel Landau, *Noda' Bi-Yhudah.* 2 vols. Reprint edition, Jerusalem, 1969.

Langermann. Y. Tzvi Langermann, "Gersonides on the Magnet and the Heat of the Sun." *Studies on Gersonides,* ed. Gad Freudenthal, pp. 267–84. Leiden, 1992.

Lasker, "Ha-Ḥeit." Daniel Lasker, "Ha-Ḥeit ha-Qadmon ve-Khaparato le-fi Ḥasdai Crescas," *Da'at* 20 (1988):127–35.

Lasker, *Philosophical Polemics.* Daniel Lasker, *Jewish Philosophical Polemics Against Christianity in the Middle Ages.* New York, 1977.

Lea, *Auricular Confession.* Henry Charles Lea, *A History of Auricular Confession and Indulgences in the Latin Church.* 3 vols. Philadelphia, 1896.

Lerner. R. E. Lerner, *The Heresy of the Free Spirit.* Berkeley and Los Angeles, 1972.

Lesnick. Daniel Lesnick, *Preaching in Medieval Florence: The Social World of Franciscan and Dominican Spirituality.* Athens, GA, 1989.

Levi ibn Habib, *Responsa. She'elot u-Teshuvot ha-RaLBaH.* Lemberg, 1865.

Levi, *Divrei Shelomoh.* Solomon ben Isaac Levi (Shelomoh le-Veit ha-Levi), *Divrei Shelomoh.* Venice, 1596.

Levin. Israel Levin, *'Al Mavet: Ha-Qinah 'al ha-Met be-Shirat ha-Ḥol ha-'Ivrit bi-Sefarad.* Tel Aviv, 1973.

Levy and Cantera. Raphael Levy and Francisco Cantera, eds., *The Beginning of Wisdom: An Astrological Treatise by Abraham ibn Ezra.* Baltimore, London, Paris, 1939.

Lieberman. Saul Lieberman, *Sheqi'in.* Jerusalem, 1970.

Liebes, *Zohar.* Yehudah Liebes, *Studies in the Zohar.* Albany, 1993.

Liebschutz. H. Liebschutz, "The Significance of Judaism in Peter Abelard's Dialogue," *JJS* 12 (1961):1–18.

Lille. Alan of Lille (Alanus de Insulis), *The Art of Preaching,* trans. Gillian R. Evans. Kalamazoo, 1981.

Llull. *Raimundi Lulli Opera Latina,* ed. Frederick Stegmuller, vol. 3. Palma de Mallorca, 1961.

Luntshitz, *'Ir.* Ephraim Luntshitz, *'Ir Gibborim.* Lublin, 1884.

Luntshitz, *'Olelot.* Ephraim Luntshitz, *'Olelot Efrayim.* Reprint edition, Tel Aviv, 1975.

MacKay. Angus MacKay, *Money, Prices and Politics in Fifteenth-Century Castile.* London, 1981.

Mahan. J. Alexander Mahan, *Maria Theresa of Austria.* New York, 1932.

MaHaRaL. *Sifrei MaHaRaL mi-Prag.* 11 vols. New York, 1969.

MaHaRIL. Jacob ben Moses Moelln, *Sefer MaHaRIL.* Shklov, 1796.

Mahler. Raphael Mahler, *Divrei Yemei Yisra'el: Dorot Aharonim.* 7 vols. Merhavia, 1954.

Maimonides, *Code.* Moses Maimonides, *Mishneh Torah.* 16 vols. Jerusalem, 1957–1965.

Maimonides, *Epistles.* Abraham Halkin and David Hartman, eds., *Crisis and Leadership: Epistles of Maimonides.* Philadelphia, 1985.

Maimonides, *Guide.* Moses Maimonides, *Guide of the Perplexed,* ed. M. Friedlander. 3 vols. in 1, New York, 1946.

Maimonides, *Millot ha-Higayon.* Moses Maimonides, *Millot ha-Higayon,* ed. Leon Roth. Jerusalem, 1965.

Maimonides, *Mitzvot. Sefer ha-Mitzvot le-ha-RaMBaM.* New York, 1956.

Maimonides, *Responsa. Teshuvot ha-RaMBaM,* ed. Joshua Blau. 3 vols. Jerusalem, 1958.

Marcus, *Jew.* Jacob Marcus, *The Jew in the Medieval World.* Cincinnati, 1990.

Marcus, *Piety.* Ivan Marcus, *Piety and Society: The Jewish Pietists of Medieval Germany.* Leiden, 1981.

Math. Moses Math, *Matteh Mosheh.* Frankfurt, 1720.

McManamon. John McManamon, *Funeral Oratory and the Cultural Ideals of Italian Humanism.* Chapel Hill, NC, 1989.

McNeill and Gamer. John McNeill and Helena Gamer, *Medieval Handbooks of Penance.* New York, 1938.

Méchoulan, "Spinoza." Henri Méchoulan, "Spinoza et Morteira au carrefour du socianisme," *REJ* 135 (1976):51–65.

Méchoulan, "Visite." Henri Méchoulan, "A propos de la visite de Fréderic-Henri, Prince d'Orange, à la synagogue d'Amsterdam." *Lias* 5 (1978):81–86.

Medieval Rhetoric. Readings in Medieval Rhetoric, ed. J. M. Miller, M. H. Prosser, T. W. Benson. Bloomington, IN, 1973.

Me'iri, *Tehillim.* Menahem Me'iri, *Perush ha-Me'iri le-Sefer Tehillim,* ed. Joseph Cohn. Jerusalem, 1936.

Me'iri, *Teshuvah.* Menahem Me'iri, *Ḥibbur ha-Teshuvah,* ed. Judah Horeb. Jerusalem, 1961.

Melamed, "Erets Yisra'el." Abraham Melamed, "Erets Yisra'el ve-ha-Te'oriah ha-Aqlimit ba-Maḥshavah ha-Yehudit," in *Erets Yisra'el ba-Hagut ha-Yehudit bi-Ymei ha-Beinayim,* ed. Moshe Halamish and Aviezer Ravitzky, pp. 52–78. Jerusalem, 1991.

Melamed, *Mefarshei ha-Miqra.* Ezra Melamed, *Mefarshei ha-Miqra.* 2 vols. Jerusalem, 1975.

Melamed, *Parashiyot.* Ezra Melamed, *Parashiyot me-Aggadot ha-Tanna'im.* Jerusalem, 1955.

Melnick. Ralph Melnick, *From Polemics to Apologetics: Jewish-Christian Rapprochement in 17th Century Amsterdam.* Assen, 1981.

Menasseh, *Conciliator.* Menasseh ben Israel, *The Conciliator,* trans. E. D. Lindo. London, 1842.

Menasseh, *Nishmat.* Menasseh ben Israel, *Nishmat Ḥayyim.* Leipzig, 1862.

Mendelssohn. Moses Mendelssohn, *Gesammelte Schriften.* 7 vols. Leipzig, 1843–45.

Messer Leon. *The Book of the Honeycomb's Flow,* by Judah Messer Leon, ed. Isaac Rabinowitz. Ithaca, 1983.

Mevorakh, "Review." Barukh Mevorakh, Review of Azriel Shochat, *'Im Ḥillufei Tequfot, Kiryat Sefer* 37 (1961–62):150–55.

Mevorakh, "Ma'asei ha-Hishtadlut." Barukh Mevorakh, "Ma'asei ha-Hishtadlut be-Eiropah le-Meni'at Gerusham shel Yehudei Bohemiah u-Moraviah 1744–1745," *Zion* 28 (1963):125–64.

Meyer. Michael A. Meyer, *The Origins of the Modern Jew: Jewish Identity and European Culture in Germany 1749–1824.* Detroit, 1967.

Michaud. Claude Michaud, "Laudatio et Carmen Post Mortem: Nachrufe auf Maria Theresia in Frankreich und Belgien," in *Österreich im Europa der Aufklärung,* 2 vols., 2:673–700. Vienna, 1985.

Midrash Rabbah. The Midrash Rabbah. 5 vols. London, Jerusalem, 1977.

Modena, *Autobiography.* Leon Modena, *The Autobiography of a Seventeenth-Century Venetian Rabbi,* ed. Mark Cohen. Princeton, 1988.

Modena, *Midbar.* Leon Modena, *Midbar Yehudah.* Venice, 1602.

Modena, *Ziqnei.* Leon Modena, *She'elot u-Teshuvot Ziqnei Yehudah,* ed. Shlomo Simonsohn. Jerusalem, 1957.

Moore, *Origins.* R. I. Moore, *The Origins of European Dissent.* Oxford, 1985.

Morpurgo. Elia Morpurgo, *Orazione Funebre in Occasione della Morte dell' Eroina della Germania S. S. C. R. A. M. Maria Theresa Imperadrice, e Regina ec. ec. Gorizia,* 1781.

Morteira 1645. Saul Levi Morteira, *Giv'at Sha'ul.* Amsterdam, 1645.

Morteira 1912. Saul Levi Morteira, *Giv'at Sha'ul.* Warsaw, 1912.

Moscato. Judah Moscato, *Nefutsot Yehudah.* Warsaw, 1871.

Muneles. Otto Muneles, *Bibliographical Survey of Jewish Prague.* Prague, 1952.

Müntzer. *The Basic Writings of Thomas Müntzer,* ed. Michael Baylor. London and Toronto, 1993.

Nave. Penina Nave, *Yehudah Aryeh mi-Modena, Leqet Ketavim.* Jerusalem, 1968.

Nelli. Rene Nelli, *L'érotique des troubadours.* Toulouse, 1963. *New Catholic Encyclopedia.* The *New Catholic Encyclopedia.* 18 vols. New York, 1967–89.

Netanyahu. Benzion Netanyahu, *The Marranos of Spain.* New York, 1966.

Nigal. "Derashotav shel Shemu'el Yehudah Katzenellenbogen," *Sinai* 36 (1971–72):79–85.

Nissim ben Reuben, *Derashot. Derashot ha-RaN le-Rabbenu Nissim ben Reuben Gerundi*, ed. Aryeh (Leon) Feldman. Jerusalem, 1974.

Nissim ben Reuben, *Ḥiddushim. Ḥiddushei ha-RaN 'al Masekhet Rosh Hashanah*. Jerusalem, 1960.

Noonan. John Noonan, *Contraception*. Cambridge, MA, 1966.

Oberman. Heiko Oberman, *The Roots of Anti-Semitism in the Age of Renaissance and Reformation*. Philadelphia, 1984.

Odber de Baubeta. Patricia Anne Odber de Baubeta, "Towards a History of Preaching in Medieval Portugal," *Portuguese Studies* 7 (1991):1–18.

Oldenbourg. Zoe Oldenbourg, *Massacre at Montségur*. New York, 1961; from the French edition of 1959.

O'Malley. John O'Malley, *Praise and Blame in Renaissance Rome*. Durham, NC 1979.

Origen. Origen, In *Genesim Homiliae*. *PG* 12:146–262.

Oshry. Ephraim Oshry, *Shu"t Mi-ma'amaqim*. 2 vols. New York, 1963.

Otsar Tehillot. *Otsar Tehillot Yisra'el*, ed. Israel Saharov. 14 vols. Tel Aviv, 1956–78.

Owst, *Literature*. G. R. Owst, *Literature and Pulpit in Medieval England*. New York, 1961.

Owst, *Preaching*. G. R. Owst, *Preaching in Medieval England*. New York, 1965.

Pachter, "Demuto." Mordechai Pachter, "Demuto shel ha-ARI be-Hesped she-Hispido R. Shemu'el Uceda," *Zion* 37 (1972):22–40.

Pagis, *Ḥiddush u-Masoret*. Dan Pagis, *Ḥiddush u-Masoret be-Shirat ha-Ḥol*. Jerusalem, 1976.

Passamaneck. Stephen Passamaneck, *Insurance in Rabbinic Law*. Edinburgh, 1974.

Patai. Raphael Patai, *The Jewish Alchemists*. Princeton, 1994.

Paton. B. T. Paton, *Custodians of the Civic Conscience: Preaching Friars and the Communal Ethos in Late Medieval Siena*. Oxford, 1989.

Patzig. G. Patzig, *Aristotle's Theory of the Syllogism*. Dordrecht, 1968.

Petry. Ray C. Petry, ed., *No Uncertain Sound*. Philadelphia, 1948.

Philo, *On Abraham*. Philo, *On Abraham*, in *The Loeb Classical Library Philo*, vol. 6. Cambridge, MA and London, 1935.

Pick. Robert Pick, *Empress Maria Theresa: The Earlier Years, 1717–1757*. New York, 1966.

Pieterse, *Bet Haim*. Wilhelmina Pieterse, *Livro de Bet Haim do Kahal Kados de Bet Yahacob*. Assen, 1970.

Piekarz, *Bi-Ymei Tsemiḥat*. Mendel Piekarz, *Bi-Ymei Tsemiḥat ha-Ḥasidut*. Jerusalem, 1978.

Piekarz, *Ide'ologiyah*. Mendel Piekarz, *Bein Ide'ologiyah le-Metsi'ut*. Jerusalem, 1994.

Pieterse, *Barrios*. Wilhelmina Pieterse, *Daniel Levi de Barrios als Geschiedschrijver*. Amsterdam, 1968.

Polen, *Holy Fire*. Nehemia Polen. *The Holy Fire: The Teachings of Rabbi Kalonymus Kalman Shapira, the Rebbe of the Warsaw Ghetto*. Northvale, NJ, 1994.

Poliakov, *Bankers*. Leon Poliakov, *Jewish Bankers and the Holy See*. London and Boston, 1977; from the French edition of 1965.

Portaleone. Abraham Portaleone, *Shiltei Gibborim*. Jerusalem, 1970.

Prescott. William Prescott, *History of the Reign of Ferdinand and Isabella*. 3 vols. Philadelphia, 1868.

Quay. Paul M. Quay, "Angels and Demons: The Teaching of IV Lateran," *Theological Studies* 42 (1981):20–45.

Rabinowitz. Isaac Rabinowitz, ed. and trans., *The Book of the Honeycomb's Flow*, by Judah Messer Leon. Ithaca, 1983.

RaLBaG, *Megillot*. Levi ben Gershom, *Perush 'al Hamesh Megillot*. Koenigsberg, 1860.

RaLBaG, *Torah. Perush ha-RaLBaG 'al ha-Torah.* Venice, 1547; reprint edition, New York, 1958.

RaMBaN. *Kitvei Rabbenu Mosheh ben Nahman,* ed. Hayyim Chavel, 2 vols. Jerusalem, 1963.

RaMBaN, *Writings. RaMBaN: Writings and Discourses,* ed. Charles Chavel. 2 vols. New York, 1978.

Ravitzky, *'Al Da'at ha-Maqom.* Aviezer Ravitzky, *'Al Da'at ha-Maqom.* Jerusalem, 1991.

Ravitzky, "Derekh Ḥaqiratah." Aviezer Ravitzky, "'Al Derekh Ḥaqiratah shel ha-Pilosofiah ha-Yehudit bi-Ymei ha-Beinayim," *Jerusalem Studies in Jewish Thought* 1 (1981):7–22.

Ravitzky, *Derashat ha-Pesah.* Aviezer Ravitzky, *Derashat ha-Pesah le-R. Hasdai Crescas u-Mehqarim be-Mishnato ha-Pilosofit.* Jerusalem, 1989.

Ravitzky, "Hitpaṭḥut." Aviezer Ravitzky, "Hitpaṭḥut Hashqafotav shel R. Ḥasdai Crescas bi-She'elat Ḥofesh ha-Ratson," *Tarbiz* 51 (1982):445–69.

Ravitzky, "Ketav." Aviezer Ravitzky, "Ketav Nishkaḥ le-R. Ḥasdai Crescas," *Kiryat Sefer* 51 (1976):705–11.

Ravitzky, "Miracles." Aviezer Ravitzky, "The Anthropological Theory of Miracles in Medieval Jewish Philosophy," in *Studies in Medieval Jewish History and Literature,* Vol. 2, ed. Isadore Twersky, pp. 231–72. Cambridge, MA, 1984.

Ravitzky, "Zehuto." Aviezer Ravitzky, "Zehuto ve-Gilgulav shel Ḥibbur Pilosofi she-Yuhas le-R. Mikha'el ben Shabbetai Balbo," *Kiryat Sefer* 56 (1981):153–63.

Regev, "Derashot." Shaul Regev, "Derashot le-Haggadah shel Pesaḥ, la-Mo'adim, u-le-Shab-batot: Sarid mi-Khetuv Yad le-Hakham Sefaradi Lo Noda'," *Asufot* 8 (1994):227–40.

Regev, "Re'iyat." Shaul Regev, "Re'iyat Atsilei Benei Yisra'el (Shemot 24:9–11) ba-Pilosofiyah ha-Yehudit bi-Ymei ha-Beinayim," *Jerusalem Studies in Jewish Thought* 4 (1984–85): 281–302.

Regev, "Teshuvah." Shaul Regev, "Derashot 'al ha-Teshuvah le-Rabbi Yosef ibn Shem Tov," *Asufot* 5 (1991):183–211.

Rembaum. Joel Rembaum, "Medieval Jewish Criticism of the Doctrine of Original Sin," *AJS Review* 7–8 (1982–83):353–82.

Renan, "Écrivains." Ernst Renan, "Les écrivains juifs français du xive siècle," in *Histoire lit-téraire de la France,* vol. 31. Paris, 1893.

Revah. I. S. Revah, *Spinoza et Juan de Prado.* The Hague, 1959.

Richler. Benjamin Richler, "Ketavim Bilti-Yedu'im shel Rabbi Yehudah Aryeh mi-Modena. *Asufot* 7 (1993):157–72.

Rivlin. Bracha (Ardos) Rivlin, *'Arevim Zeh la-Zeh ba-Ghetto ha-Italqi.* Jerusalem, 1991.

Robert of Flamborough. Robert of Flamborough, *Liber poenitentialis,* ed. J. J. Francis Firth. Toronto, 1971.

Roider, *Austria.* Karl Roider, *Austria's Eastern Question 1700–1790.* Princeton, 1982.

Roider, *Maria Theresa.* Karl Roider, *Maria Theresa.* Englewood Cliffs, NJ, 1973.

Rosenberg, "Exile." Shalom Rosenberg, "Exile and Redemption in Jewish Thought in the Six-teenth Century: Contending Conceptions," in *Jewish Thought in the Sixteenth Century,* ed. Bernard Cooperman, pp. 399–430. Cambridge, MA, 1983.

Rosenberg, "Parshanut." Shalom Rosenberg, "Ha-Parshanut ha-Pilosofit le-Shir ha-Shirim: He'arot Mavo," *Tarbiz* 59 (1990): 133–51.

Rosenberg, "Sefer ha-Hata'ah." Shalom Rosenberg, "*Sefer ha-Hata'ah* le-R. Yosef ibn Kaspi," *'Iyyun* 32 (1983):275–95.

Rosenberg and Manekin. Shalom Rosenberg and Bezalel Manekin, "Yafet be-Oholei Shem:

Perush Themistius le-Sefer ha-Heqesh," *Jerusalem Studies in Jewish Thought* 9 (1990):267–74.

Rosenthal. Gilbert Rosenthal, *Banking and Finance Among Jews in Renaissance Italy.* New York, 1962.

Rosenzweig. Israel Rosenzweig, *Hogeh Yehudi mi-Qets ha-Renesans.* Tel Aviv, 1972.

Rosner. Fred Rosner, *Moses Maimonides' Glossary of Drug Names.* Philadelphia, 1979.

Roth, *Conversos.* Norman Roth, *Conversos, Inquisition, and the Expulsion of the Jews from Spain.* Madison, WI, 1995.

Roth, "Elegy." Cecil Roth, "A Hebrew Elegy on the Martyrs of Toledo, 1391," *JQR* 39 (1948):135–50.

Roth, "European Jewry." Cecil Roth, "European Jewry in the Dark Ages," *HUCA* 23 (1950–51) Part 2:151–69.

Roth, "Lopez Rosa." Cecil Roth, "Lopez Rosa," in *EJ*, 11:491.

Roth, *Magna Bibliotheca.* Cecil Roth, ed., *Magna Bibliotheca Anglo-Judaica: A Bibliographical Guide to Anglo-Jewish History.* London, 1937.

Roth, *Marranos.* Cecil Roth, *A History of the Marranos.* New York and Philadelphia, 1959.

Roth, *Menasseh.* Cecil Roth, *Menasseh ben Israel.* Philadelphia, 1934.

Roth, *Renaissance.* Cecil Roth, *The Jews in the Renaissance.* Philadelphia, 1959.

Rothenberg. Gunther Rothenberg, *Napoleon's Great Adversaries: The Archduke Charles and the Austrian Army.* Bloomington, 1981.

Rouse and Rouse. R. Rouse and M. Rouse, *Preachers, Florilegia and Sermons.* Toronto, 1979.

Rowland. Ingrid Rowland, "Egidio da Viterbo's Defense of Pope Julius II, 1509 and 1511," in *De Ore Domini: The Preacher and Word in the Middle Ages,* ed. Thomas Amos, Eugene Green, Beverly Kienzle, pp. 235–60. Kalamazoo, 1989.

Ruderman, "Exemplary Sermon." David Ruderman, "An Exemplary Sermon from the Class-rom of a Jewish Teacher in Renaissance Italy," *Italia* 1 (1978):7–38.

Ruether. Rosemary Ruether, *Faith and Fratricide: The Theological Roots of Anti-Semitism.* New York, 1974.

Rusconi. Roberto Rusconi, *Predicazione e vita religiosa nella società italiana: Da Carlo Magno alla controriforma.* Turin, 1981.

Russell, *Lucifer.* Jeffrey Burton Russell, *Lucifer: The Devil in the Middle Ages.* Ithaca, 1984.

Saadia, *Emunot ve-De'ot.* Saadia Gaon, *Sefer Emunot ve-De'ot,* trans. Judah ibn Tibbon. Jerusalem, 1972.

Saba. Abraham Saba, *Tseror ha-Mor.* Reprint edition, Tel Aviv, 1975.

Sadek. Vladimir Sadek, "La chronique hébraique de l'histoire des juifs pragois de la deuxième moitié du 18e siècle," *Judaica Bohemia* 1 (1965): 59–68.

Salomon, "Excommunication." H.P. Salomon, "La vraie excommunication de Spinozo," in *Forum Litterarum—Miscelanea de Estudos Literarios, Linguisticos e Historicos oferecido a J. J. van den Besselaar,* pp. 181–99. Amsterdam, 1984.

Salomon, "Myth." H. P. Salomon, "Myth or Anti-Myth? The Oldest Account Concerning the Origin of Portuguese Judaism at Amsterdam," *LIAS* 16 (1989):275–316.

Salomon, *Portrait.* H. P. Salomon, *Portrait of a New Christian: Fernao Alvares Melo (1569–1632).* Paris, 1982.

Salomon, Tratado. Saul Levi Morteira, *Tratado da verdade da lei de Moises,* ed. with introduction by H. P. Salomon. Coimbra, 1988.

Samuel ben Hofni, *Torah. Perush ha-Torah le-Rav Shemu'el ben Hofni Ga'on,* ed. Aaron Greenbaum. Jerusalem, 1979.

Saperstein, "Art Form." Marc Saperstein, "The Sermon as Art-Form: Structure in Morteira's *Gib'at Sha'ul*," *Prooftexts* 3 (1983):243–61.

Saperstein, "Bedersi's Commentary." "Selected Passages from Yedaiah Bedersi's Commentary on the Midrashim," in *Studies in Medieval Jewish History and Literature*, Vol. 2, ed. Isadore Twersky, pp. 423–40. Cambridge, MA, 1984.

Saperstein, *Decoding*. Marc Saperstein, *Decoding the Rabbis: A Thirteenth-Century Commentary on the Aggadah*. Cambridge, MA, 1980.

Saperstein, *Jewish Preaching*. Marc Saperstein, *Jewish Preaching 1200–1800*. New Haven, 1989.

Saperstein, "Stories." Marc Saperstein, "Stories in Jewish Sermons (The 15th–16th Centuries)," *Proceedings of the Ninth World Congress of Jewish Studies*, Division C, pp. 101–108. Jerusalem, 1986.

Saperstein, "Treatise." Marc Saperstein, "Saul Levi Morteira's Treatise on the Immortality of the Soul," *Studia Rosenthaliana* 25 (1991):131–48.

Schama. Simon Schama, *The Embarrassment of Riches: An Interpretation of Dutch Culture in the Golden Age*. Berkeley and Los Angeles, 1988.

Schatz Uffenheimer. Rivka Schatz Uffenheimer, *Hasidism as Mysticism: Quietistic Elements in Eighteenth-Century Hasidic Thought*, trans. Jonathan Chipman. Jerusalem and Princeton, 1993; from the Hebrew edition of 1980.

Schechterman. Deborah Schechterman, "Sugyat ha-Ḥeit ha-Qadmon ve-ha-Parshanut le-Divrei ha-RaMBaM ba-Hagut ha-Yehudit ba-Me'ot ha-Shelosh 'Esreh ve-ha-Arba' 'Esreh," *Da'at* 20 (1988):65–90.

Schirmann, "Pulmus." Hayyim Schirmann, "Ha-Pulmus shel Shelomoh Bonafed be-Nikhbedei Saragossa." *Qovetz 'al Yad* 4 (14) (1946):9–64.

Schirmann, *Shirah*. Hayyim Schirmann, *Ha-Shirah ha-Ivrit bi-Sefarad u-vi-Provens*. 2 vols in 4. Jerusalem and Tel Aviv, 1961.

Schmitz. R.-P. Schmitz, *'Aqedat Jishaq*. Hildesheim, 1979.

Schochet. Elijah Schochet, *Rabbi Joel Sirkes*. Jerusalem, 1971.

Scholem, "Ḥaqirot." Gershom Scholem, "Ḥaqirot Ḥadashot 'al R. Abraham ben Eliezer Halevi," *Kiryat Sefer* 7 (1930–31):149–65.

Scholem, *Kabbalah*. Gershom Scholem, *On the Kabbalah and Its Symbolism*. New York, 1965.

Scholem, *Major Trends*. Gershom Scholem, *Major Trends in Jewish Mysticism*. New York, 1941.

Scholem, *Meḥqarim*. Gershom Scholem, *Meḥqarim u-Meqorot le-Toledot ha-Shabta'ut ve-Gilguleha*. Jerusalem, 1982.

Scholem, *Origins*. Gershom Scholem, *The Origins of the Kabbalah*, ed. R. J. Z. Werblowsky. Philadelphia, 1987; from the German edition of 1962.

Scholem, *Sabbatai Ṣevi*. Gershom Scholem, *Sabbatai Sevi: The Mystical Messiah*. Princeton, 1973; from the Hebrew edition of 1957.

Schuerer. Oskar Schuerer, *Prag: Kultur, Kunst, Geschichte*. Munich, 1935.

Schwartz, "Yetsi'at Mitsrayim." Dov Schwartz, "Derashah be-'Inyan Yetsi'at Mitsrayim le-Rabbi Vidal Yosef de la Caballeria," *Asufot* 7 (1993):261–80.

Sefer ha-Ḥinukh. *Sefer ha-Ḥinukh*, ed. Hayyim Chavel. Jerusalem, 1962.

Sefer Ḥasidim (Bologna). *Sefer Ḥasidim*. Jerusalem, 1966.

Sefer Ḥasidim (Parma). *Sefer Ḥasidim*, ed. Jehuda Wistinetzki. Frankfurt am Main, 1924.

Seibt. Ferdinand Seibt, ed., *Die Juden in den böhmischen Ländern*. Munich and Vienna, 1983.

Selihot. *Selihot la-Ashmurot ha-Boqer ke-fi Minhag Q'Q Sefaradim*. Venice, 1735.

Septimus. Bernard Septimus, *Hispano-Jewish Culture in Transition.* Cambridge, MA, 1982.

Sermoneta, "Dante." Joseph Sermoneta, "Dante Alighieri," *EJ.* 5:1295–96.

Shalom. Abraham Shalom, *Neveh Shalom.* Venice, 1575.

Shatzmiller, "Kefirah." Joseph Shatzmiller, "Ha-Kefirah ha-Albigensit be-'Einei ha-Yehudim Benei ha-Zeman," in *Tarbut ve-Ḥevrah be-Toledot Yisra'el bi-Ymei ha-Beinayim: Qovets Ma'amarim le-Zikhro shel Hayyim Hillel Ben-Sasson,* ed. Robert Bonfil, Menahem Ben Sasson, and Joseph Hacker, pp. 333–52. Jerusalem, 1989.

Shatzmiller, *Shylock.* Joseph Shatzmiller, *Shylock Reconsidered: Jews, Moneylending, and Medieval Society.* Berkeley and Los Angeles, 1990.

Shazar. Zalman Shazar, *Ha-Tiqvah li-Shenat HaTaQ.* Jerusalem, 1970.

Shem Tov, *Derashot.* Shem Tov ben Joseph ibn Shem Tov, *Derashot.* Salonika, 1525; reprinted Jerusalem, 1973.

Shochat, "Beirurim." Azriel Shochat, "Beirurim be-farashat ha-Pulmus ha-Rishon 'al Sifrei ha-RaMBaM," *Zion* 36 (1971):25–60.

Shochat, *Ḥillufei.* Azriel Shochat, '*Im Ḥillufei Tequfot: Reshit ha-Haskalah be-Yahadut Germanya.* Jerusalem, 1960.

Shulvass. Moses Shulvass, *The Jews in the World of the Renaisaance.* Leiden, 1973.

Siddur ha-Ge'onim. Siddur ha-Ge'onim ve-ha-Mequbalim ve-ha-Ḥasidim, ed. Bentsiyon Mosheh Vainshtok. 17 vols. Jerusalem, 1970–78.

Siete Partidas. Las Siete Partidas del Rey Don Alfonso el Sabio. Vol. 1, *Partida Primera.* Madrid, 1807.

Silver. Abba Hillel Silver, *A History of Messianic Speculation in Israel.* Boston, 1959.

Simonsohn. Shlomo Simonsohn, *History of the Jews in the Duchy of Mantua.* Jerusalem, 1977.

Sirat. Collette Sirat, *A History of Jewish Philosophy in the Middle Ages.* New York, 1985; from the French edition of 1983.

Smalley. Beryl Smalley, *English Friars and Antiquity in the Early Fourteenth Century.* Oxford, 1960.

Smith. Hilary Dansey Smith, *Preaching in the Spanish Golden Age.* Oxford, 1978.

Soloveitchik, "Ta'arikh." Haym Soloveitchik, "Le-Ta'arikh Hibburo shel 'Sefer Ḥasidim'," in *Tarbut ve-Ḥevrah be-Toledot Yisra'el bi-Ymei ha-Beinayim: Qovets Ma'amarim le-Zikhro shel Ḥayyim Hillel Ben-Sasson,* ed. Robert Bonfil, Menahem Ben Sasson, and Joseph Hacker, pp. 383–88. Jerusalem, 1989.

Soloveitchik, "Three Themes." Haym Soloveitchik, "Three Themes in the *Sefer Hasidim,*" *AJS Review* 1 (1976):311–57.

Sonne. Isaiah Sonne, "Leon Modena and the Da Costa Circle in Amsterdam," *HUCA* 21 (1948):1–28.

Sperber. Daniel Sperber, *Minhagei Yisra'el.* 2 vols. Jerusalem, 1989–91.

Spiegel. Shalom Spiegel, *The Last Trial.* Philadelphia, 1967.

Spinoza. Benedict de Spinoza, *A Theologico-Political Treatise and A Political Treatise,* trans. R. H. M. Elwes. New York, 1955.

Spitzer, "Derashot." Solomon Spitzer, "Derashot ve-Dinim be-Hilkhot Pesaḥ le-Rabbenu Ya'aqov Weil." *Moriah* 11:5–6 (1982):21–30.

Steinschneider. Moritz Steinschneider, *Die Hebraeischen Übersetzungen des Mittelalters und die Juden als Dolmetscher.* Berlin, 1893.

Stiernotte. Alfred B. Stiernotte, ed., *Frederick May Eliot: An Anthology.* Boston, 1959.

Storrs. Richard Storrs, *Bernard of Clairvaux.* New York, 1893.

Stout. Harry Stout, *The New England Soul: Preaching and Religious Culture in Colonial New England.* Oxford, 1986.

Stow, *Catholic Thought.* Kenneth Stow, *Catholic Thought and Papal Jewry Policy.* New York, 1977.

Taku. Moses Taku, "Ketav Tamim," *Otsar Nehmad* 3 (1960):58–99.

Talmage, "Apples of Gold." Frank Talmage, "Apples of Gold: The Inner Meaning of Sacred Texts in Medieval Judaism," in *Jewish Spirituality from the Bible through the Middle Ages,* ed. A. Green. 2 vols., 2:313–55. New York, 1986–87.

Talmage, *David Kimhi.* Talmage, *David Kimhi: The Man and the Commentaries.* Cambridge, MA, 1975.

Talmage, *Disputation.* Frank Talmage, *Disputation and Dialogue.* New York, 1975.

Talmage, "Hebrew Polemical Treatise." Frank Talmage, "A Hebrew Polemical Treatise: Anti-Cathar and Anti-Orthodox," *Harvard Theological Review* 60 (1967):323–38.

Talmage, *Kitvei Pulmus.* Frank Talmage, *Kitvei Pulmus le-Profiat Duran.* Jerusalem, 1981.

Talmage, "Rationalist Tradition." Frank Talmage, "David Kimhi and the Rationalist Tradition," *HUCA* 39 (1968):177–218.

Taylor. Larissa Taylor, *Soldiers of Christ: Preaching in Late Medieval and Reformation France.* New York and Oxford, 1993.

Tenenti. Alberto Tenenti, *Sense de la mort et amour de la vie.* L'Harmattan, 1983

Tetel. Marcel Tetel, Ronald Witt, and Rona Geffen, eds., *Life and Death in Fifteenth-Century Florence.* Durham, NC, 1989.

Thomas de Chobham, *Summa de arte praedicandi,* ed. Franco Morenzoni. Brepols, 1988.

Thorndike, *Magic.* Lynn Thorndike, *A History of Magic and Experimental Science.* 8 vols. New York, 1923–54.

Thorndike, *Scot.* Lynn Thorndike, *Michael Scot.* London, 1965.

Three Jewish Philosophers. Three Jewish Philosophers, ed. Hans Lewy, Alexander Altmann, and Isaak Heinemann. New York and Philadelphia, 1960.

Tishby, *Ḥiqrei Qabbalah.* Isaiah Tishby, *Ḥiqrei Qabbalah u-Sheluhotehah.* 3 vols. Jerusalem, 1982–93.

Tishby, *Netivei.* Isaiah Tishby, *Netivei Emunah u-Minut.* Jerusalem, 1982.

Tishby, *Wisdom.* Isaiah Tishby, *The Wisdom of the Zohar.* 3 vols. Oxford, 1989.

Toaff. Ariel Toaff, *The Jews in Medieval Assisi.* Florence, 1979.

Todros ha-Levi, *Gan ha-Meshalim. Gan ha-Meshalim ve-ha-Ḥiddot (Diwan Don Todros ha-Levi Abu al-'Afia),* ed. David Yellin. 2 vols. Jerusalem, 1932–36.

Todros ha-Levi, *Otsar ha-Kavod.* Todros ben Joseph Ha-Levi Abulafia, *Otsar ha-Kavod.* Satmar, 1926.

Trachtenberg. Joshua Tractenberg, *The Devil and the Jews: The Medieval Conception of the Jew and Its Relation to Modern Antisemitism.* Reprint edition, Philadelphia, 1983.

Tractate "Mourning." The Tractate "Mourning", ed. and trans. Dov Zlotnick. New Haven, 1966.

Trautner-Kromann. Hanne Trautner-Kromann, *Shield and Sword: Jewish Polemics against Christianity and the Christians in France and Spain from 1100–1500.* Tübingen, 1993.

Trebitsch. Abraham Trebitsch, *Qorot ha-'Ittim.* Lemberg, 1851.

Twersky, *Maimonides Reader.* Isadore Twersky, *A Maimonides Reader.* New York, 1972.

Twersky, *Rabad.* Isadore Twersky, *Rabad of Posquières.* Revised edition, Philadelphia, 1980.

Vega. Alvares Vega, *Het Beth Haim van Ouderkerk.* Amsterdam, 1975.

Weinberg, "Preaching in the Venetian Ghetto: The Sermons of Leon Modena," in *Preachers of the Italian Ghetto,* ed. David Ruderman, pp. 105–28.

Weinzierl-Fischer. Erika Weinzierl-Fischer, "Die Bekämpfung der Hungersnot in Böhmen 1770–1772 durch Maria Theresia und Joseph II," *Mitteilungen des Österreichischen Staatsarchivs* 7 (1954): 478–514.

Weiss, *Studies.* Joseph Weiss, *Studies in Eastern European Jewish Mysticism.* Oxford, 1985.

Weissman. Ronald Weissman, *Ritual Brotherhoods in Renaissance Florence.* New York, 1982.

Werblowsky, Karo. R. J. Z. Werblowsky, *Joseph Karo: Lawyer and Mystic.* Philadelphia, 1977.

Whicher. George Whicher, *The Goliard Poets.* New York, 1959.

Wijnhoven. Johanan Wijnhoven, "The Zohar and the Proselyte," in *Texts and Responses: Studies Presented to N. N. Glatzer,* pp. 120–40. Leiden, 1975.

Wilken, *Chrysostom.* Robert L. Wilken, *John Chrysostom and the Jews.* Berkeley, Los Angeles, 1983.

Wilken, *Land.* Robert Wilken, *The Land Called Holy.* New Haven, 1992.

Williams. Arthur Lukyn Williams, *Adversus Judaeos.* Cambridge, Eng., 1935.

Wills. Lawrence Wills, "The Form of the Sermon in Hellenistic Judaism and Early Christianity," *HTR* 77 (1984):277–99.

Wind. Solomon Wind, *Rabbi Yehezkel Landau.* Jerusalem, 1961.

Wiznitzer. A Wiznitzer, "The Merger Agreement and Regulations of Congregation Talmud Tora of Amsterdam 1638–39." *Historia Judaica* 20 (1958):109–32.

Wolff. Philippe Wolff, "The 1391 Pogrom in Spain: Social Crisis or Not?" *Past and Present* 50 (1967):4–18.

Wolfson, *Crescas.* Harry Wolfson, *Crescas' Critique of Aristotle.* Cambridge, MA, 1979.

Wolfson, *Studies.* Harry Wolfson, *Studies in the History of Philosophy and Religion,* 2 vols., ed. Isadore Twersky and George Williams. Cambridge, MA, 1973–77.

Wright. William Wright, *Serf, Seigneur and Sovereign.* Minneapolis, 1966.

Yabetz, *Hasdei ha-Shem.* Joseph Yabetz, *Hasdei ha-Shem.* Brooklyn, 1934.

Yabetz, *Or ha-Ḥayyim.* Joseph Yabetz, *Or ha-Ḥayyim.* Lublin, 1912.

Yerushalmi, "Professing Jews." Yosef Hayim Yerushalmi, "Professing Jews in Post-Expulsion Spain and Portugal," in *Salo W. Baron Jubilee Volume.* 3 vols., 2:1023–58. New York, 1974.

Yerushalmi, *Haggadah.* Yosef Hayim Yerushalmi, *Haggadah and History.* Philadelphia, 1975.

Yerushalmi, *Lisbon Massacre.* Yosef Hayim Yerushalmi, *The Lisbon Massacre of 1506 and the Royal Image in the Shebet Yehudah.* Cincinnati, 1976.

Yerushalmi, *Spanish Court.* Yosef Hayim Yerushalmi, *From Spanish Court to Italian Ghetto. Isaac Cardoso: A Study in Seventeenth-Century Marranism and Jewish Apologetics.* New York, 1971.

Yovel. Yirmiahu Yovel, *Spinoza and Other Heretics.* 2 vols. Princeton, 1989.

Zahalon. *A Guide for Preachers on Composing and Delivering Sermons: The Or ha-Darshanim of Jacob Zahalon,* ed. Henry Sosland. New York, 1987.

Zarfati. Joseph ben Hayyim Zarfati, *Yad Yosef.* Amsterdam, 1700.

Zohar Ḥadash. Zohar Ḥadash, Warsaw, 1885; reprint Jerusalem, 1978.

Zunz. Yom Tov (Leopold) Zunz, *Ha-Derashot be-Yisra'el,* ed. Hanokh Albeck. Jerusalem, 1974. Translation of *Die gottesdienstlichen Vorträge der Juden, historisch entwickelt.* 2nd edition, Frankfurt am Main, 1892.

Index of Passages Cited

General Index